Rick Steves'®

SPAIN

2009

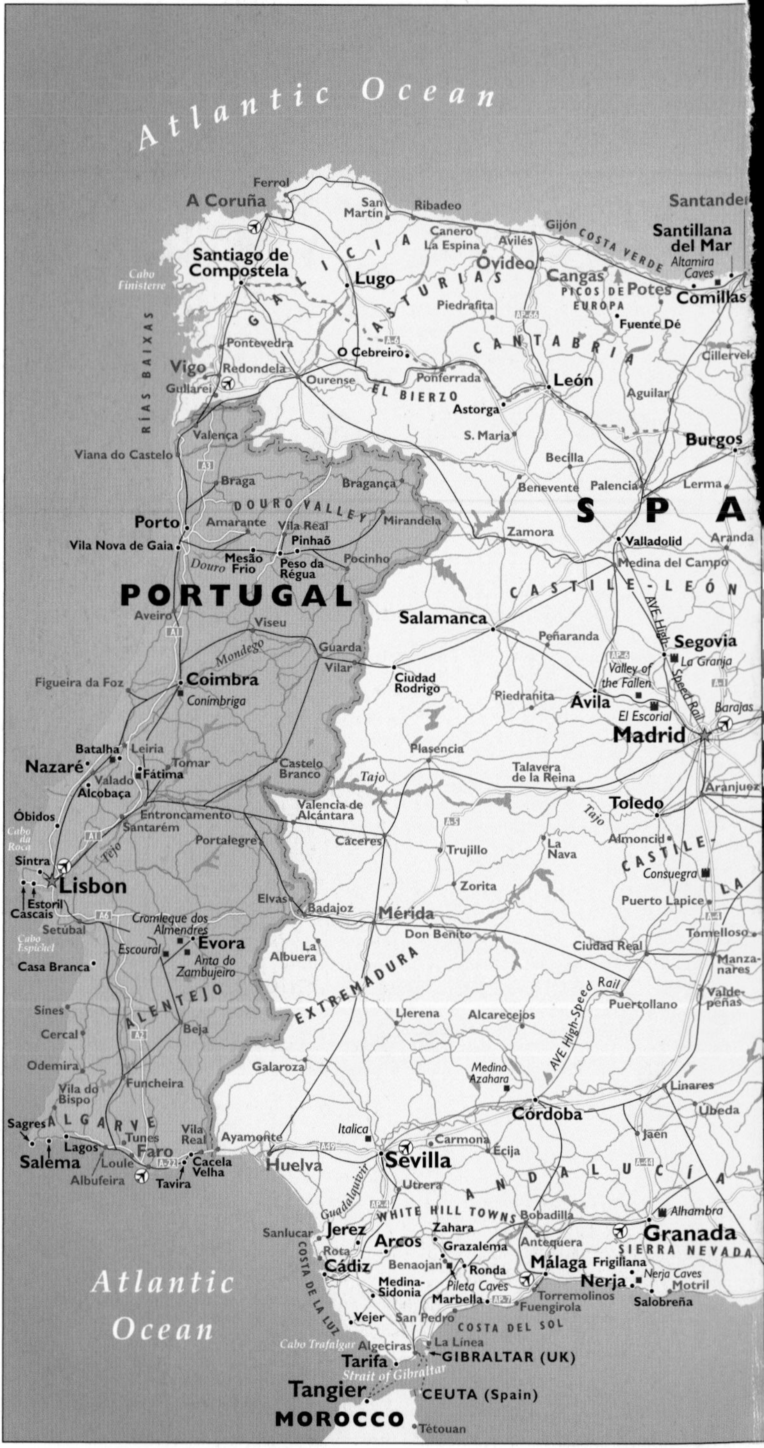

Atlantic Ocean
Ferrol
A Coruña
San Martín
Ribadeo
Santander
Gijón
COSTA VERDE
Santillana del Mar
Altamira Caves
Canero
La Espina
Avilés
Santiago de Compostela
Cabo Finisterre
GALICIA
Lugo
Ovideo
ASTURIAS
Cangas
PICOS DE EUROPA
Potes
Comillas
Piedrafita
Fuente Dé
RÍAS BAIXAS
Pontevedra
O Cebreiro
CANTABRIA
Cillervelo
Vigo
Redondela
Ourense
Ponferrada
León
Gullarei
EL BIERZO
Aguilar
Astorga
Valença
S. Maria
Burgos
Viana do Castelo
Becilla
Braga
Bragança
Benevente
Palencia
Lerma
DOURO VALLEY
SPA
Porto
Amarante
Vila Real
Mirandela
Zamora
Vila Nova de Gaia
Pinhaõ
Valladolid
Aranda
Douro
Mesão Frio
Peso da Régua
Pocinho
Medina del Campo
PORTUGAL
CASTILE-LEÓN
Aveiro
Viseu
Salamanca
AVE High-Speed Rail
Mondego
Guarda
Peñaranda
Segovia
La Granja
Vilar
Ciudad Rodrigo
Valley of the Fallen
Figueira da Foz
Coimbra
Conímbriga
Piedrahita
Ávila
El Escorial
Barajas
Madrid
Batalha
Leiria
Plasencia
Nazaré
Tomar
Castelo Branco
Valado
Fátima
Talavera de la Reina
Alcobaça
Tajo
Aranjuez
Óbidos
Entroncamento
Valencia de Alcántara
Toledo
Cabo da Roca
Santarém
Tajo
Portalegre
Cáceres
Almoncid
Sintra
Tejo
Trujillo
La Nava
CASTILE-LA
Lisbon
Consuegra
Estoril
Cascais
Zorita
Elvas
Badajoz
Mérida
Puerto Lapice
Setúbal
Cromleque dos Almendres
Cabo Espichel
Escoural
Évora
Don Benito
Tomelloso
Anta do Zambujeiro
La Albuera
Ciudad Real
Casa Branca
Manzanares
EXTREMADURA
ALENTEJO
Valdepeñas
Sines
Puertollano
Beja
Llerena
Alcarecejos
Cercal
Odemira
Galaroza
Medina Azahara
Funcheira
Vila do Bispo
Linares
Córdoba
Úbeda
Sagres
ALGARVE
Italica
Jaén
Vila Real
Ayamonte
Carmona
Tunes
Lagos
Salema
Faro
Loulé
Cacela Velha
Huelva
Sevilla
Écija
Albufeira
Tavira
Guadalquivir
Utrera
ANDALUCÍA
WHITE HILL TOWNS
Bobadilla
Alhambra
Sanlucar
Jerez
Zahara
Granada
Arcos
Grazalema
Antequera
SIERRA NEVADA
Rota
Cádiz
Benaojan
Ronda
Málaga
Frigiliana
Nerja
Nerja Caves
Motril
Medina-Sidonia
Pileta Caves
Torremolinos
COSTA DE LA LUZ
Marbella
Fuengirola
Salobreña
Vejer
San Pedro
COSTA DEL SOL
Cabo Trafalgar
Algeciras
La Línea
Tarifa
GIBRALTAR (UK)
Strait of Gibraltar
Tangier
CEUTA (Spain)
MOROCCO
Tétouan
Atlantic Ocean

SPAIN
Freeway
Major Rail Line
Camino de Santiago (Ancient Pilgrimage Route)
Airport
Tarifa Recommended Location
Elda Just Passing Through
National Park/Natural Wonder
Ruin, Museum, other Point of Interest
Castle, Monument, Palace
0 50 100 km
0 50 100 mi
To Plymouth, England
To Portsmouth, England
To Paris
To Lyon and Paris
To Nice
Bay of Biscay
FRANCE
Bordeaux
Libourne
St. Emilion
DORDOGNE
Périgueux
Brive-la-Gaillarde
Sarlat
Le Buisson
Beynac
Aurillac
Cahors
Rodez
DUNE DU PILAT
AQUITAINE
Agen
Montauban
Millau
Albi
Toulouse
Castres
Dax
St. Jean-de-Luz
Biarritz
Bayonne
Hendaye
Irun
San Sebastián
Lekeitio
Bilbao
Bilbao Guggenheim Museum
Guernica
BASQUE
St. Jean-Pied-du-Port
Pau
Tarbes
Lourdes
CIRQUE DE GAVARNIE
LANGUEDOC
Minerve
Carcassonne
Narbonne
Foix
Perpignan
Collioure
Cerbère
Portbou
Cadaqués
Figueres
Dalí Museum
Girona
Tossa
COSTA BRAVA
ANDORRA
Andorra la Vella
La Tour
Puigcerda
Miranda de Ebro
Vitoria
Puente de la Reina
Pamplona
Canfranc
Laguardia
Haro
RIOJA
Logroño
Santo Domingo de la Calzada
NAVARRE
Castejón
PYRENEES
Jaca
Torla
Ainsa
ORDESA NAT'L PARK
Huesca
Barbastro
ARAGÓN
Ebro
Sto. Domingo de Silos
Soria
Duero
Zaragoza
AVE High-Speed Rail
Lérida
CATALUNYA
Montserrat
Mataró
Barcelona
El Prat de Llobregat
Vilafranca
Sitges
Tarragona
COSTA DORADA
Delta del Ebro
Almazan
Siguenza
Calatayud
AVE High-Speed
Daroca
Molina
Montalbán
Alcañiz
Tortosa
Monreal
Guadalajara
Sacedon
Morella
Vinarós
Teruel
Cuenca
Torrebaja
Castelló de la Plana
Alcazar
MANCHA
Motilla
Requena
Sagunto
Valencia
Sotuélamos
Albacete
Alzira
Gandia
Dénia
Jávea
Alcoy
Alcaraz
Elche
Jumilla
Elda
Benidorm
Alicante
MURCIA
Caravaca
Murcia
COSTA BLANCA
Cúllar Baza
Lorca
Cartagena
La Manga
Mojacar
Almería
Mediterranean Sea
BALEARIC ISLANDS
MALLORCA
Palma
CABRERA
IBIZA
Ibiza
FORMENTERA
Ferries to Menorca

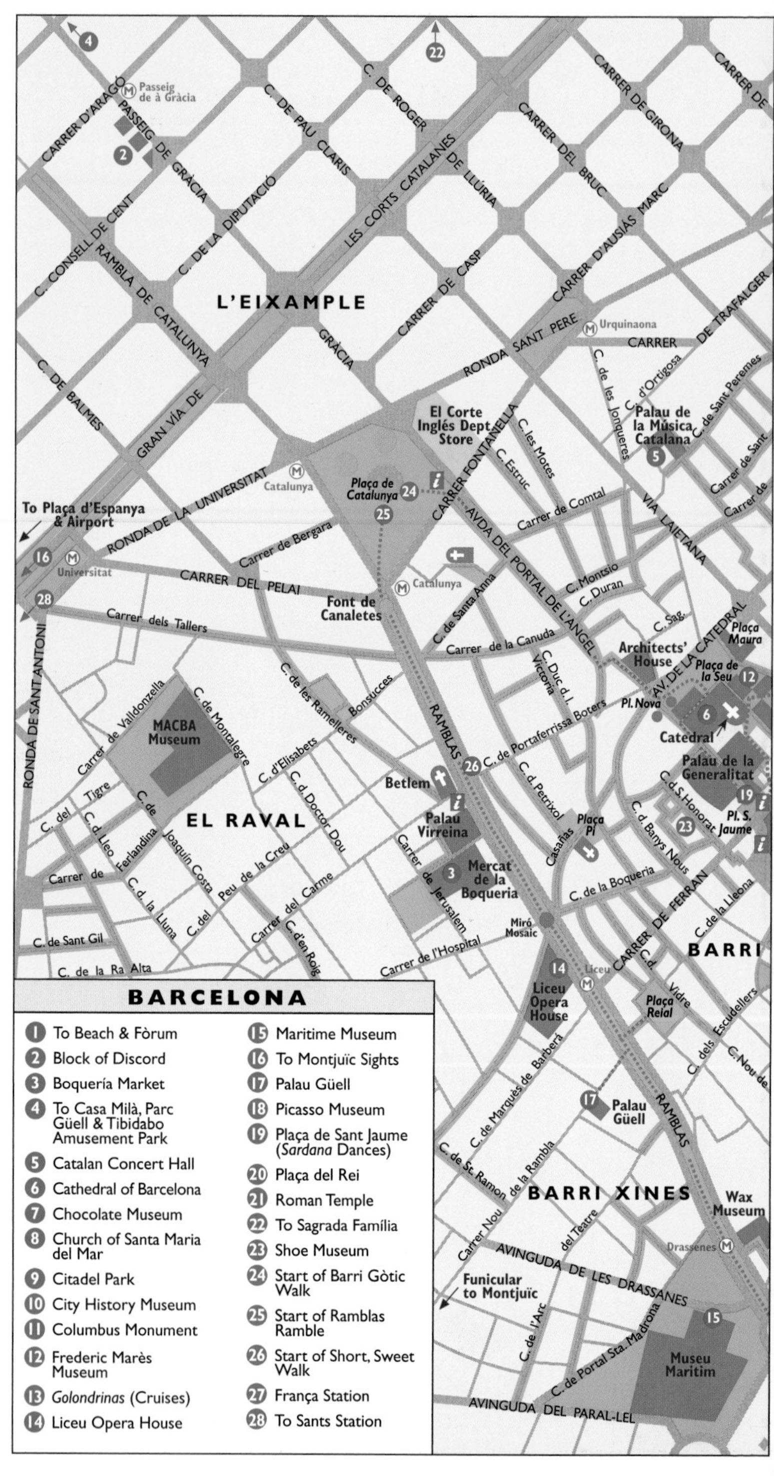
BARCELONA
1 To Beach & Fòrum
2 Block of Discord
3 Boquería Market
4 To Casa Milà, Parc Güell & Tibidabo Amusement Park
5 Catalan Concert Hall
6 Cathedral of Barcelona
7 Chocolate Museum
8 Church of Santa Maria del Mar
9 Citadel Park
10 City History Museum
11 Columbus Monument
12 Frederic Marès Museum
13 Golondrinas (Cruises)
14 Liceu Opera House
15 Maritime Museum
16 To Montjuïc Sights
17 Palau Güell
18 Picasso Museum
19 Plaça de Sant Jaume (Sardana Dances)
20 Plaça del Rei
21 Roman Temple
22 To Sagrada Família
23 Shoe Museum
24 Start of Barri Gòtic Walk
25 Start of Ramblas Ramble
26 Start of Short, Sweet Walk
27 França Station
28 To Sants Station
L'EIXAMPLE
EL RAVAL
BARRI XINES
BARRI
Passeig de à Gràcia
Carrer d'Aragó
Passeig de Gràcia
C. de Pau Claris
C. de Roger de Llúria
Carrer de Girona
Carrer del Bruc
Carrer de
Les Corts Catalanes
C. Consell de Cent
Rambla de Catalunya
C. de la Diputació
Carrer d'Ausiàs Marc
Carrer de Casp
Urquinaona
Carrer de Trafalger
Ronda Sant Pere
C. de Balmes
Gran Vía de
El Corte Inglés Dept Store
Carrer Fontanella
C. les Motes
C. Estruc
C. de les Jonqueres
C. d'Ortigosa
Palau de la Música Catalana
C. de Sant Peremes
Carrer de Sant
Catalunya
Plaça de Catalunya
Ronda de la Universitat
To Plaça d'Espanya & Airport
Universitat
Carrer de Bergara
Carrer del Pelai
Avda del Portal de l'Angel
Carrer de Comtal
Via Laietana
C. Montsio
C. Duran
Font de Canaletes
Carrer dels Tallers
C. de Santa Anna
Carrer de la Canuda
C. Sag.
Architects' House
Av. de la Catedral
Plaça Maura
Plaça de la Seu
Ronda de Sant Antoni
C. de les Ramelleres
Bonsuccs
Ramblas
C. Duc d. l. Victoria
Pl. Nova
Catedral
Carrer de Valldonzella
MACBA Museum
C. de Montalegre
C. d'Elisabets
C. de Portaferrissa
Boters
Palau de la Generalitat
C. d. Doctor Dou
Betlem
C. d. Petrixol
C. d.S.Honorat
Pl. S. Jaume
C. del Tigre
C. d. Leo
C. de Ferlandina
Joaquín Costa
Palau Virreina
Plaça Pi
C. d. Banys Nous
Carrer de
C. d. la Lluna
C. del Peu de la Creu
Carrer de Jerusalem
Mercat de la Boqueria
Casañas
C. de la Boqueria
Carrer de Ferran
C. de la Lleona
C. de Sant Gil
C. del Carme
Carrer d'en Roig
Miró Mosaic
Carrer de l'Hospital
C. de la Ra Alta
Liceu
Liceu Opera House
C. d. Vidre
Plaça Reial
C. dels Escudellers
C. Nou de
C. de Marquès de Barberà
Palau Güell
C. de St. Ramon
de la Rambla
Wax Museum
Carrer Nou
del Teatre
Drassenes
Avinguda de les Drassanes
Funicular to Montjuïc
C. de l'Arc
C. de Portal Sta. Madrona
Museu Marìtim
Avinguda del Paral-lel

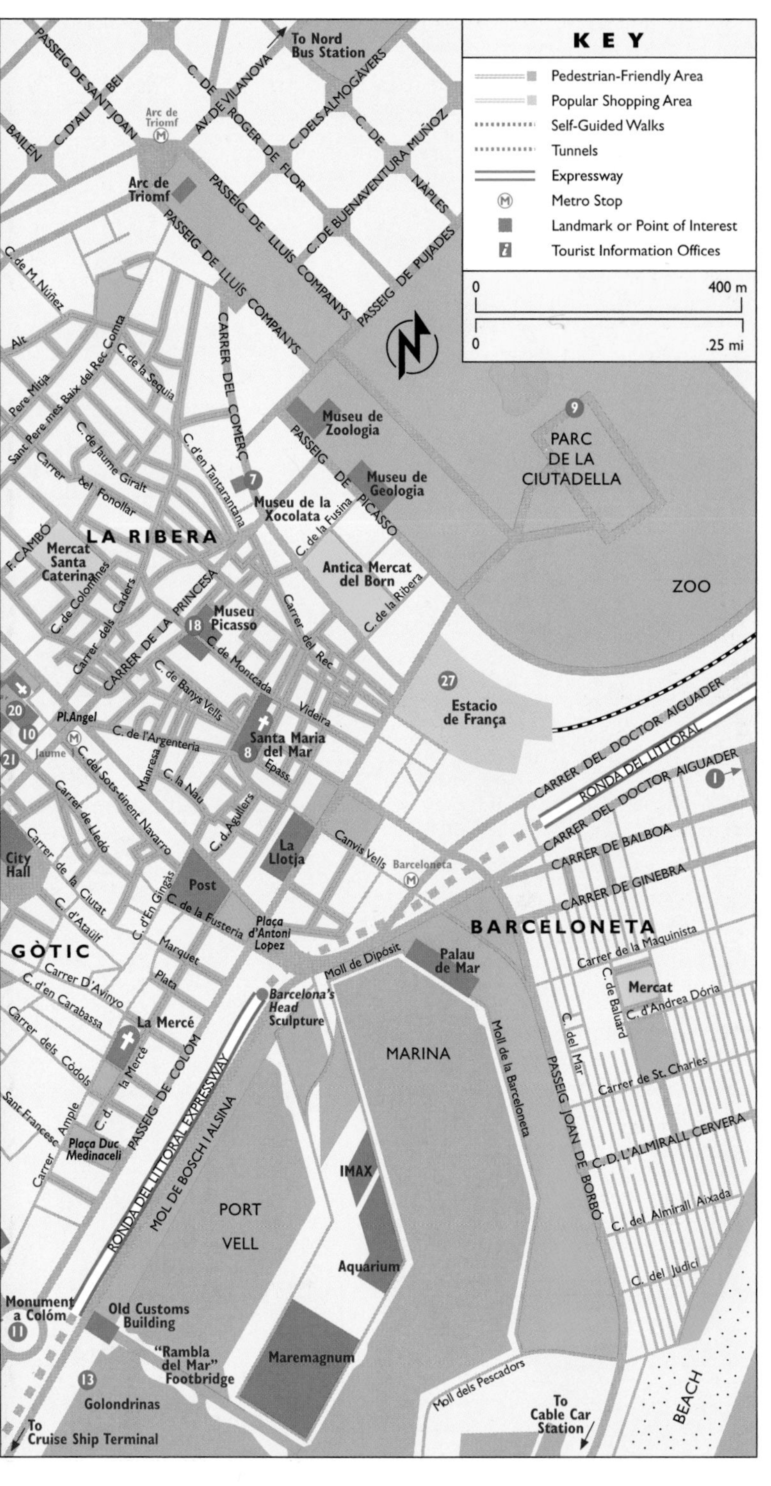
KEY
Pedestrian-Friendly Area
Popular Shopping Area
Self-Guided Walks
Tunnels
Expressway
Metro Stop
Landmark or Point of Interest
Tourist Information Offices
0
400 m
0
.25 mi
To Nord Bus Station
PASSEIG DE SANT JOAN
C. D'ALI BEI
BAILÉN
Arc de Triomf
Arc de Triomf
C. DE VILANOVA
AV. DE VILANOVA
C. DE ROGER DE FLOR
C. DELS ALMOGÀVERS
C. DE NÀPLES
C. DE BUENAVENTURA MUÑOZ
PASSEIG DE LLUÍS COMPANYS
PASSEIG DE LLUÍS COMPANYS
PASSEIG DE PUJADES
CARRER DEL COMERÇ
C. de M. Núñez
Alt
Pere Mitjà
Sant Pere mes Baix del Rec Comtal
C. de la Sequia
C. de Jaume Giralt
Carrer del Fonollar
C. d'en Tantarantana
Museu de Zoologia
Museu de Geologia
PASSEIG DE PICASSO
Museu de la Xocolata
C. de la Fusina
PARC DE LA CIUTADELLA
LA RIBERA
F. CAMBÓ
Mercat Santa Caterina
C. de Colomines
Carrer dels Caders
CARRER DE LA PRINCESA
Antica Mercat del Born
C. de la Ribera
ZOO
Museu Picasso
C. de Montcada
Carrer del Rec
C. de Banys Vells
Videira
Estacio de França
Pl.Angel
C. de l'Argenteria
Santa Maria del Mar
Jaume I
C. del Sots-tinent Navarro
Manresa
C. la Nau
Epass.
CARRER DEL DOCTOR AIGUADER
RONDA DEL LITORAL
CARRER DEL DOCTOR AIGUADER
CARRER DE BALBOA
Carrer de Lledó
City Hall
Carrer de la Ciutat
C. d.Agullers
La Llotja
Canvis Vells
Barceloneta
CARRER DE GINEBRA
Post
C. d'En Gingàs
C. de la Fusteria
C. d'Ataülf
Plaça d'Antoni Lopez
BARCELONETA
GÒTIC
Marquet
Moll de Diposit
Palau de Mar
Carrer de la Maquinista
Carrer D'Avinyo
Plata
C. de Balluard
Mercat
C. d'Andrea Dória
C. d'en Carabassa
Barcelona's Head Sculpture
La Mercé
C. del Mar
Carrer dels Còdols
C. d. la Mercé
PASSEIG DE COLÓM
MARINA
Moll de la Barceloneta
PASSEIG JOAN DE BORBÓ
Carrer de St. Charles
Sant Francesc
Ample
Carrer
Plaça Duc Medinaceli
RONDA DEL LITORAL EXPRESSWAY
MOL DE BOSCH I ALSINA
IMAX
C. D. L'ALMIRALL CERVERA
PORT VELL
C. del Almirall Aixada
Aquarium
C. del Judici
Monument a Colóm
Old Customs Building
"Rambla del Mar" Footbridge
Maremagnum
Moll dels Pescadors
To Cable Car Station
BEACH
Golondrinas
To Cruise Ship Terminal

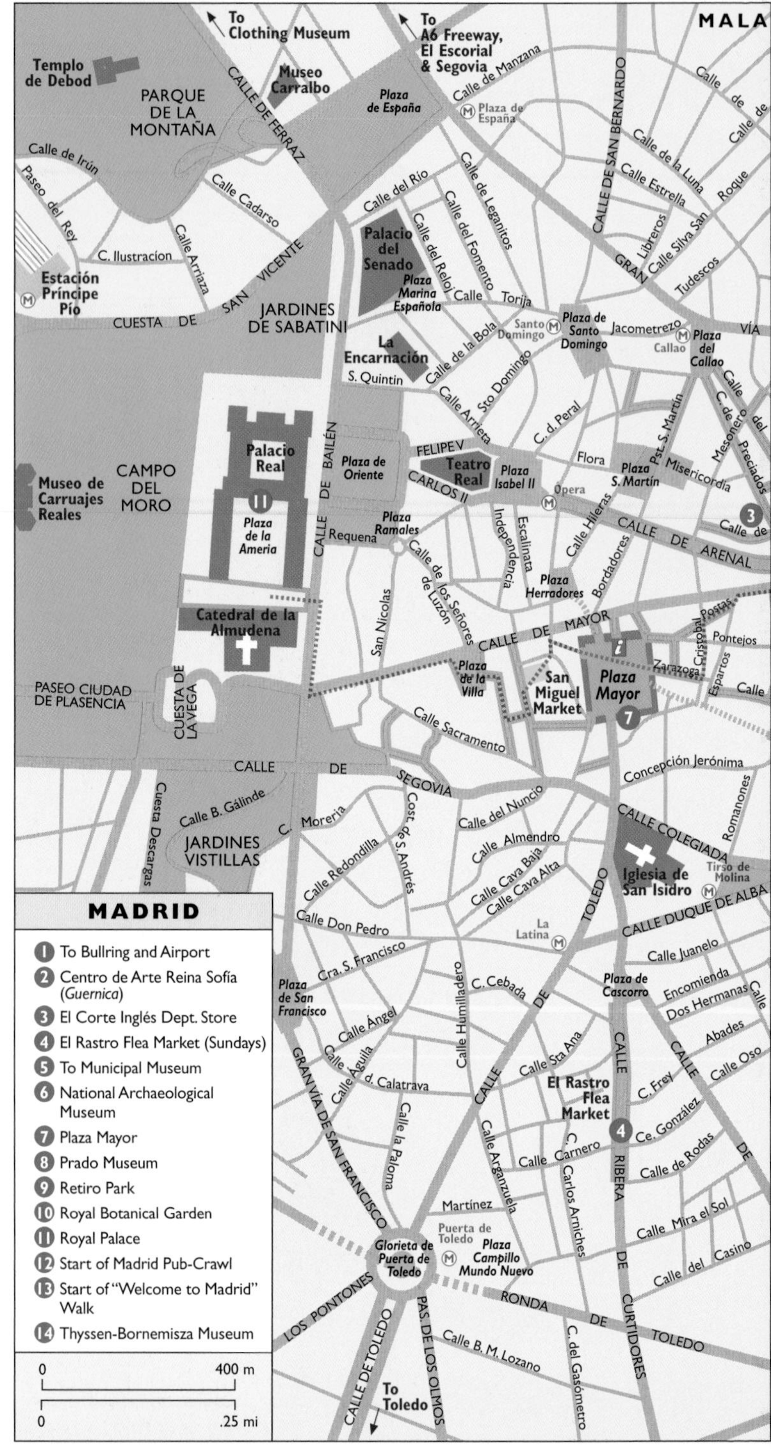

MADRID
1 To Bullring and Airport
2 Centro de Arte Reina Sofía (*Guernica*)
3 El Corte Inglés Dept. Store
4 El Rastro Flea Market (Sundays)
5 To Municipal Museum
6 National Archaeological Museum
7 Plaza Mayor
8 Prado Museum
9 Retiro Park
10 Royal Botanical Garden
11 Royal Palace
12 Start of Madrid Pub-Crawl
13 Start of "Welcome to Madrid" Walk
14 Thyssen-Bornemisza Museum
0 400 m
0 .25 mi
To Clothing Museum
To A6 Freeway, El Escorial & Segovia
To Toledo
Templo de Debod
Museo Carralbo
Parque de la Montaña
Plaza de España
Palacio del Senado
La Encarnación
Jardines de Sabatini
Estación Príncipe Pío
Palacio Real
Plaza de Oriente
Teatro Real
Plaza Isabel II
Campo del Moro
Museo de Carruajes Reales
Plaza de la Ameria
Catedral de la Almudena
Plaza Mayor
San Miguel Market
Plaza de la Villa
Plaza de Santo Domingo
Plaza del Callao
Plaza S. Martín
Plaza Herradores
Plaza Ramales
Jardines Vistillas
Iglesia de San Isidro
Plaza de San Francisco
Plaza de Cascorro
El Rastro Flea Market
Glorieta de Puerta de Toledo
Plaza Campillo Mundo Nuevo
Calle de Segovia
Calle de Mayor
Calle de Arenal
Calle de Bailén
Gran Vía
Calle de Toledo
Gran Vía de San Francisco
Ronda de Toledo
Calle Ribera de Curtidores
Calle Duque de Alba
Calle Colegiada
Cuesta de San Vicente
Calle de Ferraz
Calle de San Bernardo

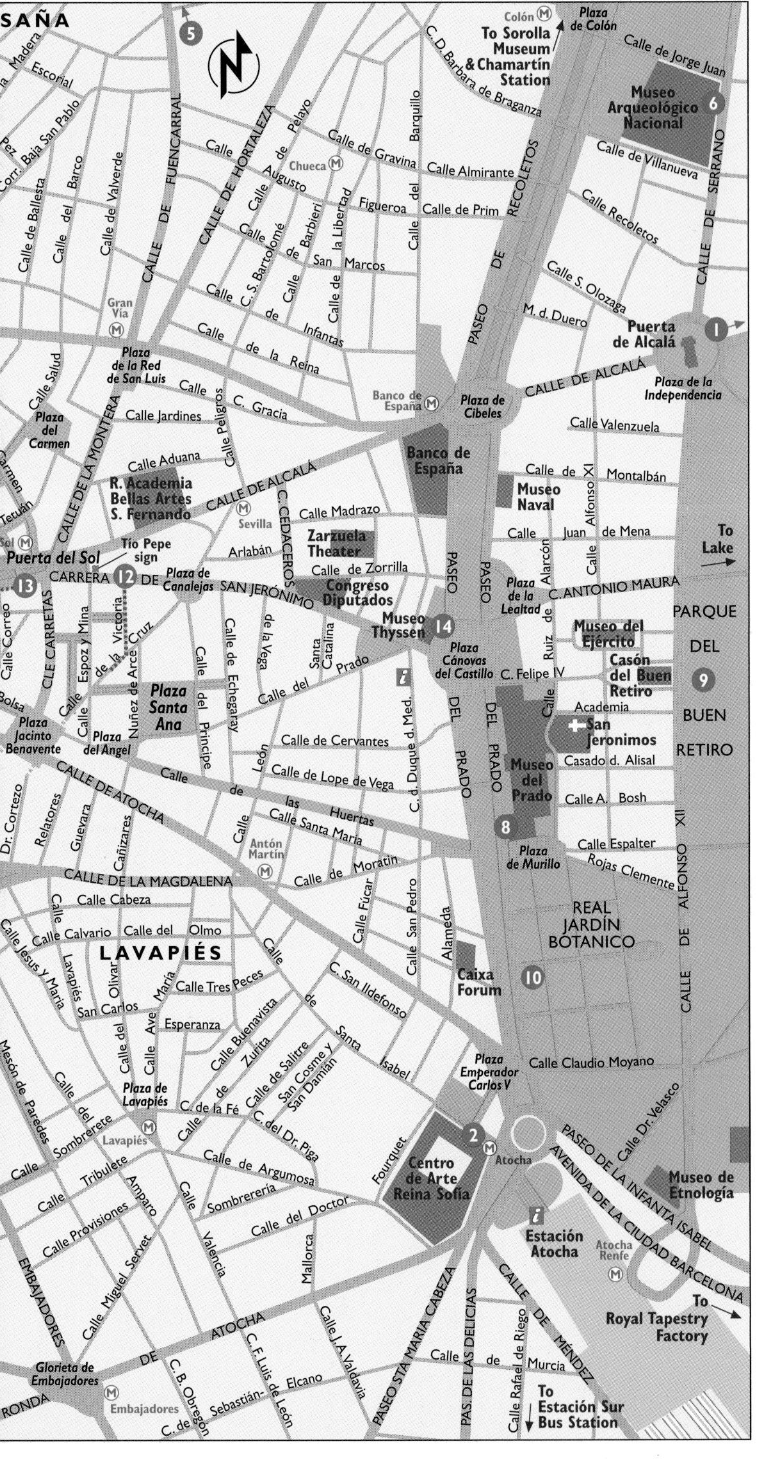

SAÑA
To Sorolla Museum & Chamartín Station
Plaza de Colón
Museo Arqueológico Nacional
Puerta de Alcalá
Plaza de la Independencia
Plaza de Cibeles
Banco de España
Museo Naval
R. Academia Bellas Artes S. Fernando
Zarzuela Theater
Congreso Diputados
Tío Pepe sign
Puerta del Sol
Plaza de Canalejas
Museo Thyssen
Plaza Cánovas del Castillo
Plaza de la Lealtad
Museo del Ejército
Casón del Buen Retiro
PARQUE DEL BUEN RETIRO
To Lake
San Jeronimos
Museo del Prado
Plaza Santa Ana
Plaza Jacinto Benavente
Plaza del Angel
Plaza de Murillo
REAL JARDÍN BOTANICO
LAVAPIÉS
Caixa Forum
Plaza Emperador Carlos V
Plaza de Lavapiés
Centro de Arte Reina Sofía
Estación Atocha
Museo de Etnología
To Royal Tapestry Factory
Glorieta de Embajadores
To Estación Sur Bus Station

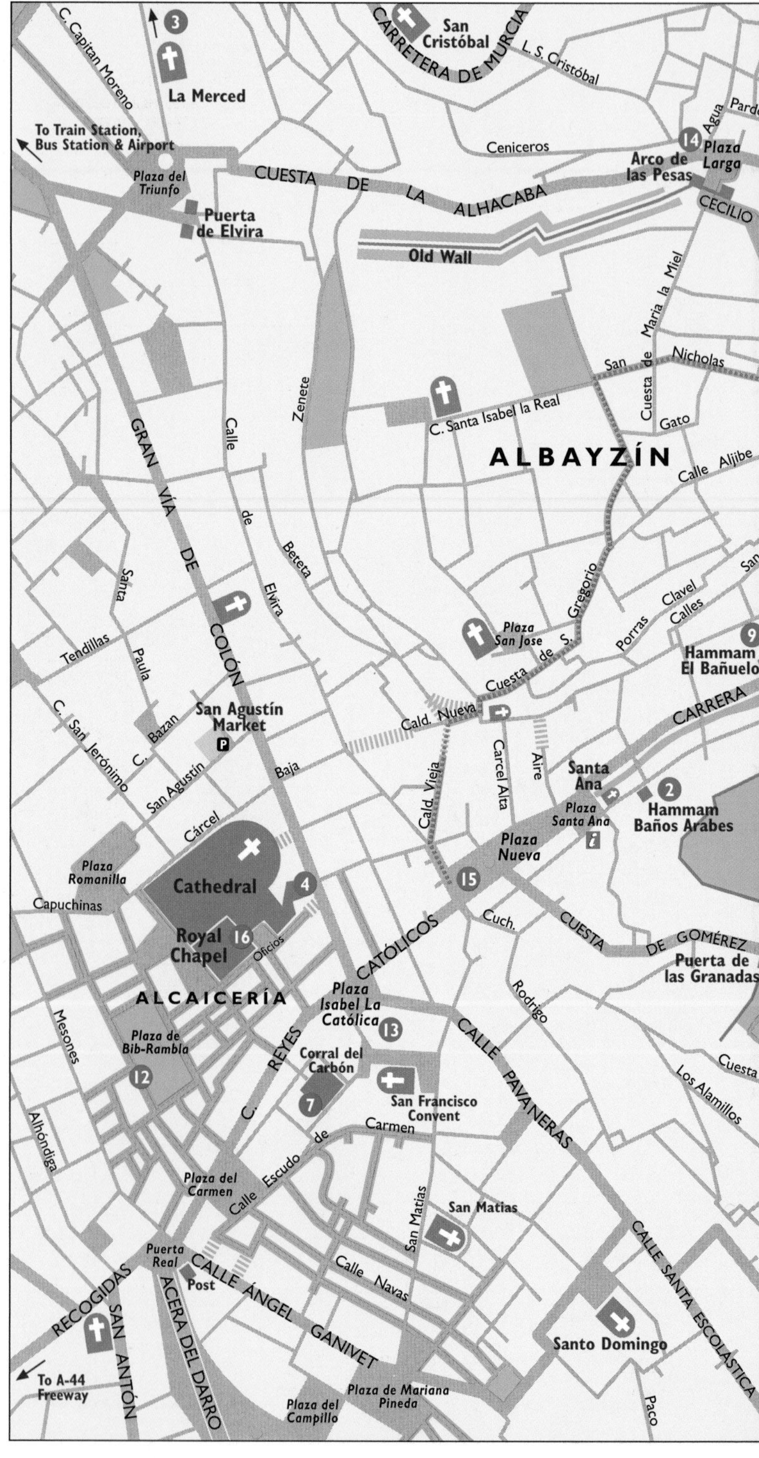

C. Capitan Moreno
La Merced
To Train Station, Bus Station & Airport
Plaza del Triunfo
Puerta de Elvira
CUESTA DE LA ALHACABA
Old Wall
San Cristóbal
CARRETERA DE MURCIA
L. S. Cristóbal
Ceniceros
Agua
Pardo
Plaza Larga
Arco de las Pesas
CECILIO
Cuesta de Maria la Miel
San Nicholas
Gato
C. Santa Isabel la Real
ALBAYZÍN
Calle Aljibe
Zenete
Calle de Elvira
Beteta
GRAN VÍA DE COLÓN
Santa Paula
Tendillas
C. San Jerónimo
Bazan
C.
San Agustín Market
San Agustín
Baja
Cárcel
Cald. Nueva
Cald. Vieja
Cuesta de S. Gregorio
Plaza San Jose
Porras
Clavel
Calles
San
Hammam El Bañuelo
CARRERA
Carcel Alta
Aire
Santa Ana
Plaza Santa Ana
Hammam Baños Arabes
Plaza Nueva
Plaza Romanilla
Cathedral
Capuchinas
Royal Chapel
Oficios
ALCAICERÍA
CATÓLICOS
Cuch.
CUESTA DE GOMÉREZ
Puerta de las Granadas
Rodrigo
Plaza Isabel La Católica
C. REYES
Mesones
Plaza de Bib-Rambla
Corral del Carbón
San Francisco Convent
CALLE PAVANERAS
Cuesta
Los Alamillos
Alhóndiga
Calle Escudo de Carmen
Plaza del Carmen
San Matias
Puerta Real
Post
CALLE ÁNGEL GANIVET
Calle Navas
CALLE SANTA ESCOLASTICA
Santo Domingo
RECOGIDAS
SAN ANTÓN
ACERA DEL DARRO
To A-44 Freeway
Plaza de Mariana Pineda
Plaza del Campillo
Paco

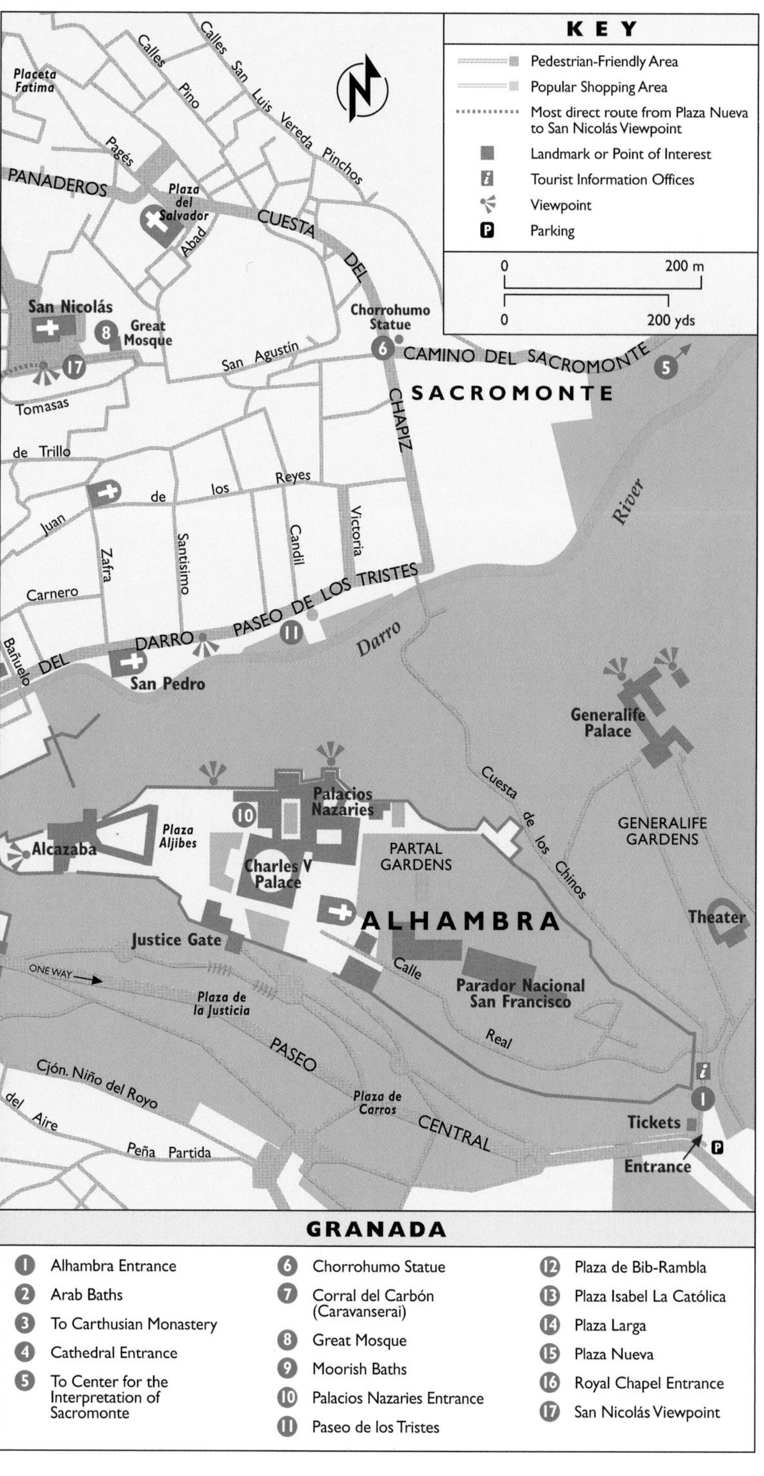

KEY
Pedestrian-Friendly Area
Popular Shopping Area
Most direct route from Plaza Nueva to San Nicolás Viewpoint
Landmark or Point of Interest
Tourist Information Offices
Viewpoint
Parking
0
200 m
0
200 yds
Placeta Fatima
Calles
Calles
Pino
San Luis
Vereda
Pinchos
Pagés
PANADEROS
Plaza del Salvador
Abad
CUESTA
DEL
CHAPIZ
San Nicolás
Great Mosque
Chorrohumo Statue
San Agustín
CAMINO DEL SACROMONTE
SACROMONTE
Tomasas
de Trillo
Reyes
de
los
Juan
Zafra
Santisimo
Candil
Victoria
River
Carnero
PASEO DE LOS TRISTES
DARRO
DEL
Bañuelo
Darro
San Pedro
Generalife Palace
Palacios Nazaries
Plaza Aljibes
Alcazaba
Charles V Palace
PARTAL GARDENS
Cuesta de los Chinos
GENERALIFE GARDENS
ALHAMBRA
Theater
Justice Gate
ONE WAY
Calle
Real
Parador Nacional San Francisco
Plaza de la Justicia
PASEO
CENTRAL
Plaza de Carros
Cjón. Niño del Royo
del Aire
Peña Partida
Tickets
Entrance
GRANADA
1 Alhambra Entrance
2 Arab Baths
3 To Carthusian Monastery
4 Cathedral Entrance
5 To Center for the Interpretation of Sacromonte
6 Chorrohumo Statue
7 Corral del Carbón (Caravanserai)
8 Great Mosque
9 Moorish Baths
10 Palacios Nazaries Entrance
11 Paseo de los Tristes
12 Plaza de Bib-Rambla
13 Plaza Isabel La Católica
14 Plaza Larga
15 Plaza Nueva
16 Royal Chapel Entrance
17 San Nicolás Viewpoint

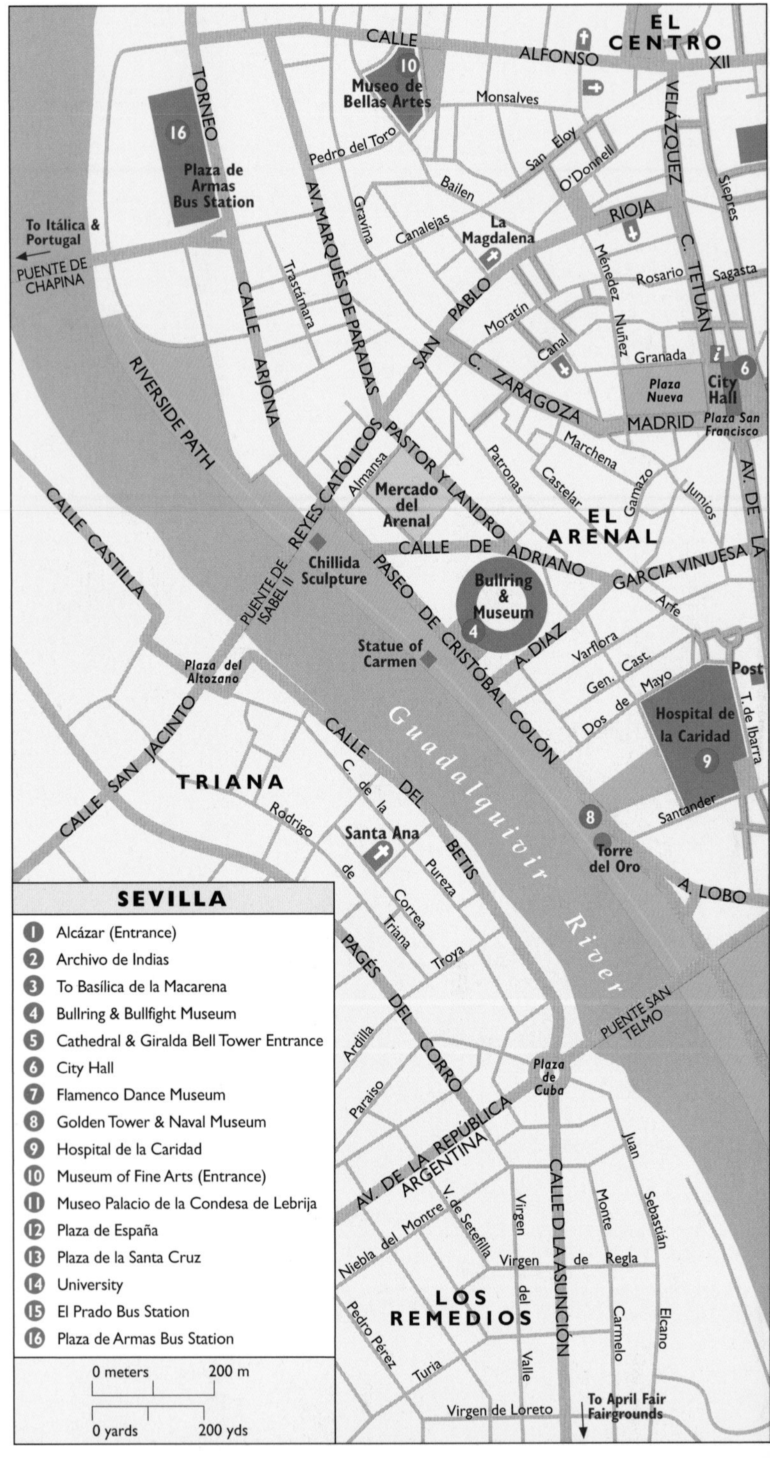

SEVILLA
1 Alcázar (Entrance)
2 Archivo de Indias
3 To Basílica de la Macarena
4 Bullring & Bullfight Museum
5 Cathedral & Giralda Bell Tower Entrance
6 City Hall
7 Flamenco Dance Museum
8 Golden Tower & Naval Museum
9 Hospital de la Caridad
10 Museum of Fine Arts (Entrance)
11 Museo Palacio de la Condesa de Lebrija
12 Plaza de España
13 Plaza de la Santa Cruz
14 University
15 El Prado Bus Station
16 Plaza de Armas Bus Station
0 meters
200 m
0 yards
200 yds
EL CENTRO
EL ARENAL
TRIANA
LOS REMEDIOS
Museo de Bellas Artes
Plaza de Armas Bus Station
To Itálica & Portugal
PUENTE DE CHAPINA
La Magdalena
Plaza Nueva
City Hall
Plaza San Francisco
Mercado del Arenal
Chillida Sculpture
Bullring & Museum
Statue of Carmen
Hospital de la Caridad
Post
Torre del Oro
Plaza del Altozano
Santa Ana
Plaza de Cuba
Guadalquivir River
To April Fair Fairgrounds
CALLE ALFONSO XII
TORNEO
Monsalves
Pedro del Toro
AV. MARQUÉS DE PARADAS
Gravína
Bailen
San Eloy
O'Donnell
VELÁZQUEZ
Siepres
RIOJA
Canalejas
C. TETUÁN
Sagasta
Rosario
Ménedez Nuñez
Trastámara
CALLE ARJONA
SAN PABLO
Moratín
Canal
Granada
C. ZARAGOZA
MADRID
RIVERSIDE PATH
REYES CATÓLICOS
PASTOR Y LANDRO
Almansa
Patronas
Marchena
Castelar
Gamazo
Jumios
AV. DE LA
CALLE DE ADRIANO
GARCIA VINUESA
Arfe
PUENTE DE ISABEL II
PASEO DE CRISTÓBAL COLÓN
A. DIAZ
Varflora
Gen. Cast.
Dos de Mayo
T. de Ibarra
Santander
A. LOBO
CALLE CASTILLA
CALLE SAN JACINTO
CALLE DEL BETIS
C. de la Pureza
Rodrigo de Triana
Correa
Troya
PAGÉS DEL CORRO
Ardilla
Paraíso
PUENTE SAN TELMO
AV. DE LA REPÚBLICA ARGENTINA
Niebla del Montre
V. de Setefilla
Virgen de Regla
Virgen del Valle
CALLE D LA ASUNCIÓN
Monte Carmelo
Juan Sebastián Elcano
Pedro Pérez
Turia
Virgen de Loreto

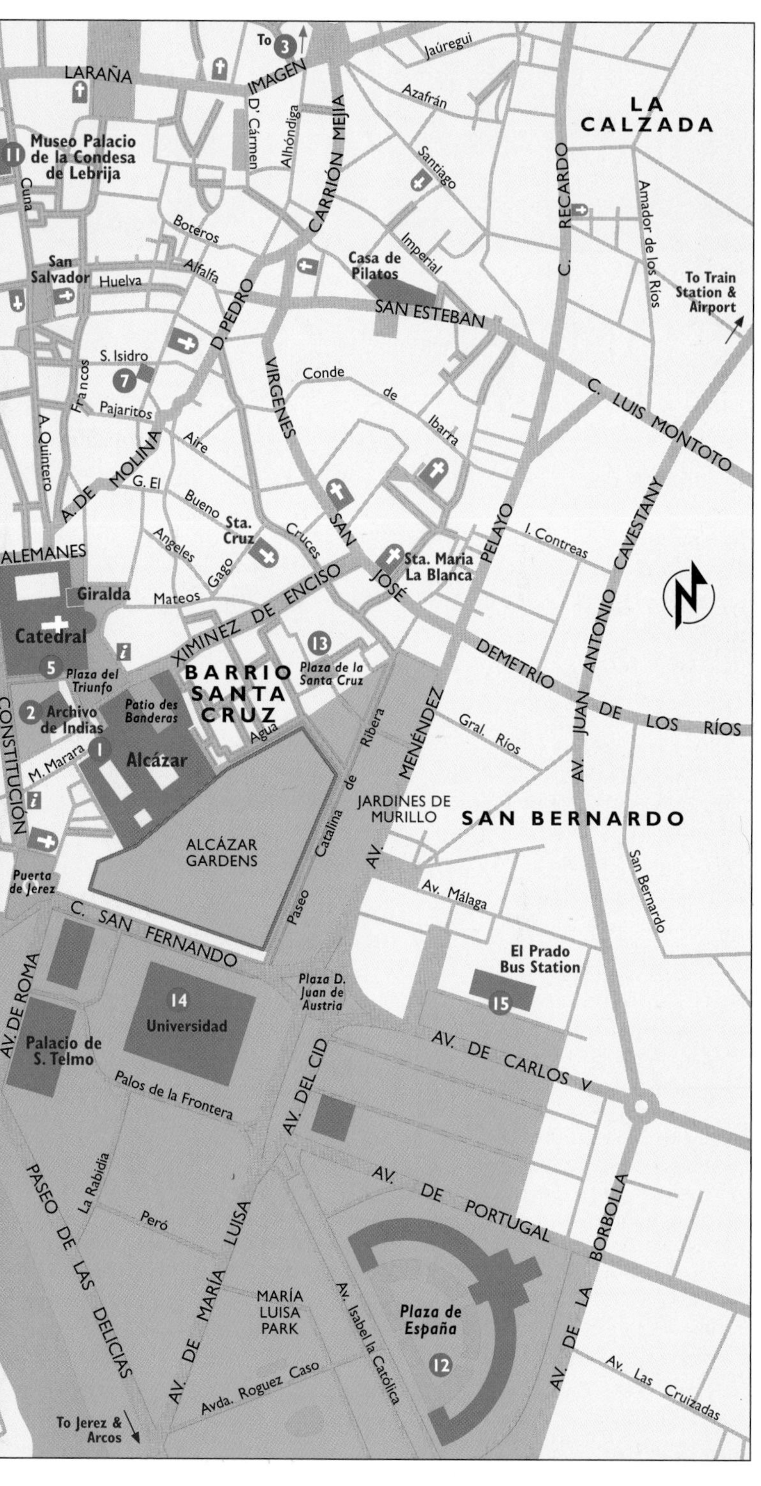

To 3
LARAÑA
IMAGEN
Jaúregui
Azafrán
LA CALZADA
Museo Palacio de la Condesa de Lebrija
11
D' Cármen
Alhóndiga
CARRIÓN MEJIA
Santiago
C. RECARDO
Amador de los Ríos
Cuna
Boteros
Imperial
San Salvador
Huelva
Alfalfa
Casa de Pilatos
To Train Station & Airport
D. PEDRO
SAN ESTEBAN
S. Isidro
7
Francos
VIRGENES
Conde de Ibarra
C. LUIS MONTOTO
Pajaritos
A. Quintero
Aire
A. DE MOLINA
G. El Bueno
Sta. Cruz
SAN JOSÉ
PELAYO
I. Contreas
JUAN ANTONIO CAVESTANY
Angeles
Cruces
ALEMANES
Gago
Sta. Maria La Blanca
Giralda
Mateos
XIMINEZ DE ENCISO
Catedral
DEMETRIO DE LOS RÍOS
5
Plaza del Triunfo
BARRIO SANTA CRUZ
13
Plaza de la Santa Cruz
CONSTITUCIÓN
2
Archivo de Indias
Patio des Banderas
Agua
MENÉNDEZ
Gral. Ríos
1
M. Marara
Alcázar
Paseo Catalina de Ribera
AV.
JARDINES DE MURILLO
SAN BERNARDO
ALCÁZAR GARDENS
Puerta de Jerez
Av. Málaga
San Bernardo
C. SAN FERNANDO
El Prado Bus Station
Plaza D. Juan de Austria
15
AV. DE ROMA
14
Universidad
AV. DE CARLOS V
Palacio de S. Telmo
Palos de la Frontera
AV. DEL CID
La Rabidia
AV. DE PORTUGAL
PASEO DE LAS DELICIAS
Peró
AV. DE MARÍA LUISA
MARÍA LUISA PARK
Av. Isabel la Católica
Plaza de España
12
AV. DE LA BORBOLLA
Avda. Roguez Caso
Av. Las Cruizadas
To Jerez & Arcos

CONTENTS

Spain

España

Like a grandpa bouncing a baby on his knee, Spain is a mix of old and new, modern and traditional. For the tourist, Spain means bullfights, massive cathedrals, world-class art, Muslim palaces, vibrant folk life, whitewashed villages, and bright sunshine. Yes, you'll find those things...but the country's special charm lies in its people and their unique lifestyle. Spain has a richness of history, of culture, and of people that has little to do with GDP. From the stirring *sardana* dance in Barcelona to the sizzling rat-a-tat-tat of flamenco in Sevilla, this country creates its own beat amid the heat.

Spain's diverse landscape and history (a blend of Roman, Muslim, and Christian) have forged a country with a wide variety of regions, languages, and customs. If you fly over Spain, you'll see that much of the country's center is a parched, red-orange desert. But Spain's topography resembles a giant upside-down bowl, with the high, flat, dry central plateau and a coastal lip. The north is mountainous and rainy; the south is hilly and hot. Ringing it all is 2,000 miles of coastline.

Spain's geography makes it less a centralized nation than a collection of distinct regions. In the central plain sits the urban island of Madrid, a region unto itself. Just south is Toledo, a medieval showpiece and melting-pot city with Christian,

Muslim, and Jewish roots. Farther south is Andalucía, a region formerly ruled by Muslims, now home to sleepy, sun-baked *pueblos blancos* (whitewashed hill towns). Spain's south coast, the Costa del Sol, is a palm-tree jungle of beach resorts, casinos, time-share condos, discos, and sunburned Brits on holiday. Along the Mediterranean coast (to the east), Spain has an almost Italian vibe, and Barcelona and Catalunya keep one eye cocked towards trends sailing in from the rest of Europe. Tourism is huge here. With 40 million inhabitants, Spain entertains 50 million visitors annually.

To the north is the Basque Country, which combines sparkling beaches, cutting-edge architecture, and proudly feisty locals. From here, gregarious modern-day pilgrims follow the Camino de Santiago westward across the parched north of Spain into mellow and lush Galicia, where moss-covered churches and tree-strewn rolling hillsides beckon. Beyond its contiguous lands, Spain clings to the last of its far-flung holdings: a few Mediterranean islands (including Menorca, Mallorca, and Ibiza), Ceuta in Morocco, and the distant Canary Islands.

"Castilian"—what we call "Spanish"—is spoken throughout the country. But Catalans (around Barcelona) speak their own Romance language, Catalan. The Galicians speak Galego. And in the far north, the Basques keep alive the ancient tongue of Euskara. A fringe group of separatist Basques (with their notorious and unpopular terrorist wing, ETA) has lobbied hard and sometimes violently for self-rule. But every region in Spain has its own dialect, customs, and (often half-hearted) separatist movement. Each region also hosts local festivals, whether parading Virgin Mary statues through the streets, running in front of a pack of furious bulls, or pelting each other with tomatoes. People think of themselves first and foremost as Basques, Catalans, Andalusians, Galicians, Leonese, and so on...and only second as Spaniards.

Spain is in Europe, but not *of* Europe—it has a unique identity and history, thanks largely to the Pyrenees Mountains that physically isolate it from the rest of the Continent. For more than 700 years (711–1492), Spain's dominant culture was Muslim, not Christian. And after a brief Golden Age financed by New World gold (1500–1600), Spain retreated into three centuries of isolation (1600–1900). Spain's seclusion contributed to the creation of unusual customs—bullfights, flamenco dancing, and a national obsession with ham. Even as other countries opened up to each other in the 20th century, the fascist dictator Francisco Franco virtually sealed off Spain from the rest of Europe's democracies. But since Franco's death in 1975, Spaniards have almost swung to the opposite extreme, becoming wide open to new trends and technologies. (For more on Spanish history, see page 643.)

Spaniards are proud and stoic. They can be hard to get to

Spain Almanac

Official Name: It's officially the Reino de España (Kingdom of Spain), but locals just call it España.

Population: 40.5 million. Most speak the official national language of Castilian, but 17 percent speak Catalan, 7 percent Galego, and 2 percent Euskara (the Basque language). The country is 94 percent Roman Catholic.

Latitude and Longitude: 40ºN and 4ºW (similar latitude to New York City).

Area: 195,000 square miles (15 percent bigger than California). This includes the Canary and Balearic Islands, and small enclaves in Morocco. Spain's long-standing claim to Gibraltar remains a nagging dispute with Britain.

Geography: The interior of Spain is a high, flat plateau (the Meseta Central), with hot, dry summers and harsh winters. Surrounding the plateau are mountains (including the Pyrenees in the north) and 2,000 miles of coastline.

***Agua Agua* Everywhere:** A leader in hydropower and irrigation, Spain, for its size, has more man-made lakes from dams (about 1,400) than any other country. Still, the average Spaniard uses one-third less energy than the average American. Spain's 1,800 rivers are mostly small, less than 50 miles long. The 600-mile Tajo River (a.k.a. Tagus in English, or Tejo in Portuguese) runs westward from Toledo through Portugal to the Atlantic. The Guadalquivir irrigates Andalucía and makes Sevilla an ocean-going port city.

Biggest Cities: Madrid (3.2 million; and at more than 2,000 feet in altitude, it's Europe's highest capital), Barcelona (1.6 million), Valencia (810,000), and Sevilla (700,000). Spaniards are urban dwellers—only one in five lives outside a metropolitan area.

Economy: The Gross Domestic Product is $1.4 trillion (about the same as the state of New York). The GDP per capita is $33,700 (New York's is $46,600). Major moneymakers include tourism, clothes, shoes, olives, wine, oranges, machine parts, and ships.

Government: Guided symbolically by King Juan Carlos I, Spain is a parliamentary monarchy. José Luis Rodríguez Zapatero is the left-of-center prime minister. Some of the 600-plus legislators (in two houses) are elected directly, some by regional bodies or political parties. The country is divided into 19 autonomous regions (e.g., Andalucía, Catalunya, Castile-La Mancha, and Madrid).

Flag: Spain's flag has three horizontal bands of red, yellow, and red. To the left of center is the coat of arms—a shield with a crown, framed by the Pillars of Hercules that symbolically flank the Straits of Gibraltar.

Soccer: The two perennial powerhouses in "la Liga" (the League) are Real Madrid and FC Barcelona.

The Average José: The average Spaniard is 40 years old, will live to age 79, and resides in a home with one car and one TV. Almost half of Spaniards use the Internet, and one in 10 owns a cat. The average Spaniard has one mobile phone, 1.3 kids, and sleeps 40 minutes less every night than the typical European.

know—but once you've made that connection, you've got a friend for life. The Spanish people have long had a reputation as thrifty, straightforward, and unpretentious. Traditionally, their lives revolved around the Catholic Church and the family. Young adults tended to live at home until they got married—even into their late 20s. Spaniards prided themselves on their nonmaterialistic values, owning just one car and one TV, and living in small urban apartments instead of giant suburban houses. The notorious "machismo" culture of domineering men ruled.

But Spain's old ways have changed very quickly in the nearly three and a half decades since Franco. While the vast majority of Spaniards are still nominally Catholic, the country is at the forefront of liberal reforms in abortion and gay marriage. Spain's extreme religiosity has been replaced by an extreme secularism. The old hierarchy of aristocrats, peasants, priests, and old ladies in black has become democratic and hang-loose. The allure of consumerism, status symbols, and easy credit means that many Spanish people now save (or borrow) for high-fashion clothes, second cars, and summer chalets. And yet, in spite of its recent economic boom, Spain remains affordable for visitors.

Even as the country plunges into the 21st century, some things never change. Daily lives focus on friends and family, as they always have.

Many people (especially in rural areas) still follow the siesta schedule, which emphasizes a big midday meal with the family. Spaniards tend to have a small, quick breakfast, grab a late-morning sandwich to tide them over, then gather with friends and family for the siesta. From around 1:00 to 4:00 p.m., many businesses close as people go home for lunch, to socialize, and maybe to grab a quick nap. The siesta is not so much a time to sleep as it is the opportunity for everyone to shut down their harried public life, and enjoy good food and the comfort of loved ones.

In the cool of the evening, Spain comes back to life. Whole families pour out of their apartments to stroll through the streets and greet their neighbors—a custom called the paseo. Even the biggest city feels like a rural village. People stop into bars for a drink or to watch a big soccer match on TV. They might order a bite to eat, enjoying appetizers called tapas. Around 22:00 (10:00 p.m.) in the heat of summer, it's finally time for a light dinner. Afterwards, even families with young children might continue their paseo or attend a concert. Spaniards are notorious night owls. Many clubs and restaurants don't even open until after midnight. Dance clubs routinely stay open until the sun rises, and young people stumble out bleary-eyed and head for work. The antidote for late nights? The next day's siesta.

Spanish food is hearty and unrefined. Remember that Spain is not Mexico—you'll find no tacos, Tabasco, or tequila. (Even things that sound Mexican can be very different—for example, a *tortilla* is an omelet.) Major meals feature meat (such as roast suckling pig) or seafood. Popular regional foods are gazpacho (cold tomato soup) and paella (seafood and meat cooked with saffron-flavored rice). Spaniards snack between meals on tapas. Most bars offer a variety of these appetizers served hot or cold. A few small plates of olives, chorizo (sausage), grilled shrimp, Russian salad, or deep-fried nuggets can add up to a multi-course meal.

The most treasured delicacy in Spain is *jamón*—cured ham that is sliced thin and served cold. Bars proudly hang pigs' legs on their walls as part of the decor. Like connoisseurs of fine wine, Spaniards debate the merits of different breeds of pigs, what part of the pig they're eating, what the pig has eaten, and the quality of curing.

Drinking is part of the Spanish meal, and part of the social ritual. Spain produces large quantities of wine, especially their spicy red Rioja, made from the *tempranillo* grape. (For more on Spanish drinks, see page 25.)

For a country its size, Spain has produced an astonishing number of talented artists with distinctive styles—from El Greco's mystical religiosity to the sober realism of Diego Velázquez. (Madrid's Prado Museum is a veritable showcase of European Renaissance art, bought with the spoils from

the New World.) Francisco Goya painted the Golden Age in decline. In the 20th century, Pablo Picasso shattered the art world, then pasted it back together by inventing Cubism. Later, he painted *Guernica,* an epic snapshot of Spain's horrific Civil War. It's one of the most powerful antiwar paintings ever created (now displayed in Madrid). Salvador Dalí created a surreal juxtaposition of old and new, while his fellow Catalan Joan Miró picked up the Surrealist baton and ran with it. Spain carries on this rich tradition today, with a thriving contemporary arts scene.

In music, Spain continues its long tradition of great guitarists—classical, flamenco, and Gipsy Kings–style "new flamenco." In dance, you'll find the fiery flamenco (from Andalucía) and the stately do-si-do of the *sardana* (from Catalunya). Contemporary film includes works by the director Pedro Almodóvar, who explores changing family and social roles as Spain moves from its conservative past to its wide-open future. And there's one contemporary Spaniard whose works will be known and appreciated for generations to come: Santiago Calatrava, an architect who designs buildings and bridges for the 21st century.

While you can see some European countries by just passing through, Spain is a destination. Learn its history and accept it on its own terms. Gain (or just fake) an appreciation for cured ham, dry sherry, and bull's-tail soup, and the Spaniards will love you for it. If you go, go all the way. Immerse yourself in Spain.

INTRODUCTION

This book gives you all the information and opinions necessary to wring the maximum value out of your limited time and money. If you plan a month or less in Spain, this book is all you need.

Experiencing Spain's culture, people, and natural wonders economically and hassle-free has been my goal for three decades of traveling, tour guiding, and writing. With this book, I pass on to you the lessons I've learned, updated for 2009.

Rick Steves' Spain 2009 is a tour guide in your pocket, with a balanced, comfortable mix of exciting cities and cozy towns, topped off with an exotic dollop of Morocco. It covers the predictable biggies and stirs in a healthy dose of "Back Door" intimacy. Along with seeing a bullfight, the Prado, and flamenco, you'll greet pilgrims at Santiago de Compostela, visit a bull bar in Madrid, and buy cookies from cloistered nuns in a sun-parched Andalusian town. I've been selective, including only the most exciting sights and experiences. Rather than listing Spain's countless whitewashed Andalusian hill towns, I recommend the top stops: Arcos de la Frontera and Ronda.

The best is, of course, only my opinion. But after spending half of my adult life researching Europe, I've developed a sixth sense for what travelers enjoy.

About This Book

This book is organized by destination. Each destination is covered as a mini-vacation on its own, filled with exciting sights and homey, affordable places to stay. In the following chapters, you'll find these sections:

Top Destinations in Spain

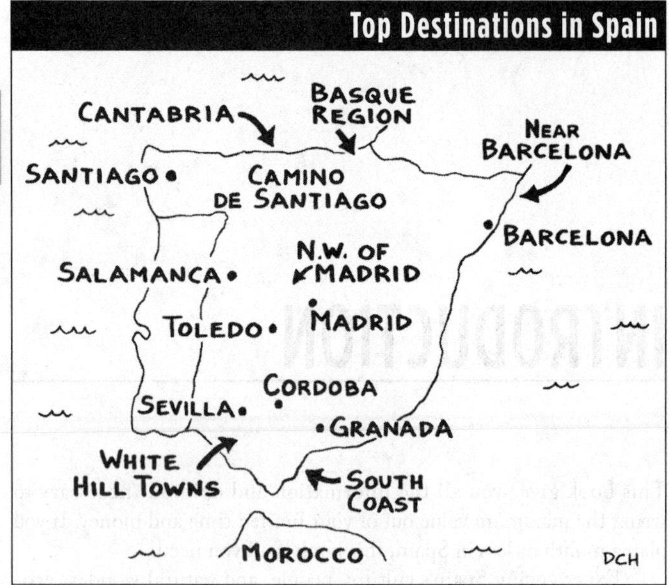

Planning Your Time suggests a schedule with thoughts on how to best use your limited time.

Orientation includes tourist information, tips on public transportation, local tour options, helpful hints, and easy-to-read maps designed to make the text clear and your arrival smooth.

Sights, described in detail, are rated:

▲▲▲—Don't miss;
▲▲—Try hard to see;
▲—Worthwhile if you can make it;
No rating—Worth knowing about.

Self-Guided Walks take you through interesting neighborhoods, with a personal tour guide in hand.

Sleeping describes my favorite hotels, from budget deals to cushy splurges.

Eating serves up good-value restaurants, ranging from inexpensive take-out joints to fancier options.

Transportation Connections outlines your options for traveling to destinations by bus and train. In car-friendly regions, I've included route tips for drivers.

History and Culture gives you a quick overview of Spanish history, art, architecture, and the tradition of bullfighting.

The **appendix** is a traveler's tool kit, with a handy packing checklist, recommended books and films, instructions on how to use the telephone, and useful phone numbers. You'll find detailed information on trains and driving, along with a climate chart, festival list, hotel reservation form, and Spanish survival phrases.

Browse through this book, choose your favorite destinations, and link them up. Then have a *maravilloso* trip! Traveling like a temporary local, you'll get the absolute most out of every mile, minute, and euro. As you visit places I know and love, I'm happy you'll be meeting my favorite Spanish people.

PLANNING

Trip Costs

Five components make up your trip cost: airfare, surface transportation, room and board, sightseeing and entertainment, and shopping and miscellany.

Airfare: A basic round-trip flight from the US to Barcelona or Madrid should cost \$900 to \$1,600, depending on where you fly from and when you go. Smaller budget airlines provide bargain service from several European capitals to many cities in Spain (see "Cheap Flights" on page 677 for details). Always consider saving time and money in Europe by flying "open jaw" (into one city and out of another; e.g., into Barcelona and out of Santiago de Compostela, or Lisbon, Portugal).

Surface Transportation: For a three-week whirlwind trip of all my recommended destinations, allow \$550 per person for second-class trains and buses (\$750 for first-class trains). For a three-week car rental, tolls, gas, and insurance, allow \$875 per person (based on two people sharing). Car rental or leases are cheapest if arranged from the US. Train passes are normally available only outside of Europe. You may save money by simply buying tickets as you go (see "Transportation," page 667, for more details on car rental, rail trips, and bus travel).

Room and Board: You can thrive in Spain on \$90 a day per person for room and board. This allows \$10 for lunch, \$20 for dinner, and \$60 for lodging (based on two people splitting the cost of a \$120 double room that includes breakfast). That's doable. If you've got more money, I've listed great ways to spend it. Students and tightwads do it on \$30 a day (\$15 per hostel bed, \$15 for meals and snacks).

Sightseeing and Entertainment: In big cities, figure about \$14 per major sight (Barcelona's Picasso Museum, Madrid's Prado), \$4 for minor ones (climbing church towers), and about \$30–45 for splurge experiences (flamenco, bullfights). An overall average of \$15 a day works for most. Don't skimp here. After all, this category is the driving force behind your trip—you came to sightsee, enjoy, and experience Spain.

Shopping and Miscellany: Figure roughly \$2 per coffee, beer, ice-cream cone, and postcard. Shopping can vary in cost from nearly nothing to a small fortune. Good budget travelers find that this category has little to do with assembling a trip full of lifelong and wonderful memories.

Whirlwind Three-Week Trip of Spain

Day	Plan	Sleep in
1	Arrive in Barcelona	Barcelona
2	Barcelona	Barcelona
3	AVE train to Madrid	Madrid
4	Madrid	Madrid
5	Day trip to El Escorial/Valley of Fallen	Madrid
6	Toledo	Toledo
7	AVE train to Sevilla	Sevilla
8	Sevilla	Sevilla
9	To Arcos	Arcos
10	To Tarifa	Tarifa
11	Day trip to Morocco	Tarifa
12	To Nerja via Gibraltar	Nerja
13	To Granada	Granada
14	Granada	Granada
15	To Segovia	Segovia
16	To Salamanca via Ávila	Salamanca
17	Salamanca	Salamanca
18	To Santiago	Santiago
19	Santiago	Santiago
20	To Cantabria	Santillana or Comillas
21	To San Sebastián via Bilbao	San Sebastián
22	San Sebastián	San Sebastián

This itinerary is designed to be done by public transportation, but can be done by car with a few variations. Spain's long distances make the option of flying for at least a portion of the trip worth considering. If you rent a car, it's best for the White Hill Towns (southern Spain), El Escorial/Valley of the Fallen (northwest of Madrid), and Cantabria (northern Spain), where sparse public transportation limits the efficiency of your sightseeing. To mix car and train transportation, consider getting a Spain Rail & Drive pass.

If you're a fan of Salvador Dalí's art, or if you want to make a pilgrimage to the holy site of Montserrat, allot an extra day for Barcelona for day trips. If you want more Moorish sights, stay another day in Sevilla to make a side-trip to Córdoba (45 min on AVE high-speed train). If you're not interested in day-tripping to Tangier, Morocco, you could skip Tarifa and go to Ronda instead. To allow time to explore Gibraltar, add an extra day between Tarifa (or Ronda) and Nerja. If you're exploring the Camino de

Santiago by car, consider reversing the above itinerary to start in San Sebastián, and figure on adding several days to a week to your trip.

The suggested itinerary assumes you'll fly "open jaw" into Barcelona and out of San Sebastián. If you're returning to Barcelona or Madrid from San Sebastián, it's roughly an eight-hour train ride (night train possible) or a one-hour flight. Or you can cross into France and take the six-hour TGV train to Paris for more adventures!

Two-Week Itineraries: You can end the three-week route (described above) a week early by returning to Madrid from Salamanca and saving northern Spain for another trip.

Here's another alternative, which could include a few car days in southern Spain near the end of your trip: Start in Barcelona (stay two days); train to Madrid (stay five days total, with two days in Madrid and three for side-trips to Toledo, El Escorial, and Segovia or Ávila); train to Granada (two days); bus to Nerja (one day, could rent car here); both Ronda and Arcos for drivers, or just Ronda by train (two days); to Sevilla (drop off car, two days); and then train to Madrid and fly home.

Sightseeing Priorities

Depending on the length of your trip, here are my recommended priorities:

3 days: Madrid and Toledo
6 days, add: Sevilla, Granada
10 days, add: Barcelona, Andalucía (White Hill Towns)
13 days, add: Costa del Sol, Morocco
15 days, add: Salamanca, Segovia
17 days, add: Santiago de Compostela
21 days, add: Basque Region (San Sebastián and Bilbao), Cantabria (northern Spain)
25 days, add: Camino de Santiago (by car)

This includes nearly everything on the map on page 5.

When to Go

Spring and fall offer the best combination of good weather, light crowds, long days, and plenty of tourist and cultural activities.

July and August are the most crowded and expensive in the coastal areas, and less crowded but uncomfortably hot and dusty in the interior. Air-conditioning is worth the splurge. During these steamy months, lunch breaks can be long, especially in Andalucía.

Off-season, roughly November through March, expect sights to have shorter hours, lunchtime breaks, and fewer activities. Confirm your sightseeing plans locally, especially when traveling off-season.

For weather specifics, see the climate chart on page 680 of the appendix.

Travel Smart

Your trip to Spain is like a complex play—easier to follow and really appreciated on second viewing. While no one does the same trip twice to gain that advantage, reading this book in its entirety before your trip accomplishes much the same thing.

Design an itinerary that enables you to visit museums and festivals (see page 678) on the right days. Note the days when sights are closed. Saturdays are virtually weekdays, with earlier closing hours. Sundays have similar pros and cons as they do for travelers in the US: Special events and weekly markets pop up, sightseeing attractions are generally open, banks and some shops are closed, public transportation options are fewer, and there's no rush hour. Rowdy evenings are rare on Sundays.

Be sure to mix intense and relaxed periods in your itinerary. To maximize rootedness, minimize one-night stands. Every trip (and every traveler) needs at least a few slack days. Pace yourself. Assume you will return.

Reread this book as you travel, and visit local tourist information offices. Upon arrival in a new town, lay the groundwork for a smooth departure; write down the schedule for the train or bus you'll take

Major Holidays and Weekends

Popular places are even busier on weekends...and inundated on three-day weekends, when hotels, trains, and buses can get booked up before, during, and after the actual holiday. Plan ahead and reserve your accommodations and transportation (particularly for AVE trains) well in advance. Note that religious holidays are big in Spain.

In 2009, be prepared for big crowds during these holiday periods: Holy Week and Easter weekend (April 5–12); April Fair in Sevilla (April 28–May 3); the San Isidro festival in Madrid (May 15); Labor Day and Ascension weekend (May 1–4); Pentecost weekend (May 30–June 1); Assumption weekend (Aug 15–17); Spain National Day (Oct 12); Constitution Day, followed closely by the Feast of the Immaculate Conception, plus the weekend (Dec 6-9); and the winter holidays (Dec 20–Jan 6). Look out for local holidays that fall on a Tuesday or Thursday—the Spanish will often make it into a *puente*, meaning they'll take Monday or Friday off as well to have a four-day weekend.

For a list of festivals, see page 678 of the appendix.

when you depart. Use taxis in the big cities, bring along a water bottle, and linger in the shade.

Plan ahead for laundry, picnics, and Internet stops. Get online at Internet cafés or at your hotel to research transportation connections, confirm events, check the weather, and get directions to your next destination. Buy a phone card and use it for reservations, reconfirmations, and double-checking hours.

Connect with the culture. Set up your own quest for the best main square, paella, cloister, tapas bar, or whatever. Enjoy the friendliness of the Spanish people. Slow down and ask questions—most locals are eager to point you in their idea of the right direction. Keep a notepad in your pocket for organizing your thoughts. Wear your money belt, and learn the local currency and how to estimate prices in dollars. Those who expect to travel smart, do.

PRACTICALITIES

Red Tape: You need a passport—but no visa or shots—to travel in Spain or Morocco. You may be denied entry into certain countries if your passport is due to expire within six months of your ticketed date

Know Before You Go

Your trip is more likely to go smoothly if you plan ahead.

Be sure that your **passport** is valid at least six months after your ticketed date of return to the US. If you need to get or renew a passport, it can take up to two months (for more on passports, see www.travel.state.gov).

Book your rooms well in advance if you'll be traveling during any major **holidays** (see "Major Holidays and Weekends," page 7).

Call your **debit and credit card companies** to let them know the countries you'll be visiting, so that they'll accept (and not deny) your international charges. Confirm your daily withdrawal limit; consider asking to have it raised so you can take out more cash at each ATM stop. Ask about international transaction fees.

If you're taking an **overnight train,** especially to international destinations and you need a sleeping berth *(litera)*—and you must leave on a certain day—consider booking it well in advance, even though it may cost more. All high-speed trains in Spain require a seat reservation, but it's usually possible to make arrangements in Spain just a few days ahead unless it's a holiday weekend. (For more on train travel, see page 668.)

If you're planning on **renting a car** in Spain, you'll need an International Driver's Permit (IDP), available at your local AAA office ($15 plus two passport photos; www.aaa.com).

Since **airline carry-on restrictions** are always changing, visit the Transportation Security Administration's website (www.tsa.gov/travelers) for an up-to-date list of what you can bring on the plane with you...and what you have to check. Remember to arrive with plenty of time to get through security.

Reservations for Sights: If you'll be visiting Granada's Alhambra, consider making ticket reservations in advance. You can make reservations upon arrival in Spain (ideally before you reach Granada), but I mention it here for those who like to nail things down before they leave home. For more information, see page 430 of the Granada chapter. You'll also need reservations to visit the Salvador Dalí house near Cadaqués (see page 107).

of return. Get it renewed if you'll be cutting it close. Pack a photocopy of your passport in your luggage in case the original is lost or stolen.

Time: In Spain—and in this book—you'll use the 24-hour clock. It's the same through 12:00 noon, then keep going: 13:00, 14:00, and so on. For anything over 12, subtract 12 and add p.m. (14:00 is 2:00 p.m.).

Spain, like most of continental Europe, is generally six/nine hours ahead of the East/West Coasts of the US. The exceptions are the beginning and end of Daylight Saving Time: Europe "springs forward" the last Sunday in March (two weeks after most of the US), and "falls back" the last Sunday in October (one week before the US). Moroccan time can run up to two hours earlier than Spanish time. For a handy online time converter, try www.timeanddate.com/worldclock.

Business Hours: For visitors, Spain is a land of strange and frustrating schedules. Many businesses respect the afternoon siesta. When it's 100 degrees in the shade, you'll understand why.

The biggest museums stay open all day. Smaller ones often close for a siesta. Shops are generally open from 9:00 to 13:00 and from 16:00 to 20:00, longer in touristy places. Small shops are often open on Saturday only in the morning, and are closed all day Sunday. Banks are generally open Monday through Friday from 9:00 to 14:00.

Watt's Up? Europe's electrical system is different from North America's in two ways: the shape of the plug (two round prongs) and the voltage of the current (220 volts instead of 110 volts). For your North American plug to work in Europe, you'll need an adapter, sold inexpensively at travel stores in the US. As for the voltage, most newer electronics or travel appliances (such as hair dryers, laptops, and battery chargers) automatically convert the voltage—if you see a range of voltages printed on the item or its plug (such as "110–220"), it'll work in Europe. Otherwise, you can buy a converter separately in the US (about $20).

News: Americans keep in touch via the *International Herald Tribune* (published almost daily via satellite throughout Europe). Every Tuesday, the European editions of *Time* and *Newsweek* hit the stands with articles of particular interest to European travelers. Sports addicts can get their daily fix online or from *USA Today.* Good websites include www.iht.com, www.europeantimes.com and http://news.bbc.co.uk.

Theft Alert: Thieves target tourists throughout Spain, especially in Barcelona, Madrid, Granada, and Sevilla. While hotel rooms are generally safe, thieves break into cars, snatch purses, and pick pockets. Thieves zipping by on motorbikes grab handbags from pedestrians or even from cars in traffic (by reaching through open car windows at stoplights). A fight or commotion is created to enable pickpockets to work unnoticed. Be on guard, use a money belt, and treat any disturbance around you as a smoke screen for theft. Don't believe any "police officers" looking for counterfeit bills. Drivers should read the tips on page 676. When traveling by train, keep your luggage in sight and get a *litera* (berth in an attendant-monitored sleeping car) for safety on overnight trips.

Just the FAQs, Please

Whom do I call in case of emergency?
In Spain, dial 091 for police help and 112 in a medical emergency. In Morocco, dial 19 for police.

What if my credit card is stolen?
Act immediately. See "Damage Control for Lost Cards," page 12, for instructions.

How do I make a phone call to, within, and from Europe?
For detailed dialing instructions, refer to page 663.

How can I get tourist information about my destination?
Spain has a national tourist information office in the US, as well as a network of local offices (see page 655 for specifics on both). Note that Tourist Information is abbreviated **TI** in this book.

What's the best way to pack?
Light. For a recommended packing list, see page 682.

Does Rick have other materials that will help me?
For more on Rick's guidebooks, public television series, free audio tours, public radio show, guided tours, travel bags, accessories, and railpasses, see page 656.

Are there any updates to this guidebook?
Check www.ricksteves.com/update for changes to the most recent edition of this book.

Can you recommend any good books or movies for my trip?
For suggestions, see pages 659–661.

MONEY

Cash from ATMs

Throughout Europe, cash machines (ATMs) are the standard way for travelers to get local currency. Travelers checks are a waste of time (long waits at slow banks) and a waste of money (in fees).

Bring plastic—credit and/or debit cards—along with several hundred dollars in hard cash as an emergency backup. It's smart to bring two cards, in case one gets demagnetized or eaten by a temperamental machine.

To use a cash machine (called a *cajero automático*) to withdraw money from your account, you'll need a debit card (ideally with a Visa or MasterCard logo for maximum usability), plus a PIN code. Know your PIN code in numbers; there are only numbers—no letters—on European keypads.

Do I need to speak some Spanish?
Many Spanish people—especially those in the tourist trade, and in big cities—speak English. Still, many people don't, and you'll get better treatment if you learn and use Spanish pleasantries. For a list of survival phrases, see page 685.

Do you have information on driving, train travel, and flights?
See "Transportation," on page 667.

How much do I tip?
Relatively little. For tips on tipping, see page 13.

Will I get a student or senior discount?
Not likely. Discounts for sights are not listed in this book because they are generally limited to European residents and countries that offer reciprocal deals (the US does not).

How can I get a VAT refund on major purchases?
See the details on page 13.

How do I calculate metric amounts?
Europe uses the metric system. A liter is about a quart, four to a gallon. A kilometer is six-tenths of a mile. I figure kilometers to miles by cutting them in half and adding back 10 percent of the original (120 km: 60 + 12 = 72 miles, 300 km: 150 + 30 = 180 miles). For more metric conversions, see page 680.

Before you go, verify with your bank that your card will work overseas, and alert them that you'll be making withdrawals in Europe; otherwise, the bank may not approve transactions if it perceives unusual spending patterns.

Try to take out large sums of money to reduce your per-transaction bank fees. If the machine refuses your request, try again and select a smaller amount (some cash machines won't let you take out more than about €150—don't take it personally) or try a different machine.

To keep your cash safe, use a money belt—a pouch with a strap that you buckle around your waist like a belt, and wear under your clothes. Thieves target tourists. A money belt provides peace of mind, allowing you to carry lots of cash safely. Don't waste time every few days tracking down a cash machine—withdraw a week's worth of money, stuff it in your money belt, and travel!

Credit and Debit Cards

For purchases, Visa and MasterCard are more commonly accepted than American Express. Just like at home, credit or debit cards work easily at larger hotels, restaurants, and shops, but smaller businesses prefer payment in local currency (in small bills—break large bills at a

Exchange Rate

I list prices in euros for Spain.

1 euro (€) = about $1.50

To convert prices in euros to dollars, add about 50 percent: €20 = about $30, €50 = about $75. (You can check www.oanda.com for the most up-to-date exchange rates and to print a cheat sheet.) Just like the dollar, the euro is broken down into 100 cents. You'll find coins ranging from €0.01 to €2, and bills from €5 to €500.

Gibraltar uses pounds (£) but also takes euros; you'll get a better exchange rate using pounds (£1 = about $2).

For Morocco, I list prices in dirhams (the official currency; 8 dirhams = about $1), although euros and dollars are usually accepted.

bank or larger store).

Credit and debit cards—whether used for purchases or ATM withdrawals—often come with additional, tacked-on "international transaction" fees of up to 3 percent plus $5 per transaction. To avoid unpleasant surprises, call your bank or credit-card company before your trip to ask about these fees.

Damage Control for Lost Cards

If you lose your credit, debit, or ATM card, you can stop people from using your card by reporting the loss immediately to the respective global customer-assistance centers. Call these 24-hour US numbers collect: Visa (410/581-9994; toll-free number in Spain is 900-991-124), MasterCard (636/722-7111), and American Express (623/492-8427).

At a minimum, you'll need to know the name of the financial institution that issued you the card, along with the type of card (classic, platinum, or whatever). Providing the following information will allow for a quicker cancellation of your missing card: full card number, whether you are the primary or secondary cardholder, the cardholder's name exactly as printed on the card, billing address, home phone number, circumstances of the loss or theft, and identification verification (your birth date, your mother's maiden name, or your Social Security number—memorize this, don't carry a copy). If you are the secondary cardholder, you'll also need to provide the primary cardholder's identification-verification details. You can generally receive a temporary card within two or three business days in Europe.

If you promptly report your card lost or stolen, you typically won't be responsible for any unauthorized transactions on your account, although many banks charge a liability fee of $50.

Tipping

Tipping in Spain isn't as automatic and generous as it is in the US, but for special service, tips are appreciated, if not expected. As in the US, the proper amount depends on your resources, tipping philosophy, and the circumstances, but some general guidelines apply.

Restaurants: In most restaurants, a service charge *(servicio incluido)* is generally included in the bill, though it's customary to tip 5 percent extra for good service. If service is not included *(servicio no incluido),* tip up to 10 percent. Leave the tip on the table. It's best to tip in cash even if you pay with your credit card. Otherwise the tip may never reach your server. If you order a meal at a counter, don't tip.

Taxis: To tip the cabbie, round up. Spanish people rarely give tips in taxis, unless it's to round up to the next full euro (if the fare is €4.85, they'll give €5). If the cabbie hauls your bags and zips you to the airport to help you catch your flight, you might want to toss in a little more. But if you feel like you're being driven in circles or otherwise ripped off, skip the tip.

Special Services: It's thoughtful to tip a couple of euros to someone who shows you a special sight and who is paid in no other way. Tour guides at public sites sometimes hold out their hands for tips after they give their spiel; if I've already paid for the tour, I don't tip extra, though some tourists do give a euro or two, particularly for a job well done. I don't tip at hotels, but if you do, give the porter a euro for carrying bags and leave a couple of euros in your room at the end of your stay for the maid if the room was kept clean. In general, if someone in the service industry does a super job for you, a tip of a couple of euros is appropriate...but not required.

When in doubt, ask. If you're not sure whether (or how much) to tip for a service, ask your hotelier or the tourist information office; they'll fill you in on how it's done on their turf.

Getting a VAT Refund

Wrapped into the purchase price of your Spanish souvenirs is a Value-Added Tax (VAT) of about 16 percent. If you purchase more than €90 (about $135) worth of goods at a store that participates in the VAT-refund scheme, you're entitled to get most of that tax back. Getting your refund is usually straightforward and, if you buy a substantial amount of souvenirs, well worth the hassle. If you're lucky, the merchant will subtract the tax when you make your purchase. (This is more likely to occur if the store ships the goods to your home.) Otherwise, you'll need to:

Get the paperwork. Have the merchant completely fill out the necessary refund document, *Bordereay de Vente a l'Exportation,* also called a "cheque." You'll have to present your passport at the store.

Get your stamp at the border or airport. Process your cheque(s) at your last stop in the EU (e.g., at the airport) with the customs agent who deals with VAT refunds. It's best to keep your purchases in your carry-on for viewing, but if they're too large or dangerous (such as knives) to carry on, track down the proper customs agent to inspect them before you check your bag. You're not supposed to use your purchased goods before you leave. If you show up at customs wearing your new flamenco outfit, officials might look the other way—or deny you a refund.

Collect your refund. You'll need to return your stamped document to the retailer or its representative. Many merchants work with services, such as Global Refund (www.globalrefund.com) or Premier Tax Free (www.premiertaxfree.com), which have offices at major airports, ports, or border crossings. These services, which extract a 4 percent fee, can refund your money immediately in your currency of choice or credit your card (within two billing cycles). If the retailer handles VAT refunds directly, it's up to you to contact the merchant for your refund. You can mail the documents from home, or quicker, from your point of departure (using a stamped, addressed envelope you've prepared or one that's been provided by the merchant)—and then wait. It could take months.

Customs for American Shoppers

You are allowed to take home $800 worth of items per person duty-free, once every 30 days. The next $1,000 is taxed at a flat 3 percent. After that, you pay the individual item's duty rate. You can also bring in duty-free a liter of alcohol (slightly more than a standard-size bottle of wine; you must be at least 21), 200 cigarettes, and up to 100 non-Cuban cigars. Food in cans or sealed jars is permissible as long as no meat is included. Some, but not all, types of cheese are allowed. Fresh fruits and vegetables are prohibited. Note that you'll need to carefully pack any bottles of wine and other liquid-containing items in your checked luggage, due to the three-ounce limit on liquids in carry-on baggage. To check customs rules and duty rates before you go, visit www.cbp.gov, and click on "Travel," then "Know Before You Go."

SIGHTSEEING

Sightseeing can be hard work. Use these tips to make your visits to Spain's finest sights meaningful, fun, fast, and painless.

Plan Ahead

Set up an itinerary that allows you to fit in all your must-see sights. For a one-stop look at opening hours, see the "At a Glance" sidebars for the bigger cities. Most sights keep stable hours, but you can easily confirm the latest by calling the local TI.

Don't put off visiting a must-see sight—you never know when a place will close unexpectedly for a holiday, strike, or restoration.

If you'll be visiting during a holiday, find out if a particular sight will be open by phoning ahead or visiting its website.

When possible, visit key museums first thing (when your energy is best) and save other activities for the afternoon. Hit the highlights first, then go back to other things if you have the stamina and time.

Depending on the sight, there are ways to avoid crowds. This book offers tips on specific sights. In general, try visiting the sight very early, at lunch, or very late. Evening visits (when possible) are usually peaceful with fewer crowds.

Read ahead. To get the most out of the self-guided tours and sight descriptions in this book, read them before you visit. Several cities offer sightseeing passes that are worthwhile values for serious sightseers; plan ahead.

At the Sight

All sights have rules, and if you know about these in advance, they're no big deal.

Some important sights use metal detectors or conduct bag searches that will slow your entry.

At churches—which generally offer interesting art (usually free) and a cool, welcome seat—a modest dress code (no bare shoulders or shorts) is encouraged.

Most museums require you to check daypacks and coats. They'll be kept safely. If you have something you can't bear to part with, stash it in a pocket or purse. If you don't want to check a small backpack, carry it (at least as you enter) under your arm like a purse. From a guard's point of view, a backpack is generally a problem while a purse is not.

Photography is often banned at major sights. Look for signs or ask. If cameras are allowed, flashes or tripods are usually not. Flashes damage oil paintings and distract others in the room. Even without a flash, a handheld camera will take a decent picture (or you can buy postcards or posters at the museum bookstore). Video cameras are usually allowed.

Some museums have special exhibits in addition to their permanent collection. Some exhibits are included in the entry price, while others come at an extra cost. Occasionally you have to pay even if you don't want to see the exhibit.

Many sights rent audioguides, which offer dry-but-useful recorded descriptions in English (about $7.50). If you bring along your own pair of headphones and a Y-jack, two people can share one audioguide and save. Guided tours in English (usually $9 and widely ranging in quality) are most likely to occur during peak season.

Expect changes—paintings can be on tour, on loan, out sick, or shifted at the whim of the curator. To adapt, pick up any available free floor plans as you enter, and ask museum staff if you can't find a particular painting. Say the title or artist's name, or point to the photograph in this book, and ask, "*¿Dónde está?*" (dohn-day ay-stah; meaning, "Where is?").

Some important sights have an on-site café or cafeteria (usually a good place to rest and have a snack or light meal). The WCs are free and generally clean.

Museums have bookstores selling postcards and souvenirs. Before you leave, scan the postcards and thumb through the biggest guidebook (or skim its index) to be sure you haven't overlooked something that you'd like to see.

Most sights stop admitting people 30–60 minutes before closing time, and some rooms close early (generally about 45 minutes before the actual closing time). Guards usher people out, so don't save the best for last.

Every sight or museum offers more than what is covered in this book. Use this information as an introduction—not the final word.

SLEEPING

Spain offers some of the best accommodation values in Western Europe. Most places are government-regulated, with posted prices. While prices are low, street noise is high (Spaniards are notorious night owls). Always ask to see your room first. Check the price posted on the door, consider potential night-noise problems, ask for another room, or bargain down the price. You can request *con vista* (with a view), or *tranquilo* or *callado* (quiet). In most cases, view rooms come with street noise. Most of the year, prices are soft.

In the interest of smart use of your time, I favor hotels (and restaurants) handy to your sightseeing activities. Rather than list hotels scattered throughout a city, I describe my favorite couple of neighborhoods and recommend the best accommodations values in each, from $15 bunks to $330 suites.

All rooms have sinks with hot and cold water. Rooms with private bathrooms are often bigger and renovated, while the cheaper rooms without bathrooms often will be dingier and/or on the top floor. Any room without a bathroom has access to a bathroom on the corridor. You can usually save time by paying your bill the evening before you leave, instead of paying in the busy morning, when the reception desk is crowded with tourists who want to pay up, ask questions, or check in.

Sleep Code

(€1 = about $1.50, country code: 34)

To help you sort easily through these listings, I've divided the rooms into three categories based on the price for a standard double room with bath:

$$$ Higher Priced
$$ Moderately Priced
$ Lower Priced

To pack maximum information into minimum space, I use the following code to describe accommodations in this book. Prices listed are per room, not per person.

When there is a range of prices in one category, that means the price fluctuates with the season: high season (*alta*, July–Sept), shoulder season (*media*, roughly April–June and Oct), and low season (*baja*, Nov–March). The prices and seasons are posted at or near the hotel desk. In resort areas, prices go way up in high season. In Spain, some hotels include the 7 percent I.V.A. tax in the room price; others tack it onto your bill.

S = Single room (or price for one person in a double).
D = Double or twin. Double beds are usually big enough for nonromantic couples.
T = Triple (generally a double bed with a single).
Q = Quad (usually two double beds).
b = Private bathroom with toilet and shower or tub.
s = Private shower or tub only (the toilet is down the hall).

According to this code, a couple staying at a "Db-€140" hotel would pay a total of €140 (about $210) for a double room with a private bathroom. You can assume a hotel takes credit cards unless you see "cash only" in the listing. Unless otherwise noted, hotel staff speak basic English and breakfast is included.

Types of Accommodations

Hotels: Don't judge hotels by their bleak and dirty entryways. Landlords, stuck with rent control, often stand firmly in the way of hardworking hoteliers who'd like to brighten up their buildings.

Any regulated place will have a complaint book *(libro de reclamaciones).* A request for this book will generally prompt the hotelier to solve your problem to keep you from writing a complaint.

Hotels are officially prohibited from using central heat before November 1 and after April 1 (unless it's unusually cold); prepare for cool evenings if you travel in spring and fall. Summer can be extremely hot. Consider air-conditioning, fans, and noise (since you'll want your window open), and don't be shy about asking for ice at the fancier hotels. Many rooms come with mini-refrigerators (if it's noisy at night, unplug it). Conveniently, expensive business-class hotels in big, non-resort cities often drop their prices in July and August, just when the air-conditioned comfort they offer is most important.

Most hotel rooms with air-conditioners come with control sticks (like a TV remote, sometimes requires a deposit) that generally have the same symbols and features: fan icon (click to toggle through wind power from light to gale); louver icon (choose steady air flow or waves); snowflake and sunshine icons (heat or cold, depending on season); clock ("O" setting: run *X* hours before turning off; "I" setting: wait *X* hours to start); and the temperature control (20° or 21° Celsius is the normal sleeping temperature).

Historic Inns: Spain has luxurious, government-sponsored, historic inns called *paradores.* These are often renovated castles, palaces, or monasteries, many with great views and stately atmospheres. While full of Old World character, they are usually run in a sterile, bureaucratic way. These are pricey (doubles $100–240), but can be a good deal for younger people (30 and under) and seniors (60 and over), who often get discounted rates; for details, bonus packages, and family deals, see www.parador.es. If you're not eligible for any deals, you'll get a better value by sleeping in what I call (and list in this book as) "poor man's *paradores*"—elegant, normal places that offer double the warmth and Old World intimacy for half the price.

Rooms in Private Homes: You'll find rooms in private homes, typically in touristy areas where locals decide to open up a spare room and make a little money on the side. These rooms are usually as private as hotel rooms, often with separate entries. Especially in resort towns, the rooms might be in small apartment-type buildings. Ask for a *cama, habitación,* or *casa particular.* They're cheap ($15–30 per bed without breakfast) and usually a good experience.

Hostels and Campgrounds: Spain has plenty of youth hostels and campgrounds, but considering the great bargains on other accommodations, I don't think they're worth the trouble and usually don't cover them in this book. *Hostales* and *pensiones* are easy to find, inexpensive, and, when chosen properly, a fun part of the Spanish cultural experience. If you're on a starvation budget or just prefer camping or hosteling, plenty of information is available in the Let's Go guidebook (see page 658), through the national tourist office, and at local TIs.

Phoning

To call Spain, you'll need to know its country code: 34. To call Spain from the US or Canada, dial 011-34-local number. If calling Spain from another European country, dial 00-34-local number.

Making Reservations

Given the quality of the gems I've found for this book, I'd recommend that you reserve your rooms in advance, particularly if you'll be traveling during peak season. Book several weeks ahead, or as soon as you've pinned down your travel dates. Note that some national holidays jam things up and merit your making reservations far in advance (see "Major Holidays and Weekends" sidebar, page 7).

To make a reservation in advance, contact hotels directly by email, phone, or fax. Email is the clearest and most economical way to make a reservation. In addition, many hotel websites now have online reservation forms. If phoning from the US, be mindful of time zones (see page 8). Most hotels listed are accustomed to English-only travelers. To ensure you have all the information you need for your reservation, use the form in this book's appendix (also at www.ricksteves.com/reservation).

When you request a room in writing for a certain time period, use the European style for writing dates: day/month/year. Hoteliers need to know your arrival and departure dates. For example, a two-night stay in July would be "2 nights, 16/07/09 to 18/07/09." Consider in advance how long you'll stay; don't just assume you can extend your reservation for extra days once you arrive.

If you don't get a reply to your email or fax, it usually means the hotel is already fully booked. If the response from the hotel gives its room availability and rates, it's not a confirmation. You must tell them that you want that room at the given rate.

For more spontaneity, you can make reservations as you travel, calling hotels a few days to a week before your visit. If you prefer the flexibility of traveling without any reservations at all, you'll have greater success snaring rooms if you arrive at your destination early in the day. When you anticipate crowds, call hotels around 9:00 on the day you plan to arrive, when the hotel clerk knows who'll be checking out and just which rooms will be available. If you encounter a language barrier, ask the fluent receptionist at your current hotel to call for you.

Whether you're reserving from home or on the road, the hotelier will sometimes request your credit-card number for a one-night deposit. You can email your credit-card information (I do), but it's safer to share that personal info via phone call, fax, or secure online reservation form (if the hotel has one on its website).

If you must cancel your reservation, it's courteous to do so with as much advance notice as possible (simply make a quick phone call or send an email). Family-run hotels and B&Bs lose money if they turn away customers while holding a room for someone who doesn't show up. Understandably, some hotels bill no-shows for one night. Hotels in larger cities sometimes have strict cancellation policies: For example, you might lose a deposit if you cancel within two weeks of your reserved stay, or you might be billed for the entire visit if you leave early. Ask about cancellation policies before you book.

Always reconfirm your room reservation a few days in advance from the road. If you'll be arriving after 17:00, let them know. Don't have the tourist office reconfirm rooms for you; they'll take a commission.

On the small chance that a hotel loses track of your reservation, bring along a hard copy of their emailed or faxed confirmation.

EATING

Spanish cuisine is hearty and served in big, inexpensive portions. You can eat well in restaurants for €15.

The Spanish eating schedule—lunch from 13:00–16:00, dinner after 21:00—frustrates many visitors. Most Spaniards eat one major meal of the day—lunch *(almuerzo)* at 14:00, when stores close, schools let out, and people gather with their friends and family for the siesta. Because most Spaniards work until 19:30, supper *(cena)* is usually served at about 21:00 or 22:00. And, since few people want a heavy meal that late, many Spaniards build a light dinner out of appetizer portions called tapas.

Don't buck this system. Generally, no self-respecting *casa de comidas* ("house of eating"—when you see this label, you can bet it's a good, traditional eatery) serves meals at American hours.

In addition, the Spanish diet—heavy on ham, deep-fried foods (usually fried in olive oil), more ham, weird seafood, and ham again—can be brutal on Americans more accustomed to salads, fruit, and grains.

Survival Tips: To get by in Spain, either adapt yourself to the Spanish schedule and cuisine, or scramble to get edible food in between. Have an early light lunch at a bar. Many Spaniards have a *bocadillo* (sandwich) at about 11:00 to bridge the gap between their coffee-and-roll breakfast and lunch at 14:00 (hence the popularity of fast-food sandwich chains such as Pans & Company). Besides *bocadillos,* bars often have slices of *tortilla española* (potato omelet) and fresh-squeezed orange juice.

Then, either have your main meal at a restaurant at 15:00, followed by a light tapas snack for dinner later; or reverse it, having a tapas meal in the afternoon, followed by a late restaurant dinner. Either way, tapas in bars are the key (see page 22).

The key to getting your veggies at restaurants is to order two courses, because the first course generally has a green option. Resist the cheese-and-ham appetizers and instead choose first-course menu items such as creamed vegetable soup, *parrillada de verduras* (sautéed vegetables), or *ensalada mixta* (no Spaniard ever eats only a salad, so they tend to be small and simple—just iceberg lettuce, tomatoes, and maybe olives and tuna; if it's only a salad you're after, try a fast-food joint such as McDonald's). Main courses such as meats or fish are usually served with only a garnish, not a side of vegetables. Fruit isn't normally served for breakfast or as a snack—it's a dessert. After-meal dessert menus usually have a fruit option.

Breakfast

Hotel breakfasts are generally handy, optional, and pricey (€6). Start your day instead with a Spanish flair at a corner bar or at a colorful café near the town market hall (and pay just €2–3). Ask for the *desayunos* (breakfast special, usually only available until noon), which can include coffee, a roll (or sandwich), and juice for one price—much cheaper than ordering them separately. In Andalucía, get your morning protein with the *mollete con jamón y aceite,* a soft roll of bread with Spanish ham and finger-licking good olive oil (sometimes comes with cheese, too). If you like a Danish and coffee in American greasy-spoon joints, you must try the Spanish equivalent: greasy, cigar-shaped fritters called *churros* (or the thicker *porras*) that you dip in warm chocolate pudding.

Here are some key words for breakfast:

café solo	shot of espresso
café con leche	espresso with hot milk
té	tea
zumo de fruta	fruit juice
zumo de naranja (natural)	orange juice (freshly squeezed)
pan	bread
tortilla española	potato omelet (standard dish cooked fresh each morning, served in cheap slices)
sandwich (tostado)	Wonder bread (toasted)
...con jamón/queso/mixto	...with ham/cheese/both
...mixto con huevo	...with ham and cheese topped by an over-easy egg
croissant a la plancha	grilled croissant slathered with butter

Restaurants

In restaurants, don't expect "My name is Carlos and I'll be your waiter tonight" cheery service. Service is often *serio*—it's not friendly or unfriendly...just white-shirt-and-bowtie proficient.

Although not fancy, Spanish cuisine comes with an endless variety of regional specialties. Two famous Spanish dishes are paella and gazpacho. Paella features saffron-flavored rice as a background for whatever the chef wants to mix in—seafood, sausage, chicken, peppers, and so on. While paella is heavy for your evening meal,

Ordering Tapas

You can often just point to what you want, say *por favor,* and get your food, but these words will help you learn the options and fine-tune your request.

Tapas Terms

pincho	bite-size portion (not always available)
pinchito	tiny *pincho*
tapas	snack-size portions
ración	larger portions—half a meal, occasionally available in a smaller version called a "1/2 *ración*" *(media-ración)*
frito	fried
...a la plancha	grilled
¿Cuánto cuesta una tapa?	How much per tapa?

Sandwich Words

canapé	tiny open-faced sandwich
pulguitas	small closed baguette sandwich
montadito	baguette slice with the tapa "mounted" on top
bocadillos	baguette sandwiches, cheap and basic, a tapa on bread
flautas	sandwich made with flute-thin baguette
pepito	yet one more word for a little sandwich

Typical Tapas

aceitunas	olives
almendras	almonds
atún	tuna
bacalao	cod
banderilla	small skewer of spicy, pickled veggies—eat all at once for the real punch (it's named after the spear matadors use to spike the bull)
bombas	fried meat and potatoes ball
boquerones	fresh anchovies marinated in olive oil, vinegar, and garlic
calamares fritos	fried squid rings
caracoles	snails (May–Sept)
cazón en adobo	salty, marinated dogfish
champiñones	mushrooms
croquetas de...	breaded and fried béchamel (made of flour and milk), usually with chunks of *jamón* (ham)
empanadillas	pastries stuffed with meat or seafood

ensalada rusa	potato salad with lots of mayo, peas, and carrots
espinacas (con garbanzos)	spinach (with garbanzo beans)
gambas (a la plancha, al ajillo)	shrimp (grilled, with garlic)
gazpacho	cold soup, made with tomato, bread, garlic, and olive oil
guiso	stew
mejillones	mussels
paella	rice dish with saffron, seafood, meat, and/or chicken
pan	bread
patatas bravas	fried chunks of potato with spicy tomato sauce
pescaditos fritos	assortment of fried little fish
picos	little breadsticks
pimiento (relleno)	peppers (stuffed)
pisto	mixed sautéed vegetables
pulpo	octopus
queso	cheese (or a beautiful woman)
queso manchego	sheep-milk cheese
rabas	squid tentacles
rabo de toro	bull-tail stew
revuelto de...	scrambled eggs with...
...setas	...wild mushrooms
tabla serrana	hearty plate of mountain meat and cheese
tortilla española	potato omelet
tortilla de jamón/queso	potato omelet with ham/cheese
variado fritos	typical Andalusian mix of various fried fish

Cured Meats *(Charcutería)*

salchichón	sausage
jamón ibérico	best ham, from acorn-fed baby pigs
jamón serrano	cured ham
chorizo	spicy sausage
lomo	pork tenderloin

Typical Desserts

flan de huevo	crème caramel
arroz con leche	rice pudding
helados (variados)	ice cream (various flavors)
fruta de la estación	fruit in season
queso	cheese

jump (like everyone else in the bar) at the opportunity to snare a small plate of paella when it appears hot out of the kitchen in a tapas bar. Avoid the paella shown in pretty pictures on a separate menu—it's from the microwave. Gazpacho, an Andalusian specialty, is a chilled soup of tomatoes, bread chunks, and spices—refreshing on a hot day and commonly available in the summer. Spanish cooks love garlic and olive oil. The cheapest meal is simply a *bocadillo de jamón* (ham-on-French-bread sandwich), sold virtually everywhere.

For a budget meal in a restaurant, try a *plato combinado* (combination plate), which usually includes portions of one or two main dishes, a vegetable, and bread for a reasonable price; or the *menú del día* (menu of the day, also known as *menú turístico*), a substantial three- to four-course meal that usually comes with a carafe of house wine.

Tapas Bars

You can eat well any time of day in tapas bars. Tapas are small portions, like appetizers, of seafood, salads, meat-filled pastries, deep-fried tasties, and on and on—normally displayed under glass at the bar.

Tapas typically cost about €2, up to €10 for seafood. Most bars push larger portions called *raciones* (dinner plate–sized) rather than smaller tapas (saucer-sized). Ask for the smaller tapas portions or a *media-ración* (listed as 1/2 *ración* on a menu), though many bars simply don't serve anything smaller than a *ración*.

Eating and drinking at a bar is usually cheapest if you eat or drink at the counter *(barra)*. You may pay a little more to eat sitting at a table *(mesa)* and still more for an outdoor table *(terraza)*. Locate the price list (often posted in fine type on a wall somewhere) to know the menu options and price tiers. In the right place, a quiet snack and drink on a terrace on the town square is well worth the extra charge. But the cheapest seats sometimes get the best show. Sit at the bar and study your bartender—he's an artist.

Be assertive or you'll never be served. *Por favor* (please) grabs the guy's attention. Don't worry about paying until you're ready to leave (he's keeping track of your tab). To get the bill ask: "*¿La cuenta?*" (or *la dolorosa*—meaning literally "the sadness"—always draws a confused laugh). Bars come with a formidable language barrier. A small working vocabulary is essential for tapas proficiency (see page 22), and will help you eat better, too.

Chasing down a particular bar for tapas nearly defeats the purpose and spirit of tapas—they are impromptu. Just drop in at any lively place. I look for the noisy spots with piles of napkins and food debris on the floor (go local and toss your trash, too), lots of locals, and the TV blaring. Popular television-viewing includes bullfights and soccer games, American sitcoms, and Spanish interpretations of soaps and silly game shows (you'll see Vanna Blanco). While tapas are served all day, the real action begins late—21:00 at the earliest. But for beginners, an earlier start is easier and comes with less commotion.

Get a fun, inexpensive sampler plate. Ask for *una tabla de canapés variados* to get a plate of various little open-face sandwiches. Or ask for a *surtido de* (an assortment of...) *charcutería* (a mixed plate of meat) or *queso* (cheese). *Un surtido de jamón y queso* means a plate of different hams and cheeses. Order bread and two glasses of red wine on the right square—and you've got a romantic (and €10) dinner for two.

Spanish Drinks

Spain is one of the world's leading producers of grapes and that means lots of excellent wine: both red *(tinto)* and white *(blanco)*. Major wine regions include Valdepeñas, Penedès (Cabernet-style wines from near Barcelona), Rioja (spicy, lighter reds from the *tempranillo* grape, from the high plains of northern Spain), and Ribera del Duero (northwest of Madrid). For quality wine, ask for *crianza* (old), *reserva* (older), or *gran reserva* (oldest).

Sherry, a fortified wine from the Jerez region, is a shock to the taste buds if you're expecting a sweet dessert drink. It ranges from dry *(fino)* to sweet *(dulce)*—Spaniards drink the *fino* and export the *dulce*. *Cava* is Spain's answer to champagne. Sangria (a punch of red wine mixed with fruit slices) is popular and refreshing.

To get a small draft beer, ask for a *caña* (KAHN-yah). Spain's bars often serve fresh-squeezed orange juice *(zumo de naranja natural)*. For something completely different, try *horchata de chufas*, a sweet, milky beverage made from chufa nuts (a.k.a. earth almonds). If ordering mineral water in a restaurant, request a *botella grande de agua* (big bottle). They push the more profitable small bottles.

Here are some words to help you quench your thirst:

agua con/sin gas	water with/without bubbles
un vasito de agua	glass of tap water
una jarra de agua	pitcher of tap water
refresco	soft drink (common brands are Coca-Cola; Fanta—*limón* or *naranja;* and Schweppes—*limón* or *tónica*)
vino tinto/blanco de la casa	house red/white wine

How Was Your Trip?

Were your travels fun, smooth, and meaningful? If you'd like to share your tips, concerns, and discoveries, please fill out the survey at www.ricksteves.com/feedback. I value your feedback. Thanks in advance—it helps a lot.

un tinto	small glass of house red wine
chato	small glass of house wine
tinto de verano	lighter sangria (more popular with locals than sangria)
vermú	vermouth
mucho cuerpo	full-bodied
afrutado	fruity
seco	dry
dulce	sweet
cerveza	beer
caña	small glass of draft beer
doble, tubo	tall glass of beer
¡Salud!	Cheers!

TRAVELING AS A TEMPORARY LOCAL

We travel all the way to Europe to enjoy differences—to become temporary locals. You'll experience frustrations. Certain truths that we find "God-given" or "self-evident," such as cold beer, ice in drinks, bottomless cups of coffee, hot showers, and bigger being better, are suddenly not so true. One of the benefits of travel is the eye-opening realization that there are logical, civil, and even better alternatives. A willingness to go local ensures that you'll enjoy a full dose of Spanish hospitality.

If there is a negative aspect to the image the Spanish have of Americans, it's that we are big, loud, aggressive, impolite, rich, superficially friendly, and a bit naive.

Given our reluctance to work with the world on climate change issues, Europeans don't respond well to Americans complaining about being too hot or too cold. Bring a sweater in winter, and in summer, be prepared to sweat a little like everyone else.

While Spaniards look bemusedly at some of our Yankee excesses—and worriedly at others—they nearly always afford us individual travelers all the warmth we deserve.

Judging from all the happy feedback I receive from travelers who have used this book, it's safe to assume you'll enjoy a great, affordable vacation—with the finesse of an independent, experienced traveler.

Thanks, and *buen viaje!*

BACK DOOR TRAVEL PHILOSOPHY

From *Rick Steves' Europe Through the Back Door*

Travel is intensified living—maximum thrills per minute and one of the last great sources of legal adventure. Travel is freedom. It's recess, and we need it.

Experiencing the real Europe requires catching it by surprise, going casual..."Through the Back Door."

Affording travel is a matter of priorities. (Make do with the old car.) You can travel—simply, safely, and comfortably—nearly anywhere in Europe for $120 a day plus transportation costs (allow less for Spain and more for big cities). In many ways, spending more money only builds a thicker wall between you and what you came to see. Europe is a cultural carnival, and, time after time, you'll find that its best acts are free and its best seats are the cheap ones.

A tight budget forces you to travel close to the ground, meeting and communicating with the people, not relying on service with a purchased smile. Never sacrifice sleep, nutrition, safety, or cleanliness in the name of budget. Simply enjoy the local-style alternatives to expensive hotels and restaurants.

Extroverts have more fun. If your trip is low on magic moments, kick yourself and make things happen. If you don't enjoy a place, maybe you don't know enough about it. Seek the truth. Recognize tourist traps. Give a culture the benefit of your open mind. See things as different but not better or worse. Any culture has much to share.

Of course, travel, like the world, is a series of hills and valleys. Be fanatically positive and militantly optimistic. If something's not to your liking, change your liking. Travel is addictive. It can make you a happier American as well as a citizen of the world. Our Earth is home to six and a half billion equally important people. It's humbling to travel and find that people don't envy Americans. Europeans like us, but, with all due respect, they wouldn't trade passports.

Globe-trotting destroys ethnocentricity. It helps you understand and appreciate different cultures. Regrettably, there are forces in our society that want you dumbed down for their convenience. Don't let it happen. Thoughtful travel engages you with the world—and it's more important than ever these days. Travel changes people. It broadens perspectives and teaches new ways to measure quality of life. Rather than fear the diversity on this planet, travelers celebrate it. Many travelers toss aside their hometown blinders. Their prized souvenirs are the strands of different cultures they decide to knit into their own character. The world is a cultural yarn shop, and Back Door travelers are weaving the ultimate tapestry. Join in!

BARCELONA

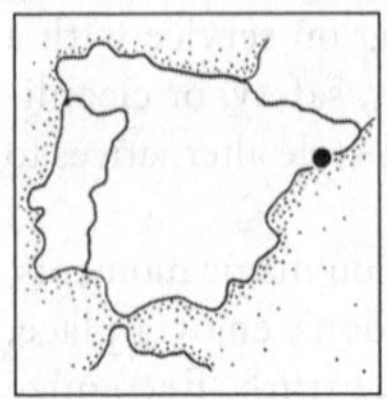

Barcelona is Spain's second city, and the capital of the proud and distinct region of Catalunya. With Franco's fascism now ancient history, Catalan flags wave once again. And the local language and culture are on a roll in Spain's most cosmopolitan and European corner.

Barcelona bubbles with life in its narrow Barri Gòtic alleys, along the grand boulevards, and throughout the chic, grid-planned, new part of town, called Eixample. While Barcelona had an illustrious past as a Roman colony, Visigothic capital, 14th-century maritime power, and—in more modern times—a top Mediterranean textile and manufacturing center, it's most enjoyable to throw out the history books and just drift through the city. If you're in the mood to surrender to a city's charms, let it be in Barcelona.

Planning Your Time

Located in the far northeast corner of Spain, Barcelona makes a good first or last stop for your trip. With the new AVE train, Barcelona is only three hours away from Madrid. Or you could sandwich Barcelona between flights. From the US, it's as easy to fly into Barcelona as it is to land in Madrid, Lisbon, or Paris. Those renting a car can cleverly start here, fly or train to Madrid, and see Madrid and Toledo, all before picking up their car—saving on several days' worth of rental fees.

On the shortest visit, Barcelona is worth one night, one day, and an evening flight or train ride out. The Ramblas is two different streets by day and by night. Stroll it from top to bottom in the evening and again the next morning, grabbing breakfast on a stool in a market café. Wander the Barri Gòtic (BAH-ree GOH-teek), see the cathedral, and have lunch in the Eixample (eye-SHAM-plah). The

Barcelona Overview

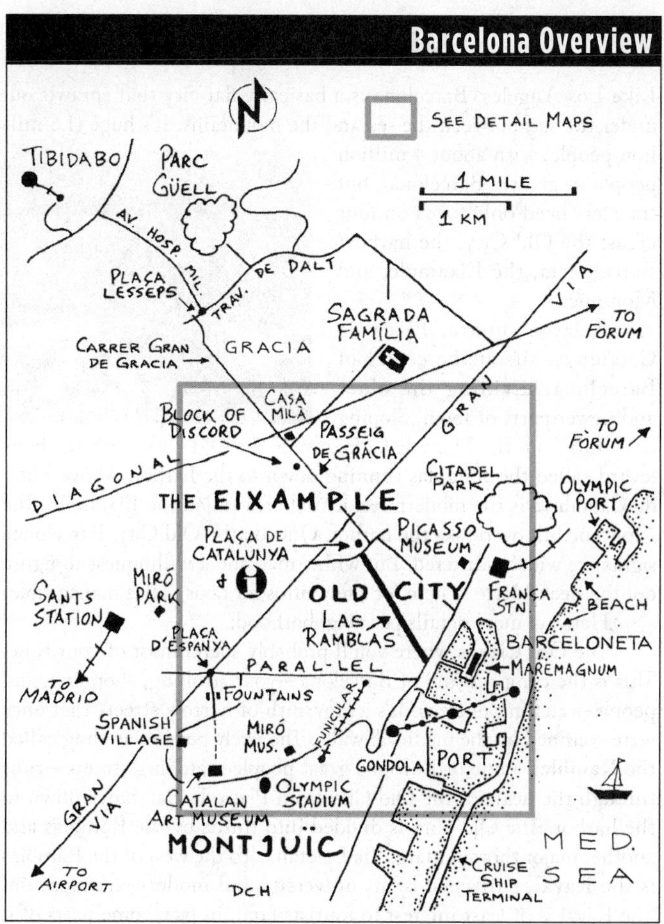

top two sights in town, Antoni Gaudí's Sagrada Família church and the Picasso Museum, are usually open until 20:00 during the summer (Picasso closed Mon). The illuminated Magic Fountains on Montjuïc make a good finale for your day.

Of course, Barcelona in a day is insane. To better sample the city's ample charm, spread your visit over two or three days. With two days, you could divide-and-conquer the town geographically: one day for the Barri Gòtic (Ramblas, cathedral area, Picasso Museum); and another for the Eixample and Gaudí sights (Casa Milà, Sagrada Família, Parc Güell). Do Montjuïc on whichever day you're not exhausted (if any).

With more time, several tempting day trips lie nearby—see the Near Barcelona chapter for tips on Montserrat, Sitges, and the Salvador Dalí sights at Figueres and Cadaqués.

ORIENTATION

Like Los Angeles, Barcelona is a basically flat city that sprawls out under the sun between the sea and the mountains. It's huge (1.6 million people, with about 4 million people in greater Barcelona), but travelers need only focus on four areas: the Old City, the harbor/Barceloneta, the Eixample, and Montjuïc.

A large square, Plaça de Catalunya, sits at the center of Barcelona, dividing the older and newer parts of town. Sloping downhill from the Plaça de Catalunya is the Old City, with the boulevard called the Ramblas running down to the harbor. Above Plaça de Catalunya is the modern residential area called the Eixample. The Montjuïc hill overlooks the harbor. Outside the Old City, Barcelona's sights are widely scattered. But with a map and a willingness to figure out the sleek Metro system (or a few euros for taxis), all is manageable.

Here are more details per neighborhood:

The **Old City** is where you'll probably spend most of your time. This is the compact soul of Barcelona—your strolling, shopping, and people-watching nucleus. It's a labyrinth of narrow streets that once were confined by the medieval walls. The lively pedestrian drag called the **Ramblas**—one of Europe's great people-watching streets—runs through the heart of the Old City from Plaça de Catalunya down to the harbor. The Old City is divided into thirds by the Ramblas and another major thoroughfare, Via Laietana. To the west of the Ramblas is the **Raval,** enlivened by its university and modern-art museum. The Raval is of least interest to tourists (and, in fact, some parts of it are quite seedy and should be avoided). Far better is the **Barri Gòtic** (Gothic Quarter), between the Ramblas and Via Laietana, with the cathedral as its navel. To the east of Via Laietana is the trendy **Ribera** district (a.k.a. "El Born"), centered on the Picasso Museum and the Church of Santa Maria del Mar.

The **harborfront** has been energized since the 1992 Olympics. A pedestrian bridge links the Ramblas with the modern **Maremagnum** shopping/aquarium complex. On the peninsula across the harbor is **Barceloneta,** a traditional fishing neighborhood that's home to some good seafood restaurants and a string of sandy beaches. Beyond Barceloneta, a man-made beach, several miles long, leads east to a new commercial and convention district called the **Fòrum.**

North of the Old City, beyond the bustling hub of Plaça de Catalunya, is the elegant **Eixample** district—its grid plan softened by cut-off corners. Much of Barcelona's Modernista architecture is found

Cheap Tricks in Barcelona

- Arriving by train? Save time, hassle, and the cost of a Metro ride by finding out if your train stops at any of the handy downtown stations (such as Passeig de Gràcia or Plaça de Catalunya). But remember that AVE trains from Madrid stop only at the Sants station.
- If connecting to cities elsewhere in Spain, don't overlook budget flights—which can be cheaper and faster than the train or bus (for tips, see page 677).
- For getting around the city, skip taxis and the Tourist Bus, and instead use the excellent network of Metro and buses. The T10 Card (10 rides for €7.20) makes the system super-cheap—each ride costs €0.72 instead of €1.30 for an individual ticket.
- If visiting the cathedral, be sure to go when it's free, between 8:00-12:45 (13:45 on Sun) or 17:15-19:30; at other times, you'll pay €5 to see exactly the same thing. Also note that several interesting sights around the cathedral (such as the Deacon's House and Roman Temple) are free to enter. Not far away, in La Ribera, the Church of Santa Maria del Mar is also free.
- One of Barcelona's most delightful Modernista sights, Antoni Gaudí's Parc Güell, is free and an enjoyable place to relax. Some expensive Gaudí sights (such as Casa Milà, Casa Batllò, and the Sagrada Família) can be just as interesting (and free) from the outside. For a free glimpse at a Gaudí interior, visit Palau Güell (though it may begin charging admission as newly renovated rooms re-open).
- Some museums have certain days and times when they don't charge admission: Picasso Museum (first Sun of month), Catalan Art Museum (first Sun of month), and Frederic Marès Museum (Wed afternoon).
- When tapas-hopping, note that trendy, upscale neighborhoods—such as the Eixample and La Ribera—come with higher prices. For a cheaper and more characteristic meal, find a blue-collar neighborhood (such as Carrer de la Mercè, described on page 93).

here (see sidebar on Modernisme, page 65). To the north is the **Gràcia** district, and beyond that, Antoni Gaudí's **Parc Güell.**

The large hill overlooking the city to the west is **Montjuïc,** home to a variety of attractions including some excellent museums (Catalan Art, Joan Miró) and the Olympic Stadium.

Apart from your geographical orientation, you'll need to orient yourself linguistically to a language distinct from Spanish. While Spanish ("Castilian") is widely spoken, the native tongue in this region is Catalan—nearly as different from Spanish as Italian (see the sidebar on page 38).

Tourist Information

Barcelona's TI has several branches. The main one is at **Plaça de Catalunya** (daily 9:00–21:00, under the main square near recommended hotels—look for red sign, tel. 932-853-832). Other convenient branches include at the top of the **Ramblas** (daily 9:00–21:00, at #115); **Plaça de Sant Jaume** just south of the cathedral (Mon–Fri 9:00–20:00, Sat 10:00–20:00, Sun 10:00–14:00); **Plaça d'Espanya** (daily July–Sept 10:00–20:00, Oct–June 10:00–16:00); the **airport** (daily 9:00–21:00, offices in both terminals A and B); **Sants train station** (Mon–Fri 8:00–20:00, Sat–Sun 8:00–14:00, near track 6); **Nord bus station** (daily July–Sept 9:00–21:00, Oct–June 9:00–15:00); and more. Throughout the summer, young, red-jacketed tourist-info helpers appear in the most touristy parts of town. The central information number for all TIs is 932-853-834 (www.barcelonaturisme.cat).

At any TI, pick up the free city map (can be hard to read—consider springing €1 for a better one), the small Metro map, and the free quarterly *See Barcelona* guide (practical information on museum hours, restaurants, transportation, history, festivals, and so on). The monthly *Barcelona Metropolitan* magazine and quarterly *What's On Barcelona* (both free and in English) have timely and substantial coverage of topics and events. The TI is a handy place to buy tickets for the Tourist Bus (described in "Getting Around Barcelona," page 36). Some TIs (at Plaça de Catalunya, Plaça de Sant Jaume, and the airport) also provide a room-booking service.

The main TI, at Plaça de Catalunya, offers guided walks (described under "Tours," page 37). Its Modernisme desk gives out a handy route map showing all the Modernista buildings and offers a discount package (€12 for a great guidebook and 20 percent discounts to many Modernisme sites—worthwhile if going beyond my big three; for €18 you'll also get a guidebook to Modernista bars and restaurants).

The **all-Catalunya TI** works fine for the entire region and even Madrid (Mon–Sat 10:00–19:00, Sun 10:00–14:00, on Plaça de Joan Carlos I, at the intersection of Diagonal and Passeig de Gràcia, Passeig de Gràcia 107, tel. 932-388-091).

Articket Card: You can get into seven art museums and their temporary exhibits with this ticket, including the recommended Picasso Museum, Casa Milà, Catalan Art Museum, and Fundació Joan Miró (€20, valid for six months, sold at TIs and participating museums, www.articketbcn.org). If you're planning to go to three or more of the museums, this time-saver pays for itself. To skip the ticket-buying line at a museum, show your Articket Card (to the ticket-taker, at the info desk, or at the group entrance), and they'll help you get your entrance ticket pronto.

Barcelona Card: This card covers public transportation (buses, Metro, Montjuïc funicular, and *golondrina* harbor tour) and includes free admission to minor sights and discounts on major sights (€25/2 days, €30/3 days, €34/4 days, €40/5 days, sold at TIs and El Corte Inglés department store).

Arrival in Barcelona

By Train: Virtually all trains end up at Barcelona's Sants train station (described below). But be aware that many trains also pass through other stations en route, such as **França station** (between the Ribera and Barceloneta neighborhoods), or the downtown **Passeig de Gràcia** or **Plaça de Catalunya** stations (which are also Metro stops—and very close to most of my recommended hotels). Figure out which stations your train stops at, and get off at the one most convenient to your hotel. (AVE trains from Madrid go only to Sants station.)

Sants station is vast and sprawling, but manageable. In the large lobby area under the upper tracks, you'll find a TI, ATMs, a world of handy shops and eateries, and a classy, quiet Sala Euromed lounge for travelers with first-class reservations (TV, free drinks, study tables, and coffee bar). Sants is the only Barcelona station with luggage storage (small bag-€3/day, big bag-€4.50/day, must go through security check, daily 5:30–23:00, follow signs to *consigna,* at far end of hallway from tracks 13–14).

There's also a long wall of ticket windows. Figure out which is right for you before you wait in line (all are labeled in English). Generally, the first stretch (on the left, windows 1–8) are for local trains, such as to Sitges; the next group (windows 9–21) are for advance tickets for long-distance trains; farther to the right are information windows (22–26)—go here first if you're not sure which window you want; and those at the right end (windows 27–31) sell tickets for long-distance trains leaving today. Attendants are often standing by to help you find the right line. If you know what you want, there are also automated train-ticket vending machines.

To get into downtown Barcelona from Sants station, simply follow signs for the Metro. The L3 (green) line—described under "Getting Around Barcelona" on page 36—zips you directly to a number of useful points in town, including all of my recommended hotels.

If departing from the downtown **Passeig de Gràcia station,** where three Metro lines converge with the rail line, you might find the underground tunnels confusing. You can't access the RENFE station directly from some of the entrances. Use the northern entrances to this station (rather than the southern "Consell de Cent" entrance, which is closest to Plaça de Catalunya).

By Plane: Barcelona's **El Prat de Llobregat Airport,** eight miles southwest of town, has three terminals: A, B, and C. The bigger terminals A and B each have a post office, pharmacy, left-luggage office, plenty of good cafeterias in the gate areas, and ATMs (avoid the gimmicky machines before the baggage carousels; instead, use the bank-affiliated ATMs at the far-left end of the arrivals hall as you face the street). Airport info tel. 902-404-704.

You have two options for getting downtown cheaply and quickly: The **Aerobus** (#A1) stops immediately outside the arrivals lobby of all three terminals and takes you in about 30 minutes to downtown, where it makes several stops, including Plaça d'Espanya, Plaça de Catalunya (near many of my recommended hotels), and Passeig de Gràcia (near more hotels; every 6 min, from airport 6:00–1:00 in the morning, from downtown 5:30–24:15, buy €4.05 ticket from machine or from driver). The line to board the bus can be very long, but—thanks to the high frequency of buses—it moves fast.

The second option is the RENFE **train,** which involves more walking. Walk down the long, orange-roofed overpass between terminals A and B to reach the station (line 10, 2/hr at about :29 and :59 after the hour, 20 min to Sants station, 25 min to Passeig de Gràcia station—near Plaça de Catalunya and many recommended hotels, 30 min to França station; €2.60 or covered by T10 Card, which you can purchase at automated machines at the airport train station—for details see "Getting Around Barcelona," page 36).

A **taxi** between the airport and downtown costs about €25.

Some budget airlines, including Ryanair, use **Girona-Costa Brava Airport,** located 60 miles north of Barcelona near Girona. Sagalés buses link to Barcelona (departures timed to meet flights, 70 min, €12, tel. 935-931-300 or 902-361-550, www.sagales.com). You can also take a Sagalés bus (hourly, 25 min, €2.50) or a taxi (€20) to Girona, where you can catch a train to Barcelona (at least hourly, 70 min, €7). A taxi between the Girona airport and Barcelona will cost at least €120. Airport info tel. 972-186-600.

By Car: Barcelona's parking fees are outrageously expensive (the one behind Boquería market charges upwards of €25/day). You won't need a car in Barcelona because the taxis and public transportation are so good.

Helpful Hints

Theft Alert: You're more likely to be pickpocketed here—especially on the Ramblas—than about anywhere else in Europe. Most of the crime is nonviolent, but muggings do occur. Leave valuables in your hotel and wear a money belt.

Street scams are easy to avoid if you recognize them. Most common is the too-friendly local who tries to engage you in conversation by asking for the time, talking sports, asking whether you speak English, and so on. Beware of thieves posing as lost tourists who ask for your help. A typical street gambling scam is the pea-and-carrot game, a variation on the shell game. The people winning are all ringers, and you can be sure that you'll lose if you play. Also beware of groups of women aggressively selling carnations, people offering to clean off a stain from your shirt, and people picking things up in front of you on escalators. If you stop for any commotion or show on the Ramblas, put your hands in your pockets before someone else does. Assume any scuffle is simply a distraction by a team of thieves. Crooks are inventive, so keep your guard up. Don't be intimidated...just be smart.

Some areas feel seedy and can be unsafe after dark; I'd avoid the southern part of the Barri Gòtic (basically the two or three blocks directly south and east of Plaça Reial—though the strip near the Carrer de la Mercè tapas bars is better), and I wouldn't venture too deep into the Raval (just west of the Ramblas). One block can separate a comfy tourist zone from the junkies and prostitutes.

US Consulate: It's at Passeig Reina Elisenda 23 (passport services Mon–Fri 9:00–13:00, closed Sat–Sun, tel. 932-802-227).

Emergency Phone Numbers: General emergencies—112, police—092, ambulance—061 or 112.

Pharmacy: A 24-hour pharmacy is near La Boquería market at #98 on the Ramblas.

Laundry: Several self-service launderettes are located around the Old City. **Wash 'n Dry** is on the edge of the tourist zone, near a seedy neighborhood just down the street past the Palau Güell (self-service: wash-€5/load, dry-€2/load, daily 7:00–22:00; full-service: €15/load, Mon–Fri 9:00–14:00 & 17:00–20:00, closed Sat–Sun; Carrer Nou de la Rambla 19, tel. 934-121-953).

Internet Access: EasyInternetcafé—with piles of computers, zippy and cheap access, FedEx and UPS pickup, disc-burning, drinks, and munchies—has two central locations (both open daily 8:30–24:00): One is half a block west of Plaça de Catalunya on Ronda Universitat, behind the Subway sandwich counter at #35; and the other is near the seedy bottom of the Ramblas at #31.

Bike Rental: Biking is a joy in Citadel Park and along the beach (suggested route described on page 63)—but it's stressful in the city center, where pedestrians and cars rule. There are plenty of bike rental places around Citadel Park and La Ribera's Church of Santa Maria del Mar. The handy **Un Cotxe Menys** ("One Car Less"), near the Church of Santa Maria del Mar (50 yards behind the flame memorial), gives out maps and proposed biking routes (€5/hr, €11/4 hrs, daily 10:00–19:00, leave €150 or photo ID for deposit, Esparteria 3, tel. 932-682-105, www.bicicletabarcelona.com);

they also lead bike tours (see "Tours," next page). To rent a bike on the Barceloneta beach, consider **Biciclot** (€6/hr, €13/3 hrs, €18/24 hrs; summer Mon–Thu 10:00–15:00 & 16:00–20:00, Fri–Sun 10:00–15:00 & 16:00–21:00; off-season Sat–Sun only; on the sand 300 yards from Olympic Village towers at Passeig Maritime 33, tel. 932-219-778). Closer to downtown, **Barcelona Rent-A-Bike** is three blocks downhill from Plaça de Catalunya (€6/2 hrs, €10/4 hrs, €15/24 hrs, daily 9:00–20:00, inside the courtyard at Carrer dels Tallers 45, tel. 933-171-970).

Getting Around Barcelona

By Public Transit: Barcelona's Metro, among Europe's best, connects just about every place you'll visit. Rides cost €1.30. Given the excellent Metro service, it's unlikely you'll take a local bus (also €1.30), although I've noted the places where the bus makes sense. The T10 Card for €7.20 gives you 10 rides and is a great deal (shareable, good for all Metro and local bus lines as well as the separate FGC line and RENFE train lines, including trains to the airport). Full-day and multi-day passes are also available (€5.50/1 day, €10/2 days, €14.30/3 days, €18.30/4 days, €21.70/5 days). Automated machines at the Metro entrance have English instructions and sell all types of tickets (though these can be temperamental about accepting payment—nearby ticket windows are staffed during working hours).

Pick up the free Metro map (at any TI) and study it to get familiar with the system. There are several color-coded lines, but most useful for tourists is the **L3 (green) line**—if you're sticking to my recommended sights and neighborhoods, you'll barely have use for any other. Handy city-center stops on this line include (in order):

Sants Estació (main train station);

Espanya (Plaça d'Espanya, with access to the lower part of Montjuïc and trains to Montserrat);

Paral-lel (funicular to top of Montjuïc);

Drassanes (bottom of the Ramblas, near Maritime Museum, Maremagnum mall, and the cable car up to Montjuïc);

Liceu (middle of the Ramblas, near the heart of the Barri Gòtic and cathedral);

Plaça de Catalunya (top of the Ramblas and main square with TI, airport bus, and lots of transportation connections);

Passeig de Gràcia (classy Eixample street at the Block of Discord; also connection to L2/purple line to Sagrada Família and L4/yellow line—described below);

Diagonal (Gaudí's Casa Milà); and

Lesseps (where you can walk or catch bus #24 to Gaudí's Parc Güell).

The **L4 (yellow) line,** which crosses the L3 (green) line at Passeig de Gràcia, is also useful. Helpful stops along here include **Jaume I** (between the Barri Gòtic/cathedral and La Ribera/Picasso Museum) and **Barceloneta** (at the south end of the Ribera, near the harbor action).

When you enter the Metro, first look for your line number and color, then follow signs to take that line in the direction you're going. Insert your ticket into the turnstile (with the arrow pointing in), then reclaim it. Once on board, most trains have handy Metro-line diagrams with dots that light up next to upcoming destinations. Because the lines cross each other multiple times, there can be several ways to make any one journey. Watch your valuables. (If I were a pickpocket, I'd set up shop along the made-for-tourists L3/green line.)

By Tourist Bus: The handy Tourist Bus (Bus Turístic) offers three multi-stop circuits in colorful double-decker buses that go topless in sunny weather. The two-hour red route covers north Barcelona (most Gaudí sights), the two-hour blue route covers south Barcelona (Barri Gòtic, Montjuïc), and the shorter, 40-minute green route covers the beaches and Fòrum. All have headphone commentary (44 stops, daily 9:00–22:00 in summer, 9:00–21:00 in winter, buses run every 5-25 min, most frequent in summer, no green route Oct-mid-March). Ask for a brochure (includes good city map) at the TI or at a pick-up point. One-day (€20) and two-day (€26) tickets, which you can buy on the bus or at the TI, include 10–20 percent discounts on the city's major sights and walking tours, which will likely save you half the cost of the Tourist Bus.

By Taxi: Barcelona is one of Europe's best taxi towns. Taxis are plentiful (there are more than 10,000) and honest (whether they like it or not—the light on top shows which tariff they're charging). They're also reasonable (€2 drop charge, €1 per kilometer, these "*Tarif 2*" rates are in effect 7:00–21:00, pay higher "*Tarif 1*" rates off-hours, luggage-€1/piece, other fees posted in window). Save time by hopping a cab (figure €4 from Ramblas to Sants station). To save even more time, make a point to cross the street if necessary to catch taxis heading in the appropriate direction.

TOURS

Walking Tours—The TI at Plaça de Catalunya offers great guided walks through the **Barri Gòtic** in English only (€11, daily at 10:00, 2 hours, groups limited to 35, departs from the TI, buy your ticket 15 minutes early at the TI desk—not from the guide—in summer call ahead to reserve). A local guide will explain the medieval story of

"You're not in Spain, You're in Catalunya!"

This is a popular nationalistic refrain you might see on T-shirts or stickers around town. Catalunya is *not* the land of bullfighting and flamenco that many visitors envision when they think of Spain (best to wait until you're in Madrid or Sevilla for those).

The region of Catalunya—with Barcelona as its capital—has its own language, history, and culture, and the people have a proud, independent spirit. Historically, Catalunya ("Cataluña" in Spanish, sometimes spelled "Catalonia" in English) has often been at odds with the central Spanish government in Madrid. The Catalan language and culture were discouraged or even outlawed at various times in Spanish history, as Catalunya often chose the wrong side in wars and rebellions against the kings in Madrid. In the Spanish Civil War (1936–1939), Catalunya was one of the last pockets of democratic resistance against the military coup of the fascist dictator Francisco Franco, who punished the region with four decades of repression. During that time, the Catalan flag was banned—but locals vented their national spirit by flying their football team's flag instead.

Three of Barcelona's monuments are reminders of Franco-era suppression: Citadel Park (Parc de la Ciutadella) was originally a much-despised military citadel, constructed in the 18th century to keep locals in line. The Castle of Montjuïc, built for similar reasons, has been the site of numerous political executions, including hundreds during the Franco era. The Sacred Heart Church atop Tibidabo, completed under Franco, was meant to atone for the sins of Barcelonans during the Spanish Civil War—the main sin being opposition to Franco. Although rivalry between Barcelona

the city as you walk from Plaça de Catalunya through the cathedral neighborhood, finishing at the City Hall on Plaça de Sant Jaume. The TI also offers a **Picasso** walk, taking you through the streets of his youth and early career and finishing in the Picasso Museum (€15, includes museum admission, Tue–Sun at 10:30, 2 hrs plus museum visit). There are also **gourmet** walks (€15, Fri and Sat at 11:00, 2 hrs) and **Modernisme** walks (€11, Fri and Sat June–Sept at 18:00, Oct–May at 16:00, 2 hrs). All tours depart from the TI at Plaça de Catalunya.

Bike Tours—Several companies run bike tours around Barcelona. **Un Cotxe Menys** ("One Car Less") organizes three-hour, English-

and Madrid has calmed down in recent times, it rages any time the two cities' football clubs meet.

To see real Catalan culture, look for the *sardana* dance (described on page 55) or an exhibition of *castellers*. These teams of human-castle builders come together for festivals throughout the year to build towers of flesh that can reach more than 50 feet high, topped off by the bravest member of the team—a child! The Gràcia festival in August and the Mercè festival in September are good times to catch the *castellers*.

The Catalan language is irrevocably tied to the history and spirit of the people here. Since the end of the Franco era in the mid-1970s, the language has made a huge resurgence. Now most school-age children learn Catalan first and Spanish second. Although Spanish is understood here (and the basic survival words are the same), Barcelona speaks Catalan.

Here are the essential Catalan phrases:

English	**Catalan**	**Pronounced**
Hello	*Hola*	OH-lah
Please	*Si us plau*	see oos plow
Thank you	*Gracies*	GRAH-see-es
Goodbye	*Adéu*	ah-DAY-oo
Exit	*Sortida*	sor-TEE-dah
Long live Catalunya!	*¡Visca Catalunya!*	BEE-skah kah-tah-LOON-yah

Most place-names in this chapter are listed in Catalan. Here's a pronunciation guide:

Plaça de Catalunya	PLAS-sah duh cat-ah-LOON-yah
Eixample	eye-SHAM-plah
Passeig de Gràcia	PAH-sage duh grass-EE-ah
Catedral	KAH-tah-dral
Barri Gòtic	BAH-ree GOH-teek
Montjuïc	MOHN-jew-eek

only bike tours daily at 11:00 (April–mid-Sept also Fri–Mon at 16:30). Your guide leads you from sight to sight, mostly on bike paths and through parks, with a stop-and-go commentary (€22 includes bike rental and a drink, reservations not necessary, just show up at Plaça de Sant Jaume, next to the TI, tel. 932-682-105, www.biketoursbarcelona.com, also see bike-rental listing on page 35).

Local Guides—The Barcelona Guide Bureau is a co-op with about 20 local guides who give personalized four-hour tours starting at €202 (per person price drops as group gets bigger); **Joana Wilhelm** and **Carles Picazo** are excellent (Via Laietana 54, tel. 932-682-422 or 933-107-778, www.bgb.es). **Jose Soler** is a great and fun-to-be-with

Barcelona at a Glance

▲▲▲**Ramblas** Barcelona's colorful, gritty pedestrian thoroughfare. **Hours:** Always open. See page 41.

▲▲▲**Picasso Museum** Extensive collection offering insight into the brilliant Spanish artist's early years. **Hours:** Tue-Sun 10:00-20:00, closed Mon. See page 56.

▲▲▲**Sagrada Família** Gaudí's remarkable, unfinished cathedral. **Hours:** Daily April-Sept 9:00-20:00, Oct-March 9:00-18:00. See page 68.

▲▲**City History Museum** One-stop trip through town history, from Roman times to today. **Hours:** April-Sept Tue-Sat 10:00-20:00, Sun 10:00-15:00, closed Mon; Oct-March Tue-Sat 10:00-14:00 & 16:00-19:00, Sun 10:00-15:00, closed Mon. See page 55.

▲▲**Catalan Concert Hall** Best Modernista interior in Barcelona. **Hours:** 50-minute English tours daily every hour 10:00-15:00, plus frequent concerts. See page 60.

▲▲**Casa Milà** Barcelona's quintessential Modernista building, the famous melting-ice-cream Gaudí creation. **Hours:** Daily March-Oct 9:00-20:00, Nov-Feb 9:00-18:30. See page 66.

▲▲**Catalan Art Museum** World-class collection of this region's art, including a substantial Romanesque collection. **Hours:** Tue-Sat 10:00-19:00, Sun 10:00-14:30, closed Mon. See page 78.

▲**Maritime Museum** Housed in an impressive medieval shipyard, it's a sailor's delight. **Hours:** Daily 10:00-19:45. See page 51.

▲**Columbus Monument** Elevator ride to the best easy view in town. **Hours:** Daily 9:00-20:30. See page 52.

local guide who enjoys tailoring a walk through his hometown to your interests (€195/half-day per group, mobile 615-059-326, www.pepitotours.com, info@pepitotours.com).

SELF-GUIDED WALKS

Most visitors to Barcelona spend much of their time in the twisty, atmospheric Old City. These two walks will give meaning to your wandering. The first begins at Barcelona's main square and leads you down the city's main drag through one of Europe's best public spaces: the Ramblas. The second walk starts at the same square, but guides

▲**Cathedral of Barcelona** Colossal Gothic cathedral ringed by distinctive chapels. **Hours:** Daily 8:00–19:30. See page 52.

▲**Sardana Dances** Patriotic dance where proud Catalans join hands in a circle. **Hours:** Every Sun at 12:00, usually also Sat at 18:00. See page 55.

▲**Church of Santa Maria del Mar** Catalan Gothic church in La Ribera, built by wealthy medieval shippers. **Hours:** Daily 9:00–13:30 & 16:30–20:00. See page 61.

▲**Block of Discord** Noisy block of competing Modernista facades by Gaudí and his rivals. **Hours:** Always viewable. See page 67.

▲**Parc Güell** Colorful park at the center of an unfinished Gaudí-designed housing project. **Hours:** Daily 10:00–20:00. See page 73.

▲**Palau Güell** Exquisitely curvy Gaudí interior. **Hours:** Tue–Sat 10:00–14:30, closed Sun–Mon. See page 68.

▲**Fundació Joan Miró** World's best collection of works by Catalan modern artist Joan Miró. **Hours:** July–Sept Tue–Sat 10:00–20:00, until 19:00 Oct–June, Thu until 21:30, Sun 10:00–14:30, closed Mon. See page 77.

▲**Magic Fountains** Lively fountains near Plaça d'Espanya. **Hours:** May–Sept 21:00–23:30, no shows Mon–Wed; Oct–April Fri–Sat 19:00–21:00, no shows Sun–Thu. See page 79.

▲**Barcelona's Beach** Fun-filled, man-made stretch of sand reaching from the harbor to the Fòrum. **Hours:** Always open. See page 63.

you into the heart of the Barri Gòtic, to the neighborhood around Barcelona's impressive cathedral.

▲▲▲The Ramblas Ramble: From Plaça de Catalunya down the Ramblas

Barcelona's central square and main boulevard exert a powerful pull. Many visitors spend the majority of their time doing laps on the Ramblas. While the allure of the Ramblas is fading (as tacky tourist shops and fast-food joints replace its former elegance), this is still a fun people zone that offers a good introduction to the city. See it, but be sure to venture farther afield. Here's a top-to-bottom orientation walk.

Plaça de Catalunya: This vast central square divides old and new Barcelona. It's also the hub for the Metro, bus, airport shuttle, and Tourist Bus (red northern route leaves from El Corte Inglés—described below; blue southern route leaves from the west, or Ramblas, side of the square). Overlooking the square, the huge **El Corte Inglés** department store offers everything from bonsai trees to a travel agency, plus one-hour photo developing, haircuts, and cheap souvenirs (Mon–Sat 10:00–22:00, closed Sun, pick up English directory flier, supermarket in basement, ninth-floor terrace cafeteria/restaurant has great city view—take elevator from entrance nearest the TI, tel. 933-063-800). Across the square from El Corte Inglés is **FNAC,** a French department store popular for electronics, music, and books (on west side of square—behind blue Tourist Bus stop; Mon–Sat 10:00–22:00, closed Sun).

Four great boulevards radiate from Plaça de Catalunya: the Ramblas; the fashionable Passeig de Gràcia (top shops, noisy with traffic); the cozier, but still fashionable, Rambla de Catalunya (most pedestrian-friendly); and the stubby, shop-filled, and delightfully traffic-free Avinguda Portal de l'Angel. Homesick Americans can even find a Hard Rock Café. Locals traditionally start or end a downtown rendezvous at the venerable Café Zürich (at the corner near the Ramblas).

• *Cross the street from the café to...*

❶ The Top of the Ramblas: Begin your ramble 20 yards down at the ornate fountain (near #129). More than a Champs-Elysées, this grand boulevard takes you from rich (at the top) to rough (at the port) in a one-mile, 30-minute stroll. You'll raft the river of Barcelonan life past a grand opera house, elegant cafés, retread prostitutes, brazen pickpockets, power-dressing con men, artists, street mimes, an outdoor bird market, great shopping, and people looking to charge more for a shoeshine than what you paid for the shoes.

Grab a bench and watch the scene. Open up your map and read some history into it: You're about to walk right across medieval Barcelona, from Plaça de Catalunya to the harbor. Notice how the higgledy-piggledy street plan of the medieval town was contained within the old town walls—now gone, but traced by a series of roads named Ronda (meaning "to go around"). Find the Roman town,

From Plaça de Catalunya down the Ramblas

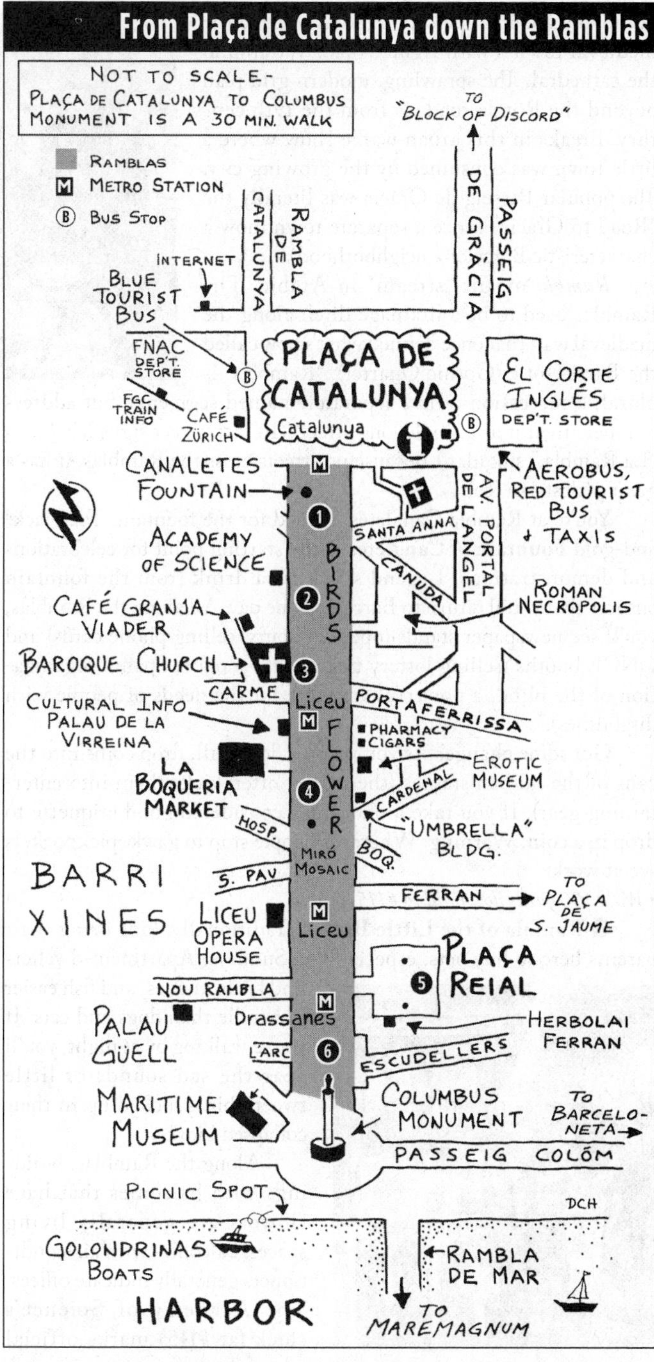

occupying about 10 percent of what became the medieval town—with tighter roads yet around the cathedral. The sprawling, modern grid plan beyond the Ronda roads is from the 19th century. Breaks in this urban waffle show where a little town was consumed by the growing city. The popular Passeig de Gràcia was literally the "Road to Gràcia" (once a separate town, now a characteristic Barcelona neighborhood).

Rambla means "stream" in Arabic. The Ramblas used to be a drainage ditch along the medieval wall that once defined what's now called the Barri Gòtic (Gothic Quarter). "Ramblas" is plural, a succession of five separately named segments, but address numbers treat it as a single long street. (In fact, street signs label it as "La Rambla," singular.) Because no streets cross the Ramblas, it has a great pedestrian feel.

You're at Rambla Canaletes, named for the fountain. The black-and-gold **Fountain of Canaletes** is the starting point for celebrations and demonstrations. Legend says that a drink from the fountain ensures that you'll return to Barcelona one day. All along the Ramblas, you'll see newspaper stands (open 24 hours, selling phone cards) and ONCE booths (selling lottery tickets that support Spain's organization of the blind, a powerful advocate for the needs of people with disabilities).

Got some change? As you wander downhill, drop coins into the cans of the human statues (the money often kicks them into entertaining gear). If you take a photo, it's considered good etiquette to drop in a coin. Warning: Wherever people stop to gawk, pickpockets are at work.

• *Walk 100 yards downhill to #115 and the...*

❷ **Rambla of the Little Birds:** Traditionally, kids bring their parents here to buy pets, especially on Sundays. Apartment-dwellers find birds, turtles, and fish easier to handle than dogs and cats. If you're walking by at night, you'll hear the sad sounds of little tweety birds locked up in their collapsed kiosks.

Along the Ramblas, buildings with balconies that have flowers are generally living spaces; balconies with air-conditioners generally indicate offices. The Academy of Science's clock (at #115) marks official

Barcelona time—synchronize. The Carrefour Express supermarket (at #113, Mon–Sat 10:00–22:00, closed Sun) has cheap groceries.

A recently discovered **Roman necropolis** is in a park across the street from the bird market, 50 yards behind the big, modern Citadines Hotel (go through the passageway at #122). Local apartment-dwellers blew the whistle on contractors, who hoped they could finish their building before anyone noticed the antiquities they had unearthed. Imagine the tomb-lined road leading into the Roman city of Barcino 2,000 years ago.

• *Another 50 yards takes you to Carrer del Carme (at #105), and a...*

❸ **Baroque Church:** The big Betlem church fronting the boulevard is Baroque, unusual in Barcelona. Note the Baroque-style sloping roofline, ball-topped pinnacles, and the scrolls above the entrance. While Barcelona's Gothic age was rich (with buildings to prove it), the Baroque age hardly left a mark. (The city's importance dropped when New World discoveries shifted lucrative trade to ports on the Atlantic.)

For a sweet treat, head down the narrow lane behind the church (going uphill parallel to the Ramblas about 30 yards) to **Café Granja Viader** (see page 89), which has specialized in baked and dairy delights since 1870. (For more sweets, follow "A Short, Sweet Walk"—on page 98—which begins at the intersection in front of the church.)

• *Continue down the boulevard, stroll through the Ramblas of Flowers to the Metro stop marked by the red* M *(near #96), and...*

❹ **La Boquería:** This lively produce market at #91 is an explosion of chicken legs, bags of live snails, stiff fish, delicious oranges, and sleeping dogs (Mon–Sat 8:00–20:00, best mornings after 9:00, closed Sun). Originally outside the walls (as many medieval markets were), it expanded into the colonnaded courtyard of a now-gone monastery. Wander around—as local architect Antoni Gaudí used to—and gain inspiration. The Francesc Conserves shop sells 25 kinds of olives (straight in, near back on right, 100-gram minimum). Full legs of ham *(jamón serrano)* abound; *Paleta Ibérica de Bellota* are the best, and cost about €120 each (see "Sampling *Serrano* Ham," page 290). Beware: *Huevos del toro* are bull testicles—surprisingly inexpensive...and oh so good. Drop by a café for an *espresso con leche* or breakfast (*tortilla española*—potato omelet).

For a quick bite, visit the **Pinotxo Bar** (just to the right as you enter the market, see listing on page 90), where animated Juan and his family are busy feeding shoppers. (Getting Juan to crack a huge smile and a thumbs-up for your camera makes a great shot...and he loves it.) The stools nearby are a fine perch for enjoying both your coffee and the people-watching. The market and lanes nearby are busy with tempting little eateries (see page 90).

• *Now turn your attention across the boulevard.*

The **Museum of Erotica** is your standard European sex museum (€7.50, daily 10:00–22:00, across from market at #96).

To the left, at #100, **Gimeno** sells cigars (appreciate the dying art of cigar boxes). Go ahead, do something forbidden in America but perfectly legal here...buy a Cuban (little singles for less than €1). Tobacco shops sell stamps and phone cards—and plenty of bongs and marijuana gear (the Spanish approach to pot is very casual).

Fifty yards farther, underfoot in the center of the Ramblas, find the much-trod-upon **anchor mosaic**—a reminder of the city's attachment to the sea. Created by noted abstract artist Joan Miró, it marks the midpoint of the Ramblas. (The towering Columbus Monument in the distance—hidden by trees—is at the end of this walk.)

Continue a few more steps down to the **Liceu Opera House.** From the Opera House, cross the Ramblas to Café de l'Opera for a beverage (#74). This bustling café, with Modernista (that is, old-timey) decor and a historic atmosphere, boasts that it's been open since 1929, even during the Spanish Civil War.

• *Continue down the Ramblas to #46; turn left down an arcaded lane (Correr de Colom) to a square filled with palm trees...*

❺ Plaça Reial: This elegant Neoclassical square has a colonial (or maybe post-colonial) ambience. It comes complete with old-fashioned taverns, modern bars with patio seating, a Sunday coin and stamp market (10:00–14:00), Gaudí's first public works (the two colorful helmeted lampposts), and characters who don't need the palm trees to be shady. **Herbolari Ferran** is a fine and aromatic shop of herbs, with fun souvenirs such as top-quality saffron, or *safra* (Mon–Fri 9:30–14:00 & 16:30–20:00, closed Sat–Sun, downstairs at Plaça Reial 18—to the right as you enter the square). The small streets stretching toward the water from the square are intriguing, but less safe.

Back on the other side of the Ramblas, **Palau Güell** offers an enjoyable look at a Gaudí interior (Carrer Nou de la Rambla 3, partly closed for renovation, see page 68). This apartment was the first of

Gaudí's innovative buildings, with a parabolic front doorway that signaled his emerging nonrectangular style.

• *Continue farther downhill on the Ramblas.*

❻ **Bottom of the Ramblas:** The neighborhood on the right-hand side, Barri Xines, is the world's only Chinatown with nothing even remotely Chinese in or near it. Named for the prejudiced notion that Chinese immigrants go hand-in-hand with poverty, prostitution, and drug dealing, the neighborhood's actual inhabitants are poor Spanish, North African, and Roma (Gypsy) people. At night, the Barri Xines is frequented by prostitutes, many of them transvestites, who cater to sailors wandering up from the port. Prostitution is nothing new here. Check out the thresholds at #22 and #24 (along the left side of the Ramblas)—with holes worn long ago by the heels of anxious ladies.

The bottom of the Ramblas is marked by the city's giant medieval shipyards (on the right, now the impressive Maritime Museum) and the Columbus Monument (both are described on page 52). And just beyond the Columbus Monument, **La Rambla del Mar** ("Rambla of the Sea") is a modern extension of the boulevard into the harbor. A popular wooden pedestrian bridge—with waves like the sea—leads to Maremagnum, a soulless Spanish mall with a cinema, huge aquarium, restaurants (including the recommended Tapasbar Maremagnum; see page 91), and piles of people. Late at night, it's a rollicking youth hangout. It's a worthwhile stroll.

The Barri Gòtic: From Plaça de Catalunya to the Cathedral

Barcelona's Barri Gòtic, or Gothic Quarter, is a bustling world of shops, bars, and nightlife packed between hard-to-be-thrilled-about 14th- and 15th-century buildings. The section near the port is generally dull and seedy. But the area around the cathedral is a tangled-yet-inviting grab-bag of undiscovered courtyards, grand squares, schoolyards, Art Nouveau storefronts, baby flea markets on Thursdays, musty junk shops, classy antique shops (on Carrer de la Palla), street musicians strumming Catalan folk songs, and balconies with domestic jungles behind wrought-iron bars. Go on a cultural scavenger hunt. Write a poem. This self-guided walk gives you a structure, covering the main sights and offering a historical overview before you get lost.

• *Start on Barcelona's bustling main square...*

Plaça de Catalunya: This square is the center of the world for seven million Catalan people. The square (described at the start of my Ramblas self-guided walk, above) is decorated with the likenesses of

Barcelona's Barri Gòtic

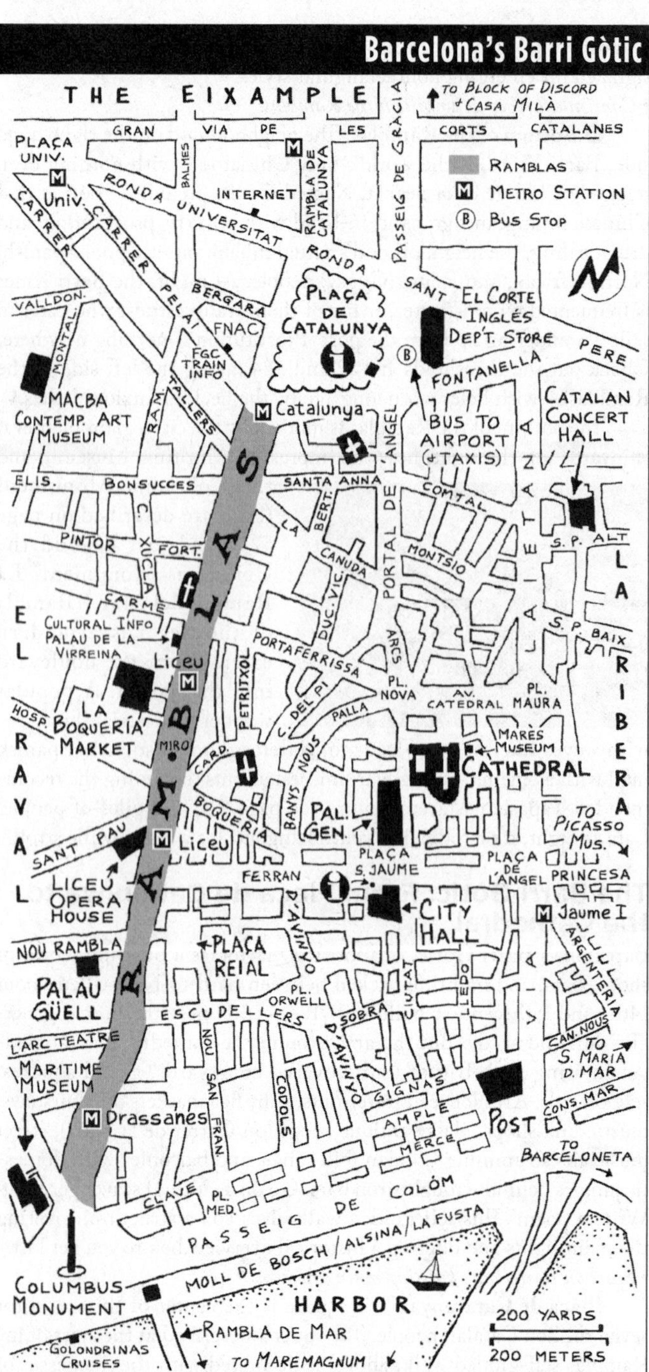

important Catalans. From here, walls that contained the city until the 19th century arc around in each direction to the sea. Looking at your map of Barcelona, you'll see a regimented waffle design—except for the higgledy-piggledy old town corralled by these walls.

The city grew with its history. Originally a Roman town, Barcelona was ruled by the Visigoths from the fall of Rome until 714, when the Moors arrived (they were, in turn, sent packing by the French in 801—because their stay was cut so short, there are few Moorish-style buildings here). Finally, in the 10th century, the Count of Barcelona unified the region, and the idea of Catalunya came to be. The area between Plaça de Catalunya and the old Roman walls (circling the smaller ancient town, down by the cathedral) was settled by churches, each a magnet gathering a small community outside the walls (or "extra muro"). Around 1250, when these "extra muro" communities became numerous and strong enough, the king agreed to invest in a larger wall, and Barcelona expanded. This outer wall was torn down in the 1850s and replaced by a series of circular boulevards (named Rondas).

• *From Plaça de Catalunya's TI, head downhill, crossing the busy street into a broad pedestrian boulevard called...*

Avinguda Portal de l'Angel: This boulevard is named "Gate of the Angel" for the gate in the medieval wall—crowned by an angel—that once stood here. The angel kept the city safe from plagues and bid voyagers safe journey as they left the security of the city. Imagine the fascinating scene here at the Gate of the Angel, where Barcelona stopped and the wilds began.

Walking down the Avinguda Portal de l'Angel, consider an optional detour a half-block right on **Carrer de Santa Anna,** where a lane on the right leads into a courtyard facing one of those "extra muro" churches, with a fine cloister and simple, typically Romanesque facade.

Continuing down the main boulevard, you reach a fork in the road with a blue-and-yellow-tiled **fountain.** This was once a freestanding well—in the 17th century, it was the last watering stop for horses before leaving town. Take the left fork to the cathedral (past the Architects' House with its Picasso-inspired frieze).

Enter the square, where you'll stand before two bold **towers**—the remains of the old Roman wall that protected a smaller Barcino, as the city was called in ancient times. The big stones that make up the base of the towers are actually Roman. The wall stretches left of the towers, incorporated into the Deacon's House (which you'll enter from the other side later).

• *The sights from here on are located on the map on*

page 53. Walk around—past the modern bronze letters BARCINO *and the mighty facade of the cathedral (which we'll enter momentarily)—and go inside the...*

Deacon's House: Visitors are welcome inside this mansion, which today functions as the city archives (its front door faces the wall of the church). It's a good example of a Renaissance nobleman's palace. Notice how the century-old palm tree seems to be held captive by urban man. Inside you can see the Roman stones up close. Upstairs affords a good view of the cathedral's exterior—textbook Catalan Gothic (plain and practical, like this merchant community) next to textbook Romanesque (the smaller, once freestanding, more humble church adjacent on the right—which you'll visit entering from the church's cloister later).

• *Exit the house to the left and follow the lane. You'll emerge at the entrance to the...*

Cathedral of Barcelona (Catedral de Barcelona): This huge house of worship is worth a look. Its vast size, peaceful cloister, and many ornate chapels—each one sponsored by a local guild—are impressive. For a self-guided tour, see the "Cathedral of Barcelona" listing on page 52.

• *After visiting the cathedral's cloister, exit and walk to the tiny lane ahead on the right (far side of the statue, Carrer de Montjuïc del Bisbe). This leads to the cute...*

Plaça Sant Felip Neri: This square serves as the playground of an elementary school bursting with youthful energy. The Church of Sant Felip Neri, which Gaudí attended, is still pocked with bomb damage from the Civil War. As a stronghold of democratic, anti-Franco forces, Barcelona saw a lot of fighting. The shrapnel that damaged this church was meant for the nearby Catalan government building (Palau de la Generalitat, described below).

Study the medallions on the wall. Guilds powered the local economy, and the carved reliefs here show that this building must have housed the shoemakers. In fact, on this square you'll find a fun little Shoe Museum (see page 55).

• *Circle the block back to the cathedral's cloister and take a right, walking along Carrer del Bisbe next to the huge building (on the right) stretching all the way to the next square...*

Palau de la Generalitat: For nearly 600 years, this place has been the home of the Catalan government. Through good times and bad, the Catalan spirit has survived, and this building has housed its capital.

• *Continue along Carrer del Bisbe to...*

Plaça de Sant Jaume (jow-mah): This stately central square of the Barri Gòtic, once the Roman forum, has been the seat of city government for 2,000 years. Today the two top governmental buildings in Catalunya face each other: the Barcelona City Hall (Ajuntament; free but open to the public only Sun 10:00–13:30) and the seat of the autonomous government of Catalunya (Palau de la Generalitat, described above). It always flies the Catalan flag (red and yellow stripes) next to the obligatory Spanish one. From these balconies, the nation's leaders (and soccer heroes) greet the people on momentous days.

• *Take two quick left turns from the corner of Carrer Bisbe (just 10 yards away), and climb Carrer del Paridís. Follow this street as it turns right, but pause when it swings left, at the summit of...*

"Mont" Tàber: A millstone in the corner marks ancient Barcino's highest elevation, a high spot in the road called Mount Tàber. A plaque on the wall says it all: "Mont Tàber, 16.9 meters." Step into the courtyard for a peek at a surviving corner of the imposing **Roman temple** (Temple Roma d'August), which once stood here on Mont Tàber, keeping a protective watch over Barcino (free, well-explained on wall in English, daily 10:00–14:00 & 16:00–20:00).

• *Continue down Carrer del Paridís back to the cathedral, take a right, and go downhill about 100 yards to...*

Plaça del Rei: The Royal Palace sat on this "King's Square" (a block from the cathedral) until Catalunya became part of Spain in the 15th century. Then it was the headquarters of the local Inquisition. In 1493, a triumphant Christopher Columbus, accompanied by six New World natives (whom he called "Indians") and several pure-gold statues, entered the Royal Palace. King Ferdinand and Queen Isabel rose to welcome him home, and they honored him with the title "Admiral of the Oceans."

• *Your tour is over. Nearby, just off Plaça del Rei, is another sight—the City History Museum (described on page 55). And the Frederic Marès Museum is just up the street (toward the cathedral entrance; see page 56). Or simply wander and enjoy Barcelona at its Gothic best.*

SIGHTS

Barcelona's Old City

I've divided Barcelona's Old City sights into three neighborhoods: near the harbor, at the bottom of the Ramblas; the cathedral and nearby (Barri Gòtic); and the Picasso Museum and nearby (La Ribera).

On the Harborfront, at the Bottom of the Ramblas

▲Maritime Museum (Museu Marítim)—Barcelona's medieval shipyard, the best preserved in the entire Mediterranean, is now an impressive museum covering the salty history of ships and navigation from the 13th to the 20th centuries. Riveting for nautical types, and interesting for anyone, its modern and beautifully presented exhibits will put you in a seafaring mood. The museum's cavernous halls evoke the 14th-century days when Catalunya was a naval and shipbuilding power, cranking out 30 huge galleys a winter. As in the US today, military and commercial ventures mixed and mingled as Catalunya built its trading empire. The excellent included audioguide tells the story and explains the various seafaring vessels displayed—including an impressively huge and richly decorated royal galley (€6.50, €7.20 combo-ticket includes Columbus Monument, daily 10:00–19:45, last entry at 19:00, breezy courtyard café, Avinguda de la Drassanes, tel. 933-429-920).

▲Columbus Monument (Monument a Colóm)—Marking the point where the Ramblas hits the harbor, this 200-foot-tall monument built for an 1888 exposition offers an elevator-assisted view from its top. The tight four-person elevator takes you to the glassed-in observation area at the top for congested but fine views (€2.30, daily 9:00–20:30). It was here in Barcelona that Ferdinand and Isabel welcomed Columbus home after his first trip to America. It's ironic that Barcelona would so honor the man whose discoveries ultimately led to its downfall as a great trading power.

***Golondrinas* Cruises**—At the harbor near the foot of the Columbus Monument, tourist boats called *golondrinas* offer two different, unguided tours. The shorter version goes around the harbor in 35 minutes (€5.50, daily on the hour 11:30–19:00, every 30 min mid-June–mid-Sept, sometimes does not run Nov–April—call ahead, tel. 934-423-106). The longer, 90-minute tour goes up the coast to the new Fòrum complex and back (€11.50, can disembark at Fòrum in summer only, about 7/day, daily 11:30–19:30).

▲Cathedral of Barcelona

Most of the construction on Barcelona's vast cathedral (Catedral de Barcelona) took place in the 14th century, during the glory days of the Catalan nation. The facade was humble, so in the 19th century, the proud local bourgeoisie redid it in a more ornate Neo-Gothic style.

Cost, Hours, Location: Strangely, even though the cathedral is free to enter daily 8:00–12:45 (13:45 on Sun) and 17:15–19:30, you must pay €5 to enter between 12:45–17:15 (tel. 933-151-554). The dress code is strictly enforced; don't wear tank tops, short shorts, or short skirts.

Getting There: The huge, can't-miss-it cathedral is in the center of the Barri Gòtic,

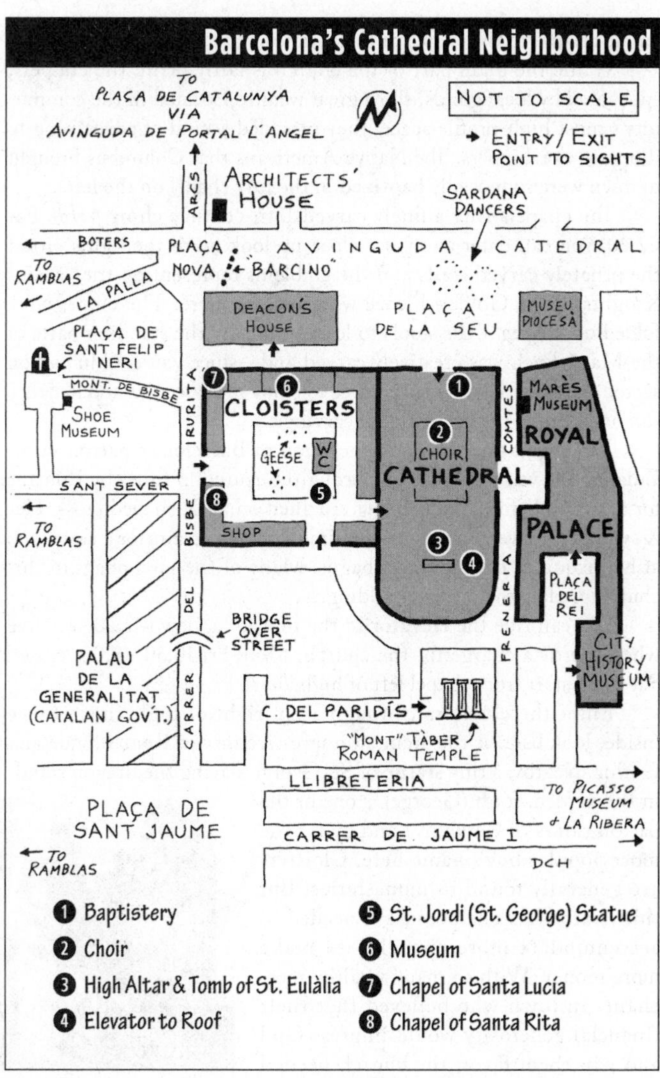

on Plaça de la Seu. For an interesting way to reach the cathedral from Plaça de Catalunya, and some commentary on the surrounding neighborhood, see my self-guided walk of the Barri Gòtic on page 47.

➲ **Self-Guided Tour:** Though the cathedral is Gothic and supported by buttresses, it has smooth outside walls. That's because the supporting buttresses are on the inside, providing walls for 28 richly ornamented chapels. This, along with the interior's open and spacious feeling, is typical of Catalan Gothic. Typical of all medieval churches, the cathedral has an "ambulatory" plan—allowing worshippers to amble around to the chapel of their choice.

While the main part of the church is fairly plain, the **chapels,** sponsored by local guilds, show great wealth. Located in the community's most high-profile space, they provided a kind of advertising to illiterate worshippers. The Native Americans that Columbus brought to town were supposedly **baptized** in the first chapel on the left.

The chapels ring a finely carved 15th-century **choir** *(coro)*. For €2.20, you can enter and get a close-up look (with the lights on) of the ornately carved stalls and the emblems representing the various Knights of the Golden Fleece who once sat here. The chairs were folded up, giving VIPs stools to lean on during the standing parts of the Mass. Each was creatively carved and—since you couldn't sit on sacred things—the artists were free to enjoy some secular and naughty fun here. Study the upper tier of carvings.

The **high altar** sits upon the tomb of Barcelona's patron saint, Eulàlia. She was a 13-year-old local girl tortured 13 times by Romans for her faith before finally being crucified on an X-shaped cross. Her X symbol is carved on the pews. Climb down the stairs for a close look at her exquisite marble sarcophagus. Many of the sarcophagi in this church predate the present building.

You can ride the **elevator** to the roof for a view (€2.20—or free when there's a charge for the church, Mon–Fri 10:30–18:00, closed Sat–Sun, start from chapel left of high altar).

Enter the **cloisters** (through arch, right of high altar). Once inside, look back at the arch, an impressive mix of Romanesque and Gothic. Nearby, a tiny **statue** of St. George slaying the dragon stands in the garden. Jordi (George) is one of the patron saints of Catalunya and by far the most popular boy's name here. Cloisters are generally found in monasteries. But this church has one because it needed to accommodate more chapels—to make more money. With so many wealthy merchants in town who believed that their financial generosity would impress God and win them favor, the church needed more private chapel space. Merchants wanted to be buried close to the altar, and their tombs also spill over into the cloister. On the pavement stones, as in the chapels, notice the symbols of the trades or guilds: scissors, shoes, bakers, and so on.

Long ago the resident **geese**—there are always 13, in memory of Eulàlia—functioned as an alarm system. Any commotion would get them honking, alerting the monk in charge. They honk to this very day.

From the statue of St. Jordi, circle to the right (past a WC hidden on the left). The skippable little €2 **museum** (far corner) is one plush

Sardana Dances

The patriotic *sardana* dances are held at the cathedral (every Sun at 12:00, usually also Sat at 18:00). Locals of all ages seem to spontaneously appear. For some, it's a highly symbolic, politically charged action representing Catalan unity—but for most, it's just a fun chance to kick up their heels. Participants gather in circles after putting their things in the center—symbolic of community and sharing (and the ever-present risk of theft). All are welcome, even tourists cursed with two left feet.

Holding hands, dancers raise their arms—slow-motion *Zorba the Greek*-style—as they hop and sway gracefully to the music. The band *(cobla)* consists of a long flute, tenor and soprano oboes, strange-looking brass instruments, and a tiny bongo-like drum *(tambori)*. The rest of Spain mocks this lazy circle dance, but considering what it takes for a culture to survive within another culture's country, it is a stirring display of local pride and patriotism. The event lasts between one and two hours.

room with a dozen old religious paintings. Just beyond the museum in the corner, built into the outside wall of the cloister, is the dark, barrel-vaulted, Romanesque **Chapel of Santa Lucía,** a small church that predates the cathedral. People hoping for good eyesight (Santa Lucía's specialty) leave candles outside. Farther along the cloister, the **Chapel of Santa Rita** (her forte: impossible causes) usually has the most candles.

In the Barri Gòtic, near the Cathedral

For an interesting route from Plaça de Catalunya to the cathedral neighborhood, see my self-guided walk of the Barri Gòtic on page 47. And if you're in town on a weekend, don't miss the *sardana* dances (see above).

Shoe Museum (Museu del Calçat)—Shoe-lovers enjoy this two-room shoe museum, watched over by a we-try-harder attendant. The huge shoes at the entry are designed to fit the foot of the Columbus Monument at the bottom of the Ramblas (€2.50, Tue–Sun 11:00–14:00, closed Mon, 1 block beyond outside door of cathedral cloister, behind Plaça de G. Bachs on Plaça Sant Felip Neri, tel. 933-014-533).

▲▲City History Museum (Museu d'Història de la Ciutat)—Walk through the history of the city with the help of an included audioguide. First watch the fine nine-minute introductory video in the small theater (playing alternately in Catalan, Spanish, and English)—it's worth viewing in any language. Then take an elevator down 65 feet (and 2,000 years—see the date spin back as you descend) to stroll the streets of Roman Barcelona. You'll see sewers, models of domestic life, and bits of an early-Christian church. Finally, an exhibit in the 11th-century count's palace shows you Barcelona through the Middle Ages (€6; April–Sept Tue–Sat 10:00–20:00, Sun 10:00–15:00, closed Mon; Oct–March Tue–Sat 10:00–14:00 & 16:00–19:00, Sun 10:00–15:00, closed Mon; Plaça del Rei, enter on Vageur street, tel. 932-562-122).

Frederic Marès Museum (Museu Frederic Marès)—This eclectic collection of local artist (and pack-rat) Frederic Marès sprawls around a peaceful courtyard through several old Barri Gòtic buildings. The biggest part of the collection is sculpture, from ancient times to the early 20th century. But even more interesting is Marès' vast collection of items he found representative of everyday life in the 19th century—rooms upon rooms of fans, stamps, pipes, and other bric-a-brac, all lovingly displayed. There are also several sculptures by Frederic Marès himself, and temporary exhibits (€4.20, free Wed afternoon; open Tue–Sat 10:00–19:00, Sun 10:00–15:00, closed Mon; Plaça de Sant Iu 5–6, tel. 932-563-500, www.museumares.bcn.cat). The delightfully tranquil courtyard café offers a nice break, even if you're not going to the museum.

▲▲▲Picasso Museum (Museu Picasso)

This is the best collection in the country of the work of Spaniard Pablo Picasso (1881–1973), and—since he spent his formative years (age 14–21) in Barcelona—it's the best collection of his early works anywhere. By seeing his youthful, realistic art, you can more fully appreciate the artist's genius and better understand his later, more challenging art. The collection is scattered through several connected Gothic palaces, six blocks from the cathedral in the Ribera district (for more on this area, see "In La Ribera, near the Picasso Museum," below).

Cost, Hours, Location: €9, free on first Sun of month, open Tue–Sun 10:00–20:00, closed Mon, Montcada 15–23, ticket office at #21, Metro: Jaume I, tel. 932-563-000, www.museupicasso.bcn.cat. The ground floor has a required bag check, as well as a handy array of other services (bookshop, WC, and cafeteria).

Crowd-Beating Tips: There's almost always a line, but it moves quickly (you'll rarely wait more than an hour to get in). The busiest time is from when it opens until about 13:00 (worst on Tuesdays); generally the later in the afternoon you visit, the fewer the crowds. If you have an Articket Card (see page 32), you can skip the line by going to the group entrance.

Hungry? The museum itself has a good café. The Textil Café, hiding in a beautiful and inviting museum courtyard across the street, is an ideal place to sip a *café con leche* or eat a light meal (€5–10 salads, couscous, and quiche fare; Tue–Sun 10:00–24:00, closed Mon, 30 yards from Picasso Museum at Montcada 12–14, tel. 932-682-598; also hosts jazz concerts Sunday nights 21:00–23:00 weather permitting—usually not in winter, stand for free or pay €5 cover to sit). And just down the street is a neighborhood favorite for tapas, El Xampanyet (see page 95).

Background: Picasso's personal secretary amassed a huge collection of his work and bequeathed it to the city. Picasso, happy to have a fine museum showing off his work in the city of his youth, added to the collection throughout his life. (Sadly, since Picasso vowed never to set foot in a fascist, Franco-ruled Spain, and died two years before Franco, the artist never saw the museum.)

➲ **Self-Guided Tour:** While the rooms are sometimes rearranged, the collection (291 paintings) is always presented chronologically. With the help of thoughtful English descriptions for each stage (and blue-shirted guards who don't let you stray), it's easy to follow the evolution of Picasso's work. The room numbers—though not exact—can help you get oriented in the museum. You'll see his art evolve in these stages:

Room 1—Boy Wonder, Age 12–14, 1895–1897: Pablo's earliest art is realistic and serious. A budding genius emerges at age 12 as Pablo moves to Barcelona and gets serious about art. Even this young, his portraits of grizzled peasants show great psychological insight and flawless technique. You'll see portraits of Pablo's first teacher, his father *(El Padre del Artista)*. Displays show his art-school work. Every time Pablo starts breaking rules, he's sent back to the standard classic style. The assignment: Sketch nude models to capture human anatomy accurately. Early self-portraits (1896, 1897) show the self-awareness of a blossoming intellect (and a kid who must have been a handful in junior high school). When Pablo was 13, his father quit painting to nurture his young prodigy. Look closely at the portrait of his mother *(Retrato de la Madre del Artista)*. Pablo, then age 15, is working on the fine details and gradients of white in her blouse and the expression in her cameo-like face. Notice the signature. Spaniards keep both parents' surnames, with the father's first, followed by the mother's: Pablo Ruiz Picasso. Pablo was closer to his mom than his dad. Eventually he kept just her name.

Room 2—Adolescence, Developing Talent: During a short trip to Málaga, Picasso dabbles in Impressionism (otherwise unknown in

Spain at the time). Later, as a 15-year-old, Pablo dutifully enters art-school competitions. His first big work—while forced to show a religious subject (*Primera Comunión,* or *First Communion,* Room 7)—is more an excuse to paint his family. Notice his sister Lola's exquisitely painted veil. This painting was heavily influenced by local painters.

Room 3—Early Success: *Ciencia y Caridad (Science and Charity),* which won second prize at a fine-arts exhibition, got Picasso the chance to study in Madrid. Now Picasso conveys real feeling. The doctor (Pablo's father) represents science. The nun represents charity and religion. From her hopeless face and lifeless hand, it seems that Picasso believes nothing will save this woman from death. Pablo painted a little perspective trick: Walk back and forth across the room to see the bed stretch and shrink. Three small studies for this painting, hanging in the back of the room, show how this was an exploratory work. The frontier: light.

Picasso travels to Madrid for further study. Finding the stuffy fine-arts school in Madrid stifling, Pablo hangs out in the Prado Museum and learns by copying the masters. Notice his nearly perfect copy of Felipe IV by Diego Velázquez. Having absorbed the wisdom of the ages, in 1898, Pablo visits Horta de San Juan, a rural Catalan village, and finds his artistic independence. Poor and without a love in his life, he returns to Barcelona.

Room 4—Barcelona Freedom, 1900: Art Nouveau is the rage. Upsetting his dad, Pablo quits art school and falls in with the avant-garde crowd. These bohemians congregate daily at Els Quatre Gats ("The Four Cats," slang for "a few crazy people"—a popular restaurant to this day). Further establishing his artistic freedom, he paints portraits—no longer of his family...but of his new friends. Still a teenager, Pablo puts on his first one-man show.

Rooms 5–7—Paris, 1900–1901: Nineteen-year-old Picasso arrives in Paris, a city bursting with life, light, and love. Dropping the paternal surname Ruiz, Pablo establishes his commercial brand name: "Picasso." Here, the explorer Picasso goes bohemian and befriends poets, prostitutes, and artists. He paints Impressionist landscapes like Claude Monet, cancan dancers like Toulouse-Lautrec, still lifes like Paul Cézanne, and bright-colored Fauvist works like Henri Matisse. (*La Espera*—with her bold outline and strong gaze—pops out from the Impressionistic background.) It was Cézanne's technique of "building" a figure with "cubes" of paint that inspired Picasso to soon invent Cubism.

Temporary Exhibits: As if to cleanse the museum-goer's palate before plunging into the major stuff, you'll now walk through some temporary exhibits.

Room 8—Blue Period, 1901–1904: The bleak Paris weather, the suicide of his best friend, and his own poverty lead Picasso to his "Blue Period." He cranks out piles of blue art just to stay housed and fed. With blue backgrounds (the coldest color) and depressing subjects, this period was revolutionary in art history. Now the artist is painting not what he sees but what he feels. The touching portrait of a mother and child, *Desamparados* (*Despair*, 1903), captures the period well. Painting misfits and street people, Picasso, like Velázquez and Toulouse-Lautrec, sees "the beauty in ugliness." Back home in Barcelona, Picasso paints his hometown at night from rooftops *(Azoteas de Barcelona)*. Still blue, here we see proto-Cubism...five years before the first real Cubist painting.

Room 9—Rose Period, 1904–1907: The woman in pink *(Retrato de la Señora Canals)*, painted with classic "Spanish melancholy," finally lifts Picasso out of his funk, moving him out of the blue and into a happier "Rose Period" (of which this museum has only the one painting).

Room 11—Cubism, 1907–1920: Pablo's invention in Paris of the shocking Cubist style is well-known—at least I hope so, since this museum has no true Cubist paintings. In the age of the camera, the Cubist gives just the basics (a man with a bowl of fruit) and lets you finish it.

Also in Rooms 9 and 10—Eclectic, 1920–1950: Picasso is a painter of many styles. In *Mujer con Mantilla* (Room 9), we see a little post-Impressionistic Pointillism in a portrait that looks like a classical statue. After a trip to Rome, he paints beefy women, inspired by the three-dimensional sturdiness of ancient statues. To Spaniards, the expressionist horse symbolizes the innocent victim (Room 10). In bullfights, the horse—clad with blinders and pummeled by the bull—has nothing to do with the fight. To Picasso, the horse symbolized the feminine, and the bull, the masculine. Picasso would mix all these styles and symbols—including this image of the horse—in his masterpiece *Guernica* (in Madrid's Centro de Arte Reina Sofía—see page 332) to show the horror and chaos of modern war.

From here, follow signs to Rooms 12–14.

Rooms 12–14—Picasso and Velázquez, 1957: Notice the small print of Velázquez's *Las Meninas* (in Madrid's Prado). Picasso, who

had great respect for Velázquez, painted more than 50 interpretations of this painting that many consider the greatest painting by anyone, ever. These two Spanish geniuses were artistic equals. Picasso seems to enjoy a relationship with Velázquez. Like artistic soulmates, they spar and tease. He dissects Velázquez, and then injects playful uses of light, color, and perspective to horse around with the earlier masterpiece. In the big black-and-white canvas, the king and queen (reflected in the mirror in the back of the room) are hardly seen, while the self-portrait of the painter towers above everyone. The two women of the court on the right look like they're in a tomb—but they're wearing party shoes. In these rooms, see the fun Picasso had playing paddleball with Velázquez's masterpiece—filtering Velázquez's realism through the kaleidoscope of Cubism.

All his life, Picasso said, "Paintings are like windows open to the world." In Room 14, we see the French Riviera—with simple black outlines and Crayola colors, Picasso paints sun-splashed nature and the joys of the beach. He died with brush in hand, still growing. To the end, Picasso continued exploring and loving life through his art. As a child, he was taught to paint as an adult. Now, as an old man (with little kids of his own and also-childlike artist Marc Chagall for a friend), he paints like a child.

Rooms 15–16—Ceramics, 1947: As a wrap-up, walk through 41 ceramic works Picasso made during his later years.

In La Ribera, near the Picasso Museum

There's more to the Ribera neighborhood than just the Picasso Museum. While the nearby waterfront Barceloneta district was for the working-class sailors, La Ribera housed the wealthier shippers and merchants. Its streets are lined with their fine mansions—which, like the much-appreciated Church of Santa Maria del Mar, were built with shipping wealth.

La Ribera (also known as "El Born") is separated from the Barri Gòtic by Via Laietana, a four-lane highway built through the Old City in the early 1900s to alleviate growing traffic problems. From the Plaça de l'Angel (with the nearest Metro stop—Jaume I), cross this busy street to enter an up-and-coming zone of lively and creative restaurants and nightlife. The Carrer de l'Argenteria ("Goldsmiths Street"—streets in La Ribera are named after the workshops that used to occupy them) runs diagonally from the Plaça de l'Angel straight down to the Church of Santa Maria del Mar. The Catalan Concert Hall is to the north.

▲▲Catalan Concert Hall (Palau de la Música Catalana)—This concert hall, finished in 1908, features my favorite Modernista interior in town (by Lluís Domènech i Muntaner). Inviting arches lead you into the 2,138-seat hall. A kaleidoscopic skylight features a choir singing around the sun, while playful carvings and mosaics celebrate music and Catalan culture. Admission is by tour only and starts with a relaxing 12-minute video (€10, 50-min tours in English run daily every hour 10:00–15:00, tour times may change based on performance schedule, about 6 blocks northeast of cathedral, tel. 932-957-200, www. palaumusica.org).

The catch: You must buy your ticket in advance to get a spot on an English guided tour (tickets available up to 7 days in advance—ideally buy yours at least 2 days before, sometimes available the day before).

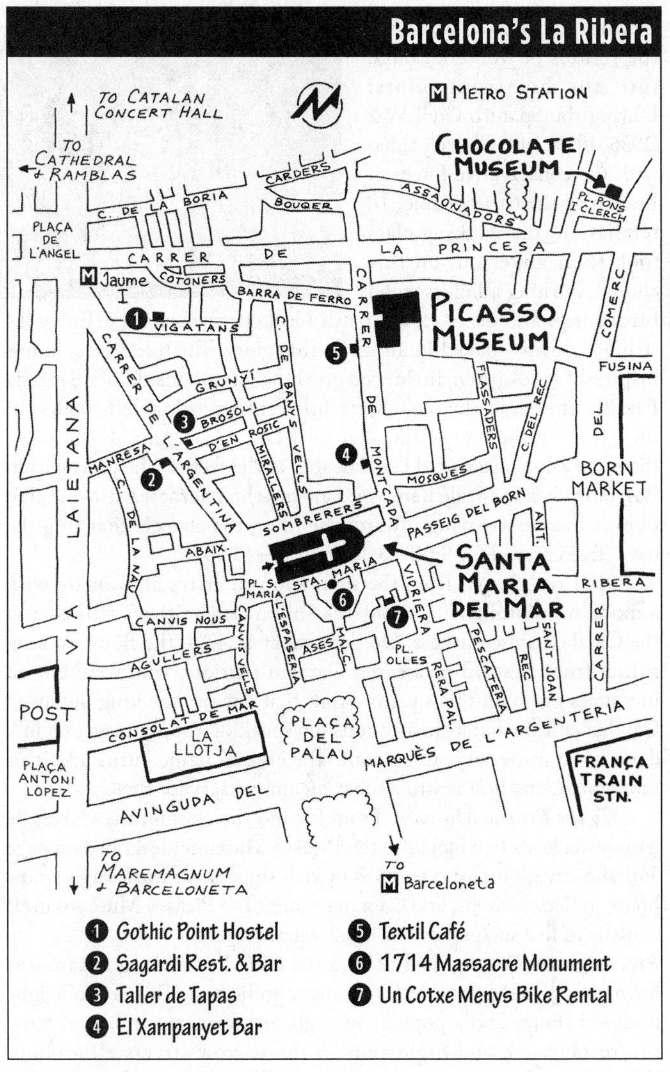

You can buy the ticket in person at the concert hall box office (open daily 9:30–15:30); by phone with your credit card (tel. 902-485-475); or online via the concert hall website (www. palaumusica.org).

It might be easier to get tickets for a **concert** (300 per year, tickets for some performances as cheap as €7, see website for details).

▲Church of Santa Maria del Mar—This church is the proud centerpiece of La Ribera. "Del Mar" means "of the sea," and that's where the money came from. The proud shippers built this church in only 55 years, so it has a harmonious style considered pure Catalan

Gothic. As you step in, notice the figures of workers carved into the big front doors. During the Spanish Civil War (1936–1939), the Church sided with the conservative forces of Franco against the people. In retaliation, the working class took their anger out on this church, burning all of its wood furnishings and decor (carbon still blackens the ceiling). Today it's stripped down—naked in all its Gothic glory. The tree-like columns inspired Gaudí (their influence on the columns inside his Sagrada Família church is obvious). Sixteenth-century sailors left models of their ships at the foot of the altar for Mary's protection. Even today, there remains a classic old Catalan ship at the feet of Mary. As within Barcelona's cathedral, here you can see the characteristic Catalan Gothic buttresses flying inwards, defining the chapels that ring the nave (free entry, daily 9:00–13:30 & 16:30–20:00).

Exit the church from the side, and you arrive at a square with a modern **monument** to a 300-year-old massacre that's still part of the Catalan consciousness. On September 11, 1714, the Bourbon king ruling from Madrid massacred Catalan patriots, who were buried in a mass grave on this square. From that day on, the king outlawed Catalan culture and its institutions (no speaking the language, no folk dances, no university, and so on). The eternal flame burns atop this monument, and 9/11 is still a sobering anniversary for the Catalans.

To the Picasso Museum: From behind the church, the Carrer de Montcada leads two blocks to the Picasso Museum (described on page 56). The street's mansions—built by rich shippers centuries ago—now house galleries, shops, and even museums. The Picasso Museum itself consists of five such mansions laced together.

Passeig del Born—Just behind the church, this long square was formerly a jousting square (as its shape indicates). This is the neighborhood center and a popular springboard for exploring tapas bars, fun restaurants, and nightspots in the narrow streets all around. Wandering around here at night, you'll find piles of inviting and intriguing little restaurants (I've listed my favorites in "Eating," page 88). Enjoy a glass of wine on the square facing the church, or consider renting a bike here for a pedal down the beach promenade to the Fòrum (described on next page).

Chocolate Museum (Museu de la Xocolata)—This museum, only a couple of blocks from the Picasso Museum (and near Citadel Park—see below), is a delight for chocolate-lovers. Operated by the local confectioners' guild, it tells the story of chocolate from Aztecs to Europeans via the port of Barcelona, where it was first unloaded and processed. But the history lesson is just an excuse to show off a series of remarkably ornate candy sculptures. These works of edible art—which change every year but often include such Spanish themes as Don Quixote or bullfighting—begin as store-window displays for Easter or Christmas. Once the holiday passes, the confectioners bring the sculptures here to be enjoyed (€4, Mon and Wed–Sat 10:00–19:00, Sun 10:00–15:00, closed Tue, Carrer Comerç 36, tel. 932-687-878, www.museuxocolata.com).

Near the Waterfront, East of the Old City and Harbor

Citadel Park (Parc de la Ciutadella)—Barcelona's biggest, greenest park, originally the site of a much-hated military citadel, was transformed in 1888 for a World's Fair (Universal Exhibition). The stately Triumphal Arch at the top of the park, celebrating the removal of the citadel, was built as the main entrance. Inside, you'll find wide pathways, plenty of trees and grass, a zoo, and museums of geology and zoology. Barcelona, one of Europe's most densely populated cities, suffers from a lack of real green space. This park is a haven, and especially enjoyable on weekends when it teems with happy families. Enjoy the ornamental fountain that the young Antoni Gaudí helped design, and consider a jaunt in a rental rowboat on the lake in the center of the park. Check out the tropical Umbracle greenhouse and the Hivernacle winter garden, which has a pleasant café-bar (daily 8:00–20:00, Metro: Arc de Triomf, east of França train station).

▲Barcelona's Beach, from Barceloneta to the Fòrum—Barcelona has created a summer tourist beach trade by building a huge stretch of beaches east from the town center. Before the 1992 Olympics, this area was an industrial wasteland nicknamed the "Catalan Manchester." Not anymore. The industrial zone was demolished and dumped into the sea, while sand was dredged out of the sea bed to make the pristine beaches locals enjoy today. The scene is great for sunbathing and for an evening paseo before dinner. It's like a resort island—complete with lounge chairs, volleyball, showers, bars, WCs, and bike paths.

Bike the Beach: For a break from the city, rent a bike (in La Ribera or Citadel Park—for details, see "Helpful Hints," page 35) and take the following little ride: Explore Barcelona's "Central Park"—Citadel Park—filled with families enjoying a day out (described earlier). Then roll through Barceloneta (an artificial peninsula, once the home of working-class sailors and shippers). From the Barceloneta beach, head west to the Olympic Village, where the former apartments for 13,000 visiting athletes now house permanent residents. The village's symbol, Frank Gehry's striking "fish," shines brightly in the sun. A bustling night scene keeps this stretch of harborfront busy until the wee hours. From here you'll come to a series of man-made, crescent-shaped beaches, each with trendy bars and cafés. If you're careless (down by Platja de la Mar Bella), you might find yourself pedaling through people working on an all-over tan. In the distance, you see the huge solar panel marking the site of the Fòrum shopping and convention center (described below).

The Fòrum—The original 1860 vision for Barcelona's enlargement continued the boulevard called Diagonal right to the sea. They finally realized this goal nearly a century and a half later, with the opening of the Fòrum. Go here for a taste of today's Barcelona: nothing Gothic, nothing quaint, just big and modern—a mall and a convention center. In 2004, Barcelona hosted the "Forum of the Cultures," an attempt to create a world's fair that recognized not states, but peoples. Roma (Gypsies), Basques, Māoris, Native Americans, and Catalans all assembled here in a global celebration of cultural diversity, multiculturalism, peace, and sustainability.

The Fòrum also tries to be an inspiration for environmental engineering. Waste is burned to create heat. The giant solar panel creates perfectly clean and sustainable energy. The festival was a moderate success and might be repeated as a bash for this planet's "nations without states." Local government officials hoped the event—like other "expos"—would goose development...and it did. Barcelona now has a new modern part of town.

You can get out to the Fòrum by bike, bus, or taxi via the long and impressive new beach. Or the Metro zips you there in just a few minutes from the center (L4/yellow line, Fòrum station). Once there, browse around the modern shopping zone.

The Eixample: Modernisme and Antoni Gaudí

Wide sidewalks, hardy shade trees, chic shops, and plenty of Art Nouveau fun make the Eixample a refreshing break from the Old City. Uptown Barcelona is a unique variation on the common grid-plan city. Barcelona snipped off the building corners to create light and spacious eight-sided squares at every intersection. For the best Eixample example, ramble Rambla de Catalunya (unrelated to the more famous Ramblas) and pass through Passeig de Gràcia (described below, Metro for Block of Discord: Passeig de Gràcia, or Metro for Casa Milà: Diagonal).

The 19th century was a boom time for Barcelona. By 1850, the city was busting out of its medieval walls. A new town was planned to follow a grid-like layout. The intersection of three major thoroughfares—Gran Via, Diagonal, and Meridiana—would shift the city's focus uptown.

Modernisme

The Renaixensa (Catalan cultural revival) gave birth to Modernisme (Catalan Art Nouveau) at the end of the 19th century. Barcelona is its capital. Its Eixample neighborhood shimmers with the colorful, leafy, flowing, blooming shapes of Modernisme in doorways, entrances, facades, and ceilings.

Meaning "a taste for what is modern"—things like streetcars, electric lights, and big-wheeled bicycles—this free-flowing organic style lasted from 1888 to 1906. Breaking with tradition, artists experimented with glass, tile, iron, and brick. The structure was fully modern, using rebar and concrete, but the decoration was a clip-art collage of nature images, exotic Moorish or Chinese themes, and fanciful Gothic crosses and knights to celebrate Catalunya's medieval glory days. It's Barcelona's unique contribution to the Europe-wide Art Nouveau movement. Modernisme was a way of life as Barcelona burst into the 20th century.

Antoni Gaudí (1852-1926), Barcelona's most famous Modernista artist, was descended from four generations of metalworkers, a lineage of which he was quite proud. He incorporated ironwork into his architecture and came up with novel approaches to architectural structure and space.

Two more Modernista architects famous for their unique style are Lluís Domènech i Muntaner and Josep Puig i Cadafalch. You'll see their work on the Block of Discord.

The Eixample, or "Expansion," was a progressive plan in which everything was made accessible to everyone. Each 20-block-square district would have its own hospital and large park, each 10-block-square area would have its own market and general services, and each five-block-square grid would house its own schools and day-care centers. The hollow space found inside each "block" of apartments would form a neighborhood park.

While much of that vision never quite panned out, the Eixample was an urban success. Rich and artsy big shots bought plots along the grid. The richest landowners built as close to the center as possible. For this reason, the best buildings are near the Passeig de Gràcia. While adhering to the height, width, and depth limitations, they built as they pleased—often in the trendy new Modernista style.

For many visitors, Modernista architecture is Barcelona's main draw. (The TI even has a special desk set aside just for Modernisme-seekers—see above.) And one name tops them all: **Antoni Gaudí** (1852–1926). Barcelona is an architectural scrapbook of Gaudí's galloping gables and organic curves. A devoted Catalan and Catholic, he immersed himself in each project, often living on-site. At various times, he called Parc Güell, Casa Milà, and the Sagrada Família home.

First I've covered the main Gaudí attractions close to the Old City. Two more—the Sagrada Família and Parc Güell—are farther afield, but worth the trip. And since many visitors do those two sights together, I've included tips on how to connect them.

Gaudí Sights near the Old City

▲▲Casa Milà (La Pedrera)—This Gaudí exterior laughs down on the crowds filling Passeig de Gràcia. Casa Milà, also called La Pedrera ("The Quarry"), has a much-photographed roller coaster of melting-ice-cream eaves. This is Barcelona's quintessential Modernista building and Gaudí's last major work (1906–1910) before dedicating his final years to the Sagrada Família.

You can visit three sections of Casa Milà: the apartment, attic, and rooftop (€8, includes good audioguide, daily March–Oct 9:00–20:00, Nov–Feb 9:00–18:30, Passeig de Gràcia 92, Metro: Diagonal, tel. 902-400-973).

As you enter, choose the 75-minute audioguide (which offers more listening options than the 30-minute version; either one included in admission). Then head upstairs. Two elevators take you up to either the apartment or the attic. Normally you're directed to the apartment, but if you arrive late in the day, go to the attic elevator first, then climb right up to the rooftop, to make sure you have enough time to enjoy Gaudí's works and the views.

The typical, fourth-floor **apartment** is decorated as it might have been when the building was first occupied, by middle-class urbanites (a 7-minute video explains Barcelona society at the time). Notice Gaudí's clever use of the atrium to maximize daylight in all of the apartments.

The **attic** houses a sprawling multimedia "Gaudí Space," tracing the history of the architect's career with models, photos, and videos of his work. It's all displayed under distinctive parabola-shaped arches. While evocative of Gaudí's style in themselves, the arches are formed this way partly to support the multi-level roof above. This area was also used for ventilation, helping to keep things cool in summer and warm in winter. Tenants had storage spaces and did their laundry up here.

From the attic, a stairway leads to the fanciful, undulating, jaw-dropping **rooftop,** where 30 chimneys play volleyball with the clouds.

Casa Milà or Casa Batllò?

These two Antoni Gaudí houses offer a similar, up-close look at Modernista architecture. Casa Batllò's rooftop is smaller, all on one level, and less impressive than the expansive rooftop at Casa Milá. But the unfurnished Casa Batllò is less of a museum and better allows the architecture to speak for itself. If choosing one, Casa Milà is cheaper and has the better rooftop, but Gaudí fans will find both worthwhile.

Back at the **ground level** of Casa Milà, poke into the dreamily painted original entrance courtyard. The first floor hosts free art exhibits.

Concerts: During July, a rooftop concert series called "Pedrera by Night" features live music—jazz, flamenco, tango—a glass of *cava,* and the chance to see the rooftop illuminated (€12, 22:00–24:00, tel. 902-400-973).

Hungry? Stop by the recommended La Bodegueta, a long block away (daily lunch special, see "Eating" on page 88).

▲Block of Discord—Four blocks from Casa Milà, you can survey a noisy block of competing late 19th-century facades. Several of Barcelona's top Modernista mansions line Passeig de Gràcia (Metro: Passeig de Gràcia). Because the structures look as though they are trying to outdo each other in creative twists, locals nicknamed the block between Consell de Cent and Arago the "Block of Discord."

First (at #43) and most famous is Gaudí's **Casa Batllò,** with skull-like balconies and a tile roof that suggests a cresting dragon's back; Gaudí based the work on the popular legend of St. Jordi (George) slaying the dragon. The house—a rival of Casa Milà (described above)—can also be toured (€16.50, daily 9:00–20:00, may close early for special events, tel. 932-160-306, www.casabatllo.cat). You'll see the main floor (with a funky mushroom-shaped fireplace nook), the blue-and-white-ceramic-slathered atrium, the attic (more parabolic arches), and the rooftop, all with the help of a good audioguide. It's pricey, but the interior is even more fanciful and over-the-top than Casa Milà's. There's barely a straight line in the house. By the way, if you're tempted to snap your photos from the middle of the street, be careful—Gaudí died under a streetcar.

Next door, at **Casa Amatller** (#41), check out architect Josep Puig i Cadafalch's creative mix of Moorish- and Gothic-inspired architecture and iron grillwork, which decorates a step-gable like those in the Netherlands.

On the corner (at #35), **Casa Lleó Morera** has a wonderful interior highlighted by the dining room's fabulous stained glass. The architect, Lluís Domènech i Muntaner, also did the Catalan Concert Hall (you'll notice similarities).

La Rita restaurant, just around the corner on Carrer Arago, serves a fine three-course lunch for a great price from 13:00 (see "Eating," page 88).

▲Palau Güell—Just as the Picasso Museum reveals a young genius on the verge of a breakthrough, this early Gaudí building (completed in 1890) shows the architect taking his first tentative steps toward what would become his trademark curvy style. The parabolic-arch doorways, viewable from the outside, are the first clue that this is not a typical townhouse. In the midst of an extensive renovation, only part of the house is open to the public: the main floor and the Neo-Gothic cellar (which was used as a stable—notice the big carriage doors in the back and the rings on some of the posts used to tie up the horses). By 2010, they hope to have more of the house open...and start charging admission (free, Tue–Sat 10:00–14:30, closed Sun–Mon, a half-block off the Ramblas at Carrer Nou de la Rambla 3–5, tel. 933-173-974, www.palauguell.cat). Even if the rooftop is open, I'd skip it if you plan to see the more interesting one at Casa Milà (described on page 66).

▲▲▲Sagrada Família (Holy Family Church)

Gaudí's most famous and persistent work is this unfinished landmark church. He worked on the Sagrada Família from 1883 to 1926. Since then, construction has moved forward in fits and starts. Even today, the half-finished church is not expected to be completed for another quarter-century. (But over 30 years of visits, I've seen considerable progress.) The temple is funded exclusively by private donations and entry fees, which is another reason its completion has taken so long. Your admission helps pay for the ongoing construction.

Cost, Hours, Location: €10, daily April–Sept 9:00–20:00, Oct–March 9:00–18:00, Metro: Sagrada Família puts you right on the doorstep—exit toward *Pl de la Sagrada Família,* tel. 932-073-031, www.sagradafamilia.cat.

Crowd-Beating Tips: The ticket line can be very long (up to about 30–45 minutes at peak times). It's least crowded right when the church opens (9:00–10:00) and worst at high noon. You can call ahead to pre-purchase tickets (tel. 902-101-212, buy tickets with credit card, then pick them up when you arrive).

Tours: The 50-minute English tours cost €4 (April–Oct daily at 11:00 and 13:00, Nov–March usually Fri–Mon only, same times). Or rent the good 70-minute audioguide (also €4).

Elevators: Two different elevators take you partway up the towers for a great view of the city and a gargoyle's-eye perspective of the loopy church. Each one costs €2.50 (pay as you board elevator). The **Passion facade elevator** takes you 215 feet up, where you can climb higher if you want; then an elevator takes you back down. The **Nativity facade elevator** is similar, but you can also cross the dizzying bridge between the towers—and you must walk all the way down. (Some people prefer the Nativity elevator despite the additional climbing because it offers close views of the facade that Gaudí actually worked on.) For the climbing sections, expect the spiral stairs to be tight, hot, and congested. Lines for both elevators can be very long (up to a 2-hour wait at the busiest times); signs along the stanchions give an estimated wait time.

The Construction Project: There's something powerful about an opportunity to feel a community of committed people with a vision working on a church that will not be finished in their lifetime (as was standard in the Gothic age). Local craftsmen often cap off their careers by spending a couple of years on this exciting construction site. The church will trumpet its completion with 18 spires: A dozen "smaller" 330-foot spires (representing the apostles) will stand in groups of four and mark the three entry facades of the building. Four taller towers (dedicated to the four Evangelists) will surround the two tallest, central towers: a 400-foot-tall tower of Mary and the grand 550-foot Jesus tower, which will shine like a spiritual lighthouse—visible even from out at sea. A unique exterior ambulatory will circle the building, like a cloister turned inside out. If there's any building on earth I'd like to see, it's the Sagrada Família...finished.

➲ **Self-Guided Tour:** To get a good rundown, follow this commentary.

• *Begin facing the western side of the church (where you'll enter).*

Passion Facade: It seems strange to begin with something that Gaudí had nothing to do with...but that's where they put the entrance. When Gaudí died in 1926, only the stubs of four spires stood above the building site. The rest of the church has been inspired by Gaudí's vision but designed and executed by others. Gaudí knew he wouldn't live to complete the church and recognized that later architects and artists would rely on their own muses for inspiration. This artistic freedom was amplified in 1936, when Civil War shelling burned many of Gaudí's blueprints. Judge for yourself how the recently completed and controversial Passion facade by Josep María Subirachs (b. 1927) fits with Gaudí's original formulation (which you'll see downstairs in the museum).

Subirachs' facade is full of symbolism from the Bible. The story of Christ's Passion unfolds in the shape of a Z, from bottom to top. Find the stylized Alpha and Omega over the door; Jesus—hanging on the cross—with an open book (the word of God) for hair; and the grid of numbers adding up to 33 (Jesus' age at the time of his death). The distinct face of the man below and just left of Christ is a memorial to Gaudí.

Now look high above: The figure perched on the bridge between the towers is the soul of Jesus, ascending to heaven. The colorful ceramic caps of the towers symbolize the miters (formal hats) of bishops.

Grand and impressive as this seems, keep in mind it's only the *side* entry to the church. The nine-story apartment flat to the right will be torn down to accommodate the grand front entry. The three facades—Passion, Nativity, and Glory—will chronicle Christ's life from birth to death to resurrection.

• *We'll enter the church later. For now, look right to find the...*

School: Gaudí built this school for the children of the workers building the church. Now it houses an exhibit focusing on the architect's use of geometric forms. You'll also see a classroom and a replica of Gaudí's desk as it was the day he died, and a model for the proposed Glory facade...the next big step.

• *Leaving the school, turn right and go down the ramp under the church, into the...*

Museum: Housed in what is someday intended to be the church's crypt, the museum runs underground from the Passion facade to the Nativity facade. The first section tells the chronological story of the Sagrada Família. Look for the replicas of the pulpit and confessional that Gaudí, the micro-manager, designed for his church. As you wander through the plaster models used for the church's construction, you'll notice that they don't always match the finished product—these are ideas, not blueprints set in stone. Photos show the construction work as it was when Gaudí died in 1926 and how it's progressed over the years. See how the church's design is a fusion of nature, architecture, and religion. The columns seem light, with branches springing forth and capitals that look like palm trees.

Modernista Sights

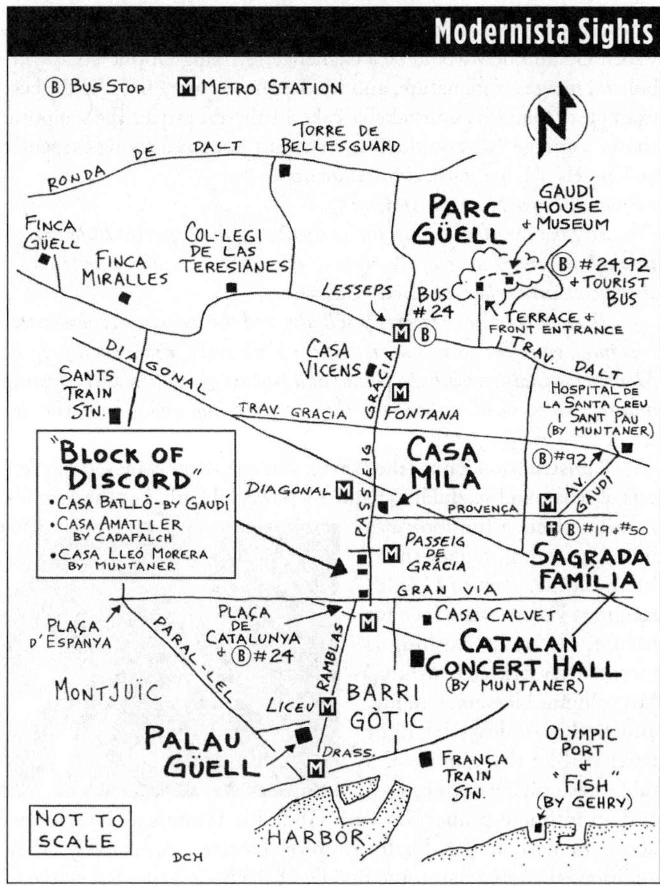

Walking down the long passage to the other side of the church, you'll pass under a giant plaster model of the nave (you'll see the real thing soon). Find the hanging model showing how Gaudí used gravity to calculate the perfect parabolas incorporated into the church design (the mirror above this model shows how the right-side-up church is derived from this). Nearby, you'll find some original Gaudí architectural sketches in a dimly lit room and a worthwhile 20-minute movie (generally shown in English at :50 past each hour).

Then you'll peek into a busy workshop for making plaster models of the planned construction, just as Gaudí used—he found these helpful for envisioning the final product in 3-D. The museum wraps up with an exhibit on the design and implementation of the Passion facade.

• *Climb up the ramp and hook left to see the...*

Nativity Facade (east side): This, the only part of the church essentially finished in his lifetime, shows Gaudí's original vision.

(Cleverly, this was built and finished first to inspire financial support, which Gaudí knew would be a challenge.) Mixing Gothic-style symbolism, images from nature, and Modernista asymmetry, it is the best example of Gaudí's unmistakable cake-in-the-rain style. The sculpture shows a unique twist on the Nativity, with Jesus as a young carpenter and angels playing musical instruments.

• *From here, you have two options:*

To take the elevator up the Nativity facade (described above), go through the small door to the right of the main door. The line stretches through an area called the Rosary Cloister.

To enter the church (where you'll also find the Passion facade elevator entrance), go in the door to the left of the main entry. First you'll pass the Montserrat Cloister, with the ***Gaudí and Nature*** *exhibition that compares nature, waves, shells, mushrooms, the ripple of a leaf, and so on to Gaudí's work. Then you'll enter the...*

Construction Zone (the Nave): The cranking cranes, rusty forests of rebar, and scaffolding require a powerful faith, but the Sagrada Família offers a fun look at a living, growing, bigger-than-life building. Part of Gaudí's religious vision was a love for nature. He said, "Nothing is invented; it's written in nature." His columns blossom with life, and little windows let light filter in like the canopy of a rain forest, giving both privacy and an intimate connection with God. The U-shaped choir hovers above the nave, tethered halfway up the columns. A relatively recent addition—hanging out in the middle of the back wall—is a statue of Barcelona's patron saint, St. Jordi (George of dragon-slaying fame). At the far end of the nave, you'll see the line to take the elevator up the Passion facade.

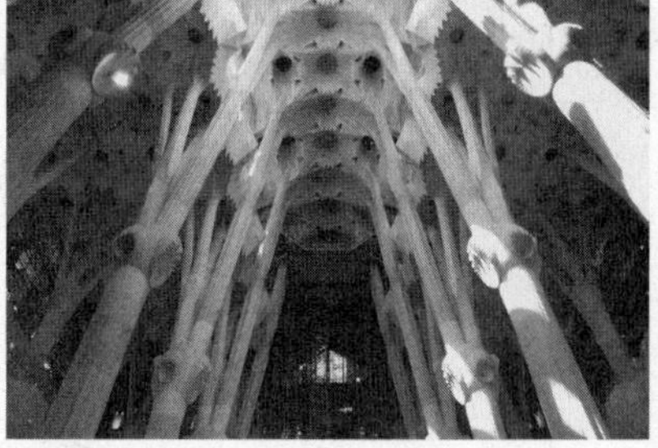

Currently, the construction is focused on two major tasks: stabilizing the existing nave (which has been rattled by vibrations from the Metro and new AVE train line underground); and eventually adding the third, biggest entry—the Glory facade. They're also in the process of replacing the temporary, clear windows with stained-glass ones. The final phase is the central tower (550 feet tall), which, it's estimated, will require four underground support pylons, each consisting of 8,000 tons of cement.

Gaudí lived on the site for more than a decade and is buried in a Neo-Gothic 19th-century crypt (which is where the church began). His tomb is sometimes viewable from the museum, but will likely be closed to the public through 2009. There's a move afoot to make Gaudí a saint. Perhaps someday, his tomb will be a place of pilgrimage.

Gaudí—a faithful Catholic whose medieval-style mysticism belied his Modernista architecture career—was certainly driven to greatness by his passion for God. When undertaking a lengthy project, he said, "My client"—meaning God—"is in no hurry."

Scenic Connection to Parc Güell: If your next stop is Parc Güell (see below), and you don't want to spring for a taxi, try this route: With the Nativity facade at your back, walk to the near-left corner of the park across the street. Then cross the street to reach the diagonal Avinguda Gaudí (between the Repsol gas station and the KFC). From here, you'll follow the funky lampposts four blocks gradually uphill (about 10 min) along a pleasant, shaded, café-lined pedestrian street (Avinguda Gaudí). When you reach the striking Modernista-style Hospital de la Santa Creu i Sant Pau (designed by Lluís Domènech i Muntaner), cross the street and go up one block (left) on St. Antonio Maria Claret street to catch bus #92, which will take you to the side entrance of Parc Güell.

From the Sagrada Família, you could also get to Parc Güell by taking the Metro to Lesseps, then bus #24 (described below), but that involves two changes...and less scenery.

More Bus Connections: From the Sagrada Família, bus #19 makes an easy 15-minute journey to the Old City (stops near the cathedral and La Ribera district); bus #50 goes from the Sagrada Família to Montjuïc, skipping the funicular but taking you past all the sights (see "Getting to Montjuïc," page 75).

▲Parc Güell

Gaudí fans enjoy the artist's magic in this colorful park. Gaudí intended this 30-acre garden to be a 60-residence housing project—a kind of gated community. As a high-income housing development, it flopped. But as a park, it's a delight, offering another peek into the eccentric genius of Gaudí. Notice the mosaic medallions that say "park" in English, reminding folks that this is modeled on an English garden.

Cost and Hours: Free, daily 10:00–20:00, tel. 932-130-488.

Getting There: From Plaça de Catalunya, the red Tourist Bus or bus #24 will leave you at the park's side entrance, or a €6 taxi will drop you at the main entrance. From elsewhere in the city, you can take a Metro-plus-bus combination: Go by Metro to the Lesseps stop. To avoid the tiring, uphill 20-minute walk to the park, don't follow the *Parc Güell 1300 metros* sign; instead, exit left out of the Metro station, cross the streets Princep d'Astúries and Gran de Grácia, and catch bus #24 (on Gran de Grácia), which takes you to the park's side entrance in less than 10 minutes. For a more scenic approach (on bus #92) from the Sagrada Família, see the previous page.

➲ **Self-Guided Tour:** This tour assumes you're arriving at the front/main entrance (by taxi). If you're instead arriving by bus at the side entrance, walk straight ahead through the gate to find the terrace with colorful mosaic benches, then walk down to the stairway and front entrance.

As you wander the park, imagine living here a century ago—if this gated community had succeeded and was filled with Barcelona's wealthy.

Front Entrance: Entering the park, you walk by Gaudí's wrought-iron gas lamps (1900–1914). His dad was a blacksmith, and he always enjoyed this medium. Two gate houses made of gingerbread flank the entrance. One houses a good bookshop, while the other is home to the skippable Center for Interpretation of Parc Güell (Centre d'Interpretació), which shows Gaudí's building methods plus maps, photos, and models of the park (€2.30, daily 11:00–15:00, tel. 933-190-222); the Gaudí House and Museum, described below, is better.

Stairway and Columns: Climb the grand stairway, past the famous ceramic dragon fountain. At the top, dip into the "Hall of 100 Columns," designed to house a produce market for the neighborhood's 60 mansions. The fun columns—each different, made from concrete and rebar, topped with colorful ceramic, and studded with broken bottles and bric-a-brac—add to the market's vitality.

As you continue up (on the left-hand staircase), look left, down the playful "pathway of columns" that support a long arcade. Gaudí drew his inspiration from nature, and this arcade is like a surfer's perfect tube.

Terrace: Once up top, sit on a colorful bench—designed to fit your body ergonomically—and enjoy one of Barcelona's best views. Look for the Sagrada Família church in the distance. Gaudí was an engineer as well. He designed a water-catchment system by which rain hitting this plaza would flow into and through the columns from the market below, and power the park's fountains.

When considering the failure of Parc Güell as a community development, also consider that it was an idea a hundred years ahead of its time. Back then, high-society ladies didn't want to live so far from the cultural action. Today, the surrounding neighborhoods are some of the wealthiest in town, and a gated community here would be a big hit.

Gaudí House and Museum: This pink house with a steeple, standing in the middle of the park (near the side entrance), was actually Gaudí's home for 20 years, until his father died. His humble artifacts are mostly gone, but the house is now a museum with some quirky Gaudí furniture and a chance to wander through a model home used to sell the others. While small, it offers a good taste of what could have been (€4, daily April–Sept 10:00–20:00, Oct–March 10:00–18:00).

Montjuïc

Montjuïc ("Mount of the Jews"), overlooking Barcelona's hazy port, has always been a show-off. Ages ago it had an impressive fortress. In 1929, it hosted an international fair, from which most of today's sights originated. And in 1992, the Summer Olympics directed the world's attention to this pincushion of attractions once again.

I've listed these sights by altitude, from highest to lowest; if you're visiting all of them, do them in this order so that most of your walking is downhill (though for selective sightseers, the Fundació Joan Miró and Catalan Art Museum are the most worthwhile). Note that if you want to visit only the Catalan Art Museum, you can just take the Metro to Plaça d'Espanya and ride the escalators up (with some stairs, as well) to the museum.

Getting to Montjuïc: You have several options. The simplest is to take a **taxi** directly to your destination (about €7 from downtown).

Buses from various points in the city take you up to Montjuïc, including public bus #55 (from Plaça de Catalunya, next to Caja de Madrid building), public bus #50 (from the corner of Gran Via and Passeig de Gràcia, or from the Sagrada Família), and the blue Tourist Bus.

A **funicular** takes visitors from the Paral-lel Metro stop up to Montjuïc (covered by a Metro ticket, every 10 min, 9:00–22:00). You can easily reach this funicular by **Metro** (take it to the Paral-lel stop, then follow signs for *Parc Montjuïc* and the little funicular icon—you can enter the funicular directly without using another ticket, number of minutes until next departure posted at start of entry

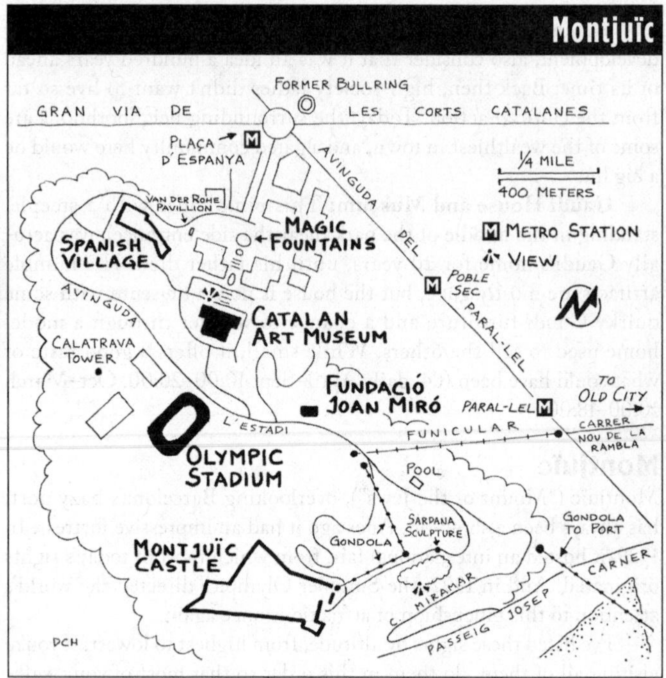

tunnel). From the top of the funicular, turn left and walk two minutes to the Joan Miró museum, six minutes to the Olympic Stadium, or ten minutes to the Catalan Art Museum.

From the port, the most scenic way to Montjuïc is via the **gondola,** called the 1929 Transbordador Aereo (€9.50 one-way, €12.50 round-trip, 3/hr, daily 10:45–19:00, until 20:00 in June–Sept).

Getting Around Montjuïc: Up top, the bus marked *Parc de Montjuïc* (#PM) loops between the sights. There are two routes: The blue line starts at Plaça d'Espanya and goes to the Catalan Art Museum, the Joan Miró museum, the funicular, and the Castle of Montjuïc; the red line comes up from Drassanes, at the bottom of the Ramblas. The blue Tourist Bus also does a circuit around the top of Montjuïc.

Castle of Montjuïc—The castle offers great city views from its fortress and a military museum (€3, Tue–Sun 9:30–20:00, closed Mon). The seemingly endless museum houses a dull collection of guns, swords, and toy soldiers. An interesting section on the Spanish-American War of 1898 covers Spain's valiant fight against American aggression (from Spain's perspective). Unfortunately, there are no English descriptions. Those interested in Jewish history will find a fascinating collection of ninth-century Jewish tombstones.

The castle itself has a fascist past rife with repression. It was built in the 18th century by the central Spanish government to keep an eye on Barcelona and stifle citizen revolt. When Franco was in power, the castle was the site of hundreds of political executions.

Getting There: To spare yourself the hike up to the museum, take the **gondola** from just above the upper station of the Montjuïc funicular (€5.70 one-way, €7.90 round-trip, June–Sept daily 10:00–21:00, until 19:00 April–May and Oct, until 18:00 Nov–March).

▲Fundació Joan Miró—Showcasing the talents of yet another Catalan artist, this museum has the best collection of Joan Miró art

anywhere. You'll also see works by other Modern artists (such as *Mercury Fountain* by the American sculptor Alexander Calder). If you don't like abstract art, you'll leave here scratching your head, but those who love this place are not faking it...they understand the genius of Miró and the fun of abstract art.

As you wander, consider this: Miró believed that everything in the cosmos is linked—colors, sky, stars, love, time, music, dogs, men, women, dirt, and the void. He mixed childlike symbols of these things creatively, as a poet uses words. It's as liberating for the visual artist to be abstract as it is for the poet: Both can use metaphors rather than being confined to concrete explanations. Miró would listen to music and paint. It's interactive, free interpretation. He said, "For me, simplicity is freedom."

Here are some tips to help you enjoy and appreciate Miró's art: 1) meditate on it; 2) read the title (for example, *The Smile of a Tear*); 3) meditate on it again. Repeat the process until you have an epiphany. There's no correct answer—it's pure poetry. Devotees of Miró say they fly with him and don't even need drugs. You're definitely much less likely to need drugs if you take advantage of the wonderful audioguide, well worth the €4 extra charge (€8, July–Sept Tue–Sat 10:00–20:00, until 19:00 Oct–June, Thu until 21:30, Sun 10:00–14:30, closed Mon, 200 yards from top of funicular, Parc de Montjuïc, tel. 934-439-470, www.bcn.fjmiro.es). The museum has a cool cafeteria, café, and bookshop.

Olympic and Sports Museum (Museu Olímpic i de l'Esport)—This new attraction rides the coattails of the stadium across the street (see next listing). You'll twist down a timeline-ramp that traces the history of the Olympic Games, interspersed with random exhibits about various sports. Downstairs you'll find exhibits designed to test your athleticism, a play-by-play rehash of the '92 Barcelona Olympiad, a commemoration of Juan Antonio Samaranch (a Spaniard and influential president of the IOC for two decades), a sports media exhibit, and a schmaltzy movie collage. High-tech but still hokey, the museum is worth the time and money only for those nostalgic for the '92 Games (€4, April–Sept Tue–Sun 10:00–20:00, Oct–March Tue–Sun 10:00–18:00, closed Mon, Avinguda de l'Estadi 60, tel. 932-925-379, http://fundaciobarcelonaolimpica.es/moe).

Olympic Stadium (Estadi Olímpic)—For two weeks in the summer of 1992, the world turned its attention to this stadium (between the Catalan Art Museum and the Fundació Joan Miró at Passeig Olímpic 17). Redesigned from an earlier 1929 version, the stadium was updated, expanded, and officially named for Catalan patriot Lluís Companys i Jover. The XXV Olympiad kicked off here on July 25, when an archer dramatically lit the Olympic torch—which still stands high at the end of the stadium overlooking the city skyline—with a flaming arrow. Over the next two weeks, Barcelona played host to the thrill of victory (mostly at the hands of Magic Johnson, Michael Jordan, Larry Bird, and the rest of the US basketball "Dream Team") and the agony of defeat (i.e., the nightmares of the Dream Team's opponents). Hovering over the stadium is the memorable, futuristic Calatrava Communications Tower, used to transmit Olympic highlights and lowlights around the world. Aside from the memories of the medals, today's Olympic Stadium offers little to see today... except when it's hosting a match for Barcelona's soccer team, RCD Espanyol.

Spanish Village (Poble Espanyol)—This tacky five-acre model village uses fake traditional architecture from all over Spain as a shell to contain gift shops. Craftspeople do their clichéd thing only in the morning (not worth your time or €8, www.poble-espanyol.com). After hours, it's a popular local nightspot.

▲▲Catalan Art Museum (Museu Nacional d'Art de Catalunya)—The big vision for this wonderful museum is to showcase Catalan art from the 10th century through about 1930. Often called "the Prado of Romanesque art" (and "MNAC" for short), its highlight is Europe's best collection of Romanesque frescos (€8.50, includes audioguide, free first Sun of month, open Tue–Sat 10:00–19:00, Sun 10:00–14:30,

closed Mon, last entry 30 min before closing; in massive National Palace building above Magic Fountains, near Plaça d'Espanya—take escalators up; tel. 936-220-376, www.mnac.es).

As you enter, pick up a map (helpful for such a big and confusing building). The left wing is Romanesque, and the right wing is Gothic, exquisite Renaissance, and Baroque. Upstairs is more Baroque, plus modern art, photography, coins, and more.

The MNAC's rare, world-class collection of **Romanesque** art came mostly from remote Catalan village churches in the Pyrenees (saved from unscrupulous art dealers—including many Americans). The Romanesque wing features frescoes, painted wooden altar fronts, and ornate statuary. This classic Romanesque art—with flat 2-D scenes, each saint holding his symbol, and Jesus (easy to identify by the cross in his halo)—is impressively displayed on replicas of the original church ceilings and apses.

Across the way, in the **Gothic** wing, fresco murals give way to vivid 14th-century wood-panel paintings of Bible stories. A roomful of paintings (Room 34) by the Catalan master Jaume Huguet (1412–1492) deserves a look, particularly his altarpiece of Barcelona's patron saint, George.

For a break, glide under the huge dome (which once housed an ice-skating rink) over to the air-conditioned cafeteria. This was the prime ceremony room and dance hall for the 1929 International Exposition. Then, from the big ballroom, ride the glass elevator upstairs, where the **Modern** section takes you on a delightful walk from the late 1800s to about 1930—kind of a Catalan Musée d'Orsay, offering a big chronological clockwise circle from Spain's Golden Age (Zurbarán, heavy religious scenes, Spanish royals with their endearing underbites), to Symbolism and Modernisme (furniture complements the empty spaces you likely saw in Gaudí's buildings), then Impressionists, *fin de siècle* fun, and Art Deco.

Upstairs you'll also find photography (with a bit on how photojournalism came of age covering the Spanish Civil War), seductive sofas, and the chic Oleum restaurant, with vast city views (and €20 meals).

▲Magic Fountains (Font Màgica)—Music, colored lights, and huge amounts of water make an artistic and coordinated splash on summer nights at Plaça d'Espanya (20-min shows every half-hour; May–Sept Thu–Sun 21:00–23:30, no shows Mon–Wed; Oct–April Fri–Sat 19:00–21:00, no shows Sun–Thu; from the Espanya Metro station, walk toward the towering National Palace).

Away from the Center

Tibidabo—Tibidabo comes from the Latin for "to thee I shall give," the words the devil used when he was tempting Christ. It's still an enticing offer: At the top of Barcelona's highest peak, you're offered the city's oldest fun-fair (€24, erratic hours, tel. 932-117-942, www.tibidabo.es), the Neo-Gothic Sacred Heart Church, and—if the weather and air quality are good—an almost limitless view of the city and the Mediterranean.

Getting there is part of the fun: Start by taking the L7 line from the Plaça de Catalunya station (under Café Zürich) to the Tibidabo stop. (The red Tourist Bus stops here, too.) Then take Barcelona's only remaining tram—the Tramvía Blau—from Plaça John F. Kennedy to Plaça Dr. Andreu (€3.90 round-trip, 2–4/hr). From there, take the funicular to the top (€3, fare is reimbursable with paid admission, tel. 906-427-017). A special "Tibibus" runs from Plaça de Catalunya to the park every day at 10:30 (€2.50, reimbursable with paid admission).

NIGHTLIFE

Sightseeing After Dark

Refer to the *See Barcelona* guide (free from TI) and ask about the latest at a TI. Major sights open until 20:00 include the Picasso Museum (closed Mon), Gaudí's Sagrada Família (open daily, until 18:00 Oct–March), Casa Milà (daily, until 18:30 Nov–Feb), and Parc Güell (daily). On Thursday, Montjuïc's Joan Miró museum stays open until 21:30 (otherwise open July–Sept Tue–Sat until 20:00).

Many lesser sights also stay open at least until 20:00, such as La Boquería market (Mon–Sat), Columbus Monument (daily), City History Museum (Tue–Sat), Church of Santa Maria del Mar (daily), Casa Batllò (daily), Parc Güell's Gaudí House and Museum (daily April–Sept), the Castle of Montjuïc (Tue–Sat), and Citadel Park (daily). The Magic Fountains on Plaça d'Espanya make a splash on weekend evenings (Fri–Sat, plus Thu and Sun in summer). The Tourist Bus runs until 22:00 every day in summer.

Music and Entertainment

The weekly *Guía del Ocio,* sold at newsstands for €1 (or free in some hotel lobbies), is a Spanish-language entertainment listing (with guidelines for English-speakers inside the back cover; www.guiadelocio.com). The monthly *Barcelona Metropolitan* magazine and quarterly *What's On Barcelona* are also helpful (free from the TI). For music, consider a performance at Casa Milà ("Pedrera by Night" July concert series, see page 67), the Liceu Opera House (page 46), or the Catalan Concert Hall (page 60). There are many nightspots around Plaça Reial (such as the popular Jamboree).

Palau de la Virreina, an arts-and-culture TI, offers information on Barcelona cultural events—music, opera, and theater (Tue–Sat 11:00–20:00, Sun 11:00–14:30, closed Mon, Ramblas 99, see map on page 43).

SLEEPING

Book ahead. Barcelona is Spain's most expensive city. Still, it has reasonable rooms. Cheap places are more crowded in summer; fancier business-class hotels fill up in winter and offer discounts on weekends and in summer. When considering relative hotel values, in summer and on weekends you can often get modern comfort in business-class hotels for about the same price (€100) as you'll pay for ramshackle charm (and only a few minutes' walk from the Old City action). Some TI branches (including those at Plaça de Catalunya, Plaça de Sant Jaume, and the airport) offer a room-finding service, though it's cheaper to go direct. Note that prices at the Hotel Continental Barcelona and the Hotel Continental Palacete include great all-day snack-and-drink bars; several other hotels also offer free breakfasts to those who book direct with this guidebook.

Business-Class Comfort near Plaça de Catalunya

These hotels have sliding glass doors leading to plush reception areas, air-conditioning, and perfectly sterile modern bedrooms. Most are on big streets within two blocks of Barcelona's exuberant central square. As business-class hotels, they have hard-to-pin-down prices that fluctuate wildly. I've listed the average rate you'll pay. But in summer and on weekends, supply often far exceeds the demand, and many of these places cut prices to around €100—always ask for a deal.

$$$ Hotel Catalonia Albinoni, the best-located of all, elegantly fills a renovated old palace with wide halls, hardwood floors, and 74 rooms. It overlooks a thriving pedestrian boulevard in front and a quiet swimming-pool garden in back (Sb-€149, Db-€189, extra bed-€35, family rooms, back rooms have private little sun terraces and cost extra; great free buffet breakfast—normally €15/person—when you book direct, pay the full rate, and show this book in 2009; lower promotional rates in summer—but free breakfast not valid with discounts, non-smoking, air-con, elevator, pay Internet access and Wi-Fi, a block down from Plaça de Catalunya at Avinguda Portal de l'Angel 17, tel. 933-184-141, fax 933-012-631, www.hoteles-catalonia.com, albinoni.reservas@hoteles-catalonia.es).

$$$ Hotel Duques de Bergara has four stars, an elegant old entryway, splashy public spaces, slick marble and hardwood floors, 150 comfortable but nothing-fancy rooms, and a garden courtyard with a pool a world away from the big-city noise (Sb-€173, Db-€213, Tb-€243, breakfast-€15, non-smoking, air-con, elevator, pay Internet access and Wi-Fi, a half-block off Plaça de Catalunya at Carrer de Bergara 11, tel. 933-015-151, fax 933-173-442, www.hoteles-catalonia.com, duques@hoteles-catalonia.es).

Sleep Code

(€1 = about $1.50, country code: 34)
S = Single, **D** = Double/Twin, **T** = Triple, **Q** = Quad, **b** = bathroom, **s** = shower only. Unless otherwise noted, credit cards are accepted, English is spoken, and prices listed do not include the 7 percent tax or breakfast (ranging from simple €3 spreads to €25 buffets).

To help you easily sort through these listings, I've divided the rooms into three categories, based on the price for a standard double room with bath (during high season):

$$$ Higher Priced—Most rooms €150 or more.
$$ Moderately Priced—Most rooms between €100-150.
$ Lower Priced—Most rooms €100 or less.

While many of my recommendations are on pedestrian streets, night noise can be a problem (especially in cheap places, which have single-pane windows). For a quiet night, ask for "*tranquilo*" rather than "*con vista.*"

$$$ Nouvel Hotel, in an elegant, Victorian-style building on a handy pedestrian street, is less business-oriented and offers more character than the others listed here. It boasts royal lounges and 78 comfy rooms (Sb-€102, Db-€179, includes breakfast, manager Roberto promises a 10 percent discount on these prices to those booking direct via email—not their website—with this book in 2009, extra bed-€35, air-con, elevator, free Wi-Fi in lobby, Carrer de Santa Ana 20, tel. 933-018-274, fax 933-018-370, www.hotelnouvel.com, info@hotelnouvel.com).

$$ Hotel Reding, on a quiet street a five-minute walk west of the Ramblas and Plaça de Catalunya action, is a slick and sleek place renting 44 mod rooms at a very good price (Db-€120, extra bed-€35, get their best deal on the Web and then claim free breakfasts with this book in 2009—select "no breakfast" and type "free Rick Steves breakfast" in comment line, non-smoking rooms, air-con, elevator, free Internet access and Wi-Fi, near Metro: Universitat, Gravina 5–7, tel. 934-121-097, fax 932-683-482, www.hotelreding.com, reding@oh-es.com).

$$ Hotel Duc de la Victoria, with 156 rooms, is professional yet friendly, buried in the Barri Gòtic just three blocks off the Ramblas (Db-€140, bigger "superior" rooms on a corner with windows on 2 sides-€25 extra, breakfast-€15, non-smoking, air-con, elevator, free Internet access, pay Wi-Fi, Duc de la Victoria 15, tel. 932-703-410, fax 934-127-747, www.nh-hotels.com, nhducdelavictoria@nh-hotels.com).

$$ Hotel Lleó (YEH-oh) is well-run, with 89 big, bright, and comfortable rooms; a great breakfast room; and a generous lounge (Db-€130 but flexes way up with demand, can be cheaper in summer, extra bed-about €25, breakfast-€11, non-smoking rooms, air-con, elevator, free Internet access and Wi-Fi, 2 blocks west of Plaça de Catalunya at Carrer de Pelai 22, tel. 933-181-312, fax 934-122-657, www.hotel-lleo.es, reservas@hotel-lleo.es).

$$ Hotel Atlantis is solid, with 50 big, homey-yet-mod rooms and great prices for the location (Sb-€90, Db-€107, Tb-€125, refreshingly stable rates, breakfast-€9, non-smoking rooms, air-con, elevator, free Internet access and Wi-Fi, older windows let in a bit more street noise than other hotels in this category—request a quieter room in back, Carrer de Pelai 20, tel. 933-189-012, fax 934-120-914, www.hotelatlantis-bcn.com, inf@hotelatlantis-bcn.com).

Hotels with "Personality" on or near the Ramblas

These recommended places are generally family-run, with ad-lib furnishings, more character, and lower prices. Only the Jardí offers a quaint square buried in the Barri Gòtic ambience—and you'll pay for it.

$ Hotel Continental Barcelona, in a building overlooking the top of the Ramblas, offers an inviting lounge and classic, tiny-view balcony opportunities if you don't mind the noise. Its comfortable rooms come with double-thick mattresses, wildly clashing carpets and wallpaper, and perhaps one too many clever ideas (they're laden with microwaves, fridges, a "command center" of light switches, and Tupperware drawers). Choose between your own little Ramblas-view balcony (where you can eat your breakfast) or a quieter back room (Sb-€85, Db-€95, twin Db-€105, Db with Ramblas balcony-€115, extra bed-€30, 5 percent discount with this book in 2009, prices include breakfast and tax, non-smoking, air-con, elevator, free Internet access and Wi-Fi, Ramblas 138, tel. 933-012-570, fax 933-027-360, www.hotelcontinental.com, barcelona@hotelcontinental.com). J. M.'s (José Maria) free breakfast and all-day snack-and-drink bar make this a better deal than the price suggests.

$ Hostería Grau is homey, family-run, and almost alpine. Its 25 cheery, garden-pastel rooms are a few blocks off the Ramblas in the colorful university district. The first two floors have ceilings a claustrophobic seven feet high, then things get tall again (S-€35, D-€65, Db-€85, extra bed-€15; 2-bedroom family suites: Db-€95, Tb-€120, Qb-€150; slippery prices jump during fairs and big events, breakfast next door-€3–7, air-con, free Internet access and Wi-Fi, lots of stairs with no elevator, 200 yards up Carrer dels Tallers from the Ramblas at Ramelleres 27, tel. 933-018-135, fax 933-176-825, www.hostalgrau.com, reservas@hostalgrau.com, Monica).

Hotels near the Ramblas

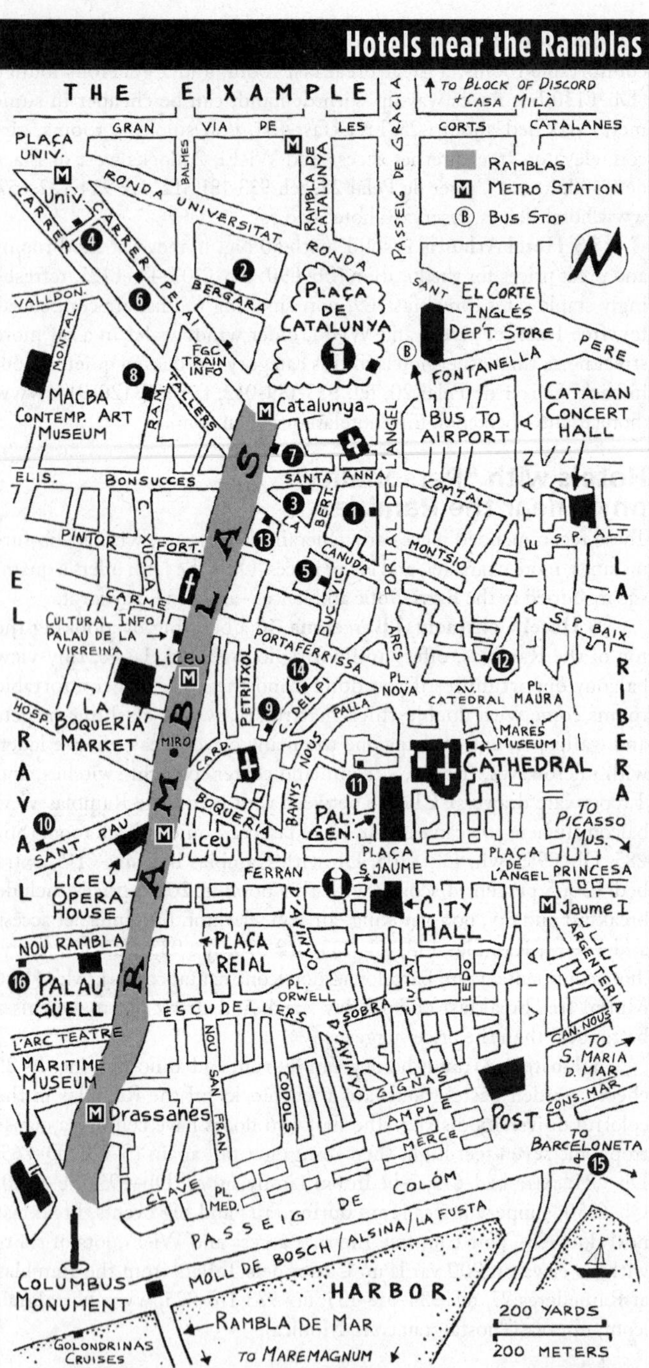

Hotels Key

❶ Hotel Catalonia Albinoni	❾ Hotel Jardí
❷ Hotel Duques de Bergara	❿ Hostal Opera
❸ Nouvel Hotel	⓫ Hotel Neri
❹ Hotel Reding	⓬ Hotel Regencia Colón
❺ Hotel Duc de la Victoria	⓭ Hostal Campi
❻ Hotels Lleó & Atlantis	⓮ Hostal Maldá
❼ Hotel Continental Barcelona	⓯ To Sea Point Hostel
❽ Hostería Grau & Barcelona Rent-A-Bike	⓰ Launderette

$ Hotel Jardí offers 40 clean, remodeled rooms on a breezy square in the Barri Gòtic. Many of the tight, plain, comfy rooms come with petite balconies (for an extra charge) and enjoy an almost Parisian ambience. It's a good deal only if you value the cute square location. Book well in advance, as this family-run place has an avid following (small basic interior Db-€79, nicer interior Db-€89, outer Db with balcony or twin with window-€95, large outer Db with balcony or square-view terrace-€106, extra bed-€12, breakfast-€6, non-smoking, air-con, elevator, some stairs, free Wi-Fi in lobby, halfway between Ramblas and cathedral at Plaça Sant Josep Oriol 1, tel. 933-015-900, fax 933-425-733, www.hoteljardi-barcelona.com, reservations@hotel jardi-barcelona.com).

$ Hostal Opera, with 70 stark rooms 20 yards off the Ramblas, is clean, institutional, and modern. The street can feel seedy at night, but it's safe, and the hotel is very secure (Sb-€49, Db-€69, no breakfast, air-con only in summer, elevator, pay Internet access, free Wi-Fi in lobby, Carrer Sant Pau 20, tel. 933-188-201, www.hostalopera.com, info@hostalopera.com).

Deep in the Barri Gòtic

$$$ Hotel Neri is chic, posh, and sophisticated, with 22 rooms spliced into the ancient stones of the Barri Gòtic overlooking an overlooked square (Plaça Sant Felip Neri) a block from the cathedral. It has big plasma-screen TVs, pricey modern art on the bedroom walls, and dressed-up people in its gourmet restaurant (Db-€265, suites-€360–425, breakfast-€21, air-con, elevator, free Wi-Fi, rooftop tanning deck, St. Sever 5, tel. 933-040-655, fax 933-040-337, www .hotelneri.com, info@hotelneri.com).

$$ Hotel Regencia Colón, one block in front of the cathedral square, offers 50 solid, well-priced rooms in a handy location (Db-€120, air-con, elevator, Carrer Sagristans 13–17, tel. 933-189-858, fax 933-172-822, www.hotelregenciacolon.com, info@hotelregenciacolon.com).

Humble, Cheaper Places Buried in the Old City

$ Hostal Campi is big, subdued, and ramshackle, but offers simple class. This easygoing, old-school spot rents 24 rooms a few doors off the top of the Ramblas (S-€32, D-€54, Db-€62, T-€74, Tb-€84, no breakfast, non-smoking rooms, lots of stairs with no elevator, pay Internet access, Canuda 4, tel. & fax 933-013-545, www.hostalcampi.com, reservas@hostalcampi.com, friendly Margarita and Nando).

$ Hostal Maldá rents the best cheap beds I found in the old center. With 25 rooms above a small shopping mall near the cathedral, it's a time-warp—quiet and actually charming—but does not take reservations (though you can try calling a day before). It generally remains full through the summer, but it's worth a shot (S-€15, D-€30, T-€45, lots of stairs with no elevator, 100 yards up Carrer del Pi from delightful Plaça Sant Josep Oriol, Carrer del Pi 5, tel. 933-173-002). Good-natured Aurora doesn't speak English, but Delfi, who works only half the year, does.

Youth Hostels in the Center of Town

A wonderful chain of well-run and centrally located youth hostels provides €20–26 dorm beds in 4- to 14-bed coed rooms with €2 sheets and towels, free Internet access, Wi-Fi, breakfast, lockers (B.Y.O. lock, or buy one here), and plenty of opportunities to meet other backpackers. They're open 24 hours but aren't party hostels, so they enforce quiet after 23:00. Visit their websites to choose the neighborhood you like: Eixample, Barri Gòtic, or near the beach.

$ Centric Point Hostel is a huge new place renting 430 cheap beds at what must be the best address in Barcelona (bar, kitchen, Passeig de Gràcia 33, tel. 932-151-796, fax 932-461-552, www.centricpointhostel.com). See map on page 87.

$ Gothic Point Hostel rents 150 beds in the trendy Ribera district a block from the Picasso Museum (roof terrace, Carrer Vigatans 5, tel. 932-687-808, www.gothicpoint.com). See map on page 61.

$ Sea Point Hostel has 70 beds on the beach nearby (Plaça del Mar 4, tel. 932-247-075, www.seapointhostel.com). See map on page 84.

In the Eixample

For an uptown, boulevard-like neighborhood, sleep in the Eixample, a 10-minute walk from the Ramblas action.

$$ Hotel Granvía, filling a palatial 1870s mansion, offers Botticelli and chandeliers in the public rooms; a sprawling, peaceful sun patio; and 54 spacious, comfy rooms. Its salon is plush and royal, making the hotel an excellent value for romantics (Sb-€80, Db-€130 or €110 July–Aug, Tb-€150, these rates promised with this book in 2009 when you reserve directly by phone or email—not on their website—and mention my name, breakfast-€11, request a quiet

Hotels and Restaurants in Barcelona's Eixample

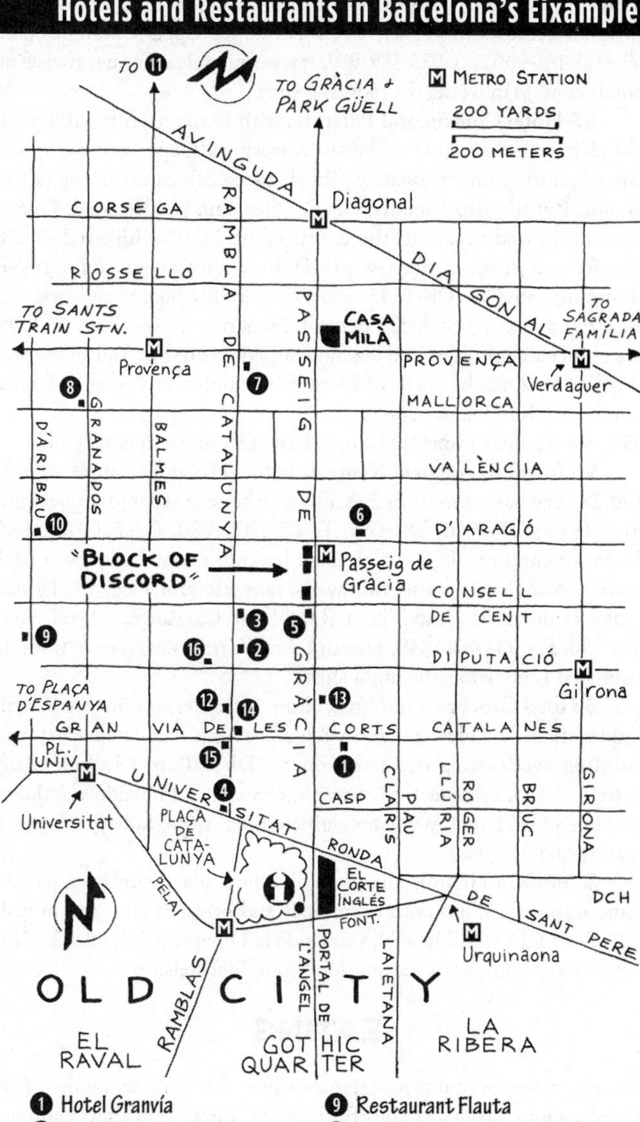

1. Hotel Granvía
2. Hotel Continental Palacete
3. Hostal Residencia Neutral
4. Hotel Ginebra
5. Centric Point Hostel
6. La Rita Restaurant
7. La Bodegueta
8. Restaurante la Palmera
9. Restaurant Flauta
10. Rest. de Degustacio Cincsentits
11. To Hofmann
12. El Racó
13. "Qu Qu" Quasi Queviures
14. Ciudad Condal Cerveceria
15. La Tramoia
16. Somnio Hostel

room if street noise bothers you, non-smoking, air-con, elevator, free Internet access and Wi-Fi, Gran Via de les Corts Catalanes 642, tel. 933-181-900, fax 933-189-997, www.nnhotels.com, hgranvia@nnhotels.com, Juan works the morning shift).

$$ Hotel Continental Palacete, with 19 rooms, fills a 100-year-old chandeliered mansion. With flowery wallpaper and cheap but fancy furniture under ornately gilded stucco, it's gaudy in the city of Gaudí. But it's also friendly, clean, quiet, and well-located. Guests have unlimited access to the extravagant, "cruise-inspired" fruit, veggie, and drink buffet—worth factoring into your comparison-shopping (Sb-€97, Db-€132, €35–45 more for bigger and brighter view rooms, extra bed-€45, 5 percent discount with this book in 2009, prices include breakfast and tax, non-smoking, air-con, Internet access and Wi-Fi, 2 blocks north of Plaça de Catalunya at corner of Carrer Diputació, Rambla de Catalunya 30, tel. 934-457-657, fax 934-450-050, www.hotelcontinental.com, palacete@hotelcontinental.com).

$ Hostal Residencia Neutral, with a classic Eixample address and 28 very basic rooms, is a family-run time-warp and a fine value (tiny S-€35, Ds-€60, Db-€65, Ts-€75, Tb-€80, Qs-€80, Qb-€85, €8 continental breakfast in pleasant breakfast room, request a back room to avoid street noise, thin walls, fans, elevator, elegantly located 2 blocks north of Gran Via at Rambla de Catalunya 42, tel. 934-876-390, fax 934-876-848, hostalneutral@arrakis.es, owner Ramón, animated Lino works the night shift).

$ Hotel Ginebra is minimal, clean, and quiet considering its central location. The Herrera family rents 12 rooms in a dated apartment building overlooking the main square (Db-€70, or €80 June–Aug, extra bed-€15, breakfast-€3, air-con, elevator, Rambla de Catalunya 1/3, tel. 933-171-063, www.hotelginebra.net, info@hotelginebra.net, Juan speaks English).

$ Somnio Hostel, an innovative new place run by a pair of American expats, has both dorm beds and private rooms (dorm bed-€23, S-€40, D-€72, Db-€80, Carrer de la Diputació 251, tel. 932-725-308, www.somniohostels.com, info@somniohostels.com).

EATING

Barcelona, the capital of Catalan cuisine—featuring seafood—offers a tremendous variety of colorful eateries. Because of their common struggles, Catalans seem to have an affinity for Basque culture—so you'll find a lot of Basque tapas places here, too. (For more on Basque food, see page 123.) Most of my listings are lively spots with a busy tapas scene at the bar, along with restaurant tables for *raciones*. A regional specialty is *pa amb tomaquet* (pah ahm too-MAH-kaht), bread topped with a mix of crushed tomato and olive oil.

I've listed mostly practical, characteristic, colorful, and afford-

able restaurants. My recommendations are grouped by neighborhood—along the Ramblas; in the Barri Gòtic; in the Ribera neighborhood; and in the Eixample—followed by some budget options scattered throughout the city. And for dessert, I've suggested "A Short, Sweet Walk" (see page 98). The city is thriving with trendy and chic new eateries, and foodies will do well to get local advice or explore the Ribera area for a fine dinner. Many restaurants close in August (or July), when the owners take a vacation. It's deadly to your Barcelona experience to eat too early—if a place feels touristy, come back later and it may be a thriving local favorite.

Along the Ramblas

Within a few steps of the Ramblas, you'll find handy lunch places, an inviting market hall, a slew of vegetarian options, and a giant tapas bar.

Lunching Simply yet Memorably near the Ramblas

While these places are enjoyable for a lunch break between your Ramblas sightseeing, many are also open for dinner. For locations, see the map on page 92.

Taverna Basca Irati serves 40 kinds of hot and cold Basque *pintxos* for €1.70 each. These are open-faced sandwiches—like sushi on bread. Muscle in through the hungry local crowd. Get an empty plate from the waiter, and then help yourself. Every few minutes, a waiter prances proudly by with a platter of new, still-warm munchies. Grab one as they pass by...it's addictive. You pay on the honor system: You're charged by the number of toothpicks left on your plate when you're done. Wash it down with €2–3 glasses of Rioja (full-bodied red wine), Txakolí (sprightly Basque white wine), or *sidra* (apple wine) poured from on high to add oxygen and bring out the flavor (daily 11:00–24:00, a block off the Ramblas, behind arcade at Carrer Cardenal Casanyes 15, Metro: Liceu, tel. 933-023-084).

Restaurant Elisabets is a happy little neighborhood eatery packed with antique radios and popular with locals for its "home-cooked," three-course €10 lunch special. Stop by for lunch, survey what those around you are enjoying, and order what looks best (Mon–Sat 7:30–23:00, closed Sun, lunch special served 13:00–16:00, otherwise only €3 tapas—not full meals, 2 blocks west of Ramblas on far corner of Plaça Bonsucces at Carrer Elisabets 2, tel. 933-175-826, run by Pilar).

Café Granja Viader is a quaint time-capsule place, family-run since 1870. They boast about being the first dairy business to bottle and distribute milk in Spain. This feminine-feeling place—specializing in baked and dairy delights, toasted sandwiches, and light meals—is ideal for a traditional breakfast. Or indulge your sweet tooth: Try a glass of *orxata* (or *horchata*—*chufa* nut milk, summer only), *llet mallorquina* (Majorca-style milk with cinnamon, lemon, and sugar), *crema catalana* (crème brûlée, their specialty), or *suis* ("Swiss"—hot chocolate with a snowcap of whipped cream). *Mel y mato* is fresh cheese with honey...very Catalan. It's a block off the Ramblas behind El Carme church (Tue–Sat 9:00–13:45 & 17:00–20:45, Mon 17:00–20:45 only, closed Sun, Xucla 4, tel. 933-183-486).

Picnics: Shoestring tourists buy groceries at **El Corte Inglés** (Mon–Sat 10:00–22:00, closed Sun, supermarket in basement, Plaça de Catalunya) and **Carrefour Express supermarket** (Mon–Sat 10:00–22:00, closed Sun, Ramblas 113).

In and near La Boquería Market

Try eating at La Boquería market at least once (#91 on the Ramblas). Like all farmers markets in Europe, this place is ringed by colorful, good-value eateries. Lots of stalls sell fun take-away food—especially fruit salads and fresh-squeezed fruit juices. There are several good bars around the market busy with shoppers munching at the counter (breakfast, tapas all day, coffee). The market, and most of the eateries listed here (unless noted), are open Monday through Saturday from 8:00 until 20:00 (though things get very quiet after about 16:00) and closed on Sunday.

Pinotxo Bar is just to the right as you enter the market. It's a great spot for coffee, breakfast (spinach tortillas, or whatever's cooking with toast), or tapas. Fun-loving Juan and his family are La Boquería fixtures. Grab a stool across the way to sip your drink with people-watching views. Have a Chucho?

Kiosko Universal is popular for its great prices on wonderful fish dishes. As you enter the market from the Ramblas, it's all the way to the left on the first alley. If you see people waiting, ask who's last in line *("¿El último?")*. You'll eat immersed in the spirit of the market (€13 fixed-price lunches with different fresh-fish options from 12:00–16:00, better before 12:30 but always packed, tel. 933-178-286).

Restaurant la Gardunya, at the back of the market, offers tasty meat and seafood meals made with fresh ingredients bought directly from the market (€13 fixed-price lunch includes wine and bread, €16 three-course dinner specials don't include wine, €10–20 à la carte dishes, Mon–Sat 13:00–16:00 & 20:00–24:00, closed Sun, mod seating indoors or outside watching the market action, Carrer Jerusalem 18, tel. 933-024-323).

Bar Terrace Restaurant Ra is a lively terrace immediately behind the market (at the right end of the big parking lot) with outdoor tables filled by young, trendy, happy eaters. At lunch they serve one great salad/pasta/wine meal for €11. If you feel like eating a big salad under an umbrella...this is the place (€9-15 à la carte dishes, daily 10:00–12:30 & 13:30–16:00 & 21:00–24:00, fancier menu at night, mobile 615-959-872).

Vegetarian Eateries near Plaça de Catalunya and the Ramblas

Biocenter, a Catalan soup-and-salad restaurant popular with local vegetarians, takes its cooking very seriously and feels a bit more like a real restaurant than most (€8-9.50 lunch specials include soup or salad and plate of the day, Mon–Sat 13:00–17:00, Thu–Sat also 20:00–23:00, closed Sun, 2 blocks off the Ramblas at Pintor Fortuny 25, Metro: Catalunya, tel. 933-014-583).

Juicy Jones is a tutti-frutti vegan/vegetarian eatery with colorful graffiti decor, a hip veggie menu (served downstairs), groovy laid-back staff, and a stunning array of fresh-squeezed juices served at the bar. Pop in for a quick €3 "juice of the day." For lunch, you can get the Indian-inspired €6 *thali* plate, the €6.25 plate of the day, or an €8.50 meal including one of the two plates plus soup or salad and dessert (daily 13:00–24:00, also tapas and salads, Carrer Cardenal Casanyes 7, tel. 933-024-330). There's another location on the other side of the Ramblas (Carrer Hospital 74).

Out at Sea, at the Bottom of the Ramblas

Tapasbar Maremagnum is a big, rollicking, sports-bar kind of tapas restaurant, great for large groups. It's a fun way to end your Ramblas walk, featuring breezy harbor views and good local food with an emphasis on the sea. Go here not for the tapas, but to make the Maremagnum scene (daily 11:00–24:00, a 10-minute stroll past the Columbus Monument straight out the dock on Moll d'Espanya, tel. 932-258-180).

In the Barri Gòtic

These eateries populate Barcelona's atmospheric Gothic Quarter, near the cathedral. Choose between a sit-down meal at a restaurant, or a string of very old-fashioned tapas bars. For locations, see the map on next page.

Dining (Real Restaurants) in the Barri Gòtic

Café de l'Academia is a delightful place on a pretty square tucked away in the heart of the Barri Gòtic—but patronized mainly by the neighbors. They serve "honest cuisine" from the market with Catalan

Barcelona's Barri Gòtic Restaurants

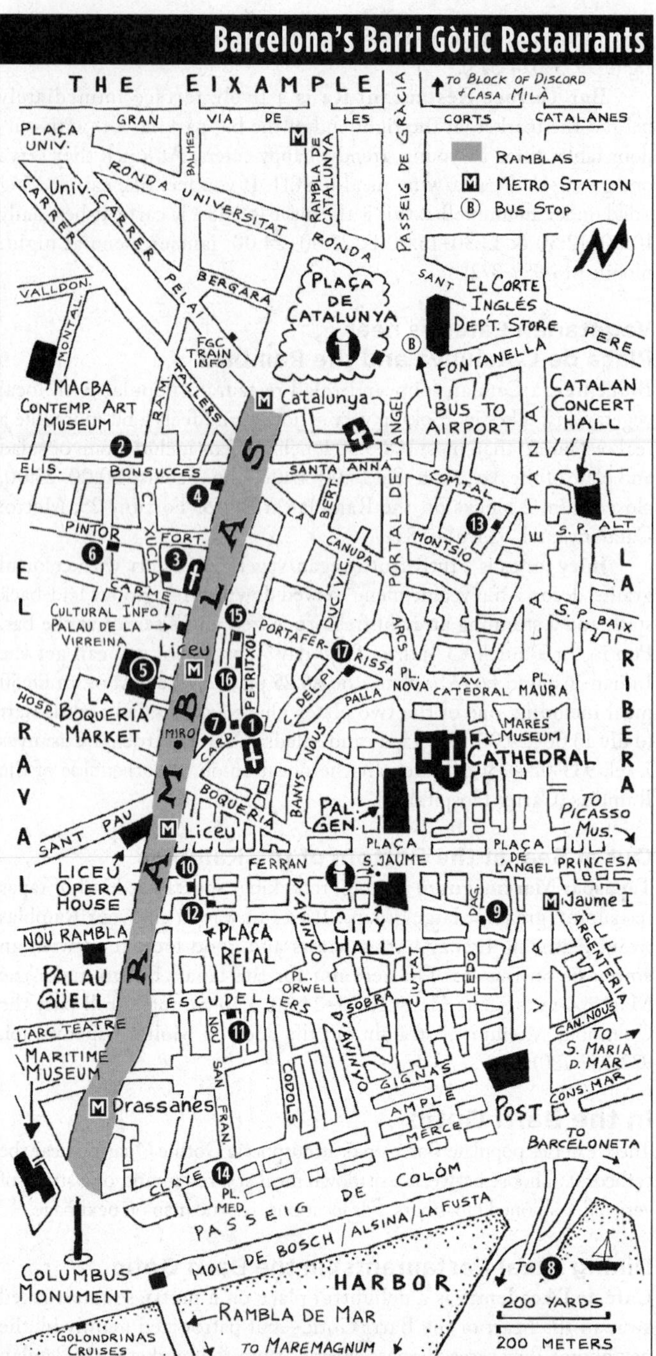

Restaurant Key

1 Taverna Basca Irati	10 La Crema Canela
2 Restaurant Elisabets	11 La Fonda
3 Café Granja Viader	12 Les Quinze Nits
4 Supermarket	13 La Dolça Herminia
5 La Boquería Market Eateries	14 Carrer de la Mercè Tapas Bars
6 Biocenter Veggie Rest.	15 Casa Colomina
7 Juicy Jones	16 Granja La Pallaresa
8 To Tapasbar Maremagnum	17 Fargas Chocolate Shop
9 Café de l'Academia	

roots. The candlelit, air-conditioned interior is rustic yet elegant, with soft jazz, flowers, and modern art. And if you want to eat outdoors on a convivial, mellow square...this is it (€10–12 first courses, €12–15 second courses, fixed-price lunch for €10 at the bar or €14 at a table, Mon–Fri 13:30–16:00 & 20:30–23:30, closed Sat–Sun, near the City Hall square, off Carrer de Jaume I up Carrer Dagueria at Carrer Lledo 1, tel. 933-198-253).

Popular Chain Restaurants: Barcelona enjoys a chain of several bright, modern restaurants, all with different names. These five are a hit for their modern, artfully presented Spanish and Mediterranean cuisine, crisp ambience, and unbeatable prices. Because of their three-course €9 lunches and €16–20 dinners (both with wine), all are crowded with locals and in-the-know tourists (all open daily 13:00–15:45 & 20:30–23:30, unless otherwise noted). My favorite of the bunch is **La Crema Canela,** which feels cozier than the others and is the only one that takes reservations (30 yards north of Plaça Reial at Passatge de Madoz 6, tel. 933-182-744). The rest are notorious for long lines at the door—arrive 30 minutes before opening, or be prepared to wait. The next two (along with La Crema Canela) are within a block of the Plaça Reial, and the third is near the Catalan Concert Hall: **La Fonda** (Carrer dels Escudellers 10, tel. 933-017-515—as this is very close to a seedy stretch of street, approach it from the Ramblas rather than from Plaça Reial); **Les Quinze Nits** (on Plaça Reial at #6—you'll see the line, tel. 933-173-075); and **La Dolça Herminia** (2 blocks toward Ramblas from Catalan Concert Hall at Carrer de les Magdalenes 27, tel. 933-170-676). The fifth restaurant in the chain, **La Rita,** is described later under "Restaurants in the Eixample."

Tapas on Carrer de la Mercè in the Barri Gòtic

Barcelona boasts great *tascas*—colorful local tapas bars. Get small plates (for maximum sampling) by asking for "tapas," not the bigger "*raciones.*" Glasses of *vino tinto* go for about €0.50. While trendy uptown restaurants are safer, better-lit, and come with English menus and less grease,

these places will stain your journal. The neighborhood's dark, the regulars are rough-edged, and you'll get a glimpse of a crusty Barcelona from before the affluence hit. Try *pimientos de padrón*—Russian roulette with peppers that are lightly fried in oil and salted...only a few are jalapeño-spicy. At the cider bars, it's traditional to order *queso de cabrales* (a traditional, very moldy blue cheese) and spicy chorizo (sausage)...ideally prepared *al diablo* ("devil-style")—soaked in wine, then flambéed at your table.

From the bottom of the Ramblas (near the Columbus Monument), hike east along Carrer Clave. Then follow the small street that runs along the right side of the church (Carrer de la Mercè), stopping at the *tascas* that look fun. For a montage of edible memories, wander Carrer de la Mercè west to east and consider these spots, stopping wherever looks most inviting. I've listed ye olde dives, but there are many trendy places here as well. Most of these places close down around 23:00.

La Pulpería (at #16), with a bit less character than the others, eases you into the scene with fried fish, octopus, and *patatas bravas*, all with Galician Ribeiro wine. A few steps down the street, at **Casa del Molinero** (#13), you can sauté your chorizo *al diablo*. It's great with *pa amb tomaquet* (tomato bread). Farther down at the corner (#28), **La Plata** keeps things wonderfully simple, serving extremely cheap plates of sardines (€1.70), little salads (€1.50), and small glasses of keg wine (less than €1). **Tasca el Corral** (#17) serves mountain favorites from northern Spain by the half-*ración* (see their list), such as *queso de cabrales* and chorizo *al diablo* with *sidra* (apple wine sold by the €5 bottle). **Sidrería Tasca La Socarrena** (#21) offers hard cider from Asturias in €5 bottles with *queso de cabrales* and chorizo. At the end of Carrer de la Mercè, **Cerveceria Vendimia** slings tasty clams and mussels (hearty *raciones* for €4–6 a plate—they don't do smaller portions, so order sparingly). Sit at the bar and point to what looks good. Their *pulpo* (octopus) is more expensive and is the house specialty. Carrer Ample and Carrer Gignas, the streets parallel to Carrer de la Mercè inland, have more refined bar-hopping possibilities.

In the Ribera District, near the Picasso Museum

La Ribera, the hottest neighborhood in town, sparkles with eclectic and trendy as well as subdued and classy little restaurants hidden in the small lanes surrounding the Church of Santa Maria del Mar. While I've listed a few well-established tapas bars that are great for light meals, to really dine, simply wander around for 15 minutes and pick the place that tickles your gastronomic fancy. I think anyone saying they know what's best in this area is kidding themselves—it's changing too fast and the choices are too personal. One thing's for sure: There are a lot of talented and hardworking restaurateurs with plenty to offer. Consider starting your evening off with a glass of fine wine at one of the *enotecas* on the square facing the Church of Santa Maria del Mar. Sit back and admire the pure Catalan Gothic architecture. My first four listings are all on the main drag, Carrer de l'Argenteria. For locations, see the map on page 61.

Sagardi offers a wonderful array of Basque goodies—tempting *pinchos* and *montaditos* at €1.70 each—along its huge bar. Ask for a plate and graze (just take whatever looks good). You can sit on the square with your plunder for €0.50 per tapa extra. Wash it down with Txakolí, a Basque white wine poured from the spout of a huge wooden barrel into a glass as you watch. When you're done, they'll count your toothpicks to tally your bill (daily 12:00–24:00, Carrer de l'Argenteria 62–64, tel. 933-199-993).

Sagardi Euskal Taberna, hiding behind the thriving Sagardi tapas bar (described above), is a mod, rustic, and minimalist woody restaurant committed to serving Basque T-bone steaks and grilled specialties with only the best ingredients. Crisp and friendly service and a big open kitchen with sizzling grills contribute to the ambience. Reservations are smart (€10–15 first courses, €15–25 second courses, plan on €45 for dinner, daily 13:00–16:00 & 20:00–24:00, Carrer de l'Argenteria 62, tel. 933-199-993).

Taller de Tapas ("Tapas Workshop") is an upscale, trendier tapas bar and restaurant that dishes up well-presented, sophisticated morsels and light meals in a medieval-stone yet mod setting. Pay 10 percent more to sit on the square. Elegant but a bit stuffy, it's favored by local office workers who aren't into the Old World Gothic stuff. Four plates will fill a hungry diner for about €20 (Mon–Sat 8:30–24:00, Sun 12:00–24:00, Carrer de l'Argenteria 51, tel. 932-688-559).

El Xampanyet, a colorful family-run bar with a fun-loving staff (Juan Carlos, his mom, and the man who may be his father), specializes in tapas and anchovies. Don't be put off by the seafood from a tin...Catalans like it this way. A *sortido* (assorted plate) of *carne* (meat) or *pescado* (fish) with *pa amb tomaquet* (bread with crushed-tomato spread) makes for a fun meal. While it's filled with tourists during the sightseeing day, this is a local favorite after dark. The scene is great but—especially during busy times—it's tough without Spanish skills. When I asked about the price, Juan Carlos said, "Who cares? The ATM is just across the street." Plan on spending €20 for a meal with wine (same price at bar or table, Tue–Sat 12:00–16:00 & 19:00–23:30, Sun 12:00–16:00 only, closed Mon, a half-block beyond the Picasso Museum at Montcada 22, tel. 933-197-003).

In the Eixample

The people-packed boulevards of the Eixample (Passeig de Gràcia and Rambla de Catalunya) are lined with appetizing eateries featuring breezy outdoor seating. Choose between a real restaurant or an upscale tapas bar. For locations, see the map on page 87.

Restaurants in the Eixample

La Rita is a fresh and dressy little restaurant serving Catalan cuisine near the Block of Discord. Their lunches (three courses with wine for €8, served Mon–Fri from 13:00–15:45) and dinners (€15, à la carte, daily 20:30–23:30) are a great value. Like its four sister restaurants—described under "Dining (Real Restaurants) in the Barri Gòtic," above—it takes no reservations and its prices attract long lines, so arrive just before the doors open...or wait (a block from Metro: Passeig de Gràcia, near corner of Carrer de Pau Claris and Carrer Arago at Arago 279, tel. 934-872-376).

La Bodegueta is an unbelievably atmospheric below-street-level bodega serving hearty wines, homemade vermouth, *anchoas* (anchovies), tapas, and *flautas*—sandwiches made with flute-thin baguettes. Its daily €10.50 lunch special of three courses with wine is served 13:00–16:00. A long block from Gaudí's Casa Milà, this makes a fine sightseeing break (Mon–Sat 8:00–24:00, Sun 19:00–24:00, at intersection with Provenza, Rambla de Catalunya 100, Metro: Diagonal, tel. 932-154-894).

Restaurante la Palmera serves a mix of Catalan, Mediterranean, and French cuisine in an elegant yet smoky room with bottle-lined walls. The smoke keeps out the tourists. This place offers great food, service, and value—for me, a very special meal in Barcelona. They have three zones: the classic main room, a more forgettable adjacent room, and a few outdoor tables. I like the classic room. Reservations are smart (€10 plates, creative €14 six-plate *degustation* lunch, Tue–Sat 13:00–15:45 & 20:30–23:15, closed Sun–Mon, Enric Granados 57, at the corner with Mallorca, tel. 934-532-338).

Restaurant Flauta fills two floors with enthusiastic eaters (I like the ground floor best). It's fresh and modern, with a fun, no-stress menu featuring €5 small plates, creative €4 *flauta* sandwiches, and a €10 three-course lunch deal including a drink. Good €2.30 wines by the glass are listed on the blackboard. This is a place to order high on the menu for a fine, moderately priced meal (Mon–Sat 13:00–24:00, closed Sun, fun-loving and helpful staff recommends the fried vegetables, no reservations possible, just off Via Diputació at Aribau 23, tel. 933-237-038).

Restaurant de Degustacio Cincsentits ("Taste Treats for the Five Senses"), with only about 30 seats, is my gourmet recommendation. It's a chic, minimal, smoke-free place where all the attention goes to the fine service and elegantly presented dishes. It's run by Catalans who lived in Canada (so there's absolutely no language barrier) and serve avant-garde cuisine inspired by Catalan traditions and ingredients. Their €65 *degustation menu* is an unforgettable extravaganza. Reservations are required (Tue–Sat 13:30–15:00 & 20:30–23:00, Mon 13:30–15:00 only, closed Sun, near Carrer d'Aragó at Aribau 58, tel. 933-239-490).

El Racó is a local favorite for "creative Mediterranean cuisine"—pasta, pizza, crêpes, and salads (about €6–9 each) in a modern, lively, cavernous-but-bright, air-conditioned setting (daily 13:00–24:00, Rambla de Catalunya 25, tel. 933-175-688).

A Bit Farther Out: **Hofmann** is a renowned cooking school with an excellent if pricey restaurant serving modern Mediterranean market cuisine. Dress up and dine in intimate rooms papered with photos of famous patrons. The four-course, €39 lunches are made up of just what the students are working on that day—so there's no choice (watch the students as they cook). Dinners can easily cost twice as much (à la carte). Save room (and euros) for the incredible desserts. Reserve long in advance, because locals love this place (Mon–Fri 13:30–15:15 & 21:00–23:15, closed Sat–Sun and Aug, 4 blocks northwest of Casa Milà at La Granada del Penedès 14-16, tel. 932-187-165, www.hofmann-bcn.com).

Fancy Tapas Bars in the Eixample

Many trendy and touristic tapas bars in Eixample offer a cheery welcome and slam out the appetizers. These three are my favorites.

Quasi Queviures (**"Qu Qu"** for short) serves upscale tapas, sandwiches, or the whole nine yards—classic food served fast from a fun menu with modern decor and a high-energy sports-bar ambience. It's bright, clean, and not too crowded. Walk through their enticing kitchen to get to the tables in back. Committed to developing a loyal following, they claim, "We fertilize our local customers with daily specialties" (€2–3 tapas, €5 dinner salads, €7 plates, prices 17 percent higher on the terrace, daily 8:00–24:00, between Gran Via and Via Diputació at Passeig de Gràcia 24, tel. 933-174-512).

Ciudad Condal Cerveceria brags that it serves the best *montaditos* (€2–3 little open-faced sandwiches) and beers in Barcelona. It's an Eixample favorite, with an elegant bar and tables plus good seating out on the Rambla de Catalunya for all that people-watching action. It's classier than Qu Qu and packed after 21:00, when you'll likely need to put your name on a list and wait. While it has no restaurant-type menu, the list of tapas and *montaditos* is easy, fun, and comes with a great variety (including daily specials). This place is a cut above your normal tapas bar, but with reasonable prices (most tapas around €4–5, daily until 24:00, facing the intersection of Gran Via and Rambla de Catalunya at Rambla de Catalunya 18, tel. 933-181-997).

La Tramoia, at the opposite corner, serves piles of cheap *montaditos* and tapas at its ground-floor bar and at nice tables inside and out. If Ciudad Condal Cerveceria is jammed up, you're more likely to find a seat here. The brasserie-style restaurant upstairs bustles with happy local eaters enjoying grilled meats (€6–10 plates), but I'd stay downstairs for the €4 tapas (open daily, also facing the intersection of Gran Via and Rambla de Catalunya at Rambla de Catalunya 15, tel. 934-123-634).

Budget Options Around Town

Sandwiches: Bright, clean, and inexpensive sandwich shops proudly hold the cultural line against the fast-food invasion hamburgerizing the rest of Europe. Catalan sandwiches are made to order with crunchy French bread. Rather than butter, locals prefer *tomaquet* (a spread of crushed tomatoes). You'll see two big local chains (Pans & Company and Bocatta) everywhere, but these serve mass-produced McBaguettes ordered from a multilingual menu. I've had better luck with hole-in-the-wall sandwich shops—virtually as numerous as the chains—where you can see exactly what you're getting.

Kebabs: Kebab places are a good, super-cheap standby. A favorite, **Maoz Falafel,** lets you create the falafel of your dreams for €4 (just off the City Hall square at Plaça de Sant Jaume 7).

A Short, Sweet Walk

Let me propose this three-stop dessert (or, since these places close well before the traditional Barcelona dinnertime, a late-afternoon snack). You'll try a refreshing glass of *orxata,* munch some *churros con chocolate,* and visit a fine *xocolateria,* all within a three-minute walk of each other in the Barri Gòtic just off the Ramblas. Start at the corner of Carrer Portaferrissa midway down the Ramblas. For the best atmosphere, begin your walk at about 18:00. For locations, see the map on page 92.

***Orxata* at Casa Colomina:** Walk down Carrer Portaferrissa to #8 (on the right). Casa Colomina, founded in 1908, specializes in homemade *torrons*—a variation of nougat made with almond, honey, and sugar, brought to Spain by the Moors 1,200 years ago. Three different kinds are sold in big €10 slabs: *blando, duro,* and *yema*—soft, hard, and yolk (€2 smaller chunks also available). In the summer, the shop also sells ice cream and the refreshing *orxata* (or *horchata*—a drink made from the *chufa* nut). Order a glass and ask to see and eat a *chufa* nut (a.k.a. earth almond or tiger nut; Mon–Sat 10:00–20:30, Sun 12:30–20:30, tel. 933-122-511).

***Churros con Chocolate* at Granja La Pallaresa:** Continue down Carrer Portaferrissa, taking a right at Carrer Petrixol to this fun-loving *xocolateria.* Older, elegant ladies gather here for the Spanish equivalent of tea time—dipping their greasy *churros* into pudding-thick cups of hot chocolate (€4.10 for five *churros con chocolate,* Mon–Fri 9:00–13:00 & 16:00–21:00, Sat–Sun 9:00–13:00 & 17:00–21:00, Carrer Petritxol 11, tel. 933-022-036).

Homemade Chocolate at Fargas: For your last stop, head for the ornate Fargas chocolate shop (Mon–Fri 9:30–13:30 & 16:00–20:00, Sat 10:00–14:00 & 16:00–20:00, closed Sun; continue down Carrer Petritxol to the square, hook left through the two-part square, and then left up Carrer del Pi; it's on the corner of Portaferrissa and Carrer del Pi, tel. 933-020-342). Since the 19th century, gentlemen with walking canes have dropped by here for their chocolate fix. Founded in 1827, this is one of the oldest and most traditional chocolate places in Barcelona. If they're not too busy, ask to see the old chocolate mill (*"¿Puedo ver el molino?"*) to the right of the counter. They sell even tiny quantities (one little morsel) by the weight—don't be shy. A delicious chunk of the crumbly, semi-sweet house specialty costs €0.45 (tray by the mill). The tempting bonbons in the window cost about €1 each.

TRANSPORTATION CONNECTIONS

From Barcelona by Train: Unless otherwise noted, all of these trains depart from the Sants station; however, some trains also stop at other stations more convenient to the downtown tourist zone: França station, Passeig de Gràcia, or Plaça de Catalunya. Figure out if your train stops at these stations (and board there) to save yourself the trip to Sants.

The new **AVE train to Madrid** has shaved hours off that journey, making it faster than flying (when you consider that you're zipping from downtown to downtown). The train departs frequently (2/hr) in the morning, and about hourly in the afternoon and evening. The nonstop train is a little more expensive (€125, 3 hrs) than the slightly slower train that makes a few stops and adds about a half-hour (€106, 3.5 hrs). Regular reserved AVE tickets can be pre-purchased at www.renfe.es and picked up at the station. If you have a railpass, you'll pay only a reservation fee of €25 for first class, which includes a meal (€15 second class, buy at any train station in Spain). Passholders can't reserve online through RENFE but you can make the reservation at www.raileurope.com for delivery before leaving the US ($17 in second class, $40 in first class).

By Train to: Sitges (4/hr, 35–40 min, €2.60), **Montserrat** (departs from Plaça d'Espanya, hourly, 1.5 hrs, €14.50 round-trip, includes cable car or rack train to monastery—see details on page 112), **Figueres** (hourly, 2 hrs, €15 round-trip), **Sevilla** (3/day—one fast, 6.5 hrs, €129; one slow, 12 hrs, €58; and one night train, 10 hrs, €85), **Granada** (1/day Wed, Fri, and Sun only, 11.5 hrs, €57; also 1 night train/day, 12 hrs, €58), **Salamanca** (8/day, 6–7.5 hours, change in Madrid from Atocha station to Chamartín station via Metro; 1 direct/day,

11 hrs), **San Sebastián** (3/day—one fast, 6 hrs, €59; one slow, 8.5 hrs, €39; one night train/day except Sat, 10 hrs, €50), **Málaga** (3/day—one fast, 6.5 hrs, €130; one slow, 13 hrs, €59; and one night train, 13 hrs, €59), **Lisbon** (no direct trains, head to Madrid and then catch night train to Lisbon, 17 hrs, about €130), **Nice** (1/day via Montpelier, about €100; cheaper connections possible with multiple changes including Cerbère), **Avignon** (5/day, less on weekends, 6–9 hrs, about €40, or about €65 for change in Montpellier), **Paris** (3/day, 9 hrs, 1–2 changes; 1 night train/day, 12 hrs, about €130, or €45 with railpass, reservation mandatory). Train info: tel. 902-240-202, www.renfe.es.

By Bus to: Madrid (14/day, 8 hrs, €27—a fraction of the AVE train price, departs from Nord bus station at Metro: Arc de Triomf on line 1, bus info tel. 902-260-606, Alsa bus company tel. 902-422-242), **Salamanca** (2/day, 11 hrs, Alsa buses), **Cadaqués** (3/day, 60 min, €4.50). Sarfa buses serve all the **coastal resorts** (tel. 902-302-025, www.sarfa.com). For bus schedules, see www.barcelonanord.com.

By Plane: Check the reasonable flights from Barcelona to Sevilla or Madrid. Vueling is Iberia's most popular discount airline (e.g., Barcelona–Madrid flights as low as €30 if booked in advance, tel. 902-333-933, www.vueling.com). Iberia (tel. 902-400-500, www.iberia.com) and Air Europa (tel. 902-401-501 or 932-983-907, www.aireuropa.com) offer €80 flights to Madrid. Also, for flights to other parts of Europe, consider British Airways (tel. 902-111-333, www.britishairways.com), easyJet (tel. 902-299-992, www.easyjet.com), and Ryanair (www.ryanair.com). Most use Barcelona's **El Prat de Llobregat Airport** (tel. 902-404-704), but Ryanair uses an airport 60 miles away called **Girona-Costa Brava** (tel. 972-186-600). Information on both airports can be found on the official Spanish airport website, www.aena.es.

For details on getting between either airport and downtown Barcelona, see "Arrival in Barcelona—By Plane," page 34.

NEAR BARCELONA

Figueres • Cadaqués • Sitges • Montserrat

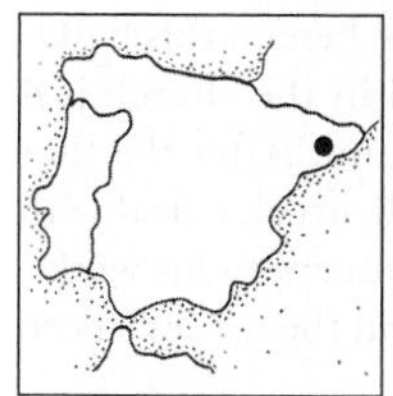

Four fine sights are day-trip temptations from Barcelona. Fans of Surrealism can combine a fantasy in Dalí-land with a classy but sleepy port-town getaway by spending a day or two in Cadaqués (pictured above), with a stop at the Dalí Theater-Museum in Figueres (an hour from Cadaqués and two hours from Barcelona). For the consummate day at the beach, head 45 minutes south to the charming and free-spirited resort town, Sitges. And pilgrims with hiking boots head an hour into the mountains for the most sacred spot in Catalunya: Montserrat.

Figueres

The town of Figueres (feeg-YEHR-ehs)—conveniently connected by train to Barcelona—is of sightseeing interest only for its Salvador Dalí Theater-Museum. In fact, the entire town seems Dalí-dominated.

Getting to Figueres: Figueres is an easy day trip from Barcelona, or a handy stopover en route to France (trains between Barcelona and France stop in Figueres). Trains to Figueres from Barcelona depart from Sants Station or from the RENFE station at Metro: Passeig de Gràcia (hourly, 2 hours, €15 round-trip). For bus connections to Cadaqués, see page 106.

Arrival in Figueres: From the train station, simply follow *Museu Dalí* signs (and the crowds) for the 15-minute walk to the museum.

SIGHTS

▲▲▲Dalí Theater-Museum (Teatre-Museu Dalí)

This is *the* essential Dalí sight—and, if you like Dalí, one of Europe's most enjoyable museums, period. Inaugurated in 1974, the museum is a work of art in itself. Ever the entertainer and promoter, Dalí personally conceptualized, designed, decorated, and painted it to showcase his life's work. The museum fills a former theater and is the artist's mausoleum (his tomb is in the crypt below center stage). It's also a kind of mausoleum to Dalí's creative spirit.

Dalí had his first public art showing at age 14 here in this building when it was a theater, and he was baptized in the church just across the street. The place was sentimental to him. After the theater was destroyed in the Spanish Civil War, Dalí struck a deal with the mayor: Dalí would rebuild the theater as a museum to his works, Figueres would be put on the sightseeing map...and the money's been flowing in ever since.

Even from the outside—painted pink, studded with golden loaves of bread, and topped with monumental eggs and a geodesic dome—the building exudes Dalí's outrageous public persona.

Cost, Hours, Information: €11; July–Sept daily 9:00–20:00; June daily 9:30–18:00; Oct and March–May Tue–Sun 9:30–18:00, closed Mon; Nov–Feb Tue–Sun 10:30–18:00, closed Mon; last entry 45 minutes before closing, tel. 972-677-500, www.salvador-dali.org. The free bag check has your bag waiting for you at the exit.

Coin-Op Tip: Much of Dalí's art is movable and coin-operated—bring a few €0.20 and €0.50 coins.

Visiting the Museum: The museum has two parts—the theater/mausoleum and the "Dalí's Jewels" exhibit in an adjacent building. There's no logical order for a visit (that would be un-Surrealistic). And, naturally, there's no audioguide. Dalí said there are two kinds of visitors: those who don't need a description, and those who aren't worth a description.

➲ **Self-Guided Tour:** At the risk of offending Dalí, I've written this loose commentary to attach some meaning to your visit.

Stepping into the **theater** (with its audience of statues), face the stage—and Dalí's unmarked crypt. You know how you can never get a cab when it's raining? Pop a coin into Dalí's personal 1941 Cadillac, and it rains inside the car. Look above, atop the tire tower: That's the boat enjoyed by Dalí and his soulmate, Gala—his emotional

Near Barcelona

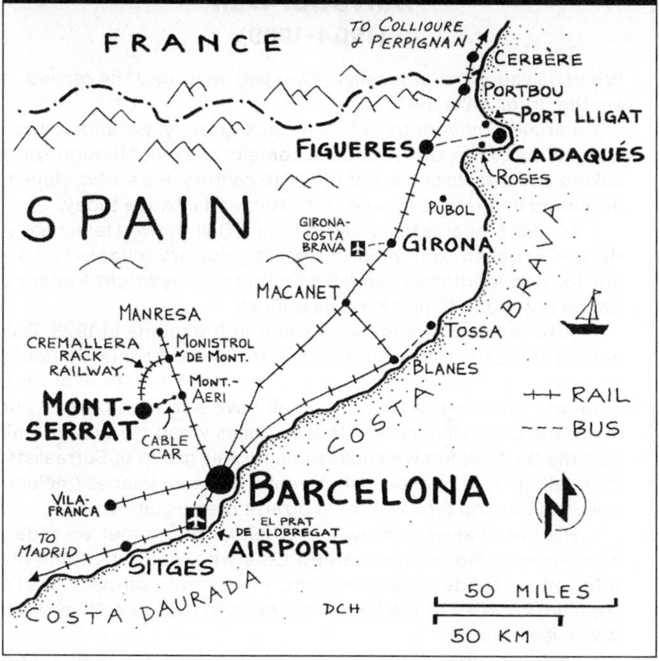

life-preserver, who kept him from going overboard. When she died, so did he (for his last seven years). Blue tears made of condoms drip below the boat.

Up on the **stage,** squint at the big digital Abraham Lincoln, and president #16 comes into focus. Approach the painting to find that Abe's facial cheeks are Gala's butt cheeks. Under the painting, a door leads to the **Treasures Room,** with the greatest collection of actual Dalí original oil paintings in the museum. (Many of those you see on the walls are prints.) You'll see Cubist visions of Cadaqués and dreamy portraits of Gala. Crutches—a recurring Dalí theme—represent Gala, who kept him supported whenever a meltdown threatened.

The famous **Homage to Mae West room** is a tribute to the sultry seductress. Dalí loved her attitude. Saying things like, "Why marry and make one man unhappy, when you can stay single and make so many so happy?" Mae West was to conventional morality what Dalí was to conventional art. Climb to the vantage point

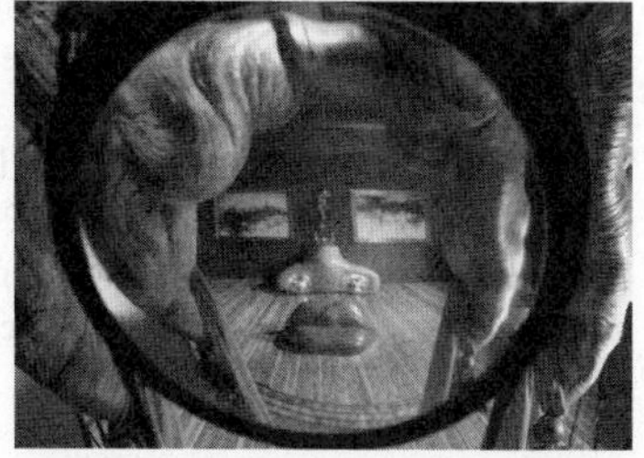

Salvador Dalí
(1904–1989)

When Salvador Dalí was asked, "Are you on drugs?" he replied, "I am the drug... take me."

Labeled by various critics as sick, greedy, paranoid, arrogant, and a clown, Dalí produced some of the most thought-provoking and trailblazing art of the 20th century. His erotic, violent, disjointed imagery continues to disturb and intrigue today.

Born in Figueres to a well-off family, Dalí showed talent early. He was expelled from Madrid's prestigious art school—twice—but formed longtime friendships with the playwright Federico García Lorca and filmmaker Luis Buñuel.

After a breakthrough art exhibit in Barcelona in 1925, Dalí moved to Paris. He hobnobbed with fellow Spaniards Pablo Picasso and Joan Miró, and with a group of artists exploring Sigmund Freud's theory that we all have a hidden part of our mind, the unconscious "id," that surfaces when we dream. Dalí became the best-known spokesman for this group of Surrealists, channeling his id to create photorealistic dream images (melting watches, burning giraffes) set in bizarre dreamscapes.

His life changed forever in 1929, when he met an older, Russian, married woman named Gala who would become his wife, muse, model, manager, and emotional compass. Dalí's popularity spread to the US, where he (and Gala) weathered the WWII years.

In his prime, Dalí's work became less Surrealist and more classical, influenced by past masters of painted realism (Velázquez, Raphael, Ingres) and by his own study of history, science, and religion. He produced large-scale paintings of historical events (e.g., Columbus discovering America, the Last Supper)

where the sofa lips, fireplace nostrils, painting eyes, and drapery hair come together to make the face of Mae West.

Dalí's art can be playful, but also disturbing. He was passionate about the dark side of things, but, with Gala for balance, he managed never to go off the deep end. Unlike Pablo Casals (the Catalan cellist) and Pablo Picasso (another local artist), Dalí didn't go into exile under Franco's dictatorship. Pragmatically, he accepted both Franco and the Church, and was supported by the dictator. Apart from the occasional *sardana* dance (see page 55), you won't find a hint of politics in Dalí's art.

Wander around. You can spend hours here, wondering, is it real or not real? Am I crazy, or is it you? Beethoven is painted with squid ink applied by a shoe on a stormy night. Jesus is made with candle smoke and an eraser. It's fun to see the Dalí-ization of art classics.

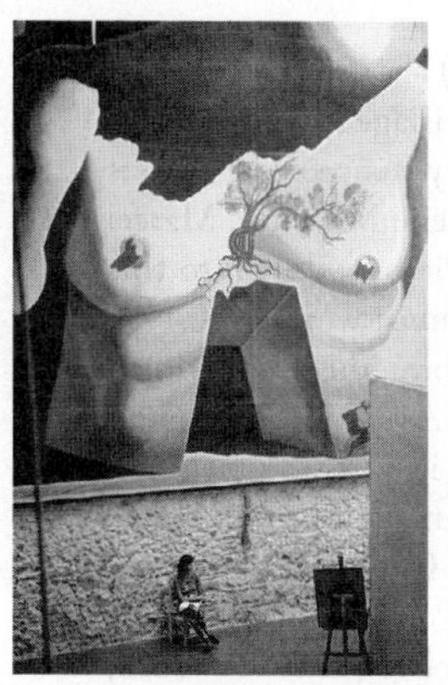

that were collages of realistic scenes floating in a surrealistic landscape, peppered with thought-provoking symbols.

Dalí—an extremely capable technician—mastered many media, including film. *An Andalusian Dog* (*Un Chien Andalou,* 1929, with Luis Buñuel) was a cutting-edge montage of disturbing, eyeball-slicing images. For Alfred Hitchcock, he designed the big-eye backdrop for the dream sequence of *Spellbound* (1945). He made jewels for the rich and clothes for Coco Chanel, wrote a novel and an autobiography, and pioneered what would come to be called "installations." He also helped develop "performance art" by showing up at an opening in a diver's suit or by playing the role he projected to the media—as a super-confident, waxed-mustached artistic genius.

In later years, Dalí's over-the-top public image contrasted with his ever-growing illness, depression, and isolation. He endured the scandal of a dealer overselling "limited editions" of his work. When Gala died in 1982, Dalí retreated to his hometown, living his last days in the Torre Galatea of the Theater-Museum complex, where he died of heart failure.

Dalí's legacy as an artist includes his self-marketing persona, his exceptional ability to draw, his provocative pairing of symbols, and his sheer creative drive.

Dalí, like so many modern artists, was inspired by the masters—especially Velázquez.

The former theater's **smoking lounge** is a highlight, with portraits of Gala and Dalí (with a big eye, big ear, and a dark side) bookending a Roman candle of creativity. The fascinating ceiling painting shows the feet of Gala and Dalí as they bridge earth and the heavens. Dalí's drawers are wide open and empty, indicating that he gave everything to his art.

Leaving the theater, keep your ticket and pop into the adjacent **"Dalí's Jewels"** exhibit. It shows sketches and paintings of jewelry Dalí designed, and the actual pieces jewelers made from those surreal visions: a mouth full of pearly whites, a golden finger corset, a fountain of diamonds, and the breathing heart. Explore the ambiguous perception worked into the big painting entitled *Apotheosis of the Dollar.*

Cadaqués

Since the late 1800s, Cadaqués (kah-dah-KEHS) has served as a haven for intellectuals and artists alike. The fishing village's craggy coastline, sun-drenched colors, and laid-back lifestyle inspired Fauvists such as Henri Matisse and Surrealists such as René Magritte, Marcel Duchamp, and Federico García Lorca. Even Picasso, drawn to this enchanting coastal haunt, painted some of his Cubist works here.

Salvador Dalí, raised in nearby Figueres, brought international fame to this sleepy Catalan port in the 1920s. As a kid, Dalí spent summers here in the family cabin, where he was inspired by the rocky landscape that would later be the backdrop for many Surrealist canvases. In 1929, he met his future wife, Gala, in Cadaqués. Together, they converted a fisherman's home in nearby Port Lligat into their semi-permanent residence, dividing their time between New York, Paris, and Cadaqués. And it was here that Dalí did his best work.

In spite of its fame, Cadaqués is mellow and feels off the beaten path. If you want a peaceful beach-town escape near Barcelona, this is a good place. From the moment you descend into the town, taking in whitewashed buildings and deep blue waters, you'll be struck by the port's tranquility and beauty. Join the locals playing chess or cards at the cavernous Casino Coffee House (harborfront, with games and Internet access). Have a glass of *vino tinto* or *cremat* (a traditional rum-and-coffee drink served flambé-style) at one of the seaside cafés. Savor the lapping waves, brilliant sun, and gentle breeze. And, for sightseeing, the reason to come to Cadaqués is the Salvador Dalí House, a 20-minute walk from the town center at Port Lligat.

Tourist Information: The TI is at Carrer Cotxe 2 (July–Sept Mon–Sat 9:00–21:00, Sun 10:00–13:00, less off-season, tel. 972-258-315).

Getting to Cadaqués

Reaching Cadaqués is very tough without a car. There are no trains and only a few buses a day.

By Car: It's a twisty drive from Figueres (figure 45–60 min). In Cadaqués, drivers should park in the big lot just above the city—don't try to park near the harborfront. To reach the Salvador Dalí House, follow signs near Cadaqués to Port Lligat (easy parking).

By Bus: Cadaqués is connected by Sarfa buses to **Figueres** (3/day, 60 min, €4.50) and to **Barcelona** (2/day, more in July–Aug, 2.5 hours, €20). Bus info: Barcelona tel. 902-302-025, Cadaqués tel. 972-258-713, Figueres tel. 972-674-298, www.sarfa.com.

SIGHTS

In Port Lligat, near Cadaqués

▲▲▲Salvador Dalí House (Casa Museu Salvador Dalí)—Once Dalí's home, this house gives fans a chance to explore his labyrinthine compound. This is the best artist's house I've toured in Europe. It shows how a home can really reflect the creative spirit of an artistic genius and his muse. The ambience both inside and out is perfect for a Surrealist hanging out with his creative playmate. The bay is ringed by sleepy islands. Fishing boats are jumbled on the beach. After the fishermen painted their boats, Dalí asked them to clean their brushes on his door—creating an abstract work of art he adored (which you'll see as you line up to get your ticket).

The interior is left almost precisely as it was in 1982, when Gala died and Dalí moved out. See Dalí's studio (the clever easel cranks up and down to allow the artist to paint while seated, as he did eight hours a day); the bohemian-yet-divine living room (complete with a mirror to reflect the sunrise onto their bed each morning); the phallic-shaped swimming pool, which was the scene of orgiastic parties; and the painter's study (with his favorite moustaches all lined up). Like Dalí's art, his home is offbeat, provocative, and fun.

Cost and Hours: €10; mid-June–mid-Sept daily 9:30–21:00; mid-March–mid-June and mid-Sept–early Jan Tue–Sun 10:30–18:00, closed Mon; closed early Jan–mid-March. Last tour departs 50 minutes before closing.

Touring the House: Reservations are mandatory—call or go online ahead to book a time (tel. 972-251-015, www.salvador-dali.org). Only 8–10 people are allowed in (no large groups) every 10 minutes. In summer, book a week in advance. You must arrive 30 minutes early to pick up your ticket, or they'll sell it. Once inside, there are five sections, each with a guard who gives you a brief explanation in English, and then turns you loose for a few minutes. The entire visit takes 50 minutes. While you wait, enjoy the 15-minute video that plays in the waiting lounge (with walls covered in Dalí media coverage) just across the lane from the house.

Getting There: Parking is free nearby. There are no buses or taxis. The house is a 20-minute, one-mile walk over the hill from Cadaqués to Port Lligat. (The path, which cuts across the isthmus, is much shorter than the road.)

Sleep Code

(€1 = about $1.50, country code: 34)
S = Single, **D** = Double/Twin, **T** = Triple, **Q** = Quad, **b** = bathroom, **s** = shower only. Unless otherwise noted, credit cards are accepted and English is spoken.

To help you easily sort through these listings, I've divided the rooms into two categories, based on the price for a standard double room with bath (during high season):

$$ Higher Priced—Most rooms €75 or more.
$ Lower Priced—Most rooms less than €75.

SLEEPING

$$ Hotel Llané Petit, with 37 spacious rooms (half with view balconies), is a small, resort-like hotel with its own little beach, a 10-minute walk south of the town center (Db-€130 mid-July–Aug, €115 in shoulder season, €82 in winter; €10 more for seaview rooms, air-con, elevator, Dr. Bartomeus 37, tel. 972-251-020, fax 972-258-778, www.llanepetit.com, info@llanepetit.com). Book direct with this guidebook to get a free €12 breakfast (not valid on weekends and mid-July–Aug).

$ Hotel Nou Estrelles is a big, concrete exercise in efficient, economic comfort facing the bus stop, a few blocks in from the waterfront. With 15 rooms, it's family-run and a great value (Db-€82 in high season, €68 in shoulder season, €55 in winter; extra bed-€10, breakfast-€7, air-con, elevator, Carrer Sant Vicens, tel. 972-259-100, www.hotelnouestrelles.com, nouestrelles@yahoo.es, Emma).

$ Hostal Marina is a cheap, low-energy place, with 27 rooms and a great location a block from the harborfront main square (D-€40, Db-€50, balcony rooms-€10 extra, cheaper off-season, no breakfast, no elevator, no English, Riera 3, tel. 972-159-091).

EATING

There are plenty of eateries along the beach. A lane called Carrer Miguel Rosset (across from Hotel La Residencia) also has several places worth considering. At **Casa Anita** you'll sit with others around a big table, and enjoy house specialties such as *calamares a la plancha* (grilled squid) and homemade *helado* (ice cream). Finish your meal with a glass of sweet Muscatel (closed Mon, Calle Miquel Rosset 16, tel. 972-258-471, Juan and family).

Sitges

Sitges (SEE-juhz) is one of Catalunya's most popular resort towns. Because the town beautifully mingles sea and light, it's long been an artists' colony. Here you can still feel the soul of the Modernistas... in the architecture, the museums, the salty sea breeze, and the relaxed rhythm of life.

Today's Sitges is a world-renowned vacation destination among the gay community. Despite its jet-set status, the Old Town has managed to retain its charm. With a much slower pulse than Barcelona, Sitges is an enjoyable break from the big city.

Getting to Sitges: Southbound trains depart Barcelona from Sants Station (take train on the green line toward Sant Vincenç de Calders, 4/hr, 35–40 min, €2.60 each way). Closer to Barcelona's city center, you can catch this same train at the Passeig de Gràcia RENFE station.

ORIENTATION

Tourist Information

The **main TI** is a couple of blocks northwest of the train station (mid-June–mid-Sept Mon–Sat 9:00–20:00, closed Sun; mid-Sept–mid-June Mon–Fri 9:00–14:00 & 16:00–18:30, closed Sat–Sun; Sínia Morera 1, phone number for all TIs: 902-103-428, www.sitgestur.com).

There are more convenient branch kiosks in front of the **train station** (mid-June–mid-Sept daily 9:00–13:00 & 17:00–21:00, closed off-season) and down at the start of the **beach promenade** (mid-June–mid-Sept Mon–Sat 10:00–14:00 & 16:00–20:00, Sun 10:00–14:00; mid-Sept–mid-June Sun–Thu 10:00–14:00, Fri–Sat 10:00–14:00 & 16:00–19:00).

At any TI, pick up the good map (with info on sights on the back) and brochures for any museums that interest you. The TI can also help you find a room.

Arrival in Sitges

From the train station, exit straight ahead (past a TI kiosk—open in summer) and walk down Carrer Francesc Gumà. When it dead-ends, continue right onto Carrer de Jesús, which takes you to the town's tiny main square, Plaça del Cap de la Villa. (Keep an eye out for directional signs.) From here, turn right down Carrer Major ("Main Street"), which leads you past the old market hall (now an art gallery) and the town hall, to a beautiful terrace next to the main church. From here, you can poke into the Old Town or take the grand staircase down to the beach promenade.

SIGHTS

Sitges basically has two attractions: Its tight-and-tiny Old Town (with a few good museums) and its long, luxurious beaches.

Old Town—Take time to explore the old town's narrow streets. They're crammed with cafés, boutiques, and all the resort staples.

The focal point, on the waterfront, is the 17th-century, Baroque-style **Sant Bartomeu i Santa Tecla Church.** The terrace in front of the church will help you get the lay of the land.

As an art town, Sitges has seen its share of creative people—many of whom have left their mark in the form of appealing museums. Walking along the water behind the church, you'll find two of the town's three museums (€3.50 each or €6.40 combo-ticket for all three, same hours for all three museums: July–Sept Tue–Sat 9:30–14:00 & 16:00–19:00, Sun 10:00–15:00; Oct–June Tue–Sat 9:30–14:00 & 15:30–18:30, Sun 10:00–15:00; closed Mon year-round). The **Museu Maricel** displays the eclectic artwork of a local collector, including some Modernista works. The museum also shows off works by local Sitges artists, and a collection of maritime-themed works. The **Museu Cau Ferrat** bills itself as a "temple of art," as collected by local intellectual Santiago Rusiñol. In addition to paintings and drawings, you'll find iron work, glass, and ceramics. Also on this square, you'll see **Palau Maricel**—a sumptuous old mansion that's sometimes open to the public for concerts in the summer (ask at TI).

The third museum, **Museu Romàntic**—offering a look at 19th-century bourgeois lifestyles in an elegant mansion—is a few blocks up (one block west of main square: head out of the square on the main pedestrian street, then take the first right turn, to Sant Gaudenci 1). Inside, amidst gilded hallways, you'll find a collection of more than 400 dolls.

Beaches—Nine beaches, separated by breakwaters, extend about a mile southward from town. Stroll down the seaside promenade, which stretches from the town to the end of the beaches. Anyone can enjoy the sun, sea, and sand; or you can rent a beach chair to relax like a pro. About halfway, the crowds thin out, and the last three beaches are more intimate and cove-like. Along the way, restaurants and *chiringuitos* (beachfront bars) serve tapas, paella, and drinks.

If you walk all the way to the end, you can continue inland to enjoy the nicely landscaped **Terramar Gardens** (Jardins de Terramar; free, daily mid-June–mid-Sept 10:30–20:30, mid-Sept–mid-June 9:00–19:00).

SLEEPING

Because it's an in-demand resort, hotel values are not much better here than in Barcelona (especially in summer). But if you prefer a swanky beach town to a big city, consider these options. Note that this is a party town, so expect some noise after hours (request a quiet room). I've listed peak-season prices (roughly mid-July–mid-Aug); these drop substantially off-season. The first one is on the beach, while the other two are old villas with colorful tile floors a few blocks into the town.

$$ Hotel Celimar, with 26 small but modern rooms, occupies a classic Modernista building facing the beach (Db-€150, €20 extra for sea view, check website for latest prices, air-con, free Wi-Fi, elevator, Paseo de la Ribera 20, tel. 938-110-170, fax 938-110-403, www.hotelcelimar.com, info@hotelcelimar.com).

$$ Hotel Romàntic is family-run, old-fashioned-elegant, and quirky. Its 78 rooms (including some in the annex, Hotel de la Renaixença) are nothing special, but the whole place feels classic and classy—especially the plush lounge and bar (S-€65, Sb-€85, D-€100, Db-€115, €10 extra for balcony, includes breakfast, no air-con or elevator, pay Wi-Fi, Sant Isidre 33, tel. 938-948-375, fax 938-114-129, www.hotelromantic.com, romantic@hotelromantic.com).

$$ El Xalet (as in "Chalet") is of a similar vintage, with a little less style and lower prices. They have 11 rooms in the main hotel and another 12 in their annex Hotel Noucentista up the street—both in fine old Modernista buildings (Db-€100, €25 extra for suite, includes breakfast, air-con, free Wi-Fi, Carrer Illa de Cuba 35, tel. 938-110-070, fax 938-945-579, www.elxalet.com, info@elxalet.com).

Montserrat

Montserrat—the "serrated mountain"—rockets dramatically up from the valley floor northwest of Barcelona. With its unique rock formations, a dramatic mountaintop monastery (also called Montserrat), and spiritual connection with the Catalan people and their struggles, it's a popular day trip. This has been Catalunya's most important pilgrimage site for a thousand years.

Hymns explain how the mountain was carved by little angels with golden saws. Geologists blame nature at work.

Once upon a time, there was no mountain. A river flowed here, laying down silt that hardened into sedimentary layers of hard rock. Ten million years ago, the continents shifted, and the land around the rock massif sank, exposing this series of peaks that reach upwards to 4,000 feet. Over time, erosion pocked the face with caves and cut vertical grooves near the top, creating the famous serrated look.

The monastery is nestled in the jagged peaks at 2,400 feet, but it seems higher because of the way the rocky massif rises out of nowhere. The air is certainly fresher than in Barcelona. In a quick day trip, you can view the mountain from its base, ride a funicular up to the top of the world, tour the basilica and museum, touch a Black Virgin's orb, hike down to a sacred cave, and listen to Gregorian chants by the world's oldest boys' choir.

Montserrat's monastery is Benedictine, and its 30 monks carry on its spiritual tradition. Since 1025, the slogan *"ora et labora"* ("prayer and work") has pretty much summed up life for a monk here.

The Benedictines welcome visitors—both pilgrims and tourists—and offer this travel tip: Please remember that the most important part of your Montserrat visit is not enjoying the architecture, but rather discovering the religious, cultural, historical, social, and environmental values that together symbolically express the life of the Catalan people.

Getting to Montserrat

Barcelona is connected to the valley below Montserrat by a convenient train; from there, a cable car or rack railway takes you up to the mountaintop (your choice). Both options cost the same and take about the same amount of time (1.5–1.75 hours each way from downtown Barcelona to the monastery). For ticket options, see the sidebar on opposite page. Driving or taking the bus round out your options.

Train Plus Cable Car or Rack Railway

By Train: Trains leave hourly from Barcelona's Plaça d'Espanya to Montserrat. Take the Metro to Espanya, then follow signs showing a picture of a train to the FGC (Ferrocarrils de la Generalitat de Catalunya) underground station. Once there, look for train line R5 (direction: Manresa, departures at :36 past each hour).

You'll ride about an hour on the train. As you reach the base of the mountain, you have two options, outlined below: Get out at Montserrat-Aeri for the cable car, or continue another few minutes to the next stop—Monistrol de Montserrat (or simply "Monistrol de M.")—for the rack railway. (You'll have to make this decision when you buy your ticket in Barcelona—see the sidebar on opposite page.)

By Cable Car, at the Montserrat-Aeri Stop: Departing the train,

Tickets to Montserrat

Various combo-tickets cover your journey to Montserrat, as well as some of the sights you'll visit there. All begin with the train from Barcelona's Plaça d'Espanya, and cover either the cable car or rack railway—you'll have to specify one or the other when you buy the ticket (same price for either option). You can't go one way and come back the other, unless you pay extra (about €5) for the leg that's not included in your ticket.

The basic option is to buy a **train ticket** to Montserrat (€14.50 round-trip, includes the cable car or rack railway to monastery, Eurailpass not valid, tel. 932-051-515, www.fgc.es). Note that if you buy this ticket in Barcelona, then decide at Montserrat that you want to use the funiculars, you can buy a €7.45 ticket covering both funiculars at the TI or at either funicular.

If you plan to do some sightseeing once at Montserrat, it makes sense to spend a little more on one of two combo-tickets from the train company: The €21 **Trans Montserrat** ticket includes your Metro ride in Barcelona to the train station, the train trip, the cable car or rack railway, unlimited trips on the two funiculars at Montserrat, and entrance to the audiovisual presentation. The €35 **Tot Montserrat** ticket includes all of this, plus the good Museum of Montserrat and a self-service lunch.

If you plan to do it all, you'll save at least €5 with either of these combo-tickets. You can buy any of these tickets at the automated machines at Barcelona's Plaça d'Espanya station (tourist officials are standing by in the morning to help you figure it out). But buying the ticket at the station doesn't let you use your included Metro ride *to* the station. Instead, buy the ticket in advance at the Plaça de Catalunya TI in Barcelona, or at the uncrowded FGC La Molina office next to Plaça de Catalunya (Mon–Fri 10:00–14:00 & 16:30–20:30, Sat 10:00–14:00, closed Sun, see map on page 43 for location, Pelai 17–39 Triangle, tel. 933-664-553, helpful Anna).

follow signs to the cable-car station (€5 one-way, €8 round-trip, included with your train or combo-ticket, 4/hr, 5-min trip, daily March–Oct 9:40–14:00 & 14:35–19:00, Nov–Feb 10:40–14:00 & 14:35–18:00—note the lunch break). Because the cable car is smaller than the train, don't linger or you might have to wait for the next car. On the way back down, departures from the monastery at :40 past the hour make the Barcelona-bound trains leaving at :48 past the

hour. In summer, the last efficient departure is at 18:40 (off-season at 17:40). Although there's a later cable-car departure from the monastery (at 19:00, or 18:00 off-season), it entails almost an hour-long wait for the next Barcelona-bound train.

By Rack Railway (Cremallera), at the Monistrol de Montserrat Stop: From this stop, you can catch the Cremallera rack railway up to the monastery (€4.60 one-way, €7.30 round-trip, cheaper off-season, included with your train or combo-ticket, hourly, 20-min trip, www.cremallerademontserrat.com). On the return trip, this train departs the monastery at :15 past the hour (:22 past the hour on winter weekdays), allowing you to catch the Barcelona-bound train leaving Monistrol de Montserrat at :44 past the hour. The last convenient connection back to Barcelona leaves the monastery at 18:15 (or 20:15 in July–Aug). Confirm the schedule when you arrive, as specific times tend to change year to year. Note that there is one intermediate stop on this line (Monistrol-Vila, at a large parking garage), but—going in either direction—you want to stay on until the end of the line.

Cable Car or Rack Train? For the sake of scenery and fun, I enjoy the little German-built cable car more than the rack railway. Departures are more frequent (4/hr rather than hourly on the railway), but because the cable car is small, you might have to wait a while to get on. Paying the extra €5 to do both (explained in the "Tickets to Monserrat" sidebar on previous page) isn't worthwhile.

Other Options

By Car: Once drivers get out of Barcelona (Road #82, then C-55), it's a short 30-minute drive to the base of the mountain, then a 10-minute series of switchbacks to the actual site (where you can find parking for €5 per day). It may be easier to park your car down below and ride the cable car up.

By Bus: One bus per day connects downtown Barcelona directly to the monastery at Montserrat (departs from Viriat Street near Barcelona's Sants station daily at 9:15, returns from the monastery to Barcelona at 18:00 in June–Sept or at 17:00 in Oct–May, €4.85 one-way, one-hour trip depending on traffic). However, since the other options are scenic, fun, and relatively easy, the only reason to take this bus is to avoid transfers.

ORIENTATION

When you arrive at the base of the mountain, look up the rock face to find the cable-car line, the monastery near the top, and the tiny building midway up (marking the Sacred Cave).

However you make your way up to the Montserrat monastery, it's easy to get oriented once you arrive at the top. Everything is within a few minutes' walk of your entry point. All of the transit options converge at the big train station: the rack railway and cable car down to the valley, and (above those) both funicular stations (one up to the ridgetop, the other down to the Sacred Cave trail). Across the street is the TI, and above that (either straight up via the stairs, or up the ramp around the left side) is the main square. To the right of the station, a long road leads along the cliff to the parking lot; a humble farmers' market along here sells produce.

Crowd-Beating Tips: Arrive early or late, as tour groups mob the place midday. Crowds are less likely on weekdays and worst on Sundays.

Tourist Information

The square below the basilica houses a helpful TI, right across from the train station (daily from 9:00, closes just after last train heads down—roughly 18:15, or 20:15 in July–Aug, tel. 938-777-701, www.montserratvisita.com). Pick up the free map and get your questions answered. A good audioguide, available only at the TI, describes the general site and basilica (€5, includes book). If you're a hiker, buy a hiking brochure here. Trails offer spectacular views (on clear days) to the Mediterranean and even (on clearer days) to the Pyrenees.

The audiovisual center (upstairs from the TI) offers some cultural and historical perspective. The lame interactive exhibition—nowhere near as exciting as the mountains and basilica outside—includes computer touch-screens and a short 20-minute video in English, covers the mountain's history, and gives a glimpse into the daily lives of the monastery's resident monks (€2, covered by Trans Montserrat and Tot Montserrat combo-tickets, same hours as TI).

SELF-GUIDED SPIN-TOUR

From the monastery's main square, Plaça de Santa Maria, face the main facade and take this spin tour, moving from right to left: Like a good pilgrim, face Mary, the centerpiece of the facade. Below her to the left is St. Benedict, the sixth-century monk who established the rules that came to govern Montserrat's monastery. St. George, the symbol of Catalunya, is on the right (amid victims of Spain's Civil War).

Five arches line the base of the church. The one on the far right leads pilgrims to the high point of any visit, the Black Virgin (a.k.a. La Moreneta). The center arch leads into the basilica, and the arch second from left directs you to a small votive chapel filled with articles representing prayer requests or thanks.

Left of the basilica, the delicate arches mark the old monks' cloister. Below that are four trees the monks plant, hoping to harvest only their symbolism (palm = martyrdom, cypress = eternal life, olive = peace, and laurel = victory). Next to the trees is a public library

The History of Montserrat

The first hermit monks built huts at Montserrat around A.D. 900. By 1025, a monastery was founded. The Montserrat Escolania, or Choir School, soon followed, and is considered to be the oldest music school in Europe (they still perform—see "Choir Concert" on page 119).

Legend has it that in medieval times, some shepherd children saw lights and heard songs coming from the mountain. They traced it to a cave (now called the Sacred Cave, or Santa Cova), where they found the Black Virgin statue (La Moreneta), making the monastery a pilgrim magnet.

In 1811, Napoleon's invading French troops destroyed Montserrat's buildings, though the Black Virgin survived, hidden away by monks. Then, in the 1830s, the Spanish royalty—tired of dealing with pesky religious orders—dissolved the monasteries and convents.

But in the 1850s, the monks returned as part of Catalunya's (and Europe's) renewed Romantic appreciation for all things medieval and nationalistic. (Montserrat's revival coincided with other traditions born out of rejuvenated Catalan pride: the much-loved Football Club Barcelona, Barcelona's Palace of Catalan Music, and even the birth of local sparkling wine, *cava*.) Montserrat's basilica and monastery were reconstructed and became, once more, the strongly beating spiritual and cultural heart of the Catalan people.

Then came Franco, who wanted a monolithic Spain. To him, Montserrat represented Catalan rebelliousness. During Franco's rule, the *sardana* dance was still illegally performed here (but with a different name), and literature was published in the outlawed Catalan language. In 1970, 300 intellectuals demonstrating for more respect for human rights in Spain were locked up in the monastery for several days by Franco's police.

But now Franco is history. The 1990s brought another phase of rebuilding (after a forest fire and rain damage), and the Montserrat community is thriving once again, unafraid to display its pride for the Catalan people, culture, and faith.

and peaceful reading room. The big archway is the private entrance to the monastery. Then comes the modern hotel and, below that, the modern, white museum. Other buildings provide cells for pilgrims. The Sant Joan funicular lifts hikers up to the trailhead (you can see the tiny building at the top). From there, you can take a number of fine hikes (described later in this section). Another funicular station descends to the Sacred Cave. And, finally, five arches separate statues of founders of the great religious orders. Step over to the arches for a commanding view (on a clear day) of the Llobregat River, meandering all the way to the Mediterranean.

SIGHTS AND ACTIVITIES

Basilica—Although there's been a church here since the 11th century, the present church was built in the 1850s, and the facade only dates from 1968. The decor is Neo-Romanesque, so popular with the Romantic artists of the late 19th century. The basilica itself is ringed with interesting chapels, but the focus is on the Black Virgin sitting high above the main altar.

Montserrat's top attraction is **La Moreneta,** the small wood statue of the Black Virgin, discovered in the Sacred Cave in the 12th century. Legend says she was carved by St. Luke (the Gospel writer and supposed artist), brought to Spain by St. Peter, hidden away in the cave during the Moorish invasions, and miraculously discovered by shepherd children. (Carbon dating says she's 800 years old.) While George is the patron saint of Catalunya, La Moreneta is its patroness, having been crowned as such by the pope in 1881. "Moreneta" is usually translated as "black" in English, but the Spanish name actually means "tanned." The statue was originally lighter, but darkened over the centuries from candle smoke, humidity, and its original varnish darkening with age. Pilgrims shuffle down a long and ornate passage leading alongside the church for their few moments alone with the virgin (free, daily 8:00–10:30 & 12:00–18:30, plus in summer 19:30–20:15, www.abadiamontserrat.net). The church itself has longer hours and daily services (Mass at 11:00, vespers at 18:45).

Join the line of pilgrims (along the right side of the church). Though Mary is behind a protective glass case, the royal orb she cradles in her hands is exposed. Pilgrims touch Mary's orb with one hand and hold their other hand up to show that they accept Jesus. Newlyweds in particular seek Mary's blessing.

Immediately after La Moreneta, turn right into the delightful Neo-Romanesque prayer chapel, where worshippers sit behind the Virgin and continue to pray. The ceiling painted in the Modernista style in 1898 by Joan Llimona shows Jesus and Mary high in heaven. The trail connecting Catalunya with heaven seems to lead through these serrated mountains. The figures depicted lower are people symbolizing Catalan history and culture.

You'll leave by walking along the Ave Maria Path (along the outside of the church), which thoughtfully integrates nature and the basilica. Thousands of colorful votive candles are all busy helping the devout with their prayers. Before you leave the inner courtyard and head out into the main square, pop into the humble little room with the many votive offerings where people leave personal belongings (wedding dresses, baby's baptism outfits, wax replicas of body parts in need of healing, and so on) as part of a prayer request or as a thanks for divine intercession.

Museum of Montserrat—The bright, shiny, and cool collection of paintings and artifacts was mostly donated by devout Catalan Catholics. While it's nothing really earth-shaking, you'll enjoy an air-conditioned wander past lots of antiquities and fine artwork. Head upstairs first to see some lesser-known works by the likes of Picasso, El Greco, Caravaggio, Monet, Renoir, Pissarro, Degas, John Singer Sergeant, and some local Modernista artists. One gallery shows how artists have depicted the Black Virgin of Montserrat over the centuries in many different styles. There's even a small Egyptian section, with a sarcophagus and mummy. Down on the main floor, you'll see ecclesiastical gear, a good icon collection, and more paintings, including—at the very end—a Dalí painting, some Picasso sketches and prints, and a Miró (€6.50, covered by Tot Montserrat combo-ticket, good €1 audioguide; July–Aug daily 10:00–19:00; Sept–June Mon–Fri 10:00–17:45, Sat–Sun 10:00–19:00; tel. 938-777-745).

Sant Joan Funicular—This funicular climbs 820 feet above the monastery in five minutes (€4.15 one-way, €6.60 round-trip, covered by Trans Montserrat and Tot Montserrat combo-tickets, goes every 20 min, more with demand). At the top of the funicular, you are at the starting point of a 20-minute walk that takes you to the Sant Joan Chapel (follow sign for *Ermita de St. Joan*). Other hikes also begin at the trailhead by the funicular (get details from TI before you ascend; basic map with suggested hikes posted by upper funicular station). For a quick and easy chance to get out into nature, simply ride up and follow the most popular hike, a 45-minute, mostly downhill loop through mountain scenery back to the monastery. For this route, go left from the funicular station; the trail—marked *Monestir de Montserrat*—will first go up to a rocky crest before heading downhill.

Sacred Cave (Santa Cova)—The Moreneta was originally discovered in the Sacred Cave (or Sacred Grotto), a 40-minute hike down from the monastery (then another 50 minutes back up). The path (c. 1900) was designed by devoted and patriotic Modernista architects, including Gaudí and Josep Puig i Cadafalch. It's lined with Modernista statues depicting scenes from the life of Christ. While the original Black Virgin statue is now in the basilica, a replica sits in the cave. A three-minute funicular ride cuts 20 minutes off the hike (€1.70

one-way, €2.70 round-trip, covered by Trans Montserrat and Tot Montserrat combo-tickets, goes every 20 min, more with demand).

If you're here on a late afternoon, check the funicular schedule before you head into the Sacred Cave to make sure you don't miss the final ride down. Missing the last ride could mean catching a train back to Barcelona later than you had planned.

Choir Concert—Montserrat's Escolania, or Choir School, has been training voices for centuries. Fifty young boys, who live and study in the monastery itself, make up the choir, which performs daily except Saturday (Mon–Fri at 13:00, Sun–Thu at 18:45, and Sun also at 12:00, choir on vacation late June–late Aug). The boys sing for only 10 minutes, the basilica is jam-packed, and you'll likely actually see almost nothing. Also note that if you attend the evening performance, you'll miss the last funicular down the mountain.

SLEEPING

An overnight here gets you monastic peace and a total break from the modern crowds. There are ample rustic cells for pilgrim visitors, but tourists might prefer this place:

$$ Hotel Abat Cisneros, a three-star hotel with 82 rooms and all the comforts, is low-key and appropriate for a sanctuary (Sb-€38–61, Db-€65–101, price depends on season, includes breakfast, half- and full-board available, elevator, pay Internet access, tel. 938-777-701, fax 938-777-724, www.abadiamontserrat.cat, reserves@larsa-montserrat.cat).

EATING

Montserrat is designed to feed hordes of pilgrims and tourists. You'll find a cafeteria along the main street (across from the train station) and more eateries (including a grocery store and bar with simple sandwiches) where the road curves on its way up to the basilica. Or pack a picnic from Barcelona.

BASQUE COUNTRY

Euskal Herria

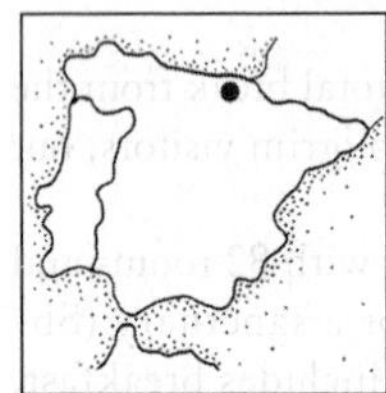

Straddling two nations on the Atlantic Coast—stretching about 100 miles from Bilbao, Spain, north to Bayonne, France—lies the ancient, free-spirited land of the Basques. The Basque Country is famous for its sunny beaches and scintillating modern architecture...and for its feisty, industrious natives. It's also simply beautiful: Bright, white, chalet-style homes with deep-red-and-green shutters scatter across lush, rolling hills, the Pyrenees Mountains soar high above the Atlantic, and surfers and sardines share the waves.

Insulated from mainstream Europe for centuries, the plucky Basques have just wanted to be left alone for more than 7,000 years. An easily crossed border separates the French *Pays Basque* from the Spanish *País Vasco,* allowing you to sample both sides from a single base (in Spain, I prefer fun-loving San Sebastián; in France, I hang my hat in cozy St. Jean-de-Luz).

Much unites the Spanish and French Basque regions: They share a cuisine, Union Jack–style flag (green, red, and white), and common language (Euskara), spoken by about a half-million people. (Virtually everyone also speaks Spanish or French.) And both have been integrated by their respective nations, sometimes forcibly. The French Revolution quelled French Basque ideas of independence; 130 years later, Spain's Generalísimo Francisco Franco attempted to tame his own separatist-minded Basques.

But over the last generation, things have started looking up. The long-suppressed Euskara language is enjoying a resurgence. And, as the European Union celebrates regions rather than nations, the Spanish and French Basques are feeling more united. This heavily industrialized region is enjoying a striking 21st-century renaissance. In Spain, the dazzling new architecture of the Guggenheim Bilbao

Cheap Tricks in the Basque Country

In San Sebastián

- Most of San Sebastián's best attractions—exploring the Old Town, poking around the Bretxa Public Market, strolling the promenade, hiking up Monte Urgull, and basque-ing (er, basking) on the beach—are free.
- *Pintxo* bar-hopping (i.e., tapas) is a cheap way to eat. Many tapas here are practically gourmet-quality, and since they're small, you can maximize variety.

In Guernica

- If visiting the two museums in town (Peace Museum and Basque Country Museum), buy the €5.25 combo-ticket to save €1.25 over individual admissions. The third sight in town—the Assembly House and Oak Tree—is free.

In Bilbao

- Skip taxis. The designed-for-tourists EuskoTran tram system is a cheap and easy way to shrink this spread-out city, connecting the train stations, bus station, big parking garage, Guggenheim Museum, and Old Town for just €1.15 per ride (€3.15 for all day—worthwhile if you're seeing it all).
- While the interior of the Guggenheim Museum is worth seeing, the exterior is even more striking. Save €12.50 and take a slow walk around the museum's perimeter, including across the river. Or, if you're paying to enter anyway, borrow the included audioguide that describes the exterior.

In St. Jean-de-Luz

- As a resort town, St. Jean-de-Luz offers many free ways to spend time—most notably relaxing on the beach. The town's only real sight, the St. Jean-Baptiste Church, is free to enter.
- Nearby, the beach resort of Biarritz is also easy to enjoy for free.

modern-art museum and the glittering resort of San Sebastián are drawing enthusiastic crowds. And in France, long-ignored cities such as Bayonne and the surfing mecca of Biarritz are being revitalized. At the same time, traditional small towns—like Spain's Lekeitio and Hondarribia, and France's St. Jean-de-Luz and nearby mountain villages—are also thriving, making the entire region colorful, fun, welcoming...and unmistakably Basque.

Planning Your Time

One day is enough for a quick sample of the Basque Country, but two or three days lets you breathe deep and hold it in. Where you go depends on your interests: Spain or France? Cities (such as Bilbao,

Bayonne, and San Sebastián) or resorts (including St. Jean-de-Luz, Biarritz, and...San Sebastián)?

If you want to slow down and focus on Spain, spend one day relaxing in San Sebastián and the second side-tripping to Bilbao (and possibly to Guernica and Lekeitio, especially if you have a car).

Better yet, take this easy opportunity to dip into France. Sleep in one country, then side-trip into the other, devoting one day to Spain (San Sebastián and maybe Bilbao), and a second day to France (St. Jean-de-Luz, Bayonne, and maybe Biarritz).

Wherever you go, most of your sightseeing will be cultural, scenic, and culinary; in Basque Country, museum-going takes a backseat to relaxing.

Getting Around the Basque Country

The tourist's Basque Country—from Bilbao to Bayonne—stays close to the coastline. Fortunately, everything is connected by good roads and public transportation.

By Bus and Train: From San Sebastián, the bus is the best way to reach Bilbao (and from there, Guernica and Lekeitio). To go between San Sebastián and France, a train—with a transfer in Hendaye—is your best bet (2/hr, takes 1 hour between San Sebastián and St. Jean-de-Luz; faster but less frequent by bus: 2/day direct, 45 min). Once in France, the three main towns (St. Jean-de-Luz, Bayonne, Biarritz) are connected by bus (trains also zip between St. Jean-de-Luz and Bayonne). Specific connections are explained in each section.

Note that a few out-of-the-way areas—Spain's Lekeitio and Bay of Biscay, France's Basque villages of the interior—are impractical by public transportation...but wonderful by car.

By Car: San Sebastián, Bilbao, St. Jean-de-Luz, Biarritz, and Bayonne are connected by a convenient expressway, called A-8 in Spain and A-63 in France (rough timings: Bilbao to San Sebastián, 1.25 hrs; San Sebastián to St. Jean-de-Luz, 45 min; St. Jean-de-Luz to Biarritz or Bayonne, 30 min).

Language Warning: For the headers throughout this chapter, I've listed place names using the Spanish or French spelling first and the Euskara spelling second. In the text, I use the spelling that prevails locally. While most people refer to towns by their Spanish or French names, road signs list places in the national language and in Euskara. The Spanish or French version is sometimes scratched out by independence-minded locals, so you might have to navigate by Euskara names.

Also note that in terms of linguistic priority (e.g., museum information), Euskara comes first, Spanish and French second, and English a distant fourth...and it sometimes doesn't even make the cut.

Basque Country

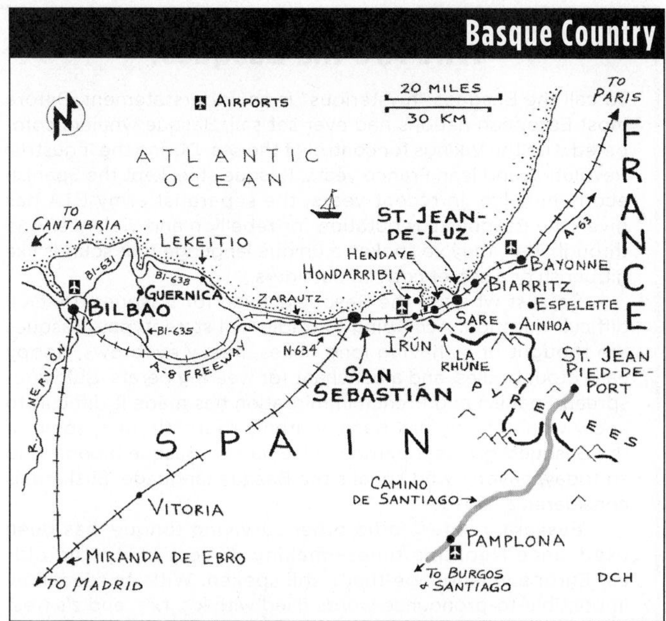

Cuisine Scene in Basque Country

Mixing influences from the mountains, sea, Spain, and France, Basque food is reason enough to visit the region. The local cuisine—dominated by seafood, tomatoes, and red peppers—offers some spicy dishes, unusual in most of Europe. While you'll find similar specialties throughout the Basque lands, Spain is still Spain and France is still France. Here are some dishes you're most likely to find in each area.

Spanish Basque Cuisine: Hopping from bar to bar sampling *pintxos*—the local term for tapas—is a highlight of any trip (for details, see sidebar on page 141). On menus, you'll see *bacalao* (salted cod), best when cooked *à la bizkaina* (with tomatoes, onions, and roasted peppers); *merluza* (hake, a light whitefish prepared in a variety of ways); and *chipirones en su tinta* (squid served in their own black ink). Carnivores will find beef (*chuletas,* steaks) and lamb (*chuletillas,* lamb chops). Local brews include *sidra* (hard apple cider) and *txakolí* (cha-koh-LEE, a local light, sparkling white wine—often theatrically poured from high above the glass for aeration).

French Basque Cuisine: The red peppers (called *piments*) hanging from homes in small villages end up in *piperade,* a dish that combines peppers, tomatoes, garlic, ham, and eggs. Look for anything "Basque-style" (*basquaise*)—cooked with tomato, eggplant, red pepper, and garlic. Don't leave without trying *ttoro* (tchoo-roh), a seafood stew that is

Who Are the Basques?

To call the Basques "mysterious" is an understatement. Before most European nations had ever set sail, Basque whalers competed with the Vikings for control of the sea. During the Industrial Revolution and lean Franco years, Basque steel kept the Spanish economy alive. In recent years, the separatist army ETA has given the Basques a reputation for rebellion and violence. And through it all, they've spoken a unique language that sounds like gibberish or a secret code to outsiders.

So, just who are the Basques? Even for Basques, that's a difficult question. According to traditional stereotypes, Basques are thought of as having long noses, heavy eyebrows, floppy ears, stout bodies, and a penchant for wearing berets. But widespread Spanish and French immigration has made it difficult to know who actually has Basque ethnic roots. (In fact, some of the Basques' greatest patriots have had no Basque blood.) And so today, anyone who speaks the Basque language, Euskara, is considered a "Basque."

Euskara, related to no other surviving tongue, has been used since Neolithic times—making it, very likely, the oldest European language that's still spoken. With its seemingly impossible-to-pronounce words filled with k's, tx's, and z's (rest rooms are *gizonak* for men and *emakumeak* for women), Euskara makes speaking French suddenly seem easy. (Some tips: *tx* is pronounced "ch," while *tz* is pronounced "ts." Other key words: *kalea* is "street," and *ostatua* is a cheap hotel.) Kept alive as a symbol of Basque cultural identity, Euskara is typically learned proudly as a second or third language. Many locals can switch effortlessly from Euskara to Spanish or French. Basques wave their language like a flag—look for Euskara street signs, menus, and signs in shops.

The Basque economy has historically been shaped by three factors: the sea, agriculture, and iron deposits.

Basque sailors were some of the first and finest in Europe, as they built ever-better boats to venture farther and farther into the Atlantic in search of whales. (These long journeys were made possible by the invention of *bacalao*—dried, salted cod that could last for months to sustain whalers.) By the year 1000, Basque sailors were chasing whales a thousand miles from home, in the Norwegian fjords. Despite lack of physical evidence, many historians surmise that the Basques must have sailed to the Americas before Christopher Columbus.

When the "Spanish" era of exploration began, Basques continued to play a key role, as sailors and shipbuilders. Columbus' *Santa María* was likely Basque-built, and his crew included many Basques. History books teach that Ferdinand Magellan was the first to circumnavigate the globe, with the footnote that he was killed partway around. Who took over the ship for the rest of the journey, completing the circle? The Basque sailor Juan Sebastián de Elcano. And a pair of well-traveled Catholic priests, known for their far-reaching missionary trips that led to founding the Jesuit order, were also Basques: St. Ignatius of Loyola and St. Francis Xavier.

Later, the Industrial Age swept Europe, gaining a foothold in Iberia when the Basques began using their rich iron deposits to make steel. Pioneering Basque industrialists set the tempo as they dragged Spain into the modern world. Cities such as Bilbao were heavily industrialized, sparking an influx of workers from around Spain (which gradually diluted Basque blood in the Basque Country).

The independence-minded Basques are notorious for their stubbornness. In truth, as a culturally and linguistically unique island surrounded by bigger and stronger nations, the Basques have learned to compromise. Historically Basques have remained on good terms with outsiders, so long as their traditional laws, the *Fueros*, were respected. While outdated, the *Fueros* continue to symbolize a self-governance that the Basques hold dear. It is only when foreign law has been placed above the *Fueros*—as many of today's Basques feel Spanish law does—that the people become agitated.

In recent years, most news of the Basques—especially in Spain—has been made by the terrorist organization ETA. (ETA stands for the Euskara phrase *Euskadi Ta Askatasuna*, or "Basque Country and Freedom"; *eta* also means "and" in Euskara.) ETA has been blamed for more than 800 deaths since 1968. The violence ebbs and flows, but ETA tends to focus on political targets, and their activities go largely unnoticed by tourists. While many people in Basque Country would like a greater degree of autonomy from Madrid, only a tiny minority supports ETA.

This is only a first glimpse into the important, quirky, and fascinating Basque people. To better understand the Basques, there's no better book than Mark Kurlansky's *The Basque History of the World*—essential pre-trip reading for historians.

Basque Country's answer to bouillabaisse and cioppino. *Marmitako* is a hearty tuna stew. Local cheeses come from Pyrenean sheep's milk *(pur brebis),* and the local ham *(jambon de Bayonne)* is famous throughout France. After dinner, try a shot of *izarra* (herbal-flavored brandy). To satisfy your sweet tooth, look for *gâteau basque,* a local tart filled with cream or jams, or chocolates from Bayonne. Hard apple cider is the locally made beverage, but the region's wine, Irouleguy, isn't worth its price.

Spanish Basque Country
(El País Vasco)

Four of the seven Basque territories lie within Spain. Many consider Spanish Basque culture to be feistier and more colorful than the relatively integrated French Basques—you'll hear more Euskara spoken here than in France.

For 40 years, the figure of Generalísimo Franco loomed large over the Spanish Basques. Franco depended upon Basque industry to keep the floundering Spanish economy afloat. But even as he exploited the Basques economically, he so effectively blunted Basque culture that the language was primarily Spanish by default. Franco kicked off his regime by offering up the historic Basque town of Guernica as target practice to his ally Hitler's air force. The notorious result—the wholesale slaughter of innocent civilians—was immortalized by Pablo Picasso's mural *Guernica.*

But Franco is long gone, and today's Basques are looking to the future. The iron deposits have dried up, prompting the Basques to reimagine their rusting cities for the 21st century. True to form, they're rising to the challenge. Perhaps the best example is Bilbao, whose iconic Guggenheim Museum—built on the former site of an industrial wasteland—is the centerpiece of a bold new skyline.

San Sebastián is the heart of the tourist's *País Vasco,* with its sparkling beach picturesquely framed by looming green mountains and a charming old town with gourmet *pintxos* (tapas) spilling out of every bar. On-the-rise Bilbao is worth a look for its landmark Guggenheim and its atmospheric Old Town. For small-town fun, drop by the fishing village of Lekeitio (near Bilbao) and little Hondarribia near the French border. And for history, Guernica has some intriguing museums.

This chapter focuses on Basque destinations on or near the ocean. Some inland Basque towns and cities—including Pamplona—are covered in the Camino de Santiago chapter.

San Sebastián / Donostia

Shimmering above the breathtaking bay of La Concha, elegant and prosperous San Sebastián (Donostia in Euskara) has a favored location with golden beaches, capped by twin peaks at either end, and a cute little island in the center. A delightful beachfront promenade runs the length of the bay, with an intriguing Old Town at one end and a smart shopping district in the center. It has 180,000 residents and almost that many tourists in high season (July–Sept). With a romantic setting, a soaring statue of Christ gazing over the city, and a late-night lively Old Town, San Sebastián has a Rio de Janeiro aura. While the "sightseeing" isn't too compelling, the scenic city provides a pleasant introduction to Spain's Basque Country. And as a culinary capital of Spain, it dishes up some of the top tapas anywhere.

In 1845, Queen Isabel II's doctor recommended she treat her skin problems by bathing here in the sea. (For modesty's sake, she would go inside a giant cabana that could be wheeled into the surf—allowing her to swim far from prying eyes, never having to set foot on the beach.) Her visit mobilized Spain's aristocracy, and soon the city was on the map as a seaside resort. By the turn of the 20th century, San Sebastián was the toast of the belle époque, and a leading resort for Europe's beautiful people. Before World War I, Queen María Cristina summered here and held court in her Miramar Palace overlooking the crescent beach (the turreted, red-brick building partway around the bay). Hotels, casinos, and theaters flourished. Even Franco enjoyed 35 summers in a place he was sure to call San Sebastián, not Donostia.

Planning Your Time

San Sebastián's sights can be exhausted in a few hours, but it's a great place to be on vacation for a full, lazy day (or longer). Stroll the two-mile-long promenade and scout the place you'll grab to work on a tan. The promenade leads to a funicular that lifts you to the Monte Igueldo viewpoint. After exploring the Old Town and port, walk up to the hill of Monte Urgull. With more time, art-lovers can venture to the Chillida-Leku Museum on the outskirts. A key ingredient of any visit to San Sebastián is enjoying tapas in the Old Town bars.

ORIENTATION

The San Sebastián that we're interested in surrounds Concha Bay (Bahía de la Concha). It can be divided into three areas: Playa de la Concha (best beaches), the shopping district (called Centro), and the

skinny streets of the grid-planned Old Town (called Parte Vieja, to the north of the shopping district). Centro, just east of Playa de la Concha, has beautiful turn-of-the-20th-century architecture, but no real sights. A busy drag called Alameda del Boulevard (or just "Boulevard") separates the Centro from the Old Town, and is also where you'll find the TI.

It's all bookended by mini-mountains: Monte Urgull to the north and east, Monte Igueldo to the south and west. The river (Río Urumea) divides central San Sebastián from the district called Gros (which—contrary to its name—is actually quite nice, with a lively night scene and surfing beach).

Tourist Information

San Sebastián's TI, conveniently located right on the Boulevard, has information on city and regional sights, as well as bus and train schedules. Pick up the free map and the *Holiday Guide* booklet, which has English descriptions of the three walking tours—the Old Town/Monte Urgull walk is best (July–Sept Mon–Sat 8:30–20:00, Sun 10:00–14:00 & 15:30–19:00; Oct–June Mon–Sat 9:00–13:30 & 15:30–19:00, Sun 10:00–14:00; Boulevard 8, tel. 943-481-166, www.sansebastianturismo.com). Skip the **San Sebastián Card** unless you plan to use the bus a lot (€10 for 3 days of free bus transport plus minor sightseeing discounts).

Arrival in San Sebastián

Neither train station has luggage storage. Near the bus station, you can check bags at the Alsa ticket office; downtown, try the CyberWorld Internet café (€3/4 hrs, €5/8 hrs, €8/24 hrs, daily 11:00–13:00 & 16:00–22:00, Aldamar 3, tel. 943-420-651).

By Train: If you're coming on a regional Topo train from Hendaye/Hendaia on the French border, get off at the **EuskoTren station** (end of the line, called Amara). It's a level 15-minute walk to the center: Exit the station and walk across the long plaza, then veer left and walk eight blocks down Calle Easo (toward the statue of Christ hovering on the hill) to the beach. The Old Town will be ahead on your right, with Playa de la Concha to your left. To speed things up, catch bus #21, #26, or #28 along Calle Easo and take it to the Boulevard stop, near the TI at the bottom of the Old Town.

If you're arriving by train from elsewhere in Spain (or from France with a transfer in Irún), you'll get off at the main **RENFE station.** It's just across the river from the Centro shopping district. To reach the Old Town and most recommended hotels, cross the fancy,

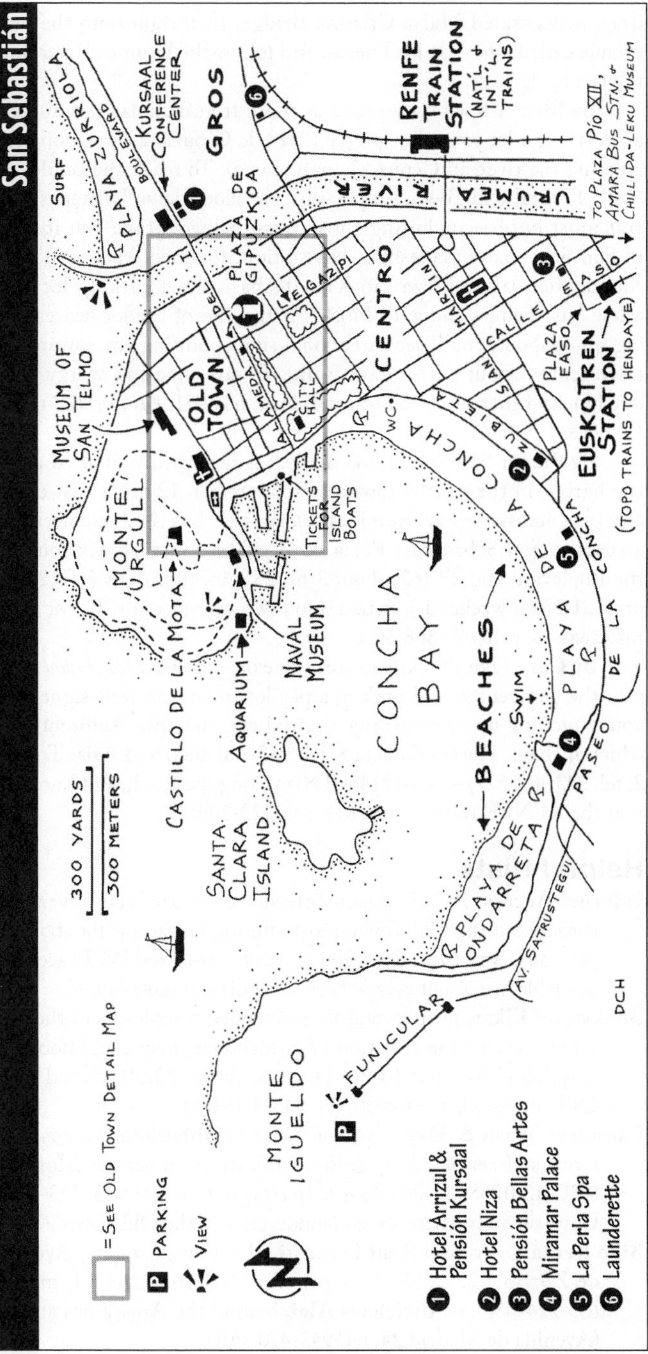
San Sebastián
= See Old Town Detail Map
Parking
View
1 Hotel Arrizul & Pensión Kursaal
2 Hotel Niza
3 Pensión Bellas Artes
4 Miramar Palace
5 La Perla Spa
6 Launderette
300 Yards
300 Meters
Monte Igueldo
Funicular
Santa Clara Island
Castillo de la Mota
Monte Urgull
Museum of San Telmo
Aquarium
Naval Museum
Tickets for Island Boats
Concha Bay
Beaches
Swim
Playa de Ondarreta
Av. Satrustegui
Playa de la Concha
Paseo de la Concha
Old Town
Alameda
City Hall
Plaza de Gipuzkoa
Centro
San Martin
Calle San
Plaza Easo
Calle Easo
Euskotren Station
(Topo trains to Hendaye)
Gros
Kursaal Conference Center
Playa Zurriola
Boulevard
Surf
Renfe Train Station
(Nat'l + Int'l Trains)
Urumea River
To Plaza Pío XII, Amara Bus Stn. + Chillida-Leku Museum
W.C.
DCH

dragon-decorated María Cristina Bridge, turn right onto the busy avenue called Paseo de los Fueros, and follow the Urumea River until the last bridge.

By Bus: A few buses—such as those from Hondarribia and the airport—can let you off at pretty Plaza de Gipuzkoa (first stop after crossing the river, in Centro shopping area). To reach the Boulevard (with TI) and Old Town, simply walk one block down Legazpi street. But most buses—including those from Bilbao—take you instead to San Sebastián's makeshift "bus station" (dubbed Amara) at a big roundabout called Plaza Pío XII. It's basically a parking lot with a few bus shelters and a TI kiosk. At the end of the lot nearest the big roundabout, you'll see directional signs pointing you toward the town center (about a 30-minute walk). To save time and energy, walk one block in that direction to catch local bus #21, #26, or #28 to the Boulevard stop, near the TI at the start of the Old Town.

By Plane: San Sebastián's airport is beautifully situated along the harbor in the nearby town of Hondarribia, 12 miles east of the city (just across the bay from France). An easy bus (#I-2) connects the airport to San Sebastián's Plaza de Gipuzkoa, just a block south of the Boulevard and TI (€2, about 3/hr, 25 min, runs daily 7:45–20:20, until 21:20 on weekends). A taxi into town costs about €30. For flight information, call 943-668-500.

By Car: Take the Amara freeway exit, follow *centro ciudad* signs into the city center, and park in a pay lot (many are well-signed). If you're picking up or returning a rental car, the "Big Autorental"—which includes Hertz (Zubieta 5, tel. 943-461-084) and Avis (Triunfo 2, tel. 943-461-527)—is near Hotel Niza along the beach, and Europcar is at the RENFE train station (tel. 943-322-304).

Helpful Hints

Internet Access: A half-dozen Internet cafés are well-advertised throughout the Old Town, most offering fast access for about €2 per hour. And these days, government-subsidized Wi-Fi access is available just about everywhere (including at most hotels).

Bookstore: Elkar, near several recommended restaurants in the Old Town, has a wide selection of guidebooks, maps, and books in English (Mon–Sat 10:00–14:00 & 16:00–20:00, closed Sun, Calle Fermín Calbetón 30, tel. 943-420-080).

Laundry: Wash & Dry is in the Gros neighborhood, across the river (self-service daily 8:00–22:00, drop-off service Mon–Fri 9:30–13:00 & 16:00–20:00, Iparragirre 6, tel. 943-293-150). Unfortunately, there are no launderettes in the Old Town.

Bike Rental: Try **Bici Rent Donosti** (also rents scooters, Avenida de Zurriola 22, 3 blocks across the river from the TI, mobile 655-724-458), or **Bicicletas Alai,** behind the Amara bus station (Avenida de Madrid 24, tel. 943-470-001).

Getting Around San Sebastián

By Bus: Along the Boulevard at the bottom edge of the Old Town, you'll find a line of public buses ready to take you anywhere in town; give any driver your destination, and he'll tell you the number of the bus to catch (€1.20, pay driver).

Some handy bus routes: #21, #26, and #28 connect the Amara bus and EuskoTren stations to the TI (get off at the Boulevard stop); #16 begins at the Boulevard/TI stop, goes along Playa de la Concha and through residential areas, and eventually arrives at the base of the Monte Igueldo funicular. The TI has a good bus-route map (or see www.ctss.es).

By Taxi: Taxis start at €3, then charge €0.50 per kilometer. You can't hail a taxi on the street—you must call one (tel. 943-404-040 or 943-464-646) or find a taxi stand (most convenient along the Boulevard).

TOURS

The TI runs English-language **walking tours** of the Old Town (Parte Vieja), Monte Urgull, and Centro (€5, 90 min, July–Aug daily at 10:00, Sept–June weekends only at 11:00, confirm schedule with TI). The TI also rents **audioguides** (€10/2 hrs).

Gabriella Ranelli, an American who's lived in San Sebastián for 20 years, is a **local guide** specializing in culinary tours. She can take you on a sightseeing spin around the Old Town, along with a walk through the market and best *pintxo* bars (€135/half-day, €180/day, more for driving into the countryside, mobile 609-467-381, www.tenedortours.com, info@tenedortours.com). She also does cooking classes, where you shop at the market then cook up some tasty *pintxos* of your own (€115 per person for a small group).

Two tour options on wheels (following a similar route around the bay) are available, but most travelers won't find them necessary in this walkable city: The **"txu-txu"** tourist train (€4.50, daily July–mid-Sept 11:00–21:00, mid-Sept–June 11:00–13:00 & 14:00–19:00, 40-min round-trip, tel. 943-422-973); and the **Donosti Tours** hop-on, hop-off bus tour (follows two different routes—one along the bay and the other around the city; €12/route, or €14 for both, about 1 hour each, ticket good for 24 hours, leaves from Victoria Eugenia theater on the Boulevard, tel. 696-429-847).

SIGHTS AND ACTIVITIES

▲▲Old Town (Parte Vieja)

Huddled in the shadow of its once-protective Monte Urgull, the Old Town is where San Sebastián was born about 1,000 years ago. The grid plan of streets hides heavy Baroque and Gothic churches, surprise plazas, and fun little shops, including venerable pastry stores, rugged produce markets, Basque-independence souvenir shops, and seafood-to-go delis. "THC shops" offer the latest from the decriminalized marijuana scene in Spain—adults are allowed to grow two plants. Be sure to wander out to the port to see the fishing industry in action (described below).

The highlight of the Old Town is its array of incredibly lively tapas bars—though here, these snacks are called *pintxos* (PEEN-chohs; see "Eating").

▲Plaza de la Constitución—The Old Town's main square is where bullfights used to be held. Notice the seat numbering on the balconies: Even if you owned an apartment here, the city retained rights to the balconies, which it could sell as box seats. (The residents could peek over the paying customers' shoulders.)

Above the clock, notice the seal of San Sebastián: A merchant ship with sails billowing in the wind. The city was granted trading rights by the crown—a reminder of the Basque Country's importance in Spanish seafaring.

Inviting café tables spill into the square from all corners. But one thing you won't see are the "private eating clubs" on this square (and others that dot the city center). Basque society is matrilineal and very female-oriented. A husband brings home his paycheck and hands it directly to his wife, who controls the house's purse-strings (and everything else). Basque men felt they needed a place where they could congregate and play "king of the castle." They formed eating clubs, where members could reserve a table to cook for their friends. While the clubs used to be exclusively male, women are now allowed as invited guests...but never in the kitchen, which remains the men's domain.

Museum of San Telmo—This humble museum will likely be closed for renovation through 2010. When open, it displays exhibits and paintings in rooms arranged around the peaceful cloister of a former Dominican monastery. There are a few exhibits on Basque folk life, and a small collection of 19th- and 20th-century paintings by Basque artists that offers an interesting peek into the spirit, faces, and natural beauty of this fiercely independent region (other featured artists include El Greco and Rubens; Plaza Zuloaga 1, tel. 943-481-580).

▲Bretxa Public Market (Mercado de la Bretxa)—Wandering through the public market is a fun way to get in touch with San Sebastián and with Basque culture. The big, white market building on the Boulevard has been converted into a modern shopping mall inside, but the fish and meat market still thrives underground (enter by going down escalators in smaller glass building behind the market hall; most stalls open Mon–Fri 8:00–14:00 & 17:00–20:00, Sat 8:00–14:00 only, Plaza de Sarriegi).

At the bottom of the escalator, notice the **fish stall** on the left (marked *J. Ma. Mujika*). In the case, you'll see different cuts of *bacalao* (cod). Entire books have been written about the importance of cod to the evolution of seafaring in Europe. The fish could be preserved in salt to feed sailors on ever-longer trips into the North Atlantic, allowing them to venture beyond the continental shelf (where they could catch fresh fish). Cod was also popular among Catholic land-lubbers on Fridays. Today cod remains a Basque staple. People still buy the salted version, which must be soaked for 48 hours (and the water changed three times) to become edible. If you're in a rush, you can buy de-salted cod...for a price.

Continue into the market and turn left down the meat aisle, checking out the different types of ham. The best ham in this region (and in all of France) comes from across the border, in Bayonne. Then enter the fresh fish market—often with the catch of the day set up in cute little scenes.

Head back up to street level and cross the street to the **Ailor Lasa Gaztategi** cheese shop (Mon–Fri 8:30–14:00 & 17:15–20:00, Sat 8:30–14:30, closed Sun, Aldamar 12, tel. 943-430-354). Pass the fragrant piles of mushrooms at the entrance and head back to the display case, showing off the Basque specialty of *idiazábal*—raw sheep's milk cheese. Notice the wide variety, which depends on the specific region it came from, whether it's smoked or cured, and for how long it's been cured *(curación)*. If you're planning a picnic, this is a very local (and expensive) ingredient.

SAN SEBASTIÁN

The Port

At the west end of the Old Town, protected by Monte Urgull, is the port. To reach the first three sights, take the passage through the wall at the appropriately named Calle Puerto, and jog right along the level, portside Paseo del Muelle. You'll pass fishing boats unloading the catch of the day (with hungry locals looking on), salty sailors' pubs, and fisher-folk mending nets. Also along this strip are the Naval Museum and the Aquarium. The trails to the top of Monte Urgull are just above this scene, near Santa María Church (or climb up the stairs next to the aquarium).

Cruise—Small boats cruise from the Old Town's port to the island in the bay (Isla Santa Clara), where you can hike the trails and have lunch at the lone café, or pack a picnic before setting sail (€8 round-trip; departures hourly on the hour 12:00–13:00 & 16:00–20:00, boats don't run Oct–May).

Naval Museum (Museo Naval)—This museum's two floors of exhibits describe the seafaring city's history, revealing the intimate link between the Basque culture and the sea. The well-presented exhibit changes each year. As the closest thing to a Basque culture museum the city has, this is quite good, but suffers from a lack of English information (€1.20, free on Thu, ask if they have any English info at entry, Tue–Sat 10:00–13:30 & 16:00–19:30, Sun 11:00–14:00, closed Mon, just before aquarium at Paseo del Muelle 24, tel. 943-430-051).

▲Aquarium—San Sebastián's aquarium is small and expensive, but surprisingly good. Exhibits include a history of the sea, a collection of naval vessels, models showing various drift-netting techniques, a petting tank filled with nervous fish, a huge whale skeleton, and a 45-foot-long tunnel that allows you to look up at floppy rays and menacing sharks (€10, €6 for kids under 13, some English explanations; July–Aug daily 10:00–21:00; Easter–June and Sept Mon–Fri 10:00–20:00, Sat–Sun 10:00–21:00; Oct–Easter Mon–Fri 10:00–19:00, Sat–Sun 10:00–20:00; at the end of Paseo del Muelle at Carlos Blasco de Imaz Plaza 1, tel. 943-440-099, www.aquariumss.com).

▲Monte Urgull—The once-mighty castle (Castillo de la Mota) atop the hill deterred most attackers, allowing the city to prosper in the Middle Ages. The museum located within the castle, featuring San Sebastián history, is mildly interesting. The best views from the hill are not from the statue of Christ, but from the ramparts on the left side (as you face the hill), just above the port's aquarium. **Café El Polvorín,** nestled in the park, is a friendly place with salads, sandwiches, and good sangria.

A new walkway allows you to stroll the mountain's entire perimeter near sea level. This route is continuous from Hotel Parma to the aquarium, and offers an enjoyable after-dinner wander. You can also walk a bit higher up over the port (along the white railing)—called the *paseo de las curas,* or "priest's path," where the clergy could stroll unburdened by the rabble in the streets below. These paths are technically open only from sunrise to sunset (daily May–Sept 8:00–21:00, Oct–April 8:00–19:00), but you can often access them later.

The Beach

▲▲La Concha Beach and Promenade—The shell-shaped Playa de la Concha, the pride of San Sebastián, has one of Europe's loveliest stretches of sand. Lined with a two-mile-long promenade, it allows even backpackers to feel aristocratic. While pretty empty off-season, in summer, sunbathers pack its shores. But year-round, it's surprisingly

devoid of eateries and money-grubbing businesses. There are free showers, and *cabinas* provide lockers, showers, and shade for a fee. For a century, the lovingly painted wrought-iron balustrade that stretches the length of the promenade has been a symbol of the city; it shows up on everything from jewelry to headboards. It's shaded by tamarisk trees, with branches carefully pruned into knotty bulbs—another symbol of the city.

The Miramar palace and park, which divides the crescent in the middle, was where Queen María Cristina held court when she summered here. Her royal changing rooms are used today as inviting cafés, restaurants, and a fancy spa.

La Perla Spa—The spa attracts a less royal crowd today and appeals mostly to visitors interested in sampling "the curative properties of the sea." You can enjoy its Talasso Fitness Circuit, featuring a hydrotherapy pool, relaxation pool, panoramic Jacuzzi, cold-water pools, seawater steam sauna, dry sauna, and a relaxation area. For those seriously into spas, they offer additional services, from Dead Sea mud wraps to massages to day-long "personalized programs" (€21 for 1.75-hour fitness circuit, €27 for 3-hour circuit, daily 8:00–22:00, caps sold and towels rented, bring or buy a swimsuit, on the beach at the center of the crescent, Paseo de la Concha, tel. 943-458-856, www.la-perla.net).

More Sights

Monte Igueldo—For commanding city views (if you ignore the tacky amusements on top), ride the funicular up Monte Igueldo, a mirror image of Monte Urgull. The views over San Sebastián, along the coast, and into the distant green mountains, are sensational day or night. The entrance to the funicular is on the road behind the tennis club on the far western end of Playa de Ondarreta, which extends from Playa de la Concha to the west (funicular-€2.30 round-trip; July–mid-Sept daily 10:00–22:00; April–June and mid-Sept–Oct daily 11:00–20:00; Nov–March Mon–Tue and Thu–Fri 11:00–18:00, Sat–Sun 11:00–20:00, closed Wed). If you drive to the top, you'll pay €1.70 to enter. The #16 bus takes you here from the Old Town in about 10 minutes, stopping at the funicular station.

Kursaal Conference Center—These two Lego-like boxes (just east and across the river from the Old Town, in Gros) mark the spot of what was once a grand casino, torn down by Franco to discourage gambling. Many locals wanted to rebuild it as it once was, in a similar style to the turn-of-the-20th-century buildings in the Centro. But, in an effort to keep up with the postmodern trends in Bilbao, city leaders opted instead for Rafael Moneo's striking contemporary design. The complex is supposed to resemble the angular rocks that make up the town's breakwater. The Kursaal houses a theater, conference facilities, some gift shops and travel agencies, and a restaurant.

Near San Sebastián: Chillida-Leku Museum

Eduardo Chillida (1924–2002), a popular Basque sculptor, is the focus of this enjoyable museum on the outskirts of town. Chillida worked rough, heavy materials (such as iron and marble) into huge but delicate-seeming abstract sculptures. You might not have heard of Chillida, but you've likely seen his big, blocky works, which decorate cities around Spain and throughout Europe. In San Sebastián, among the rocks at the west end of the beachfront promenade, you'll find one of Chillida's most famous works: the "wind combs" *(peine del viento)*.

The museum has three parts: The entry area shows a 45-minute loop film of the artist at work; the grounds—with beautiful, grassy rolling hills and trees—display his larger works, mostly of iron or rose marble; and a 16th-century farmhouse—which the artist renovated expressly for this purpose—shows off some of his smaller works (of bronze, felt, clay, alabaster, and so on).

As you explore, notice the way Chillida began with imposing chunks of media, then carved passages into them to allow light and air to penetrate an otherwise impenetrable block. This has the unexpected effect of making big, clumsy things seem light and graceful. Most of his works are carved from a single piece. The artist believed that works should be unique and evolve organically—he'd contemplate the medium and listen to what it had to say before carving it up. As you stroll the grounds surveying the works, imagine both the intense pressure and the delicate touch required to persuade these materials to become art.

Because it takes some effort to get here, the museum is best for people who know Chillida and appreciate his work. Art-lovers in the region to visit the Guggenheim might find this to be the perfect complement.

Cost and Hours: €8.50, good €4 audioguide; July–Aug Mon–Sat

10:30–20:00, Sun 10:30–15:00; Sept–June Wed–Mon 10:30–15:00, closed Tue; Barrio Jáuregui 66, Hernani, tel. 943-336-006, www.eduardo-chillida.com.

Getting There: It's on the edge of San Sebastián, about a €10 taxi ride from the Old Town. You can also take bus #G-2 from near the Perla Spa along the beach (2/hr, €1.25).

SLEEPING

Rates in San Sebastián fluctuate with the season. When you see a range, the top end is for summer (roughly July–Sept), and the low end is for the shoulder season (May–June and Oct); outside of these times, you'll pay even less. Since breakfast is often not included, I've recommended some good options elsewhere in town (see "Eating").

In or Near the Old Town

$$$ Hotel Parma is a business-class place with 27 fine rooms and family-run attention to detail and service. It stands on the edge of the Old Town, away from the bar-scene noise, and overlooks the river and a surfing beach (Sb-€63–86, windowless interior Db-€93–130, view Db-€113–44, air-con, modern lounge, pay Internet access, free Wi-Fi, Paseo de Salamanca 10, tel. 943-428-893, fax 943-424-082, www.hotelparma.com, hotelparma@hotelparma.com; Iñaki, Pino, and Maider).

$$ Pensión Edorta ("Edward") elegantly mixes wood, brick, and color into 12 modern, stylish rooms (S/D-€40–60, Sb/Db-€60–80, extra bed-€20–25, elevator, Calle Puerto 15, tel. 943-423-773, fax 943-433-570, www.pensionedorta.com, info@pensionedorta.com).

$ Pensión Amaiur is a flowery and inviting place buried deep in the Old Town, with great-value rooms. Kind Virginia gives the justifiably popular *pensión* a homey warmth—and it's absolutely spotless. Her 13 colorful, cozy rooms share seven bathrooms (S-€28–42, quiet interior D-€38–50, exterior D-€45–60, T-€60–80, Q-€75–95, family room, kitchen facilities, pay Internet access, free Wi-Fi, next to Santa María Church at Calle 31 de Agosto 44, tel. 943-429-654, www.pensionamaiur.com, amaiur@telefonica.net).

$Hotel Adore Plaza, run by young and energetic Santi, offers bright and good-value rooms overlooking the Old Town's centerpiece, Plaza de la Constitución. If Santi isn't around, his parents offer a warm, friendly welcome. Seven rooms—four with balconies and views of the plaza, and three interior rooms with less noise—share four bathrooms (D-€50–60, one Db-€65–75, T-€66–81, Q-€80–100, includes tax, elevator, free Wi-Fi, Plaza de la Constitución 6, tel. & fax 943-422-270, mobile 610-521-092 or 610-521-532, www.adoreplaza.com, adoreplaza@yahoo.es).

Sleep Code

(€1 = about $1.50, country code: 34)
S = Single, **D** = Double/Twin, **T** = Triple, **Q** = Quad, **b** = bathroom, **s** = shower only. You can assume these places accept credit cards and speak English unless otherwise noted. Breakfast is generally not included (unless noted). This code applies to this chapter's listings in both Spain and France. The word *ostatua* (which you'll see throughout the Basque Country) means "pension."

To help you sort easily through these listings, I've divided the rooms into three categories based on the price for a standard double room with bath in peak season:

$$$ Higher Priced—Most rooms €90 or more.
$$ Moderately Priced—Most rooms between €60-90.
$ Lower Priced—Most rooms €60 or less.

Across the River, in Gros

The pleasant Gros district—San Sebastián's "uptown"—is marked by the super-modern, blocky Kursaal conference center. The nearby beach is popular with surfers. These hotels are less than a 10-minute walk from the Old Town.

$$$ Hotel Arrizul is new and fresh, with sleek, mod decor in each of its 12 rooms (Sb-€65–88, Db-€99–129, breakfast-€6, air-con, elevator, free Wi-Fi, Peña y Goñi 1, tel. 943-322-804, fax 943-326-701, www.arrizulhotel.com, info@arrizulhotel.com).

$$ Pensión Kursaal has 10 basic but colorful rooms (Db-€63–82, elevator, pay Internet, free Wi-Fi, Peña y Goñi 2, tel. 943-292-666, fax 943-297-536, www.pensionesconencanto.com, kursaal@pensionesconencanto.com).

On the Beach

$$$ Hotel Niza, set in the middle of Playa de la Concha, is understandably often booked well in advance. Half of its 40 rooms (some with balconies) overlook the bay. From its chandeliered and plush lounge, a classic elevator takes you to its comfortable, pastel rooms with wedding-cake molding (tiny interior Sb-€58–64, Db-€123–139, view rooms cost the same—requests with reservation considered...but no promises, extra bed-€22, only streetside rooms have air-con, great buffet breakfast-€11, free Internet access and Wi-Fi, parking-€14/day—must reserve in advance, Zubieta 56, tel. 943-426-663, fax 943-441-251, www.hotelniza.com, niza@hotelniza.com). The breakfast room has a sea view and doubles as a bar with light snacks throughout the day (Bar Biarritz, daily 7:30–24:00, food service ends at 22:30). The cheap and cheery restaurant downstairs, called La Pasta Gansa,

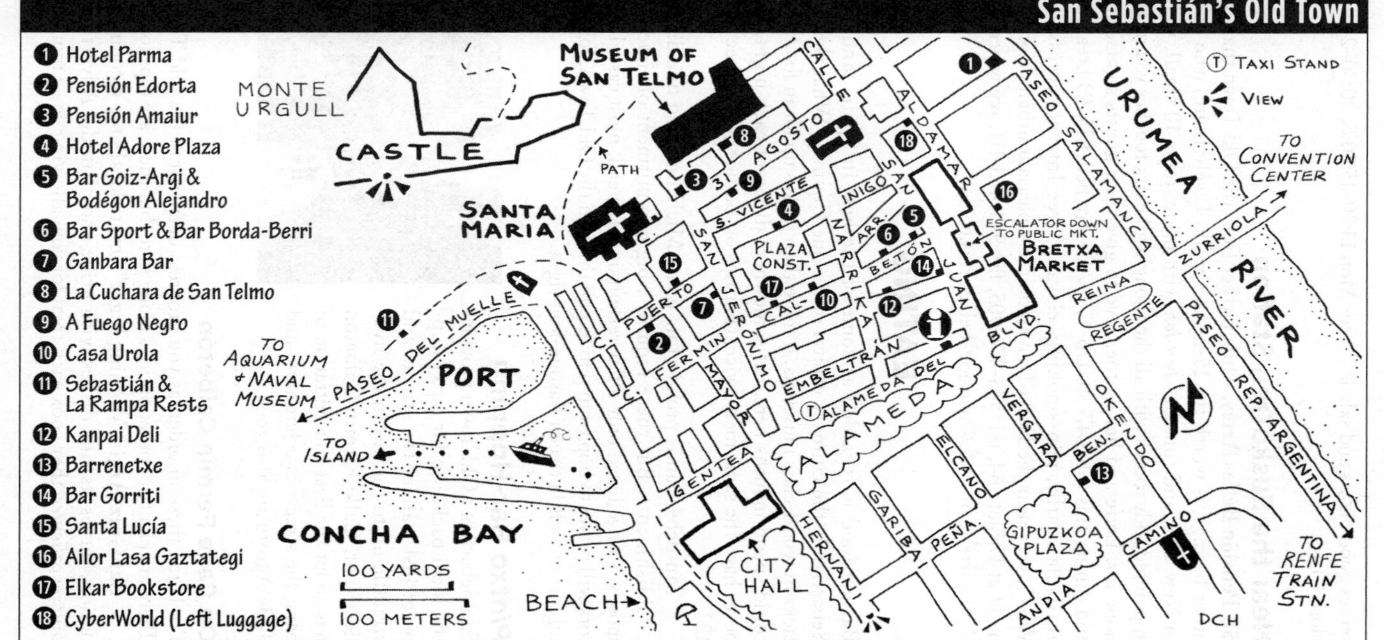

SAN SEBASTIÁN

serves good pizzas and salads (Wed–Mon 13:30–15:30 & 20:30–24:00, closed Tue).

Near the EuskoTren Station

$$ Pensión Bellas Artes, while farther from the Old Town than my other listings, is worth the 15-minute walk. Lively Leire, who lived in New York and runs her *pensión* with pride, rents 10 small, well-appointed, tidy rooms with all the thoughtful extra touches you might hope for. Leire and her mother love to give their guests sightseeing and dining tips (Sb-€47–58, Db-€72–79, extra bed-€35, €3 breakfast available nearby, non-smoking, elevator, free Internet access and Wi-Fi, very near the EuskoTren station in a pleasant urban neighborhood at Urbieta 64, tel. 943-474-905, fax 943-463-111, www.pension-bellasartes.com, info@pension-bellasartes.com).

EATING

Basque food is regarded as some of the best in Spain...and San Sebastián is the culinary capital of Basque Country. What the city lacks in world-class museums, it more than makes up for in food. You could spend months here, eat somewhere different each night, and never have the same meal twice. (For tips on Basque cuisine, see page 123.)

San Sebastián is proud of its many Michelin-rated fine dining establishments. But these require a big commitment of time and money, so I've listed only a few restaurants. Instead, most casual visitors will prefer to hop from pub to pub through the Old Town, following the crowds between Basque-font signs.

Pintxo Bar-Hopping

San Sebastián's Old Town provides the ideal backdrop for tapas-hopping; just wander the streets and straddle up to the bar in the liveliest spot. Calle Fermín Calbetón has about the best concentration of bars; the streets San Jerónimo and 31 de Agosto are also good.

On Calle Fermín Calbetón

I've listed these in order, as you progress deeper into the Old Town. There are plenty of other options along here, but these are top-notch.

Bar Goiz-Argi ("Morning Light"), every local's top recommendation, serves its tiny dishes with pride and attitude. Advertising *pintxos calientes,* they cook each treat for you, allowing you a montage

Do the *Txiquiteo* Tango

Txiquiteo (chih-kee-TAY-oh) is the word for hopping from bar to bar, enjoying characteristically small sandwiches and tiny snacks (*pintxos,* PEEN-chohs) and glasses of wine. Local competition drives small bars to lay out the most appealing array of *pintxos*, and the selection is amazing. Watch the locals to see what they're eating and find out what's best. But don't get carried away at one place—there will be more you'll want to try at the next bar.

Later in the evening, the best spreads get picked over (20:30 is prime time). As the night progresses, bars get more crowded and bartenders bounce around. If you can't get the bartender's attention to serve you a particular *pintxo*, don't be shy—just grab it and a napkin, and munch away. Most bars operate on the honor system, so keep a mental note of the number of tapas you've eaten.

If you want a meal instead of *pintxos*, note that some bars—even ones that look only like bars from the street—have attached restaurants (usually with an entrance from the bar). If you're hungry, ask if there's a restaurant.

of petite gourmet snacks. Try their *tartaleta de txangurro* (spider-crab spread on bread) or their wonderful shrimp kebab. Wash it all down with a glass of whichever wine you like—open bottles are clearly priced and displayed on the shelf. You stand at the bar since there are no chairs (closed Mon–Tue, Calle Fermín Calbetón 4, tel. 943-425-204).

At **Bar Sport,** they may offer to *calentar* (heat up) some of your selections, such as the toothpick-towering *jamón* and mushroom *pintxo*. They have a few tables, but don't expect service. Order at the bar and take it to your table...if you're lucky enough to get one (daily, Calle Fermín Calbetón 10, tel. 943-426-888).

Bar Borda-Berri (loosely "Mountain Hut"), a couple doors down, features a more low-key ambience and top-quality €3 *pintxos*. There are only a few items at the bar; check out the chalkboard menu for today's options (ask for English translation), order, and they'll make it fresh. The specialty here is melt-in-your-mouth beef cheeks *(carrillera de tenera)* in a tangy sauce (closed Mon, Calle Fermín Calbetón 12, tel. 943-430-342).

Other *Pintxo* Bars in the Old Town

Ganbara serves little croissant-sandwich *pintxos,* and also heaps of peppers and mushrooms—whatever's in season—on its bar. They'll sauté you a tasty *ración* for a steep price; for example, a plate of grilled *hongos a la plantxa*—grilled giant mushrooms—will run you about €13 (closed Mon, San Jerónimo 21, tel. 943-422-575).

La Cuchara de San Telmo, with cooks taught by a big-name Basque chef, is a cramped place that devotes as much space to its thriving kitchen as its bar. It has nothing precooked and set on the bar—you order your mini-gourmet plates with a spirit of adventure from the constantly changing blackboard. Their foie gras with apple jelly is rightfully famous (€3 *pintxos,* closed Mon, tucked away on a lonely alley called Santa Corda behind Museum of San Telmo at 31 de Agosto #28, tel. 943-420-840).

A Fuego Negro is cool and upscale compared to the others, with a hip, slacker vibe and a blackboard menu of *pintxos* and drinks (closed Mon, 31 de Agosto #31, mobile 650-135-373).

Sit-Down Restaurants

Bodégon Alejandro is a good spot for modern Basque cuisine in a dark and traditional setting (3-course fixed-price meal-€35, from 13:00 and 20:30, closed Mon–Tue except in Aug, no dinner Sun, in the thick of the Old Town on Calle Fermín Calbetón 4, tel. 943-427-158).

Casa Urola, a block away, is a fine option for a traditional, sit-down Basque meal (more expensive, €16–22 entrées, from 13:00 and 20:00, reservations smart, Calle Fermín Calbetón 20, tel. 943-423-424).

Seafood along the Port: For seafood with a salty sailor's view, check out the half-dozen hardworking, local-feeling restaurants that line the harbor on the way to the aquarium. Along here, locals like **Sebastián** (more traditional, closed Tue) and **La Rampa** (more upscale, closed Tue afternoon and all day Wed).

Picnics and Take-Out

A picnic on the beach or atop Monte Urgull is a tempting option. These places are a memorable place to assemble a bang-up spread.

Kanpai, a high-quality deli serving Basque and international cuisine, offers tempting, well-presented food. Davíd (who runs the place with his mother) carefully crafts each dish. Step up to the display case and get something "to go" for an easy and tasty picnic, or enjoy it at one of their little tables, and ask them to *calentar*—heat it up (€10 three-course meal offered Mon–Fri only, fancier foods on weekends, also wine-tastings, open daily 10:00–15:00 & 17:00–21:00, San Lorenzo 4, tel. 943-423-884).

Explore the **Bretxa Public Market** at Plaza de Sarriegi (described on page 132).

Upscale picnickers can tempt their tastebuds at **Barrenetxe** for an amazing array of breads, prepared foods, and some of the best desserts in town. In business since 1699, the somewhat formal service is justified (open daily, hours vary but always closed Sun afternoon, Plaza de Guipúzcoa 9, tel. 943-424-482).

Breakfast

If your hotel doesn't provide breakfast—or even if it does—consider one of these places. The first is a traditional stand-up bar, while the second is a greasy spoon.

Bar Gorriti, delightfully local, is packed with market workers and shoppers starting their busy day. You'll stand at the bar and choose a hot-off-the-grill *tortilla* (omelet) sandwich and other goodies (€2 each). This and a cup of coffee makes for an energizing and very Basque breakfast (bar open long hours daily, breakfast served 6:30–10:00, facing the side of the big white market building at San Juan 3, tel. 943-428-353).

Santa Lucía, a 1950s-style diner, is ideal for a cheap Old Town breakfast or *churros* break (*churros* are like deep-fried, sweet French fries that can be dipped in pudding-like hot chocolate). Photos of two dozen different breakfasts decorate the walls, and plates of fresh *churros* with sugar keep patrons happy. Grease is liberally applied to the grill...from a squeeze bottle. To counteract this place's heart-attack potential, get a glass of O.J., fresh-squeezed by the clever machine (daily 8:00–21:00, Calle Puerto 6, tel. 943-425-019).

TRANSPORTATION CONNECTIONS

By Train

Remember that San Sebastián has two train stations: RENFE and EuskoTren (described in "Arrival in San Sebastián," page 128). The station you use depends on your destination.

RENFE Station: This station handles long-distance destinations within Spain (most of which require reservations). Connections include **Irún** (12/day, 25 min), **Hendaye,** France (9/day, 30 min), **Madrid** (3/day, 5–7 hrs), **Burgos** (4/day, 3–3.5 hrs), **León** (1/day, 5 hrs), **Pamplona** (3/day, 2 hrs), **Salamanca** (1/day, 6 hrs), **Vitoria** (5/day, 1.75 hrs), **Barcelona** (3/day–one fast, 6 hrs; one slow, 8.5 hrs; 1 night train/day except Sat, 10 hrs), and **Santiago de Compostela** (1/day, 11 hrs, final destination A Coruña).

EuskoTren Station: If you're going into France, it's best to take the regional Topo train (which leaves from the EuskoTren station) over the French border into **Hendaye** (2/hr, 30 min, departs EuskoTren station at :15 and :45 after the hour 6:15–21:45). From Hendaye, connect to France's SNCF network, including **Paris** (from Hendaye: 4/day, 5.5 hrs, or 8.5-hr night train, reservations required). Unfortunately,

San Sebastián's EuskoTren station doesn't have information on Paris-bound trains from Hendaye (except sometimes in summer). Don't buy the Spanish ticket too far in advance—EuskoTren tickets to Hendaye must be used within two hours of purchase (or else they expire).

Also leaving from San Sebastián's EuskoTren station are slow regional trains to destinations in Spain's Basque region, including **Bilbao** (hourly, €10.50 round-trip ticket saves €2, 2.25–2.75 hrs—the bus is faster; EuskoTren info: tel. 902-543-210, www.euskotren.es). Although the train ride from San Sebastián to Bilbao takes twice as long as the bus, it passes through more interesting countryside. The Basque Country shows off its trademark green and gray: lush green vegetation and gray clouds. It's an odd mix of heavy industrial factories, small homegrown veggie gardens, streams, and every kind of livestock you can imagine.

By Bus

There is no real bus station in San Sebastián—it's more a congregation of bus parking spots next to the big Hotel Amara Plaza, at the roundabout called Plaza Pío XII (on the river, four blocks south of EuskoTren station). The "station" is called Amara (for the neighborhood it's in). Some schedules are posted at various stops, but confirm departure times and buy your tickets in advance at any of the bus companies with offices on either side of the block north of the station area (toward downtown, along Avenida de Sancho el Sabio and Paseo de Vízcaya). Pesa, which serves St. Jean-de-Luz and Bilbao, is located on the same side as the "station," at Avenida de Sancho el Sabio 33 (tel. 902-101-210, www.pesa.net). The Alsa office—which serves Madrid, Burgos, and León, and also has baggage storage—is at Paseo de Vízcaya 16 (tel. 902-422-242, www.alsa.es).

From San Sebastián, buses go to **Bilbao** (get ticket from Pesa office, 2/hr, hourly on weekends, 6:30–22:00, 1.25 hrs, €9.20, departs from Amara; morning buses fill with tourists, commuters, and students, so consider buying your ticket the day before; once in Bilbao, buses leave you at Termibús stop with easy tram connections to the Guggenheim modern-art museum), **Pamplona** (La Roncalesa office, 8/day, 1 hr, €6.50), **León** (Alsa office, 1/day, 6 hrs, €28), **Madrid** (Alsa office, 8/day, 6 hrs direct, otherwise 7 hrs, €30–42; same bus stops at **Burgos**), and **Barcelona** (Vibasa office, 2/day and 1 at night, 7.5 hrs, €27).

To visit **Hondarribia** (described on page 160), you can catch bus #I-2 much closer to the center at Plaza Gipuzkoa (1 block south of TI; about 3/hr, 30 min, €2, same bus goes to airport en route to Hondarribia).

Buses to French Basque Country: A bus goes from San Sebastián's Amara bus station to **St. Jean-de-Luz** (Mon–Sat only, 2/day at 9:00 and 14:30, 45 min, €4.20 one-way, €7.50 round-trip, get ticket from Pesa office, runs only 1/week off-season), then continues directly to **Biarritz** (1.25 hrs from San Sebastián) and **Bayonne** (1.5 hrs from San Sebastián).

Between San Sebastián and Bilbao: The Bay of Biscay

Between the two Spanish Basque cities of San Sebastián and Bilbao is a beautiful countryside of rolling green hills and a scenic, jagged coastline that looks almost Celtic. Aside from a scenic joyride, this area merits a visit for the cute fishing and resort town of Lekeitio.

Route Tips for Drivers

San Sebastián and Bilbao are connected in about an hour and a quarter by the A-8 expressway (the toll between the cities is about €7.50). While speedy and scenic, this route is nothing compared to some of the free, but slower, back roads connecting the two towns.

If side-tripping from San Sebastián to Bilbao, you can drive directly there on A-8 in the morning. But coming home to San Sebastián, consider this more scenic route: Take A-8 until the turnoff for Guernica, then head up into the hills on BI-635. After visiting Guernica (described on page 147), follow signs along the very twisty road to Lekeitio (about 40 min). Leave Lekeitio on the road just above the beach; after crossing the bridge, take the left fork and follow BI-3428 to Ondarroa (with a striking modern bridge and nice views back into the steep town), Mutriku, and Deba to hug the coastline east to San Sebastián. There's a fine photo-op pull-out as you climb along the coast just after Deba. Soon after, you'll have two opportunities to get on the A-8 (blue signs) for a quicker approach to San Sebastián; but if you've enjoyed the scenery so far, stick with the coastal road (white signs, N-634) through Zumaia and Getaria, rejoining the expressway at Zarautz.

Lequeitio / Lekeitio

A small fishing port with an idyllic harbor and a fine beach, Lekeitio (leh-KAY-tee-oh) is just over an hour by bus from Bilbao and an easy stop for drivers. It's protected from the Bay of Biscay by a sand spit that leads to the lush and rugged little San Nicolás Island. Hake boats fly their Basque flags and proud Basque locals black out the Spanish translations on street signs.

Lekeitio is a teeming resort during July and August (when its population of 7,000 triples as big-city Basque folks move in to their vacation condos), and it's a backwater fishing village the rest of the year. It's isolated from the modern rat race by its location down a long, windy little road.

While sights are humble here, the 15th-century St. Mary's Parish Church is a good example of Basque Gothic, with an impressive altarpiece (Mon–Sat 8:00–12:00 & 17:00–19:30, closed Sun). The town's back lanes are reminiscent of old days when fishing was the only industry. Fisherwomen sell their husbands' catches each morning from about 10:30 along the port. The golden crescent beach is as inviting as the sandbar, which—at low tide—challenges you to join the seagulls out on San Nicolás Island.

Getting There: Buses connect Lekeitio with **Bilbao** (hourly, 1.25 hrs; same bus stops at **Guernica**, 40 min) and **San Sebastián** (4/day Mon–Fri, 2/day Sat–Sun, 1.25 hrs). But this stop is most logical for those with a car. Drivers can park most easily in the lot near the bus station. Exit the station left, walk along the road, then take the first right (down the steep, cobbled street) to reach the harbor. There is no luggage storage in town.

Tourist Information: The TI faces the fish market next to the harbor (July–Aug daily 10:00–14:00 & 16:00–20:00; Sept–June Tue–Sat 10:30–13:30 & 16:00–19:00, Sun 10:00–14:00, closed Mon; tel. 946-844-017).

Sleeping: **$$ Emperatriz Zita Hotel** is the obvious best bet for your beach-town break. It's named for Empress Zita (who lived here in exile after her Habsburg family lost World War I and was booted from Vienna). While Zita's mansion burned down, this 1930s rebuild still has a belle époque aristocratic charm, solid classy furniture in 42 spacious rooms, real hardwood floors, and an elegant spa in the basement. Located on the beach a few steps from the harbor, with handy free parking and a view restaurant, it's a fine value (Sb-€46–59, Db-€60–77, Db suite-€90–107, views—ask for *vistas del mar*—are worth the extra €6, high prices are for mid-June–mid-Sept and Fri–Sat all year, extra bed-€20, breakfast-€8, elevator, free Wi-Fi, Santa Elena Etorbidea, tel. 946-842-655, fax 946-243-500, www.aisiahoteles.com, zita@aisiahoteles.com). The hotel also has a thermal seawater pool, Jacuzzi, and full-service spa (all available at reasonable prices).

Eating: Although it's sleepy in the off-season, the harbor promenade is made-to-order in summer for a slow meal or a tapas crawl.

Restaurante Zapirain, hiding in the narrow streets a few blocks up from the harbor, is a local favorite for fancy seafood. This cozy, white-tablecloth eatery fills one small room with 10 tables of happy eaters (€15 starters, €20 main dishes, closed Tue, Igualdegi 3, tel. 946-840-255).

Guernica / Gernika

The workaday market town of Guernica (GEHR-nee-kah) is near and dear to Basques and pacifists alike. This is the site of the Gernikako Arbola (oak tree of Gernika), which marked the assembly point where the regional Basque leaders, the Lords of Bizkaia, met through the ages to assert their people's freedom. Long the symbolic heart of Basque separatism, it was also a natural target for Franco (and his ally Hitler) in the Spanish Civil War—resulting in an infamous bombing raid that left the town in ruins (see "The Bombing of Guernica"), as immortalized by Picasso in his epic work *Guernica*. Today, Guernica—while nothing special at first glance—holds some of the Basque Country's more compelling museums. And Basque bigwigs have reclaimed the town as a meeting point—they still elect their figurehead leader on that same ancient site under the oak tree.

ORIENTATION

Guernica is small (about 15,000 inhabitants) and compact, focused on its large market hall (Monday market 9:00–14:00).

Arrival in Guernica

Drivers will find a handy parking lot near the train tracks at the end of town. Buses drop off along the main road skirting the town center. No matter where you enter, the TI is well-signed (look for yellow *i* signs)—head there first to get your bearings.

Tourist Information

The TI is in the town center (Mon–Sat 10:00–14:00 & 16:00–19:00—no lunch break in summer, Sun 10:00–14:00, Artekalea 8, tel. 946-255-892, www.gernika-lumo.net). Pick up the free, good town map. If you'll be visiting both the Peace Museum and the Basque Country Museum, buy the €5.25 combo-ticket here.

SIGHTS

I've arranged Guernica's sights in the order of a handy sightseeing loop from the TI.

• *Exit the TI to the left, cross the street, and walk up the left side of the square, where you'll find the...*

▲Gernika Peace Museum—Because of the brutality of the Guernica bombing, and the powerful Picasso painting that documented the atrocities of war, the name "Guernica" has become synonymous with pacifism. This thoughtfully presented exhibit has taken a great tragedy of 20th-century history and turned it into a compelling cry for peace in our time. Borrow the English translations at the entry, request an English showing of the movie upstairs, and head up through the two-floor exhibit. The first floor begins by considering different ways of defining "peace." You'll then enter an apartment and hear Begoña describe her typical Guernica life in the 1930s...until the bombs dropped (a mirror effect shows you the devastating aftermath). You'll exit into an exhibit about the town's history, with a special emphasis on the bombing. Finally, a 10-minute movie shows grainy footage of the destruction, and ends with a collage of peaceful reconciliations in recent history—in Ireland, South Africa, Guatemala, Australia, and Berlin. On the second floor, Picasso's famous painting is superimposed on three transparent panels to highlight different themes. The exhibit concludes with a survey of the recent history of conflicts in the Basque Country (€4; July–Aug Tue–Sat 10:00–20:00, Sun 10:00–15:00, closed Mon; Sept–June Tue–Sat 10:00–14:00 & 16:00–19:00, Sun 10:00–14:00, closed Mon; Foru Plaza 1, tel. 946-270-213, www.peacemuseum guernica.org).

• *Continue uphill to the big church. At the road above the church, you can turn right and walk a block and a half to find a tile replica of* **Picasso's Guernica** *(left-hand side of the street). Or you can head left to find the next two attractions...*

▲Basque Country Museum (Euskal Herria Museoa)—This well-presented, newly renovated exhibit offers a good overview of Basque culture and history. Follow the suggested route and climb chronologically up through Basque history, with the help of an included audioguide. You'll find exhibits about traditional Basque architecture and landscape, and a region-by-region rundown of the Basque Country's seven parts. One interesting map shows Basque emigration over the centuries—including to the US. The top floor is the most engaging, highlighting Basque culture: sports, dances, cuisine, myths and legends, music, and language, plus a wrap-around movie featuring images of a proud people living the Basque lifestyle (€3, Tue–Sat 10:00–14:00 & 16:00–19:00, Sun 11:00–15:00, closed Mon, Allendesalazar 5, tel. 946-255-451).

The Bombing of Guernica

During the Spanish Civil War, Guernica was the site of one of history's most reviled wartime acts.

Monday, April 26, 1937, was market day, when the town was filled with farmers and peasants from the countryside selling their wares. At about four-forty in the afternoon, a German warplane appeared ominously on the horizon, and proceeded to bomb bridges and roads surrounding the town. Soon after, more planes arrived. Three hours of relentless saturation bombing followed, as the German and Italian air forces pummeled the city with incendiary "firebombs." People running through the streets or along the green hillsides were strafed with machine-gun fire. As the sun fell low in the sky and the planes finally left, hundreds—or possibly thousands—had been killed, and many more wounded. (Because Guernica was filled with refugees from other besieged towns, nobody is sure how many perished.)

Hearing word of the attack in Paris, Pablo Picasso—who had been commissioned to paint a mural for the 1937 world's fair—was devastated at the news of what had gone on in Guernica. Inspired, he painted what many consider the greatest antiwar work of art, ever. (For more on this great painting, now displayed in Madrid, see page 332.)

Why did the bombings happen? Reportedly, Adolf Hitler wanted an opportunity to try out his new saturation-bombing attack strategy (these days, we'd call it "shock and awe"). Francisco Franco, who was fed up with the independence-minded Basques, offered up their historic capital as a candidate for the experiment.

There's no doubt that Guernica, a gateway to Bilbao, was strategically located. But historians believe most of the targets here were far from strategic. Why attack so mercilessly, during the daytime, on market day, when innocent casualties would be maximized? Like the famous silent scream of Picasso's *Guernica* mother, this question haunts pacifists everywhere to this day.

▲▲Gernika Assembly House and Oak Tree—In the Middle Ages, the meeting point for the Basque general assembly was under the old oak tree on the gentle hillside above Guernica. The tradition continues today, as the tree stands at the center of a modest but interesting complex celebrating Basque culture and self-government (free, daily 10:00–14:00 & 16:00–18:00, until 19:00 in summer, on Allendesalazar, tel. 946-251-138).

As you enter the grounds, the **old trunk** in the small colonnade dates from the 1700s. Basque traditions have lived much, much longer than a single tree's life span. When one dies, it's replaced with a new one. This is the oldest surviving trunk.

Once inside the big building, the exhibit has three parts. The **stained-glass window room** features a gorgeous ceiling rife with Basque symbolism. The elderly leader stands under the oak holding a book with the "Old Law" *(Lege Zarra).* These are the *Fueros,* which the Basques lived by for centuries. Below him are groups representing the three traditional skills of this industrious people: sailors and fishermen; miners and steelworkers; and farmers. Behind them all is a classic Basque landscape: on the left is the sea, and on the right are rolling green hills dotted with red-and-white homes.

Out back, a tribune surrounds the fateful **oak tree.** This little fella is from 2005, planted here when the earlier one "finished out its life cycle" after standing here for nearly a century and a half. This tree is a descendant of that one, and (supposedly) of all the trees here since ancient times. This is where Basque leaders have met in solidarity across the centuries. In the Middle Ages, after Basque lands became part of Castile, Castilian kings came here to pledge respect to the old Basque laws. When Basque independence came under fire in the 19th century, patriots rallied by singing a song about this tree ("Ancient and holy symbol / Let thy fruit fall worldwide / While we gaze in adoration / Upon thee, our blessed tree"). After the 1937 bombing, in which this tree was miraculously unscathed, hundreds of survivors sought refuge under its branches. Today, although official representatives in the Spanish government are elected at the polls, the Basques choose their figurehead leader, the Lehendakari ("First One"), in this same spot.

Finally, the **assembly chamber** is like a mini-parliament for the region of Bizkaia ("Vízcaya" in Spanish, "Biscay" in English; one of the seven Basque territories). Notice the holy water and the altar—a sign that there's no separation of church and state in Basque politics. The paintings show the Lords of Bizkaia swearing allegiance to the *Fueros.*

TRANSPORTATION CONNECTIONS

Guernica is well-connected to **Bilbao** (1–2 trains/hr to Bilbao's Atxuri station, 40 min; also 2 buses/hr, 40 min) and to **Lekeitio** (hourly buses, 40 min). Connections are much less on weekends. The easiest way to connect to San Sebastián is via Bilbao, though you can also get there on the slow Topo train (transfer in Lemoa).

GUERNICA

Bilbao / Bilbo

In recent years, Bilbao (bil-BOW, rhymes with "cow") has seen a transformation like no other Spanish city. Entire sectors of the industrial city's long-depressed port have been cleared away to allow construction of a new opera house, convention center, and the stunning Guggenheim Museum.

Bilbao feels at once like a city of the grim industrial past...and of an exciting new future. It mingles beautiful but crumbling old buildings; eyesore high-rise apartment blocks; brand-new, super-modern additions to the skyline (such as the Guggenheim); and, draping the lush green hillsides on the horizon all around, typical whitewashed Basque homes with red roofs. Bilbao enjoys a vitality and well-worn charm befitting its status as a regional capital of culture and industry.

Planning Your Time

For most visitors, the Guggenheim is the main draw (and many could spend the whole day just there). But with a little more time, it's also worth hopping on a tram to explore the atmospheric Old Town (Casco Viejo).

Don't bother coming to Bilbao on Monday, when virtually all its museums—including the almighty Guggenheim—are closed (except in July–Aug).

ORIENTATION

When you're in the center, Bilbao feels smaller than its population of 500,000. The city, nestled amidst green hillsides, hugs the Bilbao River as it curves through town. The Guggenheim is more or less centrally located near the top of that curve; the bus station is to the west; the Old Town (Casco Viejo) and train stations are to the east; and a super-convenient (and actually enjoyable-to-ride) green tram called the EuskoTran ties it all together.

Tourist Information

Bilbao's handiest TI is next to the Guggenheim (July–Aug Mon–Sat 10:00–19:00, Sun 10:00–18:00; Sept–June Tue–Fri 11:00–18:00, Sat 11:00–19:00, Sun 11:00–15:00, closed Mon; Avenida Abandoibarra 2, tel. 944-710-301, www.bilbao.net). There are also branches at the airport and at Arriaga Theater near the Old Town. Pick up a city map and the bimonthly *Bilbao Guide.* If you're interested in something beyond the Guggenheim, ask about walking tours and grab the museum brochure (describing museums dedicated to everything from bullfighting and seafaring to sports and Holy Week processionals).

Arrival in Bilbao

Most travelers—whether arriving by train, bus, or car—will want to go straight to the museum. Thanks to a perfectly planned tram system (EuskoTran), this couldn't be easier. From any point of entry, simply buy a €1.15 single-ride ticket at a user-friendly green machine (€3.15 for an all-day pass), hop on a green-and-gray tram, enjoy the Muzak, and head for the Guggenheim stop (there's only one line so you can't get lost, trams come every 10–15 min, www.euskotran.es). When you buy your ticket, validate it immediately at the machine (follow the red arrow), since you can't do it once on board.

The Metro system, designed by prominent architect Lord Norman Foster, is a work of art... but not practical for most visitors.

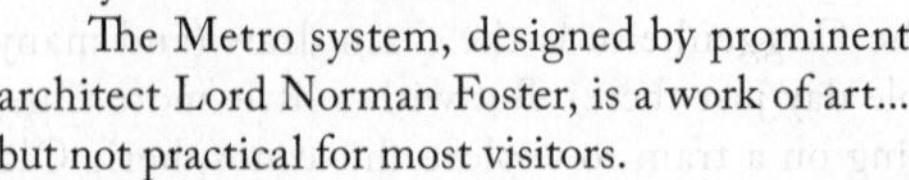

If you get lost, ask: "*¿Dónde está el museo Guggenheim?*" (DOHN-day ay-STAH el moo-SAY-oh "Guggenheim").

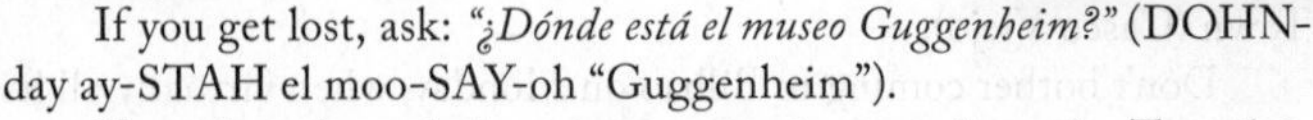

Note that the only luggage storage in town is at the Termibús station (not at either train station).

By Train: Bilbao's **RENFE station** (trains from most parts of Spain) is on the river in central Bilbao. The train station is on top of a small shopping mall. To reach the tram to the Guggenheim, descend into the stores. Leave from the exit marked *Hurtado de Amézaga,* and go right to find the BBK bank. Enter, find the *Automatikoa* door on the right, and buy your ticket at the green machine marked *Abando* (the machine is mixed in with a bunch of ATMs). Leave the bank and continue right around the corner. Validate your ticket at the machines at the tram stop before boarding the tram marked *Basurto.*

Trains coming from San Sebastián arrive at the riverside **Atxuri station,** southeast of the museum. Buy and validate your ticket, hop on a tram (direction: Basurto), and follow the river to the Guggenheim stop.

By Bus: Buses stop at the **Termibús station** on the western edge of downtown, about a mile southwest of the museum. The station has luggage lockers and a left-luggage desk (€2/bag, Mon–Fri 7:00–22:00, Sat 8:00–21:00, Sun 7:00–21:00). The tram (San Mamés station) is on the road just below the station—look for the steel *CTB* sign, buy and validate a ticket at the machine, and hop on the tram (direction: Atxuri) to Guggenheim.

By Plane: Bilbao's compact, modern, user-friendly airport is about six miles north of downtown. Everything branches off of a light-and-air-filled main hall, designed by prominent architect Santiago

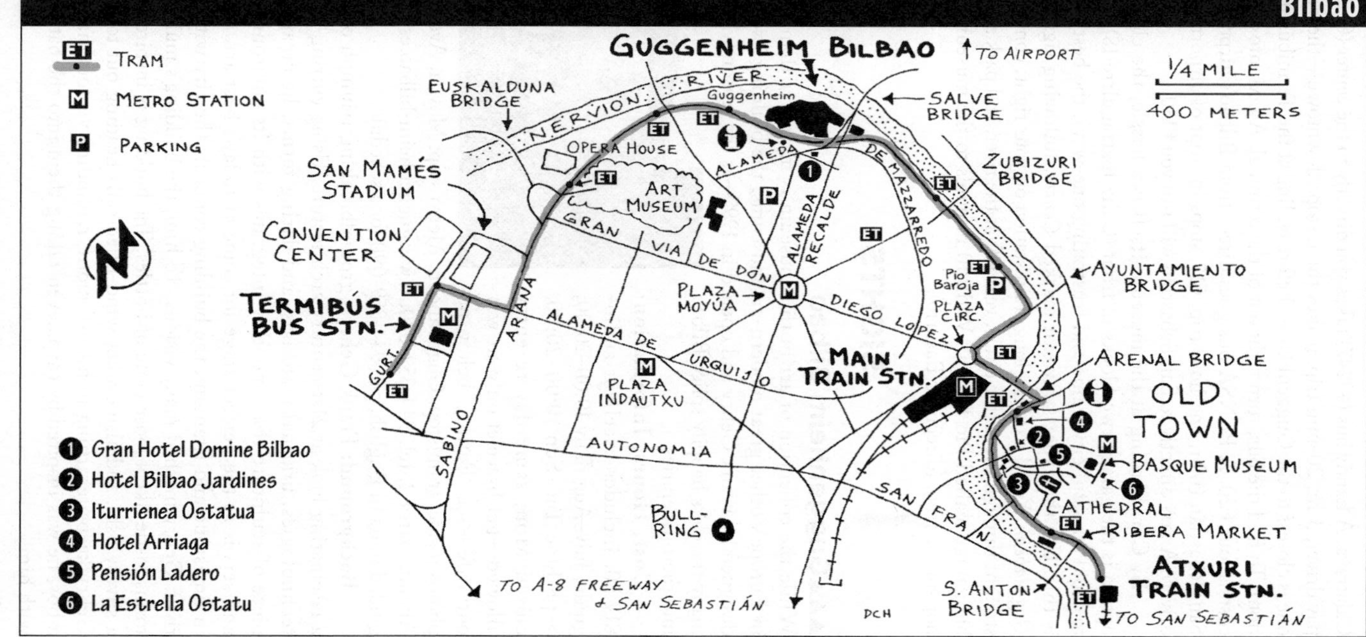
Bilbao
TRAM
METRO STATION
PARKING
GUGGENHEIM BILBAO
TO AIRPORT
1/4 MILE
400 METERS
EUSKALDUNA BRIDGE
RIVER
NERVION
Guggenheim
SALVE BRIDGE
OPERA HOUSE
ALAMEDA
ZUBIZURI BRIDGE
SAN MAMÉS STADIUM
ART MUSEUM
DE MAZZARREDO
ALAMEDA RECALDE
CONVENTION CENTER
GRAN VIA DE DON
AYUNTAMIENTO BRIDGE
Pío Baroja
PLAZA MOYÚA
PLAZA CIRC.
DIEGO LOPEZ
TERMIBÚS BUS STN.
ARANA
ALAMEDA DE
URQUIJO
MAIN TRAIN STN.
ARENAL BRIDGE
OLD TOWN
GURT.
PLAZA INDAUTXU
SABINO
AUTONOMIA
BASQUE MUSEUM
SAN FRAN.
CATHEDRAL
RIBERA MARKET
BULL-RING
ATXURI TRAIN STN.
S. ANTON BRIDGE
TO A-8 FREEWAY & SAN SEBASTIÁN
DCH
TO SAN SEBASTIÁN
1 Gran Hotel Domine Bilbao
2 Hotel Bilbao Jardines
3 Iturrienea Ostatua
4 Hotel Arriaga
5 Pensión Ladero
6 La Estrella Ostatu

Calatrava. A handy bus (#3247) takes you directly to the center (€1.25, pay driver, 3/hr, 20-min trip, makes three stops downtown—the first one is closest to the Guggenheim—before ending at the Termibús station). To find the bus, turn right out of the terminal. A taxi into town costs about €20. A PENSA bus goes direct from Bilbao's airport to San Sebastián (1/hr, one-hour trip, €15, stops in front of airport, pay driver). A taxi directly to San Sebastián will run you €150.

By Car: Parking at the museum itself is a hassle; the closest option is the garage two blocks in front (Calle Iparraguirre 18). But to avoid stressful city traffic and frustrating one-ways, the best plan is this: Use the expressway exit marked *Centro,* following signs to *Guggenheim.* You'll pass the long train station on your right; continue straight through the traffic circle, veer left at the river, and park at the big garage (called Pío Baroja). Walk 10 minutes to the museum, or hop on the tram (direction: Basurto).

SIGHTS

▲▲▲Guggenheim Bilbao

While the collection of art in this museum is no better than that in Europe's other great modern-art museums, the building itself—designed by Frank Gehry and opened in 1997—is the reason why so many travelers happily splice Bilbao into their itineraries.

Cost, Hours, Information: €12.50, includes excellent audioguide; July–Aug daily 10:00–20:00; Sept–June Tue–Sun 10:00–20:00, closed Mon; same-day re-entry allowed—get bracelet on your way out; café—see "Eating," below, no photos inside, tram stop: Guggenheim, Metro stop: Moyua, Avenida Abandoibarra 2, tel. 944-359-080, www.guggenheim-bilbao.es. For guided tours in English, call 944-359-090 for a schedule.

Background: Frank Gehry's groundbreaking triumph offers a fascinating look at 21st-century architecture. Using cutting-edge technologies, unusual materials, and daring forms, he created a piece of sculpture that smoothly integrates with its environment and serves as the perfect stage for some of today's best art. Clad in limestone and titanium, the building connects the city with its river. Gehry meshed many visions. To him, the building's multiple forms jostle like a loose crate of bottles. The building is inspired by a silvery fish...and also evokes wind-filled sails heading out to sea. Gehry keeps returning to his fish motif, reminding visitors that, as a boy, he was inspired by carp...even taking them into the bathtub with him.

➲ **Self-Guided Tour:** The audioguide will lead you room-by-room through the collection, but this information will get you started.

Guarding the main entrance is artist Jeff Koons' 42-foot-tall **West Highland Terrier.** Its 60,000 plants and flowers, which blossom in concert, grow through steel mesh. A joyful structure, it brings viewers back to their childhood...perhaps evoking humankind's relationship to God...or maybe it's just another notorious Koons hoax. One thing is clear: It answers to "Puppy."

Descend to the **main entrance.** After buying your ticket, be sure to pick up the free audioguide that explains Gehry's architecture in vivid detail and describes the exhibits (both permanent and temporary). Also pick up the English brochure explaining the architecture and museum layout (at the information desk) and the monthly bulletin detailing the art currently on display.

After presenting your ticket, enter the **atrium.** This acts as the heart of the building, pumping visitors from various rooms on three levels out and back, always returning to this central area before moving on to the next. The architect invites you to caress the sensual curves of the walls. There are virtually no straight lines (except the floor). Notice the sheets of glass that make up the elevator shaft—overlapping each other like a fish's scales. The various glass and limestone panels are each unique, designed by a computer and shaped by a robot...as will likely be standard in constructing the great buildings of the future.

From the atrium, step out onto the riverside **terrace.** The "water garden" lets the river symbolically lap at the base of the building. This pool is home to two unusual sculptures (which appear occasionally throughout the day): a five-part "fire fountain" (notice the squares in the pool to the right) and a "fog sculpture" that billows up from below.

Still out on the terrace, notice the museum's commitment to public spaces: On the right, a grand **staircase** leads under a big green bridge to a tower; the effect wraps the bridge into the museum's grand scheme. The 30-foot-tall **spider,** called *Maman* ("Mommy"), is a French artist's depiction of her mother: She spins a beautiful and delicate web of life...which is used to entrap her victims. (It makes a little more sense if you understand that the artist's mother was a weaver. Or maybe not.)

Gehry designed the vast **ground floor** mainly to house often-huge modern-art installations. Computer-controlled lighting adjusts for different exhibits. Surfaces are clean and bare, so you can focus on the art.

Speaking of which...because this museum is part of the Guggenheim "family" of museums, the **collection** perpetually rotates among the sister Guggenheim galleries in New York, Venice, and Berlin. The best approach to your visit is simply to immerse yourself in a modern-art happening, rather than to count on seeing a particular piece or a specific artist's works.

Twenty galleries occupy three floors. Use the handy touch-screens scattered throughout the museum to figure out exactly where you are and what's left to see, since the organic floor plan can be confusing. If you've always confused Klimt with Matisse, be sure to visit the *espacio didáctico* (learning area) on the third floor for its brilliantly concise timeline of all major art movements since the mid-19th century.

Or, if you're not turned on by this kind of art, just rattle around the inside of the remarkable building for a while. Especially around the atrium, every angle morphs the building into a whole new experience.

A great way to fully enjoy the **exterior** is to take a circular stroll up and down each side of the river, along the handsome promenade and over the two modern pedestrian bridges. (After you tour the museum, you can borrow a free "outdoor audioguide" to learn more—but it doesn't take you across the river.) The building's skin—shiny, metallic, with a scale-like texture—is made of thin titanium, carefully created to give just the desired color and reflective quality. The external appearance tells you what's inside: the blocky limestone parts contain square-shaped galleries, while the titanium sections hold nonlinear spaces.

As you look out over the rest of the city, think of this: Gehry designed his building to reflect what he saw here in Bilbao. Now other architects are, in turn, creating new buildings that complement his. It's an appealing synergy for this old city.

Old Town (Casco Viejo)

Bilbao's Old Town is worth a stroll, with tall, narrow lanes lined with thriving shops and tapas bars. Because the weather is wetter here than in many other parts of Spain (hence the green hillsides), the little balconies that climb the outside walls of buildings are glassed in, creating cozy little breakfast nooks. Approaching on the tram, hop off at the Arriaga stop, near the dripping-Baroque riverfront theater of the same name. From here, it's a short stroll into the twisty Old Town.

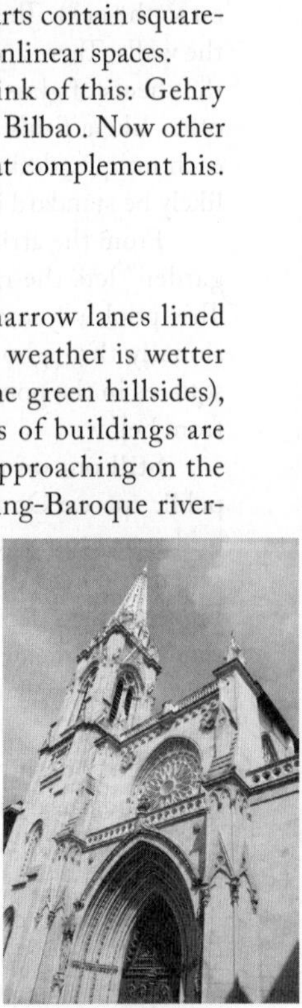

Whether you want to or not, you'll eventually wind up at Old Bilbao's centerpiece, the **Santiago Cathedral,** a 14th-century Gothic church with a tranquil interior that's recently been scrubbed clean inside and out (free, €1 to dip into cloister, Mon–Sat 10:00–13:00 & 17:00–19:30, closed Sun).

Various museums (including those dedicated to diocesan art and the Holy Week processions) are in or near the Old Town, but on a quick visit only one is worth considering...

Basque Museum (Euskal Museoa)—As a leading city of Spain's Basque region, it's fitting that Bilbao would have a museum dedicated to its unique culture. Unfortunately, the almost complete lack of English leaves the exhibits, much like the Basques themselves, shrouded in mystery. Around a ground-floor cloister, you'll see old stone monuments. The first floor delves into the Basque cultural heritage, displaying ceramics, guns, looms, and other tools. Special emphasis is given to nautical artifacts from this seafaring people; Basque settlers in the American West; and the pastoral lifestyles of rural Basques. The top floor is dedicated to archaeology, with exhibits about old tools and settlements (€3, Tue–Sat 11:00–17:00, Sun 11:00–14:00, closed Mon, Miguel de Unamuno Plaza 4, tel. 944-155-423, www.euskal-museoa.org).

SLEEPING

(€1 = about $1.50, country code: 34)
Bilbao merits an overnight stay. Even those who are only interested in the Guggenheim find that there's much more to see in this historic yet quickly changing city. Unless otherwise noted, the 7 percent tax is not included in the prices listed below.

Near the Guggenheim Museum

$$$ Gran Hotel Domine Bilbao is *the* place for wealthy modern-art fans looking for a handy splurge. It's right across the street from the Guggenheim, with decor (by a prominent Spanish designer) clearly inspired by Gehry's masterpiece. The hotel is gathered around an atrium with a giant "stone tree" and other artsy flourishes. Its 145 plush rooms are distinctly black, white, steel, and very postmodern (standard Db-€135, museum-view "executive" rooms for €20 more, rates can vary widely—can be much higher during conferences and cheaper during summer, no breakfast, non-smoking rooms, air-con, elevator, free Internet and Wi-Fi, great museum-view breakfast terrace, Alameda Mazarredo 61, tel. 944-253-300, fax 944-253-301, www.granhoteldominebilbao.com, recepcion.domine@hoteles-silken.com).

In the Old Town

To reach the Old Town, take the tram to the Arriaga stop. Note that the rates at these places can fluctuate by about €5 from season to season; I've listed the average rate.

$$ Hotel Bilbao Jardines, a fresh new place buried in the Old Town, is the most hotelesque option, with 32 modern but basic rooms (Sb-€58, Db-€75, cheaper off-season, breakfast-€4.50, quieter rooms in back, air-con, elevator, free Wi-Fi, Calle Jardines 9, tel. 944-794-210, fax 944-794-211, www.hotelbilbaojardines.com, info@hotelbilbaojardines.com).

$ Iturrienea Ostatua, on a pedestrian street in the Old Town, is a tidy pension renting 21 rooms packed with brick, stone, and antiques (Sb-€50, Db-€60, twin Db-€66, Tb-€80, prices include tax, €10–15 more July–Aug, breakfast-€8, free Wi-Fi, Santa María 14, tel. 944-161-500, fax 944-158-929, www.iturrieneaostatua.com, info@iturrieneaostatua.com). From the main train station, cross the bridge and go past the big theater. Where the river bends, turn left and walk a block and a half up quaint Santa María street.

$ Hotel Arriaga offers 21 traditional but well-maintained rooms and a spirited reception (Sb-€48, Db-€60, extra bed-€11, some rooms overlook a busy street—request a quiet back room, free Wi-Fi, parking-€11, Ribera 3, tel. 944-790-001, fax 944-790-516). As you cross the bridge from the station, it's just behind the big theater of the same name.

$ Pensión Ladero, renting ramshackle but cheap rooms, is a fine budget option in the Old Town. They don't accept reservations, but you can call when you arrive to check availability (S-€24, D-€36, T-€53, Q-€63, up 4 flights of stairs; 7 rooms up a very tight spiral staircase share 1 bathroom, while 11 rooms use the other 3 bathrooms on the main floor; cash only, Lotería 1, tel. 944-150-932, www.pensionladero.es). You'll find the *pensión* just before the cathedral at the center of the Old Town. This is a better value than the more prominent Pensión Roquefer across the street.

BILBAO

$ La Estrella Ostatu has 26 simple but neat rooms up a twisty staircase near the Basque Museum (Sb-€35, Db-€60 in summer including tax, cheaper off-season, breakfast-€3–4, María Muñoz 6, tel. 944-164-066, fax 944-150-731, www.laestrellaostatu.com, laestrellabilbao@yahoo.es, just enough English spoken).

EATING

Near the Guggenheim Museum

The easiest choice is the good cafeteria in the museum itself (upper level, separate entry above museum entry; Tue–Sun 9:00–21:00, closed Mon, €15 lunch deal offered 13:00–15:15). The streets in front of the museum have a handful of both sit-down and carry-out eateries (cafés, pizzerias, sandwich shops) to choose from.

In the Old Town

Bilbao has a thriving restaurant and tapas-bar scene. For pointers on Basque food, see page 123. You'll find the best options on three streets near the cathedral. Most restaurants around the Old Town advertise a fixed-price lunch for around €10.

Perro street is tops for the tasty little tapas called *pintxos* (PEEN-chohs). This is the place to do a tapas-bar crawl. Along here, Bar Irrintzi (open daily, at #8) and Gatz Bar (closed Sun afternoon, at #10) have the best reputation, but locals also enjoy Santa María and Kasko (all of these are within a few yards of each other).

Ventas Shops

Dancing between France and Spain and along the foothills of the Pyrenees, you'll see many signs for *ventas* (from the Spanish *vender,* "to sell"). Follow one of these signs to a cultural detour. Originally used as contraband outposts, *ventas* shops operate as a café, bar, restaurant, grocery store, gas station, cheap boutique, and more. Most are lost in the hills and hard to find, and many still don't have signs—locals just know where they are. Today, they are legal in a borderless Europe, and they still offer inexpensive products. Customers are mostly the French Basque, who cause traffic jams on weekends driving to the border to do cheap shopping or fill the gas tank. In most *ventas,* gas is cheaper by 25 percent, cigarettes and alcohol leave by the case, and the Spanish, French, and Euskara languages mingle as locals enjoy a coffee or beer among hanging garlands of cheap hams.

Santa María street is better for a sit-down restaurant meal. Browse the menus and interiors and choose your favorite. Well-regarded options include three places virtually next door to each other (at #4): Egiluz (€10 meals, closed Tue afternoon and all day Wed); Río-Oja (€8 specialties, focus on shareable traditional dishes called *kazuelitas,* closed Mon); and Rotterdam (€10–15 meals).

Finally, more eateries abound on **Jardines street,** including the popular Breton (meals and *pintxos,* at #11, closed Mon).

TRANSPORTATION CONNECTIONS

From Bilbao by Bus to: San Sebastián (2/hr, hourly on weekends, 6:00–22:30, 1.25 hrs, arrives at San Sebastián's Amara station), **Guernica** (2/hr, 40 min), **Lekeitio** (hourly, 1.25 hrs), **Burgos** (4–5/day, 2 hrs), **Santander** (hourly, 90 min, transfer there to bus to **Santillana del Mar** or **Comillas**—see Cantabria chapter). These buses depart from Bilbao's Termibús station.

By RENFE Train to: Madrid (2/day, 6 hrs), **Barcelona** (2/day, 6.5–9.25 hrs), **Burgos** (5/day, 3 hrs), **Salamanca** (1/day, 5.5 hrs), **León** (1/day, 5 hrs), **Santiago de Compostela** (1/day, 11 hrs). Remember, these trains leave from the RENFE station, across the river from the Old Town. Note that in a few years, a planned new train line will connect Bilbao to other cities in a snap (30 min to San Sebastián, 2.25 hrs to Madrid, 5.5 hrs to Paris)—but it's still slow trains for now.

By EuskoTren to: San Sebastián (hourly, long and scenic 2.25–2.75-hr trip to San Sebastián's EuskoTren station, €6.20), **Guernica** (1–2/hr, 40 min). These trains depart from Bilbao's Atxuri station, just beyond the Old Town.

Between San Sebastián and St. Jean-de-Luz: Hondarribia

Just 45 minutes apart by car, San Sebastián and St. Jean-de-Luz bridge the Spanish and French Basque regions. Between them you'll find the functional towns of Irún (Spain), Hendaye (France)...and the delightful hill town of Hondarribia, which is worth a visit if you have time to spare.

Fuenterrabía / Hondarribia

For a taste of small-town *País Vasco,* dip into this enchanting, seldom-visited town (commonly known by its Euskara name rather than the Spanish version, Fuenterrabía). Much smaller and easier to manage than San Sebastián, and also closer to France (across the picturesque Bay of Txingudi from Hendaye), Hondarribia allows travelers a stress-free opportunity to enjoy Basque culture. While it's easy to think of this as a border town (between France and Spain), culturally it's in the middle of Basque Country.

The town comes in two parts: the lower port town and the historic, balcony-lined streets of the hilly and walled upper town. The upper town, which feels quite manicured, is a delightful place to poke around if you have time. The main square is fronted by Charles V's austere, oddly squat castle (now a parador inn—see below). You can follow the TI's self-guided tour of the old town (English brochure available) or just lose yourself within the walls to explore the plazas.

In the modern lower town, straight shopping streets serve a local clientele, and a pleasant walkway takes strollers along the beach.

Arrival in Hondarribia: Drivers can use the metered parking by the port (marked with blue lines, prepay for parking at machine). Buses into town stop near the TI.

Tourist Information: The TI is located where the lower town and the upper town meet, two blocks up from the port on Jabier Ugarte 6 (July–Sept daily 10:00–14:00 & 15:00–19:00; Oct–June Mon–Fri 9:00–13:30 & 16:00–18:30, Sat–Sun 10:00–14:00; tel. 943-645-458).

Sleeping: Accommodations are pricey here, but it's a nice small-town alternative to San Sebastián. **$$$ Parador El Emperador,** with 36 rooms housed in a former imperial fortress, is the town's splurge (Sb-€165, Db-€205, elevator, free Wi-Fi, Plaza de Armas 14, tel. 943-645-500, fax 943-642-153, www.parador.es, hondarribia@parador.es).

It Happened at Hendaye

If taking the train between the Spanish and French Basque regions, you'll change trains at the nondescript little Hendaye station. While it seems innocent enough, this was a site of a fateful meeting between two of Europe's most notorious 20th-century dictators.

In the days before World War II, Adolf Hitler and Francisco Franco maintained a diplomatic relationship. But after the fall of France, they decided to meet secretly in Hendaye to size each other up. On October 23, 1940, Hitler traveled through Nazi-occupied France, then waited impatiently on the platform for Franco's delayed train. The over-eager Franco hoped the Führer would invite him to join in a military alliance with Germany (and ultimately share in the expected war spoils).

According to reports of the meeting, Franco was greedy, boastful, and misguided, leading Hitler to dismiss him as a buffoon. Franco later spun the situation by claiming that he had cleverly avoided being pulled into World War II. In fact, his own incompetence is what saved Spain. Had Franco made a better impression on Hitler here at Hendaye, it's possible that Spain would have entered the war...which could have changed the course of Spanish, German, and European history.

Tourists are allowed to have sangria in the *muy* cool bar, though the terraces are for guests only. **$$$ Hotel San Nicolas,** facing the parador from across the square, offers a more affordable alternative, with 18 nicely appointed rooms (many with views) above a smoky local café (Sb-€70–90, Db-€90–100, higher price is for mid-July–mid-Sept, can be even cheaper Mon–Thu outside of summer, breakfast not included, elevator, free Wi-Fi, Plaza de Armas 6, tel. 943-644-278, fax 943-646-217, www.hotelsannikolas.com, info@hotelsannikolas.com).

TRANSPORTATION CONNECTIONS

From Hondarribia by Bus to: San Sebastián (about 3/hr, 30 min on express bus, departs from near TI—same bus also stops at airport; or twice as long on local public bus), **Hendaye** on the French border (2/hr, 20 min, June–Sept only). A bus stop in Hondarribia is across from the post office, one block below the TI.

By Boat to: Hendaye (4/hr in summer, 2/hr off-season, 10 min, runs about 11:00–19:00 or until dark).

French Basque Country
(Le Pays Basque)

Compared to their cousins across the border, the French Basques seem French first and Basque second. (But don't tell them that.) You'll see less Euskara writing here. But these destinations have their own special spice, mingling Basque and French influences with beautiful rolling countryside and gorgeous beaches. If you've been traveling in Spain, consider visiting (or even sleeping in) France for a change of pace. Your taste buds will thank you.

My favorite home base here is the central, comfy, and manageable resort village of St. Jean-de-Luz. It's a stone's throw to Bayonne (with its big-city bustle and fine Basque museum) and the snazzy beach town of Biarritz. A drive inland rewards you with a panoply of adorable French Basque villages. And St. Jean-de-Luz is a nice, relaxing place to "come home" to, with its mellow ambience, fine strolling atmosphere, and good restaurants.

St. Jean-de-Luz / Donibane Lohizune

St. Jean-de-Luz (san zhahn-duh-looz) sits happily off the beaten path, cradled between its small port and gentle bay. Pastry shops serve Basque specialties, and store windows proudly display berets (a Basque symbol). Ice-cream lickers stroll traffic-free streets, while soft, sandy beaches tempt travelers to toss their itineraries into the bay. The knobby little mountain La Rhune towers above the festive scene. Locals joke that if it's clear enough to see La Rhune's peak, it's going to rain, but if you can't see it, it's raining already.

The town has precious little of sightseeing importance. But it's a fine base for exploring the Basque Country, and a relaxing beach and port town that provides the most enjoyable dose of Basque culture in France. In July and August, the town fills with French tourists from the north—especially the first two weeks of August, when it's practically impossible to find a room without a reservation made long in advance.

ORIENTATION

St. Jean-de-Luz's old city lies between the train tracks, the Nivelle River, and the Atlantic. The main traffic-free street, rue Gambetta, channels walkers through the center, halfway between the train tracks and the ocean. The small town of Ciboure, across the river, holds

Dipping into France

If you're heading from Spain to France, you don't have to worry about border stops or currency changes (both countries use the euro). But here are a few other practicalities:

Phones: France's telephone country code is 33. Remember that Spanish phone cards and stamps will not work in France.

Hours: France typically does not use the same "siesta" system as Spain, so shops don't close for a midafternoon break. The French eat dinner closer to the European mainstream time (around 19:00–21:00)—not quite as late as Spaniards do.

Restaurant Tips: In France, if you ask for the *menu* (muh-noo), you won't get a list of dishes; you'll get a fixed-price meal. *Menus*, which include three or four courses, are generally a good value if you're hungry: You'll get your choice of soup, appetizer, or salad; your choice of three or four main courses with vegetables; plus a cheese course and/or a choice of desserts. Service is included (*service compris* or *prix net*), but wine and other drinks are generally extra.

French Survival Phrases: While some French Basques speak Euskara, most speak French in everyday life. You'll find these phrases useful (when using the phonetics, try to nasalize the "n" sound):

Good day.	***Bonjour.***	bohn-zhoor
Mrs. / Ma'am	***Madame***	mah-dahm
Mr. / Sir	***Monsieur***	muhs-yur
Please?	***S'il vous plaît?***	see voo play
Thank you.	***Merci.***	mehr-see
You're welcome.	***De rien.***	duh ree-ahn
Excuse me.	***Pardon.***	par-dohn
Yes. / No.	***Oui. / Non.***	wee / nohn
Okay.	***D'accord.***	dah-kor
Cheers!	***Santé!***	sahn-tay
Goodbye.	***Au revoir.***	oh vwahr
women / men	***dames / hommes***	dahm / ohm
one / two / three	***un / deux / trois***	uhn / duh / twah
Do you speak English?	***Parlez-vous anglais?***	par-lay voo ahn-glay

nothing of interest.

The only sight worth entering in St. Jean-de-Luz is the church where Louis XIV and Marie-Thérèse tied the royal knot (Eglise St. Jean-Baptiste, described below). St. Jean-de-Luz is best appreciated along its pedestrian streets, lively squares, and golden, sandy beaches. The park at the far eastern end of the beachfront promenade at Pointe Ste. Barbe makes a good walking destination, with views and walking trails.

Tourist Information

The helpful TI is next to the big market hall, along the busy boulevard Victor Hugo (July–Aug Mon–Sat 9:00–19:30, Sun 10:00–13:00 & 15:00–19:00; Sept–June Mon–Sat 9:00–12:30 & 14:00–19:00, Sun 10:00–13:00—except Jan–March, when it's closed Sun; 20 boulevard Victor Hugo, tel. 05 59 26 03 16, www.saint-jean-de-luz.com or www.terreetcotebasque.com).

Arrival in St. Jean-de-Luz

By Train or Bus: From the station, take the pedestrian underpass, then walk left along the busy street. To find the TI, take the first right turn (down Labrouche); the TI is at the far end of the market hall. Or, to reach the town center (place Louis XIV) from the busy road, stay straight around the traffic circle and carry on along avenue de Verdun, then turn right at the second traffic circle.

By Car: Follow signs for *Centre-Ville*, then *Gare* and *Office de Tourisme*. Parking (except on some peak summer days) is relatively easy: You can park in the big lot next to the bus station on the main road (about a five-minute walk to most hotels), or delve deeper into town looking for a smaller parking lot (at any lot, prepay at meter during daytime, free overnight). Hotels or the TI can advise you.

By Plane: The nearest airport is in Biarritz, 10 miles to the northeast. The tiny airport is easy to navigate, with a useful TI desk (airport tel. 05 59 43 83 83, www.biarritz.aeroport.fr). To reach St. Jean-de-Luz, you can take a public bus (€3, 7/day, fewer on Sun, 30 min, tel. 05 59 26 06 99 for schedule) or a 20-minute taxi ride (about €30).

Helpful Hints

Market Days: Tuesday and Friday mornings (and summer Saturdays), the farmers' stands spill through the streets from the Les Halles covered market on boulevard Victor Hugo, and seem to give everyone a whiff of "life is good" flavor.

Supermarkets: There's a **Petit Casino** grocery on rue Gambetta, just before boulevard Thiers (Mon–Sat 8:00–12:30 & 15:30–19:30, Sun 9:00–13:00 only, tel. 05 59 26 00 41). Or try the **Les Halles** market (above).

Internet Access: Run by friendly Irish ex-pats Margaret and Peter, **Internet World** is best (July–Aug Mon–Sat 9:00–24:00, Sun 10:00–18:00; Sept–June Mon–Sat 10:00–18:00, closed Sun; 7 rue Tourasse, tel. 05 59 26 86 92).

Laundry: Laverie du Port at 5 place du Maréchal Foch (full-service for €12/load available Mon–Fri 9:30–12:30 & 14:30–19:00, Sat 9:30–13:00, closed Sun; cheaper self-service available daily 7:00–21:00).

Car Rental: Avis, at the train station, is handiest (Mon–Fri 8:00–12:00 & 14:00–18:00, Sat opens at 9:00, closed Sun, tel. 05 59 26 76 66, fax 05 55 26 19 42).

SELF-GUIDED WALK

Welcome to St. Jean-de-Luz

To get a feel for the town, take this self-guided, two-mile walk. You'll start at the port and make your way to the historic church. Allow about one hour.

Port: Begin at the little working port (at place des Corsaires, just beyond the parking lot). Pleasure craft are in the next port over. While fishing boats used to catch lots of whales, now they take in cod, sardines, tuna, and anchovies, and take out tourists (two boats advertise today's and tomorrow's mini-Atlantic cruises and fishing excursions, summer only). St. Jean-de-Luz feels cute and nonthreatening now, but in the 17th century, it was home to the Basque Corsairs. With the French government's blessing, these pirates, who worked the sea—and enriched the town—moored here.

• *After you walk the length of the port, on your right is the tree-lined...*

Place Louis XIV: The town's main square, named for the king who was married here, is a hub of action. During the summer, the bandstand features traditional Basque music at 21:00 (almost nightly July–Aug, otherwise Sun and Wed). Facing the square is the City Hall (Herriko Etchea) and the "House of Louis XIV" (in which he lived for 40 festive days in 1660). A visit to this house is worthwhile only if you like period furniture (€5, open June–mid-Oct Wed–Mon, visits by guided tour only, 2–4/day, closed Tue and mid-Oct–May—when the privately owned mansion is occupied by the same family who've had it for over three centuries, tel. 05 59 26 27 58). The king's visit is memorialized by a small black equestrian statue at the entrance of the City Hall (a miniature of the huge one that marks the center of the Versailles courtyard).

• *Opposite the port on the far side of the square is...*

Rue de la République: From place Louis XIV, this historic lane—lined with mostly edible temptations—leads to the beach. Facing the square, the shop **Macarons Adam** still bakes (according to the family recipe) the macaroons Louis XIV enjoyed during his visit. You can try one (€0.90), or sample a less historic but just as tasty *gâteau basque,* a baked tart with a cream or jam filling (€1.70). Farther down rue de la République, you'll find the **Pierre Oteiza** shop, stacked with rustic Basque cheeses and meats from mountain villages (with a few samples generally out for the tasting). You'll likely eat on this lane tonight. **Kaiku,** the town's top restaurant, fills the oldest building in St. Jean-de-Luz (with its characteristic stone lookout tower), dating from the 1500s.

• *Continue to the...*

Beach: A high embankment protects the town from storm waters, but generally the Grande Plage—which is lovingly groomed daily—is the peaceful haunt of sun-seekers and happy children. Walk the elevated promenade (to the right). Various tableaux tell history

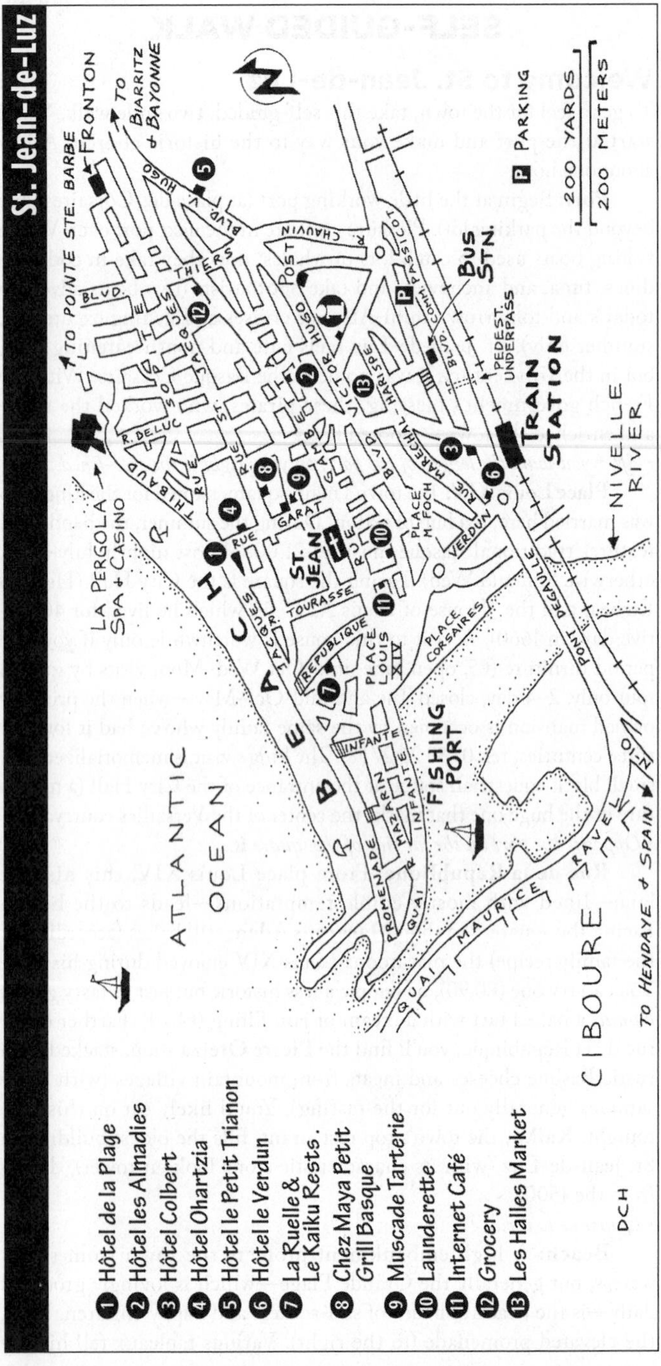

St. Jean-de-Luz
1 Hôtel de la Plage
2 Hôtel les Almadies
3 Hôtel Colbert
4 Hôtel Ohartzia
5 Hôtel le Petit Trianon
6 Hôtel le Verdun
7 La Ruelle & Le Kaiku Rests.
8 Chez Maya Petit Grill Basque
9 Muscade Tarterie
10 Launderette
11 Internet Café
12 Grocery
13 Les Halles Market
TO POINTE STE. BARBE
FRONTON
TO BIARRITZ & BAYONNE
LA PERGOLA SPA & CASINO
ATLANTIC OCEAN
BEACH
BLVD. THIERS
BLVD. V. HUGO
R. CHAUVIN
POST
R. DELUC
THIBAUD
RUE ST. JACQUES
RUE LÉON GAMBETTA
RUE GARAT
RUE VICTOR HUGO
BLVD. HARISPE
RUE MARÉCHAL FOCH
PLACE M. FOCH
BLVD. COMM. PASSICOT
PEDEST. UNDERPASS
BUS STN.
TRAIN STATION
ST. JEAN
RUE TOURASSE
JACQUES
RUE DE LA RÉPUBLIQUE
PLACE LOUIS XIV
PLACE CORSAIRES
VERDUN
PONT DEGAULLE
INFANTE
RUE MAZARIN
QUAI INFANTE
PROMENADE
FISHING PORT
QUAI MAURICE RAVEL
NIVELLE RIVER
CIBOURE
TO HENDAYE & SPAIN
200 YARDS
200 METERS
P PARKING
DCH

in French. Storms (including a particularly disastrous one in 1749) routinely knocked down buildings until Napoleon III built the three breakwaters in the 1800s.

• *Stroll past the late Art Deco–style La Pergola, which houses a casino and the Hélianthal spa center (entrance around back), and overlooks the beach. Anyone in a white robe strolling the beach is from the spa. Beyond La Pergola is the Neo-Romantic Grand Hôtel (c. 1900), with an inviting terrace for a coffee break. From here, dive back into town until you reach the bustling...*

Rue Gambetta: Turn right and circle back to your starting point, following the town's lively pedestrian shopping street. You'll notice many stores selling the renowned *linge Basque*—cotton linens such as tablecloths, napkins, and dishcloths, in the characteristic Basque red, white, and green.

• *Just before place Louis XIV, you'll see the town's main church...*

Eglise St. Jean-Baptiste: The marriage of Louis XIV and Marie-Thérèse put St. Jean-de-Luz on the map, and this church is where it all took place. The ultimate in political marriages, the knot tied between Louis XIV and Marie-Thérèse in 1660 also cinched a reconciliation deal between Europe's two most powerful countries. The king of Spain, Philip IV—who lived in El Escorial Palace—gave his daughter in marriage to the king of France, who lived in Versailles. This marriage united Europe's two largest palaces, which helped end a hundred years of hostility and forged an alliance that enabled both to focus attention on other matters (like England). Little St. Jean-de-Luz was selected for its 15 minutes of fame because it was roughly halfway between Madrid and Paris, and virtually on the France–Spain border. The wedding cleared out both Versailles and El Escorial palaces, as anyone who was anyone attended this glamorous event.

The church, centered on the pedestrian street rue Gambetta, seems modest enough from the exterior...but step inside (daily 8:00–12:00 & 14:00–18:00). The local expertise was in shipbuilding, so the ceiling resembles the hull of a ship turned upside down. The dark wood balconies running along the nave segregated the men from the women and children (men went upstairs until the 1960s) and were typical of Basque churches. The number of levels depended on the importance of the church, and this church, with three levels, is the largest Basque church in France. The three-foot-long paddle-wheel ship hanging in the center was a gift from Napoleon III's wife, Eugènie. It's a model of an ill-fated ship that had almost sunk just offshore when she was on it. The 1670 Baroque

Pelota

In keeping with their seafaring, shipbuilding, and metalworking heritage, Basque sports are often feats of strength: Who can lift the heaviest stone? Who can row the fastest and farthest?

But the most important Basque sport of all is *pelota*—similar to what you might know as jai alai. Players in white pants and red scarves or shirts use a long, hook-shaped wicker basket (called a *txistera* in Euskara, *chistera* in French, *remonte* in Spanish) to whip a ball (smaller and far bouncier than a baseball) back and forth off walls at more than 150 miles per hour. This men's-only game can be played with a wall at one or both ends of the court. Most matches are not professional, but betting on them is common. It can also be played without a racket—this slow-motion handball version is used as a starter game for kids.

It seems that every small Basque town has two things: a church and a *pelota* court (called *frontón*). While some *frontóns* are simple and in poor repair, others are freshly painted as a gleaming sign of local pride.

The TI in St. Jean-de-Luz sells tickets and has a schedule of matches throughout the area; you're more likely to find a match in summer (21:00, almost daily July–mid-Sept, afternoon matches sometimes on Sat–Sun). The professional *cesta punta* matches on Tuesdays and Fridays often come with Basque folkloric halftime shows.

altar feels Franco-Spanish and features 20 French saints. Locals call it the finest in Basque Country. Drop €1 in the box to see it light up. The place has great acoustics, and the 17th-century organ is still used for concerts (€10, mostly in summer, ask for schedule and buy tickets at TI). As you leave the church, turn left to find the bricked-up doorway—the church's original entrance. It was sealed after the royal marriage (shown on the wall to the right in a photo of a painting) to symbolize a permanent closing of the door on troubles between France and Spain.

SLEEPING

(€1 = about $1.50, country code: 33, * = French hotel rating system, 0–4 stars)

Hotels are a good value here. The higher prices are for peak season (generally June–Sept). In winter, some prices drop below those I've listed. Most hoteliers speak English. Breakfast costs extra, except for my first listing. Those wanting to eat and sleep for less will do slightly better just over the border, in San Sebastián.

$$$ Hôtel de la Plage* has the best location, right on the ocean. Its 22 rooms, 16 with ocean views, have a lively, yellow-and-blue, modern nautical decor (Db-€88–118, ocean view Db-€118–158, prices fluctuate with demand, family rooms, includes breakfast, air-con, elevator, Wi-Fi, garage-€12, 33 rue Garat, tel. 05 59 51 03 44, fax 05 59 51 03 48, www.hoteldelaplage.com, reservation@hoteldelaplage.com, run by friendly Pierre, Yannik, and Frederic).

$$$ Hôtel les Almadies*, on the main pedestrian street, is a bright boutique hotel with seven flawless rooms, comfy public spaces with clever modern touches, a pleasant breakfast terrace, and an owner who cares (Sb-€75–105, Db-€90–130, higher prices are for rooms with tubs, request room with little balcony for no extra charge, child's bed-€20, buffet breakfast-€11, free Wi-Fi, parking-€9, 58 rue Gambetta, tel. 05 59 85 34 48, fax 05 59 26 12 42, www.hotel-les-almadies.com, hotel.lesalmadies@wanadoo.fr, Monsieur and Madame Hargous will charm you with their Franglish).

$$$ Hôtel Colbert*, a Best Western, has 34 modern, tastefully appointed rooms across the street from the train station (Sb-€75–119, Db-€80–128, €10 extra for bigger "superior" rooms, breakfast-€13, air-con, elevator, free Wi-Fi, 3 boulevard du Commandant Passicot, tel. 05 59 26 31 99, fax 05 59 51 05 61, www.hotelcolbertsaintjeandeluz.com, contact@ hotelcolbertsaintjeandeluz.com).

$$ Hôtel Ohartzia** ("Souvenir"), one block off the beach, is comfortable, clean, peaceful, and characteristic, with the most charming facade I've seen. It comes with 17 simple but well-cared-for rooms and generous, homey public spaces. The highlight for me is the bird-chirping, flower-petaled garden in the back; the higher prices listed here are for the four rooms with bathtubs and views over this little Eden (mid-July–Sept Sb/Db-€79–89, April–mid-July Sb/Db-€68–72, Oct–March Sb/Db-€60–68, extra bed-€15, 28 rue Garat, tel. 05 59 26 00 06, fax 05 59 26 74 75, www.hotel-ohartzia.com, hotel.ohartzia@wanadoo.fr). Their desk is technically open only 8:00–20:00, but owners Madame and Monsieur Audibert (who speak little English) live in the building; their son Benoît speaks good English.

$$ Hôtel le Petit Trianon**, on a major street, is simple and traditional, with 26 nicely appointed rooms and accommodating staff (July–Sept Sb/Db-€75; mid-March–June and Oct–mid-Nov Sb-€58,

Db-€62; even less off-season, air-con, free Wi-Fi on lower floors, garage-€10, 56 boulevard Victor Hugo, tel. 05 59 26 11 90, fax 05 59 26 14 10, www.hotel-lepetittrianon.com, lepetittrianon@wanadoo.fr). To get a room over the quieter courtyard, ask for *côté cours* (coat-ay coor).

$ Hôtel le Verdun, above a dreary restaurant facing the train station, rents 11 basic rooms (the cheapest beds in town). It's often full off-season, when it houses seasonal laborers (D-€28–40, Ds-€33–50, Db/Tb-€45–65, €5 breakfast at downstairs café, 13 avenue de Verdun, tel. 05 59 26 02 55, www.hotel-leverdun.com, hotel.leverdun@wanadoo.fr, Henri).

EATING

St. Jean-de-Luz restaurants are known for offering good-value, high-quality cuisine. You can find a wide variety of eateries in the old center. For forgettable food with unforgettable views, choose from several places overlooking the beach. Most places serve from 12:15 to 14:00, and from 19:15 on. Remember, in France, *menu* means fixed-price, multi-course meal.

The traffic-free rue de la République, which runs from place Louis XIV to the ocean promenade, is lined with hardworking restaurants (two of which are recommended below). Places are empty at 19:30, but packed at 20:30. Making a reservation, especially on weekends or in summer, is wise. Consider a fun night of bar-hopping for dinner in San Sebastián instead (an hour away in Spain, described on page 127).

La Ruelle serves good, traditionally Basque cuisine—mostly seafood—in two tight little rooms jam-packed with tables, happy eaters, and kitschy Basque decor. André and his playful staff obviously enjoy their work, which gives this popular spot a relaxed and fun ambience. Portions are huge; their €18 *ttoro* (seafood stew) easily feeds two (€18–23 *menus,* closed Tue–Wed Oct–May, 19 rue de la République, tel. 05 59 26 37 80).

Le Kaiku is *the* gastronomic experience in town. They serve modern cuisine, specializing in "wild" (rather than farmed) seafood. The place is dressy, but offers a good time (*menus* for €35, €50, and €70; closed Tue–Wed, 17 rue de la République, tel. 05 59 26 13 20).

Chez Maya Petit Grill Basque serves hearty traditional Basque cuisine. Their €16 *ttoro* was a highlight of my day. They have €20 and €29 *menus,* but à la carte is more interesting. If you stick around in warm weather, you'll see the clever overhead fan system kick into action (closed all day Wed and Thu morning, 2 rue St. Jacques, tel. 05 59 26 80 76).

Fast and Cheap: Try the take-away crêpe stands on rue Gambetta. For a sit-down salad or a tart—either sweet or savory—consider **Muscade Tarterie** (€7–10 per slice, daily July–Aug, closed Mon Sept–June, 20 rue Garat, tel. 05 59 26 96 73).

TRANSPORTATION CONNECTIONS

The train station in St. Jean-de-Luz is called St. Jean-de-Luz-Ciboure. Its clever departure board displays lights next to any trains leaving that day. Buses leave from the green building across the street. There is reduced bus and rail service on Sundays and off-season.

From St. Jean-de-Luz by Train to: Bayonne (hourly, 25 min), **St. Jean-Pied-de-Port** (4/day, 6/day in summer, 1.5 hrs, transfer in Bayonne), **Paris** (4 direct/day, 5.5 hrs), **Bordeaux** (11/day, 2 hrs), **Sarlat** (4/day, 4 hrs, transfer in Bordeaux), **Carcassonne** (5/day, 6 hrs, transfers likely in Bayonne and Toulouse).

By Train to San Sebastián: First, take the 10-minute train to the French border town of Hendaye (Gare SNCF stop, about 10/day). Or get to Hendaye by bus (3/day, 35 min); check the schedule to see which leaves first.

Leave the Hendaye station to the right, and look for the light-blue EuskoTren building, where you'll catch the commuter train into San Sebastián (2/hour, generally at :03 and :33 after the hour 7:00–22:00, 30-min trip—faster but less frequent by bus). This milk-run train is known as the Topo ("Mole") train, since it goes underground part of the time.

By Bus: A Spanish bus runs to **San Sebastián** (2/day direct, Mon–Sat only, 45 min, runs only 1/week off-season, info in Spain tel. 902-101-210). Local bus #26 connects St. Jean-de-Luz either to **Bayonne** or **Biarritz** almost hourly. Confusingly, this one bus can run two different routes (one to Bayonne, the other to Biarritz Centre, 40 min to either one)—check the destination carefully. Another bus connects St. Jean-de-Luz to **Sare** (Mon–Tue and Thu–Fri 4/day, Wed 2/day, Sat 1/day, none Sun, 30 min).

By Taxi to: San Sebastián will cost you about €75 for up to four people, but it's convenient (tel. 05 59 26 10 11 or 06 25 76 97 69).

By Excursion Bus: The TI has information and sells tickets for popular day-trip excursions, including **Guggenheim Bilbao** (€35 round-trip, includes €12.50 museum admission, Wed only, departs 9:30 from bus terminal next to train station, returns 19:30). Other day trips are available (Ainhoa, Espelette, St. Jean-Pied-de-Port, and San Sebastián) on different days of the week.

Route Tips for Drivers

A one-day side-trip to both Bayonne and Biarritz is easy from St. Jean-de-Luz. These three towns form a sort of triangle (depending on traffic, each one is less than a 30-minute drive from the other). Hop on the autoroute to Bayonne, sightsee there, then take the N-10 road into Biarritz. Leaving Biarritz, continue along the coastal N-10. In Bidart, watch (on the right) for the town's proud *frontón* (*pelota* court). Consider peeling off to go into the village center of Guéthary, with another *frontón*. If you're up for a walk on the beach, cross the little bridge in Guéthary, park by the train station, and hike down to the walkway along the surfing beach (lined with cafés and eateries). When you're ready to move on, you're a very short drive from St. Jean-de-Luz.

Bayonne / Baiona

To feel the urban pulse of French Basque Country, visit Bayonne—modestly but honestly nicknamed "your anchor in the Basque Country" by its tourist board. With frequent, fast connections with St. Jean-de-Luz (25 min by train, 40 min by bus), Bayonne makes an easy half-day side-trip.

Come here to browse through Bayonne's atmospheric and well-worn yet lively Old Town, and to admire its impressive Museum of Basque Culture. Known for establishing Europe's first whaling industry and for inventing the bayonet, Bayonne is more famous today for its ham *(jambon de Bayonne)* and chocolate.

Get lost in Bayonne's Old Town. In pretty Grand Bayonne, tall, slender buildings, decorated in Basque fashion with green-and-red shutters, climb above cobbled streets. Make sure to stroll the streets around the cathedral and along the banks of the smaller Nive River, where you'll find the market (Les Halles).

ORIENTATION

Bayonne's two rivers, the grand Adour and the petite Nive, divide the city into three parts: St. Esprit, with the train station; and the more interesting Grand Bayonne and Petit Bayonne, which together make up the Old Town.

Tourist Information

The TI is in a modern parking lot a block off the mighty Adour River, on the northeastern edge of Grand Bayonne. They have very little in English other than a map and a town brochure (Mon–Fri 9:00–18:30, Sat 10:00–18:00, closed Sun except 10:00–13:00 in July–Aug, place des Basques, tel. 08 20 42 64 64).

Arrival in Bayonne

By Train: The TI and Grand Bayonne are a 10-minute walk from the train station: Walk straight out of the station, cross the traffic circle, and then cross the imposing bridge (pont St. Esprit). Once past the big Adour River, continue across a smaller bridge (pont Mayou), which spans the smaller Nive River. Stop on pont Mayou to orient yourself: You just left Petit Bayonne (left side of Nive River). Ahead of you is Grand Bayonne (spires of cathedral straight ahead, TI a few blocks to the right). The Museum of Basque Culture is in Petit Bayonne, facing the next bridge up the Nive River.

By Car and Bus: The handiest parking is also where buses arrive in Bayonne: next to the TI at the modern parking lot on the edge of Grand Bayonne. To reach the town center from here, first walk with the busy road on your left to the big park. Then turn right and walk with the park on your left-hand side. After a few blocks, you'll see atmospheric streets leading up to the cathedral on your right; if you continue straight, you'll reach the bridge over the Nive River called pont Mayou (described above).

To reach this parking lot, **drivers** take the *Bayonne Sud* exit from the autoroute, then follow green *Bayonne Centre* signs, then white *Centre-Ville* signs (with an *i* for tourist information). You'll see the lot on your right. In high season, when this lot can be full, use one of the lots just outside the center (follow signs to *Glain* or *Porte d'Espagne* as you arrive in town), then catch the little orange *navette* (shuttle bus) to get into the center (free, find route maps posted at stops in town, every 7 min, Mon–Sat 7:30–19:30, closed Sun).

SIGHTS

Museum of Basque Culture (Musée Basque)—This superb museum (in Petit Bayonne, facing the Nive River at pont Marengo) explains French Basque culture from cradle to grave—in French, Euskara, and Spanish. The only English you'll read is "do not touch" (unless you buy their informative English booklet for €5). Artifacts and videos take you into traditional Basque villages and sit you in the front row of time-honored festivals (€5.50, July–Aug daily 10:00–18:30, also open and free Wed evenings 18:30–21:30; Sept–June Tue–Sun 10:00–18:30, closed Mon; last entry one hour before closing, 37 quai des Corsaires, tel. 05 59 59 08 98, www.musee-basque.com).

On the ground floor, you'll begin by walking through some 16th-century gravestones, then see a display of carts and tools used in rural life. Look for the *laiak*—distinctive forked hoes used to work the ground. At the end of this section, you'll watch a grainy film on Basque rural lifestyles.

The next floor up begins by explaining that the house *(etxea)* is the building-block of Basque society. More than just a building, it's a social institution—Basques are named for their house, not vice versa. You'll see models and paintings of Basque houses, then domestic items, a giant door, kitchen equipment, and furniture (including a clever combination bench-table, near the fireplace). After an exhibit on Basque clothing, you'll move into the nautical life, with models, paintings, and actual boats. The little door leads to a model of the port of Bayonne in 1805, back when it was a highly strategic walled city.

Upstairs, you'll learn that the religious life of the Basques was strongly influenced by the Camino de Santiago pilgrim trail, which passes through their territory. One somber room explains Basque funeral traditions. The section on social life includes a video of Basque dances (typically accompanied by flute and drums). These are improvised, but according to a clearly outlined structure—not unlike a square dance. The prominence given to the sport of *pelota* (see sidebar on page 168) indicates its importance to these people. One dimly lit room shows off several types of baskets *(chistera),* gloves, and balls used for the game, and videos show how these items are made. The museum wraps up with a brief lesson on the region's history from the 16th to the 20th centuries, including exhibits on the large Jewish population here (who had fled from a hostile Spain) and the renaissance of Basque culture in the 19th century.

Cathédrale Ste. Marie—Bankrolled by the whaling community, this cathedral sits dead-center in Grand Bayonne and is worth a peek (free, Mon–Sat 10:00–11:45 & 15:00–17:45, Sun 15:30–18:00). Find the unique keystones on the ceiling along the nave, then circle behind the church to find the peaceful 13th-century cloisters (free, daily 9:00–12:30 & 14:00–17:00, until 18:00 mid-May–mid-Sept).

Sweets Shops—With no more whales to catch, Bayonne turned to producing mouthwatering chocolates and marzipan; look for shops on the arcaded rue du Port Neuf (running between the cathedral and the Adour River).

Ramparts—The ramparts around Grand Bayonne are open for walking and great for picnicking (access from park at far end of TI parking lot). However, the ramparts do not allow access to either of Bayonne's castles—both are closed to the public.

EATING

Le Bayonnais, next door to the Museum of Basque Culture, serves traditional Basque specialties à la carte. Sit in the blue-tiled interior or out along the river (€15–25 main dishes, €16 lunch *menu,* closed Sun–Mon, quai des Corsaires 38, tel. 05 59 25 61 19).

La Cidrerie Txotx (pronounced "choch") has a Spanish-bodega ambience under a chorus line of hams. Or you can sit outside, along the river just past the market hall (€7–10 Basque tapas or €12–16 *plats*, daily, 49 quai Jauréguiberry, tel. 05 59 59 16 80).

A la Bolée serves up €6–9 sweet and savory crêpes in a cozy atmosphere along the side of the cathedral (daily, 10–11 place Pasteur, tel. 05 59 59 18 75).

If the weather is good, consider gathering a **picnic** from the pedestrian streets and head for the park around the ramparts below the *Jardin Botanique* (benches galore).

TRANSPORTATION CONNECTIONS

From Bayonne, you can reach **St. Jean-de-Luz** by bus (#26, almost hourly, 40 min) or by train (hourly, 25 min). To **Biarritz**, the bus is best (take the unfortunately named "STAB" bus #1 to reach Biarritz Centre, departs every 10 min, takes 20 min). There's also a train from Bayonne up to **St. Jean-Pied-du-Port** (4/day, 6/day in summer, 1 hr). Bus #23 takes you to the inland Basque villages of **Espelette** and **Ainhoa** (4/day Mon–Fri only, none Sat–Sun, 25 min to Espelette, 35 min to Ainhoa).

Biarritz / Biarritz

A glitzy resort town steeped in the belle époque, Biarritz (BEE-ah-ritz) is where the French Basques put on the ritz. In the 19th century, this simple whaling harbor became, almost overnight, a high-class aristocrat-magnet dubbed the "beach of kings." While St. Jean-de-Luz and Bayonne are more fully French and more fully Basque, the made-for-international-tourists, jet-set scene of Biarritz is not without its charms. Perched over a popular surfing beach, anchored by grand hotels and casinos, hemmed in by jagged and picturesque rocky islets at either end, and watched over by a lighthouse on a distant promontory, Biarritz offers perhaps the most picturesque stretch of the French Basque coastline.

ORIENTATION

Biarritz feels much bigger than its population of 30,000. The town sprawls, but virtually everything we're interested in lines up along the waterfront: the beach, promenade, hotel and shopping zone, and TI.

Arrival in Biarritz

By Car: Drivers follow signs for *Centre-Ville,* then carefully track signs for specific parking garages. The most central garages are called *Grande Plage, Casino, Bellevue,* and *St. Eugénie.* Signs in front of each one tell you if it's full *(complet),* in which case, move on to the next one.

By Bus: Buses stop at "Biarritz Centre," a parking lot next to the TI (STAB buses to/from Bayonne stop along the side of the lot, while buses to/from St. Jean-de-Luz stop at the end of the lot). If you're taking a bus, be aware that some stop at the outskirts of town—only take one to "Centre."

Don't bother taking the **train** to or from Biarritz, as the station is about two miles from the tourist area (buses #2 and #9 connect the train station to the city center).

There is no baggage storage in Biarritz.

Tourist Information

The TI is in a little pink castle two blocks up from the beach (just above the beach and casino, hiding behind the City Hall/*hôtel de ville*—look for signs). Pick up the free map and get details on any sightseeing that interests you (July–Aug daily 9:00–19:00; Sept–June Mon–Fri 9:00–18:00, Sat–Sun 10:00–17:00; Square d'Ixelles, tel. 05 59 22 37 10, www.biarritz.fr).

SIGHTS

There's little of "sightseeing" value in Biarritz. The TI can fill you in on the town's four museums (Marine Museum—described below; Chocolate Planet and Museum—intriguing, but a long walk from the center; Oriental Art Museum—large and diverse collection of art from across Asia; and Biarritz Historical Museum—really?).

Your time is best spent strolling along the various levels that climb up from the sea. From the TI, you can do a loop: First head west on the lively **pedestrian streets** that occupy the plateau above the water, which are lined with restaurants, cafés, and high-class, resorty "window-licking." (Place Georges Clemenceau is the grassy "main square" of this area.)

Work your way out to the point with the **Marine Museum** (Musée de la Mer). The most convenient of Biarritz's attractions, this pricey museum/aquarium wins the "best rainy-day option" award, with a tank of seals and a chance to get face-to-teeth with live sharks (€8, hours vary based on season, daily April–Oct, closed Mon Nov–March, tel. 05 59 22 33 34, www.museedelamer.com).

Whether or not you're visiting the museum, it's worth hiking down to the entrance, then wandering out on the walkways that connect the big offshore rocks. These lead to the so-called **Virgin**

Rock (Rocher de la Vierge), topped by a statue of Mary. Spot any surfers? Europe generally isn't known for its surfing... but Biarritz is the exception.

From here, stick along the water as you head back toward the TI. After a bit of up and down over the rocks, don't miss the trail down to **Fishermen's Wharf** (Port des Pêcheurs), a little pocket of salty authenticity that clings like barnacles to the cliff below the hotels. The remnants of an aborted construction project from the town's glory days, this little fishing settlement of humble houses and rugged jetties seems to faintly echo the Basque culture that thrived here before the glitz hit. Many of the houses have been taken over by the tourist trade (gift shops and restaurants).

Continuing along the water (and briefly back up to street level), make your way back to the town's centerpiece, the **big beach** (Grande Plage). Dominating this inviting stretch of sand is the Art Deco casino, and the TI is just above that. If you haven't yet taken the time on your vacation to splash, wade, or stroll on the beach...now's your chance.

TRANSPORTATION CONNECTIONS

Biarritz is connected by bus #26 to **St. Jean-de-Luz** (nearly hourly, 40 min). Buses run by the company called "STAB" take you to **Bayonne** (#1, departs every 10 min, takes 20 min).

Villages in the French Basque Country

Traditional villages among the green hills, with buildings colored like the Basque flag, offer the best glimpse at Basque culture. Cheese, hard cider, and *pelota* players are the primary products of these villages, which attract few foreigners but many French summer visitors. Most of these villages have welcomed pilgrims bound for Santiago de Compostela since the Middle Ages. Today's hikers trek between local villages or head into the Pyrenees. The most appealing villages lie in the foothills of the Pyrenees, spared from beach-scene development.

Use St. Jean-de-Luz as your base to visit the Basque sights described below. For information on another French Basque village a bit farther away—St. Jean-Pied-de-Port (Donibane Garazi)—see page 186 in the Camino de Santiago chapter. You can reach some of these places by public transportation, but the hassle outweighs the rewards.

Do a circuit of these towns in the order they're listed here (and, with time, also add St. Jean-Pied-de-Port at the end). Assuming you're driving, I've included route instructions, as well.

• *From St. Jean-de-Luz, follow signs for* Ascain, *then* Sare. *On the road toward Sare, you'll pass the station for the train up to...*

La Rhune / Larrun

Between the villages of Ascain and Sare, near the border with Spain, a small cogwheel train takes tourists to the top of La Rhune, the region's highest peak (2,969 feet). You'll putt-putt up the hillside for 30 minutes in an open-air train car to reach panoramic views of land and sea (€14 round-trip for adults, €8 for kids, runs mid-March–mid-Nov, departures weather-dependent—so the trip is worthless if it's not clear, departures every 35 min when busiest in July–Aug, tel. 05 59 54 20 26, www.rhune.com).

• *Continue along the same road to...*

Sare / Sara

Sare, which sits at the base of the towering mountain La Rhune, is among the most picturesque villages—and the most touristed. It's easily reached from St. Jean-de-Luz by bus or car. The small TI is on the main square (Mon–Fri 9:30–12:30 & 14:00–18:00, Sat 9:30–12:30, closed Sun, tel. 05 59 54 20 14). Nearby is a cluster of hotels and the town church (which has an impressive interior, with arches over the altar and Basque-style balconies lining the nave). At the far end of the square is the town's humble *frontón*.

• *Leaving Sare, first follow signs for* St. Pée, *then watch for the turnoff to...*

Ainhoa / Ainhoa

Ainhoa is a colorful, tidy, picturesque one-street town that sees fewer tourists (which is a good thing). Its chunks of fortified walls and gates mingle with red-and-white, half-timbered buildings. The 14th-century church—with a beautiful golden *retable* (screen behind the altar)—and the *frontón* (*pelota* court) share center stage.

Ainhoa is also a popular starting point for hikes into the hills. For a spectacular village-and-valleys view, drive five minutes (or walk 90 sweaty minutes) up the steep dirt road to the Chapelle de Notre-Dame d'Aranazau ("d'Aubepine" in French). Start in the parking lot directly across the main street from the church, then head straight uphill. Follow signs for *oratoire,* then count the giant white crosses to the top.

• *As you leave Ainhoa, you'll have to backtrack the way you came in to find the road to...*

Espelette / Ezpeleta

Espelette won't let you forget that it's the capital of the region's AOC red peppers *(piments d'Espelette),* with strands of them dangling like good-luck charms from many houses and storefronts. After strolling the charming, cobbled center, wander downhill at the end of town to find the town church and the well-restored château and medieval tower, which now houses the town hall, an exhibition, and the TI (Mon–Fri 8:30–12:30 & 14:00–18:00, Sat 9:30–12:30, closed Sun, tel. 05 59 93 95 02).

Sleeping and Eating: For a good regional meal, consider the **$ Hôtel Euzkadi** restaurant, with a *muy* Spanish ambience (€25–32 *menus,* daily 12:30–14:00 & 19:30–21:00, closed Mon–Sun off-season, 285 Karrika Nagusia, tel. 05 59 93 91 88). The hotel has 27 rooms with modern touches and a swimming pool (Sb-€41–43, Db-€52–65, air-con, elevator, free Wi-Fi, www.hotel-restaurant-euzkadi.com).

• *From Espelette, if you have time, you can simply follow signs to* St. Jean-Pied-de-Port *(see page 186).*

THE CAMINO DE SANTIAGO

St. Jean-Pied-de-Port • Pamplona • Burgos • León • O Cebreiro • Lugo

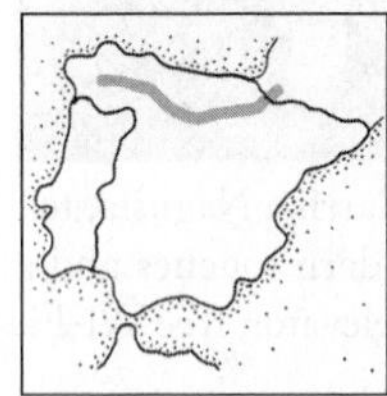

The Camino de Santiago—the "Way of St. James"—is Europe's best pilgrimage route. Since the Middle Ages, humble pilgrims have trod hundreds of miles across the north of Spain to pay homage to the remains of St. James in his namesake city, Santiago de Compostela. After several lonely centuries, today the route has been rediscovered, and more and more pilgrims are traveling—by foot, bike, and horse—along this ancient pathway.

While dedicating a month of your life to walk the Camino is admirable, you might not have that kind of time. But with a car (or public transportation), any traveler can use the Camino as a sightseeing spine—a string of worthwhile cities, towns, and countryside sights—and an opportunity to periodically "play pilgrim."

Begin in the French foothills of the Pyrenees, in the Basque village of St. Jean-Pied-de-Port. Twist up and over rugged Roncesvalles Pass into Spain, and on to Pamplona—the delightful, Basque-flavored capital of Navarre, famous for its Running of the Bulls. From here, head west through the fertile hills of Navarre to the vineyards of La Rioja, then across the endless wheat fields and rough, arid plains of northern Castile to Burgos and León, with their beautiful dueling Gothic cathedrals—one a riot of architectural styles, the other gracefully simple but packed with stained glass. As the path crosses into Galicia near the time-passed, stony mountain village of O Cebreiro, the terrain changes, becoming lush and green. This last leg of the journey, in Galicia, is the most popular: Pilgrims pass simple farms, stone churches, moss-covered homes with slate roofs, apple orchards, flocks of sheep, dense forests of oak, sweet chestnut, and eucalyptus... and plenty of other pilgrims. Just before Santiago, the ancient walled Roman city of Lugo is a worthwhile detour for car travelers.

Camino de Santiago Overview

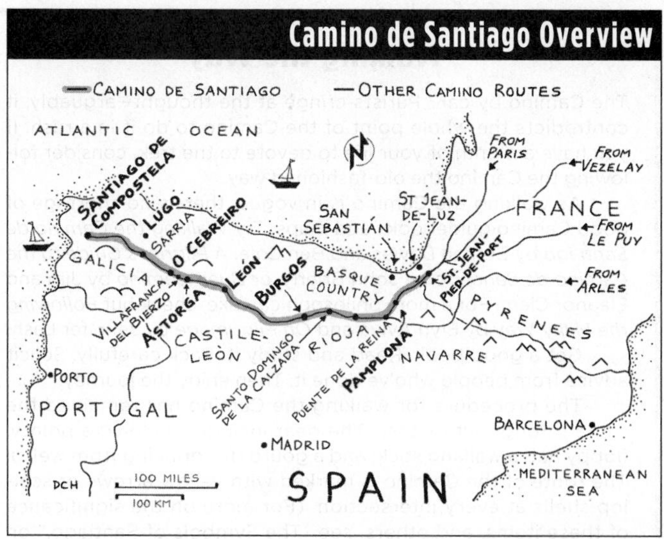

Whether undertaken for spiritual edification or sightseeing pleasure, the Camino de Santiago ties together some of Spain's most appealing landscape, history, architecture, and people.

Getting Around the Camino de Santiago

By Car: This chapter is geared for car pilgrims who want to trace the Camino and linger at the highlights. Directions marked by • are designed for drivers (with specific route tips, road numbers, and directional signs). To supplement these instructions, it's essential to get a good road map (most TIs can give you a free map covering just their province, or you can buy a better one by Michelin or Mapa Total for about €6). Driving the full Camino nonstop would take about 12 hours. Assuming you're taking the most direct (expressway/*autovía*) route, figure these estimated times for specific legs of the Camino by car (these times don't take into account stops or detours, such as the La Rioja Wine Loop):

- St. Jean-Pied-de-Port to Pamplona—1.5 hrs
- Pamplona to Burgos—3.5 hrs
- Burgos to León—2 hrs
- León to Astorga—1 hr
- Astorga to O Cebreiro—1.5 hrs
- O Cebreiro to Lugo—1 hr
- Lugo to Santiago—1.5 hrs

Many freeways are marked *Autovía Camino de Santiago* to keep you on track. But be warned that *Camino de Santiago* directional signs in small towns can be misleading, since they're sometimes intended for foot pilgrims, not drivers—navigate by town names and road numbers instead.

Walking the Way

The Camino by car? Purists cringe at the thought—arguably, it contradicts the whole point of the Camino to do it in a rush. If you have a month of your life to devote to the trek, consider following the Camino the old-fashioned way.

As walking the Camino is in vogue, there's no shortage of good Camino guidebooks and maps. Try *Walking the Camino de Santiago* by Bethan Davies and Ben Cole, *A Pilgrim's Guide to the Camino de Santiago* by John Brierly, or *Buen Camino* by Jim and Eleanor Clem. For a more philosophical take, check out *Following the Milky Way* by Elyn Aviva and *On Pilgrimage* by Jennifer Lash.

Get a good book. Read and study it. Pack carefully. Solicit advice from people who've done it. Then enjoy the journey.

The procedure for walking the Camino has remained the same throughout history. The gear includes a cloak; a pointy, floppy hat; a walking stick; and a gourd (for drinking from wells). The route of the Camino is marked with yellow arrows or scallop shells at every intersection. (For more on the significance of these items, and others, see "The Symbols of Santiago," on page 190.)

Early in the journey, pilgrims buy their "credential" *(credencial)*—a sort of passport, which they get stamped and dated at churches and lodgings along the way. (They can also show it to stay at cheap *refugios* and to get a reduced pilgrim's rate at many museums and churches en route.) At the end, they present their stamped credential in Santiago and receive a special certificate called a *compostela*. Only those who meet the two principal criteria qualify: You must do the pilgrimage for "spiritual" reasons; and you must walk at least the last 100 kilometers (about 62 miles, roughly from Sarria) or ride your bike or horse the last 200 kilometers (124 miles) into Santiago.

Doing the entire French Road from the border to Santiago takes about four to six weeks on foot (averaging 12–15 miles per day, with an occasional rest day—32 days is a typical Camino). Bikers can do it in about two weeks. Many of the trails, originally dirt paths, are now being paved. The journey itself is a type of hut-hopping: At regular intervals along the route (about every 5–10 miles), pilgrims can get a bunk for the night at humble little hostels called *albergues* (ahl-BEHR-gehs), *refugios* (reh-FOO-hee-ohs), or *hospitales* (oh-spee-TAH-lehs). Some of these are run by the government (€5–10 per bunk, closer to €3 in Galicia, even if

they're "free" a donation is requested; no reservations taken—first-come, first-served, with priority given to credential-holding pilgrims arriving on foot). Others are privately run (typically a bit more expensive—€10-20—and sometimes take reservations). A wide variety of other accommodations are available for those who prefer more comfort, ranging from simple *hostales* to grand hotels and paradors (I've listed my favorites in this chapter).

What began as a religious trek to atone for one's sins has evolved into a journey undertaken by anyone—spiritual or secular—who just wants some time to think. While some pilgrims do the trip for "fun," those who take it seriously caution that it's one of the most wrenching things you can do. After a few weeks on the Camino, many pilgrims begin to develop a telltale limp...you'll notice it getting more pronounced as you move west. (There's a reason old pilgrim hostels are sometimes called "hospitals.")

But there are worse things than blisters and sore muscles. The Camino can take a psychological toll on pilgrims. Trudging step after step across endless plains toward an ever-receding horizon, you're forced to introspection. Religious or not, you can't help but come to terms with your regrets, demons, "sins," or anything else that's on your conscience.

This process of self-reflection is symbolized by picking up a small stone somewhere early on the Camino, then depositing it at the Iron Cross near the end of the trek (see page 230)—releasing yourself from whatever's been weighing you down. The absolution of sins that awaited medieval pilgrims isn't so different from the "find myself" motives of today's iPhone-toting tourists. Whether you're pardoned by the Church, or simply allow yourself to let go of what's been nagging you, it's liberating all the same.

On a lighter note, a wonderful pilgrim camaraderie percolates along the length of the Camino, as a United Nations of vagabonds—young and old—swap stories and tips. Driving, on foot, or on bike, you'll keep crossing paths with the same pilgrims again and again...the guy who checked in before you at the hotel last night is at the cathedral with you the next morning. Along the way, the standard greeting (like a Jacobean "Happy Travels") is *"Buen Camino!"*

No matter how you get to Santiago, you'll share in the jubilation pilgrims have felt through the ages when—four miles out of town—the spires of the cathedral come into view.

Cheap Tricks on the Camino de Santiago

- If you're a credentialed pilgrim, you can walk the Camino cheaply—beds cost only €3-10 per night, grub is hearty and affordable, churches and museums often offer discounted admission, and the locals have spent centuries perfecting their pilgrim hospitality.
- Even if you're not an official pilgrim, you can enjoy some of the same deals (such as cheap meals). Inexpensive accommodations geared for pilgrims (though not official municipal ones) often also accept non-pilgrims.
- **Pamplona**'s Running of the Bulls is free, and many backpackers don't even bother with accommodations (sleep in the parks, shower at the public washrooms on Calle Hilarión Eslava).
- In **Burgos,** the Huelgas Monastery is free on Wednesdays; the Museo de Burgos is free on weekends (Sat-Sun); and the Centro de Arte is always free.
- **León**'s glorious stained-glass-filled cathedral is free to enter.
- You can enter **Astorga**'s cathedral free in the morning (9:00-11:00).
- The lost-in-a-time-warp hilltop retreat of **O Cebreiro** won't cost you a penny to visit (*pallozas* and town church are both free to enter).
- Both of **Lugo**'s main attractions—the remarkably intact town walls and the cathedral—are free.

By Public Transportation: Most of the Camino route can be done by bus and/or train. However, it can be difficult, or even impossible, to reach some of the out-of-the-way stops between the big cities (such as O Cebreiro), and there's no good, direct link from St. Jean-Pied-de-Port to Pamplona. Where feasible, I've listed train and bus connections for each of the main stops.

The Old-Fashioned Way: If you're walking or biking the entire Camino, don't rely exclusively on my coverage in this chapter (which describes the major towns and cities, but ignores so much more). Equip yourself with a good day-by-day guidebook with details on each leg, and get good advice about what to pack. For starters, see the "Walking the Way" sidebar on page 182.

Planning Your Time

Drivers begin in Basque Country (San Sebastián in Spain or St. Jean-de-Luz in France), where you can pick up your rental car. If you're in a hurry or don't plan to visit France, you can skip St. Jean-Pied-de-Port and connect easily to Pamplona from Spain's Basque Country.

Day 1: Drive through the French Basque villages (see page 177) to St. Jean-Pied-de-Port, then over Roncesvalles Pass to Pamplona. Sleep in Pamplona.

Day 2: Explore Pamplona, then drive westward to Burgos (stopping en route at Puente de la Reina, and detouring for the La Rioja Wine Loop if you have time and a healthy interest in wine). Sleep in Burgos.

Day 3: Sightsee Burgos this morning, then drive to León and dip into the cathedral there. Sleep in León—or, if you're tired of big cities, continue an hour farther to sleep in Astorga.

Day 4: Continue westward to Galicia, stopping at O Cebreiro and Lugo before arriving at Santiago de Compostela.

ORIENTATION

The term "Camino de Santiago" actually refers to several different routes, beginning in different parts of Spain, France, Portugal, and beyond. All (like this chapter) travel from east to west. The most popular has always been the so-called "French Road" (Camino Francés), which covers nearly 500 miles across northern Spain from the French border to Santiago—and that's the route described here. We'll begin in the French Basque town of St. Jean-Pied-de-Port, cross over the Pyrenees at Roncesvalles, then pass through three northern Spanish cities (Pamplona, Burgos, León), before climbing into green Galicia, ending at Santiago de Compostela.

Tourist Information: Pilgrims will find no shortage of helpful resources along the way. In addition to TIs in each town (listed in this chapter), you'll also find "Pilgrim Friend" associations and other offices (often attached to an *albergue* or *refugio*) that offer kind advice to the weary traveler.

Holy Year: The Compostela Holy Year *(Ano Xacobeo)* is celebrated in years when the Feast of St. James (July 25) falls on a Sunday—next in 2010. Traffic on the trails doubles, and the pilgrim atmosphere is even more festive.

Tours: Iberian Adventures runs guided and self-guided walking tours in English for individuals and small groups along the Camino de Santiago and in the La Rioja wine region. Company owner Jeremy Dack highlights each area's natural environment, history, culture, cuisine, and wine, and emphasizes environmental awareness and respect for local customs (mobile 620-939-116, www.iberianadventures.com, info@iberianadventures.com). Jeremy also leads hiking tours of Spain's major mountain ranges.

St. Jean-Pied-de-Port / Donibane Garazi

Just five miles from the Spanish border, the walled town of St. Jean-Pied-de-Port (sahn zhahn-pee-duh-por) is the most popular village in all the French Basque countryside. Traditionally, St. Jean-Pied-de-Port has been the final stopover in France for Santiago-bound pilgrims, who gathered here to cross the Pyrenees together and continue their march through Spain. The scallop shell of "St. Jacques" (French for "James") is etched on walls throughout the town.

Visitors to this town are equal parts pilgrims and French tourists. Gift shops sell a strange combination of pilgrim gear (such as quick-drying shirts and shorts) and Basque souvenirs. This place is packed in the summer (so come early or late).

ORIENTATION

Tourist Information

The TI, on the main road along the outside of the walled Old Town, can give you a town map (hours vary, generally July–Aug Mon–Sat 9:00–19:00, Sun 10:00–12:00; Sept–June Mon–Sat 9:00–12:00 & 14:00–18:00, Sun 10:00–12:00; maybe less in winter; tel. 08 10 75 36 71). For Camino information, you'll do better at the Pilgrim Friends Office (described below).

Arrival in St. Jean-Pied-de-Port

Parking is ample and well-signed from the main road. If arriving by **train,** exit the station to the left, then follow the busy road at the traffic circle toward the city wall.

SIGHTS

There's little in the way of sightseeing here, other than pilgrim-spotting. But St. Jean-Pied-de-Port feels like the perfect "Welcome to the Camino" springboard for the upcoming journey. Many modern pilgrims begin their Camino in this traditional spot because of its easy train connection to Bayonne, and because—as its name implies

Best Stages for a Short Walk

The Camino de Santiago is divided into stages of about 12–15 miles apiece (approximately one day's walk). Even if you're doing most of the Camino by car, consider taking an extra day or two to walk one of these recommended stages. These are scattered throughout the Camino, and listed from east to west.

Roncesvalles to Zubiri (21.5 km/13.5 miles)—This is the first stage in Spain, after the arduous trek over the Pyrenees. It's mostly (though not entirely) downhill, through rolling hills and meadows, amidst sheep and charming villages.

Puente de la Reina to Estella (19 km/12 miles)—Here the Camino becomes a bit more level and arid. This leg begins in an appealing pilgrim town, then passes through gentle farm fields and along a three-and-a-half-mile stretch of Roman road (from Cirauqui to Lorca).

Pieros to Villafranca del Bierzo (7.5 km/5 miles)—For this stretch, the Camino ascends through the hilly El Bierzo region, en route to Galicia. The last bit of this leg takes you through vineyards and vegetable patches into Villafranca, entering town at the Romanesque church of Santiago.

Ambasmestas to O Cebreiro (13.2 km/8.2 miles)—If you're not intimidated by a steep uphill hike, this leg is a gorgeous introduction to Galicia—culminating at the perfect little hilltop village.

Sarria to Portomarin (21.5 km/13.5 miles)—Because it's about 100 kilometers (62 miles) from Santiago (the minimum to qualify for a *compostela* certificate), Sarria is a popular starting point for short-haul pilgrims. From here, you can make it to Santiago in less than a week. The terrain: pretty Galicia.

("St. John at the Foot of the Pass")—it offers a very challenging but rewarding first leg: up, over, and into Spain.

Cross the old bridge over the Nive River (the same one that winds up in Bayonne) to the **Notre-Dame Gate,** which was once a drawbridge. Then head up the main walking drag, **rue de la Citadelle.** With its rosy-pink buildings and ancient dates above its doorways, this lane simply feels old. Notice lots of signs for *chambres* (rooms) and *refuges*—humble, hostel-like pilgrim bunkhouses.

Partway up, on the left at #39, look for the **Pilgrim Friends Office** (Les Amis du Chemin de Saint-Jacques, daily 7:30–12:00 & 13:30–20:30 & 21:30–22:30, tel. 05

59 37 05 09). This is where pilgrims check in before their long journey to Santiago; 32,000 pilgrims started out here last year (compared to just 4,000 a decade ago). For €2, a pilgrim can buy the official credential *(credenciel)* that she'll get stamped at each stop between here and Santiago to prove she walked the whole way and earn her *compostela* certificate. Pilgrims also receive a warm welcome, lots of advice, and help finding a bunk (the well-traveled staff swears that no pilgrim ever goes without a bed in St. Jean-Pied-de-Port).

A few more steps up, you'll pass the skippable €3 Bishop's Prison (Prison des Evêques, on the left). Continue on up to the **citadel,** dating from the mid-17th century—when this was a highly strategic location, keeping an eye on the easiest road over the Pyrenees between Spain and France. While not open to the public (as it houses a school), the grounds around this stout fortress offer sweeping views over the French Basque countryside.

SLEEPING

(* = French hotel rating system, 0–4 stars)

Lots of humble pilgrim dwellings line the main drag, rue de la Citadelle. If you're looking for a bit more comfort, consider these options.

$$ Hotel Ramuntcho** is the only real hotel option in the Old Town, located partway up rue de la Citadelle. Its 16 rooms above a restaurant are straightforward but modern (Sb-€64–74, Db-€70–79, 1 rue de France, tel. 05 59 37 03 91, fax 05 59 37 35 17, http://perso.wanadoo.fr/hotel.ramuntcho, hotel.ramuntcho@wanadoo.fr).

$$ Itzalpea, a café and tea house, rents five rooms along the main road just outside the Old Town (Db-€60–76 depending on size, includes breakfast, air-con, 5 place du Trinquet, tel. 05 59 37 03 66, fax 05 59 37

Sleep Code

(€1 = about $1.50, France country code: 33, Spain country code: 34)

S = Single, **D** = Double/Twin, **T** = Triple, **Q** = Quad, **b** = bathroom, **s** = shower only. Unless otherwise noted, credit cards are accepted and English is spoken. Breakfast is generally not included.

To help you easily sort through these listings, I've divided the rooms into three categories, based on the price for a standard double room with bath during high season (breakfast and 7 percent IVA tax not included):

$$$ Higher Priced—Most rooms €95 or more.
$$ Moderately Priced—Most rooms between €55–95.
$ Lower Priced—Most rooms €55 or less.

33 18, www.maisondhotes-itzalpea.com, itzalpea@wanadoo.fr).

$ Chambres Chez l'Habitant has five old-fashioned, pilgrim-perfect rooms along the main drag. Welcoming Maria and Jean Pierre speak limited English, but their daughter can help translate (€20 per person in D, Db, Q, or Qb, includes breakfast, 15 rue de la Citadelle, tel. 05 59 37 05 83).

TRANSPORTATION CONNECTIONS

A scenic train conveniently links St. Jean-Pied-de-Port to **Bayonne** (4/day, 6/day in summer, 1 hr), and from there to **St. Jean-de-Luz** (about 30 min beyond Bayonne). It's about a 1.25-hour drive from St. Jean-de-Luz. Unfortunately, there are no buses from St. Jean-Pied-de-Port to **Pamplona;** to connect them by public transport, you'll have to go back to Bayonne, then to San Sebastián, then catch a bus or train to Pamplona from there.

Between St. Jean-Pied-de-Port and Pamplona

The first stretch of Camino, crossing the Pyrenees from France into Spain, is among the most dramatic. While there's little in the way of civilization, it's a memorable start for the journey.

• *From St. Jean-Pied-de-Port, follow road signs to* Arnéguy *on road D-933. (But be warned that the road signs for the Camino de Santiago take a much more roundabout, high-mountain, one-lane road instead of the direct road to the border.)*

Crossing the Pyrenees: Roncesvalles (Roncevaux / Orreaga)

As you go over the stone bridge in the village of **Arnéguy,** you're also passing from France to Spain. For centuries, this bridge was the site of a delicate dance between nervous smugglers and border guards. Today you'll barely notice you've crossed a border.

The road meanders through a valley before twisting up to the pass called **Puerto de Ibañeta** (also known as the Roncesvalles Pass). This scrubby high-mountain pass is one of the Basque Country's most historic spots. The most accessible gateway through the Pyrenees between France and Spain, this pass has been the site of several epic battles. According to a popular medieval legend, Charlemagne's nephew Roland was killed fighting here. Vengeful Basque tribes, seeking retribution for Charlemagne's sacking of Pamplona, followed the army as it began its return to France—and felled the mighty Roland along this very road. Several centuries later, Napoleon used the same road to invade Spain.

The Symbols of Santiago

The pilgrim route leading to Santiago de Compostela—and the city itself—are rife with symbolism. Here are a few of the key items you'll see along the way.

- **St. James:** The Camino's namesake is also its single biggest symbol. St. James can be depicted three ways: as a pilgrim, as an apostle, and as a Crusader (slaughtering Moors). For more, see "The Three Santiagos," on page 250.
- **The Scallop Shell *(Vieira)*:** Since scallops are so abundant on the Galician coast, their shells are associated with Santiago throughout Europe. Though medieval pilgrims only carried shells with them on the return home—to prove they'd been here, and to scoop water from wells—today's pilgrims also carry them on the way *to* Santiago. The yellow sideways shell that looks like a starburst marks the route for bikers.

- **The Gourd:** Gourds were used by pilgrims to drink water and wine.
- **The Yellow Arrow:** These arrows direct pilgrims at every intersection from France to Santiago.
- **The Red Cross:** This long, skinny cross with curly ends at the top and sides, and ending in a sword blade at the bottom, represents the Knights of Santiago. This 12th-century Christian military order had a dual mission: to battle Muslim invaders while providing hospice and protection to pilgrims along the Camino de Santiago.
- **The Tomb and Star:** St. James' tomb (usually depicted as a simple coffin or box), and the stars that led to its discovery, appear throughout the city of Santiago, either together or separately.

Coming down from the pass, you reach **Roncesvalles / Orreaga** ("Valley of Pines"), which gave this area its name. This jumble of buildings surrounding a monastery is sort of a pilgrim depot, where travelers can pause to catch their collective breath after clearing the first arduous leg of the Camino. The big building on the right is a simple *refugio,* filled with bunk beds. In the afternoon, you might see pilgrims washing

their clothes at the spigots in front, then hanging them to dry amidst the cows and knobby trees out back. The big church (on the left) has a tourable cloister and museum (€4). As you leave town, you pass the first sign for Santiago de Compostela...790 kilometers (490 miles) straight ahead.

From here to Pamplona, the Camino passes through some pretty rolling hills and meadows, and several appealing villages. The first after Roncesvalles, called **Auritz / Burguete,** was supposedly Hemingway's favorite place to fish for trout when he needed to recover from a Pamplona bender.

• *Around that next bend is the first big city on the Camino: Pamplona.*

Pamplona / Iruña

Proud Pamplona, with stout old walls standing guard in the Pyrenees foothills, is the capital of the province of Navarre ("Navarra" in Spanish). At its peak in the Middle Ages, Navarre was a grand kingdom that controlled parts of today's Spain and France. (The current king of Spain, Juan Carlos, is a descendant of the French line of Navarre royalty.) After the French and Spanish parts split, Pamplona remained the capital of Spanish Navarre.

Today Pamplona feels at once affluent (with the sleek new infrastructure of a town on the rise), claustrophobic (with its warren of narrow lanes), and fascinating (with its odd traditions, rich history, and ties to Hemingway). Culturally, the city is a lively hodgepodge of Basque and *Navarro*. Locals like to distinguish between *Vascos* (people of Basque citizenship—not them) and *Vascones* (people who identify culturally as Basques—as do many *Navarros*).

And, of course, Pamplona is best known as the host of one of Spain's (and Europe's) most famous festivals: the Running of the Bulls (held in conjunction with the Fiesta de San Fermín, July 6–14). But there's more to this town than bulls—and, in fact, visiting at other times is preferable to the crowds and 24/7 party atmosphere that seize Pamplona during the festival. Contrary to the chaotic or even backwards image that its famous festival might suggest, you'll find Pamplona welcoming, sane, and enjoyable.

ORIENTATION

Pamplona has about 200,000 people. Most everything of interest is in the tight, twisting lanes of the Old Town (Casco Antiguo), centered on the main square, Plaza del Castillo. The newer Ensanche ("Expansion") neighborhood just to the south—with a sensible grid plan—holds several good hotels and the bus station.

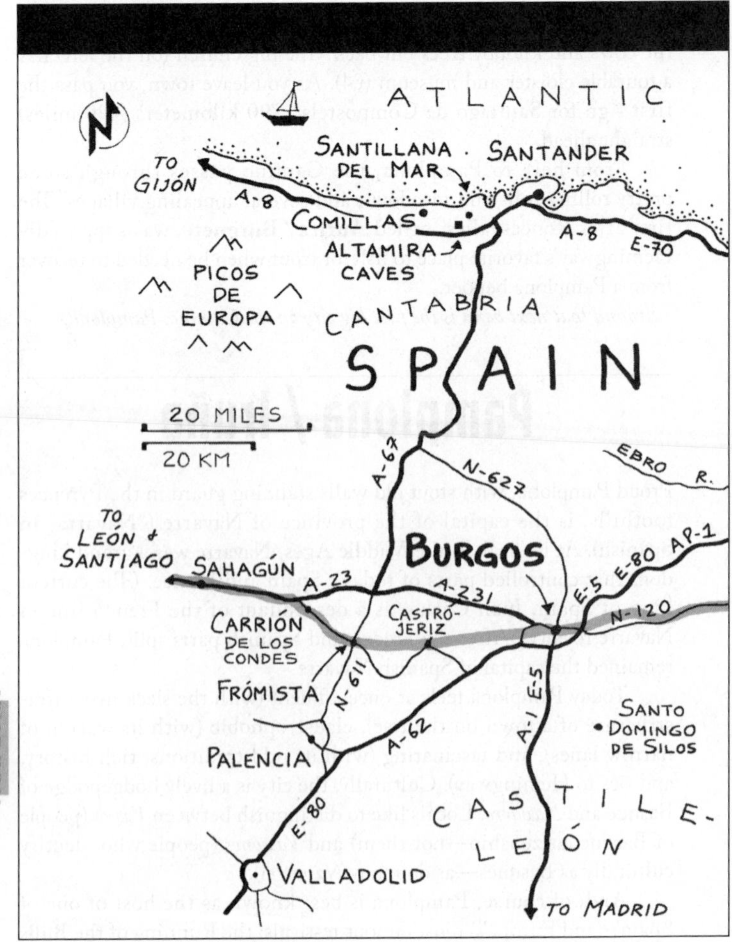

Tourist Information

Pamplona's well-organized TI overlooks a small square called Plaza de San Francisco in the heart of the Old Town. Pick up the handy map/guide and get your questions answered (Mon–Sat 10:00–14:00 & 16:00–19:00, Sun 10:00–14:00, longer hours possible July–Aug, Eslava 1, tel. 848-420-420).

Local Guide: Francisco Glaría is a top-notch guide who enjoys leading visitors through Pamplona (€140/half-day up to 4 hours, tel. 948-383-755, mobile 629-661-604, www.novotur.com, novotur@novotur.com).

Camino de Santiago: Eastern Half

Arrival in Pamplona

You can store bags at the bus station, but not at the train station.

By Bus: The sleek, new, user-friendly bus station is underground along the western edge of the Ensanche area, about a 10-minute walk from the Old Town sightseeing zone. On arrival, go up the escalator, cross the street, turn left, and walk a half-block, where you can turn right down the busy Conde Oliveto street. Along this street, you're near several of my recommended accommodations; or you can walk two blocks to the big traffic circle called Plaza Príncipe de Viana. From here, turn left up Avenida de San Ignacio to reach the Old Town.

By Train: The RENFE station is farther from the center, across the river to the northwest. It's easiest to hop on public bus #9 (every 12–20 min), which drops you at the big Plaza Príncipe de Viana traffic circle

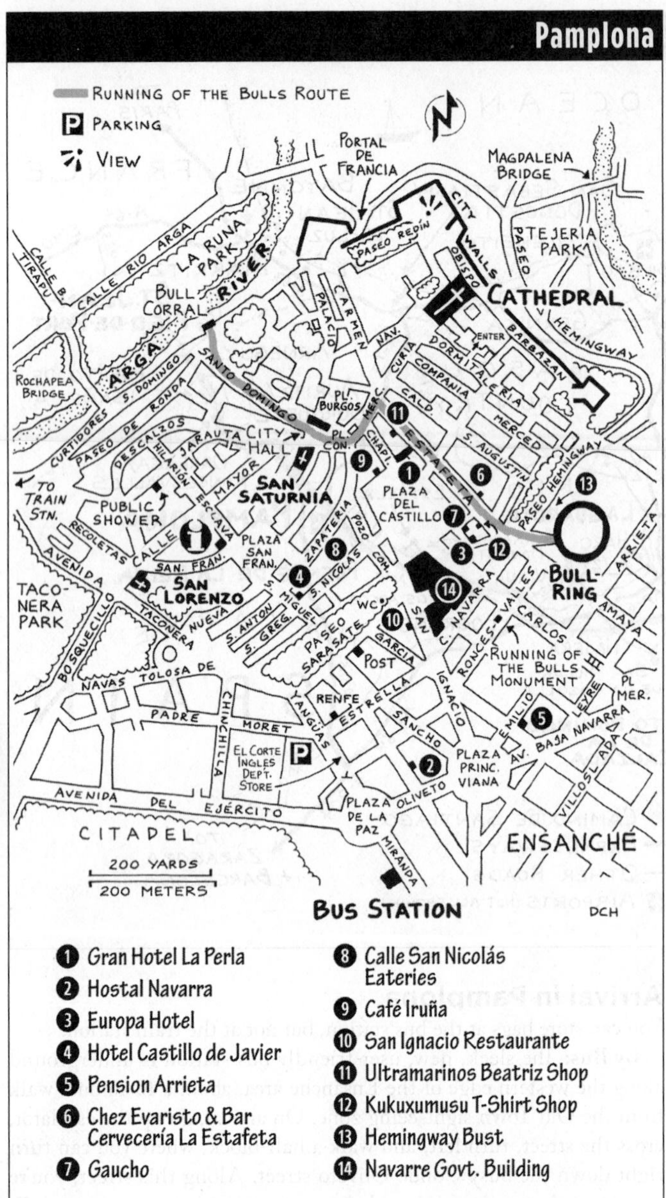
Pamplona
Running of the Bulls Route
Parking
View
Portal de Francia
Magdalena Bridge
City Walls
Paseo Redín
Tejeria Park
Paseo
Obispo
Cathedral
Enter
Barbazan
Hemingway
La Runa Park
Calle Rio Arga
Calle B. Tirapu
Bull Corral
River
Arga
Palacio
Carmen
Nav.
Curia
Dormitaleria
Compania
Rochapea Bridge
S. Domingo
Santo Domingo
Pl. Burgos
Merc.
Cald.
Merced
Curtidores
Paseo de Ronda
Descalzos
Jarauta
City Hall
Pl. Con.
Chapl.
Estafeta
S. Augustin
Paseo Hemingway
Hilarión
Mayor
San Saturnia
Plaza del Castillo
To Train Stn.
Public Shower
Escaya
Zapateria
Pozo
Recoletas
Calle
San. Fran.
Plaza San Fran.
S. Nicolas
Com.
Bull-Ring
Arrieta
Avenida
Taconera Park
San Lorenzo
S. Miguel
Navarra
Valles
Carlos
Amaya
Bosquecillo
Taconera
Nueva
S. Anton
S. Greg.
Paseo Sarasate
WC
San
C. Navarra
Garcia
Post
Ronces-
Ignacio
Running of the Bulls Monument
Navas Tolosa de
Chinchilla
Yanguas
Renfe
Estrella
Leyre
Pl. Mer.
Padre
Moret
Sancho
Emilio
El Corte Ingles Dept. Store
Plaza Princ. Viana
Av. Baja Navarra
Villosl Ada
Avenida del Ejército
Olivetó
Plaza de la Paz
Citadel
Ensanche
200 Yards
200 Meters
Miranda
Bus Station
DCH
1 Gran Hotel La Perla
2 Hostal Navarra
3 Europa Hotel
4 Hotel Castillo de Javier
5 Pension Arrieta
6 Chez Evaristo & Bar Cervecería La Estafeta
7 Gaucho
8 Calle San Nicolás Eateries
9 Café Iruña
10 San Ignacio Restaurante
11 Ultramarinos Beatriz Shop
12 Kukuxumusu T-Shirt Shop
13 Hemingway Bust
14 Navarre Govt. Building

south of the Old Town (described above).

By Car: Everything is well-marked: Simply follow the bull's-eyes to the center of town, where individual hotels are clearly signposted. There's also handy parking right at Plaza del Castillo.

By Plane: The Pamplona Airport is located about four miles outside the city (tel. 902-404-704, www.aena.es). Bus #21 connects the airport to downtown (€1, 1–2/hr, less on weekends).

SELF-GUIDED WALK

The Walking of the Tourists

Even if you're not in town for the famous San Fermín festival, you can still get a good flavor of the town by following in the foot- and hoof-steps of its participants. This walk takes you through the town center along the same route of the famous Running of the Bulls.

• *Begin in front of the...*

City Hall (Ayuntamiento): When Pamplona was just starting out, many Camino pilgrims who had been "just passing through" decided to stick around. They helped to build the city you're enjoying today, but tended to cling to their own regional groups, which squabbled periodically. So in 1423, the King of Navarre (Charles III) tore down the internal walls and built a City Hall here to unite the community. This version (Neo-Baroque, from the 18th century) is highly symbolic: Hercules demonstrates the city's strength, while the horn-blower trumpets Pamplona's greatness.

The festival of San Fermín begins and ends on the balcony of this building (with the flags). When the bulls start running, they come in this direction from the street to the left of the City Hall. Look for the line of metal circles in the pavement, used to secure barricades for the run. There are four rows, creating two barriers on each side. The inner space is for press and emergency medical care, while spectators line up along the outer barrier. This first stretch is uphill, allowing the bulls to use their strong hind legs to pick up serious momentum.

• *Follow the route of the bulls one block down Mercaderes street (next to Alexander Jewelry), until you reach the 90-degree right turn onto...*

La Estafeta Street: At this turn, the bulls—who are now going downhill—begin to lose their balance, often sliding into the barricade. (Note that if you want to visit the cathedral—described on page 199—it's just up the skinny lane called Curia from this corner.)

Once the bulls regain their footing, they charge down the middle of La Estafeta. Notice how narrow this street is: No room for

PAMPLONA

The Running of the Bulls: Fiesta de San Fermín

"A San Fermín pedimos, por ser nuestro patrón, nos guíe en el encierro, dándonos su bendición."

"We ask San Fermín, because he is our Patron, to guide us through the Running of the Bulls, giving us his blessing."

For nine days each July, a million visitors pack into Pamplona to watch a gang of reckless, sangria-fueled adventurers thrust themselves into the path of an oncoming herd of furious bulls. Locals call it *el encierro* (literally, "the enclosing"—as in, taking the beasts to be enclosed in the bullring)...but everyone else knows it as the "Running of the Bulls."

The festival begins at the City Hall on noon on July 6, with various events filling the next nine days and nights. Originally celebrated as the feast of San Fermín—who is still honored by a religious procession through town on July 7—it has since evolved into a full slate of live music, fireworks, general revelry, and an excuse for debauchery. After dark, the town erupts into a rollicking party scene. To beat the heat, participants chug refreshing sangria or *kalimotxo* (*calimocho* in Spanish)—half red wine, half cola. The town can't accommodate so many guests, so some visitors day-trip in from elsewhere (such as San Sebastián), and many young tourists simply pass out in city parks overnight (public showers are on Calle Hilarión Eslava in the Old Town).

The Running of the Bulls takes place each morning of the festival and is broadcast nationwide on live TV. The bulls' photos appear in the local paper beforehand, allowing runners to size up their opponents. If you're here to watch, stake your claim at a vantage point along the outer barrier by 6:30 or 7:00 in the morning. Don't try to stand along the inner barrier—reserved for press and medical personnel—or you'll be evicted when the action begins.

Before the run starts, runners sing a song to San Fermín (see lyrics above) three times to ask for divine guidance. Soon the bulls will be released from their pen near Cuesta Santo Domingo. From here, they'll stampede a half-mile through the town center... with thrill-seekers called *mozos* (and female *mozas*) running in front of the herd, trying to avoid a hoof or horn in the rear end.

Mozos traditionally wear white with strips of red tied around their necks and waists, and carry a newspaper to cover the bull's eyes when they're ready to jump out of the way. Two legends explain the red-and-white uniform: One says it's to honor San

Fermín, a saint (white) who was martyred (red); the other says that the runners dress like butchers, who began this tradition.

At 8:00, six bulls are set loose. The beginning of the run is marked by two firecrackers—one for the first bull to leave the pen, and another for the last bull. The animals charge down the street, while the *mozos* try to run in front of them for as long as possible before diving out of the way. The bulls are kept on course by fencing off side-streets (with openings just big enough for *mozos* to escape). Shop windows and doors are boarded up.

A bull becomes most dangerous when separated from the herd. For this reason, a few steer—who are calmer, slower, have bigger horns, and wear a bell—are released with the bulls, and a few more trot behind them to absorb angry stragglers and clear the streets. (There's no greater embarrassment in this *machismo* culture than to think you've run with a bull...only to realize later that you actually ran with a steer.)

The bulls' destination: the bullring...where they'll be ceremonially slaughtered as the day's entertainment. (For more on bullfighting, see page 651 in the appendix.)

If you're considering running with the bulls yourself, it's essential to equip yourself with specific safety information not contained in this book. Locals suggest a few guidelines: First, understand that these are very dangerous animals, and running with them is entirely at your own risk. Be as sober as possible, and wear good shoes to protect your feet from broken glass and from being stepped on by bulls and people. (Runners wearing sandals might be ejected by police.) You're not allowed to carry a backpack, as its motion could distract the bulls. If you fall, never stand up—it's better to be trampled by six bulls than to be gored by one. Ideally, try to get an experienced *mozo* to guide you on your first run.

Cruel as this all seems to the bulls—who scramble for footing on the uneven cobblestones as they rush toward their doom in the bullring—the human participants don't come out unscathed. Each year, dozens of people are gored, trampled, or otherwise injured. Over the last century, 15 runners have been killed at the event. But far more people have died from overconsumption of alcohol.

If you feel bad for the bulls—or the *mozos*—consider coming a day or two before the festival starts for the "Human Race" (a.k.a. "Running of the Nudes"), when topless and scantily clad people take to the course...with no gory results. It's part of a bullfighting protest sponsored by People for the Ethical Treatment of Animals (www.runningofthenudes.com).

The festival ends at midnight on July 14 when the townspeople congregate in front of the City Hall, light candles, and sing their sad song, *"Pobre de Mí"*: "Poor me, the Fiesta de San Fermín has ended."

barricades... no escape for *mozos.*

On days that the bulls aren't running, La Estafeta is one of the most appealing streets in Pamplona. It's home to some of the best tapas bars in town (see "Eating," on page 202). Because the Old Town was walled right up until 1923, space in here was at a premium—making houses tall and streets narrow.

Partway down the first block on the right, look for the hole-in-the-wall **Ultramarinos Beatriz** shop (at #22)—makers of the best treats in Pamplona (Mon–Fri 9:00–14:00 & 16:30–20:00, Sat 9:00–14:00, closed Sun, tel. 948-220-618). Anything with chocolate is good, but the mini-croissants are sensational. They come in two types: *garrotes de chocolate,* filled with milk chocolate; or *cabello de angel,* filled with sweet fibers (€3 for a box of six). So simple... but oh so good.

Halfway down the street, notice the alley on the right leading to the main square (we'll circle back to the square later). Farther down, near the very end of La Estafeta (on the right, at #76), look for the shop called **Kukuxumusu**—Euskara for "the kiss of a flea." These whimsical cartoon T-shirts are a local favorite. The giant digital clock outside the shop counts down to the next Running of the Bulls.

• *La Estafeta eventually leads you right to Pamplona's...*

Bullring: At the end of the run, the bulls charge down the ramp and through the red door. The bullring is used only nine days each summer (during the festival). Bullfights start at 18:00, and tickets are expensive. But the price plummets if you buy tickets from scalpers after the first or second bull. The audience at most bullfights is silent, but Pamplona's spectators are notorious for their raucous behavior. They're known to intentionally spill things on tourists just to get a reaction...if you respond with a laugh and a positive attitude, they'll respect you and you'll have the time of your life.

PAMPLONA

Look for the big bust of **Ernest Hemingway,** celebrated by Pamplona as if he were a native son. Hemingway came here for the first time during the 1923 Running of the Bulls. Inspired by the spectacle and the gore, he later wrote about the event in his bullfighting classic *The Sun Also Rises.* He said that he enjoyed seeing two wild animals running together: one on two legs, and the other on four. This literary giant put Pamplona and its humble, obscure bullfighting festival on the world map; visitors come from far and wide even today, searching for adventure in Hemingway's Pamplona. He came to his last Running of the Bulls in 1959 and reportedly regretted the attention his writing had brought to what had been a simple local festival. But the people of Pamplona appreciate "Papa" as one of their own. At the beginning of the annual festival, young people tie a red neckerchief around this statue so Hemingway can be properly outfitted for the occasion.

• *Walk a half-block along the right side of the bullring, then cross the busy street and walk a block into the pedestrian zone to the life-size...*

Running of the Bulls Monument (Monumento al Encierro): This new statue (from 2007) shows six bulls, two steer, and 10 runners in action. Find the self-portrait of the sculptor (bald, lying down, and about to be gored). The statue has quickly become a local favorite, but is not without controversy: There are 10 *mozos* but no *mozas*—where are the female runners?

• *From here, you can turn right and walk two blocks up the street to the main square...*

Plaza del Castillo: While not as grand as Spain's top squares, there's something particularly cozy and livable about Pamplona's. It's dominated by the Navarre government building (sort of like a state capitol). Several Hemingway sights surround this square. The Hotel Perla in the corner was his favorite place to stay. It recently underwent a head-to-toe five-star renovation, but they kept Hemingway's room exactly as he liked it, right down to the furniture he sat at while writing...and two balconies overlooking the bull action on Estafeta street (see listing in "Sleeping," page 201). He also was known to frequent Bar Txoko at the top of the square (as well as pretty much every other bar in town) and the venerable Café Iruña at the bottom of the square. Café Iruña actually has a separate "Hemingway Corner" room, with a life-size statue of "Papa" to pose with (see listing in "Eating," page 202).

• *You've survived the run. Now enjoy the rest of Pamplona's sights.*

SIGHTS

▲Cathedral (Catedral)

The Camino de Santiago is lined with great cathedrals, but—frankly—Pamplona's is an also-ran. Still, the cathedral does have some unique sights and a fine museum that are worth a visit.

Cost and Hours: €4.40, Mon–Fri 10:00–14:00 & 16:00–19:00 (no lunch break mid-July–mid-Sept), Sat 10:00–14:00, closed Sun, tel. 948-222-990.

➲ **Self-Guided Tour:** The cathedral—a Gothic core wrapped in a Neoclassical shell—is a bit drab from the outside. But the inside is more appealing. Head up the street to the right, follow signs for *entrada a museo,* buy your ticket, go inside, and turn right into the **museum.** The highlight here is the fascinating collection of old Mary sculptures from local village churches. Since they're displayed chronologically, you can actually watch artistic styles evolve. The earliest ones, from the 12th century, show a very stiff, uncaring Mary—she's not touching, or even looking at, the Baby Jesus, who's perched stiffly on her lap like a ventriloquist's dummy. But as women gained more power in the 13th century, we see Mary loosen up and morph into a good mother—smiling, playfully holding the orb (representing perfection), and finally (gasp!) touching her baby with her hands. In the 14th century, Mary boldly stands up and even cradles Jesus. And by the 17th century, she's looking like a real mother.

The museum is displayed in the former refectory of the monks. Find the small, attached room where you can peer up inside the five gigantic chimneys. Exiting the museum, notice the fountain at the corner of the cloister—used to wash up at mealtime.

Continue around the cloister and find the side entrance into the cathedral. Above the door, see the depiction of the Dormition (death) of Mary...with Jesus up above, returning the favor of her evolving maternity by cradling her soul like a baby.

The cathedral interior is Gothic. In the **choir,** look for the statue nicknamed "Mary of the Adopted Child." The Baby Jesus was stolen from this statue in the 16th century and replaced with a different version...which looks nothing like his mother.

The prominent **tomb** dominating the middle of the nave holds Charles III (the king of Navarre who united the disparate groups of Pamplona) and his wife. The blue fleur-de-lis pattern is a reminder that the kings of Navarre once controlled a large swath of France. Notice that Charles' face is realistic, indicating that it was sculpted while he was still alive, while his wife's face is idealized—done after she died. Around the base of the tomb, monks from various orders mourn the couple's death.

In the back-left corner chapel, find the **crucifix**—shockingly realistic for the Gothic age in which it was created (compare it to the more typical one in the next chapel over). It's said that if the dangling lock of hair touches Jesus' chest, the world will end.

Behind the cathedral (take the street through the tree-lined square along the left side of the cathedral, as you face it), don't miss the chance to see part of Pamplona's imposing **city walls**—designed to defend against potential invaders from the Pyrenees, still 80 percent intact, and now an inviting parkland. Belly up to the overlook, with views across the city's suburban sprawl. Beyond those hills on the horizon are San Sebastián and the Bay of Biscay. Camino pilgrims enter town through the gate below and on the left. This area is popular with people who are in town for the Running of the Bulls but didn't make hotel reservations. Sadly, it's not unusual for people to fall asleep on top of the wall...then roll off to their deaths.

Other Churches

As a prominent town on a pilgrim route, Pamplona has its share of other interesting churches. These two are worth a quick visit. They're both on the Camino through town; to reach them, simply head west along Calle Mayor from the City Hall Square (where the self-guided walk begins).

Church of San Saturnino—The most important pilgrim church in Pamplona, this is an architectural combination: 15th-century Gothic in front, 18th-century Baroque in back. Duck inside (free, Mon–Sat 9:15–12:30 & 18:00–20:00, Sun from 10:00). This is where pilgrims can get their credential stamped (someone's usually on duty in the pews). At the end across from where you enter, you'll see an altar with the Holy Virgin of the Camino. As you continue your journey, you'll notice that most churches along the Camino are dedicated to Mary. According to legend, when St. James himself came on a missionary trip through northern Spain, he suffered a crisis of faith around Zaragoza (not far from here). But, inspired by the Virgin, he managed to complete his journey to Galicia. Pilgrims following in his footsteps find similar inspiration from Mary today.

Church of San Lorenzo—Though San Fermín is a big name in town, he doesn't have a church of his own. But you will find him in a giant side-chapel of this church, overlooking the ring road at the edge of the Old Town (free, Mon–Fri 8:15–12:00 & 18:30–20:00, Sat–Sun 8:15–12:00 & 18:00–20:00). Enter the church and turn right down the transept to find the statue of **San Fermín,** dressed in red and wearing a gold miter (tall hat). Pamplona was founded by the Roman Emperor Pompey (hence the name) in the second century B.C. Later, a Roman general here became the first in the empire to allow Christians to worship openly. The general's son—Fermín—even preached the word himself...until he was martyred. Fermín has been the patron saint here ever since. Just below the statue's Adam's apple, squint to see a reliquary holding Fermín's actual finger. The statue—gussied up in an even more over-the-top miter and staff—is paraded around on Fermín's feast day, July 7, which was the origin of today's bull festival. This chapel is the most popular place in town for weddings.

SLEEPING

(€1 = about $1.50, country code: 34)

Because Pamplona is a business-oriented town, prices go up during the week; on weekends (Fri–Sun), you can usually score a discount. When I've listed a range, you can assume the high prices are for weekdays (Mon–Thu). All prices go way, way up for the San Fermín festival, when you must book as far in advance as possible.

$$$ Gran Hotel La Perla is the town's undisputed top splurge. Hemingway's favorite hotel, sitting right on the main square, has recently undergone a top-to-bottom five-star renovation. Its 44 rooms offer luxury at Pamplona's best address (standard Db-€230, bigger and fancier rooms-€270–450, breakfast-€25, air-con, elevator, Plaza del Castillo 1, tel. 948-223-000, fax 948-222-234, www.granhotellaperla.com, informacion@granhotellaperla.com). Well-heeled lit-lovers can drop €450 for a night in the Hemingway room, still furnished as it was when "Papa" stayed there (with a brand-new bathroom grafted on the front).

$$ Hostal Navarra is the best value in Pamplona, with 15 modern, well-maintained, clean rooms. Near the bus station, but an easy walk from the Old Town, it's well-run by Miguel (Sb-€45, Db-€60, includes tax, breakfast-€7, non-smoking, free Wi-Fi, Calle Tudela 9, tel. 948-225-164, fax 948-223-426, www.hostalnavarra.com, info@hostalnavarra.com).

$$ Europa Hotel, a few blocks off the square, offers 21 rooms with reasonable prices for its high class and ideal location (Sb-€69–78, Db-€75–89, breakfast-€9.50, non-smoking rooms, air-con, elevator, free Wi-Fi, Espoz y Mina 11, tel. 948-221-800, fax 948-229-235, www.hreuropa.com, europa@hreuropa.com). The ground-floor restaurant is a well-regarded splurge.

$$ Hotel Castillo de Javier, right on the bustling San Nicolás bar street (request a quieter back room), rents 19 simple, new-feeling rooms (Sb-€45, Db-€62, includes tax, breakfast-€4.30, air-con, elevator, free cable Internet, Calle San Nicolás 50–52, tel. 948-203-040, fax 948-203-041, www.hotelcastillodejavier.com, info@hotelcastillodejavier.com). This is a step up from the several cheap *hostales* that line the same street.

$ Pension Arrieta is an old-fashioned budget option renting 12 basic rooms in two buildings in the new part of town. Carmen and Maximo don't speak English, but their daughter does (D-€45, Db-€55, a few euros more July–Sept, Arrieta 27, tel. 948-228-459).

EATING

Tapas on La Estafeta: The best concentration of trendy tapas bars is on and near the skinny drag called La Estafeta. Along this street, you'll find **Chez Evaristo** (daily, at #69, tel. 948-207-752) and **Bar Cervecería La Estafeta** (daily, at #54, tel. 948-222-157). Around the corner, just a few steps off the main square, is the popular **Gaucho** (daily, Espoz y Mina 7, tel. 948-225-073).

Tapas on Calle San Nicolás: The narrow and slightly seedy Calle San Nicolás has more than its share of hole-in-the-wall tapas joints, with an older, more traditional clientele, and greasier, more straightforward tapas.

Café Iruña, which clings to its venerable past and its connec-

tion to Hemingway (who loved the place), serves up drinks out on the main square and food in the delightful old 1888 interior. Find the little "Hemingway's Corner" (El Rincón de Hemingway) side-eatery in back, where the bearded one is still hanging out at the bar (€13 fixed-price meal for lunch and dinner, pricier €21 Sat dinner deal, open daily, Plaza del Castillo 44, tel. 948-222-064).

San Ignacio Restaurante is a good choice for a real restaurant, with a classy upstairs dining room serving local fare (€10–15 starters, €15–20 main dishes, fixed-price meal-€15 on weekdays or €40 on weekends, open daily for lunch 13:00–15:30, Thu-Sat also dinner from 21:00, facing the back of the Navarre government building at Avenida San Ignacio 4, tel. 948-221-874).

TRANSPORTATION CONNECTIONS

Note that the bus station is closer to the Old Town than the train station, and most connections are faster by bus anyway.

From Pamplona by Bus to: Burgos (3/day, 2.5 hrs), **San Sebastián** (8/day, 1 hr), **Bilbao** (6/day, 1.75 hrs), **Madrid** (6/day, 5 hrs). For bus schedules, see www.autobusesdenavarra.com, tel. 948-203-566.

By Train to: Burgos (1/day, 2 hrs), **San Sebastián** (3/day, 2 hrs), **León** (1/day, 4 hrs), **Madrid** (4/day, 3 hrs).

From Pamplona to Burgos

The stretch of the Camino between Pamplona and Burgos is particularly appealing, with several tempting stopovers—don't rush through this section. As you finish your descent from the rugged Pyrenees, you enter the flatter, more cultivated landscape that typifies the long middle stretch of the Camino (basically from here to Galicia). The two best stops along here are the small town of Puente de la Reina (with an iconic old bridge and fun pilgrim vibes) and a potential detour for wine-lovers through La Rioja wine country.

• *Begin by taking the A-12 expressway west from Pamplona (toward Logroño). If the Puente de la Reina stop appeals to you (described below), it's a very easy detour—the exit* (Puente de la Reina norte) *is well-marked from the expressway.*

Puente de la Reina / Gares

The Camino de Santiago's two French routes converge in this cozy, sun-baked village, just one walking stage (about 12 miles) west of Pamplona. Named for a graceful 11th-century stone bridge at its center, the village retains a pilgrim's vibe (**TI** right by the bridge, Tue–Sat 10:00–13:00 & 16:00–19:00, Sun 11:00–14:00, closed Mon, tel. 948-340-845).

As you enter the town, watch (on the left) for the **Church of the Crucifixion** (Iglesia del Crucifijo), with a stork's nest on the steeple. The Knights Templar, who came to protect pilgrims from the Moors, likely founded this church in the 12th century. Inside you'll find a distinctive Y-shaped crucifix (by a German craftsman—a reminder of the rich influx of pan-European culture the Camino enjoyed). Across the street is a pilgrims' *refugio,* offering bunks and credential stamps to Camino walkers.

The most interesting sight in the town is its namesake **"Bridge of the Queen"** (which you'll see on the right as you drive across the modern bridge near the end of town). With a graceful, six-arch Romanesque design that peaks in the middle, the bridge represents life: You can't quite see where you're going until you get there. Pilgrims enjoy congregating on the riverbank under the arches of this bridge—a great place for a stretch-your-legs stop.

• *From here, you can either hop immediately back on the A-12 expressway (toward Estella) to speed along; or stick with the slower N-111 highway that connects the following Camino sights. As you pass by Estella / Lizarra (home to the imposing Romanesque Palace of the Kings of Navarre), you'll gradually begin to notice that you're entering wine country—with scrubby vegetation, red soil, and hill towns dotting the landscape.*

Even if you're on the expressway, it's worth another quick detour (again well-signed, just beyond Estella) to the fun...

Irache Monastery (Monasterio de Irache)

This monastery, sitting amidst vineyards, has a unique custom of offering free wine to pilgrims. From the parking lot near the monastery, walk down following signs for *fuente de vino* to find a faucet that dispenses free wine (daily 8:00–20:00; also one for water). The Spanish poem on the sign explains, "To drink without abusing, we invite you happily; but to be able to take it along, you must pay for the wine." In other words, pilgrims are allowed to drink as much wine as they like...provided they don't take any with them. There's even a handy webcam (www.irache.com—Hi, Mom!).

• *Continuing south, you can choose your route: To save time, zip on the A-12 expressway right to Logroño. But for a scenic and only slightly slower meander through some cute villages (El Busto, Sansol) and larger towns (Los Arcos and Viana), take the expressway only as far as Los Arcos, then follow N-111 from there.*

Either way, you'll end up at...

Logroño and La Rioja

Just before the skippable big city of Logroño, you'll cross the Ebro River. Today, as in centuries past, this river marks the end of the Basque territory (and Navarre) and the beginning of the rest of Spain. With 150,000 residents, Logroño is the largest city of La Rioja. Renowned for its robust wines, the Rioja region has historically served as a buffer between the Basques and the powerful forces to the south and east (the Moors or the Castilian Spaniards).

• *Again, choose your route from here. If you have time, and a healthy interest in wine (and vineyard scenery), detour off the Camino by heading north on A-124 to the village of Laguardia, rejoining the expressway (and the Camino) later. For this option, see the "La Rioja Wine Loop" sidebar on the next page. Otherwise, stick on the expressway to Santo Domingo de la Calzada.*

Note that west of Logroño, the expressway does a big jog to the north (AP-68, then AP-1). You'll save miles (though not necessarily time) and stick closer to the Camino if you instead take the N-120 highway from here to Burgos. Along the way is...

Santo Domingo de la Calzada

This Rioja town has a fine cathedral, oodles of historic buildings, tranquil squares, and all the trappings of a pilgrim zone (seashells in the pavement, *refugios,* vending machines, and launderettes). You'll see images of a rooster and a hen everywhere in town, thanks to a colorful local legend: A chaste pilgrim refused to be seduced by the amorous daughter of an innkeeper. For revenge, she hid a silver cup in his bed and accused him of theft. The judge, eager to hang the lad, proclaimed that the pilgrim was as dead as the roasted rooster and hen the judge was about to eat. The charred birds suddenly stood up and began to crow, saving the pilgrim from certain death.

Most of the attractions cluster in the shadow of the cathedral tower on Plaza del Santo. You can visit the **cathedral** (€3.50, Mon–Sat 9:30–13:30 & 16:00–18:30, closed Sun) or have a drink at the bar in the very atmospheric atrium lounge of the fancy

La Rioja Wine Loop

Serious wine-lovers enjoy detouring off the Camino at Logroño to visit the wine village of Laguardia, tour some unique wineries, and sample Rioja wine.

For many lovers of Spanish wines, it just doesn't get better than Rioja (ree-OH-ha). Rioja wine is a D.O.C. product, meaning that by definition it can only be produced in La Rioja region. Protected from the elements by the Cantabrian Mountains to the north (which you'll see from Laguardia), vineyards have thrived in the valley of the Ebro River since Roman times. Rioja wines (which can be red, white, or rosé) grow in a variety of soil types dominated by red clay and limestone. The reds, made primarily from the *tempranillo* grape (Spain's "noble grape"), are medium- to full-bodied in the Bordeaux style and characterized by aging in oak barrels—infusing them with overtones of vanilla. With their balance of tannins and fruitiness, red Riojas go well with grilled meats and strong cheeses like an aged *Manchego*. You'll see four types of Rioja wines, depending on how long they've been aged (from shortest to longest, and cheapest to most expensive): simply Rioja (or sometimes *cosecha*, "harvest"), Rioja Crianza, Rioja Reserva, and Rioja Gran Reserva.

Be warned that the Rioja region isn't well set up for impromptu visitors. All wine-tasting experiences prefer reservations, and most require them. Those wanting to taste on the fly might be disappointed. If you're serious about your Rioja, plan to set up here for a day or two, do some homework (www.laguardia-alava.com is helpful), and reserve at the wineries of your choice (it's best to call 2–3 days before). At very popular wineries, during the busiest time (weekends and at the October harvest), they recommend calling several weeks ahead. Although Laguardia is connected by bus to Pamplona (via Logroño), most of the experience here lies in the countryside—it's much better by car.

• *From Logroño, follow A-124 northwest (toward Vitoria, through more and more scenic vineyards, with a picturesque mountain ridge as a backdrop) to Laguardia, and park just outside the town wall.*

Laguardia is the scenic center of La Rioja wine-tasting country. This walled town—literally "The Guard," for its position watching out for potential invaders coming in from the mountains—is perched on a promontory with fine views of the surrounding region. There's not much in the way of sightseeing, but poke around a bit. Under your feet are more than 200 wine cellars *(bodegas)* where Rioja quietly ages. Only two in town are open for visitors: **El Fabulista** (€6 tasting, tel. 945-621-192) and **Carlos San Pedro** (€3.50 tasting, tel. 605-033-043); for both, you can try just dropping in, but it's better to call ahead. The **TI** can give you information on wine-tastings in town and nearby, but—again—they'll warn you that most wineries require reservations (TI open Mon–Fri 10:00–14:00 & 16:00–19:00, Sat 10:00–14:00 & 17:00–19:00, Sun 10:45–14:00, Plaza San Juan, tel. 945-600-845, www.laguardia-alava.com).

The countryside around Laguardia is blanketed with vineyards. For passing-through visitors, three wine-related attractions are worth considering. The first two are very near Laguardia, and the third is a 10-minute drive away. Note that Ysios and Marqués de Riscal are architectural gems worth dropping by to see even if you could care less about the wine:

Villa Lucía is a sort of wine-museum about La Rioja's favorite product, as well as its traditional architecture. As with everything around here, it's wise to call ahead if you want to join a tour (various programs for €6–14, Tue–Sun 10:00–14:00 & 17:00–20:00, closed Mon, watch for it in the valley right in front of Laguardia, tel. 945-600-032, www.villa-lucia.com).

Ysios is a winery with an undulating silver roof designed by the bold and prolific Spanish architect Santiago Calatrava. Winelovers enjoy the tastings and tours of the cellar, in which countless casks age under the wavy ceiling (€5; Mon–Fri at 11:00, 13:00, and 16:00; Sat–Sun at 11:00 and 13:00; call first to ensure a space, tel. 945-600-640, www.bodegasysios.com). But even from the outside, it's a worthwhile photo op for anyone (just a three-minute drive behind Laguardia, toward the mountains—behind the town, look for *Ysios* signs, you'll see the building from far off).

• *From the Laguardia area, follow signs south to* Elciego *(on A-3210) to reach...*

Marqués de Riscal, in the village of Elciego, was one of the pioneer winemakers of the Rioja wine industry. Its new winery features a distinctive hotel that could only have been designed by Frank Gehry (of Bilbao Guggenheim fame)...and it was. Gehry didn't design the tourable wine cellar (€10, closed Mon, call first, tel. 945-180-888, www.marquesderiscal.com), and his hotel isn't open to the public (Db-€400–1,000 to spend the night). But exterior views of this colorful, wavy building—improbably situated next to a humble village—merit the trip.

• *Just to the northwest is the midsized town of Haro, offering even more tasting opportunities. But if you're ready to move along, you can head south from Elciego toward Cenicero. In Cenicero, you can rejoin the AP-68 expressway, or continue down (following signs for* Nájera*) to highway N-120 to join the Camino road into Burgos.*

parador hotel, just across the square (Db-€149, tel. 941-340-300). The **TI** is just up Calle Mayor (daily 10:00–14:00 & 16:00–20:00, at #70, tel. 941-341-230).

To the southeast—but not on the Camino proper—is San Millán de la Cogolla, home to a pair of monasteries (called Yuso and Suso) where the Spanish and Euskara (Basque) languages were first written down.

• *Soon after Santo Domingo de la Calzada, you pass into the region of...*

Castile and León (Castilla y León)

Welcome to Spain's largest "state" (about the size of Indiana). If you've always wanted to see the famous plains of Spain...this is it. This vast, arid, high-altitude Meseta Central ("Inner Plateau") stretches to hilly, rainy Galicia in the northwest and all the way past Madrid to the South Coast. Those walking the entire Camino find this flat, dry stretch to be either the best part (getting away from it all with a pensive stroll) or the worst part (boring and potentially blistering-hot).

• *The next big city on the Camino is just around the bend: Burgos.*

Burgos

Burgos (BOOR-gohs) is a pedestrian-friendly city lined up along its pretty river. Apart from its epic history and urban bustle, Burgos has one major claim to touristic fame: its glorious Gothic-style cathedral, packed to the gills with centuries' worth of elaborate decorations.

Like so many towns in the north of Spain, the burg of Burgos was founded during the Reconquista to hold on to land that had been won back from the Moors. Its position on the Camino de Santiago, and the flourishing wool trade (sent to the Low Countries to become Flemish tapestries), helped it to thrive. Beginning in 1230, it became the capital of the kingdom of Castile for half a millennium (having usurped the title from León). The town's favorite son is the great 11th-century Spanish hero, El Cid (Spaniards say "el theeth"), who valiantly fought against the Moors. The 20th century saw the town decline, even as it briefly became the capital of Franco's forces during the Civil War. Later the dictator industrialized Burgos to even out the playing field (Catalunya and the Basque Country—on the political and geographical fringes of Spain—had previously been the centers of industry).

Today's Burgos feels workaday, but with a hint of elegance, as

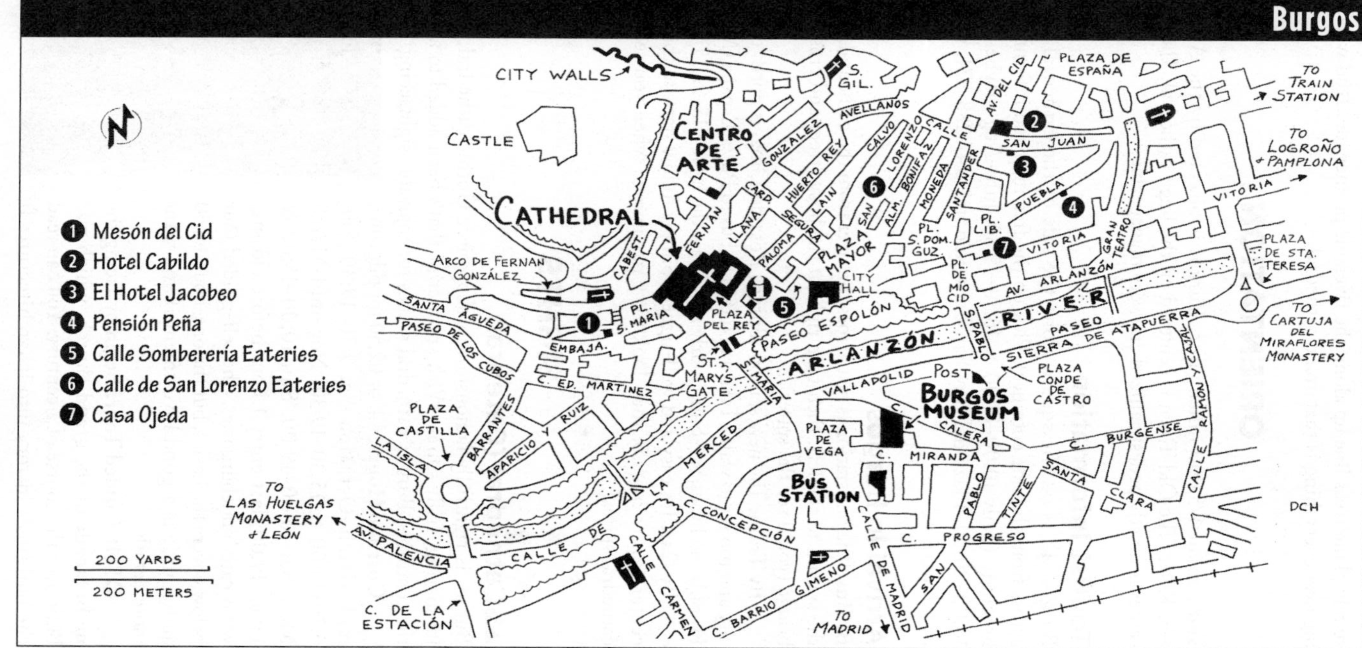
Burgos
1 Mesón del Cid
2 Hotel Cabildo
3 El Hotel Jacobeo
4 Pensión Peña
5 Calle Sombrerería Eateries
6 Calle de San Lorenzo Eateries
7 Casa Ojeda
200 YARDS
200 METERS
CITY WALLS
CASTLE
CENTRO DE ARTE
CATHEDRAL
ARCO DE FERNAN GONZÁLEZ
PLAZA MAYOR
CITY HALL
PLAZA DEL REY
ST. MARY'S GATE
PASEO ESPOLÓN
RIVER ARLANZÓN
PASEO SIERRA DE ATAPUERRA
PLAZA CONDE DE CASTRO
BURGOS MUSEUM
POST
PLAZA DE VEGA
BUS STATION
PLAZA DE CASTILLA
PLAZA DE ESPAÑA
PLAZA DE STA. TERESA
TO TRAIN STATION
TO LOGROÑO + PAMPLONA
TO CARTUJA DEL MIRAFLORES MONASTERY
TO LAS HUELGAS MONASTERY + LEÓN
TO MADRID
C. DE LA ESTACIÓN
CALLE DE MADRID
CALLE RAMÓN Y CAJAL
DCH
BURGOS

stately plane trees line up along the riverside promenade. And watching over everything is that grand cathedral.

ORIENTATION

With about 175,000 inhabitants, Burgos is bisected by the Arlanzón River. The Old Town is centered on the huge cathedral. The city center is mostly pedestrianized and very manageable.

Tourist Information

Burgos' TI is on the square along the side of the cathedral (just across from the side entrance). Pick up the free map and information brochure (daily 10:00–14:00 & 16:30–19:30, July–Aug maybe daily 10:00–20:00, Plaza del Rey San Fernando, tel. 947-288-874, www.aytoburgos.es).

Arrival in Burgos

By Bus: The bus station is just across the river from the cathedral. Exit the station to the left, then turn right at the busy street and cross the bridge (you'll see the spires).

By Train: The new station, Burgos Rosa de Lima, is north of the city and too far to walk. Take a taxi (€7) or bus to Plaza España (Mon–Fri only, no buses Sat–Sun, hourly at :15 past the hour 8:15–22:15).

By Car: It's easy and well-signed. Simply follow signs to the city center *(centro ciudad)*, then look for a pay garage when you see the cathedral spires.

SIGHTS

▲▲Cathedral (Catedral)

Burgos is rightfully famous for its showpiece Gothic cathedral, with its soaring, frilly spires. With an interior that's been added to across the centuries, Burgos' cathedral makes for enjoyable sightseeing.

Cost and Hours: €4, or €2.50 for pilgrims; mid-March–Oct Mon–Sat 9:30–19:30, Sun 9:30–15:00 & 15:30–19:30; Nov–mid-March Mon–Sat 10:00–19:00, Sun 10:00–15:00 & 15:30–19:00; last entry 1 hour before closing, www.catedraldeburgos.es. The self-guided tour below covers the basics, but the one-hour, €3.50 audioguide is a good investment if you want more details.

➲Self-Guided Tour: Begin by facing the **main facade** of the grand church, which was built over the course of a century. You can read the building's history into its architecture: It was started by French architects in the 13th century, who used a simple, graceful style similar to the famous Notre-Dame (mentally erase the tops of the spires and you'll see that famous Parisian cathedral). In the 14th century, German cathedral-builders took over, adding the flamboyant fringe to the tops of the towers (similar to the cathedral in Köln, Germany).

The entrance on this side is open only for worshippers, who have access to two chapels at the back of the cathedral (where hourly Mass takes place). Tourists head around the right side of the church to buy a ticket and enter. As you walk there, you'll realize that this "front door" facade is only one small part of the vast complex—more spires and frills lie beyond.

Buy your ticket and enter through the side door. After you show your ticket, you'll turn left and do a clockwise spin around the church, stopping at many of the 18 **chapels.** These chapels were added over many centuries, in different styles, and decorated in creative ways by a wide range of benefactors. (To aid with navigation for certain stops, I've listed the numbers that are posted for audioguide-users.) The first few chapels are just a warm-up: the Chapel of St. John of Sahagún (#6) features a Baroque relic altar and some frescoes (unusual in this church), while the Chapel of the Presentation (#8) features a painting by an Italian Renaissance master, Il Piombo.

At the back of the church, the barriers separate the worship area from the tourist zone. But look high up, just to the right of the rose window, to see the church mascot: The **"Fly-Catcher" clock** (El Papamoscas), which rings out every quarter-hour. Above the clock is a whimsical statue of its German maker, whose mouth opens and closes when the bell rings at the top of each hour. (The tourists who congregate here and crane their necks to gape up at the show seem to be imitating the clock-maker.)

Continue to the next chapel, dedicated to **St. Thecla** (#12). Here you'll find a spectacular Renaissance altar, showing the family tree of Jesus springing out of a reclining Jesse. (The sculptor included his self-portrait as one of the evangelists—find the bespectacled guy, the second from left in the bottom row.) Facing the altar is a Flemish tapestry and some original 15th-century vestments.

You've now circled back around to the transept. On your left are the sumptuous **Golden Stairs** (#13, designed by a Flemish Renaissance master who had studied under Michelangelo). On the right, you can enter the choir area. In the very center of the choir—and the very center of the cathedral, directly under the sumptuous Plateresque-style dome—is the **tomb of El Cid** (Rodericus Didaci Campidoctor) and his wife (#15). (El Cid's well-traveled remains were interred in Valencia, then in various points in Burgos, before being brought here in the early 20th century.) Take a look at the **main altar** (#16), with a fine statue of Mary slathered in silver. Also poke around the carved wooden **choir** (#17), with a giant 16th-century songbook for Gregorian chants and two organs (used only for special occasions).

Head back out into the ambulatory and ambulate around the back of the altar (#21). Notice the **stone carvings** along the wall on your right. Because they're carved from porous limestone, the carvings have deteriorated over the centuries—notice that the areas that receive the most direct sunshine look like they're melting.

Directly behind the main altar, enter the cathedral's best chapel, the **Chapel of the High Constable** (#22). Because it has its own altar, two side naves, and a choir and organ (in the back), it's been called "the cathedral within the cathedral." A high constable is a knight who won a crown in battle for his king or queen—the highest of VIPs in the Middle Ages. And yet, this chapel shows the influence not of a powerful man, but of a powerful woman. It was commissioned by the high constable's wife (who's entombed with him at the center of the chapel). She wanted the chapel decorations to demonstrate equality of the sexes (a bold statement in the late 15th century). Notice that most of the decorations on "his" side (left) are male-oriented, including the two brutes holding the coat of arms up above, and the figures on the side altar. But "her" decorations (right) are more feminine—damsels holding the coat of arms, and mostly women decorating the side altar. The yin and yang of the sexes is even suggested by the black-and-white flooring. Also notice a pair of fine paintings here (unrelated to the sexual politics): on "his" side, a beautiful Flemish depiction of a woman in a red dress (likely from the school of Hans Memling); and on "her" side, Mary Magdalene, by a favorite pupil of Leonardo da Vinci's (who probably put his own touches on the work, as well).

Continuing around, you'll enter the **cloister** (walking past the beautifully carved main sacristy, #28). The tour route takes you counterclockwise around this cloister, to a few more chapels and museum exhibits. The Corpus Christi Chapel (#26) features stairs up to the library (closed to the public) and access to the chapter house (#27), where the monks would meet. The next chapel (St. Catharine's Chapel, #28) displays a remarkable 10th-century Bible. In the same case is a copy of El Cid's pre-nup. (To protect his assets, he found a clever legal loophole to transfer ownership of all he had to his wife.)

Around the top of this room are dozens of paintings depicting centuries' worth of bishops.

Continuing to the **Chapel of St. John the Baptist and St. James** (#29), you find the cathedral's museum collection, including ecclesiastical items (such as some exquisitely detailed crosses and chalices), an emotive statue of Christ being whipped, and an altar depicting St. James the Moor-slayer (see page 247).

Finally you'll head downstairs to the **lower cloister** (#33). At the foot of the stairs is a schmaltzy portrait of El Cid, and beyond that is a model of the original Romanesque church (with the current, Gothic footprint around it for comparison). You'll also spot a large model of the entire cathedral complex... to get your bearings on all that you've just seen from the inside.

Now go in peace.

Other Sights

On a short visit, the cathedral is all that's worth seeing in Burgos. But if you're killing time here, a few other attractions might be worth a look.

Plaza Mayor and Promenade—Burgos' main square, a long block from the cathedral, is urban-feeling and strangely uninviting, with long marble benches. The stone building with two clock towers is the town hall; if you walk under here, you'll emerge at the city's delightful riverside promenade. Lined with knobby plane trees and outdoor cafés, it has an almost Provençal ambience. Going left along the promenade takes you to **Plaza del Mío Cid,** with an equestrian statue celebrating Burgos' favorite son, "My El Cid." Going right along the promenade leads you to the impressive **St. Mary's Gate,** one of six surviving entrances of this stout-walled city's original 12 gates (built in the 13th century, decorated in 16th-century Renaissance style, temporary exhibits upstairs). Passing through this gate takes you directly to the cathedral.

▲Huelgas Monastery—In addition to its grand cathedral, Burgos has a pair of impressive monasteries. The Cistercian monastery of Huelgas is the easiest to reach (though still a bit of a walk from the cathedral). Entrance is by one-hour tour only, and English tours are very rare (€5, free on Wed, open Tue–Sat 10:00–13:00 & 15:45–17:30,

Sun 10:30–14:00, closed Mon, tours depart about every 20 min, try asking your guide for some English info, tel. 947-201-630). Inside you'll see a "pantheon" of royal tombs, a Gothic cloister with Mudéjar details, a chapter house with 13th-century stained glass, and a Romanesque cloister. The highlight is a statue of St. James with an arm that could be moved to symbolically "knight" the king by placing a sword on his shoulders (since only a "saint"—or statue of a saint—was worthy of knighting royalty). Finally you'll tour a museum of rare, surviving clothes from common people (not just religious vestments) from the 13th and 14th centuries.

Getting There: It's about a 20-minute walk west of the city center, or you can take bus #5, #7, or #35 (catch the bus across the bridge from the cathedral).

The other monastery—**Cartuja de Miraflores**—is farther out of town (details at TI); seeing both Huelgas and Miraflores is redundant unless you adore monasteries.

Museums—Burgos has a few other museums that might be worth a look. On the hill behind the cathedral, the **Centro de Arte** is a contemporary art museum with temporary exhibits (free, Tue–Fri 11:30–14:00 & 17:00–21:00, Sat 11:00–14:30 & 17:00–21:00, Sun 11:00–14:30, closed Mon, tel. 947-256-550). And just across the river, near the bus station, is the **Museo de Burgos,** which celebrates the cultural heritage of Burgos province. Its five floors of painting and sculpture and two floors of archaeological exhibits ring the gorgeous courtyard of a fine old 1540 convent. The somewhat hard-to-appreciate museum hopes to display the sword of El Cid in the near future (€1.20, free Sat–Sun, €1 audioguide; July–Sept Tue–Sat 10:00–14:00 & 17:00–20:00, Sun 10:00–14:00, closed Mon; Oct–June Tue–Sat 10:00–14:00 & 16:00–19:00, Sun 10:00–14:00, closed Mon; Calle Miranda 13, tel. 947-265-875).

Near Burgos: Santo Domingo de Silos

The unassuming village of Santo Domingo de Silos—about 40 miles (an hour's drive) south of Burgos—has a fine Benedictine monastery that's become a quirky footnote in popular music. The monastery's monks are famous for their melodic Gregorian chants, which were recorded and released as the hugely popular album *Chant* in 1994. (It went on to sell six million copies.) Although the monks don't perform concerts, some of their daily services—which are free and open to the public—include chanting. The lengthy vespers *(visperas)* service is entirely chanted (daily at 19:00, 2.5 hours); there's also some chanting at the shorter Eucharist service (Mon–Fri at 9:00, Sat–Sun at 12:00). You can tour the cloister and museum (€3, open to the public Tue–Sat 10:00–13:00 & 16:30–18:00, Sun 16:30–18:00 only, closed Mon). Call to confirm before making the trip (tel. 947-390-049, www.abadiadesilos.es).

SLEEPING

(€1 = about $1.50, country code: 34)
When I've listed a price range, it fluctuates with demand; the top rates are for summer (June–Sept).

$$ Mesón del Cid enjoys Burgos' best location, gazing across a quiet square at the cathedral's front facade (full-frontal cathedral views are worth the extra €15). The 55 rooms in two buildings come with classy tile floors and old-fashioned furniture (Sb-€60–70, Db-€70–90, includes tax, breakfast-€11, air-con, elevator, free Internet access and Wi-Fi, Plaza de Santa María 8, tel. 947-208-715, fax 947-269-460, www.mesondelcid.es, mesondelcid@mesondelcid.es).

$$ Hotel Cabildo offers modern class for reasonable prices. Its lobby and 57 rooms are slick and stylish (Sb-€60–65, Db-€65–80, air-con, elevator, non-smoking rooms, free cable Internet, request quiet room, Avenida del Cid 2, tel. 947-257-840, fax 947-204-320, www.hotelcabildo.com, cabildo@hotelcabildo.com).

$$ El Hotel Jacobeo is a cheaper option, with 14 modern rooms along a lively pedestrian street (Sb-€35–40, Db-€50–60, breakfast-€4.50, free Wi-Fi, all rooms face the back—so it's quiet, San Juan 24, tel. 947-260-102, fax 947-260-100, www.hoteljacobeo.com, hoteljacobeo@hoteljacobeo.com).

$ Pensión Peña is Burgos' best budget option. Lively Loli, who speaks no English, rents eight simple but well-maintained rooms (sharing three bathrooms) in an old apartment building. Loli takes no advance reservations, but you can call in the morning to see if she has a room (S-€21–22, D-€27–28, La Puebla 18, tel. 947-206-323, mobile 639-067-089).

EATING

Tapas on Calle Sombrería: For the best tapas-bar scene, stroll along Calle Sombrería (jog right from the street that connects the cathedral area to the Plaza Mayor). **Estrella de Galicia,** with a modern, bright ambience, offers a preview of the cuisine you'll enjoy in Santiago—Galician food, wine, and beer. You can sit in the bar, in the dining room upstairs, or out on the terrace (€12 meal offered weekdays, €4–6 *raciones,* €10–15 main dishes, daily, Calle de la Paloma 35, tel. 947-276-902). Across the street, **Cervecería Morito** offers a more chaotic local ambience—one tight room with tables and a bar, or pay a little more to eat at the terrace across the street (€3 sandwiches, €5–7 *raciones,* handy photo menu, daily, Sombrería 27, tel. 947-267-555). You'll find

La Historia del Camino

The first person to undertake the Camino de Santiago was... Santiago himself. After the death of Christ, the apostles scattered to the corners of the earth to spread the Word of God. Supposedly, St. James went on a missionary trip from the Holy Land all the way to the northwest corner of Spain, which, at that point, really was the end of the world. (For more on St. James, see the sidebar on page 247.)

According to legend, St. James' remains were discovered in 813 in the town that would soon bear his name. This put Santiago de Compostela on the map, as one of three places—along with Rome and Jerusalem—where remains of apostles are known to be buried. In 951, Godescalco, the Bishop of Le Puy in France, walked to Santiago de Compostela to pay homage to the relics. As other pilgrims followed his example, the Camino de Santiago informally emerged. Then, in the 12th century, Pope Callistus II decreed that any person who walked to Santiago in a Holy Year, confessed their sins, and took communion at the cathedral would be forgiven. This opportunity for a cheap indulgence made the Camino de Santiago one of the most important pilgrimages in the world.

It's probably no coincidence that St. James' remains were "discovered" and promoted just as the Reconquista was in full swing. The Pope's decree helped to consolidate the Christians' hold over lands retaken from the Moors. Pilgrims were ideal candidates to repopulate and defend northern Spain. Many of those who made the journey to Santiago stuck around somewhere along the route (often because of privileges granted them by local rulers who needed help rebuilding). It became a self-sustaining little circle: Pilgrims came along the Camino, saw great sights, and decided to stay...to build even greater sights for the next pilgrims to enjoy.

The Christian monarchy designated an old Roman commercial road from France across northern Iberia as the "official" route, and soon churches, monasteries, hostels, hospitals, blacksmiths, and other pilgrims' services began to pop up. Religious-military orders such as the Knights of Santiago and the Knights Templar protected the route from bandits and fought alongside Christian armies against the Moorish resurgence, allowing the evolving Catholic state to gather strength in the safe haven created by the Camino.

In the Middle Ages, pilgrims came to Santiago from all over Europe—mostly from France, but also from Portugal, Italy, Britain, the Netherlands, Germany, Scandinavia, and Eastern Europe. Many prominent figures embarked on the journey, including St. Francis of Assisi, Dutch painter Jan van Eyck, and the Wife of Bath in Chaucer's *Canterbury Tales*.

This steady flow of pilgrims from around Europe inevitably resulted in a rich exchange of knowledge, art, and architecture. Even today, you'll find magnificent cathedrals along the Camino in cities such as Burgos and León, which incorporated and improved on the latest in cathedral design from France at that time.

By 1130, the trek was so popular that it prompted a French monk named Aimery Picaud (likely with the help of some ghost-writers) to pen a chronicle of his journey, including tips on where to eat, where to stay, the best way to get from place to place, and how to pack light and use a money belt. This *Codex Calixtinus* (Latin for "Camino Through the Back Door") was the world's first guidebook—the great-great-granddaddy of the one you're holding right now.

When the Moors were finally defeated in 1492, the significance of Reconquista icon St. James fell by the wayside. The discovery of the New World in the same year led both the Church and the monarchy to turn their attention across the Atlantic, and the pilgrimage began to wane. As Europe emerged from the Middle Ages, and the Black Death swept across the Continent, the Camino de Santiago was virtually forgotten. As recently as a few decades ago, only a few hardy souls still followed the route.

Then, in the late 1960s, a handful of parish priests along the Camino began working to recover the route, establishing associations of "friends of the Camino" that would eventually agree on a path and mark it. In 1982, Pope John Paul II visited Santiago de Compostela, reminding the world of the town's historic significance. In 1987, the European Union designated the Camino as Europe's first Cultural Itinerary. And after the success of the 1992 Expo in Sevilla, the Galician government decided to pour funds into reviving the tradition for the Holy Year in 1993. They made Santiago a high-profile destination and shelled out big pesetas for concerts by stars including the Rolling Stones, Bruce Springsteen, and Julio Iglesias (whose father was born in Galicia).

The plan worked, and now—aided by European Union funding—the route has enjoyed a huge renaissance of interest, with 100,000 pilgrims each year trekking to Santiago. Even Shirley MacLaine has made the journey (her book *The Camino: A Journey of the Spirit* is popular among pilgrims). Cyclists and horse riders are now joining hikers on the journey, and these days it's "in" to follow the seashells to Santiago.

more tapas bars on **Calle de San Lorenzo** (narrow lane branching off the Plaza Mayor, across the square from the town hall).

Casa Ojeda is a venerable institution that's a reliable choice for a real restaurant meal. Specializing in local Burgos cuisine, they offer seating at the bar downstairs (tapas, €6 half-*raciones*, €13 combo-plate) or in the upstairs dining room (pricier meals: €10 starters, €20–25 mains). Relax and enjoy the subdued, rapidly aging ambience (daily except Sun night, Calle Vitoria 5, tel. 947-171-256).

TRANSPORTATION CONNECTIONS

From Burgos by Bus to: Pamplona (3/day, 2.5 hrs), **León** (4/day, 2–3 hrs, Alsa), **Bilbao** (4–5/day, 2 hrs, Continental), **Santiago de Compostela** (1/day, 8.5 hrs, Alsa), **San Sebastián** (6/day, 3.5 hrs, Continental), **Salamanca** (3/day, 3.5 hrs, Alsa), **Madrid** (9/day, 3 hrs, Continental). Note that Sunday connections are very sparse.

By Train to: Pamplona (1/day, 2.25 hrs), **León** (3/day, 2 hrs), **Bilbao** (4/day, 2.5–3.5 hrs), **San Sebastián** (4/day, 3–3.5 hrs), **Salamanca** (3/day, 2.5–3 hrs), **Madrid** (7/day, 4–5 hrs).

From Burgos to León

While there are some worthwhile stops between Burgos and León, this is a good place to put some serious miles under your belt: Follow signs for the A-231 expressway and zip between the cities in less than two hours. Sticking with the true Camino—a confusing spaghetti of roads without a single, straight highway to keep you on track—takes you through a poorer, very humble countryside with few sights. Some travelers enjoy dipping into towns along here such as **Castrojeriz, Frómista,** and **Carrión de los Condes,** but on a tight itinerary, your time is better spent in Burgos or León.

León

With a delightfully compact Old Town (surrounded by ugly sprawl), León (lay-OWN) has an enjoyable small-town atmosphere. But most importantly, it has a pair of sights that serve as a textbook for medieval European art styles: Romanesque (the San Isidoro Monastery, with astonishingly well-preserved frescoes) and Gothic (the cathedral, with the best stained glass outside of France).

León means "lion" in Spanish—but in this case, the name derives from Rome's seventh legion, which was stationed here. Founded as a Roman camp at the confluence of two rivers in A.D. 68, León gradually grew prosperous because of the gold trade that passed through here

León

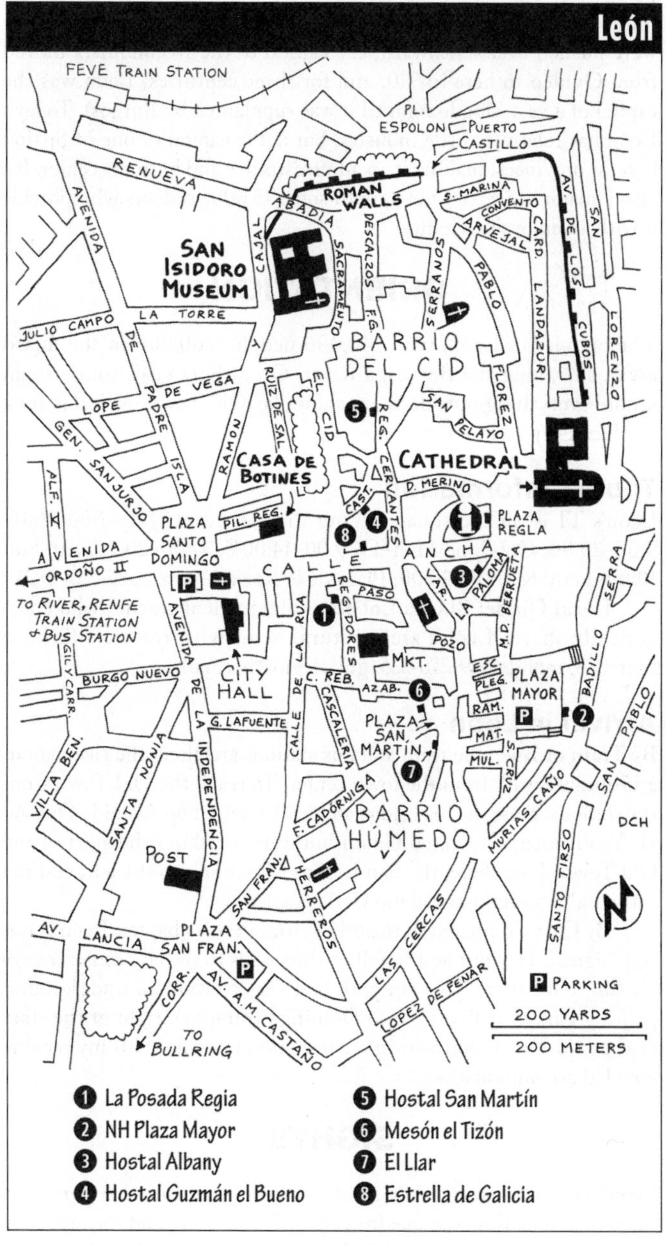

1. La Posada Regia
2. NH Plaza Mayor
3. Hostal Albany
4. Hostal Guzmán el Bueno
5. Hostal San Martín
6. Mesón el Tizón
7. El Llar
8. Estrella de Galicia

LEÓN

(mined in the Las Médulas hillsides to the west). Later, as the Moors were pushed ever southward, the capital of the Reconquista moved from Ovideo to here in 910, and for three centuries, León was the capital of a vast kingdom (until it was supplanted by Burgos). Today's León has relatively little industry, but is the capital of one of Spain's biggest provinces, making it an administrative and business center. It's also a major university town, with some 15,000 students who provide it with an enjoyable vitality.

ORIENTATION

The big city of León, with 140,000 people (200,000 in the metro area), sits along the Bernesga River. On a short visit, tourists can ignore everything outside the rectangular Old Town, which is set a few blocks up from the river.

Tourist Information

León's TI is on the square facing the cathedral (July–Sept daily 9:00–20:00; Oct–June Mon–Fri 9:00–14:00 & 17:00–20:00, Sat–Sun 10:00–14:00 & 17:00–20:00; Plaza de la Regla 3–4, tel. 987-237-082).

Local Guide: Blanca Lobete is an excellent teacher who energetically shares León's architectural gems with travelers (3-hour tour-€88, mobile 669-276-335, guiaslegio@hotmail.com).

Arrival in León

By Train or Bus: The train and bus stations are along the river, about a 15-minute walk from the town center. To reach the Old Town from the stations, cross the big bridge and walk straight up Avenida Ordoño II. You'll hit the turreted Gaudí building, marking the start of the Old Town. From here, the San Isidoro Museum is to the left, and the cathedral is straight ahead (up Calle Ancha).

By Car: Compared to the other cities in this chapter, León is not well-signed. Do your best to follow directions to the city center *(centro ciudad);* once there, you can park in a very convenient underground parking garage at Plaza Santo Domingo (€16/day), right at the start of the Old Town (and within a three-minute walk of all my recommended accommodations).

SIGHTS

León's two most worthwhile sights complement each other perfectly: the remarkable Romanesque frescoes at San Isidoro, and the gorgeous stained glass of the cathedral. While you can do these in either order, to appreciate the architectural progression it makes sense to do San Isidoro first. (If you're rushed and have time for only one, make it the cathedral.)

▲▲San Isidoro Museum (Museo de San Isidoro)

San Isidoro is an 11th-century Romanesque church that's been gradually added on to over the centuries. The church itself, due to complete a lengthy restoration in 2009, is free and always open to worshippers. But the attached museum is the real attraction. Inside you'll see a library, cloister, chapter house, and a "pantheon" of royal tombs featuring some of the most exquisite Romanesque frescoes in Spain.

Cost and Hours: €4; July–Aug Mon–Sat 9:00–20:00, Sun 9:00–14:00; Sept–June Mon–Sat 10:00–13:30 & 16:00–18:30, Sun 10:00–13:30; Plaza San Isidoro 4, tel. 987-876-161.

➲ **Self-Guided Tour:** Buy your ticket and go directly into the **Royal Pantheon** (Pantéon Real). This area, now enclosed in the middle of the complex, was once the portico in front of the west door of the church. In 2002, historians discovered the tombs of several medieval kings and queens (which are now held in the stone tombs). But who's buried here pales in comparison to the beautiful, vivid frescoes on the vaulting above them. Created in the late 11th and early 12th centuries, these frescoes have never been repainted—they're incredibly well-preserved. While most Romanesque frescoes have been moved to museums, this is a rare opportunity to see some *in situ* (where they were originally intended).

Follow along as the frescos trace the life of Christ (counterclockwise as you look up, from the front-right corner). In the scene of the Annunciation, you'll notice a sense of motion (Mary's billowing clothes) that's unusual for typically stiff and un-lifelike Romanesque art. Later, an angel appears to shepherds dressed in traditional 11th-century Leonese clothing. There's even a Leonese mastiff dog, lapping at his master's milk (while he's distracted by the angel).

In the next section, Roman soldiers carry out the gruesome slaughter of the innocents. Then, in the Last Supper, notice the bold colors. For shorthand, Romanesque artists used halos to differentiate important figures from commoners (soldiers and servants). But notice only 11 of the Apostles have halos...all but Judas (under the table). At the corner, find the rooster *(gallus),* a symbol of Jesus, who harkened the dawn of a new day for God's people. But in the next section, we see the rooster used as a different symbol—as Peter denies Christ three times before the cock crows. Also see Jesus' arrest, Simon helping Jesus carry the cross, and Pontius Pilate washing his hands of the whole business. Finally we see Jesus nailed to the cross.

The final panel, in the middle of the room, is the most artistically and thematically impressive: Jesus returning triumphant to judge the living and the dead. He's depicted here as Pantocrator ("all-powerful"). Over his shoulders are the symbols for alpha and omega, and he's surrounded by the four evangelists, depicted—according to the prophecy of Ezekiel—as animals: man, ox, eagle, and lion. The most interesting detail is the calendar running along the archway near Jesus' right hand. The 12 medallions—one for each month (labeled in Latin)—are symbolized by people's activities during that month. In January, the man closes one door (or year) while he opens the next. He proceeds to warm himself by the fire, prune, plant his crops, harvest, forage, slaughter the fattened pig, and bless his bread by the fire at Christmas. The message: Jesus is present for this entire cycle of life.

There's more to the museum. Continue into the **cloister,** where you'll find a small room with a giant 12th-century rooster weathervane that used to top the nearby tower (now replaced by a replica)—a symbol of the city.

You can also climb the tight spiral staircase (near where you came in) to the old **library** (with a giant Mozarabic Bible from 960) and the **chapter house** (displaying Romanesque reliquary chests.

Our tour is over. But for a peek at a remaining section of León's **Roman walls,** turn right out of the museum, then head right down the street.

• *For the most interesting approach to the cathedral, walk south from the San Isidoro Museum (and the surviving chunk of wall) along the busy street called Ramón y Cajal. At the roundabout (Plaza Santo Domingo), turn left. You're at the start of...*

Calle Ancha and the Old Town

This "Wide Street," which cuts through the heart of the Old Town, was widened in the mid-19th century to create an appropriate pathway to the cathedral. It was lined with grand mansions of local wealthy people who wanted to live close to God. It's only been pedestrianized for the last decade, creating a wonderful people zone.

At the start of Calle Ancha, the turreted, medieval-looking building is the **Casa de Botines**—one of few works by Antoni Gaudí outside of Catalunya (another is the Bishop's Palace in Astorga—see page 227). Now the Casa de Botines is a bank and generally not open to visitors unless there's a special exhibition. Gaudí preferred to use local materials, such as the slate roof (typical in León province). The rough stone exterior is intended to hang on to falling snow to create an atmospheric effect. Gaudí even designed the funky theft-prevention spikes on the fence

around the building. Over the door is St. George, the patron saint of Gaudí's native Catalunya. Notice the architect himself on the bench across the square, appreciating his work.

As you walk up Calle Ancha toward the cathedral, the neighborhood to the left is called **Barrio del Cid** (for a supposed former resident). The area to the right is known as the **Barrio Húmedo,** or "Wet Quarter," for all the bars that speckle its streets (see "Eating," page 226). Deep in the Barrio Húmedo is the appealing main square, or **Plaza Mayor,** overshadowed by the cathedral a few blocks over.

▲▲Cathedral (Catedral)

León's 13th-century Gothic cathedral is filled with some of the finest stained glass in all of Europe.

Cost and Hours: Free, Mon–Sat 8:30–13:30 & 16:00–19:00 (until 20:00 June–Aug), Sun 8:30–13:30 & 17:00–20:00.

➲ **Self-Guided Tour:** Take a look at the **facade.** If you've just seen Burgos' cathedral, León's—while impressive—might seem a letdown. Reserve judgment until you get inside. León's cathedral was actually built in response to the one in Burgos, to keep León on the map after Burgos wrested capital status from León in 1230. But, while Burgos' was built over two centuries, this cathedral took only about 50 years to complete. The focus was on creating a simple, purely Gothic cathedral to showcase its grand stained-glass windows. The three porticos (doorways with pointed arches) are textbook Gothic. Notice the gap between the two towers and the main facade, which allows even more light to reach those windows. This also gives the cathedral a feeling of lightness. The one exception to the pure-Gothic construction: Notice the tower on the right is a bit taller—it was capped in the 15th century with a frilly spire to keep up with what was going on in Burgos.

Now approach the **main door,** above which is a carving of the Last Judgment. Above Mary, St. Michael weighs souls to determine who is going to party with the musicians of heaven (left) or burn with the cauldrons and demons of hell (right). If you look carefully, you'll see that all of those kicking back in heaven are members of the clergy or royalty. This subtle message made the Camino de Santiago even more appealing to pilgrims: If you weren't a priest or an aristocrat, completing the Camino was your only ticket to eternal bliss.

Before entering, ponder the crucial role that **light** plays in this house of holy glass. Like all cathedrals, the main door faces the west, and the altar (at the far end) faces east—toward Jerusalem. But that also means that the sun rises behind the altar (where Jesus symbolically resides) and sets at the Last Judgment. This theme is continued again and again inside.

Speaking of which, go on in and let your eyes adjust to the light. Notice how the purely Gothic structure—extremely high, with columns and pointed arches to direct your gaze ever heavenward—really allows the stained glass to take center stage. Of all this glass (the second-most glass in any European cathedral, after Chartres in France), 70 percent is original, from the 13th to the 16th centuries.

Imagine how the light in here changes, like living inside a kaleidoscope, as the sun moves across the sky each day. Notice that the colors differ thematically in various parts of the cathedral. Above the main door, the rose window (dedicated, like the cathedral itself, to St. Mary, with 12 angels playing instruments around her) is the most colorful, as it receives the most light at the end of the day. Turning to face the front altar, notice that the glass on the left (north) side of the church, which gets less light, symbolizes darkness and obscurity—blue dominates this side. The glass on the right (south) side of the church, which is bathed in light much of the day, symbolizes brightness and has a greater variety of colors.

Now trace the layers of Gothic cathedral construction from the bottom up, as the building (like your eyes) stretches ever higher, closer to God. The lowest level is the stone foundation (with pointed archways embedded in the walls), symbolic of the mineral world. The first windows show flowers, trees, and animals—the natural world. At the top of each nature window are three medallions showing the human world: common people doing their thing—both vices and virtues.

Above this first row of windows, notice the stone gallery (used for window maintenance). It's very rare to even have windows in this section of a cathedral (in this case, replicas of coats-of-arms of nobles who funded the cathedral's construction). And the tall windows at the very top show biblical characters. On the left (north) side—the "darkness" side, before Christ—is the Old Testament; on the right (south) side—the "light" side, after Christ—is the New Testament. The two sides meet at the rose window (above the main altar) of Jesus—who is illuminated by the rising sun each morning, enlightening the entire cathedral.

If you notice **scaffolding,** it's part of a painstaking restoration of the cathedral's windows. Each piece of glass is being carefully removed from its old iron frame and reset in a brass frame. If there's scaffolding up under the main rose window, you may be able to climb up to see the work, and the window, up close (€2, entrance outside—around the left side as you face the main facade, tours every 30 min, closed Sun–Mon).

Peek into the carved wooden **choir** at the center of the nave (closed to visitors). The curved wooden part over the top of the chair is a "sounding board" *(tornavóz)*, helping voices to carry. The giant glass door replaced a solid wooden one in the early 20th century—opening up the church even more to God's light.

Head for the **transept.** Unfortunately, this part of the cathedral almost didn't survive a well-intended but botched Baroque-era reconstruction. A heavy dome placed over the transept proved too heavy for the four graceful main pillars, causing a significant chunk of the church to collapse. The transept's blue (north) rose window, featuring Christ, survives from the 13th century, while the red (south) one, with Mary, is from the 19th century.

Circling back behind the altar, you'll find a chapel with the **"White Virgin"**—the original 13th-century statue (whose face was painted white) from the front facade of the church. Note the differences between the 16th-century stained glass above the Virgin (with one large, multi-paneled scene) and the 13th- and 14th-century glass in the flanking chapels (with one scene per panel—and even tinier bits of glass).

From the left transept, you can pay €1 to enter the **cloister** (same hours as cathedral except closed Sat afternoon and all day Sun). Here you'll see some discarded, giant Baroque elements (such as turret-tops) that were added to the facade in the 16th century, and later removed because they cluttered up the architectural harmony. The cloister also offers a good view of the flying buttresses that made the stained glass structurally possible. By removing the weight from the walls and transferring it to these buttresses, medieval engineers could build higher and make larger and larger windows.

SLEEPING

(€1 = about $1.50, country code: 34)

All of these listings are inside the Old Town. If there's a range, you can assume that the high end is for summer.

$$$ La Posada Regia is a smart little hotel with 36 rooms in two buildings just off the main walking street. The old-fashioned, pleasant decor is a combination of wood beams and patches of stone (Sb-€55–65, Db-€90–120, includes breakfast, Regidores 9–11, tel. 987-213-173, fax 987-213-031, www.regialeon.com, posada@regialeon.com).

$$$ NH Plaza Mayor is the Old Town splurge, with 51 rooms right on the Plaza Mayor (some with views for no extra charge—request one). Part of a classy chain, this place offers modern four-star comfort at reasonable prices (Sb-€80–100, Db-€90–120, breakfast-€12, non-smoking rooms, air-con, elevator, pay Wi-Fi, Plaza Mayor 15, tel. 987-344-357, fax 987-215-596, www.nh-hotels.com, nhplazamayor@nh-hotels.com).

$$ Hostal Albany offers 19 very mod rooms at a good price, just a few steps off the main walking street and cathedral square (Sb-€38–49, Db-€54–65, includes tax, breakfast-€3.50, air-con, elevator, free cable Internet, Calle La Paloma 13, tel. 987-264-600, www.albanyleon.com, info@albanyleon.com).

$ Hostal Guzmán el Bueno is a simple hotel buried in the Old Town and renting 25 new-feeling rooms (Sb-€30–33, Db-€45–50, elevator, López Castrillón 6, tel. 987-231-462, www.leoncentrogotico.com/hostalguzmanelbueno, hostalguzman@hotmail.com).

$ Hostal San Martín is a fine budget option, with 12 rooms overlooking a small square in the Old Town (S-€20, Db-€40, Tb-€52, includes tax, breakfast-€2, free Wi-Fi, request quiet room in back, Plaza Torres de Omaña 1, tel. 987-875-187, fax 987-875-249, www.sanmartinhostales.com, sanmartinhostal@hotmail.com).

EATING

León is one of few Spanish cities whose bars still honor the old tradition of giving a free (if modest) tapa to anyone buying a drink. Your best bet for finding eats in León is to stroll the **Barrio Húmedo** area, south of Calle Ancha. This zone is packed with restaurants and bars offering good food and ambience. Several reliable options cluster around Plaza San Martín, including **Mesón el Tizón** (one tight room with bar in front and seating in back, order *raciones* from chalkboard menu, closed Thu, Carnicerías 1, tel. 987-256-049) and **El Llar** (tapas in bar, restaurant upstairs serves €5–10 starters and €12–15 main dishes, daily, at #9, tel. 987-254-287). Back on Calle Ancha, **Estrella de Galicia** (part of a chain) offers a foretaste of Santiago (€6–10 *raciones,* €12 daily special, €10–15 main dishes, closed Mon, Calle Ancha 20, tel. 987-240-832).

TRANSPORTATION CONNECTIONS

From León by Bus to: Astorga (1–2/hr, 50 min), **Burgos** (4/day, 2–3 hrs), **Santiago de Compostela** (8/day, 6–8 hrs), **Madrid** (11/day, 3.5 hrs). Note that all buses are run by Alsa.

By Train to: Burgos (3/day, 2 hrs), **Pamplona** (1/day, 4 hrs), **Santiago de Compostela** (1/day, 6 hrs), **Madrid** (10/day, 3–4.25 hrs).

From León to Galicia

This is arguably the most diverse stretch of the Camino. It begins in the flatness of the Meseta Central around León. Then, around Astorga, the landscape gradually becomes more varied and lush, as the Camino approaches the mountainous El Bierzo region (the northwest fringe of Castile and León). Before you know it, you're in the very Celtic-feeling terrain of Galicia.

• *Begin by making your way west, to Astorga. You can stay on the N-120 highway, or pay a €3.70 toll to zip there more quickly on the AP-71 expressway.*

Astorga

Astorga (ah-STOR-gah) sits at the intersection of two ancient roads: the Camino and a north-south trade route from Sevilla to the north coast. When León was a humble Roman camp, "Asturica" was the provincial capital. But today, the fortunes are reversed, as welcoming, laid-back, sleepy Astorga (with about 15,000 people)—just big enough to have some interesting sightseeing and good hotels and restaurants—is a nice small-town alternative to the big city of León. The main attraction here is the memorable Bishop's Palace by Antoni Gaudí.

Tourist Information: Astorga's TI shares a square with the Bishop's Palace and cathedral (daily 10:00–13:30 & 16:00–18:30 except closed Sun afternoon Nov–late June, Plaza Eduardo de Castro 5, tel. 987-618-222).

Arrival in Astorga: The **bus** station is just outside the Old Town, behind the bishop's palace. **Drivers** follow signs for *centro ciudad* and *centro urbano,* drive through the middle of town, and park in front of the TI and cathedral (to park in a blue-painted spot, prepay at the meter and put the ticket on your dashboard).

Sights: The striking **Bishop's Palace** (Palacio Episcopal), a fanciful Gothic-style castle, is one of the few buildings that Catalan architect Antonio Gaudí built outside his native land (another is now a León bank—see page 222). The palace hosts a museum about the Camino and the history of Astorga. You'll see a 17th-century statue of Pilgrim James, a few historical Camino documents, ecclesiastical gear, and a gallery of contemporary Spanish art from the surrounding region. Not as good as it should be, with little posted information (and none in English), the museum is worthwhile mostly for a chance to see a very medieval Gaudí interior (€2.50, €4 combo-ticket with cathedral museum—see below; late-March–late-Sept Tue–Sat 10:00–14:00 & 16:00–20:00, Sun 10:00–14:00, closed Mon; off-season Tue–Sat 11:00–14:00 & 16:00–18:00, Sun 11:00–14:00, closed Mon; tel. 987-616-882).

Next to (and upstaged by) the palace is Astorga's light-filled Gothic **cathedral,** with a marvelously carved choir. It's free to enter in the morning (9:00–11:00), but after 11:00 you can get in only by paying for the attached museum, which shows off a treasury collection of paintings, altarpieces, and vestments (€2.50, €4 combo-ticket with Bishop's Palace, daily April–Sept 10:00–14:00 & 16:00–20:00, Oct–March 11:00–14:00 & 15:30–18:30). Rounding out Astorga's attractions are a chocolate museum and a Roman museum.

Sleeping in Astorga: If you prefer to sleep in a small town, Astorga

is a good alternative to the big city of León (though values here are no better than in the city).

$$ Hotel Gaudí has 35 woody rooms over a restaurant across from the cathedral; some have views of the Bishop's Palace (Sb-€48–50, Db-€65–70, breakfast-€7, air-con in most rooms, elevator, free Wi-Fi, Plaza Eduardo de Castro 6, tel. 987-615-654, fax 987-615-040, www.hotelgaudiastorga.com, reservas@hotelgaudiastorga.com).

$$ Astur Hotel Plaza, which feels more business-class, has 37 rooms right on the main square. Choose between a room overlooking the square—with a clock tower that clangs every 15 minutes—or a quieter back room (Sb-€52–65, Db-€73–91, breakfast-€7, Plaza de España 2–3, tel. 987-618-900, fax 987-618-949, www.asturplaza.com,

Camino de Santiago: Western Half

asturplaza@asturplaza.com).

Eating: **Restaurante Las Termas,** a couple of blocks from the cathedral right along the Camino, is well-regarded for its food (€10 fixed-price meals, €10–16 main dishes, open Tue–Sun for lunch only 13:00–16:00, Sat for lunch and dinner, closed Mon, Calle Santiago 1, tel. 987-602-212). **Hotel Gaudí,** listed above, has an atmospheric bar with tapas and *raciones,* and a restaurant with €13–16 fixed-price meals and €10–20 main dishes (open daily).

Transportation Connections: Astorga is well-connected by bus to **León** (1–2/hr, 50 min), **Ponferrada** (hourly, 1 hr), **Villafranca del Bierzo** (4/day, 1.75 hrs), and **Lugo** (5/day, 2.25–3 hrs).

• *After Astorga, you can either zip up to Galicia on the A-6 expressway (toward Ponferrada), or stick with the Camino a bit farther south on much slower regional roads (LE-142). These two routes converge again at the small city of Ponferrada. Soon after, A-6 climbs up into the hills and to the town of Villafranca del Bierzo (described below).*

If you're sticking with the Camino, you'll be near the...

Iron Cross (Cruz de Ferro)

Near the top of Mount Irago is an iron cross atop a tall wooden pole, set in a huge pile of stones built up over the years by pilgrims unloading their "sins" brought from home (or picked up en route). It's a major landmark for Camino pilgrims, but difficult to reach for drivers (figure an hour's hike off the main road). From the cross, it's a 30-minute walk to the nearly ruined stone village of Foncebadón.

Villafranca del Bierzo

Villafranca is the capital of the westernmost part of León, El Bierzo, which is trying to build a good reputation for its wine and culinary specialties. Dubbed "Little Compostela" for its array of historical buildings, this town is set in an attractive hilly terrain strewn with grapevines, cherry trees, and vegetable patches. While hardly thrilling, Villafranca del Bierzo might be worth a quick stop (if you have time to spare) for its pilgrim ambience (TI tel. 987-540-028).

To play pilgrim, hike from the main square up to the town's stout 14th-century castle (not open to the public). Then follow signs to the Romanesque, 12th-century Church of St. James (Santiago). The church has a "gate of forgiveness" *(puerta de pardón).* If a pilgrim has come this far, falls ill, and can't continue over the rugged terrain to Santiago, he or she is pardoned anyway. (Handy loophole.) Next to the church is a funky *albergue* with oodles of pilgrim bonding. Then turn around and backtrack down into civilization (this road is actually how pilgrims arrive in the town).

• *Just after Villafranca del Bierzo on the A-6 expressway, you cross into the final region on the Camino: Galicia.*

Galicia

In its final stretch, the Camino leaves the broad expanse of the Meseta Central and climbs steeply into Galicia (gah-LEE-thee-ah). Green and hilly, Galicia shatters visitors' preconceptions about Spain. There's something vaguely Irish about Galicia—and it's not just the mossy stonework and green, rolling hills. The region actually shares a strain of Celtic heritage with its cousins across the Cantabrian Sea. People here are friendly, and if you listen hard enough, you might just hear the sound of bagpipes.

• *Shortly after entering Galicia, take the freeway exit for Pedrafita do Cebreiro. From here, follow signs to* O Cebreiro. *A well-maintained mountain road (LU-633) twists its way up to the classic Galician pilgrim village.*

O Cebreiro

An impossibly quaint hobbit hamlet perched on a ridge high above nothing, O Cebreiro (oh theh-BRAY-roh) whispers, "Welcome to Galicia." This "Galician Gimmelwald" is a time-warp into an uncomplicated, almost prehistoric past, when people lived very close to nature, in stone igloos with thatched roofs. With sweeping views across the verdant but harsh Galician landscape, O Cebreiro is constantly pummeled by some of the fiercest weather in Spain. And it's all within a five-minute drive of the freeway.

Wander around. Enjoy the remoteness. O Cebreiro smells like wood fires, manure, and pilgrim B.O. Get a snack or drink at a bar, or browse through a gift shop. A few simple townspeople (who jabber at each other in Galego—see page 237—and cock their heads quizzically when asked about newfangled inventions like email) share the town with weary pilgrims on an adrenaline high after finally reaching Galicia. The local dogs, who've known each other their whole lives, still bark at each other territorially from across the street, completely ignoring the backpackers who regularly trudge through town.

SIGHTS

▲▲***Pallozas***—From Celtic times 1,500 years ago, right up until the 1960s, the villagers of O Cebreiro lived in humble, round, stone huts with peaked thatched roofs, called *pallozas*. Three of the nine surviving *pallozas* have been turned into a loosely run museum (free, Wed-Sun 11:00–14:00 & 15:00–18:00, closed Mon–Tue; if a door of a round hut is open, poke inside). Here visitors can learn about the lifestyles of the people who lived in *pallozas* until not so long ago. Entering a *palloza,* you'll find the only "private" room in the house, belonging to the parents. Beyond that is a living area around a humble fire. (Notice there's no chimney—smoke lets itself out through the thatch.) Ponder the ancient furniture. Surrounding the fire are clever benches (which were also used as very hard beds) with pull-down counters so they could double as a table at mealtime. The big beam with the chain could be swung over the fire for cooking. Looking up, you'll see the remains of a wooden ceiling that prevented sparks from igniting the thatch. The giant black-metal spirals suspended from the ceiling were used to smoke chorizo (sausage)—very efficient. Attached to this living area is a miniature "barn" (find the barn door to outside). Animals lived on the lower level, while people slept on the upper level (which has been removed, but you can still see on the wall where the floor was once supported)—kept warm by all that livestock body heat. About a dozen people (and their animals) lived in one small hut. But thanks to the ideal insulation provided by the thatch, and the warmth from the fire and animals, it was toasty even through the difficult winter.

▲Royal St. Mary's Church (Santa María la Real)—All roads lead to the village church. Founded in the year 836—not long after the remains of St. James were found in Santiago—this pre-Romanesque building is supposedly the oldest church on the entire French Road of the Camino. The interior is surprisingly spacious, but very simple (free, daily 9:00–21:00). Notice the sunken floor: The building is actually embedded into the ground for added protection against winter storms. The desk inside stamps pilgrims' credentials and sells votive candles. The baptistery—separate from the main part

of the church, as dictated by ancient tradition—has a giant and very rough font used for immersion baptisms. In the chapel to the right of the main altar is a much-revered 12th-century golden chalice and reliquary, which holds items relating to a popular local miracle: A peasant from a nearby village braved a fierce winter snowstorm to come to this church for the Eucharist. The priest scoffed at his devotion, only to find that the host and wine had physically turned into the body and blood of Christ, staining the linens beneath them, which are now in the silver box.

EATING AND SLEEPING

(€1 = about $1.50, country code: 34)
The only businesses in town are a half-dozen very humble pub/restaurants, which feed pilgrims and other visitors hearty Galician cuisine in a smoky atmosphere. You'll see signs offering a stick-to-your-ribs €9 "pilgrim menu." Many of these places also rent a few rooms upstairs. Be warned that these rooms are very rustic, English can be tricky, and reservations are only by phone. Try **$ Hospedería San Giraldo de Aurillac** (Db-€50, 17 rooms in 3 buildings, tel. 982-367-182); **$ Casa Carolo** (D-€33, Db-€45, tel. 982-367-168); or **$ Mesón Antón** (D/Db-€38, tel. 982-151-336). The ***albergue,*** which is open only to pilgrims, is perched on a hill at the edge of town and charges €3 per bed.

• *From O Cebreiro, you've got another route decision to make.*

To stick with the Camino, you'll continue on LU-633, along twisty roads, toward Santiago. Along the way, you'll pass through some interesting larger towns: ***Sarria,*** *which is just over 100 kilometers (62 miles) from Santiago, is a popular place to begin a truncated pilgrimage (since you need to walk at least that far to earn your* compostela *certificate).* ***Portomarín*** *is a relatively new town, built only after the River Miño was flooded to create a reservoir in the 1950s. The stout and blocky late-Romanesque Church of San Juan was moved to a new site, stone by stone—and if you look closely enough, you can see how the stones were numbered to keep track of where they fit.*

I prefer the faster expressway route (backtrack to A-6, which you'll take north, following signs for A Coruña*), which offers the opportunity to dip into an appealing walled city, Lugo.*

Lugo

While not technically on the French Road of the Camino de Santiago, the midsized city of Lugo (pop. 90,000) warrants a detour for car travelers. With arguably the best-preserved Roman walls in Spain—a mile and a third long, completely encircling the town, draped with moss, and receding into the misty horizon—Lugo offers an ideal place for an evocative stroll. Lugo feels like a poor man's Santiago, with a patina of poverty and atmospherically crumbling buildings. Evocative chimneys thrust up through rickety old slate roofs. And yet, there's something proud and welcoming about the town. Aside from the walls, Lugo has a cathedral and gregarious Galician charm, making it a fine place to spend some time.

ORIENTATION

Tourist Information

The TI is a few steps up a pedestrian street off the main square, Praza Maior—look for the yellow signs (July–Aug Mon–Sat 10:00–14:00 & 16:00–20:00, Sept–June until 19:00 and closed Sun, Rúa Conde Pallares 2, tel. 982-231-361).

Arrival in Lugo

The **bus** station is just outside the town walls; once inside the Old Town, the main square and TI are a block away. The **train** station is two blocks east of the town walls. **Drivers** follow signs to *centro ciudad* and *centro urbano*. Once you enter the town walls, parking garages are signed.

SIGHTS

The town's **Roman walls** (Murallas Romanas) are free and always open, providing a kind of circular park where locals and visitors can stroll at rooftop level. You can access the walls at various points around town (there are stairs near most of the gates where traffic enters the Old Town), and it takes about 45 minutes to walk the entire way around. With less time, the most interesting stretch is along the west side of town: Walk up the ramp behind the cathedral and turn right, watching behind you for tingly views of the walls and cathedral spires.

Lugo's **cathedral** is vast, dark, and dusty, with a glittering silver altarpiece (free, daily 8:00–20:30, €2 to enter cloister). While it's a fine cathedral, it pales in comparison to Santiago's. Lugo also has a provincial museum and a Roman museum.

SLEEPING

(€1 = about $1.50, country code: 34)

Sleeping in Lugo is worth considering to break the long journey to Santiago from Cantabria or León. Budget *hostales* cluster just southeast of the town walls (near the bus station). The following two hotels are the only ones inside the Old Town.

$$$ Pazo Orban e Sangro is the town splurge, renting 12 rooms with hardwood floors, flat-screen TVs, and luxurious furnishings. It's just inside the town walls near the cathedral (Db-€100–120, includes breakfast, air-con, elevator, free cable Internet, Travesía do Miño, tel. 982-240-217, fax 982-245-645, www.pazodeorban.es, info@pazodeorban.es).

$$ Hotel Méndez Núñez, right in the heart of the Old Town, has a classy old lobby, a medieval-feeling lounge, and 70 rooms with worn furniture but new bathrooms (Sb-€50, Db-€60, breakfast-€6, air-con, elevator, free Internet access and Wi-Fi, Calle Reina 1, tel. 982-230-711, fax 982-229-738, www.hotelmendeznunez.com, hotel@hotelmendeznunez.com).

TRANSPORTATION CONNECTIONS

Lugo is connected by bus to **Santiago de Compostela** (7/day, 1.5–2 hrs, run by Empresa Freire), **Astorga** (5/day, 2.25–3 hrs, run by Alsa), and **León** (2/day, 4 hrs, run by Alsa).

• *After Lugo, the end is in sight. You have one final route decision to make: The fastest way (about 1.5 hrs to Santiago) is to stick with the A-6 expressway north to A Coruña, then pay €5 to take the AP-9 tollway back south to Santiago. But if you'd like to rejoin the Camino for the last stretch—following in the footsteps (or tire treads) of a millennium of pilgrims—follow signs from Lugo toward* Ourense *(on N-540/N-640, about 20–30 min longer than expressway option). In Guntín, split off on N-547 and head for Santiago de Compostela.*

However you arrive, turn the page to enjoy one of Europe's great pilgrim cities.

Buen Camino!

SANTIAGO DE COMPOSTELA

The best destination in the northwestern province of Galicia, Santiago de Compostela might well be the most magical city in Spain. This place has long had a powerful and mysterious draw on travelers—as more than a thousand years' worth of pilgrims have trod the desolate trail across the north of Spain just to peer up at the facade of its glorious cathedral.

But there's more to this city than pilgrims and the remains of St. James. Contrary to what you've heard, the rain in Spain does *not* fall mainly on the plain—it falls in Galicia. This "Atlantic Northwest" of Spain is like the Pacific Northwest of the United States: hilly, lush terrain that enjoys far more precipitation than the interior, plus dramatic coastal scenery, delicious seafood, fine local wines, and an easygoing ambience. The Spanish interior might be arid, but the northwest requires rain gear. Even the tourists here have a grungy vibe: Packs of happy hippie pilgrims seek to find themselves while hiking the ancient Camino de Santiago from France (described in the previous chapter). Santiago has a generally festive atmosphere, as travelers from every corner of the globe celebrate the end of a long journey.

Planning Your Time

Santiago's biggest downside is its location: a very long car, train, or bus trip from any other notable stop in Spain (though its airport is well-connected to other Spanish cities). But if you decide to visit, you—like a millennium's worth of pilgrims before you—will find it's worth the trek. You can get a good feel for Santiago in a day, but a second day relaxing on the squares makes the long trip here more worthwhile.

The city has one real sight: the cathedral, with its museum and the surrounding squares. The rest of your visit is for munching

Galego

Like Catalunya and the Basque Country, Galicia has its own distinctive language. Galego (called *gallego* in Spanish, and sometimes called "Galician" in English) is a mix between Spanish and Portuguese. Historically, Galego was closer to Portuguese. But Queen Isabel imported the Spanish language to the region in the 15th century, and ever since, the language has gradually come to sound more and more like Spanish. In an attempt at national unity, Franco banned Galego in the mid-20th century (along with Catalan and the Basque language, Euskara). During these trying times, Galicians spoke Spanish in public—and Galego at home. Since the end of the Franco era, Galego is a proud part of this region's cultural heritage. Street signs and sight names are posted in Galego, and I've followed suit in this chapter.

If you don't speak Spanish, you'll hardly notice a difference. Most apparent is the change in articles: *el* and *la* become *o* and *a*—so the big Galician city La Coruña is known as "A Coruña" around here. You'll also see a lot more *x*'s, which are pronounced "sh" (such as "Xacobeo," shah-koh-BAY-oh, the local word for St. James' pilgrimage route). The Spanish greeting *buenos días* becomes *bos días* in Galego. The familiar *plaza* becomes *praza*. And if you want to impress a local, say *graciñas* (grah-THEEN-yahs)—a super-polite thank you.

seafood, pilgrim-watching, and killing time in small museums. The highlight of a visit just may be hanging out on the cathedral square at about 10:00 to welcome pilgrims completing their long journey.

With more time, you could consider side-tripping to two other destinations in Galicia: Lugo and O Cebreiro (described in the Camino de Santiago chapter).

ORIENTATION

Santiago is built on hilly terrain, with lots of ups and downs. The tourist's Santiago is small: You can walk across the historic center, or Zona Monumental, in about 15 minutes. There you'll find the city's centerpiece—the awe-inspiring cathedral—as well as several other churches, a maze of pretty squares, a smattering of small museums, a bustling restaurant scene, and all of my recommended hotels.

The historic center is circled by a busy street that marks the former location of the town wall (easy to see on a map). Outside of that is the commercial city

Cheap Tricks in Santiago de Compostela

- As a pilgrim mecca, Santiago's accommodations, eateries, and sights are geared for low-budget travelers. It's an affordable place to visit.
- Santiago's top sight—its cathedral—is free to enter. Attend a pilgrim Mass (also free), especially if the giant Botafumiero incense burner will be swinging.
- Virtually all of the city's other attractions—including the Museum of Pilgrimages, Galicia Dixital, the Museum of the Galician People, the Galician Contemporary Art Museum, and the market—are also free.
- Accommodations values are excellent here. Even the "cheap" places I list can be nicer than the mid-range sleeps in other cities.

center, which is a modern, urban district called Céntrico. A 10-minute walk through Céntrico takes you to the train station.

Tourist Information

There are various tourist information facilities within a few steps of each other in the center of town (near the cathedral, on Rúa do Vilar).

For information specific to Santiago, stop by the well-organized **city TI** (daily June–Sept 9:00–21:00, Oct–May 9:00–14:00 & 16:00–19:00, Rúa do Vilar 63, tel. 981-555-129, www.santiagoturismo.com). The TI also runs walking tours and rents MP3-player audioguides (see "Tours," page 241). Santiago's several exhibition halls host temporary exhibits. Ask the TI what's going on when you're in town, and grab a free copy of the monthly *Culturall*.

On the same street is another useful office housing two separate tourist information services (both open Mon–Fri 10:00–20:00, Sat 11:00–14:00 & 17:00–19:00, Sun 11:00–14:00, Rúa do Vilar 30–32): The **Pilgrim's Information Center,** or "Xacobeo," with some information on the Camino de Santiago, especially the Galician sections; and the **Tourist Information Office of Galicia,** or Turgalicia, with general information about the region (tel. 981-584-081, www.turgalicia.es).

Arrival in Santiago de Compostela

Note that there's luggage storage at the bus station (and downtown, at Mundonet—see page 239)—but not at the train station.

By Train: Santiago's train station is on the southern edge of the modern Céntrico district. You'll find ATMs, a cafeteria, and a helpful train information office. Computer screens show upcoming departures. To reach the center of town, leave the station and walk up the grand granite staircase, jog right, cross the busy Avenida de Lugo, and walk uphill for 10 minutes on Rúa do Hórreo to Praza de Galicia. A taxi to your hotel will cost about €5.

By Bus: The bus station is about a 15-minute, mostly uphill walk northeast of the cathedral. Exit the station straight ahead (on Rúa de Ánxel Casal) and go to the roundabout called Praza da Paz. Turn left here onto Rúa da Pastoriza, which will bring you into town. To avoid the hike, I'd rather hop on local bus #5 (€0.90) and take it to the Praza de Galicia, a few steps from the historical center.

By Plane: Santiago's small airport (airport code: SCQ) is about six miles from the city center. A bus connects the airport to the bus station, then to Rúa do Doutor Teixeiro, a long block beyond Praza de Galicia at the south end of the historical center (€1.80, runs at least hourly, 20–30-min trip). A taxi into town costs about €18.

Helpful Hints

Closed Days: Many museums (except church-related ones) are closed on Mondays. The colorful produce market is closed on Sunday, slow on Monday, and busiest on Thursday and Saturday mornings.

Church Hours: The cathedral and other major churches in Santiago are open 9:00–21:00 without a siesta, while minor ones have limited visiting hours. There are special Masses for pilgrims daily at noon in the cathedral. The big Masses on Sunday are at 10:00 and noon.

Holy Year: On years that the Feast of St. James (July 25) falls on a Sunday, it's a special Compostela Holy Year (*Ano Xacobeo* in Galego)—with 25 percent more pilgrims than usual coming to Santiago, and more special services in the cathedral. But cooleth thy jets: The next one isn't until 2010.

Festivals: Late July is the main party time in Santiago, when the city hosts a world music festival and impromptu concerts all over town, and the royal family (or their representative) attends Mass in Santiago (with fireworks on July 24 and 31). The second-most important musical event in town—with several days of free concerts—occurs around Ascension (May 24 in 2009).

Internet Access: You'll see signs around the historic center. The handiest and best-equipped is **Cyber Nova 50** (Mon–Fri 9:00–24:00, Sat–Sun 10:00–23:00; faxing, phones, printing, and other services; Rúa Nova 50, tel. 981-575-188). Nearby is **Mundonet** (daily 10:00–23:00, also offers baggage storage and disc-burning, just above the other end of Rúa Nova at Rúa de Xelmírez 19). If you have a laptop, many cafés in town offer free Wi-Fi with a purchase (look for window signs).

Laundry: You'll find a self-service *lavandería* called **Axiña** a 15-minute walk from the historic center (€5.30/load self-service, €6.60 for full service, Mon–Fri 8:30–13:00 & 16:00–20:30, Sat 8:30–13:30, closed Sun and in Aug, Rúa de Ramón Cabanillas 1, tel. 981-591-323).

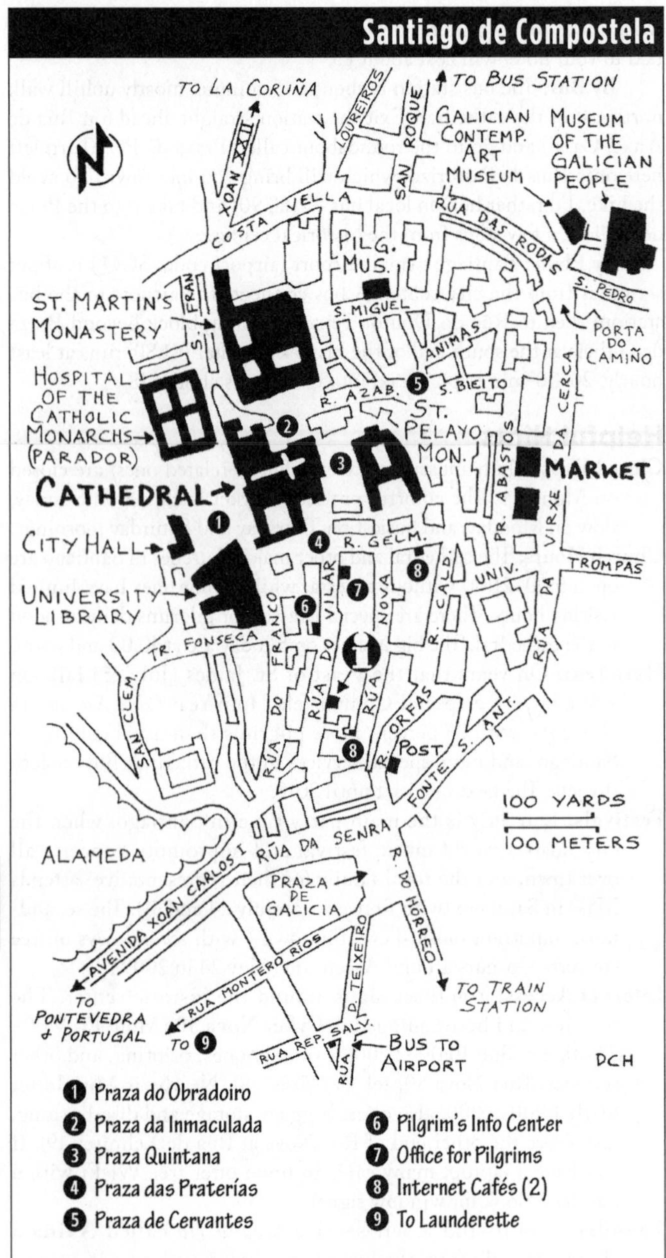

Santiago de Compostela
TO LA CORUÑA
TO BUS STATION
XOAN XXIII
LOUREIROS
SAN ROQUE
GALICIAN CONTEMP. ART MUSEUM
MUSEUM OF THE GALICIAN PEOPLE
COSTA VELLA
RÚA DAS RODAS
PILG. MUS.
S. PEDRO
S. FRAN
S. MIGUEL
ST. MARTIN'S MONASTERY
ANIMAS
PORTA DO CAMIÑO
HOSPITAL OF THE CATHOLIC MONARCHS (PARADOR)
R. AZAB.
S. BIEITO
ST. PELAYO MON.
CERCA
DA
ABASTOS
PR.
VIRXE
MARKET
CATHEDRAL
CITY HALL
R. GELM.
TROMPAS
UNIV.
UNIVERSITY LIBRARY
FRANCO
VILAR
NOVA
R. CALD.
RÚA DA
TR. FONSECA
SAN CLEM.
RÚA DO
RÚA DO
RÚA
R. ORFAS
POST
FONTE S. ANT.
100 YARDS
100 METERS
ALAMEDA
RÚA DA SENRA
R. DO HÓRREO
PRAZA DE GALICIA
AVENIDA XOÁN CARLOS I
RUA MONTERO RÍOS
P. TEIXEIRO
TO TRAIN STATION
TO PONTEVEDRA & PORTUGAL
TO 9
RUA REP. SALV.
RÚA
BUS TO AIRPORT
DCH
1 Praza do Obradoiro
2 Praza da Inmaculada
3 Praza Quintana
4 Praza das Praterías
5 Praza de Cervantes
6 Pilgrim's Info Center
7 Office for Pilgrims
8 Internet Cafés (2)
9 To Launderette

SANTIAGO

"Nunca Máis"

Galego for "never again," this message of protest appears around Santiago and Galicia. It captures the anger of local residents toward the tragic oil tanker accident in November 2002 that spilled black crude all along Spain's northern coastline. This devastating event prompted an influx of aid and volunteer support to stricken coastal regions. Locals blame "heckuva job, Brownie"-style governmental bungling for dramatically worsening the damage, and have put strong pressure on Spain to improve its environmental disaster response measures and to amend international maritime legislation to ensure it will never happen again. These words usually appear on a black field with a light-blue diagonal sash—a somber, oil-stained variation on the Galician flag, which is normally white and blue.

Shopping: Jet, the black gemstone (called *azabache* in Spanish) similar to onyx, is believed to keep away evil spirits—and to bring in tourist euros. Along with jet, the silver trade has long been important in Santiago...and continues to be a popular item for tourists. Although the Galicians are a superstitious people and have beliefs about good and bad witches, the made-in-Taiwan witches you see in souvenir shops around the city are a recent innovation. Maybe the best souvenir is a simple seashell or gourd, like the ones pilgrims carry with them along the Camino.

Best Views: There are beautiful views back toward the cathedral from the Alameda park. From the cathedral, follow Rúa do Franco to the end. Swing right into the park and continue up Paseo de Santa Susana to the viewpoint *(mirador)* along Paseo da Ferradura. There is another excellent view from the very top of the park (clearly marked on TI maps).

TOURS

The TI offers a two-hour, English-language **walking tour** that covers the cathedral and the surrounding plazas (€10, April–Oct Tue and Sun at 18:00, meet at Praza do Obradoiro, get details at the city TI). Ask about the TI's other tours, including gastronomy tours, night-time tours, and more. Or you can rent an **MP3-player audioguide** at the city TI, and follow the suggested three-hour route (€12/24-hour rental). Either tour is better than taking the silly **tourist train,** which only does a circuit around the outskirts of the old city (€5, 45 min, meet in front of the cathedral in the Praza do Obradoiro).

It's easy to visit the cathedral and nearby sights on your own with the information in this book. But if you have the extra cash, you could hire a **local guide** (for 3.5 hours: €80 Mon–Fri, €90 Sat–Sun). Patricia Furelos (mobile 630-781-795, patriciaguia@latinmail.com) and Manuel Ruzo (mobile 639-888-064, manuel@artnaturagalicia.com) are equally good, or contact the Association of Professional Guides of Galicia (tel. 981-569-890, fax 981-553-329, guiasgalicia@ctv.es).

SIGHTS

▲▲The Cathedral

Santiago's cathedral isn't the biggest in Spain, nor is it the most impressive. Yet it's certainly the most mystical, exerting a spiritual magnetism that attracts people from all walks of life and from all corners of the globe. (To more fully appreciate the pilgrim experience, before visiting the cathedral read the first part of the Camino de Santiago chapter on page 180.)

Exploring one of the most important churches in Christendom, you'll do some time travel, putting yourselves in the well-worn shoes of the millions of pilgrims who have trekked many miles to this powerful place.

• *Begin facing the cathedral's main facade, in the big square called...*

Praza do Obradoiro

Find the pavement stone with the scallop shell right in the middle of this square. For more than a thousand years, this spot has been where millions of tired pilgrims have taken a deep breath and thought to themselves: "I made it!" To maximize your chance of seeing pilgrims, be here at about 10:00—the last stop on the Camino de Santiago is two miles away, and pilgrims try to get to the cathedral in time for the 12:00 Mass. It's great fun to chat with pilgrims who've just completed their journey. They seem to be very centered and content with the experience, and tuned in to the important things in life...like taking time to talk with others. You'll likely see pilgrims arrive separately who met previously along the way, and then leave together, having reunited at the grand finale.

• *Before heading into the cathedral, take a spin around the square (start facing the cathedral).*

To your left is the **Hospital of the Catholic Monarchs** (Hostal dos Reis Católicos). Isabel and Ferdinand came to Santiago in 1501 to give thanks for successfully forcing the Moors out of Granada.

When they arrived, they found many sick pilgrims at the square. (Numerous pilgrims came to Santiago to ask for help in overcoming an illness, and the long walk here often only made their condition worse.) Isabel and Ferdinand decided to build this hospital to give pilgrims a place to recover on arrival (you'll see their coats of arms flanking the intricately carved entryway). It was free, and remained a working hospital until 1952 (many locals were actually born here)—when it was converted into a fancy parador and restaurant (see "Sleeping" and "Eating" sections). The modern white windows with the old granite facade might seem jarring—but this contrast is very common in Galicia, maximizing the brightness provided by any sunny spells in this notoriously rainy region.

Another 90 degrees to the left is the Neoclassical **City Hall** (Concello). Notice the equestrian statue up top. That's St. James, riding in from heaven to help the Spaniards defeat the Moors. All over town, Santiago's namesake and symbol—a Christian evangelist on a horse, killing Muslims with his sword—is out doing his bloody thing. See any police on the square? Santiago's cathedral, as the third most important Christian pilgrimage site in the world (after Jerusalem and Rome), would be a high-profile target for Islamic fundamentalists. It doesn't help that St. James seems to take such joy in butchering Muslims.

Completing the square (90 more degrees to the left) is the original **University** building, now just the library. Santiago has Spain's third-oldest university, with more than 30,000 students (medicine and law are especially popular).

You'll likely see Spanish school groups on the square, field-tripping from all over the country. Teachers love to use this spot for an architecture lesson, since it features four different architectural styles (starting with the cathedral and spinning left): 18th-century Baroque; 16th-century Plateresque; 18th-century Neoclassical; and 15th-century Romanesque (the facade around the university door).

• *Now take a look at the...*

Cathedral Facade

Twelve hundred years ago, a monk followed a field of stars (probably the Milky Way) to the little Galician village of San Fiz de Solovio and discovered what appeared to be the long-lost tomb of St. James.

On July 25, 813, the local bishop declared that St. James' relics had been found. They set to building a church here and named the place Santiago (St. James) de Compostela (*campo de estrellas,* or "field of stars," for the celestial bodies that guided the monk).

For the last 12 centuries, the cathedral you see today has gradually been added on to the original simple chapel. By the 11th century, the church was overwhelmed by the crowds. Construction of a larger cathedral began in 1075, and the work took 150 years. (The granite workers who built it set up shop on this very square—still called Praza do Obradoiro, literally, "Workers' Square.") Much of the design is attributed to a palace artist named Maestro Mateo, whom you'll meet a little later.

The exterior of the cathedral you see today is *not* the one that medieval pilgrims saw (though the interior is much the same). In the mid-18th century, Santiago's bishop—all fired up from a trip to Baroque-slathered Rome, and wanting to protect the original, now-deteriorating facade—decided to spruce up the building with a new Baroque facade. He also replaced the simple stonework in the interior with gaudy gold.

Scrutinize the facade. Atop the middle steeple is St. James. Beneath him is his tomb, marked by a star—one of the many symbols you'll see all over the place (see "The Symbols of Santiago" on page 190). On either side of the tomb are Theodorus and Athanasius, James' disciples who brought his body back to Santiago. On the side pillars are, to the left, James' father Zebedee, and to the right, his mother Salomé.

Don't you wish you had a miniature replica of this beautiful facade to carry around with you? Actually, you probably do. Check your pocket for a copper-colored euro coin worth €0.01, €0.02, or €0.05. There it is! Of all the churches in Spain, they chose this one as their representative in Euroland. It's even more important when you consider the significance of the images depicted on Spain's other euro coinage: a portrait of the author of *Don Quixote,* Miguel de Cervantes, Spain's greatest contributor to world literature; and the current king, Juan Carlos I. Sevilla and Toledo may have bigger cathedrals, but Santiago has the symbolism to propel its church into this powerful triumvirate.

The cathedral also houses a museum with three parts; as you face this facade, the door to the main museum is to the right, the entry to the crypt is dead ahead (under the staircase), and the door on the left leads to the Gelmírez Palace (and the cathedral rooftop, both part of the Cathedral Museum, described later in this chapter).

• *But that's for later. For now, head up the stairs to the cathedral and go inside (daily 9:00–21:00; if a service is going on, the front entrance is usually closed—enter around the side or come back later).*

As you enter, you're face-to-face with the...

Portico of Glory

Take a step back in time (remember, this used to be the main facade of the cathedral—sculpted in about 1180 by Maestro Mateo). You're a medieval pilgrim, and you've just walked 500 miles from the Frankish lands to reach this cathedral. You're here to request the help of St. James in recovering from an illness or to give thanks for a success. Maybe you've come to honor the wish of a dying relative or to be forgiven for your sins. Whatever the reason, you came here on foot.

You can't read, but you can tell from the carved images that this magnificent door represents the Final Judgment. There's Jesus, front and center, surrounded by Matthew, Mark, Luke, and John. Beside them are angels carrying tools for the Crucifixion—the cross, the crown of thorns, the spear, and a jug of vinegar. Arching above them are 24 musicians playing celestial music—each one with a different medieval instrument. Under Jesus sits St. James, and below him, a column with the genealogy of Jesus (with Mary near the top, and above her, the Holy Trinity: Father, Son, and a dove representing the Holy Spirit).

At the bases of the columns are monsters—being crushed by the glory of God. Atop the columns to the left are prophets of the Old Testament, and to the right, the apostles of the New Testament—all barefoot in the presence of God. The gang's all here. The guy with the biggest smile is Daniel.

Take an earthly diversion from your religious journey for a minute: Locals say Daniel is grinning because he's looking at the carved statue of a beautiful, voluptuous woman immediately across from him. The story continues that the priest thought she was too buxom, and instructed the sculptor to make her less shapely. He did, but the people didn't like being denied a simple pleasure. To get even, ever since, Santiago has made its popular cheese, called *tetilla,* in the shape of what they liked on the statue (you can buy the cheese at the market, listed on page 253).

Return to the spiritual plane. As a pilgrim, you would walk to the column in the middle of the entryway (try to ignore the metal bars that have recently been erected to "protect" the column from pilgrims). Squint down the nave to the end, and you'll see the stone statue of St. James that marks his tomb. Trembling with excitement at the culmination of your long journey, you'd place your hand into the well-worn finger holes on the column and bow your head, giving thanks to St. James for safe passage. Then you'd go around to the other side of the post and, at knee level, see Maestro Mateo, who carved this fine facade. What a smart guy! Kneel and tap your

head against his (or, in a pinch, against the bar) three times—to help improve your intelligence.

• *Now wander down the...*

Nave

Look up, noticing the barrel vault and the heavy, dark Romanesque design of the church. Up near the top, notice the gallery. This is where sweaty, smelly pilgrims sleep (and their animals, too). Man, it stinks in here.

• *Continue up the nave until you reach the high altar, where you'll see a thick rope hanging from a pulley system high in the dome, which is sometimes attached to the...*

Botafumeiro

This huge, silver incense burner (120 pounds and about the size of a small child) is suspended from the ceiling during special Masses (occurring about 25 times a year; ask at the TI if one is scheduled during your visit) or when a pilgrim pays about €250 to see it in action. Supposedly the custom of swinging this giant incense dispenser began in order to counteract the stench of the pilgrims. And to enhance the good mood of the congregation—already giddy for having completed the Camino de Santiago—priests were once said to add a pinch of cannabis to the mixture. After communion, eight men (called *tiraboleiros*) pull on the rope, and this huge contraption swings in a wide arc up and down the transept, spewing sweet-smelling smoke. If you're here to see it, the most impressive view is sitting or standing on either side of the main altar. From this position, the *botafumeiro* seems to whiz directly over your head. When not in use, the *botafumeiro* and a replica are kept on display in the cathedral library (see "Cathedral Museum," page 249).

• *Stand in the center of the nave, in front of the...*

Altar

You'll have to cheat with time travel for this section, since the original medieval choir and altar were replaced with this gilded Baroque piece in the 18th century (fragments of the original stone choir can be seen in the Cathedral Museum). Look all the way back, at the big gold altar, to see all three representations of St. James in one place (see "The Three Santiagos" on page 250): up top, on a white horse, is James the *Matamoros*—Moor-Slayer; below that (just under the canopy) is pilgrim James; and below that is the original stone Apostle James by

St. James

Santiago is Spanish for "St. James." James and his brother John, sons of Zebedee and Salomé, were well-off fishermen on the Sea of Galilee. One fateful day, a charismatic visionary came and said to them, "Come with me, and I will make you fishers of men." They threw down their nets and became apostles.

Along with Peter, James and John were supposedly Jesus' favorites—he called them the "sons of thunder." Some historians even think Jesus and James might have been related. (This close relationship makes James an even more appealing object of worship.)

After Jesus' death, the apostles spread out and brought his message to other lands. St. James spent a decade as a missionary bringing Christianity to the farthest reaches of the known world—which, back then, was northwest Spain. The legend goes that as soon as he returned home to the Holy Land in A.D. 44, James was beheaded by Herod Agrippa. Before his body and head could be thrown to the lions—as was the custom in those days—they were rescued by two of his disciples, Theodorus and Athanasius.

These two brought his body back to Spain in a small boat and entombed it in the hills of Galicia—hiding it carefully so it would not be found by the Roman authorities. There it lay hidden for almost eight centuries. In 813, a monk—supposedly directed by the stars—discovered the tomb, and the local bishop proudly exclaimed that St. James was in Galicia. Santiago de Compostela was born.

But is this the *real* story? Historians figure the "discovery" of the remains of St. James in Spain provided a necessary way to rally Europe against the Moors, who had invaded Spain and were threatening to continue into Europe. The "marketing" of St. James was further bolstered by his miraculous appearance, on horseback and wielding a sword, to fight for the Christian army in the pivotal battle of Clavijo during the Reconquista. With St. James *Matamoros* ("the Moor-Slayer") in Iberia, all of Europe was inspired to rise up and push the Muslims back into Africa...which they finally did in 1492. James eventually became Spain's patron saint, and for centuries Spanish armies rode into battle with the cry *"Santiago y cierra España!"* ("St. James and strike for Spain!").

Sure, the whole thing was likely a propaganda hoax to get a local populace to support a war. But yesterday's and today's pilgrims may not care whether the body of St. James actually lies in this church. The pilgrimage to Santiago is a spiritual quest powered through the ages by faith.

Maestro Mateo—still pointing down to his tomb after all these centuries.

The dome over the altar was added in the 16th century to bring some light into this dark Romanesque church.

On the columns up and down the nave and transept, notice the symbols carved into the granite. These are the markings of the masons who made the columns—to keep track of how many they'd be paid for.

• *Now head back to the Middle Ages. The finale of your long pilgrimage is just ahead. Go down the ambulatory on the left side of the altar—passing where the* botafumeiro *rope is moored to the pillar—and walk down the little stairway (see the green light, on your right) to the level of the earlier, 10th-century church and the...*

Tomb of St. James

There he is, in the little silver chest, marked by a star—Santiago. You kneel in front of the tomb and make your request or say your thanks. Then you continue through the little passage and trudge up the stairs. Turn left and wander around the ambulatory, noticing the various chapels (built by noblemen who wanted to be buried close to St. James).

• *At the very back of the church (behind the altar) is the greenish...*

Holy Door

This special door is open only during Holy Years, when pilgrims use it to access the tomb and statue of the apostle. The current door was sculpted by a local artist for the 2004 Holy Year. It shows six scenes from the life of St. James: the conversion moment when Jesus invited those Galilean fishermen to become "fishers of men"; Jesus with the 12 apostles (James is identified by his scallop shell); James doing his "fishing" in Spain; his return to Jerusalem in A.D. 44 to be beheaded; the ship taking his body back to Spain; and the discovery of James' body by the local bishop in 813. At the bottom, the little snail is the symbol of the pilgrim...slow and steady, with everything on its back.

There's one more pilgrim ritual to complete. Find the little door near where you came out from the tomb (perhaps with a line of pilgrims—10 yards away, by another green light, closed 13:30–16:00 and after 20:00). Climb the stairs under the huge babies, find Maestro Mateo's stone statue of St. James—gilded and caked with precious gems—and embrace him from behind...under the vigilant eye of a cathedral watchman, there to ensure the unholy temptation to pry loose a jewel doesn't overcome you.

• *Congratulations, pilgrim! You have completed the Camino de Santiago. Now go in peace.*

Museums at the Cathedral

Back out on the main square, you can take some time to enjoy a pair of cathedral-related museums. There are three parts: The Cathedral Museum (enter through door on the right, as you face main facade) and crypt (under the main staircase in front) share one ticket, while the Gelmírez Palace (door on the left) and rooftop are covered by a separate ticket.

▲Cathedral Museum (Museo da Catedral)—The best of the cathedral's museums, this shows off some interesting pieces from the fine treasury collection and artifacts from the cathedral's history. There's virtually no English inside, so pick up the included English guidebooklet as you enter (€5, or €3 for pilgrims; June–Sept Mon–Sat 10:00–14:00 & 16:00–20:00, Sun 10:00–14:00; Oct–May Mon–Sat 10:00–13:30 & 16:00–18:30, Sun 10:00–13:30; tel. 981-569-327).

On the ground floor, you'll find the remaining pieces of Maestro Mateo's original stone choir (stone seats for priests; these seats filled the center of the nave in the 12th century), pieced together as part of a new replica. Nearby, look for a miniature model of the choir. You'll also see fragments of Roman settlements, dating from before the tomb of St. James was discovered here.

On the first floor, find two statues of a pregnant Mary. While this theme is unusual in most of Europe, it's common in Galicia. The coin collection shows off examples of money that pilgrims brought with them from all over Europe (see the displayed map). The dirham coin in the center case is dated 387. Muhammad became a prophet in 612; therefore, this is from the year 997 on the Christian calendar.

On the second floor, you'll come to the cloister. The tombs lining the cloister floor hold the remains of priests from the cathedral. In the courtyard, you'll see a fountain (which once stood in front of the cathedral and was used by pilgrims to cleanse themselves) and the original church bells (replaced with new models in 1989). As you walk left (clockwise) around the cloister, the first door leads to the Royal Chapel, with a beautiful-smelling cedar altar that houses dozens and dozens of relics. The centerpiece (eye level) holds the remains (likely the skull) of St. James the Lesser (the *other* Apostle James). Look up to find St. James riding heroically out of the woodwork to rally all Europe to reconquer the Iberian Peninsula. This altarpiece was recarved after a fire around 1900.

Cross the hall to the treasury. Look for the painted wood altar depicting the tale of St. James—including his beheading, and his body being taken back to Galicia. The fancy solid-gold monstrance is used for carrying the communion host around the cathedral on Corpus

The Three Santiagos

You'll see three different depictions of St. James in the cathedral and throughout the city:

1. Apostle James: James dressed in typical apostle robes, often indiscernible from the other apostles (sometimes with a pilgrim's stick or shell).

2. Pilgrim James: James wearing some or all of the traditional garb of the Camino de Santiago pilgrim: a brown cloak, floppy hat, walking stick, shell, gourd, and sandals. Among pilgrims, he's the one carrying a book.

3. Crusader James, the Moor-Slayer: Centuries after his death, the Spaniards called on St. James for aid in various battles against the Moors. According to legend, St. James appeared from the heavens on a white horse and massacred Muslim foes. Locals don't particularly care for this depiction—especially these days, when the rising tide of Islamic fundamentalists could justifiably find it provocative.

Christi (the wafer sits in the little round window in the middle).

The library (near where you first entered the cloister) is where they store old books, a funky rack for reading those huge tomes ("turn pages" by spinning the rack), and the *botafumeiro* (gigantic incense burner). The next room shows how tapestries could warm a stone palace.

Go up one more floor (passing a stairwell shrine to St. Salomé—St. James' mother). If the doors are open, enjoy views from a fine balcony overlooking Praza do Obradoiro. Then walk through the collection, with some vestments and more tapestries—including some from cartoons by Rubens (first room) and Goya (last room).

After visiting the museum, consider paying a visit to the **crypt** (same ticket, under main stairs into cathedral). Since the church was built on a too-small hill, the crypt was constructed to support the part of the nave that hung over. While the crypt, under a Maestro Mateo–decorated Romanesque vault, is about as dead as its residents, it does display interesting models of the medieval musical instruments featured in the heavenly angels' combo in the Portico of Glory.

Gelmírez Palace (Pazo de Xelmírez)—Though the rooms of this now-empty medieval home (the traditional residence of the arch-

bishop) are stark and stony, the attraction here is the opportunity to walk on the rooftop of the cathedral. However, the experience offers little more than a fine view and a chance to burn your clothes at the cross—a once-common practice for pilgrims. You can visit the palace and rooftop only with a one-hour tour, which is usually in Spanish; try dropping by or calling ahead to see if an English tour is scheduled, and to reserve a spot (€10, or €8 if you bought a ticket to the Cathedral Museum, tours depart hourly 10:00–14:00 & 16:00–20:00, tel. 981-552-985, www.archicompostela.org).

Cathedral Squares

There is a square on each side of the cathedral, and all of them are lined with interesting sights and other tidbits. You've already visited Praza do Obradoiro, in the front. Here are the other three, working clockwise (to reach the first one, go up the passage—which street musicians appreciate for its acoustics—to the left as you're facing the main cathedral facade).

Praza da Inmaculada—This was the way most medieval pilgrims using the French Road actually approached the cathedral. Across the square is **St. Martin's Monastery** (Mosteiro de San Martiño Pinario), one of two monasteries that sprang up around the church to care for pilgrims. Today, it houses a museum of ecclesiastical artifacts and special exhibits. To the left of the monastery's main door is a fun multimedia exhibit called "Galicia Dixital" (see page 253).

Walk to the corner of the square with the arcade, and go to the post with the sign for Rúa Acibechería (next to the garbage can, under the streetlight). If you look to the roof of the cathedral, between the big dome and the tall tower, you can make out a small green cross. This is where the clothes of medieval pilgrims were burned when they finally arrived at Santiago. This ritual was created for hygienic reasons in an age of frightful diseases...and filthy pilgrims.

• *Continue along the arcade and around the corner, and you'll enter...*

Praza Quintana—The door of the cathedral facing this square is the Holy Door, which is only opened during Holy Years (next in 2010). There's St. James, flanked by the disciples who brought his body back to Galicia. Below them are the 12 apostles and 12 prophets. Tip: Old Testament prophets hold scrolls. New Testament apostles hold books.

Across the square from the cathedral, you'll see the huge **St. Pelayo Monastery** (Mosteiro San Paio). The windows of its cells (now used by Benedictine sisters—notice the bars and privacy screens)

face the cathedral. The church at the north end of this monastery is worth a peek. It has a frilly Baroque altar and a statue with a typical Galician theme: a pregnant Mary (to the left as you face main altar). The nuns sing at the evening vespers following the 19:30 Mass (Mon–Sat). Just off this sanctuary is the entrance to the monastery's **Sacred Art Museum** (Museo de Arte Sacra), with a small but interesting collection (€1.50, Mon–Sat 10:30–14:00 & 16:00–19:00, closed Sun, some posted English-language information). The nuns of St. Pelayo also make Galicia's best ***tarta de Santiago***—almond cake with a cross of Santiago in powdered sugar dusted on top. To buy one, exit the church to the right, head up the stairs, and walk around behind the monastery to find the entrance on Rúa San Paio de Antealtares. Once inside, go to the small window on the left (generally open Mon–Sat 9:00–14:00 & 15:00–19:00, unpredictable hours Sun).

• *Continue around to the...*

Praza das Praterías—This "Silversmiths' Square" is where Santiago's silver workers used to have their shops (and some still do). Overlooking the square is a tall **tower** that was once a fortress for keeping locals—who were fed up with high taxes—at bay, and for fending off invading enemies over the years, including Normans, Moors, English pirates, and Napoleon's army. An 18th-century bishop added the Baroque top and the bells. At the very top of the tower is a powerful light, most noticeable at night, that serves as a beacon to pilgrims.

The **cathedral door** facing this square actually combines elements of two different stone doors that were damaged over the centuries. That's why it's a hodgepodge of religious figures and motifs.

Take a look at the **fountain.** Notice the woman sitting on St. James' tomb, holding aloft a star—a typical city symbol. Under her are animals that seem to be half-horse, half-fish. This is the way that Portuguese pilgrims approached Santiago—some by land, others by sea. The mansion behind with the impressive Galician Baroque facade is very skinny—built to give the square an architectural harmony. Its centerpiece even copies the fountain's star.

Cross the street beyond the fountain (Rúa do Vilar) and on the left, you'll see the **Office for Pilgrims.** Before entering, at the gift shop next door (on the right), look for the *compostela*—the certificate issued by the office to those who can prove they finished the entire Camino—with the pilgrim's name in Latin, the date, and the priest's signature. In the shop's window is a life-size replica of the *botafumeiro,* the giant incense burner. Wander into the office (daily 9:00–21:00). Upstairs is a notice board reminiscent of pre-email days—a reminder of the friendships forged on the long trail to Santiago. Also while you're upstairs, you're likely to see weary but jubilant pilgrims receiving their "diplomas."

Other Sights

▲▲Market (Praza de Abastos)—This wonderful market, housed in Old World stone buildings, offers a fine opportunity to do some serious people-watching (Mon–Sat 8:00–14:00, closed Sun). Monday's the least interesting day, since the fishermen don't go out on Sunday. It's busiest and best on Thursday and Saturday, when villagers from the countryside come to sell things (go early).

The market was built in the 1920s (to consolidate Santiago's many small markets) in a style perfectly compatible with the medieval wonder that surrounds it. Today it offers an opportunity to get up close and personal with some still-twitching seafood. Keep an eye out for the specialties you'll want to try later—octopus, shrimp, crabs, lobsters, and expensive-as-gold *percebes* (barnacles; see sidebar on page 260). You'll also see the local *chorizo* (spicy sausage).

Grelos are a local type of turnip greens with a thick stalk and long, narrow leaves—grown only here, and often used in the *caldo galego* soup. The little green *pimientos de Padrón* (in season June–Oct) look like jalapeños, but lack the kick...sometimes.

In the cheese cases, you'll see what look like huge yellow Hershey's Kisses (or, to some, breasts). For the story on how they got this shape, see "Portico of Glory," page 245. Among typical Galician cheeses are *tetilla* (white, creamy) and *San Simón* (yellow, smoked). If you linger long enough, they'll offer you a taste.

▲Museum of Pilgrimages (Museo das Peregrinacións)—This fine museum examines various aspects of the pilgrimage phenomenon. You'll see a map of pilgrimage sites around the world, and then learn more about the pilgrimage that brings people to Santiago. There are models of earlier versions of the cathedral, explanations of the differing depictions of St. James throughout history (apostle, pilgrim, and Crusader), and coverage of the various routes to Santiago and stories of some prominent pilgrims. This well-presented place lends historical context to all of those backpackers you see in the streets. While exhibits are not described in English, the thorough info sheets available throughout the museum are well worth reading (usually free, sometimes €2.40, Tue–Fri 10:00–20:00, Sat 10:30–13:30 & 17:00–20:00, Sun 10:30–13:30, closed Mon, Rúa de San Miguel 4—but they plan to move to Praza das Praterías in 2010, tel. 981-581-558, www.mdperegrinacions.com).

Galicia Dixital—Housed in the St. Martin's Monastery, this futuristic, kid-friendly exhibit uses various kinds of technology to explore Galicia and Santiago in virtual reality. You'll visit several exhibits, accompanied by a Spanish guide (English groups unlikely, but call ahead to see if an English-speaking group is coming that you can join). First you'll take a 3-D, surround-sound tour of the squares around the cathedral (including a surprise thunderstorm). Then you go on *A Vertixe*—which means "the vertigo," as you'll soon learn. A motion-simulator 3-D "roller-coaster" ride zips you around the top of the cathedral, then underground (keep hands inside your chair, which jerks around wildly). You can don a *casco virtual* ("virtual helmet") and wander through the cathedral. Other 3-D movies include a submarine trip through Galicia's waterways for a look at sea life, and an animated tour of the cathedral with a strange little pilgrim creature. While enjoyable, you can't shake the feeling that you could step outside and see most of this stuff in person. Still, it's an enjoyable enough way to get out of the sun for an hour. It's not Disney World, but it's not bad (free, Mon–Sat 10:30–14:00 & 16:00–20:30, closed Sun; must go on one-hour guided visits, which leave about every 30 min; last visits begin at 13:00 and 19:30, tel. 981-554-048).

Museum of the Galician People (Museo do Pobo Galego)—If you're intrigued by this very traditional part of Spain, this museum will give you more insight into rural Galician life. As you tour this collection, remember that if you side-trip a few miles into the countryside, you'll find traditional lifestyles thriving even today. Beautifully displayed around an 18th-century cloister, the museum springs from a unique triple staircase, which provided privacy to various hierarchies of the monks who lived here, depending on which stairway you climbed. The collection shows off boat-building and fishing techniques, farming implements and simple horse-drawn carts, tools of trade and handicrafts (including carpentry, pottery, looms, and baskets), traditional costumes, and a collection of musical instruments, with an emphasis on the bagpipes *(gaitas)*. If the farm tools seem old-fashioned, there's a reason: Old inheritance laws mean that plots are increasingly smaller, so modern farming machinery is impractical—keeping traditional equipment alive. There's virtually no English, except for a helpful €1.50 guidebook (free entry, Tue–Sat 10:00–14:00 & 16:00–20:00, Sun 11:00–14:00, closed Mon, at northeast edge of historical center in monastery of San Domingos de Bonaval, just beyond Porta do Camiño, tel. 981-583-620, www.museodopobo.es). Behind the museum is a plush and peaceful park—once crowded with tombstones.

Next door, in the striking modern building, is the **Galician Contemporary Art Museum** (Centro Galego de Arte Contemporánea), with continually rotating exhibits—mostly by local artists (free,

Tue–Sun 11:00–20:00, closed Mon, tel. 981-546-619, www.cgac.org).

City of Culture of Galicia—This super-modern cultural complex is being built on a hillside near Santiago de Compostela. Based on an incredibly ambitious and conceptual design that's proving far more costly to implement than expected, the project is intended to put Santiago on the map as a 21st-century city (similar to Bilbao's Guggenheim). These days the complex is becoming something of a white elephant, as delays and an ever-inflating price tag are giving local residents a taste of builders' remorse. They hope to have the complex at least partly complete by the next Holy Year, 2010, with the rest done by 2012. Stay tuned (www.cidadedacultura.es).

ENTERTAINMENT

Local Street Music—You'll likely hear **bagpipes** *(gaitas)* being played in the streets of Santiago. Nobody knows for certain how this unlikely instrument caught on in Galicia, but the tradition has supposedly been passed down since the Celts lived here. Some singers use bagpipes, too, including Milladoiro (a group popular with Galicians in their 40s and 50s) and Carlos Nuñez (trendy with younger people today). Caped university students, called ***tunas***, can be seen singing traditional songs around town every night during the summer.

Galician Folk-Music Concerts—While the summertime is lively with folk-music concerts (ask for details at the TI), the rest of the year is not. One good bet is to drop by a practice session of the troupe called Cantigas e Agarimos (meets Wed and Fri at 21:30 for an hour, maybe at Rúa da Algalia de Arriba 11 or possibly playing at a nearby location—check their schedule at www.cantigaseagarimos.com). Since 1921, this group has shared the traditional Galician culture with visitors in performances throughout the year. Tall Oscar Cobos is a group leader who lived in New York City for five years. Now he's clearly found his niche as a dancer and dance teacher here in what he calls "the kingdom of far, far away."

SLEEPING

To cater to all those pilgrims, Santiago has a glut of good, cheap accommodations. Since the Camino was resurrected in 1993, new hotels are popping up all the time—many of them subsidized by the EU. There aren't many affordable big hotels in town for tour groups, so they tend to stay along the Rías Baixas (fjord-like estuaries) about an hour to the south, where beds are cheap. That means many of Santiago's visitors are day-trippers, arriving at about 10:30 and leaving in the afternoon. After dark, it's just you, the locals, the pilgrims, and St. James. High season is roughly Easter through September; most places charge more during this time. The trickiest dates to book are

Sleep Code

(€1 = about $1.50, country code: 34)
S = Single, **D** = Double/Twin, **T** = Triple, **Q** = Quad, **b** = bathroom, **s** = shower only. Unless I note otherwise, you can assume credit cards are accepted and English is spoken, but breakfast is not included. IVA tax (7 percent) is not included in these rates.

To help you easily sort through these listings, I've divided the rooms into three categories, based on the price for a standard double room with bath:

$$$ Higher Priced—Most rooms €85 or more.
$$ Moderately Priced—Most rooms between €50-85.
$ Lower Priced—Most rooms €50 or less.

Easter Sunday weekend and the Feast of St. James (July 24–25)—so if you plan to be in town around these times, reserve your rooms well ahead. When I list a range of prices, it represents low season to high season. Any single prices listed are an average (midseason). The *hostales* speak enough English to make a reservation by phone (though sometimes not much more). Don't overlook the very affordable Hostal Suso and Hospedaje Ramos, which are nicer than many of my moderately priced listings in other towns.

$$$ Hotel Virxe da Cerca is a wonderful splurge just on the edge of the historical center, across the street from the market. Its standard rooms are in a modern building, but some of its "superior" and all of its "special" historic rooms—with classy old stone and hardwoods—are in a restored 18th-century Jesuit residence. All 43 rooms surround a lush garden oasis (standard Sb-€65–85, superior Sb-€75–95, bigger "special" Sb-€85–105, standard Db-€85–105, superior Db-€95–110, bigger "special" Db-€105–130, extra bed-€15–20, breakfast-€9, beautiful glassed-in breakfast room overlooks garden, elevator, free Internet access and Wi-Fi, Rúa Virxe da Cerca 27, tel. 902-405-858, fax 981-586-925, www.pousadasdecompostela.com, info@pousadasdecompostela.com).

$$$ Altaïr Hotel is owned by the Liñares family (see Costa Vella listing, below), but caters to a different clientele. Located in a renovated three-story residence, its 11 spacious rooms and mod decor can best be described as "rustic minimalist." Exposed stone walls and open beams mixed with a sleek design provide a unique yet surprisingly affordable experience (Sb-€70–80, Db-€90–110, superior Db-€110–130, extra bed-€20, breakfast-€8, free Wi-Fi, affordable laundry service for guests, Rúa dos Loureiros 12, tel. & fax 981-554-712, www.altairhotel.net, info@altairhotel.net).

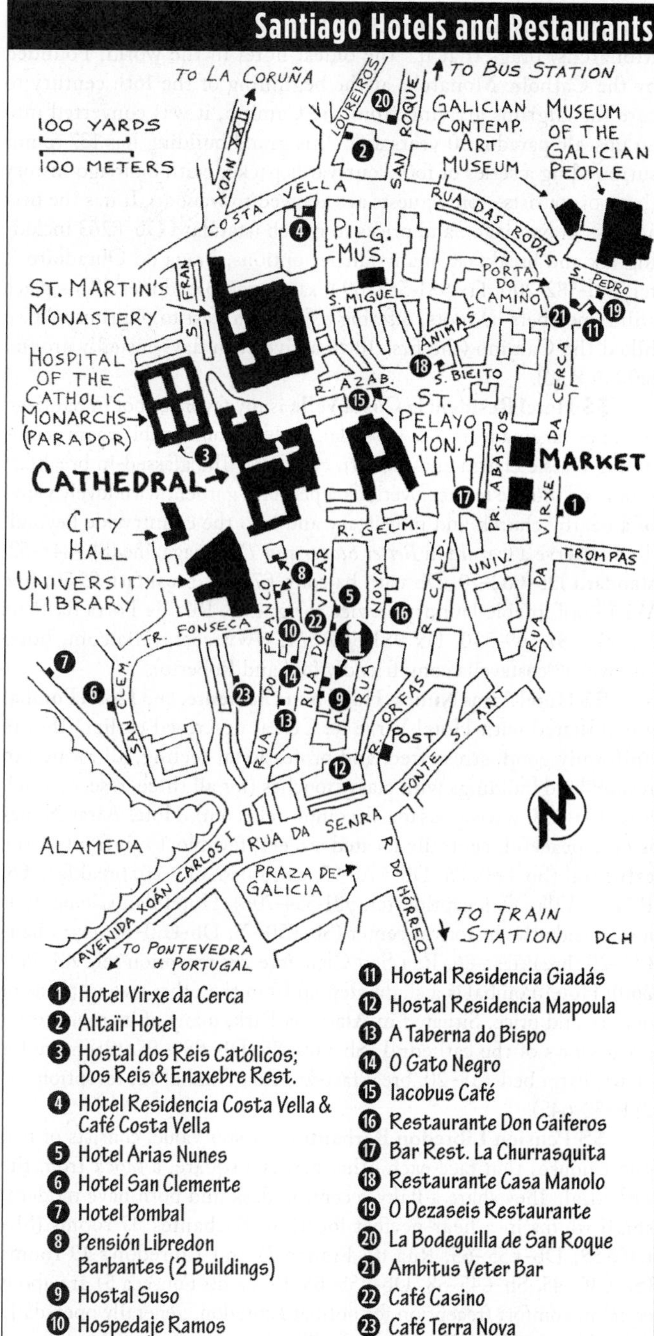
Santiago Hotels and Restaurants
TO LA CORUÑA
TO BUS STATION
100 YARDS
100 METERS
LOUREIROS
SAN ROQUE
XOAN XXIII
GALICIAN CONTEMP. ART MUSEUM
MUSEUM OF THE GALICIAN PEOPLE
COSTA VELLA
RUA DAS RODAS
PILG. MUS.
PORTA DO CAMIÑO
S. PEDRO
S. FRAN
S. MIGUEL
ST. MARTIN'S MONASTERY
ANIMAS
HOSPITAL OF THE CATHOLIC MONARCHS (PARADOR)
R. AZAB.
S. BIEITO
ST. PELAYO MON.
CERCA
DA CERCA
PR. ABASTOS
MARKET
CATHEDRAL
VIRXE
CITY HALL
R. GELM.
TROMPAS
UNIV.
UNIVERSITY LIBRARY
R. CALD.
DA
VILAR
RUA DO
NOVA
RUA
TR. FONSECA
FRANCO
DO
RUA
SAN CLEM.
R. ORFAS
POST
FONTE S. ANT
ALAMEDA
RUA DA SENRA
AVENIDA XOÁN CARLOS I
PRAZA DE GALICIA
R. DO HÓRREO
TO TRAIN STATION
TO PONTEVEDRA & PORTUGAL
DCH
1 Hotel Virxe da Cerca
2 Altaïr Hotel
3 Hostal dos Reis Católicos; Dos Reis & Enaxebre Rest.
4 Hotel Residencia Costa Vella & Café Costa Vella
5 Hotel Arias Nunes
6 Hotel San Clemente
7 Hotel Pombal
8 Pensión Libredon Barbantes (2 Buildings)
9 Hostal Suso
10 Hospedaje Ramos
11 Hostal Residencia Giadás
12 Hostal Residencia Mapoula
13 A Taberna do Bispo
14 O Gato Negro
15 Iacobus Café
16 Restaurante Don Gaiferos
17 Bar Rest. La Churrasquita
18 Restaurante Casa Manolo
19 O Dezaseis Restaurante
20 La Bodeguilla de San Roque
21 Ambitus Veter Bar
22 Café Casino
23 Café Terra Nova

$$$ Hostal dos Reis Católicos (Hospital of the Catholic Monarchs) brags that it's the oldest hotel in the world. Founded by the Catholic Monarchs at the beginning of the 16th century to care for pilgrims arriving from the Camino, it was converted into an upscale parador 50 years ago. This grand building has 137 rooms surrounding a series of four courtyards packed with Santiago history (but not tourists—only guests are allowed to wander). It has the best address in Santiago...and prices to match (standard Db-€263 including tax and breakfast, many fancier options, Praza do Obradoiro 1, tel. 981-582-200, fax 981-563-094, santiago@parador.es). This place still remembers its roots, offering a free breakfast to pilgrims who've hiked the Camino (the first 10 to arrive each day—usually around 8:00 or 8:30).

$$ Hotel Residencia Costa Vella is my favorite spot in Santiago (book as far in advance as possible), with 14 comfortable rooms combining classic charm and modern comforts. The glassed-in breakfast room and lounge terrace overlook a peaceful garden, with lovely views of a nearby church and monastery and into the countryside beyond. They deserve a feature in *Better Stones and Tiles* magazine (Sb-€48–52, standard Db-€62–70, Db with balcony-€78–87, breakfast-€5.50, free Wi-Fi, affordable laundry service for guests, Rúa da Porta da Pena 17, tel. 981-569-530, fax 981-569-531, www.costavella.com, hotel costavella@costavella.com, friendly José and Roberto).

$$ Hotel Airas Nunes, Hotel San Clemente, and **Hotel Pombal** are affiliated with Hotel Virxe da Cerca, described earlier. They're uniformly good, stress-free, and professional-feeling, all located in restored old buildings with classy touches (for all three, reserve at tel. 902-405-858, www.pousadasdecompostela.com). Hotel Airas Nunes is on a peaceful, centrally located street a few blocks in front of the cathedral (Sb-€60–85, Db-€70–95, extra bed-€15–20, breakfast-€6, Rúa do Vilar 17, reception tel. 981-554-706). Hotel San Clemente is just outside the historical center (Sb-€50–75, Db-€60–85, extra bed-€15–20, breakfast-€6, Rúa San Clemente 28, reception tel. 981-569-260). Hotel Pombal is a slight step up from the other two in terms of quality and price. Situated in Alameda Park, many of its rooms offer great views of the cathedral (Sb-€60–85, Db-€80–95, €10 more for views, extra bed-€15–20, breakfast-€6, Rúa Pombal 12, reception tel. 981-552-645).

$$ Pensión Libredon Barbantes, a lesser value, consists of two guest houses that face each other across a square, a block from the cathedral. They share a flaky reception desk and both have modern, small rooms in a near-perfect location. Barbantes' 17 rooms (Sb-€40–58, Db-€55–65, Rúa do Franco 3) and Libredon's 19 rooms (Ss-€40–45, Sb-€45–58, Db-€55–65, Praza do Fonseca 5) are about equal in comfort (reception for both at Libredon, generally open daily 9:00–22:00, tel. 981-576-520, www.libredonbarbantes.com).

$ Hostal Suso, run by the friendly Quintela family, is a great value offering 10 ridiculously cheap, new-feeling rooms around an airy atrium over a cheery—if smoky—little bar in the heart of Santiago (Sb-€18–20, Db-€35–40, breakfast-€3–5, Rúa do Vilar 65, tel. 981-586-611).

$ Hospedaje Ramos rents 10 big, tasteful, clean rooms with lots of stairs right in the center of town (Sb-€23, Db-€36, includes tax, no breakfast, Rúa da Raíña 18, tel. 981-581-859).

$ Hostal Residencia Giadás, tucked away just beyond the market, faces a tidy little square as if it owns it. The eight rooms, some with slanted floors, are simple but charming (Sb-€28–30, Db-€45–47, Tb-€60–63, elevator, next to Porta do Camiño at Praza do Matadoiro 2, tel. 981-587-071, delightful Lola and the Giadás family).

$ Hostal Residencia Mapoula offers 11 older-feeling rooms on a little lane on the edge of the historical center (Sb-€25–32, Db-€35–42, Tb-€50–55, no breakfast, elevator plus a few stairs, free Wi-Fi, laundry service available, Entremurallas 10, tel. 981-580-124, fax 981-584-089, www.mapoula.com, mapoula@mapoula.com, Manuel). Of all of my accommodations listings, this one is closest to the train station.

EATING

Santiago offers a wide range of excellent seafood (see "Galician Cuisine" sidebar). It's frustrating to try to eat before the locals do. If you find a restaurant serving before 14:00 or 21:00, you'll be all alone with a few sorry-looking tourists. Early-bird eaters should know that ordering a drink at any bar will generally get you a free tapa—Santiago is one of the few places in Spain that still honors this tradition.

Seafood and More in the Old Center

The easiest area to get your Santiago seafood fix is on two streets just south of the cathedral: **Rúa do Franco** and **Rúa do Vilar.** These lanes are lined with literally dozens of touristy seafood eateries. Even the places that seem "local" probably aren't—the Spanish-speaking clientele are mostly tourists from other parts of the country. Go for a stroll, examine the window display cases, and pop into the restaurant that looks best. You've got a wide range of options: atmospheric midrange spots; high-end, white-tablecloth splurges; and grumpy, simple, stripped-down joints actually frequented by locals. Generally, these places feel interchangeable—follow your nose.

A Taberna do Bispo is a lively Barcelona-style tavern serving *montaditos* (little €1.10 baguette slices with various toppings) at the bar, *raciones* at the tables, and good wine by the glass (daily 9:00–24:00, until 2:00 in the morning in July–Aug, Rúa do Franco 37, tel. 981-586-045). You might pick up a sandwich to go here before exploring the other Rúa do Franco options.

Galician Cuisine

Strolling through the streets of Santiago is like visiting a well-stocked aquarium: Windows proudly display every form of edible sealife, including giant toothy fish, scallops and clams of every shape and size, monstrous shrimp, and—most importantly—octopus. The fertile fjords of the Galician coast are just 20 miles away, and the region's many fishing villages keep the capital city swimming in seafood. As the seafood is so fresh, the focus here is on purity rather than sauces. The seafood is served simple—generally just steamed or grilled, and seasoned only with a little olive oil, onions, peppers, and paprika.

Tasting octopus *(pulpo)* is obligatory in Galicia; it's most often prepared *a la gallega* (also called *pulpo a feira*): After the octopus is beaten to tenderize it, then boiled in a copper pot, its tentacles are snipped into bite-size pieces with scissors. It's topped with virgin olive oil, coarse sea salt, and a mixture of sweet and spicy paprika, then served on a round wooden plate. Eat it with toothpicks, never a fork. It's usually accompanied by large hunks of country bread to sop up the olive oil, and washed down by local red *mencia* wine, often served in little saucer-like ceramic cups.

O Gato Negro is a smoky, no-frills seafood tapas bar stuck in the past and filled with loyal locals (daily 11:00–15:00 & 19:00–23:00, near Rúa do Franco at Rúa da Raíña).

Hostal dos Reis Católicos, the fancy old hospital sharing the square with the cathedral, has two fine restaurants (both downstairs). The main restaurant, **Dos Reis,** fills a former stable under a dramatic stone vault, offering international dishes—often with live piano—for €20–40 (plus a variety of interesting €35–45 fixed-price meals, and some vegetarian options). It's as atmospheric as it gets, with stiff tuxedoed service, white tablecloths, and not a hint of fun (daily 13:30–16:00 & 20:30–23:00, reservations smart, Praza do Obradoiro 1, tel. 981-582-200). A few steps away, **Enaxebre** offers a livelier, easygoing-tavern vibe, good traditional Galician food, and lower prices (€5–14 dishes, open same hours, tel. 981-050-527).

Iacobus began by offering a variety of foreign coffees—and, according to the owner, the best *churros* in Santiago—back in 1995. Success led them to open a few other branches, including one in the old center that has a good choice of wine and above-average food, including a generous selection of cheap and tasty *montaditos* and

If you're more adventurous, splurge for *percebes.* These barnacles are a delicacy; since they grow only on rocks that see a lot of dangerous waves, it takes specialists—a team of two gatherers—to harvest them; one with a rope tied to his waist, the other spotting him from above. The danger factor raises the price. You'll pay about €10 per 100 grams. Two beers and a small 100-gram plate to split makes a wonderful snack. The price includes instructions on how to eat them (twist, rip, and bite). I ask for toasted bread on the side.

Not a fan of seafood? You can slurp the *caldo galego* soup, a traditional broth that originally came from the leftover stock used to prepare an elaborate Sunday feast (cabbage or *grelos,* potatoes, and so on—not too exciting, but providing comfort on a rainy day). Also look for *pimientos de Padrón*—miniature green peppers sautéed in olive oil with a heavy dose of rock salt.

For a quick meal on the go, grab a traditional meat pie, or *empanada,* which comes *de carne* (with pork), *de bonito* or *de atún* (tuna), *de bacalao* (salted cod), *de zamburiñas* (tiny scallops), *de berberechos* (cockles)—and these days, even *de pulpo* (octopus).

And for dessert: Locals enjoy *queixo con mel* (cheese with honey) at the end of a meal. In the tourist zones, bakeries push samples of *tarta de Santiago,* the local almond cake. Historically, the cake was cooked by sisters in Santiago's convents. (You can still get it at the St. Pelayo Monastery near the cathedral—see page 251.) If you're sampling each place, don't fake like it's your first...they know the trick.

raciones. Eat at the bar or at the tables in back. It's a good value for this touristy location. End your meal with a cool, crisp *chupito de licor de hierbas*—a locally produced, Mountain Dew–colored herb liqueur (€8–15 main dishes; July–Aug daily 9:00–24:00; Sept–June Mon–Sat 9:00–24:00, closed Sun; Azabachería 5, tel. 981-582-804).

Restaurante Don Gaiferos is a classy, highly regarded splurge under a mighty stone vault (€5–10 starters, €12–24 main dishes, Tue–Sat 13:15–15:45 & 20:15–23:15, Sun–Mon in Sept–June 13:15–15:45 only, in July–Aug also 20:15–23:15, Rúa Nova 23, tel. 981-583-894).

Bar Restaurante La Churrasquita is a colorful, very local place facing the little church next to the market. At the bar, the gang watches TV and tosses things on the floor. At the little restaurant in the back, women meet after doing their market chores (€3 *bocadillos,* €6–9 *raciones;* €7, €8, and €16 meals; open all day, full meals served Mon–Sat 13:00–16:00 & 21:00–23:00, closed Sun, Plazuela de San Felix 6, tel. 981-582-657).

Restaurante Casa Manolo is where students on a tight budget go for a classy meal out. This smart little family-run eatery combines sleek contemporary design, decent Galician and Spanish food, and excellent prices. The service is rushed (which is a good thing if you're in a hurry), but the value is unbeatable (€8 fixed-price meal gives you two very generous courses, plus water, bread, and dessert; Mon–Sat 13:00–16:00 & 20:00–23:30, Sun 13:00–16:00, at the bottom of Praza de Cervantes, tel. 981-582-950).

Just Outside the Historical Center, near the Museum of the Galician People

O Dezaseis ("The Sixteen") is every local's favorite: a friendly, laid-back cellar with stone walls, heavy beams, interesting art, and old farm implements (€4–11 *raciones,* €11–13 meat and fish dishes, Mon–Sat 14:00–16:00 & 20:30–24:00, closed Sun, reservations smart, Rúa de San Pedro 16, tel. 981-564-880).

La Bodeguilla de San Roque offers enormous portions of local specialties in a relaxed neighborhood atmosphere. If the upstairs restaurant is full, have a drink at the bar to pass the time. The wine list occupies most of the menu, so order a bottle of crisp *albariño* wine to accompany your *pulpo a feira* (big €8–15 *raciones* fill two people, Mon–Fri 9:00–24:30, Sat–Sun 9:00–16:00 & 19:00–24:30, Rúa da San Roque 13, tel. 981-564-379).

Ambitus Veter Bar is a streetside, smoky place lively with locals, greasy tapas and *raciones,* and cheap *bocadillos* and meals (Mon–Fri 8:00–2:00 in the morning, Sat–Sun 10:00–2:00 in the morning, open even later Fri–Sat, Rúa Aller Ulloa 3).

Cafés

Café Costa Vella, actually the breakfast room and garden of a highly recommended hotel (see listing on page 258), is a little Eden tucked just beyond the tourist zone. The café welcomes non-guests for coffee and a relaxing break in a poetic, time-warp garden with leafy views (great €3 toasted sandwiches, plus a wide array of drinks, daily 8:00–23:00, Rúa da Porta da Pena 17, tel. 981-569-530).

Café Casino, a former private club, is a tired taste of turn-of-the-20th-century elegance with occasional live piano music. Local tour guides recommend this smoky café to their timid British groups, who wouldn't touch an octopus with a 10-foot pole (€4 *bocadillos* and sandwiches, €7–8 salads, €11 fixed-priced meal, good selection of coffees and teas, Mon–Fri 8:00–24:00, Sat–Sun 9:00–2:00 in the morning, Rúa do Vilar 35).

Café Terra Nova is a fine and friendly café three minutes' walk from the cathedral. This can be a welcoming place to hang out with expat Americans to learn more about Santiago (light food such as €3 sandwiches and wraps, Mon–Sat 10:00–23:00, March–Oct also Sun 16:00–23:00, otherwise closed Sun, free Internet access and Wi-Fi with purchase, just across from the police station at Rodrigo de Padrón 2, tel. 981-574-631).

TRANSPORTATION CONNECTIONS

From Santiago de Compostela by Train to: Madrid (2/day, 8–9.5 hrs, overnight train departs at 22:35, arrives in Madrid Chamartín at 7:45), **Salamanca** (take train to Zamora—2/day, 5 hrs—then transfer to hourly bus for 1-hr ride to Salamanca), **León** (1/day, 6 hrs), **Bilbao** (1/day direct, 11 hrs), **San Sebastián** (1/day direct, 11 hrs), **Santander** (2/day, 13 hrs, transfer in Palencia or Ávila, overnight option), **Lugo** (requires transfer in A Coruña—bus is better), **Porto,** Portugal (2/day via Vigo, 3.25 hrs). Train info: tel. 902-240-202.

By Bus to: Lugo (8/day, 2 hrs), **Madrid** (5/day, 7–9 hrs, includes night bus 21:30–6:30, arrives at Estación Sur), **Salamanca** (2/day, 1 with a transfer in Vigo, 6.5–7.5 hrs), **Astorga** (5/day, 5.5 hrs), **León** (5/day, 6–7 hrs), **Burgos** (1 night bus/day, 23:15–6:15), **Bilbao** (3/day, 2 continue to **San Sebastián,** includes 2 night buses, 9.5–12 hrs to Bilbao, 1.5 hrs more to San Sebastián), **Porto,** Portugal (2/day, 4 hrs). Bus info: tel. 981-542-416. All long-distance destinations are served by the Alsa bus company (tel. 902-422-242, www.alsa.es).

CANTABRIA

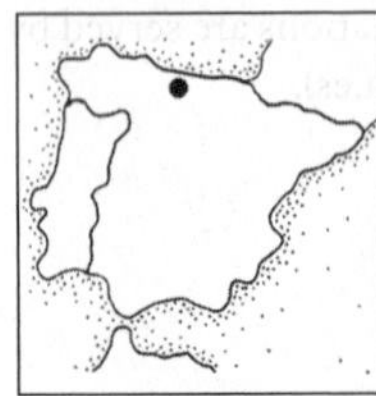

If you're connecting the Basque Country and Galicia (Santiago de Compostela) along the coast, you'll go through the provinces of Cantabria and Asturias. Both are interesting, but Cantabria (kahn-TAH-bree-ah) has a few villages and sights that are especially worth a visit. The quaint town of Santillana del Mar makes a fine home base for visiting the prehistoric Altamira Caves replica. Comillas is a pleasant beach town.

The dramatic peaks of the Picos de Europa and their rolling foothills define this region, giving it a more rugged feel than the "Northern Riviera" ambience of the Basque region. A drive through the Cantabrian countryside is rewarded with endless glimpses of charming stone homes. Though it's largely undiscovered by Americans, Cantabria is heavily touristed by Europeans in July and August, when it can get very crowded.

Planning Your Time

Cantabria doesn't rank high on the list of sightseeing priorities in Spain. Don't go out of your way to get here. However, if you're passing through, there are some charming diversions along the way. A night or two in this region breaks up the long drive from Bilbao to Santiago (figure over seven hours straight through).

Assuming you're coming from San Sebastián, this is a good plan:

Day 1: Leave San Sebastián early for the Guggenheim in Bilbao (trip takes about an hour by expressway, longer along the coast). After seeing the museum, continue on to explore (and sleep in) Santillana del Mar or Comillas. If you arrive early enough, you might have time to see the Altamira Caves (near Santillana) tonight.

Day 2: Troglodytes will want to visit the Altamira Caves replica

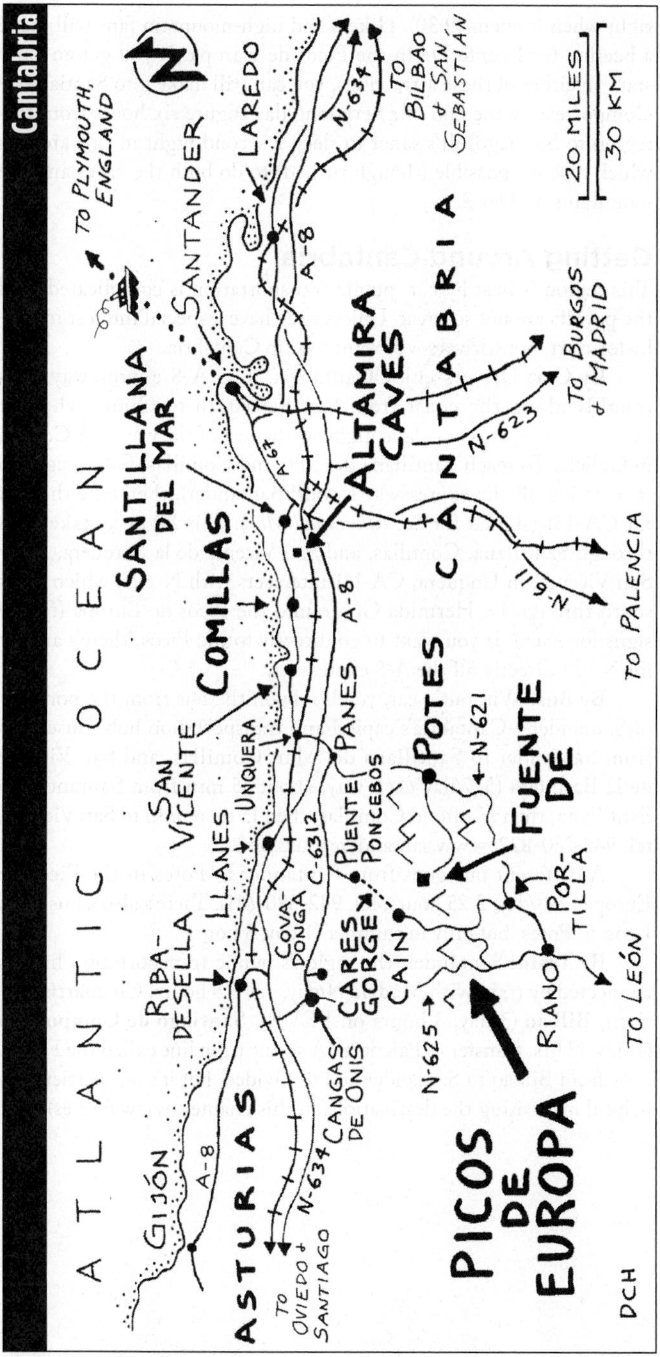

Cantabria

ATLANTIC OCEAN
TO PLYMOUTH, ENGLAND
GIJÓN
A-8
RIBA-DESELLA
LLANES
SAN VICENTE
UNQUERA
COMILLAS
SANTILLANA DEL MAR
SANTANDER
LAREDO
A-8
N-634
TO BILBAO + SAN SEBASTIÁN
A-67
ASTURIAS
TO OVIEDO + SANTIAGO
N-634
CANGAS DE ONIS
COVA-DONGA
C-6312
PANES
A-8
ALTAMIRA CAVES
N-623
TO BURGOS + MADRID
CANTABRIA
20 MILES
30 KM
CARES GORGE
PUENTE PONCEBOS
CAÍN
POTES
N-621
N-611
TO PALENCIA
N-625
FUENTE DE
POR-TILLA
RIANO
TO LEÓN
PICOS DE EUROPA
DCH

CANTABRIA

right when it opens (9:30). Hikers and high-mountain fans will make a beeline for Fuente Dé in the Picos de Europa. If you get an early start on either of these attractions, you can still make it to Santiago de Compostela by the end of a very long day (figure six hours from this region to Santiago). It's saner to sleep a second night in this area, in which case it's possible (though rushed) to do both the caves and the mountains on Day 2.

Getting Around Cantabria

This region is best by car; public transportation is complicated, and the payoffs are not so great. Unless they have a special interest in prehistoric art, non-drivers will want to skip Cantabria.

By Car: Drivers enjoy Cantabria. The A-8 expressway runs roughly along the coast from San Sebastián to Gijón, where it becomes an express two-lane highway the rest of the way to A Coruña in Galicia. To reach Santillana del Mar and Comillas, follow signs to *A-67* (a jog off the expressway toward Santander), then take the exit for CA-131 (signed for *Santillana del Mar*). This highway takes you through Santillana, Comillas, and San Vicente de la Barquera. After San Vicente, in Unquera, CA-131 intersects with N-621, which leads south through La Hermida Gorge into the Picos de Europa (follow signs for *Potes*). If you want to go directly to the Picos, there's an exit for N-621 directly off the A-8 expressway.

By Bus: Without a car, you'll rely on the bus from the port city of Santander—Cantabria's capital and transportation hub. Buses run from Santander to Santillana del Mar, Comillas, and San Vicente de la Barquera (5–7/day each way, about 35 min from Santander to Santillana, then 15 min to Comillas, then 15 more min to San Vicente, tel. 942-720-822, www.santandereabus.com).

A different bus goes from Santander to Potes in the Picos de Europa (2–3/day, 2.25 hours, tel. 942-880-611). There's also a bus from León to Potes, but only in summer (1/day, 3 hours).

By Train: Santander, the region's public transportation hub, is connected by train with **Madrid** (4/day, 4.5–5.5 hours, Chamartín station), **Bilbao** (3/day, 3 hours on FEVE), **Santiago de Compostela** (1/day, 13 hrs, transfer in Palencia). A scenic train line called the FEVE runs from Bilbao to Santander and to Ovideo, but it's not particularly helpful for visiting the destinations in this chapter (www.feve.es).

Santillana del Mar

Every guidebook imparts the same two tidbits about Santillana del Mar: One is that it's known as the "town of three lies," as it's neither holy *(santi)*, nor flat *(llana)*, nor on the ocean *(del Mar)*. The other is that the existentialist philosopher Jean-Paul Sartre once called it the "prettiest village in Spain."

The town is worth the fuss. Santillana is a proud little stone village, with charming time-warp qualities that have (barely) survived the stampede of multinational tour groups here to visit the nearby Altamira Caves. Despite it all, the town is what Spaniards would call *preciosa.*

Santillana is three cobbled streets and a collection of squares, climbing up over mild hills from where the village meets the main road. While Santillana has several sights that cater to the tourist throngs (including a much-promoted zoo), the only sight that makes a visit worthwhile—aside from the town itself—is the cave paintings of Altamira in the nearby countryside (see "Altamira Caves," on page 268).

Tourist Information: The modern TI is right at the entrance to the town (daily July–mid-Sept 9:00–21:00, off-season 9:30–13:30 & 16:00–19:00, Jesús Otero 20, tel. 942-818-251). Only residents (and guests of hotels that offer parking) are allowed to drive in the center—leave your car in the big lot by the TI (pay in-season, free off-season).

SLEEPING

Santillana makes a good home base for visiting the region and the caves. My listings are right in town; you'll find the first three places on Santillana's main square, Plaza Ramón Pelayo. The fourth is farther up, just around the corner (to the right) from the big Collegiate Church.

$$$ ***Paradores:*** Two swanky, arrogant *paradores* hold court on the main square—**Parador de Santillana** (Sb-€115, Db-€144–173 depending on amenities, breakfast-€14, Plaza Ramón Pelayo 11, tel. 942-818-000, fax 942-818-391, santillana@parador.es) and **Parador de Santillana Gil Blas** (Sb-€127, Db-€159–278 depending on amenities, breakfast-€15, same address, tel. 942-028-028, fax 942-818-391, santillanagb@parador.es).

$$ Hotel Altamira offers 32 well-priced rooms in an atmospheric 16th-century palace on the main square (Sb-€50–55, standard Db-€72–84, big Db with sitting room a worthwhile splurge at €82–100,

Sleep Code

(€1 = about $1.50, country code: 34)
S = Single, **D** = Double/Twin, **T** = Triple, **Q** = Quad, **b** = bathroom, **s** = shower only. Unless otherwise noted, English is spoken, credit cards are accepted, and tax is not included. Prices vary with season (highest July-Aug and Holy Week). I've listed shoulder- and peak-season rates.

To help you sort easily through these listings, I've divided the rooms into three categories based on the price for a standard double room with bath:

$$$ Higher Priced—Most rooms €90 or more.
$$ Moderately Priced—Most rooms between €60-90.
$ Lower Priced—Most rooms €60 or less.

20 percent more in Aug and Holy Week, cheaper Nov–March, extra bed-€20, breakfast-€8.50, Calle Cantón 1, tel. 942-818-025, fax 942-840-136, www.hotelaltamira.com, info@hotelaltamira.com).

$ Hospedaje Octavio is a fine budget option with 11 comfortable, wood-beamed rooms (Db-€30–40 depending on season, cheaper for bathroom on the hall, Plaza Las Arenas 4, tel. & fax 942-818-199, Octavio and Milagros don't speak English but their sons do).

Altamira Caves

Not far from Santillana del Mar is a replica of a cave containing some of the best examples of prehistoric art anywhere. In 1879, the young daughter of a local archaeologist discovered several 14,000-year-old paintings in a limestone cave. By the 1960s and 1970s, it became a tremendously popular tourist destination. All of the visitors got to be too much for the delicate paintings, and the cave was closed in 1979. But now a replica cave and museum have opened near the original site, allowing visitors to once again experience these pieces of prehistoric artwork, in something approximating their original setting.

Cost, Hours, Location: €2.40; May–Oct Tue–Sat 9:30–20:00, can be open even later some nights in summer, Sun 9:30–15:00, closed Mon; Nov–April Tue–Sat 9:30–18:00, Sun 9:30–15:00, closed Mon; last tour departs 30 min before closing (tel. 942-818-815, http://museodealtamira.mcu.es). The caves are on a ridge in the countryside a little over a mile southwest of Santillana del Mar. There's no public transportation to the site. To get from Santillana del Mar to the caves, it's either a 30-minute walk or a taxi ride (mobile 608-483-441). Bolder travelers hitch a ride with a friendly tour bus.

Visiting the Caves: While you can't actually visit the original caves, prehistoric-art fans will still find Altamira worth the trip. Your visit has two parts: First, there's a fine museum with good English descriptions, featuring models and reproductions of the cave dwellers who made these drawings (and their clothes, tools, and remains). Videos and illuminated pictures help bring these people to life. The second part is a 30-minute guided tour of the highly detailed replica cave. Unfortunately, English-speakers get no respect at Altamira: Posted information in English is measly, and tours in English are rare. If your guide speaks English, ask if he or she will translate the highlights for you. Otherwise, follow along with my self-guided tour, below.

Note that if all you're really interested in is the art itself, other replicas are on display in the National Archaeological Museum in Madrid (just the paintings, not the cave experience); see page 334. Remember—what you'll see at Altamira are replicas, too.

Reservations: Only 240 people are allowed to enter the replica caves each hour (20 people/tour, tours leave every 5 min—or when enough people gather, never more than a 30-min wait). This means that in the busy summer season, spaces fill up fast. In July and August, they recommend getting to the museum when it opens (9:30) to claim your tour appointment.

Better yet, make an advance reservation (no extra charge) through the bank Santander Centro Hispano—drop by a branch, or even easier, call them (tel. 902-242-424, wait through recording and ask for English-speaker). You can also make a reservation (for Tue–Sat) online using a credit card; go to http://museodealtamira.mcu.es and look for the link to the bank (in Spanish only). Request a specific date and time (one-hour window) for your tour. At the caves, pass any wait time by exploring the museum.

SELF-GUIDED TOUR

You'll begin the tour by watching a four-minute film about the various inhabitants of the cave, the discovery of the paintings in 1879, and the era of over-visitation. Then the guide leads you into the first part of the cave, where you're on your own for English information. The English descriptions that the guide eagerly points out are marginally helpful. So here's what your guide is talking about:

In the Cave

Remember that this isn't the actual cave. It's a painstaking replica (called *Neocueva,* or "Neo-cave"), achieved with special computers, so that the cave art can still be enjoyed without endangering the actual paintings. The Neo-cave also simulates the original cave's temperature, sounds, and humidity.

About 14,000 years ago, hunters, gatherers, and fishermen lived in these caves. They huddled around a fire, protected from the elements. They liked the location because of its proximity to the ocean and a river.

Excavation Site

This area displays tools used by modern scientists to dig up relics from various periods. We're talking about the Upper Paleolithic era—the time of Cro-Magnon cave people, with big hands and high foreheads. The Upper Paleolithic is divided into three periods, and this cave was inhabited, on two separate occasions, during two of those periods: the Solutrean (about 18,500 years ago) and the Magdalenian (14,000 years ago). You'll see that there are three layers to the excavation: On the bottom are artifacts from Solutrean cavemen (hunting tools and chips of flint); above that is mostly clay, with the remains of a cave bear you'll see in a few minutes; and the top layer holds hearths and tools from the Magdalenian period.

As you continue on to the next stop, you'll pass the bones of a cave bear that once lived in Altamira. Nearby, look for his paw prints.

Artists' Workshop

See the tools used by the prehistoric artists, as well as a video showing how the paintings were created. The most dramatic paintings—all the red buffaloes—were made with reddish ochre dissolved in water, outlined in black charcoal. Marrow-burning stone lamps provided light. Many of the images were engraved into the surface of the cave (using flint) before being painted. The reproductions in this Neo-cave were done using the same techniques.

Art!

Finally we reach the paintings themselves. While most tourists gasp, some hum the *Flintstones* theme.

This part of the cave has various names, including the "Great Hall," the "Polychrome Room," or even "the Sistine Chapel of Prehistoric Art." The ledge with the lights shows the floor level of the original cave. This didn't give the cavemen much room to paint, making their creations even more remarkable. Among the fauna in this room are 16 bison, a couple of running boars, some horses, and a giant deer—plus a few handprints and several mysterious symbols.

Unfortunately, the posted English information ends here. These are some of the things to look for (as your guide is pointing them out to the ooh-ing and ahh-ing Spaniards in your group):

Bumps and Cracks: Notice that the artists incorporated the ceiling's many topographical features into their creations (see the bison with the large, swollen back, or the one with the big head).

Overlap: Some paintings actually overlap onto each other. These were painted during two different eras. (The most impressive batch—including all those bison—is thought to be by the same artist.)

Detail: While a few paintings are incomplete, others are finished. Check out the bison with the highly detailed hooves and beard.

The "Old Horse": The horse with its back against the wall is probably among the oldest in the cave.

The "Great Deer": The biggest painting of all (over seven feet across) is the deer with the little black bison under his chin. Notice it's not quite in proportion; due to the tight quarters, the artist couldn't take a step back to survey his work.

Symbols: The strange hieroglyphic-like symbols scattered around the cave, called tectiforms, are difficult to interpret. Scientists have found very similar symbols in caves that were far apart, and wondered if they were some sort of primitive written language (for example, an outline of a horse with a particular symbol might explain how to set traps for hunting).

Behavior: The artists captured not only the form, but also the behavior of the animals they depicted. Notice the lowing bison; the curled-up bison; the bison turning its head; and the running boars (with the extra legs).

What's amazing about these paintings is simply that they were made by Cro-Magnon cave people. And yet, the artists had an amazing grasp of delicate composition, depicting these animals with such true-to-life simplicity. Some of them are mere outlines, a couple of curvy lines—masterful abstraction that could make Picasso jealous.

So why did they make these paintings? Nobody knows for sure. General agreement is that it's not simply for decoration, and that it must have served some religious or shamanistic purpose.

Final Cave

The most impressive paintings were discovered in a single room (whose replica you just visited). However, beyond that room, the cave extended another several hundred feet, though that area was not reproduced. As you leave this replica cave, you'll see a few more replicas—mostly carvings—that came from other parts of the original cave. Most of them are those mysterious symbols, but at the very end you'll also see three masks carved into the rock.

And with that, your cave visit is over. Yabba dabba doo!

Comillas

Just 15 minutes beyond Santillana del Mar, perched on a hill overlooking the Atlantic, you'll find quirky Comillas. Comillas presides over a sandy beach, but feels more like a hill town, with twisty lanes clambering up away from the sea. Comillas is not as undeniably charming as Santillana—it would do well to go traffic-free, as its neighbor has. But it makes for a fine home base if you prefer beach access and a more lived-in feel to touristy quaintness.

Most notably, Comillas also enjoys a surprising abundance of striking Modernista architecture. Three buildings line up along a ridge at the west end of town (just beyond the town center and parking lot, over the big park). Antoni Gaudí, Barcelona's favorite son, designed a villa here called El Capricho—now a restaurant (see below). Next door is the pointy spire of a 17th-century church, and at the end of the row is the Palace of Sobrellano, by Gaudí's mentor Joan Martorell, which hints at early Barcelona-style Modernisme. Peering back at these buildings from a parallel ridge is the huge Pontifical University building, decorated by yet another early-20th-century Catalan architect, Lluís Domènech i Muntaner. These Modernista masterpieces are compliments of Don Antonio López y López, who left Spain to find fortune in America. He returned to Barcelona (where he acquired a taste for Gaudí and company) and eventually became the Marquis of Comillas.

The beachside road below is lined with tacky tourist hotels, but the town center, up on the hill, is much more pleasant—with an odd jumble of squares surrounding the big Parochial Church.

Tourist Information: The westernmost square, Plaza Joaquín de Piélagos, is where you'll find the TI (unpredictable hours, but posted as July–Aug daily 9:00–21:00; Sept–June Mon–Sat 10:30–13:30 & 16:30–19:30, Sun 10:30–13:30; Calle Aldea 6, tel. 942-720-768).

SLEEPING

($1 = about €1.50, country code: 34)

Both of these listings are in the town center, south of the big Parochial Church, near the long, skinny, restaurant-lined Plaza de Primo de Rivera (also known as "El Corro"). The first hotel is the big red building a block off the south end of the square; the other is a few blocks above the square, on the uphill street with the blue-trimmed railing.

$$ Hotel Marina de Campíos offers 20 modern, colorful rooms, each one named for a different opera (standard Db-€65–98, "junior" Db-€80–115, "senior" Db-€120–145, higher prices are for mid-July–mid-Sept, breakfast-€7–8.50, elevator, Calle General Piélagos 14, tel. 942-722-754, fax 942-722-749, www.marinadecampios.com, reservas@marinadecampios.com).

$ Pasaje San Jorge, with 11 basic but comfortable rooms in a 100-year-old house, hovers just over the town center (Db-€55, or €70 July–Aug and Holy Week, cheaper off-season, includes breakfast, Calle Carlos Díaz de la Campa 16, tel. & fax 942-720-915, www.pasajesanjorge.com, pasajesanjorge@pasajesanjorge.com).

EATING

El Capricho is a surprising piece of Antoni Gaudí architecture hiding on a ridge above Comillas' center. The sunflower-dappled exterior alludes to Gaudí's plan for the building: His "sunflower design" attempted to maximize exposure to sunshine by arranging rooms so that they would get sun during the part of the day that they were most used. Today, the building is an exclusive-feeling restaurant serving traditional Spanish cuisine. Look around the back for the sculpture of the architect admiring his work. Don't even try to get inside if you're not eating here. Reservations are smart, especially in season (€20 entrées, €20–25 fixed-price meal, Mon–Sat 13:00–16:00 & 21:00–23:30, Sun 13:00–16:00 only; shorter hours in winter—lunch ends at 15:30 and dinner at 23:00, also closed Mon; tel. 942-720-365). There are two roads to this hard-to-find restaurant; both are at the west end of town, and both are sometimes closed. Ask locally for directions.

Near Comillas: San Vicente de la Barquera

As you continue west from Comillas, the road becomes bumpy and follows the coast, soon crossing a wide bay over a long, dramatic bridge to San Vicente de la Barquera. This salty seaside resort overlooks a boat-filled harbor, with glimpses of the dramatic Picos de Europa in the distance.

Picos de Europa

The Picos de Europa—comprising one of Spain's most popular national parks—are a relatively small stretch of cut-glass mountain peaks (the

steepest in Spain, some taller than 8,500 feet) just 15 miles inland from the ocean. These dramatic mountains are home to goats, brown bears, eagles, vultures, wallcreepers (rare birds), and happy hikers. Outdoorsy types could spend days exploring this dramatic patch of Spain, which is packed with visitors in the summer. For our purposes, we'll focus on the two most important excursions: taking the Fuente Dé funicular up to a mountaintop, and hiking the yawning chasm of the Cares Gorge.

ORIENTATION

The Picos de Europa are a patch of mountains covering an area of about 25 miles by 25 miles. They're located where three of Spain's regions converge: Cantabria, Asturias, and León. (Frustratingly, each region's tourist office pretends that the parts of the park in the other regions don't exist—so it's very hard to get information, say, about Asturias' Cares Gorge in Potes, Cantabria.) In addition to three regions, the park contains three different limestone massifs, or large masses of rock, separated by rivers.

As you venture into the Picos de Europa, pick up a good map; the green 1:80,000-scale map that you'll see is handy, featuring roads, trails, and topographical features. Serious hikers will want a guidebook (I like the Sunflower guide, published by a British company—www.sunflowerbooks.co.uk). These resources, along with a wide variety of other maps and books, are available locally.

I'll focus on the Cantabrian part of the Picos, which contains the region's most accessible and enjoyable bits: the scenic drive through La Hermida Gorge; the charming mountain town of Potes; and the sky-high views from the top of the Fuente Dé cable car. This part of the Picos is doable as a long day trip from Santillana del Mar or Comillas (but is easier if you stay in Potes). The next best activity (in León and Asturias, not

Cantabria) is the Cares Gorge hike—deeper in the park and requiring another full day.

Getting Around the Picos de Europa

The Picos de Europa are best with a car. If you don't have wheels, skip it, because bus connections are sparse, time-consuming, and frustrating (see "Getting Around Cantabria," page 266).

The A-8 expressway squeezes between the Picos and the north coast of Spain; roads branch into and around the Picos, but beware: Many of them traverse high-mountain passes—often on bad roads—and can take longer to drive through than you expect. *Puerto* means "pass" (slow going) and *desfiladero* means "gorge" (quicker but often still twisty).

Assuming you're most interested in Potes and Fuente Dé, you'll focus on the east part of the park, approaching from the A-8 expressway (or from Santillana del Mar and Comillas). You'll go through Unquera and catch N-621 into the park (follow signs for *Potes*). Wind your way through La Hermida Gorge (Desfiladero de la Hermida) en route to Potes.

The Cares Gorge can be approached from either the south (the village of Caín, deep in the mountains beyond Potes) or the north (Puente Poncebos, with easier access).

If you're really serious about tackling the region, and want to do both Fuente Dé and the Cares Gorge, the most sensible plan is this: On Day 1, drive from Comillas/Santillana del Mar to Potes and do the Fuente Dé cable car and hike (sleep in Potes); on Day 2, day-trip to the Cares Gorge hike via Caín (sleep in Potes); and on Day 3, move on to your next destination.

SIGHTS

I've arranged these sights as you'll come to them if you approach from the northeast (that is, from the expressway, Santillana del Mar, or Comillas).

Potes—This quaint mountain village, at the intersection of four valleys, is the hub of Cantabria's Picos de Europa tourist facilities. It's got an impressive old convent and a picturesque stone bridge spanning the Río Deva. It's a good place to buy maps and books. Check in at the **TI** with any travel questions (unpredictable hours, but generally July–Sept daily 10:00–14:00 & 16:00–19:00; less off-season—often closed Sun and Mon afternoons and all day Tue; Plaza de las Serna s/n, tel. 942-730-787).

Sleeping in Potes: **$ Casa Cayo** has 17 cozy rooms and a fine restaurant that overlooks the river (Sb-€35, Db-€50, Tb-€65, but these rates could go up due to major renovations, tax included but breakfast extra, closed Christmas–Feb, Calle Cántabra 6, tel. 942-730-150, fax

942-730-119, www.casacayo.com, informacion@casacayo.com).

▲▲**Fuente Dé Cable Car (Teleférico Fuente Dé)**—Perhaps the single most thrilling activity in Picos de Europa is to take the cable car at Fuente Dé. The longest single-span cable car in Europe zips you up 2,600 feet in just four ear-popping minutes, but in summer, you may have to wait more than two hours to take it. Once at the top (altitude 6,000 feet), you're rewarded with a breathtaking panorama of the Picos de Europa. The huge, pointy, Matterhorn-like peak on your right is Peña Remoña (7,350 feet). The cable-car station on top has WCs, a cafeteria (commanding views, miserable food), and a gift shop (limited hiking guides—equip yourself before you ascend).

Once you're up there, those with enough time and strong knees should consider hiking back down. From the cable-car station at the top, follow the yellow-and-white signs to *Espinama,* always bearing to the right. You'll hike gradually uphill (gain about 300 feet), then down (3,500 feet) the back side of the mountain, with totally different views than the cable-car ride up: green, rolling hills instead of sharp, white peaks. Once in Espinama, you'll continue down along the main road back to the parking lot at the base of the cable car (signs to *Fuente Dé*). Figure about four hours total (nine miles) from the top back to the bottom. Note that the trails are covered by snow into April, and sometimes even May; ask at the ranger station near Potes about conditions before you hike (see "Information," below).

Cost, Hours, Location: €14 round-trip, €8 one-way (if you're hiking down), every 30 minutes (or with demand), daily in summer 9:00–20:00, in winter 10:00–18:00, closed Jan unless weather is unseasonably good. When it's busy, there are constant departures. Note that this is a very popular destination in summer, and you may have to wait in long lines both to ascend and to descend (up to 2.5 hours in early Aug, 1 hour in late July; quieter in June, early July, and Sept—if you're concerned, call ahead to find out how long the wait is before you make the 14-mile drive from Potes). The road dead-ends at Fuente Dé, so you'll have to backtrack to return to Potes. If you're relying on public transportation, you can take the bus from Potes to Fuente Dé (2/day)—but it runs only in summer.

Information: Cable car tel. 942-736-610. The Picos de Europa National Park runs a helpful information kiosk in the parking lot during peak season (July–Aug), with handouts and advice on hikes (including the one described above). Even better, stop at the bigger National Park office on the way to Fuente Dé from Potes; about a mile after you leave Potes, look on the right for the green *Picos de*

Europa signs (daily in summer 9:00–20:00, in winter 9:00–18:00, tel. 942-730-555).

▲Cares Gorge (Garganta del Cares)—This impressive gorge hike—surrounded on both sides by sheer cliff walls, with a long-distance drop running parallel to (and sometimes under) the trail—is ideal for hardy hikers. The trail was built in the 1940s to maintain the hydroelectric canal that runs through the mountains, but today it has become an extremely popular summer-hiking destination. The trail follows the Río Cares seven miles between the towns of Caín (in the south) and Camarmeña (near Puente Poncebos, in the north). Along the way, you'll cross harrowing bridges and take trails burrowed into the rock face. Because it's deeper in the mountains and requires a good six hours (13 miles round-trip, with some ups and downs), it's best left to those who are really up for a hike and not simply passing through the Picos. Visitors who just want a glimpse will hike only partway in before heading back.

Getting There: To reach Caín from Potes, you'll drive on rough, twisty roads (N-621) over the stunning Puerto de San Gloria pass (5,250 feet, watched over by a sweet bronze deer), into a green, moss-covered gorge. Just past the village of Portilla de la Reina, turn right (following signs for *Santa Marina de Valdeón*) to reach Caín. Note that this is a very long day trip from Potes, and almost brutal if home-basing in Comillas or Santillana del Mar.

The approach to the gorge from the north (Puente Poncebos) is easier, but won't take you near Potes and Fuente Dé. You can reach Puente Poncebos via AS-114 to Las Arenas, then follow the Cares River on AS-264 to Puente Poncebos.

SALAMANCA

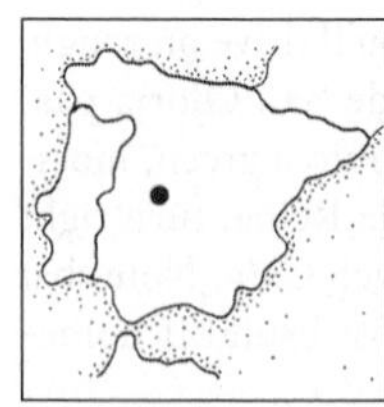

This sunny sandstone city boasts Spain's grandest plaza, its oldest university, and a fascinating history, all swaddled in a strolling, college-town ambience. Salamanca—a youthful and untouristy Toledo—is a series of monuments and clusters of cloisters. The many students help keep prices down. Take a paseo with the local crowd down Calle de Rúa Mayor and through Plaza Mayor. The young people congregate until late in the night, chanting and cheering, talking and singing. When I asked a local woman why young men all alone on Plaza Mayor suddenly break into song, she said, "Doesn't it happen where you live?"

Planning Your Time

Salamanca, with its art, university, and atmospheric Plaza Mayor, is worth a day and a night, but it is stuck out in the boonies. It's feasible as a side-trip from Madrid (it's 2.5 hours one-way from Madrid by car, bus, or train), even with a stop in Ávila on the way. If you're bound for Santiago de Compostela or Portugal, Salamanca is a natural stop.

ORIENTATION

Tourist Information

The main TI is on **Plaza Mayor** (summer: Mon–Fri 9:00–14:00 & 16:30–20:00, Sat–Sun 10:00–20:00; winter: Mon–Sat until 18:30,

Salamanca

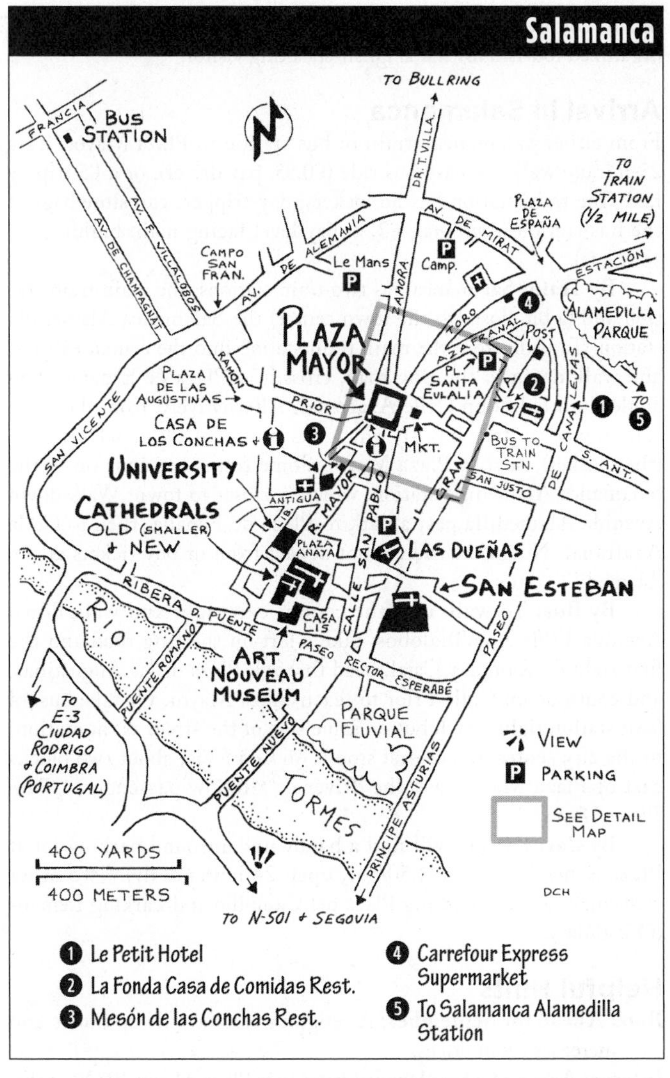

Sun until 14:00; Plaza Mayor 19, tel. 923-218-342). Pick up the free map, city brochure, and current list of museum hours. Another TI at **Casa de Las Conchas** on Calle de Rúa Mayor serves the region and province, as well as the city (July–mid-Sept Sun–Thu 9:00–20:00, Fri–Sat 9:00–21:00; mid-Sept–June daily 9:00–14:00 & 17:00–20:00; tel. 923-268-571). Summertime-only TIs spring up at the train and bus stations. The TI website (www.salamanca.es) is a good source of practical information, including a printable city-center map *(Plano de la ciudad)* and directions on how to arrive from various points in

Spain. Unfortunately, Salamanca offers relatively little in the way of organized tourism for the English-speaking visitor.

Arrival in Salamanca

From either Salamanca's train or bus station to Plaza Mayor, it's a 25-minute walk, an easy bus ride (€0.85, pay driver), or a €5 trip by taxi. The train station has no lockers; day-trippers can store bags at the bus station (*consignas;* €2, at bay level facing main building on your left).

By Train: Salamanca has two train stations: the main train station and (a bit closer to the town center) the Salamanca Alamedilla station. To walk from the main train station into the center, exit left and walk down to the ring road, cross it at Plaza de España, then angle slightly left up Calle Azafranal. Alternatively, from the main station you can take bus #1, which lets you off at Plaza del Mercado (the market), next to Plaza Mayor. Some trains continue on to the Salamanca Alamedilla station, which is closer to town: Walk down Avenida Alamedilla past a park to Plaza de España, then to Calle Azafranal. Note that you cannot depart from or buy tickets at the Alamedilla station.

By Bus: To walk into the center, exit right and walk down Avenida Filiberto Villalobos; take a left on the ring road and the first right on Ramón y Cajal, head through Plaza de las Augustinas, and continue on Calle Prior to reach Plaza Mayor. Or take bus #4 (exit station right, catch bus on same side of the street as the station) to the city center; the closest stop is on Gran Vía, about two blocks east of Plaza Mayor (ask the driver or a fellow passenger, "*¿Para Plaza Mayor?*").

By Car: Drivers will find a handy underground parking lot at Plaza Santa Eulalia (€11.50/day, open 24 hours daily). Two other convenient lots are Parking Plaza del Campillo and Parking Lemans (€13.50/day).

Helpful Hints

Book Ahead for September: A religious festival fills up hotels and increases room prices.

Internet Access: Cyberplace Internet is at Plaza Mayor 10 (Mon–Fri 11:00–24:00, Sat–Sun 12:00–24:00, first floor, tel. 923-264-281). **Navega Internet Center,** nearby, has several computers and a call center, and sells phone cards (Mon–Sat 11:00–24:00, Sun 16:00–24:00, between Plaza del Mercado and Gran Vía at Obispo Jarrín 14, tel. 923-215-447). Perhaps your most efficient Internet access is at the laundry (see below).

Laundry: It's a five-minute walk from Plaza Mayor to the self-service launderette, which also has five Internet terminals (€6.50/load for wash and dry, €2/hr for Internet access, Mon–Fri 10:00–14:00 &

16:00–20:00, Sat 10:00–14:00, closed Sun, also closed Aug 15–30, Pasaje Azafranal 18, located in passageway a half-block north of Plaza Santa Eulalia, tel. 923-260-216, helpful Juan Carlos).

Travel Agency: Viajes Salamanca books flights, trains, and some buses, including buses to Coimbra, Portugal (Calle Prior 11, tel. 923-211-414).

Local Guide: Ines Criado Velasco, a good English-speaking guide, is happy to tailor a town walk to your interests (€80/2 hrs—a special rate for readers of this book in 2009, €95/3–5 hrs, €150/day, for groups of 1–30, tel. 923-207-414, mobile 609-557-528, inescriado@yahoo.es).

SIGHTS

▲▲Plaza Mayor—Built from 1729 to 1755, this ultimate Spanish plaza is a fine place to nurse a cup of coffee (try the venerable Art Nouveau–style Café Novelty) and watch the world go by.

The town hall, with the clock, grandly overlooks the square. The Arco del Toro (built into the eastern wall) leads to the covered market. While most European squares honor a king or saint, this golden-toned square—ringed by famous Castilians—is for all the people. The square niches above the colonnade surrounding the plaza depict writers (Miguel de Cervantes), and heroes and conquistadors (Christopher Columbus and Hernán Cortés), as well as numerous kings and dictators (Francisco Franco).

Plaza Mayor has long been Salamanca's community living room. The most important place in town, it seems to be continually hosting some kind of party. Imagine the excitement of the days (until 1893) when bullfights were held in the square. Now old-timers gather here each day, remembering an earlier time when the girls would promenade clockwise around the colonnade while the boys cruised counterclockwise, looking for the perfect *queso* (cheese), as they'd call a cute dish. Perhaps the best time of all for people-watching is Sunday after Mass (13:00–15:00), when the grandmothers gather here in their Sunday best.

▲▲Cathedrals, Old and New—These cool-on-a-hot-day cathedrals share buttresses, and are both richly ornamented. You get to the old through the new. Before entering the New Cathedral, check out its ornate front door (west portal on Rúa Mayor). The **facade** is decorated Plateresque, with masonry so intricate it looks like silverwork *(plata)*. It's Spain's version of Flamboyant Gothic. At the side door

Cheap Tricks in Salamanca

- For a free, detailed audioguide, go to www.salamanca.es and click on the *ruta MP3* link. Download dramatic descriptions of the city's important sights, then copy them onto your MP3 player.
- Drinks ordered at a bar usually come with a free *pincho*, a taste of one of the larger portions of tapas. Sometimes you can even choose between several options. You can have a light meal for the price of three drinks while standing or sitting at the bar. Try Cervantes Bar, or the bar at Restaurante Comercio.
- Remember that you can linger at any bar, café, or restaurant as long as you like. Have a two-hour coffee in one of the Plaza Mayor cafés, or simply plop yourself down in the middle of the square and watch the paseo without spending a *céntimo*.
- Free sights include the New Cathedral and the Museum of the University. The University is free on Monday morning.

(around the corner to the left as you face the main entrance), look for the astronaut added by a capricious restorer in 1993. This caused an outrage in town, but now locals shrug their shoulders and say, "He's the person closest to God." I'll give you a chance to find him on your own. Otherwise, look at the end of this listing for help.

The **"New" Cathedral** was built from 1513 to 1733 and is a spacious, towering mix of Gothic, Renaissance, and Baroque. Fancy stone trim is everywhere, and the dome decoration is particularly wonderful. Occasionally the music is live, not recorded. The *coro*, or choir, blocks up half of the church (normal for Spanish Gothic), but its wood carving is sumptuous; look up to see the recently restored, elaborate organ (free, daily April–Sept 9:00–20:00, Oct–March 9:00–13:00 & 16:00–18:00).

The entrance to the **Old Cathedral** (12th-century Romanesque) is near the rear of the new one (€4.25, free English leaflet, daily April–Sept 10:00–19:30, Oct–March 10:00–12:30 & 16:00–17:30; if you attend Mass in the Old Cathedral, entry is free, but the cloister isn't). Sit in a front pew to study the altarpiece's 53 scenes from the lives of Mary and Jesus (by the Italian Florentino, 1445) surrounding a precious 12th-century statue of the Virgin of the Valley. High above, notice the dramatic Last Judgment fresco of Jesus sending condemned souls into the literal jaws of hell.

Head into the **cloister** (off the right transept) and explore the chapels, notable for their unusual tombs, ornate altarpieces, and ceilings with leering faces. If you speak Spanish, press the button on the wall at the entrance of each chapel to hear a description. In the Capilla de Santa Barbara (second on the left as you enter), you can sit like students did for their tests. During these final exams, a stern circle of professors formed around the student at the tomb of the Salamanca bishop, who founded the University of Salamanca around 1230. (The university originated with a group of teacher-priests who met in this room.)

As you continue through the cloister, you'll see the chapterhouse *(salas capitulares),* contained in three rooms on your left, with a gallery of 15th-century Castilian paintings. Next is the Capilla de Santa Catalina, with two rows of spooky saint statues and two original gargoyles from the cathedral, in the form of a seahorse and a frog. The Capilla de Anaya, farthest from the cloister entrance, has a gorgeously carved 16th-century alabaster tomb (with the dog and lion at its foot making peace—or negotiating who gets to eat the worried-looking rabbit) and a wooden, 16th-century Mudejar organ. (Mudejar is the Romanesque-Islamic style Moorish design made in Spain after the Christian conquest.)

For a fantastic view of the upper floors and terraces of both cathedrals, and a look at the inside passages with small exhibits about the cathedrals' history and architecture, visit the **tower** (marked *Jerónimos*). It was sealed after Lisbon's 1755 earthquake to create structural support and reopened in 2002. You may be able to reach the tower from inside the Old Cathedral (this entrance is open sporadically); if not, exit the cathedral to the left to find a separate entrance around the corner (€3.25 at either entrance, daily 10:00–20:00, until 18:00 in winter, last entry 45 min before closing).

Finally, go find that astronaut: He's just a little guy, about the size of a Ken-does-Mars doll, entwined in the stone trim to the left of the door, roughly 10 feet up. If you like that, check out the dragon (an arm's length below). Historians debate whether he's eating an ice-cream cone or singing karaoke.

Tourist Tram—The small tram you might see waiting at the New Cathedral does 20-minute loops throughout the town with a Spanish narration (€3.75, daily 10:00–14:00 & 16:00–20:00, departs every 20 min from cathedral, mobile 649-625-703).

▲▲University—The University of Salamanca, the oldest in Spain (est. 1230), was one of Europe's leading centers of learning for 400 years. Columbus came here for travel tips. Today, while no longer so prestigious, it's laden with history and popular with Americans, who enjoy its excellent summer program. The old lecture halls around the cloister, where many of Spain's Golden Age heroes studied, are open to the public (€4, free Mon mornings, Mon–Fri 9:30–13:30 &

16:00–19:30, Sat until 19:00, Sun 10:00–13:30, last entry 30 min before closing, enter from Calle Libreros, tel. 923-294-400, ext. 1150).

The ornately decorated grand **entrance** of the university is a great example of Spain's Plateresque style. The people studying the facade aren't art fans. They're trying to find a tiny frog on a skull that students looked to for good luck.

But forget the frog. Follow the facade's symbolic meaning. It was made in three sections by Charles V. The bottom celebrates the Catholic Monarchs. Ferdinand and Isabel saw that the university had no buildings befitting its prestige, and they granted the money for this building. The Greek script says something like "From the monarchs, this university. From the university, this tribute as a thanks."

The immodest middle section celebrates the grandson of Ferdinand and Isabel, Charles V. He appears with his queen, as well as the Habsburg double-headed eagle and the complex coat of arms of the mighty Habsburg Empire. Since this is a Renaissance structure, it features Greek and Roman figures in the shells. And, as a statement of educational independence from medieval Church control, the top shows the pope flanked by Hercules and Venus.

After paying admission, you get a free English-language leaflet full of details; to follow it, go left (clockwise around the courtyard) upon entering.

In the **Hall of Fray Luis de León,** the narrow wooden-beam tables and benches—whittled down by centuries of studious doodling—are originals. Professors spoke from the Church-threatening *cátedra,* or pulpit. It was here that freethinking brother Luis de León returned, after the Inquisition jailed and tortured him for five years for challenging the Church's control of the word of God by translating part of the Bible into Castilian. He started his first post-imprisonment lecture with, "As we were saying..." Such courageous men of truth believed the forces of the Inquisition were not even worth acknowledging.

The altarpiece in the chapel on the opposite side of the courtyard depicts professors swearing to Mary's virginity. (How did they know?) Climb upstairs for a peek into the oldest library in Spain. Outside the library, look into the courtyard at the American sequoia, brought here 150 years ago and standing all alone. Notice also the big nests in the bell tower. Storks stop here from February through August on their annual journey from Morocco to northern Europe. There are hundreds of such stork nests in Salamanca.

As you leave the university, you'll see the statue of Fray Luis de León. Behind him, to your left, is the entrance to a peaceful courtyard. Within the courtyard is the Museum of the University, notable for Gallego's fanciful 15th-century *Sky of Salamanca* (free, Tue–Sat 10:00–14:00 & 16:00–20:00, Sun 10:00–14:00, closed Mon, no photos allowed).

Can't forget about the frog? It's on the right pillar of the facade, nearly halfway up, on the leftmost of three skulls.

▲Art Nouveau Museum (Museo Art Nouveau y Art Deco)—Located in the Casa Lis, this museum—with its beautifully displayed collection of stained glass, vases, furniture, jewelry, cancan statuettes, and toy dolls—is a refreshing change of pace. Nowhere else in Spain will you enjoy an Art Nouveau collection in a building from the same era. Find the stunning sculptures of Josephine Baker and Carmen Miranda, along with lots of pieces by René Lalique. The museum is a donation of a private collection. The English brochure contains a translation of the Spanish text posted in each room of the collection (€3, mid-Oct–March Tue–Fri 11:00–14:00 & 16:00–19:00, Sat–Sun 11:00–20:00; April–mid-Oct Tue–Fri 11:00–14:00 & 17:00–21:00, Sat–Sun 11:00–21:00; closed Mon, strictly no photos—required camera check at ticket counter, between the cathedrals and the river at Calle Gibraltar 14, tel. 923-121-425, www.museocasalis.org).

Church of San Esteban—Dedicated to St. Stephen (Esteban) the martyr, this complex contains a recently restored cloister, tombs, museum, sacristy, and church. The visitors' entrance is to the right of the church entrance, which is closed except during services.

Before you enter, notice the Plateresque facade and its bas-relief of the stoning of St. Stephen. The crucifixion above is by Italian Renaissance artist Benvenuto Cellini.

After buying your ticket, walk through the cloister to the opposite corner, where signs indicate ways to the church *(iglesia)*, sacristy *(sacristía)*, choir *(coro)*, and museum *(museo)*. Head to the church first. Once inside, follow the free English pamphlet. The nave is overwhelmed by a 100-foot, 4,000-piece wood altarpiece by José Benito Churriguera (1665–1725) that replaced the original Gothic one in 1693. You'll see St. Dominic on the left, St. Francis on the right, and a grand monstrance holding the Communion wafers in the middle, all below a painting of St. Stephen being stoned. This is a textbook example of the intricately detailed churrigueresque style that influenced many South American mission buildings. Quietly ponder the dusty, gold-plated cottage cheese, as tourists shake their heads and say "too much" in their mother tongue.

Upstairs, step into the balcony choir loft for a fine overview of the nave. The staircase itself is architecturally unique, built without any interior support; the staircase is still standing, but you'll notice that when you walk, you definitely lean inward. The big spinnable book holder in the middle of the room held giant music books—large enough for all to chant from in an age when there weren't enough books for everyone.

The museum next door has temperature-controlled glass cases that preserve illustrated 14th- to 16th-century Bibles and choir books. Notice also how the curved ivory Filipino saints all look like they're carved out of an elephant's tusk. And don't miss the fascinating "chocolate box reliquaries" on the wall from 1580. Survey whose bones are collected between all the inlaid ivory and precious woods (€3, Tue 16:00–20:00, Wed–Sat 10:00–14:00 & 16:00–20:00, Sun 10:00–14:00, closed Mon, closes at 19:00 Tue–Sat in winter, last entry 45 min before closing, tel. 923-215-000).

Convento de las Dueñas—Located next door to the Church of San Esteban, the much simpler *convento* is a joy. It consists of a double-decker cloister with a small museum of religious art. Check out the stone meanies exuberantly decorating the capitals on the cloister's upper deck (€1.50, daily 10:30–12:45 & 16:30–18:45, until 17:30 in winter, no English info). The nuns sell sweets daily except Sunday (€4.50 for a small box of their specialty, *amarguillos*—almonds, egg whites, and sugar; no assortments possible even though their display box raises hopes).

Roman Bridge—Historians enjoy the low-slung Roman Bridge (Puente Romano), much of it original, spanning the Río Tormes. The *ibérico* (ancient pre-Roman) faceless bull blindly guards the entrance to the bridge; you'll find this symbol of Salamanca on every city coat of arms in town.

▲*Tuna* Music—Traditionally, Salamanca's poorer students earned money to fund their education by singing in the streets. This 15th- to 18th-century tradition survives today, as musical groups of students (representing the various faculties)—dressed in the traditional black capes and leggings—sing and strum mandolins and guitars. They serenade the public in the bars on and around Plaza Mayor. The name *tuna,* which has nothing to do with fish, refers to a vagabond student lifestyle, and later was applied to the music these students sing. They're out only on summer weeknights (singing for tips from 22:00 until after midnight), because they make more serious money performing for weddings on weekends.

SLEEPING

Salamanca, a student town, has plenty of good eating and sleeping values. All but one of my listings (Le Petit Hotel) are on or within a three-minute walk of Plaza Mayor. Directions are given from Plaza Mayor,

Sleep Code

(€1 = about $1.50, country code: 34)
S = Single, **D** = Double/Twin, **T** = Triple, **Q** = Quad, **b** = bathroom, **s** = shower only. Unless otherwise noted, credit cards are accepted, English is spoken, and the IVA tax (7 percent) and breakfast are not included.

To help you easily sort through these listings, I've divided the rooms into three categories, based on the price for a standard double room with bath during high season:

$$$ Higher Priced—Most rooms €70 or more.
$$ Moderately Priced—Most rooms between €40–70.
$ Lower Priced—Most rooms €40 or less.

assuming you are facing the building with the clock (e.g., 3 o'clock is 90 degrees to your right as you face the clock). The city is noisy on the weekends, so if you're a light sleeper, ask for an interior room.

$$$ Petit Palace Las Torres, on Plaza Mayor, is a remodeled chain hotel with 53 modern, spacious rooms (several with see-through bathroom doors), and all the amenities (Sb-€60–150, Db-€75–170, Tb-€100–220, lower prices are for non-view rooms and weekdays, higher prices are for Plaza Mayor views and weekends, 30 percent more during religious festival in Sept, breakfast-€8, air-con, elevator, pay parking at nearby Lemans lot, hotel entry just off square at Calle Concejo 4, exit Plaza Mayor at 11 o'clock, tel. 923-212-100, fax 923-212-101, www.hthotels.com, tor@hthotels.com).

$$$ Hotel Torre del Clavero has little character, but its 26 rooms are clean and contemporary. It's conveniently located between Plaza Mayor and the Church of San Esteban, across the street from the Clavero tower. Its private garage is a plus for drivers (Sb-€50–72, Db-€110–125, extra bed-€25, higher rates are for weekends and holidays, parking-€10/day; from Casa de las Conchas on Calle de Rúa Mayor, go three blocks south on Calle de Jesús to Calle del Consuelo 21, or from Gran Vía turn onto Calle de las Varillas then left onto Calle del Consuelo; tel. 923-280-410, fax 923-217-708, www.hoteltorredelclavero.com, info@hoteltorredelclavero.com).

$$ Hotel Don Juan, a block off Plaza Mayor, has 16 comfy rooms with tired carpeting and decor, and an attached restaurant (Sb-€45–53, Db-€59–72, Tb-€97, mention this book for special deals, air-con, elevator, parking in their private lot-€10/day, exit Plaza Mayor at about 5 o'clock and turn right to Quintana 6, tel. 923-261-473, fax 923-262-475, www.hoteldonjuan-salamanca.com, info@hoteldonjuan-salamanca.com, David or Livia).

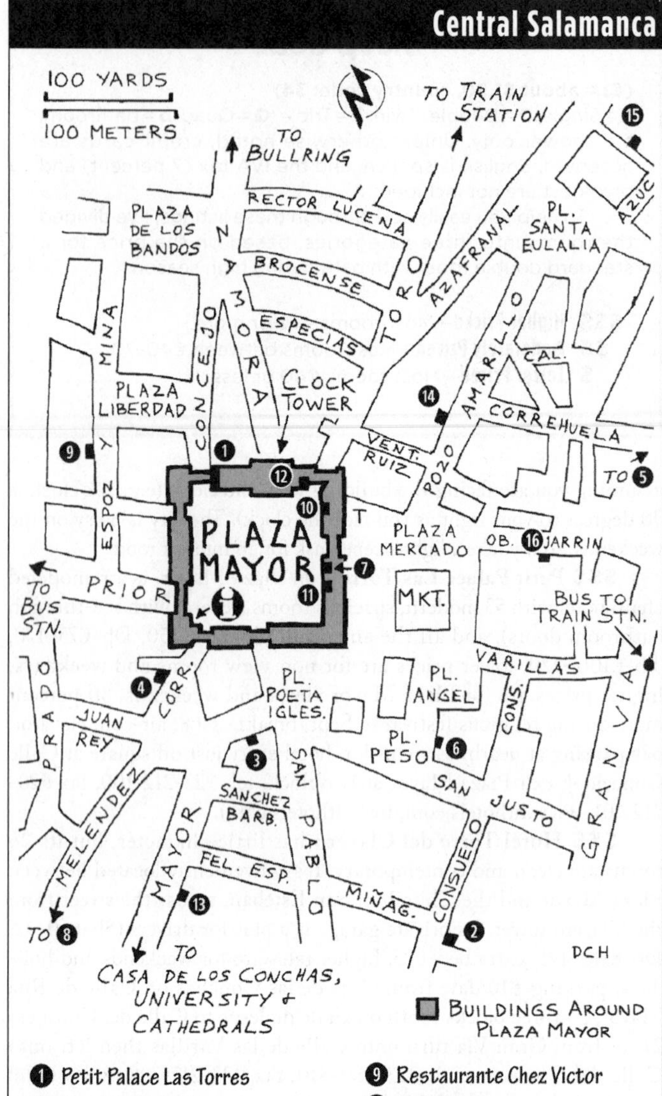

1 Petit Palace Las Torres
2 Hotel Torre del Clavero
3 Hotel Don Juan
4 Hostal Plaza Mayor
5 To Le Petit Hotel & Rest. La Fonda Casa de Comidas
6 Hostería Casa Vallejo
7 Hostal Los Angeles & Internet Café
8 To Hostal Las Vegas Centro
9 Restaurante Chez Victor
10 Café Real
11 Cervantes Bar Restaurant
12 Café Novelty
13 Mesón de las Conchas
14 Restaurante Isidro & Restaurante Comercio
15 Launderette & Internet Access
16 Internet Café

$$ Hostal Plaza Mayor, with 19 finely decorated but small rooms, has a good location a block southwest of Plaza Mayor (Sb-€30–36, Db-€50–60, Tb-€75–90, air-con, most rooms served by elevator, attached restaurant, exit Plaza Mayor at 7 o'clock, Plaza del Corrillo 20, tel. 923-262-020, fax 923-217-548, www.hostalplaza mayor.es, hostalplazamayor@hotmail.com).

$$ Le Petit Hotel, while away from the characteristic core, faces a peaceful park and a church, two blocks east of Gran Vía. It rents 23 spotless and homey yet modern rooms. The rooms with views of the church are brightest, and the fourth floor has been recently renovated—request *vista de iglesia* and *cuarta planta* (Sb-€36, Db-€49, Tb-€59, Qb-€69, breakfast-€4, cash only, air-con, elevator, desk staffed but phone not answered after 22:30, Ronda Sancti Spiritus 39, about six blocks east of Plaza Mayor; exit Plaza Mayor at 3 o'clock and continue east, turn left on Gran Vía, right on Sancti Spiritus at Banco Simeon, and left after the church; tel. 923-600-773, www.lepetithotel.net, reserve by simply calling and leaving your name and time of arrival no more than 15 days in advance, Hortensia doesn't speak English).

$$ Hostería Casa Vallejo is family-run and welcoming, with 12 rustic and renovated rooms a block away from Plaza Mayor. The attached tapas bar/restaurant is a tasty deal (Sb-€30–38, Db-€45–80, €12 each for third and fourth person, breakfast-€3, air-con, elevator, San Juan de la Cruz 3, tel. 923-280-421, fax 923-213-112, www.hosteriacasavallejo.com, info@hosteriacasavallejo.com, Amparo).

$$ Hostal Los Angeles rents 15 simple but cared-for rooms, four of which overlook the square. Stand on the balcony and inhale the essence of Spain. View rooms are popular and more expensive—when you reserve, request *"Con vista, por favor"* (S-€15–30, Sb-€25–40, D-€30–38, Db-€35–55, T-€65, Tb-€75, Q-€85, includes tax, breakfast on plaza-€5, Plaza Mayor 10, about 3 o'clock, tel. & fax 923-218-166, www.pensionlosangeles.com, info@pensionlosangeles.com, Orlando or Odalis).

$ Hostal Las Vegas Centro is clean, bright, quiet, and cheap, with 17 cozy rooms (S-€20, Sb-€24, Db-€36–40, T-€50, Tb-€55, Qb-€75, 2 blocks off Plaza Mayor, exit the square about 7 o'clock, toward cathedral at Meléndez 13, first floor, tel. & fax 923-218-749, www.lasvegascentro.net, reservas@lasvegascentro.es).

EATING

Local specialties include *serrano* ham, which is in just about everything (see "Sampling *Serrano* Ham," next page), roast suckling pig (called *tostón* around here), and *sopa de ajo,* the local garlic soup. *Patatas meneadas* (potatoes with Spanish paprika and bacon) is a simple but tasty local tapa. If you always wanted seconds at Communion, buy

Sampling *Serrano* Ham

Jamón serrano is cured in the *sierras* (mountains) of Spain. While there are many variations of this cured ham from different regions of Spain, Spanish people have a special appreciation for *jamón ibérico,* made with the back legs of black pigs fed mainly on acorns. Originating in Spain, these black pigs are fatter and happier (slaughtered much later than regular pigs). Spaniards treasure memories of grandpa thinly carving a *jamón,* supported in a *jamonero* (ham-holder) during Christmas, just as we savor the turkey-carving at Thanksgiving. To sample this delicacy without the high price tag you'll find in bars and restaurants, go to the local market, ask for 100 grams (*cien gramos de jamón ibérico extra;* about €70/kilo, so your portion will run about €7), and enjoy it as a picnic with red wine and bread.

a bag of the local specialty called *obleas*—flat wafers similar to giant Communion hosts.

Dining Well

Restaurante Chez Victor is the result of the marriage of a Castilian chef (Victor) and a French food-lover (Margarite). This family-run place, elegantly decorated with a feminine French touch and bouquets on the tables, serves modern and creative Franco/Castilian fare—perhaps your best €35–40 meal in town (Tue–Sat 14:00–15:30 & 21:00–23:30, Sun 14:00–15:30; closed Sun eve and Mon; also closed Easter week, Aug, and Christmas; air-con, Espoz y Mina 26, tel. 923-213-123).

La Fonda Casa de Comidas is a dark, woody place with solid, traditional cuisine that caters to locals. You'll happily spend about €22 for three courses (Tue–Sun 13:30–16:00 & 21:00–24:00, closed Mon, a bit smoky, reserve on weekends, 15 yards down the arcade from corner of Gran Vía and Cuesta de Sancti Spiritus at La Reja 2, tel. 923-215-712).

On Plaza Mayor and Rúa Mayor

Here you can enjoy a meal sitting on the finest square in Spain and savor some of Europe's best people-watching. The bars, with little tables spilling onto the square, serve *raciones* and €2 glasses of wine. A *ración de la casa* (house specialty of hams, sausages, and cheese), a *ración* of *patatas bravas* (chunks of potatoes with a slightly spicy tomato sauce), and two glasses of wine makes a nice dinner for two for about €25—one of the best eating values in all of Europe. For dessert, stroll with an ice cream cone from Café Novelty.

Café Real serves bar snacks in a tapas style (daily 8:30–24:00, tel. 923-210-556).

Cervantes Bar is more of a restaurant, with a wide selection of meals, €8 salads, and sandwiches. They also have an indoor section with tables that overlook Plaza Mayor from one floor up; it's a popular student hangout. Don't forget to ask for your *pincho,* a snack that comes with your drink, if you're standing at the bar (daily 10:00–24:00, tel. 923-217-213).

Café Novelty is Plaza Mayor's Art Nouveau café. It dates from 1905—and has some customers who look like they've been there since it opened. It's filled with character and literary memories. The metal sculpture depicts a famous local writer, Torrente Ballester (daily 8:00–24:00, tel. 923-214-956). Their ice cream sweetens a stroll around the plaza.

Mesón de las Conchas, on the main pedestrian drag to the cathedral, attracts a mix of locals and tourists. They offer good prices for tapas and meals—but, as is common here, they bump up tapa prices for outdoor seating (daily, bar 8:00–24:00, restaurant 12:30–16:00 & 20:00–24:00, Calle de Rúa Mayor 16, tel. 923-212-167).

Eating Simply, But Well

There are plenty of good, inexpensive restaurants between Plaza Mayor and Gran Vía, and as you leave Plaza Mayor toward Calle de Rúa Mayor. The tapas places along and around Calle de Rúa Mayor are abundant and often overrun with students.

Restaurante Isidro is a thriving local (and guidebook) favorite—a straightforward, hardworking eatery run by Alberto—offering a good assortment of fish and specialty meat dishes (€10 fixed-price meal, also à la carte €15–25 dinners, Tue–Sat 13:00–16:00 & 20:00–24:00, Sun 13:00–16:00, closed Mon, big portions, good roasts, quick and friendly service, Pozo Amarillo 19, about a block north of covered market near Plaza Mayor, tel. 923-262-848).

Restaurante Comercio, next door, has tasty food and is warmly decorated with old photos of the square. Their specialties include *sopa del obispo* (hearty soup) and oxtail stew. Consider their €10–15 fixed-price meals (also served at dinner and on weekends), the €15–20 à la carte meals, or the €5–10 *raciones* at the front bar (restaurant open Tue 13:00–16:00, Wed–Sun 13:00–16:00 & 21:00–24:00, closed Mon, tapas bar opens earlier at 10:30 & 20:00, Pozo Amarillo 23, tel. 923-260-280).

The **Pans & Company** sandwich chain is always fast and affordable, with a branch on Calle Prior across from Burger King and another on Calle de Rúa Mayor (both open daily 10:30–24:00).

Picnics: The covered *mercado* (market) on Plaza Mercado has fresh fruits and veggies (Mon–Sat 8:00–14:30, closed Sun, on east side of Plaza Mayor). A small El Arbol grocery, three blocks east of Plaza Mayor, has just the basics (Mon–Sat 9:30–21:00, closed Sun). For variety, the big Carrefour Express Supermercado is your best bet, but it's a six-block walk north of Plaza Mayor on Toro (Mon–Sat 9:30–21:30, closed Sun, across from Plaza San Juan de Sahagún and its church).

TRANSPORTATION CONNECTIONS

From Salamanca by Train to: Madrid (6/day, 2.5 hrs, Chamartín station, some are commuter trains with limited luggage space), **Ávila** (6/day, 1 hr), **Barcelona** (8/day, 6–7 hrs, change in Madrid from Chamartín Station to Atocha Station via Metro; 1 direct/day, 11.25 hrs), **Santiago** (first take hourly bus for 1-hr ride to Zamora, then transfer to train—2/day, 5 hrs—for Santiago), **Burgos** (3/day, 2.5–3 hrs), **Lisbon,** Portugal (1/day, 7 hrs, departs Salamanca station at about 4:50 in the morning, no kidding; you can catch a taxi to the train station at any hour from Plaza Mercado—a few steps east of Plaza Mayor—and from Plaza Poeta Iglesias, which is across from the big construction site, immediately south of Plaza Mayor, taxi ride costs €4 during day, €5 at night; for **Coimbra,** see below). Train info: tel. 902-240-202, www.renfe.es.

By Bus to: Madrid (€18 one way, hourly express, 2.5 hrs, arrives at Madrid's Mendez Álvaro Station, Auto-Res buses, www.auto-res.net), **Segovia** (2/day, 3 hrs; transfer in Labajos, could make a brief stop in Ávila en route, Auto-Res or La Sepulvedana buses, consider reserving a seat for the Salamanca–Labajos leg in advance), **Ávila** (4/day, 2 on weekends, 1.5 hrs, Auto-Res buses), **Ciudad Rodrigo** (nearly hourly, 1 hr, El Pilar buses), **Santiago** (2/day, 1 with a transfer in Vigo, 6.5–7.5 hrs), **Barcelona** (2/day, 11 hrs, Alsa buses), **Burgos** (3/day, 3.5 hrs, Alsa buses), **Coimbra,** Portugal (1/day, departs at 12:30, 5 hrs, one-way-€29, round-trip-€51; same bus continues to **Lisbon** in 8.25 hrs, one-way-€39, round-trip-€69; Alsa buses, tel. 913-270-540, www.alsa.es). Bus info: tel. 923-236-717 or 902-020-052 (Auto-Res).

Ciudad Rodrigo

Ciudad Rodrigo is worth a visit only if you're driving from Salamanca to Coimbra, Portugal (although buses connect Salamanca and Ciudad Rodrigo with surprising efficiency in about an hour).

This rough-and-tumble old town of 16,000 people caps a hill overlooking the Río Agueda. Spend an hour wandering among the

Salamanca Area

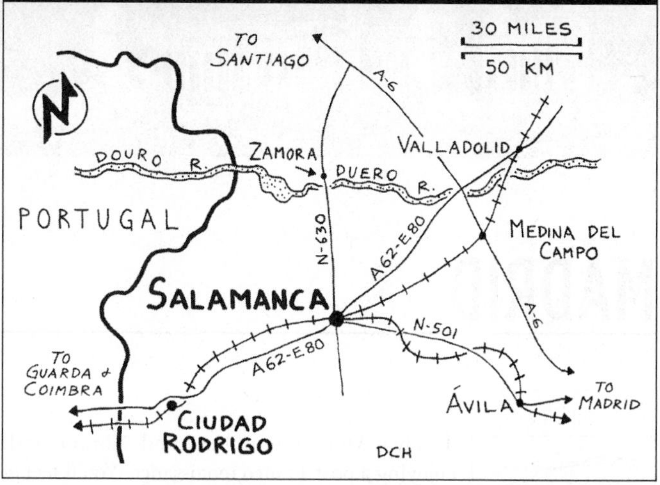

Renaissance mansions that line its streets and exploring its cathedral and Plaza Mayor. Have lunch or a snack at **El Sanatorio** (Plaza Mayor 14, tel. 923-460-024). The tapas are cheap, the crowd is local, and the walls are a Ciudad Rodrigo scrapbook, including some bullfighting that makes the Three Stooges look demure.

Ciudad Rodrigo's cathedral—pockmarked with scars from Napoleonic cannon balls—has some entertaining carvings in the choir and some pretty racy work in its cloisters. Who says, "When you've seen one Gothic church, you've seen 'em all"?

The **TI** is two blocks from Ciudad Rodrigo's Plaza Mayor, just inside the old wall near the cathedral (Mon–Fri 9:00–14:00 & 17:00–19:00, Sat–Sun 10:00–14:00 & 17:00–20:00, Plaza Ameyuelas 5, tel. 923-460-561). They can recommend a good hotel, such as Hotel Conde Rodrigo (34 rooms, Sb-€70, Db-€75, Tb-€93, air-con, elevator, Plaza San Salvador 9, tel. 923-461-404, www.conderodrigo.com, info@conderodrigo.com).

MADRID

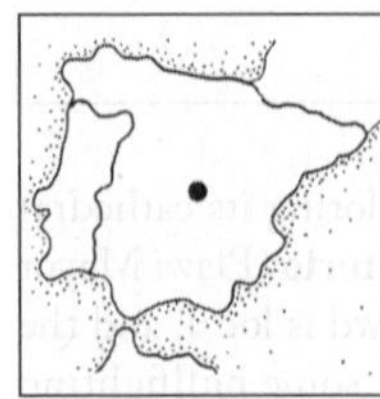

Today's Madrid is upbeat and vibrant, still enjoying a post-Franco renaissance. You'll feel it. Even the living-statue street performers have a twinkle in their eyes.

Madrid is the hub of Spain. This modern capital—Europe's highest, at more than 2,000 feet—has a population of 3.2 million. Like its people, the city is relatively young. In 1561, King Philip II decided to move the capital of his empire from Toledo to Madrid. One hundred years ago, Madrid had only 400,000 people—so the majority of today's Madrid is modern sprawl surrounding an intact, easy-to-navigate historic core.

To support their bid to host the 2012 Olympics, Madrid began some massive city-improvement building projects. Although they lost out, the construction continues as if they won. Politicians who back these projects have been rewarded both financially (locals claim some corrupt officials are getting kickbacks) and politically—residents love to see all the new squares, pedestrian streets, beltway tunnels, parks, and Metro stations popping up like wildflowers. As the city eyes another Olympics bid for 2016, construction won't let up soon. Madrid's ambitious improvement plans include the creation of a pedestrian street crossing the city from the Prado to the Royal Palace (the section from the Prado to Plaza Mayor has been completed) and a new macro-Metro station near Puerta del Sol (to accommodate a new, efficient commuter-train line due to be finished in mid-2009). By installing posts to keep cars off sidewalks, making the streets safer after dark, and restoring old buildings, Madrid is working hard to make itself more livable...and fun to visit.

Tourists are the real winners. Dive headlong into the grandeur and intimate charm of Madrid. The lavish Royal Palace, with its gilded rooms and frescoed ceilings, rivals Versailles. The Prado has Europe's top collection of paintings. The city's huge Retiro Park invites you to take a shady siesta and hopscotch through a mosaic of lovers, families, skateboarders, pets walking their masters, and expert bench-sitters. Save time for Madrid's elegant shops and people-friendly pedestrian zones. On Sundays, cheer for the bull at a bullfight or bargain like mad at a mega-size flea market. Lively Madrid has enough street-singing, bar-hopping, and people-watching vitality to give any visitor a boost of youth.

Planning Your Time

Divide your time between Madrid's top three attractions: the Royal Palace (worth a half-day), the Prado Museum (also worth a half-day), and its bar-hopping contemporary scene. On a Sunday, consider allotting extra time for the flea market (year-round) and/or a bullfight (some Sundays Easter–mid-Oct, especially during San Isidro festival mid-May).

Madrid is worth two days on even the fastest trip. I'd spend them this way:

Day 1: Take a brisk, 20-minute good-morning-Madrid walk from Puerta del Sol to the Prado (from Puerta del Sol, walk three blocks south to Plaza del Ángel, then take the pedestrian walkway to the Prado along Huertas). Spend the rest of the morning at the Prado, then take an afternoon siesta in Retiro Park, or tackle modern art at the Centro de Arte Reina Sofía (Picasso's *Guernica*) and/or the Thyssen-Bornemisza Museum. Have dinner at 20:00, with tapas around Plaza Santa Ana.

Day 2: Follow my "Welcome to Madrid" self-guided walk (see page 307), tour the Royal Palace, and have lunch near Plaza Mayor. Your afternoon is free for other sights, shopping, or a side-trip to El Escorial (last entry 18:00 April–Sept, 17:00 Oct–March, closed Mon; see next chapter). Be out at the magic hour—before sunset—when beautifully lit people fill Madrid.

Note that many top sights are closed on Monday, including the Prado, Thyssen-Bornemisza Museum, and El Escorial; sights remaining open on Monday include the Royal Palace (open daily) and Centro de Arte Reina Sofía (closed Tue). For good day-trip possibilities from Madrid, see the next two chapters (Northwest of Madrid and Toledo).

ORIENTATION

Puerta del Sol marks the center of Madrid. No major sight is more than a 20-minute walk or a €4 taxi ride from this central square. The Royal Palace (to the west) and the Prado Museum and Retiro Park (to the east) frame Madrid's historic center. This zone can be covered on foot. Southwest of Puerta del Sol is a 17th-century district with

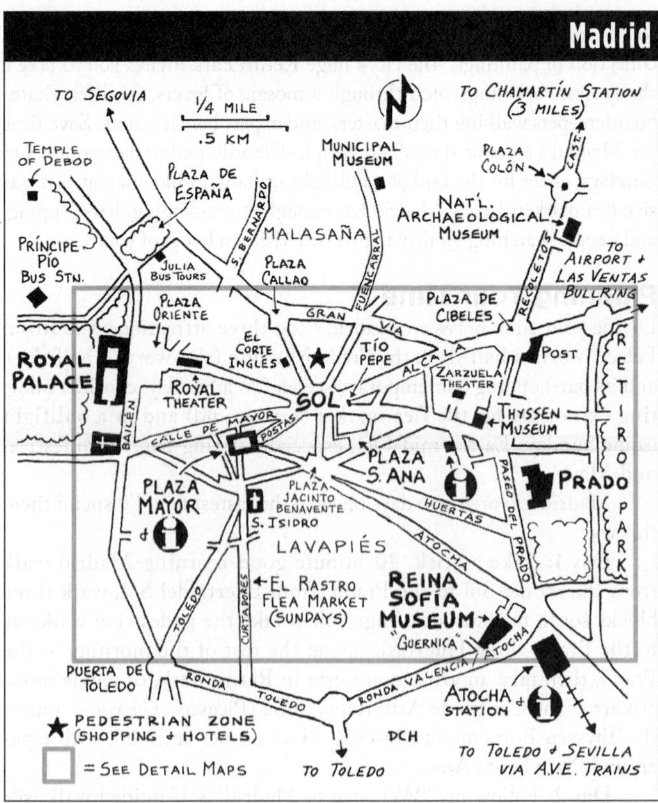

the slow-down-and-smell-the-cobbles Plaza Mayor and memories of preindustrial Spain. North of Puerta del Sol runs Calle de Gran Vía, and between the two are lively pedestrian shopping streets. Gran Vía, bubbling with shops and cinemas, leads to the modern Plaza de España. Between Puerta del Sol and the Atocha train station stretches the colorful, up-and-coming multiethnic Lavapiés district (see the "The Lavapiés District Tapas Crawl," page 355).

Tourist Information

Madrid has five TIs: on **Plaza Mayor** (daily 9:30–20:30, air-con, limited free Internet access, tel. 915-881-636); near the **Prado Museum** (Mon–Sat 8:00–20:00, Sun 9:00–14:00, Duque de Medinaceli 2, behind Palace Hotel, tel. 914-294-951); at **Chamartín train station** (near track 19–20, Mon–Sat 8:00–20:00, Sun 9:00–14:00, tel. 913-159-976); at **Atocha train station** (in the AVE side, Mon–Sat 8:00–20:00, Sun 9:00–14:00, tel. 915-284-630); and at the **airport** (at Terminal 1 in arrival hall and at Terminal 4 at baggage claim, Mon–Sat 8:00–20:00, Sun 9:00–14:00, tel. 913-058-656). During the summer, small temporary stands pop up at touristed places such as Puerta del Sol and Plaza de España. There are also two permanent stands: one in **Plaza Callao,** at the end of Calle Preciados; and another in **Plaza Cibeles,** at the beginning of Paseo del Prado—on the walkway between Banco de España and the Town Hall/Ayuntamiento (both open daily 9:30–20:00).

The general tourist information number is 915-881-636 (or pricier toll call: tel. 902-100-007; www.esmadrid.com).

At any TI, pick up a map and confirm your sightseeing plans. The TI's free *Public Transport* map is very well designed to meet travelers' needs and has the most detailed map of the center. Get this and use it. TIs have the latest on bullfights and zarzuela (light Spanish opera). Only the most hyperactive travelers could save money buying the **Madrid Card,** which covers 40 museums and the Madrid Vision bus tour (€42/24 hrs, €55/48 hrs, €68/72 hrs).

For entertainment listings, the TI's printed material is not very good. Pick up the Spanish-language weekly entertainment guide ***Guía del Ocio*** (€1, sold at newsstands) or check their complete website, www.guiadelocio.com. It lists daily live music *("Conciertos"),* museums (*"Museos"*—with the latest times and special exhibits), restaurants (an exhaustive listing), kids' activities *("Los Niños"),* TV schedules, and movies (*"V.O."* means original version, *"V.O. en inglés sub"* means a movie is played in English with Spanish subtitles rather than dubbed).

If you're heading to **other destinations in Spain,** some Madrid TIs might have free maps and brochures (ideally in English). Since many small-town TIs keep erratic hours and run out of these pamphlets, get what you can in Madrid. You can also get schedules for buses and some trains, allowing you to avoid unnecessary trips to the various stations. The TI's free and amazingly informative *Mapa de Comunicaciones España* is a road map of Spain that lists all the tourist offices and highway SOS numbers. (If they're out, ask for the route map sponsored by the Paradores hotel chain, the camping map, or the golf map.)

For tips on sightseeing, hotels, and more, visit www.madridman.com, run with passion by American Scott Martin.

Arrival in Madrid

By Train

Madrid's two train stations, Chamartín and Atocha, are both on Metro lines with easy access to downtown Madrid. (For Atocha station, use the "Atocha RENFE" Metro stop; the stop named simply "Atocha" is farther from the station.) Chamartín handles most international trains and the AVE train to Segovia. Atocha generally covers southern Spain, as well as the AVE trains to Barcelona, Córdoba, Sevilla, and Toledo. Both stations offer long-distance trains *(largo recorrido)* as well as smaller, local trains (*regionales* and *cercanías*) to nearby destinations.

Buying Tickets: You can buy tickets at the stations, at a travel agency, or online. (For all the details, see "Buying Train Tickets" on page 669 in the appendix.) Convenient travel agencies for buying tickets in Madrid include the El Corte Inglés Travel Agency at Atocha (Mon–Fri 7:00–22:00, Sat–Sun only for urgent arrangements, on ground floor of AVE side at the far end) and the El Corte Inglés department store at Puerta del Sol (see "Helpful Hints," page 300).

Traveling Between Chamartín and Atocha Stations: To travel between the two stations, you can take the Metro (line 1, 30–40 minutes, €1, see "Getting Around Madrid" on page 304), but the *cercanías* trains are faster (6/hr, 12 min, €1.15, free with railpass or any train ticket to Madrid—show it at ticket window in the middle of the turnstiles, departs from Atocha's track 2 and generally Chamartín's track 2 or 3—but check the *Salidas Inmediatas* board to be sure). In the future, the trip will get even easier—a faster Atocha-Sol-Chamartín *cercanías* line is supposed to be completed in mid-2009.

Chamartín Station

The TI is opposite track 19. The impressively large Centro de Viajes/Travel Center customer-service office is in the middle of the building. You can relax in the Sala VIP Club if you have a first-class railpass and first-class seat or sleeper reservations (near track 12, next to Centro de Viajes). Luggage storage is across the street. The station's Metro stop is also called Chamartín. (If you arrive by Metro at Chamartín, signs to *Información* lead to the lobby. Signs to *Vías* send you directly to the platforms.)

Atocha Station

The station is split in two: an AVE side (mostly long-distance trains) and a *cercanías* side (mostly local trains, nearest the Metro). These two parts are connected by a corridor of shops. Each side of the station has separate schedules and customer-service offices. The TI, which is in the AVE side, offers tourist info, but no train info (Mon–Sat 9:00–20:00, Sun 9:00–14:00, tel. 915-284-630).

There are three ticket offices at Atocha: The *cercanías* side has a small office for local trains and a big one for major trains (such as AVE). The AVE side has a pleasant, airy *Taquillas* office which also sells tickets for AVE and other long-distance trains. If the line at one office is long, check the other offices. Grab a number from a machine to get your turn in line. Or, if your departure is soon, look for "*Para hoy*" or your destination and wait directly in that line without a number. For major destinations (such as Barcelona, San Sebastián, or Córdoba), you can use your credit card to avoid the lines—look for the ATM-like touch-screen machines to the right of the entrance.

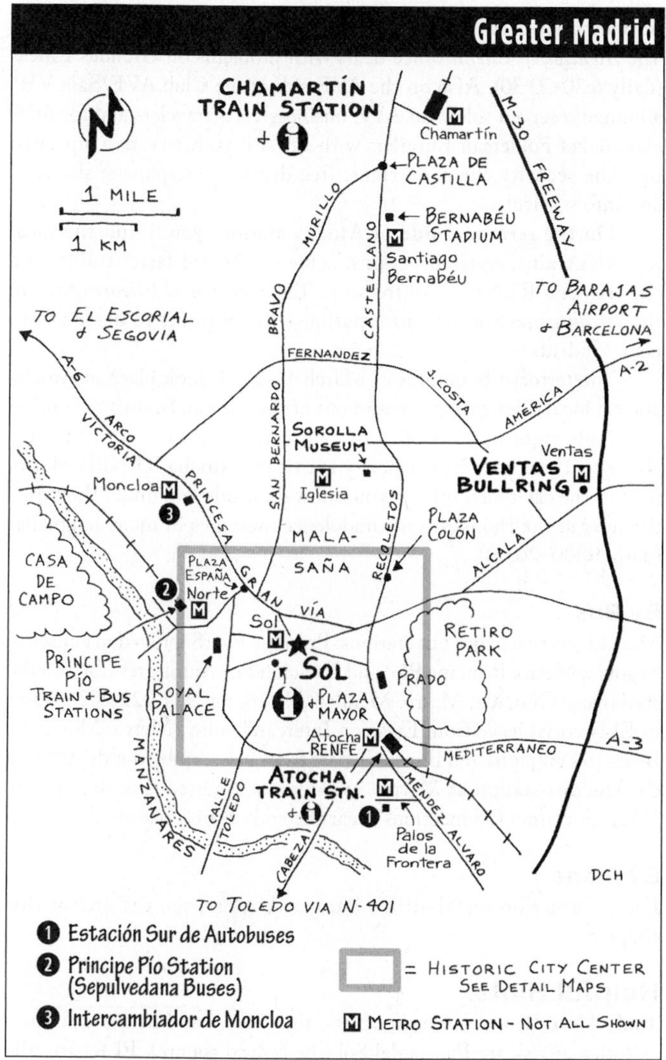

Atocha's **AVE side,** which is in the towering old-station building, is remarkable for the lush, tropical garden filling its grand hall. It has the slick AVE trains, other fast trains (Grandes Líneas), a pharmacy (daily 8:00–22:00), a cafeteria (daily 13:00–20:00), and the wicker-elegant Samarkanda restaurant (daily 13:30–16:00 & 21:00–24:00, tel. 915-309-746). Luggage storage *(consigna)* is below Samarkanda (Mon–Fri 6:00–22:20, Sat–Sun 6:30–22:20). In the departure lounge on the upper floor, TV monitors announce track numbers. For information, try the *Información* counter (daily 6:30–22:30), next to Centro

Servicios AVE (which handles only AVE changes and problems). The *Atención al Cliente* office deals with problems on Grandes Líneas (daily 6:30–23:30). Also on the AVE side is the Club AVE/Sala VIP, a lounge reserved solely for AVE business-class travelers and for first-class ticket-holders or Eurailers with a first-class reservation (upstairs, past the security check on right; free drinks, newspapers, showers, and info service).

On the ***cercanías* side** of Atocha station, you'll find the local *cercanías* trains, *regionales* trains, some eastbound faster trains, and the "Atocha RENFE" Metro stop. The *Atención al Cliente* office in the *cercanías* section has information only on trains to destinations near Madrid.

The terrorist bombings of March 11, 2004, took place in Atocha and on local lines going into and out of the station. Security is understandably tight here. A 36-foot cylindrical glass memorial towers above on the street. Near where you exit the Atocha RENFE Metro, next to the car-rental offices, you can walk inside and under the cylinder to read the thousands of condolence messages in many languages (daily 10:00–20:00).

By Bus

Madrid has two major bus stations: Príncipe Pío (Sepulvedana buses to Segovia; Metro: Príncipe Pío) and Estación Sur Autobuses (for Toledo, Ávila, and Granada; Metro: Méndez Álvaro, tel. 902-222-282). Buses to El Escorial leave from Estación Intercambiador (Metro: Moncloa). Buses to Pamplona and Burgos depart from Intercambiador de Avenida de América station at Metro: Avenida de América. For details, see "Transportation Connections" near the end of this chapter.

By Plane

For information on Madrid's Barajas Airport, see the end of this chapter.

Helpful Hints

Theft Alert: Be wary of pickpockets, anywhere, anytime. Areas of particular risk are Puerta del Sol (the central square), El Rastro (the flea market), Gran Vía (the paseo zone: Plaza del Callao to Plaza de España), the Ópera Metro station (or anywhere on the Metro), the airport, and any crowded streets. Assume a fight or any commotion is a scam to distract people about to become victims of a pickpocket. Wear your money belt. The small streets north of Gran Vía are particularly dangerous, even before nightfall. Muggings occur, but are rare. Victims of theft can call 902-102-112 for help (English spoken, once you get connected to a person).

Prostitution: Diverse by European standards, Madrid is spilling over with immigrants from South America, North Africa, and Eastern

Europe. Many young women come here, fall on hard times, and end up on the streets. While it's illegal to make money from someone else selling sex (i.e., pimping), prostitutes get away with selling it directly on the street (€27, FYI). Calle de la Montera (leading from Puerta del Sol to Plaza Red de San Luis) is lined with what looks like a bunch of high-school girls skipping out of school for a cigarette break. Again, don't stray north of Gran Vía around Calle de la Luna and Plaza Santa María Soledad—while the streets may look inviting...this area is a meat-eating flower.

Embassies: The US Embassy is at Serrano 75 (tel. 915-872-200); the Canadian Embassy is at Nuñez de Balboa 35 (tel. 914-233-250).

One-Stop Shopping: The dominant local department store is **El Corte Inglés,** which takes up several huge buildings in the commercial pedestrian zone just off Puerta del Sol (Mon–Sat 10:00–22:00, Sun 11:00–21:00, navigate with the help of the info desk near the door of the main building—the tallest building with the biggest sign, Preciados 3, tel. 913-798-000). They give out fine, free Madrid maps. In the main building, you'll find two handy travel agencies (see listing at end of this section), a post office, and a supermarket with a fancy "Club del Gourmet" section in the basement. Across the street is its Librería branch—a huge bookstore and six floors of music and home electronics, with a box office for tickets to whatever's on in town. Locals figure you'll find anything you need at El Corte Inglés.

Internet Access: There are plenty of centrally located places to check your email. Ask at any *locutorio* call center, which often have a few computers and are generally the cheapest. Near Plaza Santa Ana (and great if you're waiting for the tapas-crawl action to heat up), **La Bolsa de Minutos** has plenty of fast terminals (€2/hr), disc-burning services, and helpful staff (daily 9:30–24:00, Calle Espoz y Mina 17, tel. 915-322-622). **BBIG** has more than 100 terminals, is non-smoking, and seats casual Internet surfers apart from noisy, intense gamers (daily 9:30–24:00, at the corner of Puerta del Sol and the street that connects it to Plaza Mayor, at Mayor 1—on the second floor above Sol Park casino, tel. 915-312-364). In a pinch, there's also the noisy, smoky **Zahara,** with its clunky coin-operated computers (daily 9:00–24:00, corner of Gran Vía and Mesoneros). If you'd like to simultaneously wash clothes and surf, see "Laundry," below.

Phone Cards: You can buy cheap international phone cards at some newsstands, at Internet cafés, or at the easy-to-find *locutorio* call centers (but these are generally uncomfortable places to sit and talk). When choosing a phone card, remember that toll-free numbers start with 900, whereas 901 and 902 numbers can be expensive. Ask your hotel if they charge for the 900 number before making calls.

Madrid at a Glance

▲▲▲**Prado Museum** One of the world's great museums, loaded with masterpieces by Diego Velázquez, Francisco de Goya, El Greco, Hieronymus Bosch, Albrecht Dürer, and more. **Hours:** Tue–Sun 9:00–20:00, closed Mon. See page 319.

▲▲**Royal Palace** Spain's sumptuous, lavishly furnished national palace. **Hours:** April–Sept Mon–Sat 9:30–19:00, Sun 9:00–16:00; Oct–March Mon–Sat 9:30–18:00, Sun 9:00–15:00. See page 314.

▲▲**Puerta del Sol** Madrid's lively central square. **Hours:** Always bustling. See page 307.

▲▲**Thyssen-Bornemisza Museum** A great complement to the Prado, with lesser-known yet still impressive works and an especially good Impressionist collection. **Hours:** Tue–Sun 10:00–19:00, closed Mon. See page 329.

▲▲**Centro de Arte Reina Sofía** Modern-art museum featuring Picasso's epic masterpiece *Guernica.* **Hours:** Mon and Wed–Sat 10:00–21:00, Sun 10:00–14:30, closed Tue. See page 330.

▲▲**Bullfight** Spain's controversial pastime. **Hours:** Scattered Sundays and holidays March–mid-Oct, plus almost daily May–early June. See page 336.

▲▲**Zarzuela** Madrid's delightful light opera. **Hours:** Evenings. See page 338.

▲**Plaza Mayor** Historic cobbled square. **Hours:** Always open. See page 310.

▲**Retiro Park** Festive green escape from the city, with rental rowboats and great people-watching. **Hours:** Closes at dusk. See page 331.

▲**National Archaeological Museum** Traces the history of Iberia through artifacts, plus a replica of the Altamira Caves. **Hours:** Tue–Sat 9:30–20:00, Sun 9:30–15:00, closed Mon. See page 334.

▲**Clothing Museum** A clothes look at the 18th–21st centuries. **Hours:** Tue–Sat 9:30–19:00, Sun 10:00–15:00, closed Mon. See page 335.

▲**Chapel of San Antonio de la Florida** Church with Goya's tomb, plus frescoes by the artist. **Hours:** Tue-Fri 9:30-20:00, Sat-Sun 10:00-14:00, closed Mon. See page 335.

▲**El Rastro** Europe's biggest flea market. **Hours:** Sun 9:00-15:00, best before 11:00. See page 337.

Royal Botanical Garden A relaxing museum of plants, with specimens from around the world. **Hours:** Daily 10:00-21:00, until 18:00 in winter. See page 331.

Naval Museum Seafaring history of a country famous for its Armada. **Hours:** Tue-Sun 10:00-14:00, closed Mon and Aug. See page 331.

CaixaForum Impressive exhibit hall with free, world-class art exhibits. Hours: Daily 10:00-20:00. See page 332.

Descalzas Royal Monastery Working monastery with fine art and tapestries. **Hours:** Tue-Thu and Sat 10:30-12:30 & 16:00-17:30, Fri 10:30-12:30, Sun 11:00-13:30, closed Mon. See page 334.

Sorolla Museum Spanish painter Joaquín Sorolla's former home and studio. **Hours:** Tue-Sat 9:30-20:00, Sun 10:00-15:00, closed Mon. See page 334.

Municipal Museum Experience Madrid's history via paintings, models, and a movie. Under renovation in 2009, but some exhibits remain open to the public. **Hours:** Tue-Fri 9:30-20:00, Sat-Sun 10:00-14:00, closed Mon. See page 334.

Royal Tapestry Factory See traditional tapestries being made. **Hours:** Mon-Fri 10:00-14:00, closed Sat-Sun and Aug. See page 335.

Temple de Debod Actual ancient Egyptian temple relocated to Madrid. Hours: April-Sept Tue-Fri 10:00-14:00 & 18:00-20:00, Sat-Sun 10:00-14:00, closed Mon; Oct-March Tue-Fri 9:45-13:45 & 16:15-18:15, Sat-Sun 10:00-14:00, closed Mon. See page 335.

Cable Car Dangle over Madrid's city park. **Hours:** April-Aug daily from 12:00, Sept-March Sat-Sun only. See page 335.

Bookstores: For books in English, try **FNAC Callao** (Calle Preciados 28, tel. 915-956-100), **Casa del Libro** (English on ground floor in back, Gran Vía 29, tel. 915-212-219), and **El Corte Inglés** (guidebooks and some fiction, in its Librería branch kitty-corner from main store, fronting Puerta del Sol—see earlier listing).

Laundry: Onda Blu will wash, dry, and fold your laundry (€5.50–8.50 depending on size of load, cheaper self-service also available, change machine, Internet access, Mon–Fri 9:30–22:00, Sat–Sun 10:30–19:00, León 3, east of Plaza Santa Ana, tel. 913-695-071, Ana).

Travel Agencies: The grand department store **El Corte Inglés** has two travel agencies (air and rail tickets, but not reservations for railpass-holders, €2 fee, on first and seventh floors, Mon–Sat 10:00–22:00, Sun 11:00–21:00, just off Puerta del Sol, tel. 913-798-000).

Getting Around Madrid

If you want to use Madrid's excellent public transit, my two best tips are these: Pick up and study the fine *Public Transit* map/flier (available at TIs), and take full advantage of the cheap 10-ride Metrobus ticket deal (see below).

By Metro: The city's broad streets can be hot and exhausting. A subway trip of even a stop or two saves time and energy. Madrid's Metro is simple, speedy, and cheap (€1/ride within zone A—which covers most of the city, but not trains out to the airport; runs 6:00–1:30 in the morning, www.metromadrid.es or www.ctm-madrid.es). The 10-ride Metrobus ticket can be shared by several travelers and works on both the Metro and buses (€6.70—or €0.67 per ride, sold at kiosks, tobacco shops, and in Metro). Insert your Metrobus ticket in the turnstile (it usually shows how many rides remain on it), then retrieve it as you pass through. Stations offer free maps *(Madrid by Underground)*, but they often run out in central locations. However, there are always plenty of maps and line stops posted in hallways and on the Metro trains. Navigate by Metro stops (shown on city maps). To transfer, follow signs to the next Metro line (numbered and color-coded). The names of the end stops are used to indicate directions. Green *salida* signs point to the exit. Using neighborhood maps and street signs to exit smartly can save lots of walking. And watch out for thieves.

By Bus: City buses, while not as easy as the Metro, can be useful (€1 tickets sold on bus, or €6.70 for a 10-ride Metrobus ticket—see above; bus maps at TI or info booth on Puerta del Sol, poster-size maps are usually posted at bus stops, buses run 6:00–24:00, much less frequent *Buho* buses run all night).

By Taxi: Madrid's 15,000 taxis are reasonably priced and easy to hail. Threesomes travel as cheaply by taxi as by Metro. A ride from the Royal Palace to the Prado costs about €4. After the €1.95 drop charge, the per-kilometer rate depends on the time: *Tarifa 1* (€0.92/kilometer) should be charged Mon–Sat 6:00–22:00; *Tarifa 2* (€1.06/kilometer) is valid after 22:00 and on Sundays and holidays. If your cabbie uses anything rather than *Tarifa 1* on weekdays (shown as an isolated "1" on the meter), you're being cheated. Rates can be higher if you go outside Madrid. Other legitimate charges include the €5.25 supplement for the airport, the €2.75 supplement for train or bus stations, and €13.50 per hour for waiting. Make sure the meter is turned on as soon as you get into the cab so the driver can't tack anything onto the official rate. If the driver starts adding up "extras," look for the sticker detailing all legitimate surcharges (which should be on the passenger window).

TOURS

Madrid Vision Hop-On, Hop-Off Bus Tours—Madrid Vision offers two different hop-on, hop-off circuits of the city: historic and modern. Buy a ticket from the driver (€16/1 day, €21/2 days) and you can hop from sight to sight and route to route as you like, listening to a recorded English commentary along the way. Each route has about 15 stops and takes about 90 minutes, with buses departing every 10 or 20 minutes. The two routes intersect at the south side of Puerta del Sol and in front of Starbucks across from the Prado (daily 9:30–24:00 in summer, 10:00–19:00 in winter, tel. 917-791-888, www.madridvision.es).

LeTango Tours—Carlos Galvin, a Spaniard who speaks flawless English (and has led tours for my groups since 1998), and his wife from Seattle, Jennifer, offer private tours in Madrid and other parts of Spain. Carlos mixes a market walk in the historic center with a culinary-and-tapas crawl to get close to the Madrileños, their culture, and their food. His walk gives a fine three-hour orientation and introduction to the fascinating and tasty culture of Madrid, plus travel tips (€95 per person, 10 percent cash discount, includes tastes in the market and light tapas at the end, minimum 2 people, alcohol-free and gourmet versions available, family-friendly, price goes down with more people). They also offer guided visits to the Prado, Royal Palace, Toledo, Segovia, and El Escorial; self-guided tour packages all over Spain; and Madrid apartment rentals (tel. 913-694-752, mobile 661-752-458, www.letango.com, info@letango.com).

Private Guides—**Frederico and Cristina** are licensed local guides who lead city walks through the pedestrian streets of the historic core of Madrid. Fred, Cris, and their team offer an all-ages tour of the big museums, including the Royal Palace, the Prado, and the Reina Sofía, as well as a tapas tour. Or, if you're looking to get outside Madrid, consider their guided tour to surrounding towns (per-tour costs: Mon–Fri €160, Sat–Sun €190, 10 percent Rick Steves discount, prices don't include sight entry fees or food and drinks on the tapas tour, 3–5 hours, tel. & fax 913-102-974, mobile 649-936-222, www.spainfred.com, spainfred@gmail.com).

Inés Muñiz Martin is a good, licensed Madrileña guide who has led my tour groups (and individuals) through her hometown and the Prado for years. Inés also leads tours to nearby areas (such as El Escorial), and can customize a tour to your specific interests (€140 for up to 4 hours, €170 on weekends and holidays, these rates include discount for Rick Steves readers, transportation and museum entries extra, mobile 629-147-370, www.immguidedtours.com, info@immguidedtours.com).

Hernán Amaya Satt directs a group of licensed guides who take individuals around Madrid by foot or by car on 18 personalized tours (rates vary according to tour and number of people, 20 percent discount off official rates for Rick Steves readers, mobile 680-450-231, www.madrid-museum-tours.org, info@madrid-museum-tours.org).

Pub Crawl—British expatriate **Stephen Drake-Jones** gives entertaining, informative walks of historic old Madrid almost daily. A historian with a passion for the memory of the Duke of Wellington (the general who stopped Napoleon), Stephen is the founder and chairman of the Wellington Society. For €35, you become a member of the society for one year and get a free, two-hour tour that includes a stop along the way for local drinks and tapas (morning and afternoon departures). Or you can go on a VIP tour for €50, which includes three stops for drinks and tapas and lasts more than three hours (day and evening departures). Eccentric Stephen takes you back in time to sort out Madrid's Habsburg and Bourbon history. He likes his wine—if that's a problem, skip the tour. Tours usually start at the statue in Puerta del Sol. He also offers special tours for families, people with disabilities, and private groups; bullfight tours; multi-regional wine tastings, and day trips in the countryside (starting at €275 per couple; call 609-143-203 to confirm tour and reserve a spot, US tel. 573/301-0344, Paseo de las Delicias 75-5A, www.wellsoc.org, chairman@wellsoc.org). Members of the Wellington Society can also take advantage of Stephen's helpline (if you're in a Spanish jam, call him to translate and intervene) and assistance by email (for questions on Spain, your itinerary, and so on).

Big-Bus City Sightseeing Tours—Julia Travel offers standard guided bus tours departing from Plaza de España 7 (office open Mon–Fri 8:00–19:00, Sat–Sun 8:00–15:00, tel. 915-599-605). Their city tours include a three-hour Madrid tour with a live guide in two or three languages (€20, one stop for a drink at Hard Rock Café, one shopping stop, no museum visits, daily at 15:00, no reservation required—just show up 15 min before departure). You can tack this tour onto several others they offer, including a visit to the Santiago Bernabéu Real Madrid soccer stadium (€34, daily at 15:00, reservation required), or an excursion to the Ventas Bullring to see the *toros* (starting at €33, departure time varies, offered during bullfighting season, reservation required). If you want to hoof it, there is also a three-hour tour of the Austrias quarter and the Royal Palace (€30, Thu–Tue at 10:00, none Wed, reservation required).

Julia Travel also runs multiple day-trip tours to destinations near Madrid. The Valley of the Fallen and El Escorial tour is particularly efficient, given the lousy bus connections for this route (€47, 5 hours, makes the day trip easy—blitzing both sights with a commentary en route and no time-stealing shopping stops, Tue–Sun at 9:00, none Mon). Three trips include Toledo: one of the city itself (€39/5 hours, daily at 9:00 and 15:00, or €52/8 hours, daily at 9:15), one of Madrid and Toledo together (€50, half-day in Toledo plus panoramic 3-hour Madrid tour, daily at 9:00), and a marathon tour of El Escorial, Valley of the Fallen, and Toledo (€93, full day, Tue–Sun at 9:00, none Mon). Note that the Toledo-only full-day tours include the cathedral, but the half-day Toledo and combo-tours skip this town's one must-see sight...but not the long shopping stops, because the shops give kickbacks to the guides. And even though the buses are air-conditioned, the all-day Toledo trip is just too hot to enjoy in summer (June–Sept).

SELF-GUIDED WALK

Welcome to Madrid: From the Puerta del Sol to the Royal Palace

Connect the sights with the following commentary. Allow an hour for this half-mile walk. Begin at Madrid's central square, Puerta del Sol (Metro: Sol).

▲▲Puerta del Sol

The bustling Puerta del Sol is named for a long-gone medieval gate with the sun carved onto it. It's a hub for the Metro, buses, political demonstrations, and pickpockets.

• *Stand by the statue of King Charles III and survey the square.*

Because of his enlightened urban policies, Charles III (who ruled until 1788) is affectionately called "the best mayor of Madrid." He decorated the city squares with fine fountains, got those meddlesome Jesuits out of city government, established the public school system, made the Retiro a public park rather than a royal retreat, and generally cleaned up Madrid.

Look behind the king. The statue of the bear pawing the berry bush and the *madroño* trees in the big planter boxes are symbols of the city. Bears used to live in the royal hunting grounds outside Madrid. And the *madroño* trees produce a berry that makes the traditional *madroño* liqueur.

The king faces a red-and-white building with a bell tower. This was Madrid's first post office, established by Charles III in the 1760s. Today, it's the governor's office, though it's notorious for having been Francisco Franco's police headquarters. An amazing number of those detained and interrogated by the Franco police "tried to escape" by jumping out the windows to their deaths. Notice the hats of the civil guardsmen at the entry. It's said the hats have square backs so that the men can lean against the wall while enjoying a cigarette.

Appreciate the harmonious architecture of the buildings that circle the square. Crowds fill the square on New Year's Eve as the rest of Madrid watches the action on TV. As Spain's "Big Ben" atop the governor's office chimes 12 times, Madrileños eat one grape for each ring to bring good luck through the coming year.

• *Cross the square, walking to the governor's office.*

Look at the curb directly in front of the entrance to the **governor's office.** The scuffed-up marker is "kilometer zero," the very center of Spain. Near the entrance are two plaques expressing thanks from the regional government to its citizens for assisting in times of dire need. To the left of the entrance, a plaque on the wall honors those who helped during the terrorist bombings of March 11, 2004.

A similar plaque on the right marks the spot where the war against Napoleon started in 1808. Napoleon wanted his brother to be king of Spain. Trying to finagle this, he brought nearly the entire Spanish royal family to France for negotiations. An anxious crowd gathered outside this building awaiting word of the fate of their royals. This was just after the French Revolution, and there was a general nervousness between France and Spain. When the people of Madrid heard that Napoleon had appointed his own brother as the new king of Spain, they gathered angrily in the streets. The French guard simply massacred the mob. Painter Francisco de Goya, who worked just up the street, observed the event and captured the tragedy in his paintings *Second of May, 1808* and *Third of May, 1808,* now in the Prado (for more on Goya, see page 322).

From Puerta del Sol to Plaza Mayor

On the corner of Calle Mayor and Puerta del Sol (downhill end of Puerta del Sol, across from McDonald's) is the busy *confitería* **Salon La Mallorquina** (daily 9:00–21:15, closed mid-July–Aug). Go inside for a tempting peek at racks with goodies hot out of the oven. The shop is famous for its sweet, cream-filled *Napolitana* pastry (€1). Or sample Madrid's answer to donuts, *rosquillas* (*tontas* means "silly"—plain, and *listas* means "all dressed up and ready to go"—with icing, €0.50 each).

From inside the shop, look back toward the entrance and notice the tile above the door with the 18th-century view of Puerta del Sol. Compare this with today's view out the door. This was before the

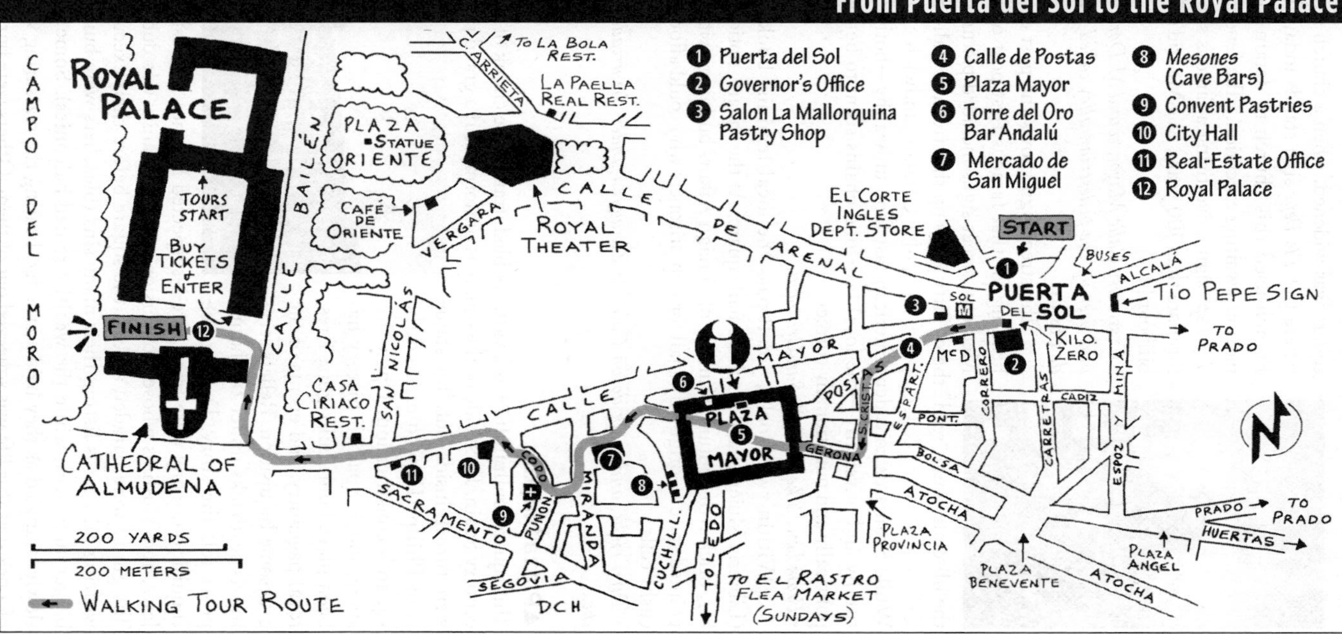
From Puerta del Sol to the Royal Palace
1 Puerta del Sol
2 Governor's Office
3 Salon La Mallorquina Pastry Shop
4 Calle de Postas
5 Plaza Mayor
6 Torre del Oro Bar Andalú
7 Mercado de San Miguel
8 Mesones (Cave Bars)
9 Convent Pastries
10 City Hall
11 Real-Estate Office
12 Royal Palace
Campo del Moro
Royal Palace
Tours Start
Buy Tickets & Enter
Finish
Cathedral of Almudena
Calle Bailén
Plaza Oriente
Statue
Café de Oriente
Vergara
Royal Theater
Arrieta
To La Bola Rest.
La Paella Real Rest.
Calle de Arenal
El Corte Ingles Dept. Store
Start
Buses
Alcalá
Tío Pepe Sign
Puerta del Sol
Sol
Kilo. Zero
To Prado
McD
Correro
Carretas
Cadiz
Mina
Espoz y Mina
Pont.
Espart.
S. Crist.
Postas
Mayor
Gerona
Plaza Mayor
Bolsa
Atocha
Plaza Provincia
Plaza Benevente
Plaza Angel
Prado
Huertas
To Prado
Calle Mayor
San Nicolás
Casa Ciriaco Rest.
Codo
Punon
Miranda
Cuchill.
Toledo
To El Rastro Flea Market (Sundays)
Sacramento
Segovia
DCH
200 yards
200 meters
Walking Tour Route

square was widened, when a church stood where the *Tío Pepe* sign stands today. The French used this church to detain local patriots awaiting execution. (The venerable *Tío Pepe* sign, advertising a famous sherry for more than 100 years, was Madrid's first billboard.)

• *Cross busy Calle Mayor, round McDonald's, and veer up the pedestrian alley called* ***Calle de Postas.***

The street sign shows the post coach heading for that famous first post office. Medieval street signs included pictures so the illiterate could "read" them. Fifty yards up the street, at Calle San Cristóbal, is Pans & Company, a popular Catalan sandwich chain. While Spaniards consider American fast food unhealthy—both culturally and physically—the local fast-food chains seem to be more politically and nutritionally correct.

• *From here, hike up Calle San Cristóbal.*

Within two blocks, you'll pass the local feminist bookshop (Librería Mujeres) and reach a small square. At the square, notice the big, brick 17th-century Ministry of Foreign Affairs building (with the pointed spire)—originally a jail for rich prisoners who could afford the cushy cells.

• *Turn right, and walk down Calle de Zaragoza under the arcade into the...*

▲Plaza Mayor

This square, built in 1619, is a vast, cobbled, traffic-free chunk of 17th-century Spain. Each side of the square is uniform, as if a grand palace were turned inside-out. The statue is of Philip III, who ordered the square's construction. Upon this stage, much Spanish history has been played out: bullfights, fires, royal pageantry, and events of the gruesome Inquisition. Reliefs serving as seatbacks under the lampposts tell the story. During the Inquisition, many were tried here—suspected heretics, Protestants, Jews, and Muslims whose "conversion" to Christianity was dubious. The guilty were paraded around the square before their execution, wearing billboards listing their many sins (bleachers were built for bigger audiences, while the wealthy rented balconies). Some were slowly strangled as they held a crucifix, hearing the reassuring words of a priest as this life was squeezed out of them. Others were burned.

The square is painted a democratic shade of burgundy—the result of a citywide vote. Since Franco's death in 1975, there's been a passion for voting here. Three different colors were painted as samples on the walls of this square, and the city voted for its favorite.

A stamp-and-coin market bustles here on Sundays from 10:00 to 14:00; on any day, it's a colorful and affordable place to enjoy a cup of coffee. Throughout Spain, lesser *plazas mayores* provide peaceful pools in the river of Spanish life. The TI (daily 9:30–20:30, wonderfully air-conditioned and with free but limited Internet access) is under the building on the north side of the square, the Casa de la Panadería, decorated with painted figures (it once housed the Bakers' Guild).

• *For some interesting, if gruesome, bullfighting lore, drop by the...*

Torre del Oro Bar Andalú

This bar is a good spot for a drink to finish off your Plaza Mayor visit (northwest corner of square, to the left of the Bakers' Guild). The bar has *Andalú* (Andalusian) ambience and an entertaining staff. Warning: They push expensive tapas on tourists. But buying a beer is safe and painless—just order a *caña* (small beer, shouldn't cost more than €2.30). The price list posted outside the door makes your costs perfectly clear. Consider taking a break at one of their sidewalk tables (or at any café/bar terrace facing Madrid's finest square). The scene is well worth the extra euro you'll pay for the drink.

The interior of the Torre del Oro bar is a temple to bullfighting, festooned with gory decor. Notice the breathtaking action captured in the many photographs. Look under the stuffed head of Barbero the bull. At eye level, you'll see a *puntilla,* the knife used to put a bull out of his misery at the arena. This was the knife used to kill Barbero. The plaque explains: weight, birth date, owner, date of death, which matador killed him, and the location. Just to the left of Barbero, there's a photo of Franco with a very famous bullfighter. This is Manuel Benítez Pérez—better known as El Cordobés, the Elvis of bullfighters and a working-class hero. At the top of the stairs to the WC, find the photo of El Cordobés and Robert Kennedy—looking like brothers. At the end of the bar in a glass case is the "suit of lights" the great El Cordobés wore in his ill-fated 1967 fight. With Franco in attendance, El Cordobés went on and on, long after he could have ended the fight, until finally the bull gored him. El Cordobés survived; the bull didn't. Find another photo of Franco with El Cordobés at the far end, to the left of Segador the bull. Under the bull is a photo of El Cordobés' illegitimate son kissing a bull. Disowned by

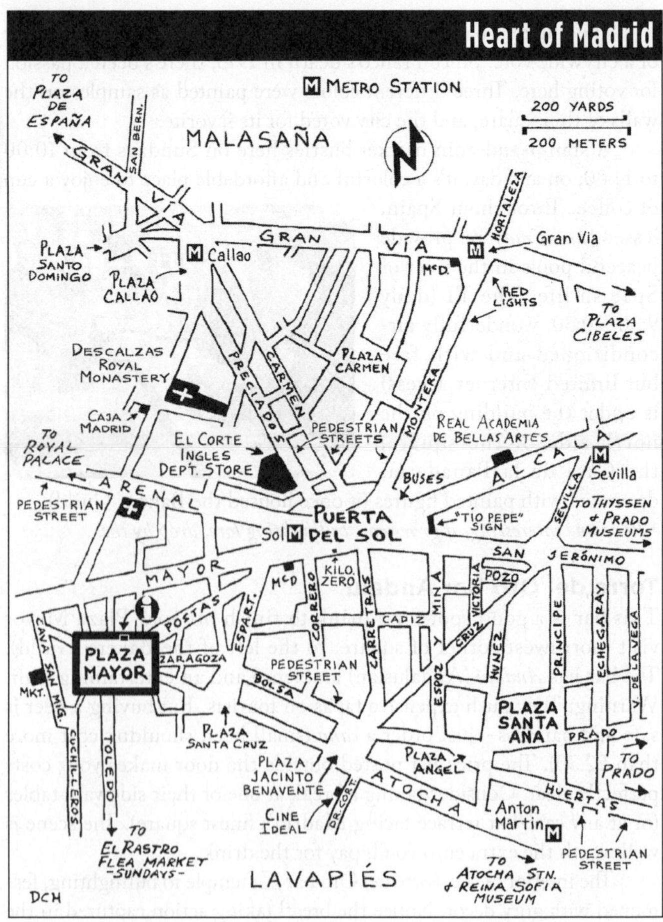

El Cordobés senior, yet still using his dad's famous name after a court battle, the new El Cordobés is one of this generation's top fighters.

Strolling from Plaza Mayor to the Royal Palace

Leave Plaza Mayor on Calle Ciudad Rodrigo (to your right as you exit the bull bar). You'll pass a series of fine turn-of-the-20th-century storefronts and sandwich joints, such as Casa Rúa, famous for their cheap *bocadillos de calamares*—fried squid-rings on a roll.

From the archway, you'll see the covered **Mercado de San Miguel** (green iron posts, on left). This historic market, closed for several years, should open again by the beginning of 2009, but it will be more of a trendy tourist stop than a place for locals to buy their veggies.

Before passing the market hall, look left down the street called Cava de San Miguel. If you like sangria and singing, come back at about 22:00 and visit one of the ***mesones*** that line the street. These cave-like bars stretch way back and get packed with locals out on cheap dates who—emboldened by sangria, the setting, and Spain—might suddenly just start singing. It's a lowbrow, electric-keyboard, karaoke-type ambience, best on Friday and Saturday nights.

• On the opposite (downhill) side of the market, follow the pedestrian lane left. At the first corner, turn right and cross the small plaza to the modern brick ***convent.***

The door on the right says *venta de dulces* (sweets for sale). To buy goodies from the cloistered nuns, buzz the *monjas* button, then wait patiently for the sister to respond over the intercom. Say "*dulces*" (DOOL-thays), and she'll let you in (Mon–Sat 9:30–13:00 & 16:00–18:30, closed Sun). When the lock buzzes, push open the door and follow the sign to *torno,* the lazy Susan that lets the sisters sell their baked goods without being seen (smallest quantity: half, or *medio,* kilo—around €6). Of the many choices (all good), *galletas* (orange shortbread cookies) are the least expensive.

• Follow Calle del Codo (where those in need of bits of armor shopped—see the street sign) uphill around the convent to Plaza de la Villa, the square where the ***City Hall*** *is located.*

The statue in the garden is of Don Bazán—mastermind of the Christian victory over the Turkish Ottomans at the naval battle of Lepanto in 1571. This pivotal battle, fought off the coast of Greece, ended the Turkish threat to Christian Europe. This square was the heart of medieval Madrid, though little remains of the 14th-century town.

From here, busy Calle Mayor leads downhill for a couple more blocks to the Royal Palace. Halfway down (on the left), at #75, a **real-estate office** *(inmobiliaria)* advertises apartments for rent (*piso* is a large apartment or condo, priced by the month—in the hundreds or low thousands of euros) and condos for sale (with six-digit prices). To roughly convert square meters to square feet, multiply by 10. Notice how, for large items, locals still think in terms of *pesetas* ("pts"), the Spanish currency before euros took over in 2002.

A few steps farther down, on a tiny square opposite the recommended Casa Ciriaco restaurant (at #84—see page 349), a statue memorializes the 1906 anarchist bombing that killed 23 people as the royal couple paraded by on their wedding day. While the crowd was throwing flowers, an anarchist (what terrorists used to be called) threw a bouquet lashed to a bomb from a balcony of #84, which was a hotel at the time. Gory photos of the event hang inside the restaurant (to the right of the entrance).

• *Continue down Calle Mayor. Within a couple of blocks, you'll come to a busy street, Calle de Bailen.*

Across the busy street is Madrid's **Cathedral of Almudena,** built between 1883 and 1993. Its exterior is a contemporary mix, and its interior is Neo-Gothic, with a refreshingly modern and colorful ceiling, glittering 5,000-pipe organ, and the 12th-century coffin (empty, painted leather on wood, in a chapel behind the altar) of Madrid's patron saint, Isidro. A humble peasant, Isidro loved the handicapped and performed miracles. Forty years after he died, this coffin was opened and his body was found miraculously preserved, which convinced the pope to canonize him as the patron saint of Madrid and of farmers, with May 15 as his feast day.

Next to the cathedral is the **Royal Palace.** Visit the palace now, using my self-guided tour (see below).

• *When you're finished, you may want to...*

Return to Puerta del Sol

With your back to the palace, face the equestrian statue of Philip IV and (beyond the statue) the Neoclassical **Royal Theater** (Teatro Real, rebuilt in 1997). On your left, the **Madrid Tower** skyscraper marks the Plaza de España. Walk behind the Royal Theater (on the right, passing Café de Oriente—a favorite with theater-goers) to another square, where you'll find the Ópera Metro stop and the mostly pedestrianized Calle de Arenal, which leads back to Puerta del Sol.

SIGHTS

▲▲Royal Palace (Palacio Real)

Europe's third-greatest palace (after Versailles and Vienna's Schönbrunn), with arguably the most sumptuous original interior, is packed with tourists and royal antiques.

After a fortress burned down on this site in the 18th century, King Philip V commissioned this huge palace as a replacement. Though he ruled Spain for 40 years, Philip V was very French. (The grandson of Louis XIV, he was born in Versailles and preferred speaking French.) He ordered this palace to be built as his own Versailles (although his wife's Italian origin had a tremendous impact on the style). It's big—more than 2,000 rooms, with tons of luxurious tapestries, a king's ransom of chandeliers, priceless porcelain, and bronze decor covered in gold leaf. While these days the royal family lives in a mansion a few miles away, this place still functions as a royal palace, and is used for formal state receptions, royal weddings,

Cheap Tricks in Madrid

- Instead of expensive city tour buses, take bus #27 on a sightseeing joyride past some major Madrid landmarks. Catch the bus in front of the Royal Botanical Garden on the Paseo del Prado and ride it to the Plaza Castilla (the end of the line). You'll pass (in order): the Prado Museum, the Neptune fountain (the Ritz and Palace hotels are on this roundabout), the Thyssen-Bornemisza Museum (on the left), the Madrid stock market and Naval Museum (on the right), the Plaza de Cibeles fountain, the Paseo de Recoletos and its lovely cafés, the National Library (on the right, before the Plaza de Colón—look for the column with the statue of Columbus pointing), then a stretch of roundabouts and businesses, the Santiago Bernabéu Real Madrid soccer stadium, and finally the Plaza de Castilla, where you'll see the two leaning KIO Towers (the crazy angle is intentional). All for just €1.
- Some major sights are free to enter at certain times (for example, the Prado is free Tue-Sat 18:00-20:00 and Sun 17:00-20:00, while the Centro de Arte Reina Sofía is free Sat afternoon after 14:30 and all day Sun). Five Madrid sights are always free: Caja Madrid, CaixaForum, National Archaeological Museum, Bullfighting Museum, and the Temple de Debod.
- If you need to quickly check your email, the TI on Plaza Mayor has limited free Internet access. All Madrid TIs have a free and informative road map of Spain, *Mapa de Comunicaciones España*.

and tourists' daydreams.

The lions you'll see throughout were symbols of power. The Bourbon kings considered previous royalty not up to European par, and this palace—along with their establishment of a Spanish porcelain works and tapestry works—was their effort to raise the bar.

Cost and Hours: €8 without a tour, €10 with a 1-hour tour (explained below); April–Sept Mon–Sat 9:30–19:00, Sun 9:00–16:00; Oct–March Mon–Sat 9:30–18:00, Sun 9:00–15:00; last entry one hour before closing. The palace can close without warning if needed for a royal function; you can call a day ahead to check (tel. 914-548-800).

Crowd-Beating Tips: The palace is most crowded on Wednesdays, when it's free for locals. Arrive early to minimize lines.

Getting There: To get to the palace from Puerta del Sol, walk down the mostly pedestrianized Calle de Arenal. If arriving by Metro, get off at the Ópera stop.

Services: At the palace, there's a WC just past the ticket booth (men will enjoy the beer-stein urinals—all the rage in Madrid).

Touring the Palace: A simple one-floor, 24-room, one-way circuit is open to the public. You can wander on your own or join an English-language tour (check time of next tour and decide as you buy your ticket; the English-language tours depart about every 20 min, not worth a long wait). The tour guides, like the museum guidebook, show a passion for meaningless data. The €2.30 audioguides are much more interesting, and they complement what I describe below (but they'd never mention beer-stein urinals). If you enjoy sightseeing cheek-to-cheek, crank up the volume and share the audioguide with your companion. The armory (€3.40, described below) and the pharmacy (included in your ticket) are in the courtyard. Photography is not allowed.

➲ **Self-Guided Tour:** If you tour the palace on your own, here are a few details beyond what you'll find on the little English descriptions posted in each room.

1. The Palace Lobby: In the old days, horse-drawn carriages would drop you off here. Today, a sign divides the visitors waiting for a tour and those going in alone. The modern black bust in the corner is of the current, very popular constitutional monarch—King Juan Carlos I.

2. The Grand Stairs: Fancy carpets are rolled down (notice the little metal bar-holding hooks) for formal occasions. At the top of the first landing, the blue-and-red coat of arms represents Juan Carlos. While Franco chose him to be his successor, J.C. knew Spain was ripe for democracy. Rather than become "Juan the Brief" (as some were nicknaming him), he turned real power over to the parliament. You'll see his (figure) head on the back of the Spanish €1 and €2 coins. At the top of the stairs (before entering first room, right of door) is a white marble bust of J.C.'s great-great-g-g-g-great-grandfather Philip V, who began the Bourbon dynasty in Spain in 1700.

3. Guard Room: The palace guards used to hang out in this relatively simple room. Notice the fine clocks. Charles IV, a great collector, amassed more than 700. The 150 displayed in this palace are all in working order. Look up, and see the first ceiling fresco in a series by the great Venetian painter Giambattista (or G. B.) Tiepolo (also see "Throne Room," below).

4. Hall of Columns: Originally a ballroom and dining room, today this space is used for formal ceremonies. (For example, this is where Spain formally joined the European Union in 1985—see plaque on far wall.) The tapestries (like most you'll see in the palace) are 17th-century Belgian, from designs by Raphael.

5. Throne Room: Red velvet walls, lions, and frescoes of Spanish scenes symbolize the monarchy in this Rococo riot. The chandeliers are the best in the house. While the room is decorated in the 18th-century style, the throne dates only from 1977. This is where the king's guests salute the king before dinner. He receives them relatively informally...standing at floor level, rather than seated up on the throne.

The ceiling fresco (1764) is the last great work by Italian master G. B. Tiepolo, who died in Madrid in 1770. This painting celebrates the days of the vast Spanish empire—upon which the sun also never set. Find the Native American (hint: follow the rainbow to the macho, red-caped conquistador).

The next several rooms were the living quarters of King Charles III (ruled 1759–1788).

6. Antechamber: The four paintings are of King Charles IV (looking a bit like a dim-witted George Washington) and his wife, María Luisa (who wore the pants in the palace)—all originals by Francisco de Goya. To meet the demand for his work, he made copies of these (which you'll see in the Prado). The clock—showing Cronus, god of time, in porcelain, bronze, and mahogany—sits on a music box. The gilded decor you see throughout the palace is bronze with gold leaf. Velázquez's famous painting *Las Meninas* (which you'll marvel at in the Prado) originally hung here.

7. Gasparini Room: This was meant to be Charles III's bedroom, but was unfinished when he died. Instead, with its painted stucco ceiling and inlaid Spanish marble floor (restored in 1992), it was the royal dressing room. It's a triumph of the Rococo style, with exotic motifs that were in vogue during that period. Note the fine stucco ceiling and the micromosaic table—a typical royal or aristocratic souvenir from any visit to Rome in the mid-1800s. The Asian influence was also trendy at the time. For a divine monarch, dressing was a public affair. The court bigwigs would assemble here as the king, standing on a platform—notice the height of the mirrors—would pull on his leotards and toy with his wig.

In the next room, the silk wallpaper is new; notice the *J.C.S.* initials of King Juan Carlos and Queen Sofía.

• *Pass through the silk room to reach...*

8. Charles III Bedroom: This room is dedicated to Charles III, known as one of the enlightened monarchs, who died here in his bed in 1788. His grandson, Ferdinand VII, commissioned the optimistic fresco on the ceiling, showing how the glories of his grandfather's virtuous life earned him a hero's welcome in heaven. Decorated in 19th-century Neoclassical style, the chandelier is in the shape of the fleur-de-lis (symbol of the Bourbon family). The thick walls separating each room hide service corridors for servants, who scurried about generally unseen.

9. Porcelain Room: The 300 separate plates that line this room were disassembled for safety during the Spanish Civil War. (Find the little screws in the greenery that hide the seams.)

The Neoclassical Yellow Room was a study for Charles III. Notice the fine chandelier, with properly cut crystal that shows all the colors of the rainbow.

10. Gala Dining Room: Up to 12 times a year, the king entertains as many as 150 guests at this bowling lane–size table, which can be extended to the length of the room. Find the two royal chairs. (Hint: With the modesty necessary for 21st-century monarchs, they are only a tad higher than the rest.) The parquet floor was the preferred dancing surface when balls were held in this fabulous room, decorated with vases from China and a fresco depicting the arrival of Christopher Columbus in Barcelona. Imagine the lighting when the 15 chandeliers (and their 900 bulbs) are fired up. The table in the next room would be lined with an exorbitantly caloric dessert buffet.

11. Cinema Room (Sala de Monedas y Medallas): In the early 20th century, the royal family enjoyed "Sunday afternoons at the movies" here. Today, this room stores glass cases filled with coins and medals.

12. Silver Room: This collection of silver tableware dates from the 19th century. The older royal silver was melted down by Napoleon's brother to help fund wars of the Napoleonic age. If you look carefully, you can see quirky royal necessities, including a baby's silver rattle.

13. Stradivarius Room: The queen likes classical music. When you perform for her, do it with these precious 350-year-old violins. About 300 Antonius Stradivarius–made instruments survive. This is the only matching quartet: two violins, a viola, and a cello. The next room was the children's room—with kid-size musical instruments.

14. China Rooms: Several collections of china from different kings (some actually from China, others from royal workshops in Europe such as Sèvres and Meissen) are displayed in this room. This room illustrates how any self-respecting royal family in Europe would have had its own porcelain works.

• *Exit to the hallway. Between statues of the giants of Spanish royal history (Isabel and Ferdinand), you'll enter the...*

15. Royal Chapel: This chapel (possibly closed for restoration in 2009) is used for private concerts and funerals. The royal coffin sits here before making the sad trip to El Escorial to join the rest of Spain's past royalty (see next chapter).

16. Queen's Boudoir: This room was for the ladies, unlike the next...

17. Billiards and Smoking Rooms: The billiards room and the smoking room were for men only. The porcelain and silk of the smoking room imitates a Chinese opium den, which, in its day, was furnished only with pillows.

18. Charles IV Bedroom: Small for a king's room, the Neoclassical, Wedgwood-like decoration stands out.

19. Fine Woods Room: Fine 18th- and 19th-century French inlaid-wood pieces decorate this room.

You'll exit down the same grand stairway you climbed 24 rooms ago. To exit, cross the big courtyard, go to the gift shop where you entered, and follow *salida* signs.

Facing the courtyard is the **armory** (€3.40), which displays the armor and swords of El Cid (Christian warrior who fought the Moors), Ferdinand (husband of Isabel), Charles V (ruler of Spain at its peak of power), and Philip II (Charles' son, who watched Spain start its long slide downward). At the exit is an air-conditioned cafeteria and a bookstore, which has a good variety of books on Spanish history.

As you leave the palace, walk around the corner to the left, along the palace exterior, to the grand yet people-friendly Plaza de Oriente. Throughout Europe, energetic governments are turning formerly car-congested wastelands into public spaces like this. Madrid's last mayor was nicknamed "The Mole" for all the digging he did. Where's all the traffic? Under your feet.

Madrid's Museum Neighborhood

Three great museums, all within a 10-minute walk of each other, cluster in east Madrid: El Prado (Europe's top collection of paintings), the Thyssen-Bornemisza Museum (a baron's collection of European art, from the old masters to the moderns), and the Centro de Arte Reina Sofía (modern art, including Picasso's famous *Guernica*).

If visiting all three museums, save a few euros by buying the ***Paseo del Arte* combo-ticket** (€14.40, buy at any of the three museums, expires in one year). Note that it's free to enter the Prado Tuesday–Saturday 18:00–20:00, and Sunday 17:00–20:00, and the Reina Sofía Saturday 14:30–21:00 and Sunday 10:00–14:30 (both are free anytime for those under 18). The Prado and Thyssen-Bornemisza are closed Monday, and the Reina Sofía is closed Tuesday.

▲▲▲Prado Museum

With more than 3,000 canvases, including entire rooms of masterpieces by superstar painters, the Prado (PRAH-doh) is overwhelming. But if you use the free English floor plan (pick up as you enter) and follow my self-guided tour (see below), you'll be impressed. The Prado is *the* place to enjoy the great Spanish painter Francisco de Goya, and it's also the home of Diego Velázquez's *Las Meninas,* considered by many to be the world's finest painting, period. In addition to Spanish works, you'll find paintings by Italian and Flemish masters, including Hieronymus Bosch's delightful *Garden of Delights* altarpiece.

Cost and Hours: €6, free Tue–Sat 18:00–20:00 and Sun 17:00–20:00, and free anytime to anyone under 18. Open Tue–Sun

Madrid's Museum Neighborhood

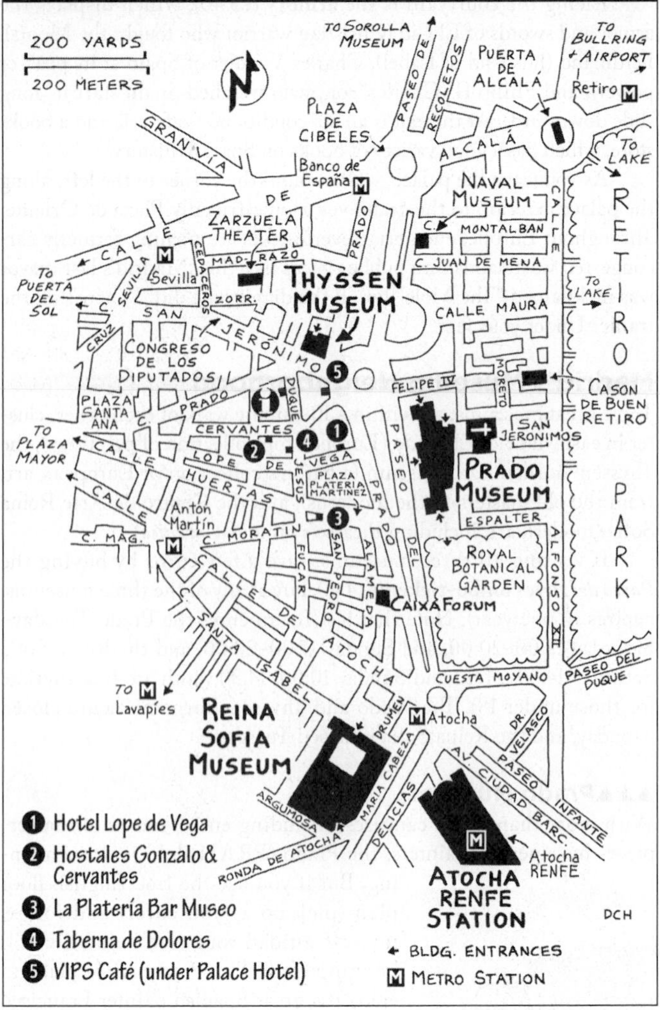

1. Hotel Lope de Vega
2. Hostales Gonzalo & Cervantes
3. La Platería Bar Museo
4. Taberna de Dolores
5. VIPS Café (under Palace Hotel)

← BLDG. ENTRANCES

M METRO STATION

9:00–20:00, closed Mon, last entry 30 min before closing.

Location: It's at the Paseo del Prado. The Banco de España and Atocha Metro stops are each a five-minute walk from the museum. Cabs picking you up at the Prado are likely to overcharge—insist on the meter.

The Prado Expansion: The museum is undergoing an extensive expansion project that will create exhibit space for many works long hidden in storage. The first extension, inaugurated in 2007, was partially constructed in the cloister of the 15th-century San Jerónimos church. This spacious addition houses a sculpture gallery and temporary exhibits, as well as a café and gift shop. Future additions in other buildings will provide space for more sculpture and decorative arts. This expansion, and any current special exhibits, may cause curators to jumble the museum's layout, making many of the directions to my self-guided tour inaccurate. Pick up a detailed map when you enter the museum, consider renting an audioguide, and enlist the help of a guard if you're unable to find a particular work of art.

Crowd-Beating Tips: Lunchtime (14:00–16:00) and weekdays are generally less crowded. It's always packed when free and on weekends; it's worth paying the entry price on other days to have your space.

Entrances: You can buy your ticket at the Goya or Veláquez entrances, but if you want tickets to any special exhibit, you must get them at the upper Goya entrance (even if the exhibit is free). There are three entrances for ticket-holders and visitors with the *Paseo del Arte* pass: Jerónimos, Goya, or Veláquez. Scope the entrances as you approach the museum to see which has the shortest line. (The Murillo entrance, the one across from the Botanical Garden, is for advance bookings such as school groups.) My self-guided tour begins at the upper Goya (north) entrance.

Tours: Take a tour, rent the €3 audioguide, buy a guidebook, or use my self-guided commentary (below). Given the ever-changing locations of paintings (making my self-guided tour tough to follow), the audioguide (with 120 paintings described) is a good investment, allowing you to wander. When you see a painting of interest, simply punch in the number and enjoy the description. You can return the audioguide at any of the exits. And, if you're on a tight budget, remember that two can crank up the volume, listen cheek-to-cheek, and share one machine.

Services and Information: Your bags will be scanned (just like at the airport) before you leave them at the free and mandatory baggage storage (no water bottles allowed inside). There's a cafeteria in the extension area by the Jerónimos entrance. Tel. 913-302-800, http://museoprado.mcu.es.

Photography: Not allowed.

➲ **Self-Guided Tour:** Thanks to Gene Openshaw for writing the following tour.

New World gold funded the Prado, the greatest painting museum in the world. You'll see world-class Italian Renaissance art (especially Titian), Northern art (Bosch, Rubens, Dürer), and Spanish

Prado Museum Overview

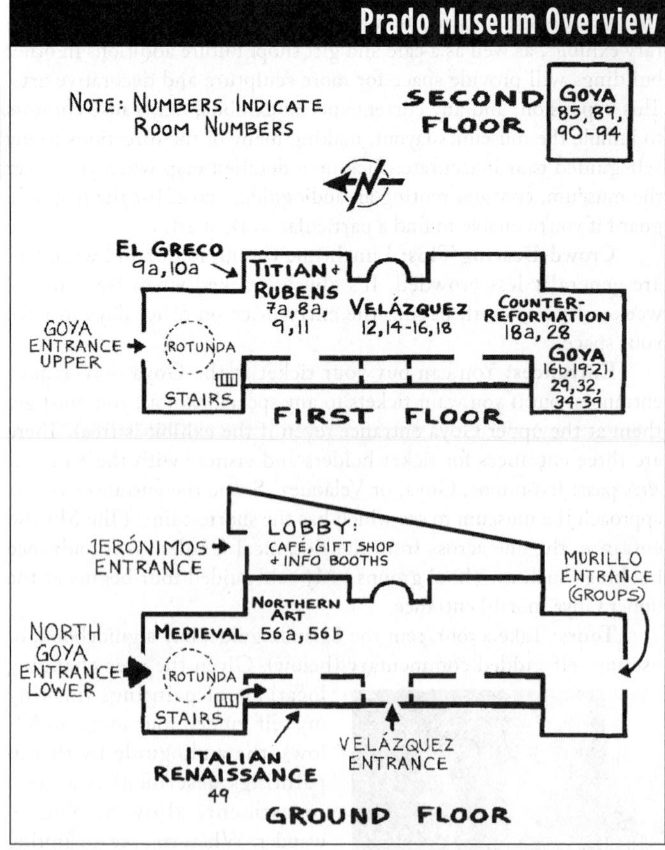

art (El Greco, Velázquez, and Goya). This huge museum is not laid out chronologically, so this tour will not be chronological. Instead, we'll hit the highlights with a minimum of walking. Remember, the Prado frequently moves its collection around. Make sure to have a map (available at entry). If you can't find a particular painting, ask.

• *Start at the Upper Goya entrance on the first floor. Go down the long main gallery. On the way, find Murillo, Room 28.*

Bartolomeo Murillo's *Immaculate Conception (La Inmaculada "de El Escorial")* puts a human face on the abstract Catholic doctrine that Mary was conceived and born free of original sin. Floating in a cloud of Ivory Soap purity, this "immaculate" virgin radiates youth and wholesome goodness. (You'll find more works by Murillo in Sevilla's Museo de Bellas Artes, page 494.)

• *At the far end of the gallery, go into the round Room 32.*

Francisco de Goya (1746–1828): Follow this complex man through the stages of his life—from dutiful court painter, to political rebel and scandal-maker, to the disillusioned genius of his "dark paintings."

The Family of Charles IV (La Familia de Carlos IV) is all decked out in their Sunday best for this group portrait. Goya himself stands to the far left, painting the court (a tribute to Velázquez in *Las Meninas*)...and revealing the shallow people beneath the royal trappings. King Charles, with his ridiculous hairpiece and goofy smile, was a vacuous, henpecked husband. His domineering queen upstages him, arrogantly stretching her swanlike neck. The other adults, with their bland faces, are bug-eyed with stupidity.

• *Find the staircase near Room 39 and head up to the second floor.*

Rooms 90–94 display canvases that were Goya's designs to make tapestries for nobles' palaces. The scenes make it clear that, while revolution was brewing in America and France, Spain's lords and ladies played—picnicking, dancing, flying kites, playing paddleball and Blind Man's Bluff, or just relaxing in the sun—the well-known *The Parasol (El Quitasol)* is in Room 85.

• *Return down the stairs to the first floor, Room 21.*

Rumors flew that Goya was fooling around with the vivacious Duchess of Alba, and he may have painted her in a scandalous pose in the two similar paintings, the *Nude Maja (La Maja Desnuda)* and *Clothed Maja (La Maja Vestida)*. A *maja* was the name for a trendy, working-class girl. Whether she's a duchess or *maja,* Goya had painted a naked lady, incurring the wrath of the Inquisition. The *Nude* stretches in a Titianesque pose to display her charms, the pale body highlighted by cool green sheets. The two paintings may have been displayed in a double frame, with the *Clothed Maja* sliding over the front to hide the Nude from Inquisitive minds.

• *Go back by the stairs still on the first floor, Room 39.*

Goya became a political liberal, a champion of democracy. He was crushed when France's hero of the Revolution, Napoleon, morphed into a tyrant and invaded Spain. On the *Second of May, 1808,*

Madrid's citizens were protesting the occupation in Puerta del Sol, when the French sent in their dreaded Egyptian mercenaries. They plow through the dense tangle of Madrileños, who have nowhere to run. The next day, the *Third of May, 1808,* the French rounded up ringleaders and executed them. The colorless firing squad—a faceless machine of death—mows them down, and they fall in bloody, tangled heaps. Goya throws a harsh, prison-yard floodlight on the main victim, who spreads his arms Christ-like to ask, "Why?"

In his 70s, Goya—disillusioned, widowed, exiled, and going deaf—retreated to a villa and smeared the walls with his "dark paintings"...dark in color and in mood. The style is considered Romantic—emphasizing emotion over beauty—but it foreshadows 20th-century Surrealism with its bizarre imagery and Expressionism, thick brushstrokes and cynical outlook.

• *To find the "dark paintings," silently flagellate yourself, then go to Rooms 34–38 (which you'll visit in reverse order).*

Dark forces convened continually in Goya's dining room, where *The Witches' Sabbath (El Aquelarre)* hung. The crones swirl in a frenzy around a dark, Satanic goat in monk's clothing who presides over the obscene rituals. The main witch exudes wild-eyed adoration and lust, while a noble lady (right of center) folds her hands primly in her lap ("I thought this was a Tupperware party!").

In the *Battle to the Death (Duelo a Garrotazos),* two giants stand face to face, buried up to their knees, and flail at each other with clubs. It's a standoff between superpowers in the never-ending cycle of war.

In *Saturn Devouring One of His Sons (Saturno),* we see Saturn—fearful that his sons would overthrow him as king of the Roman gods—eating one of them. Saturn, also known as Cronus (Time), may symbolize how time devours us all. (Either way, the painting brings new meaning to the term "child's portion.")

• *Pass by Carlos IV again and into Room 18a.*

Spanish Counter-Reformation Art: In the 1600s, when Europe was torn between Protestant and Catholic ideologies, devoted Spanish artists used images to bolster the Catholic faithful and explain abstract church doctrines. So Francisco Zurbarán's *St.*

Peter Crucified Appearing to Peter Nolasco (Aparición de San Pedro a San Pedro Nolasco) renders the mystical vision absolutely literally. Bam, there's the Apostle Peter on an upside-down cross right in front of us. Nolasco looks as shocked as we'd be.

• *Velázquez can be found in Rooms 18 and 16–14, with a grand finale in large lozenge-shaped Room 12.*

Diego Velázquez (1599–1660): Velázquez (vel-LAHTH-keth) was the photojournalist of court painters, capturing the Spanish king and his court with a blend of formal portrait and candid snapshot.

Prince Balthazar Carlos on Horseback (El Príncipe Baltasar Carlos, a Caballo) is exactly the kind of portrait Velázquez was called on to produce. The prince prances like a Roman emperor—only this "emperor" is just a cute little five-year-old acting oh so serious. Get up close and notice that his remarkably detailed costume is nothing but a few messy splotches of pink and gold paint—the proto-Impressionism Velázquez helped pioneer.

The Surrender of Breda (La Rendicion de Breda) is a piece of artistic journalism, chronicling Spain's victory over the Dutch. The defeated Dutchman starts to kneel, but the Spaniard stops him—no need to rub salt in the wound. Twenty-five lances silhouetted against the sky reinforce the optimistic calm-after-the-battle mood.

Velázquez's boss, King Philip IV, had an affair, got caught, and repented by commissioning the *Crucifixion (Cristo Crucificado)*. Christ hangs his head, humbly accepting his punishment, while Philip is left to stare at the slowly dripping blood, contemplating how long Christ had to suffer to atone for Philip's sins.

Velázquez's *The Maids of Honor (Las Meninas)* is a behind-the-scenes look at his own job. One hot summer day in 1656, Velázquez (at left, with paintbrush and Dalí moustache) stands at his easel and stares out at the people he's painting—the king and queen. They would have been standing about where we are, and we see only their reflection in the mirror at the back of the room. Their daughter (blonde hair, in center) watches her parents being painted, joined by her servants *(meninas)*, dwarfs, and the family dog. Also, at that very moment, a man happens to pass by the doorway at back and pauses to look in.

This frozen moment is lit by the window on the right, splitting the room into bright and shaded planes that recede into the distance. The main characters look right at us, making us part of the scene, seemingly able to walk around, behind, and among the characters. This is art come to life.

Velázquez's *The Drinkers (Los Borrachos)* is a cell-phone snapshot

in a blue-collar bar, with a couple of peasants mugging for a photo-op with a Greek god—Bacchus, the god of wine.

• *To find works by Titian, you will need to visit several rooms (Room 11, 7a, 8a). Start in Room 11.*

Titian (c. 1490–1576): Titian painted portraits of Spain's two Golden Age kings—both staunch Catholics—who amassed this racy collection. *Charles V on Horseback (El Emperador Carlos V en la Batalla de Muhlberg,* Room 11) rears on his horse, raises his lance, and rides out to crush an army of Lutherans. Charles, having inherited many kingdoms and baronies through his family connections, was the world's most powerful man in the 1500s.

• *Sitting amid the Titian collection (in Room 9) are works by Rubens, described below. But for now, we'll continue with Titian in Room 8a.*

Danae and the Shower of Gold (Danae Recibiendo la Lluvia de Oro), from Greek mythology, shows the princess opening her legs to receive Zeus, the lecherous king of the gods, who descends as a shower of gold. Danae is helpless with rapture, while her servant tries to catch the holy spurt with a towel.

In contrast, Charles V's son, *Philip II (Felipe II),* looks pale, suspicious, and lonely—a scholarly and complex figure. He built the austere, monastic palace at El Escorial, but also indulged himself with Titian's bevy of Renaissance Playmates.

• *Now backtrack to Room 9 to see more flesh...*

Peter Paul Rubens (1577–1640): A native of Flanders, Rubens painted Baroque-style art meant to play on the emotions, titillate the senses, and carry you away. *Diana and Her Nymphs Discovered by a*

Satyr (Diana y sus Ninfas Sorprendidas por Sátiros) ripples from left-to-right with a wave of figures, as the nymphs flee from the half-human sex predators. But Diana, queen of the hunt, turns to bravely face the satyrs with her spear. All of Rubens' trademarks are here—sex, violence, action, emotion, bright colors, fleshy bodies—with the wind-machine set on 10.

Rubens' *The Three Graces (Las Tres Gracias)* celebrate cellulite. Their ample, glowing bodies intertwine as they exchange meaningful glances. The Grace at left is Rubens' young second wife, who shows up fairly regularly in his paintings.

• *El Greco's works are nearby, in Rooms 9a and 10a.*

El Greco (1541–1614): El Greco was born in Greece (his name is Spanish for "The Greek"), trained in Venice, then settled in Toledo—60 miles from Madrid. His paintings are like Byzantine icons drenched in Venetian color and fused in the fires of Spanish mysticism. (For more on El Greco, see page 406 and visit Toledo.)

In *Christ Carrying the Cross (Cristo Abrazado a la Cruz),* Jesus accepts his fate, trudging toward death with blood running down his neck. He hugs the cross and directs his gaze along the crossbar. His upturned eyes (sparkling with a streak of white paint) lock onto his next stop—heaven.

The Adoration of the Shepherds (La Adoracion de los Pastores), originally painted for El Greco's own burial chapel in Toledo, has the artist's typical two-tiered composition—heaven above, earth below. The long, skinny shepherds are stretched unnaturally in between, flickering like flames toward heaven.

The Nobleman with His Hand on His Chest (El Caballero de la Mano al Pecho) is an elegant and somewhat arrogant man whose hand has the middle fingers touching—El Greco's trademark way of expressing elegance (or was it the 16th-century symbol for "Live long and prosper"?). The signature is on the right in faint Greek letters—"Doménikos Theotokópoulos," El Greco's real name.

• *Say hello one more time to* Las Meninas *on the way to the stairs off of Room 14. Then go down to the ground floor, Room 49.*

Italian Renaissance: During its Golden Age (the 1500s), Spain was Europe's richest country, but Italy was still the most cultured. Spain's kings loved how Renaissance artists captured a three-dimensional world on a two-dimensional canvas, bringing Bible scenes to life and celebrating real people and their emotions.

Raphael's *Christ Falls on the Way to Calvary (Caida en el Camino del Calvario)* is a study in contrasts. Below the crossbar, Christ and the women swirl in agonized passion. Above, bored soldiers mill about on the bleak hill where Jesus will die.

In the *Death of the Virgin (El Transito de la Virgen),* Mantegna masters Renaissance 3-D. The apostles mourn in a crowded room, while the floor tiles recede into the distance, creating the subconscious effect of carrying Mary's soul out the window into the serene distance.

Fra Angelico's *The Annunciation (La Anunciacion)* is half medieval piety, half Renaissance realism. In the crude Garden of Eden scene (on the left), a scrawny, sinful First Couple hovers unrealistically above the foliage, awaiting eviction. The angel's Annunciation to Mary (right side) is more Renaissance, both with its upbeat message (that Jesus will be born to redeem sinners like Adam and Eve) and in the budding photo-realism, set beneath 3-D arches. (Still, aren't the receding bars of the porch's ceiling a bit off? Painting three dimensions wasn't that easy.)

• *Continue to Room 50.*

Here you'll find Spain's medieval roots. This art features nothing but saints and Bible scenes—appropriate for a country whose extreme religious devotion was forged in seven centuries of bloody war against Muslims.

• *Backtrack to Room 49, take a left through 57b, then through 57, turn left, then right, then right again into Room 56a.*

Northern Art: Hieronymous Bosch (c. 1450–1516), in his cryptic triptych *The Garden of Delights,* relates the message that the pleasures of life are fleeting, so we'd better avoid them or we'll wind up in hell. The large altarpiece has so many interesting small figures that it helps to "frame off" small sections to catch the details. Here's the big picture: In the central panel, men on horseback ride round and round, searching for but never reaching the elusive Fountain of Youth. Others frolic in earth's "Garden," oblivious to where they came from (Paradise, left panel) and where they may end up (Hell, right panel). On the left, innocent Adam and Eve get married, with God himself performing the ceremony. The

right panel is Hell, a burning wasteland where genetic-mutant demons torture sinners. Everyone gets their just desserts, like the glutton who is eaten and re-eaten eternally. In the center, hell is literally frozen over. A creature with a broken eggshell body, tree-trunk legs, and a witch's cap stares out—it's the face of Bosch himself.

Pieter Bruegel (BROY-gull) the Elder chronicled the 16th century's violent Catholic-Protestant wars in *The Triumph of Death (El Triunfo de la Muerte)*. The painting is one big, chaotic battle, featuring skeletons attacking helpless mortals. Bruegel's message is simple and morbid: No one can escape death.

• *Find Dürer's work nearby, in Room 55b.*

Albrecht Dürer's *Self-Portrait (Autorretrato)* is possibly the first true self-portrait. The artist, age 26, is dolled up in a fancy Italian hat and permed hair. He'd recently returned from Italy and wanted to impress his fellow Germans with his sophistication. But Dürer wasn't simply vain. He'd grown accustomed, as an artist in Renaissance Italy, to being treated like a prince. Note Dürer's signature, the pyramid-shaped "A. D." (D inside the A) on the windowsill.

Dürer's *Adam and Eve* (two separate panels) are the first full-size nudes in Northern European art. Like Greek statues, they pose in their separate niches, with three-dimensional, anatomically correct bodies. This was a bold humanist proclamation that the body is good, man is good, and the things of the world are good.

• *The Prado is also good, but our tour is over. Exit through Room 55 and continue through the red-painted walls to the open space of the Prado extension, where you'll find the café, exhibit halls of the San Jerónimos cloister, and the Jerónimos exit.*

▲▲Thyssen-Bornemisza Museum

Locals call this stunning museum simply the Thyssen (TEE-sun). It displays the impressive collection that Baron Thyssen (a wealthy German married to a former Miss Spain) sold to Spain for $350 million. It's basically minor works by major artists and major works by minor artists (major works by major artists are in the Prado). But art-lovers appreciate how the good baron's art complements the Prado's collection by filling in where the Prado is weak (such as Impressionism).

Each floor is divided into two separate areas: the permanent collection (numbered rooms) and additions from the Baroness since the 1980s (lettered rooms). The museum recently opened a new wing (creating an L-shaped museum) to house even more of the Baroness' collection, including works by Impressionists (Monet's *Charing Cross Bridge*), Post-Impressionists, and Picasso.

After purchasing your high-tech barcode ticket, continue down the wide main hall past larger-than-life paintings of King Juan Carlos and Queen Sofía, alongside the Baron (who died in 2002) and his art-collecting Baroness, Carmen. Pick up two museum maps (one for numbered rooms, another for lettered rooms) at the info desk. Ascend to the top floor and work your way down, taking a delightful walk through art history. Visit the rooms on each floor in numerical and alphabetical order, from Primitive Italian (Room 1) to Surrealism and Pop Art (Room 48). Afterwards, if you're heading to Centro de Arte Reina Sofía and you're tired, hail a cab at the gate to zip straight there.

Temporary exhibits at the Thyssen often parallel those at the free **Caja Madrid** exhibit hall (Tue–Sat 10:00–20:00, closed Mon, tel. 913-792-050, www.fundacioncajamadrid.es), across from the Descalzas Royal Monastery on the Plaza San Martín.

Cost and Hours: €6 (€3 more for special exhibits); children under 12 free, Tue–Sun 10:00–19:00, closed Mon, last entry 30 min before closing.

Location: The museum is kitty-corner from the Prado at Paseo del Prado 8 in Palacio de Villahermosa (Metro: Banco de España).

Services and Information: Free baggage storage, €4 audioguide, café, shop, no photos, tel. 914-203-944, www.museothyssen.org.

▲▲Centro de Arte Reina Sofía

This former public hospital (Madrid's first) shows off an exceptional collection of modern art. The permanent collection is on the second and fourth floors; temporary exhibits are on the first and third floors. Ride the fancy glass elevator to the second floor and follow the room numbers for art chronologically displayed from 1900 to 1940. The fourth floor continues the collection, from 1940 to 1980.

The museum is most famous for Pablo Picasso's *Guernica* (second floor, Room 6), an epic painting showing the horror of modern war (see "*Guernica*" on page 332). Notice the two rooms of studies Picasso did for *Guernica,* filled with iron-nail tears and screaming mouths. *Guernica* was displayed at the Museum of Modern Art in New York City until Franco's death, and now it reigns as Spain's national piece of art. After pondering the destruction of war, visit the room furthest back from the painting (confusingly, also numbered 6) to see photos of Picasso creating this masterpiece.

The museum also houses an easy-to-enjoy collection by other

modern artists, including more of Picasso and a mind-bending room of works by Salvador Dalí (Room 10). Room 12 is a treat for movie buffs: Two films by Surrealist director Luis Buñuel (who had help from friends Dalí and the poet Federico García Lorca) play continuously. Enjoy a break in the shady courtyard before leaving.

Cost and Hours: €6, free Sat afternoon after 14:30 (less crowded after 15:00) and all day Sun, always free to those under 18 and over 65. Even if admission is free when you visit, grab a ticket anyway. The museum is open Mon and Wed–Sat 10:00–21:00, Sun 10:00–14:30, closed Tue.

Location: It's across from the Atocha Metro station at Santa Isabel 52. Exiting the Metro, walk across two big streets, Delicias and Santa María la Cabeza. At the opening into a square, look for the exterior glass elevators. There are two entrances: the old entrance (leads to permanent collection first; on Calle Sánchez Bustillo, on a big square close to the Metro stop) and the new entrance (leads to temporary exhibits first, often shorter lines; standing on the square facing the Atocha train station, turn right onto the next street—the unmarked Ronda de Atocha—and go about a block to the big, red, modern addition).

Services and Information: Good brochure, no tours in English, hardworking €4 audioguide, no photos, free baggage storage. The *librería* just outside the new addition has a larger selection of Picasso and Surrealist reproductions than the main gift shop at the entrance. Tel. 914-675-062, www.museoreinasofia.es.

Near the Prado

▲Retiro Park (Parque del Buen Retiro)—Once the private domain of royalty, this majestic park has been a favorite of Madrid's commoners since Charles III decided to share it with his subjects in the late 18th century. Siesta in this 300-acre, green-and-breezy escape from the city. At midday on Saturday and Sunday, the area around the lake becomes a street carnival, with jugglers, puppeteers, and lots of local color. These peaceful gardens offer great picnicking and people-watching. From the Retiro Metro stop, walk to the big lake (El Estanque), where you can cheaply rent a rowboat. Past the lake, a grand boulevard of statues leads to the Prado.

Royal Botanical Garden (Real Jardín Botánico)—After your Prado visit, you can take a lush and fragrant break in this sculpted park. Wander among trees from around the world. The flier in English explains that this is actually more than a park—it's a museum of plants (€2, daily 10:00–21:00, until 18:00 in winter, entry opposite Prado's Murillo/south entry, Plaza de Murillo 2).

Naval Museum (Museo Naval)—This museum tells the story of Spain's navy, from the Armada to today, in a plush and fascinating-to-boat-lovers exhibit (free, no English anywhere, Tue–Sun 10:00–14:00,

Guernica

Perhaps the single most impressive piece of art in Spain is Pablo Picasso's *Guernica*. The monumental canvas—one of Europe's must-see sights—is not only a piece of art but a piece of history, capturing the horror of modern war in a modern style.

Pablo Picasso (1881-1973), a Spaniard, was in Paris in 1937, preparing an exhibition of paintings for its world's fair. Meanwhile, a bloody Civil War was being fought in his own country. The legally elected democratic government was being challenged by traditionalist right-wing forces under Francisco Franco. Franco would eventually win and rule the country with an iron fist for three decades.

On April 27, 1937, Guernica—a proud Basque market town in northern Spain—was the target of the world's first saturation-bombing raid on civilians. Franco gave permission to his fascist ally, Hitler, to use the town as a guinea pig to try out Germany's new air force. The raid leveled the town, causing destruction that was unheard of at the time (though by 1944 it would be commonplace). For more on the town of Guernica and the bombing, see page 147.

News of the bombing reached Picasso in Paris. He scrapped earlier plans and immediately set to work sketching scenes of the destruction as he imagined it. In a matter of weeks, he put these bomb-shattered shards together into a large mural (286 square feet). For the first time, the world could see the destructive force of the rising fascist movement—a prelude to WWII.

The bombs are falling, shattering the quiet village. A

closed Mon and in August, a block north of the Prado across boulevard from Thyssen-Bornemisza Museum, Paseo del Prado 5, tel. 915-239-884, www.museonavalmadrid.com). Because this is a military facility, you'll need to show your passport to get in.

CaixaForum—Across the street from the Prado and Royal Botanical Garden, you'll find this impressive exhibit hall with funky woman looks up at the sky (far right), horses scream (center), and a man falls from a horse and dies, while a wounded woman drags herself through the streets. She tries to escape, but her leg is too thick, dragging her down, like trying to run from something in a nightmare. On the left, a bull—a symbol of Spain—ponders it all, watching over a mother and her dead baby...a modern *pietà*. A woman in the center sticks her head out to see what's going on. The whole scene is lit from above by the stark light of a bare bulb. Picasso's painting threw a light on the brutality of Hitler and Franco, and suddenly the whole world was watching.

Picasso's abstract, Cubist style reinforces the message. It's as if he'd picked up the shattered shards and pasted them onto a canvas. The black and white tones are as gritty as the black-and-white newspaper photos that reported the bombing. The drab colors create a depressing, almost nauseating mood.

Picasso chose images with universal symbolism, making the work a commentary on all wars. Picasso himself said that the central horse, with the spear in its back, symbolizes humanity succumbing to brute force. The fallen rider's arm is severed and his sword is broken, more symbols of defeat. Near the bull, the dove of peace can do nothing but cry.

The bombing of Guernica—like the entire Spanish Civil War (1936-1939)—was an exercise in brutality. As one side captured a town, it might systematically round up every man, old and young—including priests—line them up, and shoot them in revenge for atrocities by the other side.

Thousands of people attended the Paris art fair, and *Guernica* caused an immediate sensation. They could see the horror of modern war technology, the vain struggle of the Spanish Republicans, and the cold indifference of the fascist war machine. After the Paris exhibition, *Guernica* was exiled to America until Franco's death. Picasso also vowed never to return to Spain while Franco ruled. (Franco outlived him.)

With each passing year, the canvas seemed more and more prophetic—honoring not just the thousand that died in Guernica, but also the 600,000 victims of Spain's bitter Civil War, and the 80 million worldwide that perished in World War II. Picasso put a human face on what we now call "collateral damage."

architecture and an outdoor hanging garden. The forum features various activities (such as lectures), but the world-class art exhibits are the main reason to visit. You'll see them advertised around town and at the TIs, but it's worth coming here in person to find out what's on (free, daily 10:00–20:00, Paseo del Prado 36, tel. 913-307-300, www.obrasocial.lacaixa.es).

Elsewhere in Madrid

Descalzas Royal Monastery (Monasterio de las Descalzas Reales)—Madrid's most visit-worthy monastery was founded in the 16th century by Philip II's sister, Joan of Habsburg (known to Spaniards as Juana, and to Austrians as Joanna). She's buried here. The monastery's chapels are decorated with fine art, Rubens-designed tapestries, and the heirlooms of the wealthy women who joined the order (the nuns were required to give a dowry). Because this is still a working Franciscan monastery, tourists can visit only when the nuns vacate the cloister, and the number of daily visitors is limited. The scheduled tours often sell out—come in the morning to buy your ticket, even if you want an afternoon tour (€5, visits guided in Spanish or English depending on demand, Tue–Thu and Sat 10:30–12:30 & 16:00–17:30, Fri 10:30–12:30, Sun 11:00–13:30, closed Mon, Plaza de las Descalzas Reales 3, near the Ópera Metro stop and just a short walk from Puerta del Sol, tel. 914-548-700).

▲National Archaeological Museum (Museo Arqueológico Nacional)—This fine museum gives you a chronological walk through the story of Iberia on one convenient floor. With a rich collection of artifacts (but a maddening refusal to describe anything in English), it shows off the wonders of each age: Celtic pre-Roman, Roman, a fine and rare Visigothic section, Moorish, Romanesque, and beyond (always free; open Tue–Sat 9:30–20:00, Sun 9:30–15:00, closed Mon; Calle Serrano 13, Metro: Serrano or Colón, tel. 915-777-912). Outside, underground in the museum's garden, is an underwhelming replica artwork from northern Spain's Altamira Caves (big on bison), giving you a faded peek at the skill of the cave artists who created the originals 14,000 years ago. For more on the real Altamira Caves, see page 268 in the Cantabria chapter.

Sorolla Museum (Museo Sorolla)—Joaquín Sorrolla (1863–1923) is known for his portraits, landscapes, and use of light. It's a relaxing experience to stroll through the rooms of his former house and studio, especially to see the lazy beach scenes of his hometown Valencia. Take a break after your visit to reflect in the small garden in front of his house (€2.40, free on Sun, open Tue–Sat 9:30–20:00, Sun 10:00–15:00, closed Mon, General Martínez Campos, 37, Metro: Iglesia, tel. 913-101-584, http://museosorolla.mcu.es).

Municipal Museum (Museo Municipal)—Follow the history of Madrid in old paintings and models (but no English). As you enter, notice Pedro de Ribera's fine Baroque door featuring "St. James the Moor-Slayer" (described on page 247). While the museum is undergoing a major renovation through 2011, this door may be covered in scaffolding, and only certain sections of the museum may be open (free, Tue–Fri 9:30–20:00, Sat–Sun 10:00–14:00, closed Mon, Calle Fuencarral 78, Metro: Tribunal or Bilbao, tel. 917-011-863).

▲Clothing Museum (Museo del Traje)—This museum shows the history of clothing from the 18th century until today. In a cool and air-conditioned chronological sweep, the museum's one floor of exhibits includes regional ethnic costumes, a look at how bullfighting and the French influenced styles, accessories through the ages, and Spanish flappers. The only downside of this marvelous modern museum is that it's a long way from anything else of interest (€3, free Sat 14:30–19:00 and all day Sun, open Tue–Sat 9:30–19:00, Sun 10:00–15:00, closed Mon, last entry 30 min before closing, Avenida Juan Herrera 2; Metro: Moncloa and a longish walk, bus #46, or taxi; tel. 915-497-150).

▲Chapel of San Antonio de la Florida—In this simple little Neoclassical chapel from the 1790s, Francisco de Goya's tomb stares up at a splendid cupola filled with his own proto-Impressionist frescoes. He frescoed this using the same unique technique that he used for his "dark paintings." Use the mirrors to enjoy the drama and energy he infused into this marvelously restored masterpiece (free, Tue–Fri 9:30–20:00, Sat–Sun 10:00–14:00, closed Mon, Glorieta de San Antonio de la Florida, tel. 915-420-722). This chapel is a five-minute walk down Paseo de San Antonio de la Florida from Metro: Príncipe Pío (and its bus station, serving Segovia). If you're day-tripping to Segovia from Madrid, it's easy to stop by before or after your trip.

Royal Tapestry Factory (Real Fábrica de Tapices)—Have a look at traditional tapestry-making (€3.50, Mon–Fri 10:00–14:00, closed Sat–Sun and Aug, some English tours, Calle Fuenterrabia 2, Metro: Menendez Pelayo, take Gutenberg exit, tel. 914-340-550). You can actually order a tailor-made tapestry (starting at $10,000).

Temple de Debod—In 1968, Egypt gave Spain its own ancient temple. It was a gift of the Egyptian government, which was grateful for Franco's help in rescuing monuments that had been threatened by the rising Nile waters above the Aswan Dam. Consequently, Madrid is the only place I can think of in Europe where you can actually wander through an intact original Egyptian temple—complete with fine carved reliefs from 200 B.C. (free; April–Sept Tue–Fri 10:00–14:00 & 18:00–20:00, Sat–Sun 10:00–14:00, closed Mon; Oct–March Tue–Fri 9:45–13:45 & 16:15–18:15, Sat–Sun 10:00–14:00, closed Mon). Set in a romantic park that locals love for its great city views (especially at sunset), the temple—as well as its art—is well-described. Popular as the view may be, the uninspiring "grand Madrid view" only causes me to wonder why anyone would build a city here.

Cable Car (Teleférico)—For city views, ride this cable car from downtown over Madrid's sprawling city park to Casa de Campo (€3.50 one-way, €5 round-trip, April–Aug daily from 12:00, Sept–March Sat–Sun only, departs from Paseo del Pintor Rosales, a short walk from Metro: Argüelles, tel. 915-417-450, www.teleferico.com). Do an immediate round-trip to skip Casa de Campo's strange mix of rental rowboats, prostitutes, addicts, a zoo, and an amusement park. The family-friendly bits of the park are far from the cable-car terminus.

EXPERIENCES

▲▲Bullfight—Madrid's Plaza de Toros hosts Spain's top bullfights on some Sundays and holidays from March through mid-October, and nearly every day during the San Isidro festival (May through early June—often sold out long in advance). Fights start between 17:00 and 21:00 (early in spring and fall, late in summer). The bullring is at the Ventas Metro stop (a 15-min Metro ride from Puerta del Sol, tel. 913-562-200, www.las-ventas.com). For info on the "art" of bullfighting, see page 651.

Bullfight tickets range from €3.50 to €120. There are no bad seats at the Plaza de Toros; paying more gets you in the shade and/or closer to the gore. (The action often intentionally occurs in the shade to reward the expensive-ticket holders.) To be close to the bullring, choose areas 8, 9, or 10; for shade: 1, 2, 9, or 10; for shade/sun: 3 or 8; for the sun and cheapest seats: 4, 5, 6, or 7. Note these key words: *corrida*—a real fight with professionals; *novillada*—rookie matadors and younger bulls. Getting tickets through your hotel or a booking office is convenient, but they add 20 percent or more and don't sell the cheap seats. There are two booking offices; call both before you buy: at Plaza del Carmen 1 (Mon–Sat 9:30–13:00 & 16:30–19:00, Sun 9:30–13:30, tel. 915-319-131, or buy online at www.bullfighttickets madrid.com; run by English-speaking José, who also sells soccer tickets) and at Calle Victoria 3 (Mon–Fri 10:00–14:00 & 17:00–19:00, Sat–Sun 10:00–14:00, tel. 915-211-213). To save money, you can stand in the ticket line at the bullring. Except for important bullfights—or during the San Isidro festival—there are generally plenty of seats available. About a thousand tickets are held back to be sold in the five days leading up to a fight, including the day of the fight. Scalpers hang out before the popular fights at the Calle Victoria booking office. Beware: Those buying scalped tickets are breaking the law and can lose the ticket with no recourse.

For a dose of the experience, you can buy a cheap ticket and just stay to see a couple of bullfights. Each fight takes about 20 minutes, and the event consists of six bulls over two hours.

Madrid's **Bullfighting Museum** (Museo Taurino) is not as good as Sevilla's or Ronda's (free, Tue–Fri 9:30–14:30, Sun 10:00–13:00, closed Sat and Mon and early on fight days, at the back of bullring, tel. 917-251-857).

"Football"—Madrid, like most of Europe, is enthusiastic about soccer (which they call *fútbol*). The Real Madrid team plays to a spirited local crowd Saturdays and Sundays from September through May (tickets from €30—sold at bullfight box offices listed above, stadium at Metro: Santiago Bernabéu).

SHOPPING

Shoppers focus on the colorful pedestrian area between Gran Vía and Puerta del Sol. The giant Spanish department store El Corte Inglés, a block off Puerta del Sol, is a handy place to pick up just about anything you need (Mon–Sat 10:00–22:00, Sun 11:00–21:00, see page 345).

El Rastro: Europe's biggest flea market is a sight in itself and worth ▲. It's a field day for shoppers, people-watchers, and thieves (Sundays only, 9:00–15:00, best before 11:00). Thousands of stalls titillate more than a million browsers with mostly new junk. Locals have lamented the tackiness of El Rastro lately—you'll find cheap underwear and bootleg CDs, but no real treasures. Start at the Plaza Mayor, with its stamp- and coin-collectors market (see below), and head south or take the Metro to Tirso de Molina. Walk downhill, finishing at the Puerta de Toledo Metro stop. El Rastro offers a fascinating chance to see gangs of young thieves overwhelming and ripping off naive tourists with no police anywhere in sight. Seriously: Don't even bring a wallet. The pickpocket action is brutal, and tourists are targeted.

While the flea market can be a downer, Europe's biggest stamp and coin market, thriving simultaneously on Plaza Mayor, is a genteel delight. Watch the old-timers paging lovingly through each other's albums, looking for win-win trades.

Fans: Casa de Diego sells *abanicos* (fans), *mantones* (typical Spanish shawls), *castañuelas* (castanets), *peinetas* (hair combs), and umbrellas. Even if you're not in the market, it's fun to watch the women flip open their final fan choices before buying (Mon–Sat 9:30–20:00, closed Sun, Puerta del Sol 12, tel. 915-226-643).

Classical Guitars: Guitar-lovers know that the world's finest classical guitars are made in Spain. Several of the top workshops, within an easy walk of Puerta del Sol, offer inviting little showrooms with a peek at their craft and an opportunity to strum the final product. Consider the workshops of José Romero (Calle de Espoz y Mina 30, tel. 915-214-218) and José Ramirez (Calle de la Paz 8, tel. 915-314-229). Union Musical is a popular guitar shop off Puerta del Sol (Carrera de San Jerónimo 26, tel. 914-293-877). If you're shopping, be prepared to spend €1,000.

NIGHTLIFE

Disco dancers may have to wait until after midnight for the most popular clubs to even open, much less start hopping. Spain has a reputation for partying very late, not ending until offices open in the morning. If you're people-watching early in the morning, it's actually hard to know who is finishing their day and who's just starting it. Even if you're not a party animal after midnight, make a point to be out with the happy masses, luxuriating in the cool evening air between 22:00 and midnight. The scene is absolutely unforgettable.

▲▲▲Paseo—Just walking the streets of Madrid seems to be the way the Madrileños spend their evenings. Even past midnight on a hot summer night, whole families with little kids are strolling, enjoying tiny beers and tapas in a series of bars, licking ice cream, and greeting their neighbors. A good area to wander is along Gran Vía (from about Metro: Callao to Plaza de España). Or start at Puerta del Sol, and explore in the direction of Plaza Santa Ana. See "The Madrid Pub-Crawl Dinner (for Beginners)" on page 352.

▲▲Zarzuela—For a delightful look at Spanish light opera that even English-speakers can enjoy, try zarzuela. Guitar-strumming Napoleons in red capes; buxom women with masks, fans, and castanets; Spanish-speaking pharaohs; melodramatic spotlights; and aficionados clapping and singing along from the cheap seats, where the acoustics are best—this is zarzuela...the people's opera. Originating in Madrid, zarzuela is known for its satiric humor and surprisingly good music. You can buy tickets at Theater Zarzuela, which alternates between zarzuela, ballet, and opera throughout the year (€10–40, box office open 12:00–18:00 for advance tickets or until showtime for that day, Jovellanos 4, near the Prado, Metro: Sevilla or Banco de España, tel. 915-245-400, http://teatrodelazarzuela.mcu.es; to purchase online, go to the theater section of www.servicaixa.com and choose the English version). Madrid puts on live zarzuela events in the Royal Palace gardens summer evenings (ask the TI for details). The TI's monthly guide has a special zarzuela listing.

▲Flamenco—Although Sevilla is the capital of flamenco, Madrid has two easy and affordable options.

Taberna Casa Patas attracts big-name flamenco artists. You'll quickly understand why this intimate (30-table) and smoky venue is named "House of Feet." Since this is for locals as well as tour groups, the flamenco is contemporary and may be jazzier than your notion—it depends on who's performing (€31, Mon–Thu at 22:30, Fri–Sat at 21:00 and 24:00, closed Sun, 75–90 min, price includes cover and first drink, reservations smart, no flash cameras, Cañizares 10, tel. 913-690-496, www.casapatas.com). Its restaurant is a logical spot for dinner before the show (€30 dinners, Mon–Sat from 20:00). Or, since it's three blocks south of the recommended Plaza Santa Ana tapas bars, this could be your post-tapas-crawl entertainment.

Las Carboneras, more downscale, is an easygoing, folksy little place a few steps from Plaza Mayor with a nightly hour-long flamenco show (€33 includes an entry and a drink, €61 gets you a table up front with dinner and unlimited cheap drinks if you reserve ahead, manager Enrique promises a €5 per person discount if you book direct and show this book in 2009, Mon–Thu at 22:30 and often at 20:30, Fri–Sat at 20:30 and 23:00, closed Sun, earlier shows possible if a group books, reservations recommended, Plaza del Conde de Miranda 1, tel. 915-428-677).

Regardless of what your hotel receptionist may want to sell you, other flamenco places—such as Arco de Cuchilleros (Calle de los Cuchilleros 7), Café de Chinitas (Calle Torija 7, just off Plaza Mayor), Corral de la Morería (Calle de Morería 17), and Torres Bermejas (off Gran Vía)—are filled with tourists and pushy waiters.

Mesones—Just west of Plaza Mayor, the lane called Cava de San Miguel is lined with *mesones:* long, skinny, cavelike bars famous for drinking and singing late into the night. If you were to toss lowbrow locals, Spanish karaoke, electric keyboards, crass tourists, cheap sangria, and greasy calamari into a late-night blender and turn it on, this is what you'd get. It's generally lively only on Friday and Saturday, but you're welcome to pop in to several bars (such as Guitarra, Tortilla, or Boquerón) and see what you can find.

Late-Night Bars—If you're just picking up speed at midnight, and looking for a place filled with old tiles and a Gen-X crowd, power into **Bar Viva Madrid** (daily 13:00–3:00 in the morning, downhill from Plaza Santa Ana on Calle Manuel Fernández y González, tel. 914-293-640). The same street has other late-night bars filled with music. Or hike on over to **Chocolatería San Ginés** (described on page 351) for a dessert of *churros con chocolate.*

Movies—During Franco's days, movies were always dubbed into Spanish. Movies in Spain remain about the most often dubbed in Europe. To see a movie with its original soundtrack, look for *V.O.* (meaning "original version"). **Cine Ideal,** with nine screens, is a good place for the latest films in V.O. (€7.50, 5-min walk south of Puerta del Sol at Calle del Dr. Cortezo 6, tel. 913-692-518 for info). For extensive listings, see the *Guía del Ocio* entertainment guide (€1 at newsstands, www.guiadelocio.com) or a local newspaper.

SLEEPING

Madrid has plenty of centrally located budget hotels and *pensiones.* You'll have no trouble finding a sleepable double for €35, a good double for €70, and a modern, air-conditioned double with all the comforts for €100. Prices vary throughout the year at bigger hotels, but remain about the same for the smaller hotels and *hostales.* It's almost always easy to find a place. Anticipate full hotels only during May (the San Isidro festival, celebrating Madrid's patron saint with bullfights and zarzuelas—especially around his feast day on May 15) and the last week in September (conventions). In July and August, prices can be softer—ask about promotional deals. All of the accommodations I've listed are within a few minutes' walk of Puerta del Sol.

With all of Madrid's street noise, I'd request the highest floor possible. Also, twin-bedded rooms are generally a bit larger than double-bedded rooms for the same price. Madrid hoteliers rarely offer a cash discount. During slow times, drop-ins can often score a room in business-class hotels for just a few euros more than the budget hotels (which don't have prices that fluctuate as wildly with demand).

Fancier Places in the Pedestrian Zone Between Puerta del Sol and Gran Vía

Reliable and away from the seediness, these hotels are good values for those wanting to spend a little more. Their formal prices may be inflated, but some offer weekend and summer discounts when it's slow. Drivers will pay about €24 a day in garages. Use Metro: Sol for all but Hotel Opera (Metro: Ópera). For locations, see the map on next page.

$$$ Hotel Regente is big and traditional, with 154 tastefully decorated, comfortable, air-conditioned rooms, generous public spaces, a great location, and a good value (Sb-€77, Db-€102, Tb-€124,

Sleep Code

(€1 = about $1.50, country code: 34)
S = Single, **D** = Double/Twin, **T** = Triple, **Q** = Quad, **b** = bathroom, **s** = shower only. Unless otherwise noted, credit cards are accepted, English is spoken, and breakfast is *not* included. In Madrid, the 7 percent IVA tax is sometimes included in the price.

To help you easily sort through these listings, I've divided the rooms into three categories, based on the price for a standard double room with bath during high season:

$$$ Higher Priced—Most rooms €100 or more.
$$ Moderately Priced—Most rooms between €70–100.
$ Lower Priced—Most rooms €70 or less.

Madrid's Center—Hotels and Restaurants

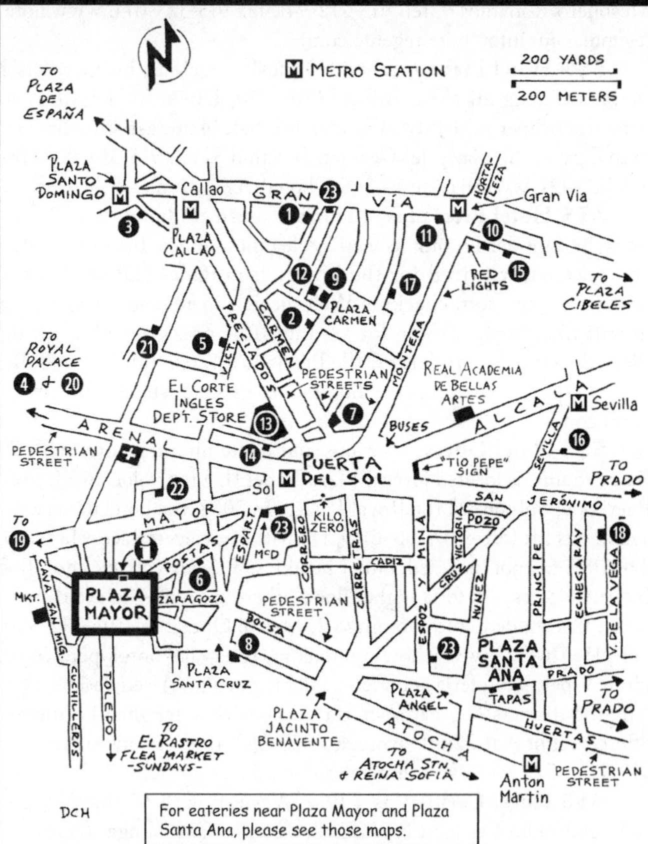

1. Hotel Regente
2. Hotel Liabeny
3. Hotel Preciados
4. To Hotel Opera
5. Hotel Carlos V
6. Petit Palace Posada del Peine
7. Hotel Europa & Cafeteria
8. Hotel Plaza Mayor
9. Hostales at Calle de la Salud 13
10. Hostal Aliste & Pension Marina Santa
11. Hostales Res. Luis XV, Jerez & Metropol
12. Restaurante Puerto Rico
13. El Corte Inglés Cafeteria
14. Casa Labra Taberna Restaurante
15. La Gloria de Montera Rest. & Fresc Co Buffet
16. La Finca de Susana
17. Artemisia II Veggie Rest.
18. Artemisia I Veggie Rest.
19. To Casa Ciriaco & La Paella Real Rest.
20. To La Bola Taberna
21. Chocolaterías Valor
22. Chocolatería San Ginés
23. Internet Cafés (3)

breakfast-€11, midway between Puerta del Sol and Plaza del Callao at Mesonero Romanos 9, tel. 915-212-941, fax 915-323-014, www.hotelregente.com, info@hotelregente.com).

$$$ Hotel Liabeny rents 220 plush, spacious, business-class rooms offering all the comforts (Sb-€110, Db-€150, Tb-€176, 10 percent cheaper mid-July–Aug and Fri–Sat, breakfast-€16, air-con, sauna, gym, off Plaza del Carmen at Salud 3, tel. 915-319-000, fax 915-327-421, www.liabeny.es, info@hotelliabeny.com).

$$$ Hotel Preciados, a four-star business hotel, has 73 fine, sleek, and modern rooms as well as elegant lounges. It's well located and reasonably priced for the luxury it provides (Db-€125–160, prices are often soft, checking Web specials in advance or dropping in will likely snag a room for around €100, breakfast-€15, just off Plaza de Santo Domingo at Calle Preciados 37, tel. 914-544-400, fax 914-544-401, www.preciadoshotel.com, preciadoshotel@preciadoshotel.com).

$$$ Hotel Opera, a serious and contemporary hotel with 79 classy rooms, is located just off Plaza Isabel II, a four-block walk from Puerta del Sol toward the Royal Palace. In 2008, the hotel underwent a mod facelift (Sb-€107, Db-€149, Db with big view terrace-€189–210, Tb-€189, tax not included, buffet breakfast-€13, air-con, elevator, free Internet access, ask for a higher floor—there are nine—to avoid street noise, Cuesta de Santo Domingo 2, Metro: Ópera, tel. 915-412-800, fax 915-416-923, www.hotelopera.com, reservas@hotelopera.com). Hotel Opera's cafeteria is understandably popular. Also consider their "singing dinners"—great operetta music with a delightful dinner—offered nightly at 22:00 (average price-€60, reservations smart, call 915-426-382 or reserve at hotel reception desk).

$$$ Hotel Carlos V is a Best Western with 67 sharp, high-ceilinged rooms, elegant breakfast, and a pleasant lounge. Its central location off Preciados pedestrian street makes it convenient—but ask for an inside room to avoid street noise (Sb-€95, standard Db-€115, larger "superior" Db with terrace-€173, Tb-€135, tax not included, breakfast-€9, air-con, non-smoking floors, elevator, Maestro Victoria 5, tel. 915-314-100, fax 915-313-761, www.hotelcarlosv.com, recepcion@hotelcarlosv.com).

$$$ Petit Palace Posada del Peine feels like part of a big modern chain (which it is), but fills its well-located old building with fresh, efficient character. Behind the ornate and sparkling Old World facade is a comfortable and modern business-class hotel with 69 rooms just a block from Plaza Mayor (Db-€100–160 depending on demand, tax not included, breakfast-€9, air-con, Calle Postas 17, tel. 915-238-151, fax 915-232-993, www.hthoteles.com, pos@hthoteles.com).

$$ Hotel Europa, with sleek marble, red carpet runners along the halls, happy Muzak charm, and an attentive staff, is a tremendous value. It rents 103 squeaky-clean rooms, many with balconies overlooking the pedestrian zone or an inner courtyard (Sb-€74, Db-€92–110, Tb-€130, Qb-€155, Quint/b-€175, tax not included, breakfast-€2–10, air-con, elevator, free Internet access, easy phone reservations with credit card, Calle del Carmen 4, tel. 915-212-900, fax 915-214-696, www.hoteleuropa.net, info@hoteleuropa.net, run by Antonio and Fernando Garaban and their helpful and jovial staff, Javi and Jim). The convenient Europa cafeteria/restaurant next door is a lively and convivial scene—fun for breakfast, and a fine value any time of day (see page 345 in "Eating").

$$ Hotel Plaza Mayor, with 34 solidly outfitted rooms, is tastefully decorated and beautifully situated a block off Plaza Mayor (Sb-€65, Db-€85, bigger Db corner room-€95, Tb-€115, buffet breakfast-€8, 5 percent discount if you reserve direct by email or fax and mention this book in 2009, air-con, elevator, Wi-Fi, Calle Atocha 2, tel. 913-600-606, fax 913-600-610, www.h-plazamayor.com, info@h-plazamayor.com).

Cheaper Bets near Puerta del Sol and Gran Vía

These accommodations are also in or near the handy pedestrian zone between Puerta del Sol and Gran Vía. The first two (Acapulco and Triana) are by far the best (and priciest). The Arcos, Aliste, and Marina Santa are your best cheap-bed options (with youth-hostel prices, yet hotel privacy).

At Calle de la Salud 13

These are all in the same building at Calle de la Salud 13, overlooking Plaza del Carmen—a little square with a sleepy, almost Parisian ambience. (The square might be a bit more bustling in 2009, thanks to the construction of a new commuter-train line nearby.)

$ Hostal Acapulco rents 16 bright rooms with air-conditioning and all the big hotel gear. The neighborhood is quiet enough that it's smart to request a room with a balcony (Sb-€49–54, Db-€59–64, Tb-€77–80, elevator, free Internet access, fourth floor, tel. 915-311-945, fax 915-322-329, hostal_acapulco@yahoo.es, Ana and Marco).

$ Hostal Triana, also a fine deal, is bigger—with 40 rooms—and offers a little less charm for a little less money (Sb-€42, Db-€55, Tb-€75, includes taxes, rooms facing the square have air-con and cost €3 extra, other rooms have fans, elevator, free Wi-Fi, first floor, tel. 915-326-812, fax 915-229-729, www.hostaltriana.com, triana@hostaltriana.com, Victor González).

$ Pension Arcos is tiny, granny-run, and old-fashioned—it's been in the Hernández family since 1936. The business cards have the new phone codes penned in, and there's no hint of email or even fax. You can reserve by phone—in Spanish—only a day in advance, and you must pay in cash. But its five rooms are clean, quiet, reasonably friendly, air-conditioned, and served by an elevator—and you step right out onto a great square. You also have access to a tiny roof terrace and a nice little lounge. If you're looking for cheap beds in a great locale, assuming you can communicate enough to reserve a room, this place is unbeatable (D-€36, Db-€40, fifth floor, air-con, tel. 915-324-994, Anuncia and Sabino).

More Cheap Sleeps

At Caballero de Gracia 6: These two *hostales* (which share the same building near Gran Vía Metro) are quiet, plain, and dreary, yet safe, on a quiet street a block past the unthreatening prostitutes of Calle de la Montera: **$ Hostal Aliste** (11 rooms, third floor, Sb-€35–38, Db-€45–48, extra bed-€20, elevator, tel. 915-215-979, h.aliste@teleline.es, Manuela's son Edward speaks English) and the humble **$ Pension Marina Santa** (nine rooms, second floor, D-€40, Db-€45, elevator, tel. 915-327-074, Lydia).

$ Hostal Residencia Luis XV is a big, plain, well-run, and clean place offering a good value. It's on a quiet eighth floor (there's an elevator). You'll find it where prostitute-lined Calle de la Montera hits noisy Gran Vía. It can be smoky, and there are no non-smoking rooms. They also run the 36-room **Hostal Jerez**—similar in every way except the name—located on the sixth floor (Sb-€45, Db-€59, Tb-€75, includes tax, air-con, elevator, Calle de la Montera 47, tel. 915-221-021, fax 915-221-350, www.hrluisxv.net, reservas@hrluisxv.net).

$ Hostal Metropol is a big, colorful, and very youthful youth hostel with 130 beds beautifully located at the noisy corner of Calle de la Montera and Gran Vía, a few minutes' walk from Puerta del Sol (bed-€18, 3–5 beds per room, always co-ed, Sb-€35, Db-€60, includes a fitted sheet and breakfast, towel not included, free Internet access, Calle de la Montera 47, first floor, tel. 915-212-935, fax 915-212-934, www.metropolhostel.com, metropol@terra.es).

Near the Prado

To locate the following three places, please see "Madrid's Museum Neighborhood" map on page 320.

$$$ Hotel Lope de Vega is your best business-class hotel value near the Prado. A four-star place that opened in 2000, it's a "cultural-themed" hotel inspired by the 17th-century writer Lope de Vega. With 60 rooms, it feels cozy and friendly for a formal business-class hotel (Sb-€115, Db-€125–145, Tb-€189, one child sleeps free, prices about 20 percent lower Fri–Sun and during most of the summer, air-con, elevator, Internet access, parking-€23/day, Calle Lope de Vega 49, tel. 913-600-011, fax 914-292-391, www.hotellopedevega.com, lopedevega@hotellopedevega.com).

At Cervantes 34: Two fine budget *hostales* are at Cervantes 34 (Metro: Anton Martín—but not handy to Metro). Both are homey, with inviting lounge areas; neither serves breakfast. **$ Hostal Gonzalo**—with 15 spotless, comfortable rooms, well-run by friendly and helpful Javier—is deservedly in all the guidebooks, so reserve in advance (Sb-€45, Db-€55, Tb-€70, air-con, elevator, third floor, tel. 914-292-714, fax 914-202-007, www.hostalgonzalo.com, hostal@hostalgonzalo.com). Downstairs, the nearly as polished **$ Hostal Cervantes** also has 15 rooms (Sb-€50, Db-€60, Tb-€75, includes tax, cheaper when slow and for longer stays, Internet access and Wi-Fi, second floor, tel. 914-298-365, fax 914-292-745, www.hostal-cervantes.com, correo@hostal-cervantes.com, Fabio).

Apartments

$$$ Raquel Román rents apartments throughout Madrid, most of which have air-conditioning and a washing machine. Review your options on the website (www.homesfortravellers.com), choose an apartment, reserve online, and pay a nonrefundable deposit (usually about 30 percent) by credit card. Upon arrival, you can pay the rest in cash or by credit card, depending on the owner of the apartment (€65–160 per night based on size and amenities, mobile 629-196-883, info@homesfortravellers.com).

EATING

In Spain, only Barcelona rivals Madrid for taste-bud thrills. You have three dining choices: a memorable, atmospheric sit-down meal in a well-chosen restaurant; a forgettable, basic sit-down meal; or a stand-up meal of tapas in a bar...or four. Many restaurants are closed in August (especially through the last half). Madrid has famously good tap water, and waiters willingly serve it free—just ask for *agua del grifo*.

Eating Cheaply North of Puerta del Sol

See the map on page 341 for locations.

Restaurante Puerto Rico fills a long, congested hall by serving good meals for great prices to smart locals (€10 three-course fixed-price meal, Mon–Sat 13:00–16:30 & 20:30–24:00, closed Sun, Chinchilla 2, between Puerta del Sol and Gran Vía, tel. 915-219-834).

Hotel Europa Cafetería is a fun, high-energy scene with a mile-long bar, traditionally clad waiters, great people-watching, local cuisine, and a fine €11 fixed-price lunch (daily 7:00–24:00, next to Hotel Europa—listed on page 342, 50 yards off Puerta del Sol at Calle del Carmen 4, tel. 915-212-900). The menu lists three price levels: bar, table, or outside, on the terrace. Though you pay a premium for the outdoor seating, it's a big hit with people-watchers.

El Corte Inglés' seventh-floor cafeteria is fresh, modern, and understated. While not particularly cheap, it's popular with locals (Mon–Sat 10:00–22:00, closed Sun, non-smoking section, just off Puerta del Sol at intersection of Preciados and Tetuán, see "One-Stop Shopping," page 301).

Casa Labra Taberna Restaurante is famous as the birthplace of the Spanish Socialist Party in 1879...and as a spot for great cod. Packed with Madrileños, it's a wonderful scene with three distinct sections: the stand-up bar (cheapest, with two lines: one for munchies, the other for drinks), a peaceful little sit-down area in back (a little more expensive but still cheap; good €6 salads), and a fancy restaurant (€20 lunches). Their tasty little €1 *Tajada de Bacalao* (cod) dishes put it on the map. The waiters are fun to joke around with (daily 11:00–15:30 & 18:00–23:00, restaurant only closed Sun, a block off Puerta del Sol at Calle Tetuán 12, tel. 915-310-081).

La Gloria de Montera Restaurante, a hip Spanish bistro with white tablecloths and a minimalist-library ambience, serves good food to locals (€8 fish and meat plates, daily 13:15–16:00 & 20:30–23:45, no reservations—arrive early or put your name on the list, a block from Gran Vía and Metro: Red de San Luis at Caballero de Gracia 10, tel. 915-234-407). Their sister restaurant, **La Finca de Susana,** is also extremely popular for the same reasons (daily 13:00–15:45 & 20:30–23:45, go early—line starts forming at about 20:00, just east of Puerta del Sol at Calle Arlabán 4, tel. 913-693-557).

Fresc Co is the place for a cheap, modern, fast, and buffet-style meal. It's a chain with a winning plan: a long, appealing salad and buffet bar with one cheap price for all-you-can-eat, including dessert and a drink (€9 lunch, €10 dinner, daily 12:30–24:00, air-con, Caballero de Gracia 8, tel. 915-216-052).

Vegetarian: **Artemisia II** is a hit with vegetarians who like good, healthy food in a smoke-free room without the typical hippie ambience that comes with most veggie places (great €11.25 three-course fixed-price lunch Mon–Fri only, open daily 13:30–16:00 & 21:00–24:00, 2 blocks north of Puerta del Sol at Tres Cruces 4, a few steps off Plaza del Carmen, tel. 915-218-721). **Artemisia I,** II's older sister, is located two blocks east of Plaza Santa Ana at Ventura de la Vega 4, off San Jerónimo (same hours, tel. 914-295-092).

On or near Plaza Mayor

Madrileños enjoy Plaza Mayor (without its high costs) by grabbing a bite to go from a nearby bar and just planting themselves somewhere on the square to eat (squid sandwiches are popular—described below). But for many tourists, dinner at a sidewalk café right on the Plaza Mayor is worth the premium price (consider Cervecería Pulpito, southwest corner of the square at #10).

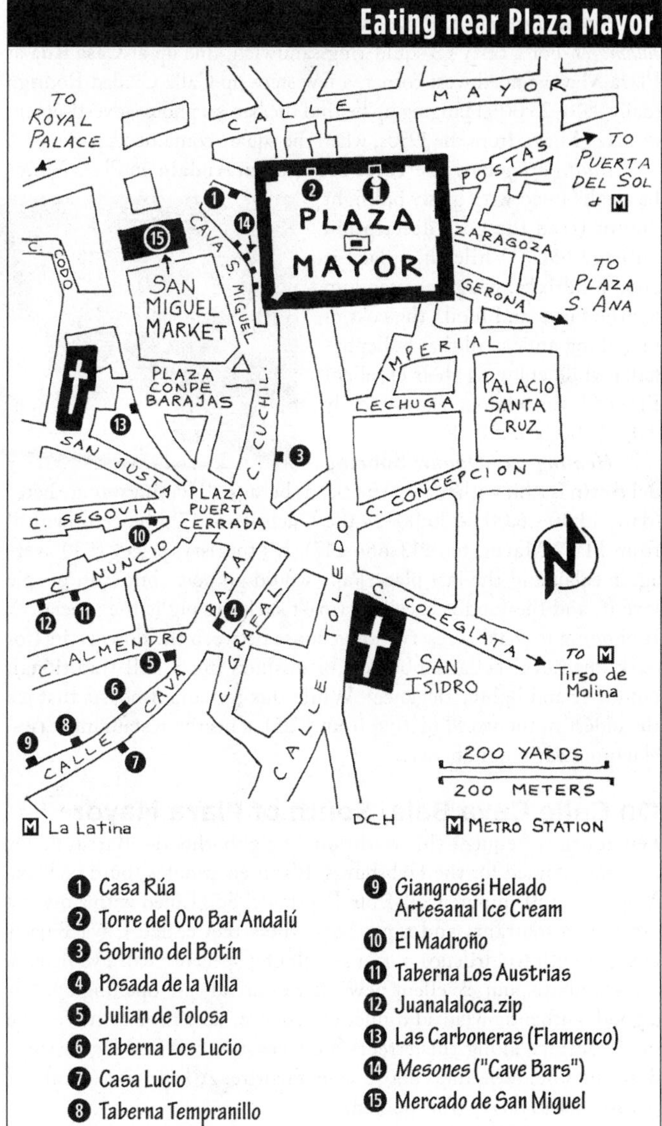
Eating near Plaza Mayor
TO ROYAL PALACE
CALLE MAYOR
POSTAS
TO PUERTA DEL SOL & M
PLAZA MAYOR
ZARAGOZA
GERONA
TO PLAZA S. ANA
C. CODO
SAN MIGUEL MARKET
CAVA S. MIGUEL
PLAZA CONDE BARAJAS
C. CUCHIL.
IMPERIAL
LECHUGA
PALACIO SANTA CRUZ
SAN JUSTA
PLAZA PUERTA CERRADA
C. SEGOVIA
C. CONCEPCION
C. NUNCIO
BAJA
C. GRAFAL
TOLEDO
C. COLEGIATA
TO M Tirso de Molina
SAN ISIDRO
C. ALMENDRO
CALLE CAVA
CALLE TOLEDO
200 YARDS
200 METERS
M La Latina
DCH
M METRO STATION
1 Casa Rúa
2 Torre del Oro Bar Andalú
3 Sobrino del Botín
4 Posada de la Villa
5 Julian de Tolosa
6 Taberna Los Lucio
7 Casa Lucio
8 Taberna Tempranillo
9 Giangrossi Helado Artesanal Ice Cream
10 El Madroño
11 Taberna Los Austrias
12 Juanalaloca.zip
13 Las Carboneras (Flamenco)
14 Mesones ("Cave Bars")
15 Mercado de San Miguel

Squid Sandwich: Plaza Mayor is famous for its *bocadillos de calamares.* For a tasty €2 squid-ring sandwich, line up at **Casa Rúa** at Plaza Mayor's northwest corner, a few steps up Calle Ciudad Rodrigo (daily 9:00–23:00). Hanging up behind the bar is a photo-advertisement of Plaza Mayor from the 1950s, when the square contained a park.

Bullfighting Bar: The **Torre del Oro Bar Andalú** on Plaza Mayor has walls lined with grisly bullfight photos (read the gory description on page 651). While this place is good for drinks, you pay a premium for the tapas and food...the cost of munching amidst all that bullephenalia while enjoying their excellent Plaza Mayor outdoor seating (daily 8:00–15:00 & 18:00–24:00).

Hemingway Haunt: **Sobrino del Botín** is a hit with many Americans because "Hemingway ate here" (daily 13:00–16:00 & 20:00–24:00, Cuchilleros 17, a block downhill from Plaza Mayor, tel. 913-664-217). It's touristy, pricey (€30 average meals), and the last place Papa would go now...but still, people love it, and the food is excellent (roast suckling pig is the specialty). If phoning to make a reservation, choose between the downstairs (for dark, medieval-cellar ambience) or upstairs (for a still-traditional, but airier and lighter elegance). While this restaurant boasts that it's the oldest in the world (dating from 1725), a nearby restaurant teases, "Hemingway never ate here."

On Calle Cava Baja, South of Plaza Mayor

Few tourists frequent this traditional neighborhood—Barrio de los Austrias, named for the Habsburgs. It's three minutes south of Plaza Mayor, or a 10-minute walk from Puerta del Sol. Lined with a diverse array of restaurants and tapas bars, the street called Cava Baja is clogged with Madrileños out in search of a special meal. I've listed a few standards, but excellent new eateries are always opening up. For a good, authentic Madrid dinner experience, take time to survey the many options along this street—between the first and last listings described below—and choose your favorite. A key wine-drinking phrase: *mucho cuerpo* (full-bodied).

Posada de la Villa serves Castilian cuisine in a 17th-century posada. This sprawling, multi-floor restaurant has dressy tables under open beams, which give it a rustic elegance. Peek into the big oven to see the baby pigs about to make some diner happy. If you're not going to Toledo or Sevilla, this is the place to try roast lamb, which is the house specialty (€30 meals, Mon–Sat 13:00–16:00 & 20:00–24:00, closed Sun and Aug, Calle Cava Baja 9, tel. 913-661-860).

Julian de Tolosa is chic, pricey, elegantly simple, and popular with natives who know good food. They offer a small, quality menu of Navarra's regional cuisine, from T-bone steak *(chuletón)* to red *tolosa* beans, in a spacious, dressy, and sane setting (€40 meals, Mon–Sat 13:30–16:00 & 21:00–24:00, Sun 13:30–16:00, Calle Cava Baja 18, tel. 913-658-210).

Taberna Los Lucio is a jam-packed bar serving good tapas, salads, *huevos estrellados* (scrambled eggs with fried potatoes), and wine. Their basement is much less atmospheric (Wed–Mon 13:00–16:00 & 20:30–24:00, Tue 20:30–24:00, Calle Cava Baja 30, tel. 913-662-984).

Casa Lucio is a favorite splurge among power-dressing Madrileños. The king and queen of Spain eat in this elegant place, but it's accessible to commoners. This could be the best place in town for a special night out and a full-blown meal (€40 for dinner, Mon–Fri and Sun 13:00–16:00 & 21:00–24:00, Sat 21:00–24:00, closed Aug, Calle Cava Baja 35; unless you're the king or queen, reserve several days in advance—and don't even bother on weekends; tel. 913-653-252).

Taberna Tempranillo, ideal for hungry wine-lovers, offers tapas and 250 kinds of wine. Wines available by the glass are listed on the board. With a phrasebook in hand or a spirit of adventure, use their fascinating menu to assemble your dream meal. It's packed and full of commotion—the crowds can be overwhelming. Arrive by 20:00 or plan to wait (Tue–Sun 13:00–15:30 & 20:00–24:00, Mon 20:00–24:00, closed Aug, Cava Baja 38, tel. 913-641-532).

Ice Cream Finale: **Giangrossi Helado Artesanal** is a popular chain considered to serve some of Madrid's best ice cream. This Giangrossi—which has a plush white leather lounge and lots of great flavors—is a fun way to finish your dining experience in this area. It's just 50 yards from the La Latina Metro stop (Cava Baja 40, tel. 902-444-130).

Near the Royal Palace

Casa Ciriaco is popular with Madrileños who appreciate good traditional cooking (€30 meals, €20 fixed-price lunch and dinner, Thu–Tue 13:30–16:00 & 20:30–24:00, closed Wed and Aug, air-con, halfway between Puerta del Sol and the Royal Palace at Calle Mayor 84—see map on page 341, tel. 915-480-620). It was from this building in 1906 that an anarchist bombed the royal couple on their wedding day (for details, see page 313). A photo of the carnage is inside the front door.

La Bola Taberna, touristy but friendly and tastefully elegant, specializes in *cocido Madrileño*—Madrid stew. The €19 stew consists of various meats, carrots, and garbanzo beans in earthen jugs. It's big enough to split—which they'll let you do, as long as the second person orders something small, like a salad. The stew is served as two courses: First you enjoy the broth as a soup, then you dig into the meat and veggies (Mon–Sat 13:00–16:00 & 20:30–23:00, closed Sun, cash only, midway between the Royal Palace and Gran Vía at Calle Bola 5—see map on page 341, tel. 915-476-930).

La Paella Real Restaurante ("Royal Paella Restaurant") is considered a top spot for "a proper paella." You'll see this saffron-rice specialty from Valencia served all over town (and it tastes best in Valencia), but paella requires a special oven and big pan in order to cook it correctly. For your paella experience, enjoy this venerable and dressy spot (€15 per person for hearty portions of paella—minimum of two, with drinks and sides figure about €20–30 per person, Mon–Sat 13:00–16:00 & 19:30–22:30, Sun 13:00–16:00, allow a good 30 min for your meal to arrive, between Puerta del Sol and the palace at Plaza de la Ópera, Arrieta 2—see map on page 341, tel. 915-420-942).

Near the Prado

Each of the three big art museums has a decent cafeteria. Or choose from these restaurants, all within a block of the Prado (for locations, see "Madrid's Museum Neighborhood" map on page 320).

La Platería Bar Museo is a hardworking little café/wine bar with a good menu for tapas, light meals, and hearty salads (listed as *raciones* and *1/2 raciones* on the chalkboard). Its tables spill onto the leafy little Plaza de Platerías de Martínez (daily 8:00–24:00, air-con, directly across busy boulevard Paseo del Prado from Atocha end of Prado, tel. 914-291-722).

Taberna de Dolores, a winning formula since 1908, is a commotion of locals enjoying €2.50 *canapés* (open-face sandwiches), tasty *raciones* of seafood, and *cañas* (small beers) at the bar or at a few tables in the back (daily 11:00–24:00, Plaza de Jesús 4, tel. 914-292-243).

VIPS is a bright, popular chain restaurant, handy for a cheap and filling salad. Engulfed in a big bookstore, this is a high-energy, no-charm eatery (daily 9:00–24:00, across the boulevard from northern end of Prado, under Palace Hotel). In 2001, Spain's first Starbucks opened next door.

Fast Food and Picnics

Fast Food: For an easy, light, cheap meal, try **Rodilla**—a popular sandwich and salad chain with a shop on the northeast corner of Puerta del Sol at #13 (Mon–Fri 9:30–23:00, Sat 9:00–23:00, Sun 11:00–23:00). **Pans & Company,** with shops throughout Madrid and Spain, offers healthy, tasty sandwiches and pre-packaged salads (daily 9:00–24:00, locations at Puerta del Sol, on Plaza Callao, at Gran Vía 30, and many more).

Breakfast in Madrid

As most hotels don't include breakfast (and many don't even serve it), you may be out on the streets first thing looking for a place. Non-touristy places only offer a hot drink and a pastry, with perhaps a potato omelet and sandwiches (toasted cheese, ham, or both). Touristy places will have a *desayuno* menu with various ham-and-eggs deals. Try *churros* once. Starbucks, a temptation for many due to its familiarity, is always nearby. Get advice from your hotel staff for their favorite breakfast place.

Picnics: The department store **El Corte Inglés** has well-stocked meat and cheese counters downstairs (Mon–Sat 10:00–22:00, Sun 11:00–21:00, see "One-Stop Shopping" on page 301).

Churros con Chocolate

Those not watching their cholesterol will want to try the deep-fried doughy treats called *churros* (or the thicker *porras*), best enjoyed by dipping them in pudding-like hot chocolate. While many *chocolaterías* offer the dunkable fritters, *churros* are most delicious when consumed fresh out of the greasy cauldron.

Chocolaterías Valor is a modern chain that does *churros* with pride and gusto. A few minutes' walk from nearly all my hotel recommendations, it's a fine place for breakfast. With a website like www.amigosdelchocolate.com, you know where their heart is (€4 *churros con chocolate,* daily 8:00–22:30, Fri–Sat until 24:00, a half-block below Plaza Callao and Gran Vía at Postigo de San Martín 7, tel. 915-229-288).

Chocolatería San Ginés is a classy institution, much beloved by Madrileños for its *churros con chocolate* (€3.20 in the morning and afternoon, €3.50 at night). Dunk your *churros* into the chocolate pudding, as locals have done here for more than 100 years. While quiet before midnight, it's packed with the disco crowd in the wee hours; the popular dance club Joy Eslava is next door (daily 22 hours a day—it's only closed between 7:00 and 9:00; from Puerta del Sol, take Calle de Arenal 2 blocks west, turn left on bookstore-lined Pasadizo de San Ginés, and you'll see the café—it's at #5; tel. 913-656-546).

Tapas

Tapa-Hopping on Calle del Nuncio (near Calle Cava Baja)

El Madroño ("The Berry Tree," a symbol of Madrid) is a fun tapas bar that preserves a bit of old Madrid. A tile copy of Velázquez's famous *Drinkers* grins from its facade. Inside, look above the stairs for photos of 1902 Madrid. Study the coats of arms of Madrid through the centuries as you try a *vermut* (vermouth) on tap and a €2 sandwich. Or ask to try the *licor de madroño;* a small glass *(chupito)* costs €1.50. While indoor seating is bright and colorful, the sidewalk tables come with great people-watching (€9 fixed-price lunch, quieter tables in the back, Tue–Sun 9:00–17:00 & 20:00–24:00, closed Mon, Plaza Puerta Cerrada 7, tel. 913-645-629).

Taberna Los Austrias, two blocks away, serves tapas, salads, and light meals on wood-barrel tables (daily 12:00–16:00 & 20:00–24:00, more formal seating in back, Calle Nuncio 17).

Juanalaloca.zip serves wine and creative tapas, such as their famous *tortilla de patatas,* a potato dish that owes much of its tastiness to an extra touch—caramelized onions. It's open late every night (€8 tapas, Tue–Fri 20:00–24:00, Sat 13:00–17:00 & 20:00–24:00, Sun 13:00–24:00, closed Mon, Calle Nuncio 17, tel. 913-654-704).

The Madrid Pub-Crawl Dinner (for Beginners)

For maximum fun, people, and atmosphere, go mobile for dinner: Do the "tapas tango," a local tradition of going from one bar to the next, munching, drinking, and socializing. Tapas are the toothpick appetizers, salads, and deep-fried foods served in most bars. Madrid is Spain's tapas capital—tapas just don't get any better. Grab a toothpick and stab something strange—but establish the prices first, especially if you're on a tight budget or at a possible tourist trap. Some items are very pricey, and most bars push larger *raciones,* rather than smaller tapas. The real action begins late (around 20:00). But for beginners, an earlier start, with less commotion, can be easier. In good old-fashioned bars, a drink comes with a free tapa. The litter on the floor is normal; that's where people traditionally toss their trash and shells (it's unsanitary to put it back on the bar). Don't worry about paying until you're ready to go. Then ask for *la cuenta* (the bill).

If done properly, a pub crawl can be a highlight of your trip. Before embarking upon this culinary adventure, study and use the tapas tips on page 22. Your ability to speak a little Spanish will get you a much better (and less expensive) experience.

Prowl the area between Puerta del Sol and Plaza Santa Ana. There's no ideal route, but the little streets (in this book's map) between Puerta del Sol, San Jerónimo, and Plaza Santa Ana hold tasty surprises. Nearby, the street Jesús de Medinaceli is also lined with popular tapas bars. Below is a six-stop tapa crawl. These places are good, but don't be afraid to make some discoveries of your own. The

more adventurous should read this crawl for ideas, and skip directly to the advanced zone (Lavapiés), described below.

• *From Puerta del Sol, walk east a block down Carrera de San Jerónimo to the corner of Calle Victoria. Across from the Museo del Jamón (Museum of Ham), you'll find...*

La Taurina Cervecería: This is a bullfighters' Planet Hollywood (daily 12:00–24:00, air-con). Wander among trophies and historic photographs. Each stuffed bull's head is named, along with his farm, awards, and who killed him. Among the many gory photos, study the first post: It's Che Guevara, Orson Welles, and Salvador Dalí, all enjoying a good fight. Around the corner, the Babe Ruth of bullfighters, El Cordobés, lies wounded in bed. The photo above and below shows him in action. I enjoyed the art. Then, inspired, I went for the *rabo de toro* (bull-tail stew, €15)—and regretted it. A good, basic dish here is *chorizos a la sidra* (spicy sausage in cider, €8) with a beer. If a fight's on, it'll be packed with aficionados gathered around the TV.

• *Across the street, just left of the Museo del Jamón, is the...*

Lhardy Pastelería: Offering a taste of Old World charm in this district of rowdy pubs, this place has been a fixture since 1839 for Madrileños wanting to duck in for a cup of soup or a light snack with a fortified wine. Step right in, and pretend you're an aristocrat back between the wars. Serve yourself. You'll pay as you leave (on the honor system). Help yourself to the silver water dispenser (free), a line of elegant bottles (each a different Iberian fortified wine: sherry, port, and so on, €2 per glass), a revolving case of meaty little pastries (€1 each), and a fancy soup dispenser (chicken broth consommé-€2, or €2.50 with a splash of sherry...local style—bottles in the corner, help yourself; Mon–Sat 9:30–15:00 & 17:00–21:30, Sun 9:30–15:00 only, non-smoking, Carrera de San Jerónimo 8).

• *Now duck into the...*

Museo del Jamón (Museum of Ham): This frenetic, cheap, stand-up bar (with famously rude service) is an assembly line of fast and simple *bocadillos* and *raciones*. It's tastefully decorated—unless you're a pig (or a vegetarian). Take advantage of the easy photo-illustrated menus that show various dishes and their prices. The best ham is the pricey *jamón ibérico*—from pigs who led stress-free lives in acorn-strewn valleys. Just point and eat, but be specific: A plate of low-end *jamón blanco* costs only €2.50, while *jamón ibérico* costs €13. For a small sandwich, ask for a *chiquito* (€0.70, or €3.10 for *ibérico*). If on a budget, don't let them sell you the *ibérico* (daily 9:00–24:00, sit-down restaurant upstairs, air-con).

• *Next, forage halfway up Calle Victoria to the tiny...*

La Casa del Abuelo: This is where seafood-lovers savor sizzling plates of tasty little *gambas* (shrimp) and *langostinos* (prawns). Try *gambas a la plancha* (grilled shrimp, €7.20) or *gambas al ajillo* (ah-HEE-yoh, shrimp version of escargot, cooked in oil and garlic and ideal for bread dipping, €8) and a €2 glass of sweet red house wine (daily 12:00–24:00, Calle Victoria 12).

• *Across the street is...*

Oreja de Oro: The "Golden Ear" is named for what it sells—sautéed pigs' ears (*oreja*, €3). While oinker ears are a Madrid specialty, this place is Galician (see "Galician Cuisine," page 260), so people also come here for *pulpo* (octopus, €12), *pimientos de Padrón* (sautéed miniature green peppers—my favorite plate of the entire crawl, €3.50), and the distinctive *ribeiro* (ree-BAY-roh) wine, served Galician-style, in characteristic little ceramic bowls (to disguise its lack of clarity).

Jaime is a frantic one-man show who somehow gets everything just right. Have fun here.

• *For a finale, continue uphill and around the corner to...*

Casa Toni: This is the spot for refreshing bowls of gazpacho—the cold tomato-and-garlic soup (€2.30, available all year but only popular when temperatures soar). Their specialties are *berenjena* (deep-fried slices of eggplant, €4.70) and *champiñones* (sautéed mushrooms, €5.20; open daily 11:30–16:00 & 18:00–23:30, closed July, Calle Cruz 14).

More Options: If you're hungry for more, and want a trendy, up-to-date, pricier tapas scene, head for Plaza Santa Ana, with lively bars spilling out onto the square. Survey the entire scene. Consider **Cervecería de Santa Ana** (tasty tapas with two zones: rowdy, circa-1900 beer-hall and classier sit-down) or **Naturbier,** a local microbrewery. **Vinoteca Barbechera,** at the downhill end of the square, has an inviting menu of tapas and fine wines by the glass (indoor and outdoor seating).

Gonzalez, a venerable gourmet cheese and wine shop with a circa 1930s interior, offers a genteel opportunity to enjoy a plate of first-class cheese or meat and a fine glass of wine with friendly service and a fun setting. Their assortment of five Spanish cheeses—more than enough for two—is a cheese-lover's treat (€10 three-course fixed-price lunch, Tue–Sat 9:00–24:00, closed Sun–Mon, three blocks past Plaza Santa Ana at Calle Leon 12, tel. 914-295-618).

The Lavapiés District Tapas Crawl (for the Adventurous)

The neighborhood called Lavapiés is emerging as a colorful magnet for people-watching. This is where the multi-ethnic tapestry of Madrid society enjoys pithy, cheap, seedy-yet-fun-loving life on the streets. Neighborhoods like this typically experience an evolution: initially they're so cheap that only the immigrants, downtrodden, and counterculture types live there. The diversity and color they bring attracts those with more money. Businesses erupt to cater to those bohemian/trendy tastes. Rents go up. Those who gave the area the colorful liveliness in the first place can no longer afford to live there. They move out...and here comes Starbucks. For now, Lavapiés is still edgy, yet comfortable enough for most.

This district has almost no tourists. Old ladies with their tired bodies and busy fans hang out on their tiny balconies as they have for 40 years, watching the scene. Shady types lurk on side streets (don't venture off the main drag, don't show your wallet or money, and don't linger on Plaza Lavapiés).

For food, you'll find all the various kinds of tapas bars described earlier in "The Madrid Pub-Crawl Dinner (for Beginners)," plus great Indian (almost all run by Bangladeshis) and Moroccan eateries. I've listed a couple of places that appealed to me...but explore your options.

I'd recommend taking the entire walk once, then backtracking and eating at the place or places that appeal to you.

From the Anton Martin Metro stop (or Plaza Santa Ana), walk down Calle Ave Maria (on its way to becoming Calle Ave Allah) to Plaza Lavapiés (where old ladies hang out with the swarthy drunks and a mosaic of cultures treat this square as a communal living room; Metro station here), and then up Calle de Lavapiés to the newly remodeled square, Plaza Tirso de Molina (Metro stop). This square was once plagued by druggies. Now with flower kiosks and a playground, it's homey and inviting. This is a fine example of the new vision for Madrid's public spaces.

On Calle Ave Maria: **Bar Melos** is a thriving dive jammed with a hungry and nubile local crowd. It's famous for its giant patty melts called *zapatillas de lacón y queso* (because they're the size and shape of a *zapatilla* or slipper, €7, feeds at least two, Ave Maria 44, smoky tables in back). **Nuevo Café Barbieri,** one of a dying breed of smoky mirrored cafés with a circa-1940 ambience, offers classical music in the afternoon and jazz in the evening. (Ave Maria 45).

On Calle de Lavapiés: At Calle de Lavapiés 44, consider a fun pair of places: **Indian Restaurant Shapla** (good €9 fixed-price meal), and **Montes Wine Bar** (countless wines open and served by the glass, good tapas, crawl under the bar to get to the WC).

TRANSPORTATION CONNECTIONS

By Train

Remember that Madrid has two main train stations: Chamartín and Atocha. At the Atocha station, AVE and other long-distance trains depart from a different area than local *cercanías* trains (for more details, see "Arrival in Madrid," page 297).

AVE Trains: Spain's AVE (AH-vay) bullet train opens up some good itinerary options. You can now get from Madrid's Atocha station to **Barcelona** in just under three hours, with trains running every 1–2 hours. The AVE train is generally faster and easier than flying (timed from downtown to downtown), but not necessarily cheaper. Basic second-class tickets are €106 one-way for most departures and €125 for the fastest, peak-time departures. First-class tickets are €153–180. Advance purchase discounts (40–60 days ahead) are available through the national rail company (RENFE), but sell out quickly. Save more by not traveling on holidays.

The AVE is also handy for visiting **Sevilla** (and, on the way, **Córdoba**). The basic Madrid–Sevilla second-class AVE fare is €67–€75, depending upon departure time (the almost-as-fast Altaria is €10 less; first-class AVE costs €135 and comes with a meal). Consider this exciting day trip to Sevilla from Madrid: 7:00–depart Madrid, 8:45–12:40-in Córdoba, 13:30–20:45-in Sevilla, 23:30-back in Madrid.

Other AVE destinations include **Toledo** (nearly hourly, 30 min, €9, from Atocha) and **Segovia** (8/day, 35 min, €9, from Chamartín station, take train going toward Valladolid). For the latest, pick up the AVE brochure at the station, or check out www.renfe.es/ave. Prices vary with times and class. Eurailpass-holders get a big discount (e.g., Madrid to Sevilla is €9 second-class, but only at RENFE ticket windows—discount not available at ticket machines). Reserve each AVE segment ahead (tel. 902-240-202 for Atocha AVE info).

Below I've listed both non-AVE and (where available) AVE trains, to help you compare your options.

From Madrid by Train to: Toledo (AVE: nearly hourly, 30 min, from Atocha), **El Escorial** (2/hr, but bus is better—see page 362), **Segovia** (AVE: 9/day, 35 min plus 20-min shuttle bus into Segovia center, from Chamartín; slower *cercanías* trains: 9/day, 2 hrs, from both Chamartín and Atocha), **Ávila** (hourly until 21:30, 90 min, more frequent connections from Chamartín than Atocha), **Salamanca** (6/day, 2.5 hrs, from Chamartín), **Santiago de Compostela** (2/day, 7.5–9 hrs, includes night train, from Chamartín), **Barcelona** (AVE: 14/day, about 3 hrs from Atocha; plus 1 night train from Chamartín, 9 hrs), **San Sebastián** (3/day, 5–6.5 hrs, from Atocha), **Pamplona** (4/day, 3 hrs, from Atocha), **Burgos** (7/day, 4–5 hrs, from Chamartín), **León** (10/day, 3–4.25 hrs, from Chamartín), **Granada** (2/day, 5 hrs, from Atocha), **Sevilla** (AVE: hourly, 2.5 hrs, departures from 16:00–19:00 can sell out far in advance; slower Altaria/Talgo trains: 2/day, 3.5 hrs; all from Atocha), **Córdoba** (AVE: 28/day, 1.75 hrs; Altaria trains: 5/day, 2 hrs; all from Atocha), **Málaga** (AVE: 12/day, 2.25–3 hrs, from Atocha), **Lisbon** (1/day departing at 22:45, 9 hrs, overnight Hotel Train from Chamartín), **Paris** (1/day, 13.5 hrs, direct overnight—a €185 Hotel Train, €160 in winter, reserve more than 15 days in advance and hope there are seats left in the €89 *oferta mini* deals, from Chamartín). General train info: tel. 902-240-202, for international journeys: tel. 902-243-402.

By Bus

Madrid has two major bus stations, connected by Metro. If you take a taxi to any bus station, you'll be charged a legitimate €2.75 supplement.

Estación Sur de Autobuses (South Bus Station): From here, you can catch buses to **Toledo** (€4.60 one-way, 2/hr, 1–1.5 hrs, Continental Auto bus company at office #45, tel. 915-272-961), **Ávila** (8/day Mon–Fri, 4/day Sat–Sun, 1.5 hrs, €11 round-trip), **Salamanca** (hourly express, 2.5 hrs, €18 one-way, run by Auto-Res, tel. 902-020-052, www.auto-res.net), **León** (11/day, 3.5 hrs, €21 one-way), **Santiago de Compostela** (5/day, 7–9 hrs, includes 24:30–9:00 night bus), and **Granada** (12/day, 5.25 hrs, €16 one-way, tel. 915-272-961). The station sits squarely on top of Metro: Méndez Álvaro (has TI, tel. 914-684-200, www.estaciondeautobuses.com).

Príncipe Pío Station: Príncipe Pío is the old North train station, which has now morphed into a trendy mall and a bus hub for local lines including **Segovia** (€6 one-way, €10 round-trip, 2/hr departing on half-hour from platforms 06 or 07, 1.25 hrs, first departure at 6:30, last return at 21:30). From Metro: Príncipe Pío, follow signs to *estación de autobuses* or follow pictures of a bus (tel. 915-598-955, www.lasepulvedana.es). Buy a ticket from the Sepulvedana window. Reservations are rarely necessary.

Intercambiador de Moncloa Station: This station, in the Moncloa Metro station, serves **El Escorial** (4/hr, 45 min; for details, see page 362). To reach the **Valley of the Fallen,** you'll first go to El Escorial, then connect on the bus from there (1/day Tue–Sun only, 15 min from El Escorial; for details, see page 362).

Intercambiador de Avenida de América Station: Located at the Avenida de América Metro, buses go to **Burgos** (9/day, 3 hrs) and **Pamplona** (6/day, 5 hrs, Continental, tel. 915-272-961, www.movelia.es).

Route Tips for Drivers

Avoid driving in Madrid. Rent your car when you depart. To leave Madrid from Gran Vía, simply follow signs for *A-6* (direction Villalba or Coruña) for Segovia, El Escorial, or the Valley of the Fallen (see next chapter for details).

It's cheapest to make car-rental arrangements before you leave home. In Madrid, consider **Europcar** (central reservations tel. 902-105-030, San Leonardo 8 office tel. 915-418-892, Chamartín station tel. 913-231-721, airport tel. 913-937-235), **Hertz** (central reservations tel. 902-402-405, Plaza de España 18, tel. 915-425-805, Chamartín station tel. 917-330-400, airport tel. 913-937-228), **Avis** (central reservations tel. 902-200-162, Gran Vía 60 tel. 915-484-204, airport tel. 913-937-223), and **National Atesa** (central reservations tel. 902-100-515). Ask about free delivery to your hotel. At the airport, most rental cars are returned at Terminal 1.

Madrid's Barajas Airport

Ten miles east of downtown, Madrid's modern airport has four terminals. Terminals 1, 2, and 3 are connected by long indoor walkways (about an 8-min walk apart), and serve airlines including Continental, Delta, Northwest, United, US Airways, Air Canada, and Spanair. The newer Terminal 4 serves airlines including Iberia, Vueling, British, and American, and also has a separate satellite terminal called T4S. In Terminal 4, it's a long way between the ticket counters and the boarding areas—signs indicate the walking times to gates. To transfer between Terminals 1–3 and Terminal 4, you can take a 10-minute shuttle bus (free, leaves every 10 min from departures level), or take the Metro (stops at Terminals 2 and 4). Make sure to allow enough time if you need to travel between terminals. For more information about navigating this massive airport, go to www.aena.es.

International flights typically use Terminals 1 and 4. At the Terminal 1 arrivals area, you'll find a helpful English-speaking **TI** (marked *Oficina de Información Turística*, Mon–Sat 8:00–20:00, Sun 9:00–14:00, tel. 913-058-656); **ATMs;** a **flight info office** (marked simply *Information* in airport lobby, open daily 24 hours, tel. 902-353-570); a **post-office** window; a **pharmacy;** lots of **phones** (buy a phone card from the nearby machine); a few scattered **Internet** terminals (small fee); **eateries;** a **RENFE office** (where you can get train info and buy long-distance train tickets, daily 8:00–21:00, tel. 902-240-202); and on-the-spot **car-rental agencies** (see above). The new, super-modern Terminal 4 offers essentially the same services.

Iberia, Spanair, and Air Europa are Spain's airlines, connecting a reasonable number of cities in Spain, as well as international destinations (ask for best rates at travel agencies). Vueling is the most popular discount airline in Iberia (e.g., Madrid–Barcelona flight as cheap as €30 if booked in advance, tel. 902-333-933, www.vueling.com).

Getting Between the Airport and Downtown

By Public Bus: Bus #200 shuttles travelers between airport Terminals 1, 2, and 3 (departing from arrivals level every 10 minutes, runs 6:00–24:00) and the Metro stop Avenida de América (northeast of the historical center) in about 20 minutes. From that Metro stop, you can connect to your hotel by taking the Metro or hopping a taxi. Bus #204 serves Terminal 4 the same way. The trip costs only €1 (buy ticket from driver; or get a shareable 10-ride Metrobus ticket for €6.70 at a tobacco shop—for more info, see "Getting Around Madrid," page 304).

By Minibus Shuttle: The AeroCity shuttle bus provides door-to-door transport in a seven-seat minibus with up to three hotel stops en route. Ask your hotel in advance if they can arrange this service for you. The €19 fee covers up to three people per trip, a good value for two or three people with luggage that they don't want to haul on public transportation. Extra passengers pay more (runs 24 hours, price includes 1 piece of luggage and 1 carry-on per person, pay driver directly in cash, toll-free tel. 900-713-583, sometimes better service at tel. 917-477-570, www.aerocity.com). They also offer a €36 private shuttle service for up to three people (your hotel can book it for you).

By Metro: The subway involves two transfers to reach the city center (€2; or add a €1 supplement to your €6.70 10-ride Metrobus ticket). The airport's futuristic "Aeropuerto T-1, T-2, T-3" Metro stop (notice the ATMs, subway info booth, and huge lighted map of Madrid) is in Terminal 2. Access the Metro at the check-in level; to reach the Metro from Terminal 1's arrivals level, stand with your back to the baggage claim, then go to your far right, up the stairs, and follow red-and-blue Metro diamond signs to the station (8-min walk). The Terminal 4 stop is the end of the line. To get to Puerta del Sol, take line #8 for 12 minutes to Nuevos Ministerios, then continue on line #10 to Tribunal, then line #1 to Puerta del Sol (30 min more total); or exit at Nuevos Ministerios and take a €5 taxi or bus #150 straight to Puerta del Sol.

By Taxi: For a taxi between the airport and downtown, allow about €25 during the day *(Tarifa 1)* or €35 at night and on Sundays *(Tarifa 2)*. For Terminal 4, add about €10. Insist on the meter. The €5.25 airport supplement is legal. There is no charge for luggage. Plan on getting stalled in traffic. For more on taxis—and corrupt cabbies—see "Getting Around Madrid," page 304.

NORTHWEST OF MADRID

El Escorial • Valley of the Fallen • Segovia • Ávila

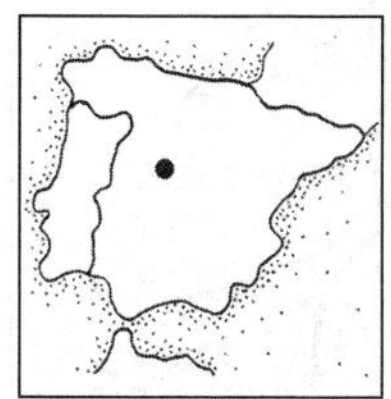

Before slipping out of Madrid, consider several fine side-trips northwest of Spain's capital city, all conveniently reached by car, bus, or train.

Spain's lavish, brutal, and complicated history is revealed throughout Old Castile. This region, where the Spanish language originated, is named for its many castles—battle scars from the long-fought Reconquista.

An hour from Madrid, tour the imposing and fascinating palace at El Escorial, headquarters of the Spanish Inquisition. Nearby at the awe-inspiring Valley of the Fallen, pay tribute to the countless victims of Spain's bloody civil war.

Segovia, with its remarkable Roman aqueduct (pictured above) and romantic castle, is another worthwhile side-trip. At Ávila, you can walk the perfectly preserved medieval walls.

Planning Your Time

See El Escorial and the Valley of the Fallen together in less than a day (but not on Monday, when both sights are closed). By car, do them en route to Segovia; by bus, make it a day trip from Madrid.

Segovia is worth a half day of sightseeing and is a joy at night. Ávila, while it has its charm, merits only a quick stop (if you're driving and in the area, 1.5 hrs from Madrid; also a logical stop on the way to Salamanca by train) to marvel at its medieval walls and, perhaps, check out St. Teresa's finger.

In total, these sights are worth two days if you're in Spain for less than a month. If you're in Spain for just a week, I'd still squeeze in a quick side-trip from Madrid to El Escorial and the Valley of the Fallen.

Northwest of Madrid

TO BURGOS & BILBAO
TO LEÓN & SANTIAGO
SEGOVIA
LA GRANJA
TO SALAMANCA
N-VI
A-6
N-110
N-603
N-501
NAVACERRADO PASS
VALLEY OF THE FALLEN
ÁVILA
C-505
SILLA DE FELIPE
EL ESCORIAL
M-505
M-40
MADRID
N-I
E-5
TO BARCELONA
BARAJAS AIRPORT
20 MILES
30 KM
DCH
E-90
A-5
N-401
RING FREEWAY
A-3
ARANJUEZ
TOLEDO
A.V.E.
E-5
A-4
TO ANDALUCÍA
AVE HIGH SPEED LINE TO SEVILLA
TO CONSUEGRA
A.V.E. RAIL
OTHER RAIL
AUTOPISTA (TOLL FREEWAY)
OTHER ROADS

El Escorial

The Monasterio de San Lorenzo de El Escorial is a symbol of power rather than elegance. This 16th-century palace, 30 miles northwest of Madrid, gives us a better feel for the Counter-Reformation and the Inquisition than any other building.

Getting to El Escorial

Most people visit El Escorial from Madrid. By public transportation, the bus is most convenient (since it gets you closer to the palace). Remember that it makes sense to combine El Escorial with a visit to the nearby Valley of the Fallen (described on page 370).

By Bus: Buses leave from the Intercambiador de Moncloa, which

Cheap Tricks

At El Escorial

Download and print out a free, detailed English guide of three architectural and historic tours through San Lorenzo del Escorial by clicking on the *Place for walks* link at www.sanlorenzoturismo.org.

In Segovia

Segovia has plenty of little Romanesque churches that are free to enter, and many have architecturally interesting exteriors that are worth a look. On your way to the main sights, keep your eyes peeled for these hidden treasures: Coming from the bus station on Avenida de Fernández Ladreda toward the center of town, you can see the San Millán church; on Plazas San Martín and San Esteban are two churches sharing their squares' names; and on the way to the Alcázar on Plaza de la Merced is the San Andrés church.

In Ávila

As you're wandering the city and you see the arched gates leading out of the old center, pop out to the other side and take in the impressive wall. Exploring sections of it from the ground may be even better than walking along it, and saves you the admission fee.

is in the basement of Madrid's Moncloa Metro stop (€3.20 one-way, buy ticket from driver, 4/hr, 45 min; in Madrid take bus #664 or slower #661 from Intercambiador's platform 30, Herranz Bus, tel. 918-969-028). The bus drops you downtown in San Lorenzo de El Escorial, a pleasant 10-minute stroll from the palace (see map): Exit the bus station from the back ramp that leads over the parked buses, turn left, and follow the newly cobbled pedestrian lane, Calle San Juan. This street veers to the right and becomes Calle Juan de Leyra. In a few short blocks, it dead-ends at Duque de Medinaceli, where you'll turn left and see the palace. Stairs lead past several decent eateries, through a delightful park, past the TI (Mon–Fri 10:00–18:00, Sat–Sun 10:00–19:00, tel. 918-905-313), and directly to the tourist entry of the immense palace/monastery.

By Train: Local trains (*cercanías* line C-8A) run twice hourly from Madrid's Atocha and Chamartín stations to El Escorial. From the station, walk 20 minutes through Casita del Príncipe park, straight up from the station. Or you can take a shuttle bus (€1, 2/hr) or a taxi (€5) to the San Lorenzo de El Escorial town center and the palace.

By Car: It's quite simple. Taxi to your car-rental office in Madrid (or ask if they'll deliver the car to your hotel). Pick up the car by 8:30 and ask for directions to highway A-6. From Gran Vía in central Madrid,

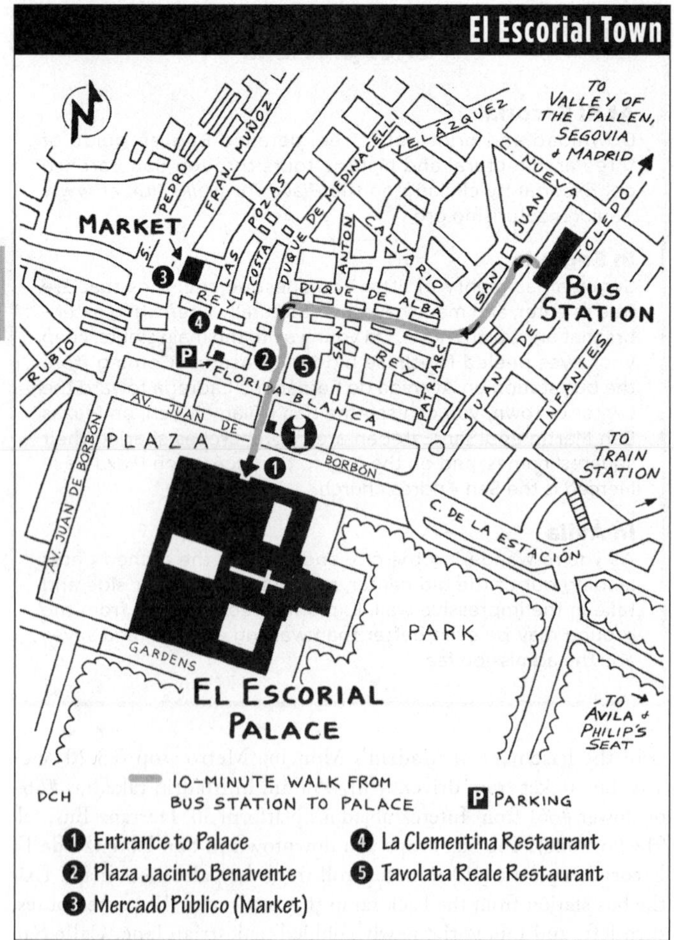

follow signs to A-6 (direction *Villalba* or *A Coruña*). The freeway leads directly out of town. Stay on A-6 past the first El Escorial exit. At kilometer 37, you'll see the cross marking the Valley of the Fallen ahead on the left. Exit 47 takes you to both the Valley of the Fallen (after a half-mile, a granite gate on right marks *Valle de los Caídos* turn-off) and El Escorial (follow signs to *San Lorenzo del Escorial*).

The nearby **Silla de Felipe** (Philip's Seat) is a rocky viewpoint where the king would come to admire his palace as it was being built. From El Escorial, follow directions to Ávila, then M-505 to Valdemorillo; look for a sign on your right after about a mile.

When you leave El Escorial for Madrid, Toledo, or Segovia, follow signs to *A-6 Guadarrama*. After about six miles, you pass the Valley of the Fallen and hit the freeway.

SIGHTS

▲▲▲Monasterio de San Lorenzo de El Escorial

Built at a time when Catholic Spain felt threatened by Protestant "heretics," the construction of this palace dominated the Spanish economy for a generation (1563–1584). Because of this bully in the national budget, Spain has almost nothing else to show from this most powerful period of her history.

Cost: The basic, unguided €8 ***visita libre* ticket** lets you tour the complex on your own (or with the help of a rentable audioguide—see below). The €10 ***visita guiada* ticket** includes a guided tour (ask for next tour in English; only sold until 90 min before closing time). If you're also going to the Valley of the Fallen, the **combo-ticket** sold here will save you some euros (€8.50 includes unguided El Escorial visit, €11 includes guided El Escorial visit, sold before 15:00 April–Sept or before 14:00 Oct–March).

Hours: April–Sept Tue–Sun 10:00–19:00, Oct–March until 18:00, always closed Mon, last entry 60 min before closing, last English tour 90 min before closing.

Information: If you opt for an unguided ticket, you'll find scant captions in English within the palace. My self-guided tour (see below) covers the basics. For more information, get the *Guide: Monastery of San Lorenzo El Real de El Escorial,* which follows the general route you'll take (€8, available at any of several shops in the palace). The audioguide rents for €2.30 (or pay €3 to get a voucher for an audioguide at the Valley of the Fallen as well). Tel. 918-905-904.

➲ **Self-Guided Tour:** The Monasterio looks confusing at first, but you simply follow the *visita* arrows and signs in one continuous walk-through. This is the general order you'll follow.

Pass through the security scanner, buy your ticket, and then continue down the hall past the *consigna* baggage check (Sala 1) to the **Chamber of the Honor Guards.** This chamber is hung with 16th-century tapestries, including fascinating copies of Hieronymus Bosch's most famous and preachy paintings (which Philip II fancied). Don't miss El Greco's towering painting of the *Martyrdom of St. Maurice.* This was the artist's first commission after arriving in Spain from Venice. It was too subtle and complex for the king, so El Greco moved on to Toledo to find work.

Continue downstairs to the fascinating **Museum of Architecture** (Museo de Arquitectura). It has long parallel corridors of fine models of the palace and some of the actual machinery and tools used to construct it. Huge stone-pinching winches, fat ropes, and rusty mortar spades help convey the immensity of this 21-year project involving 1,500 workers. At the big model, notice the complex is shaped like a grill, and recall how San Lorenzo—St. Lawrence, a Christian Spaniard martyred by pagan Romans (A.D. 258)—was

History of El Escorial

The giant, gloomy building made of gray-black stone looks more like a prison than a palace. About 650 feet long and 500 feet wide, it has 2,600 windows, 1,200 doors, more than 100 miles of passages, and 1,600 overwhelmed tourists.

Four hundred years ago, the enigmatic, introverted, and extremely Catholic King Philip II (1527–1598) ruled his bulky empire and directed the Inquisition from here. To Philip, the building embodied the wonders of Catholic learning, spirituality, and arts. To 16th-century followers of Martin Luther, it epitomized the evil of closed-minded Catholicism. To architects, the building—built on the cusp between styles—exudes both Counter-Reformation grandeur and understated Renaissance simplicity. Today, it's a time capsule of Spain's "Golden Age," packed with history, art, and Inquisition ghosts. (And at an elevation of nearly 3,500 feet, it can be friggin' cold.)

The building was conceived by Philip II to serve several purposes: as a grand mausoleum for Spain's royal family, starting with his father, Charles V (known as Carlos I in Spain); as a monastery to pray (a lot) for the royal souls; as a small palace to use as a Camp David of sorts for Spain's royalty; and as a school to embrace humanism in a way that promoted the Catholic faith.

burned to death on a grill. Throughout the palace, you'll see this symbol associated with the saint. The grill's "handle" was the palace, or residence of the royal family. The monastery and school gathered around the huge basilica.

Next, linger in the **Museum of Paintings** to consider the 15th- to 17th-century Flemish, Spanish, and Italian works. Contemplate Roger van der Weyden's *Calvary,* with mourning Mary and St. John at the feet of the crucified Christ. (It's interesting to compare it with van der Weyden's similar *Descent from the Cross,* which hangs in the Prado in Madrid.) Then pass through the peaceful and empty Courtyard of Masks to reach the **Hall of Battles** (Sala de Batallas). Its paintings celebrate Spain's great military victories—including the Battle of San Quentin over France (1557) on St. Lawrence's feast day that inspired the construction of El Escorial. The sprawling series, painted in 1590, helped teach the new king all the elements of warfare. Stroll the length for a primer on army skills.

From here, a corridor lined with various family trees (some scrawny, others lush and fecund) leads into the royal living quarters (the building's grill handle). Immediately inside the first door, find the small portrait of Philip II flanked by two large portraits of his daughters. The palace was like Philip: austere. Notice the simple floors, plain

El Escorial—Ground Floor

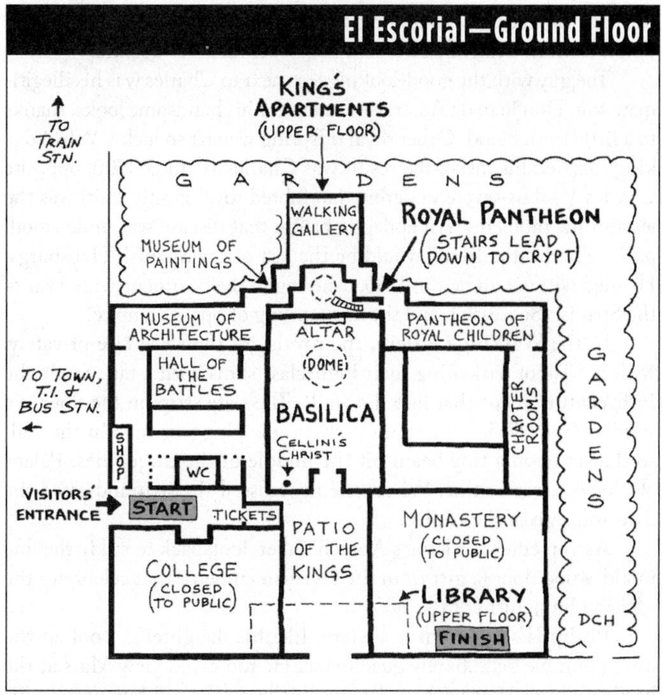

white walls, and bare-bones chandelier. This was the bedroom of one of his daughters. Notice the sheet warmer beside her bed—often necessary during the winter. Bend down to see the view from her bed...of the high altar in the basilica next door. The entire complex of palace and monastery buildings was built around that altar.

In the next room, notice the reclinable sedan chair that Philip II, thick with gout, was carried in (for seven days) on his last trip from Madrid to El Escorial. He wanted to be here when he died.

The **Audience Chamber** is now a portrait gallery filled with Habsburg royals painted by popular local artists. The portraits of unattractive people that line the walls provide an instructive peek at the consequences of mixing blue blood with more of the same blue blood (inbreeding among royals was a common problem throughout Europe in those days).

The Spanish emperor Charles V (1500–1558) is over the fireplace mantel. Charles, Philip II's dad, was the most powerful man in Europe, having inherited not only the Spanish crown, but also Germany, Austria, the Low Countries (Belgium and the Netherlands), and much of Italy. When he announced his abdication in 1555, his son Philip II inherited much of this territory...plus the responsibility of managing it. Philip's draining wars with France, Portugal, Holland, and England—including the disastrous defeat of Spain's navy, the

Spanish Armada, by England's Queen Elizabeth I (1588)—knocked Spain from its peak of power and began centuries of decline.

The guy with the good-looking legs next to Charles was his illegitimate son, Don Juan de Austria—famous for his handsome looks, thanks to a little fresh blood. Other royal offspring weren't so lucky: When one king married his niece, the result was Charles II (1665–1700, opposite Charles V). His severe underbite (an inbred royal family trait) was the least of his problems. An epileptic before that disease was understood, poor "Charles the Mad" would be the last of the Spanish Habsburgs. He died without an heir in 1700, ushering in the continent-wide War of the Spanish Succession and the dismantling of Spain's empire.

In the **Walking Gallery,** the royals got their exercise privately, with no risk of darkening their high-class skins with a tan. Study the 16th-century maps that line the walls. The slate strip on the floor is a sundial from 1755. It lined up with a (now plugged) hole in the wall so that at noon a tiny beam hit the middle of the three lines. Palace clocks were set by this. Where the ray crossed the strip indicated the date and sign of the zodiac.

As you enter the King's Antechamber, look back to study the fine inlaid-wood door (a gift from the German emperor that celebrates the exciting humanism of the age).

Philip II's bedroom is austere, like his daughter's. Look at the king's humble bed...barely queen-size. He too could view Mass at the basilica's high altar without leaving his bed. The red box next to his pillow holds the royal bedpan. But don't laugh—the king's looking down from the wall behind you. At age 71, Philip II, the gout-ridden king of a dying empire, died in this bed (1598).

From here, his body was taken to the **Royal Pantheon** (Panteón Real), the gilded resting place of 26 kings and queens...four centuries' worth of Spanish monarchy. All the kings are included—but only those queens who became mothers of kings.

There is a post-mortem filing system at work in the Pantheon. From the entrance, kings are on the left, queens on the right. (The only exception is Isabel II, since she was a ruling queen and her husband was a consort.) The first and greatest, Charles V and his Queen Isabel, flank the altar on the top shelf. Her son, Philip II, rests below Charles and opposite (only) one of Philip's four wives, and so on. There is a waiting process, too. Before a royal corpse can rest in this room, it needs to decompose for several decades. The three empty niches are already booked. The bones of the current king Juan Carlos' grandmother, Victoria Eugenia (who died in 1964), are ready to be moved in, but the staff can't explain why they haven't been transferred yet. Juan Carlos' father, Don Juan (who died in 1993), is also on the waiting list...controversially. Technically, he was never crowned king of Spain—Franco took control of Spain before Don Juan could ascend to the throne, and he was passed over for the job when Franco reinstituted the monarchy. Juan Carlos' mother is the most recent guest in the rotting room. So where does that leave Juan Carlos and Sofía? This hotel is *todo completo.*

The next rooms are filled with the tombs of lesser royals: Each bears that person's name (in Latin), relationship to the king, and slogan or epitaph. They lead to the wedding-cake **Pantheon of Royal Children** (Panteón de los Infantes) that holds the remains of various royal children who died before the age of seven (and their first Communion).

Head past the mini–gift shop and continue upstairs to the **Chapter Rooms** (Salas Capitulares). These rooms, where the monks met to do church business, are lined with big-name paintings by José Ribera, El Greco, Titian, and Velázquez. (More great paintings are in the monastery's Museum of Painting.) Continue to the final room to see some atypical Bosch paintings and the intricate, portable altar of Charles V. The **cloister** glows with bright, newly restored paintings by Pellegrino Tibaldi. Off the cloister is the **Old Church** (Iglesia Vieja), which they used from 1571 to 1586, while finishing the basilica. During that time, the bodies of several kings, including Charles V, were interred here. Among the many paintings you'll see, look for the powerful *Martyrdom of Saint Laurence* by Tiziano (Titian) above the main altar.

Follow the signs to the **basilica.** In the center of the altar wall, find the flame-engulfed grill that features San Lorenzo (the same St. Lawrence from the painting) meeting his famous death—and taking "turn the other cheek" to new extremes. Lorenzo was so cool, he reportedly told his Roman executioners: "You can turn me over now—I'm done on this side." With your back to the altar, go to the right corner for the artistic highlight of the basilica: Benvenuto Cellini's marble sculpture *The Crucifixion.* Jesus' features are supposedly modeled after the Shroud of Turin. Cellini carved this from Carrara marble for his own tomb in 1562 (according to the letters under Christ's feet).

Last comes the immense **library** *(biblioteca)*—where it's clear that education was a priority for the Spanish royalty. Savor this room. The ceiling (by Tibaldi, depicting various disciplines labeled in Latin, the lingua franca of the multinational Habsburg Empire) is a burst of color. At the far end of the room,

the elaborate model of the solar system looks like a giant gyroscope, revolving unmistakably around the Earth, with a misshapen, under-explored North America. As you leave, look back above the wooden door. The plaque warns *"Excomunión..."*—you'll be excommunicated if you take a book without checking it out properly. Who needs late fees when you hold the keys to Hell?

EATING

The **Mercado Público,** a four-minute walk from the palace, is the place to shop for a picnic (Mon–Fri 9:30–13:30 & 17:00–20:00, Sat 9:30–14:00, closed Thu and Sat afternoons and all day Sun, Calle del Rey 9).

La Clementina serves appealing tapas at their bar and full meals in the restaurant. In warm weather, their outdoor tables are a treat (daily 13:30–16:30 & 20:30–24:00, Plaza de la Constitución 9, tel. 918-901-192). Other restaurants sell *menú del día* (three-course fixed-price meals) options on nearby squares.

Tavolata Reale, serving pizza, offers a change of pace from Spanish fare (Tue–Sun 11:00–16:00 & 20:00–24:00, closed Mon, inside a mini-shopping gallery off Plaza Jacinto Benavente, tel. 918-904-591).

Valley of the Fallen

Six miles from El Escorial, high in the Guadarrama Mountains, is the Valley of the Fallen (Valle de los Caídos). A 500-foot-tall granite cross marks this immense and powerful underground monument to the victims of Spain's 20th-century nightmare—its Civil War (1936–1939).

Cost: €5, or €8.30 to include the round-trip bus from El Escorial. But if you're also visiting El Escorial, buy the combo-ticket: €8.50 includes unguided El Escorial visit, €11 includes guided El Escorial visit (sold before 15:00 April–Sept or before 14:00 Oct–March).

Hours: April–Sept Tue–Sun 10:00–19:00, Oct–March until 18:00, closed Mon, last entry 60 min before closing, basilica closes 30 min before site closes, tel. 918-905-611.

Getting There: Most visitors side-trip to the Valley of the Fallen from the nearby El Escorial. If you don't have your own wheels, the easiest way to get between these two sights is to negotiate a deal with a **taxi** (to take you from El Escorial to Valley of the Fallen, wait for you 30–60 min, and then bring you back to El Escorial, about €45 total). Otherwise, one **bus** a day (#660) connects El Escorial with the Valley of the Fallen (15 min, leaves El Escorial at 15:15, leaves Valley of the Fallen at 17:30, €8.30 round-trip includes admission to the site, or €4.30 round-trip for just the bus—if you've already bought the Escorial/Valley combo-ticket; no bus on Mon, when both sights are closed). Drivers can find tips under "Getting to El Escorial—By Car" on page 363.

Audioguide: The €2 audioguide is heavy on the theological message of the statues and tapestries, and it ignores Franco (included in €3 combo-ticket with El Escorial audioguide).

➲ **Self-Guided Tour:** Approaching by car or bus, you enter the sprawling park through a granite gate. The best views of the cross are from the bridge (but note that it's illegal for drivers to stop anywhere along this road). To the right, tiny chapels along the ridge mark the Stations of the Cross, where pilgrims stop on their hike to this memorial.

In 1940, prison workers dug 220,000 tons of granite out of the hill beneath the cross to form an underground basilica, then used the stones to erect the cross (built like a chimney, from the inside). Since it's built directly over the dome of the subterranean basilica, a seismologist keeps a careful eye on things.

The stairs that lead to the imposing monument are grouped in sets of tens, meant to symbolize the Ten Commandments (including "Thou shalt not kill"—hmm). The emotional *pietà* draped over the basilica's entrance is huge—you could sit in the palm of Christ's hand. The statue was sculpted by Juan de Ávalos, the same artist who created the dramatic figures of the four Evangelists at the base of the cross. It must have had a powerful impact on mothers who came here to remember their fallen sons.

A solemn silence and a stony chill fill the basilica. At 300 yards long, the basilica was built to be longer than St. Peter's...but the Vatican had the final say when it blessed only 262 of those yards. Many Spaniards pass under the huge, foreboding angels of fascism to visit the grave of General Franco—an unusual place of pilgrimage, to say the least.

After walking through the two long vestibules, stop at the iron gates of the actual basilica. The line of torch-like lamps adds to the shrine ambience. Franco's prisoners, the enemies of the right, dug this memorial out of solid rock from 1940 to 1959. (Though it looks like bare rock still shows on the ceiling, it's just a clever design.) The sides of the

The Spanish Civil War
(1936–1939)

Thirty-three months of warfare killed 200,000 Spaniards. Unlike America's Civil War, which split America roughly north and south, Spain's war was between classes and ideologies, dividing every city and village, and many families. It was especially cruel, with atrocities and reprisals on both sides.

The war began as a military coup to overthrow the democratically elected Republic, a government that the army and other conservative powers considered too liberal and disorganized. The rebel forces, called the Nationalists *(Nacionalistas)*, consisted of the army, monarchy, Catholic Church, big business, and rural estates, with aid from Germany, Italy, and Portugal. Trying to preserve the liberal government were the Republicans *(Republicanos)*, also called Loyalists: the government, urban areas, secularists, small business, and labor unions, with aid from the United States (minimal help) and the "International Brigades" of communists, socialists, and labor organizers.

In the summer of 1936, the army rebelled and took control of its own garrisons, rejecting the Republic and pledging allegiance to Generalísimo Francisco Franco (1892–1975). These Nationalists launched a three-year military offensive to take Spain region by region, town by town. The government ("Republicans") cobbled together an army of volunteers, local militias, and international fighters. The war pitted conservative Catholic priests against socialist factory workers, rich businessmen against radical students, sunburned farmers loyal to the old king against upwardly mobile small businessmen. People suffered. You'll notice that nearly every Spaniard in his or her 70s is very short—a product of growing up during these hungry and very difficult Civil War years.

Spain's Civil War attracted international attention. Adolf Hitler and Benito Mussolini sent troops and supplies to their fellow fascist, Franco. It was Hitler's Luftwaffe that helped Franco bomb the town of Guernica (April 1937), an event captured on canvas by Pablo Picasso (see pages 149 and 332). On the Republican side, hundreds of Americans (including Ernest Hemingway) steamed over to Spain to fight for democracy as part of the "Abraham Lincoln Brigade."

By 1939, only Barcelona and Madrid held out. But they were no match for Franco's army. On April 1, 1939, the war ended, beginning 37 years of iron-fisted rule by Franco.

monument are lined with copies of 16th-century Brussels tapestries of the Apocalypse, and side chapels contain alabaster copies of Spain's most famous statues of the Virgin Mary.

Interred behind the high altar and side chapels (marked "RIP, 1936–1939, died for God and country") are the remains of the approximately 50,000 people, both *Republicanos* and Franco's *Nacionalistas,* who lost their lives in the war. Regrettably, the urns are not visible, so it is Franco who takes center stage. His grave, strewn with flowers, lies behind the high altar. In front of the altar is the grave of José Antonio Primo de Rivera (1903–1936), the founder of Spanish fascism, who was killed by Republicans during the Civil War. Between these fascists' graves, the statue of a crucified Christ is lashed to a timber Franco himself is said to have felled. The seeping stones seem to weep for the victims.

As you leave, stare into the eyes of those angels with swords and two right wings and think about all the "heroes" who keep dying "for God and country," at the request of the latter. A Mass closes off the entire front of the basilica (altar and tombs) to the public daily from 11:00 to 12:05. The resident boys' choir (the "White Voices"—Spain's answer to the Vienna Boys' Choir) generally sings during the Mass (you can sit through the service, but not sightsee during this time).

The expansive view from the monument's terrace includes the peaceful, forested valley and sometimes snow-streaked mountains. For an even better view, consider taking a **funicular** trip—with a short commentary in English—to the base of the cross (€1.50 one-way, €2.50 round-trip, pay fare at machine, April–Sept Tue–Sun 11:00–18:30, closed Mon, 3/hr; Oct–March Tue–Sun 11:00–16:30, closed Mon, 2/hr; last ticket sold 30 min before closing; restaurant and public WC). You can hike back down in 25 minutes. If you have a car, you can drive up past the monastery and hike from the start of the trail marked *Sendero a la Cruz*.

Sleeping and Eating: Near the parking lot and bus stop at Valley of the Fallen are a small snack bar and picnic tables. Basic overnight lodging is available at the **Hospedería del Valle de los Caídos,** a 100-room monastery behind the cross (Sb-€45.50, Db-€91, includes meals, tax, and a pass to enter and leave the park after hours, tel. 918-905-494, fax 918-961-542, no English spoken). A meditative night here is good mostly for monks.

Segovia

Fifty miles from Madrid, this town of 55,000 boasts a thrilling Roman aqueduct, a grand cathedral, and a historic castle. Since the city is more than 3,000 feet above sea level and just northwest of a mountain range that leaves it exposed to northern breezes, people come here from Madrid for a break from the summer heat.

Day-Tripping from Madrid: Considering the easy train and bus connections (35 min one-way by AVE train, 2 hrs by slower train, 1.5 hrs by bus), Segovia makes a fine day trip from Madrid. The disadvantages of side-tripping are that you spend the coolest hours of the day (early and late) en route, you miss the charming evening scene in Segovia, and you'll pay more for your hotel in Madrid than in Segovia. Still, Segovia offers a rewarding and convenient break from the big-city intensity of Madrid.

ORIENTATION

Segovia is a medieval "ship" ready for your inspection. Start at the stern—the aqueduct—and stroll up Calle de Cervantes and Calle Juan Bravo to the prickly Gothic masts of the cathedral. Explore the tangle of narrow streets around playful Plaza Mayor and then descend to the Alcázar at the bow.

Tourist Information

Segovia has four TIs. The TI on Plaza Mayor covers both Segovia and the surrounding region (at #10, daily 9:00–20:00, closed for lunch 14:00–17:00 in winter, tel. 921-460-334). The TI at Plaza del Azogüejo at the base of the aqueduct specializes in Segovia and has lots of friendly staff, WCs, and a gift shop (daily 10:00–19:00, see wooden model of Segovia, tel. 921-466-720, www.aytosegovia.com). Two smaller TIs are at the bus station (behind a window, summer and weekends only 10:00–17:30) and at the AVE train station (daily 9:00–20:00, tel. 921-447-262).

Arrival in Segovia

Unfortunately, neither of the train stations nor the bus station has luggage storage. If day-tripping from Madrid, check the return schedule when you arrive here (or get one at the Segovia TI).

By Bus: It's a 10-minute walk from the bus station to the town center: Exit left out of the station, continue straight across the street, and follow Avenida Fernández Ladreda to the aqueduct.

By Train: From the **AVE train station** (called Guiomar), ride bus #11 for 20 minutes to the base of the aqueduct. To reach the center from the less-convenient ***cercanías* train station,** you can catch bus #6 or #8; take a taxi; or walk 35 minutes (start at Paseo del Conde de Sepulvedana—which becomes Paseo Ezequiel González—to the bus station, then turn right and head down Avenida Fernández Ladreda to the aqueduct).

By Car: See "Route Tips for Drivers" on page 358.

Helpful Hints

Shopping: If you buy handicrafts such as tablecloths from street vendors, make sure the item you're buying is the one you actually get; some unscrupulous vendors substitute inferior goods at the last minute. **C. B. Aljarfe** is a quality leather-goods shop (Wed–Sun 11:00–14:00 & 16:00–20:00, closed Mon–Tue, Daoiz 23, right before reaching Alcázar, Luis).

Local Guide: Elvira Valderrama Rascon, a hardworking young woman, is a good English-speaking guide (€100/half-day tour, mobile 636-227-949, elvisvalrras@yahoo.es).

SELF-GUIDED WALK

Welcome to Historic Segovia

This 15-minute walk is all downhill from the city's main square along the pedestrian-only street to the Roman aqueduct. It's most enjoyable just before dinner, when it's cool and filled with strolling locals.

Start on Segovia's inviting **Plaza Mayor**—once the scene of executions, religious theater, and bullfights with spectators jamming the balconies. In the 19th century, the bullfights were stopped. When locals complained, they were given a more gentle form of entertainment—bands in the music kiosk. Today the very best entertainment here is simply enjoying a light meal, snack, or drink in your choice of the many restaurants and cafés lining the square. The Renaissance church opposite the City Hall and behind the TI was built to replace the church where Isabel was proclaimed Queen of Castile in 1474. The symbol of Segovia is the aqueduct—find it in the seals on the Theater Juan Bravo and atop the City Hall. Head down Calle de Isabel la Católica (downhill, to right of Hotel Infanta Isabel), and tempt yourself with the pastries in the window display of the corner bakery.

Segovia

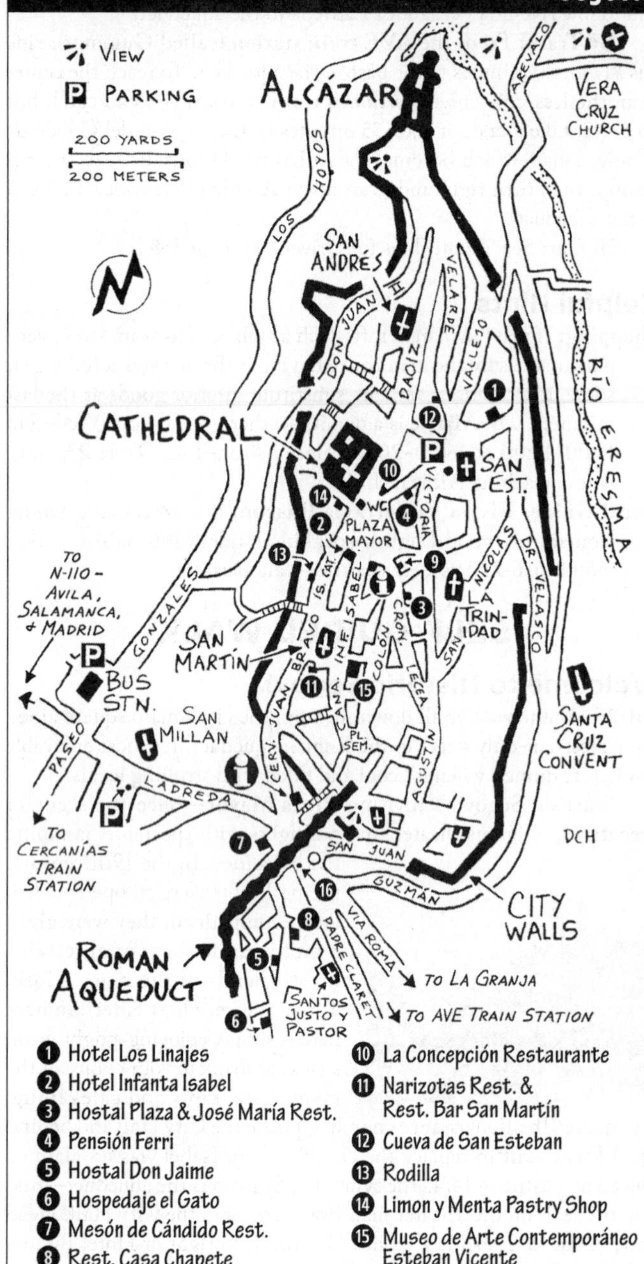

1. Hotel Los Linajes
2. Hotel Infanta Isabel
3. Hostal Plaza & José María Rest.
4. Pensión Ferri
5. Hostal Don Jaime
6. Hospedaje el Gato
7. Mesón de Cándido Rest.
8. Rest. Casa Chapete
9. Café Jeyma
10. La Concepción Restaurante
11. Narizotas Rest. & Rest. Bar San Martín
12. Cueva de San Esteban
13. Rodilla
14. Limon y Menta Pastry Shop
15. Museo de Arte Contemporáneo Esteban Vicente
16. Bus #11 to AVE Train Station

After 100 yards, at the first intersection, you'll see the Corpus Christi Convent on the right. For a donation, you can pop in to see the Franciscan church, which was once a synagogue, which was once a mosque. While sweet and peaceful, with lots of art featuring St. Francis, the church is skippable.

After another 100 yards, you come to the complicated Plaza de San Martín, a commotion of history surrounding a striking statue of Juan Bravo. When Charles V, a Habsburg who didn't even speak Spanish, took power, he imposed his rule over Castile. This threatened the local nobles, who—inspired and led by Juan Bravo—revolted in 1521. Although Juan Bravo lost the battle—and his head—he's still a symbol of Castilian pride. This statue was erected in 1921 on the 400th anniversary of his death.

On the same square, the 12th-century Church of St. Martín is Segovian Romanesque in style (a mix of Christian Romanesque and Moorish styles). The 14th-century Tower of Lozoya, behind the statue, is one of many fortified towers that marked the homes of feuding local noble families. Clashing loyalties led to mini–civil wars. In the 15th century, as Ferdinand and Isabel centralized authority in Spain, nobles were required to lop their towers. You'll see the once-tall, now-stubby towers of 15th-century noble mansions all over Segovia.

In front of the Juan Bravo statue (downhill end of square) stands the bold and bulky House of Siglo XV. Its fortified *Isabelino* style was typical of 15th-century Segovian houses. Later, in a more peaceful age, the boldness of these houses was softened with the decorative stucco work—Arabic-style floral and geometrical patterns—that you see today (for example, in the big house across the street). At Plaza del Platero Oquendo, 50 yards farther downhill on the right, you'll see a similar once-fortified, now-softened house with a cropped tower.

At the next corner, find the "house of a thousand beaks" with another truncated tower. This building, maintaining its original Moorish design, has a wall just past the door, which blocks your view from the street. This wall, the architectural equivalent of a veil, hid this home's fine courtyard—Moors didn't flaunt their wealth. Step inside; there may be art students at work and perhaps an exhibit on display.

From here, stroll 100 yards, and you'll see the Roman aqueduct, which marks the end of this walk (and is described below).

SIGHTS

▲Roman Aqueduct—Segovia was a Roman military base and needed water. Emperor Trajan's engineers built a nine-mile aqueduct to channel water from the Río Frío to the city, culminating at the Roman castle (which is the Alcázar today). The famous and exposed section of the 2,000-year-old *acueducto romano* is 2,500 feet long and 100 feet

high, has 118 arches, was made from 20,000 granite blocks without any mortar, and can still carry a stream of water. It actually functioned until the late 19th century. On Plaza del Azogüejo, a grand stairway leads from the base of the aqueduct to the top—offering close-up looks at the imposing work.

▲**Cathedral**—Segovia's cathedral, built in Renaissance times (1525–1768, the third on this site), was Spain's last major Gothic building. Embellished to the hilt with pinnacles and flying buttresses, the exterior is a great example of the final, overripe stage of Gothic, called Flamboyant. Yet the Renaissance is arriving—as evidenced by the fact that the cathedral is crowned by a dome, not a spire.

Cost and Hours: €3, free on Sun 9:30–13:15 but cathedral access only—no cloisters, open daily April–Sept 9:30–18:30, Oct–March 9:00–17:30, tel. 921-462-205.

➲ **Self-Guided Tour:** The spacious and elegantly simple interior provides a delightful contrast to the frilly exterior. The **choir** features finely carved wooden stalls from the previous church (1400s). The *catedra* (bishop's chair) is in the center rear of the choir. The many side chapels are mostly 16th-century, and come with big locking gates—a reminder that they were the private sacred domain of the rich families and guilds who "owned" them. They could enjoy private Masses here with their names actually spoken in the blessings, and a fine burial spot close to the altar. Find the **Capilla La Concepción** (a chapel in the rear that looks like a mini–art gallery). Its many 17th-century paintings hang behind a mahogany wood gate imported from colonial America. The painting *Tree of Life,* by Ignacio Ries (left of the altar), shows hedonistic mortals dancing atop the Tree of Life. As a skeletal Grim Reaper prepares to receive them into Hell (by literally chopping down the tree...timberrrr), Jesus rings a bell imploring them to wake up before it's too late. The center statue is Mary of the Apocalypse (as described in Revelations, standing on a devil and half

moon, which looks like bull's horns). Mary's pregnant and the devil licks his evil chops, waiting to devour the baby Messiah.

Opposite from where you entered, a fine door (which leads into the cloister) is crowned by a painted Flamboyant Gothic ***pietà*** in its tympanum (the statue of Jesus with a skirt, on the left, is a reminder of how prudishness from the past looks silly in the present).

The **cloisters** hold a fine little one-room museum containing French tapestries, paintings, and silver reliquaries. A glass case holds keys to the 17th-century private chapel gates. The gilded chapter room is draped with precious Flemish tapestries. Notice the gilded wagon. The Holy Communion wafer is placed in the top of this temple-like cart and paraded through town each year during the Corpus Christi festival. From the cloister courtyard, you can see the Renaissance dome rising above the otherwise Gothic rooftop.

▲Alcázar—In the Middle Ages, this fortified palace was one of the favorite residences of the monarchs of Castile, a key fortress for controlling the region. The Alcázar grew through the ages, and its function changed many times: After its stint as a palace, it was a prison for 200 years, and then a Royal Artillery School. It burned in 1862. Since the fire, it's basically been a museum.

Cost and Hours: €4 for palace, €2 for tower, daily April–Sept 10:00–19:00, Oct–March 10:00–18:00 (tower closed third Tue of month). Buy your tickets at Real Laboratorio de Chimia, facing the palace on your left. At the entrance, pass your ticket through the turnstiles on the right for the palace, or the turnstiles on the left for the tower. The 45-minute, €3 audioguide describes each room. Pick up a free English leaflet. Tel. 921-460-759.

➲ **Self-Guided Tour:** You'll enjoy a one-way route through 11 rooms, including a fine view terrace. Visit the tower afterward (€2 extra); its 152 steps up a tight spiral staircase reward you with the only 360-degree city view in town. What you see today in the Alcázar is rebuilt—a Disneyesque exaggeration of the original. Still, its fine Moorish decor and historic furnishings are fascinating. The sumptuous ceilings are accurately restored in Mudejar style, and the throne-room ceiling is the artistic highlight of the palace.

You'll see a big **mural** of Queen Isabel the Catholic being proclaimed Queen of Castile and León in Segovia's main square in 1474. The Hall of the Monarchs is lined with the busts of the 52 rulers of Castile and León who ruled during the long and ultimately successful Reconquista (711–1492): from Pelayo (the first), clockwise to Juana VII (the last). There were only seven queens during the period (the numbered ones). In this current age of Islamic extremists decapitating Christians, study the painting of St. James the Moor-Slayer—with Muslim heads literally rolling at his feet (poignantly...in the chapel). James is the patron saint of Spain. His name was the rallying cry in the centuries-long Christian crusade to push the Muslim Moors back into Africa.

Stepping onto the **terrace** (the site of the original Roman military camp, circa A.D. 100) with its vast views, marvel at the natural fortification provided by this promontory cut by the confluence of two rivers. The terrace is closed in the winter and sometimes on windy days. The Alcázar marks the end (and physical low point) of the gradual downhill course of the nine-mile-long Roman aqueduct. Can you find the mountain nicknamed *Mujer Muerta,* meaning "dead woman"?

In the **armory** (just after the terrace), find the king's 16th-century ornately carved ivory crossbow, with the hunting scene shown in the adjacent painting. The final rooms are the Museum of Artillery, recalling the period (1764–1862) when this was the Royal Artillery School. It shows the evolution of explosive weaponry, with old photos and prints of the Alcázar.

Church of Santos Justo y Pastor—This simple yet stately old church has fascinating 12th- and 13th-century frescoes filled with Gothic symbolism, plus a storks' nest atop its tower. From the base of the aqueduct, it's a short climb uphill into the newer part of town (free, Tue–Sat 11:00–14:00 & 17:00–19:00; closed Sun–Mon and when the volunteer caretaker, Rafael, needs to run an errand; located a couple of blocks from Plaza del Azogüejo). Kind old Rafael probably won't let you risk climbing the dangerous, claustrophobic bell tower for a commanding Segovia view until they've finished cleaning the pigeon poop and renovating the tower, which may take a while, as they're having trouble gathering sufficient resources to finish the job.

Museo de Arte Contemporáneo Esteban Vicente—A collection of local artist Esteban Vicente's abstract art is housed in two rooms of the remodeled remains of Henry IV's 1455 palace. Wilder than Rothko but more restrained than Pollock, his vibrant work influenced post-WWII American art. The temporary exhibits can be more interesting than the permanent collection (€2.40, free on Thu, roughly Tue–Fri 11:00–14:00 & 16:00–19:00, Sat 11:00–20:00, Sun 11:00–15:00, closed Mon).

Near Segovia

Vera Cruz Church—This 12-sided, 13th-century Romanesque church, built by the Knights Templar, once housed a piece of the "true cross" (€2, Tue–Sun 10:30–13:30 & 15:30–19:00, closed Mon and Nov, closes at 18:00 in winter, outside town beyond the castle, a 25-min walk from main square, tel. 921-431-475). There's a postcard view of the city from here, and more views follow as you continue around Segovia on the small road below the castle, labeled *ruta turística panorámica.*

▲La Granja Palace—This "little Versailles," six miles south of Segovia, is much smaller and happier than nearby El Escorial. The palace and gardens were built by the homesick French-born King Philip V, grandson of Louis XIV. Today, it's restored to its original 18th-century splendor with its royal collection of tapestries, clocks, and crystal (actually made at the palace's royal crystal factory). Plumbers and gardeners imported

from France and Italy made Philip a garden that rivaled Versailles'. The fanciful fountains feature mythological stories (explained in the palace audioguide). The Bourbon Philip chose to be buried here rather than with his Habsburg predecessors at El Escorial. His tomb is in the adjacent church, included with your ticket (€5 with Spanish-speaking guide, €4.50 without guide, April–Sept Tue–Sun 10:00–18:00, closed Mon; Oct–March Tue–Sat 10:00–13:30 & 15:00–17:00, Sun 10:00–14:00, closed Mon; tel. 921-470-019, www.patrimonionacional.es). Fourteen buses a day (fewer on weekends) make the 20-minute trip from Segovia (catch at the bus station) to San Ildefonso–La Granja. The park is free (daily 10:00–20:00, until 19:00 in winter).

SLEEPING

The best places are on or near the central Plaza Mayor. This is where the city action is: the best bars, most touristic and *típico* eateries, and the TI. During busy times—on weekends and in July and August—arrive early or call ahead.

In the Old Center, near Plaza Mayor

$$$ Hotel Los Linajes is ultra-classy, with rusticity mixed into its newly poured concrete. This poor man's parador is a few blocks beyond Plaza Mayor, with territorial views and modern, air-conditioned niceties (Sb-€78, Db-€106, big Db-€138, Tb-€127, cheaper off-season, breakfast-€10, elevator, parking-€12, Dr. Velasco 9, tel. 921-460-475, fax 921-460-479, www.loslinajes.com, hotelloslinajes@terra.es). From Plaza Mayor, take Escuderos downhill; at the five-way intersection, angle right on Dr. Velasco. Drivers, follow brown hotel signs from the aqueduct to its tight but handy garage.

$$$ Hotel Infanta Isabel, right on Plaza Mayor, is the ritziest hotel in the old town, with 38 elegant rooms, some with plaza views (Sb-€67–77, Db-€97–114 depending on room size, less in winter, breakfast on the square-€9, elevator, valet parking-€12, tel. 921-461-300, fax 921-462-217, www.hotelinfantaisabel.com, admin@hotelinfantaisabel.com).

$$ Hostal Plaza, just off Plaza Mayor, has extremely strict management, snaky corridors, and some tight squeezes. But its 28 rooms are clean and cozy (Sb-€39, D-€35, Db-€48, Tb-€65, parking-€10, Cronista Lecea 11, tel. 921-460-303, fax 921-460-305, www.hostal-plaza.com, informacion@hostal-plaza.com).

$ Pensión Ferri, half a block off Plaza Mayor, is located opposite a Guinness beer sign and within the bowels of an old mansion. This

Sleep Code

(€1 = about $1.50, country code: 34)
S = Single, **D** = Double/Twin, **T** = Triple, **Q** = Quad, **b** = bathroom, **s** = shower only. Unless otherwise noted, you can assume credit cards are accepted and English is spoken. Breakfast is generally not included.

To help you easily sort through these listings, I've divided the rooms into three categories, based on the price for a standard double room with bath during high season (breakfast and 7 percent IVA tax not included):

$$$ Higher Priced—Most rooms €85 or more.
$$ Moderately Priced—Most rooms between €30–85.
$ Lower Priced—Most rooms €30 or less.

quiet, unmarked, five-room place is cheaper than the youth hostel (S-€17, D-€24, shower-€2, cash only, Escuderos 10, tel. 921-460-957, no English spoken by laid-back Juan or Carmen, who are not about to invest in the place since retirement is just around the corner).

Outside of the Old Town, near the Aqueduct

$$ Hostal Don Jaime, opposite the Church of San Justo, is a friendly, family-run place with 38 basic, worn yet well-maintained rooms. Seven more rooms are in an annex across the street (S-€24, D-€32, Db-€45, Tb-€55, Qb-€65, breakfast-€3.50, parking-€7, Ochoa Ondategui 8; from TI at Plaza del Azogüejo, cross under the aqueduct, go right, angle left, then snake uphill for 2 blocks; tel. & fax 921-444-787, hostaldonjaime@hotmail.com).

$$ Hospedaje el Gato, a family-run place on a quiet nondescript square just outside the old town, has 10 modern, comfortable rooms (Sb-€25, Db-€40, Tb-€55, air-con, smoky bar serves breakfast and good tapas, uphill from Hostal Don Jaime and aqueduct at Plaza del Salvador 10, tel. 921-423-244, mobile 678-405-079, fax 921-438-047, hbarelgato@yahoo.es but prefer phone or fax reservations).

EATING

Look for Segovia's culinary claim to fame, roast suckling pig (*cochinillo asado:* 21 days of mother's milk, into the oven, and onto your plate—oh, Babe). It's worth a splurge here, or in Toledo or Salamanca.

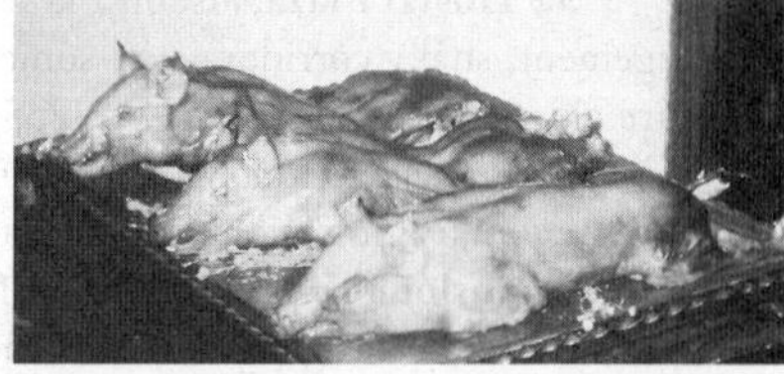

For lighter fare, try *sopa castellana*—soup mixed with

eggs, ham, garlic, and bread—or warm yourself up with the local *judiones de La Granja,* a popular soup made with flat white beans from the region.

Ponche segoviano, a dessert made with an almond-and-honey *mazapán* base, is heavenly after an earthy dinner or with a coffee in the afternoon (at the recommended Limon y Menta, described later in this section).

Roast Suckling Pig

Mesón de Cándido, one of the top restaurants in Castile, is famous for its memorable dinners. Even though it's filled with tourists, it's a grand experience. Take time to wander around and survey the photos of celebs—from King Juan Carlos to Antonio Banderas and Melanie Griffith—who've suckled here. Try to get a table in a room with an aqueduct view (figure on spending €30–35, daily 13:00–16:30 & 20:00–23:00, Plaza del Azogüejo 5, air-con, under aqueduct, call 921-428-103 for reservations, www.mesondecandido.es, candido@mesondecandido.es). Three gracious generations of the Cándido family still run the show.

José María is *the* place to pig out in the old town, a block off Plaza Mayor. While it doesn't have the history or fanfare of Cándido, locals claim this high-energy place serves the best roast suckling pig in town. It thrives with a hungry mix of tourists and locals—so reservations are usually necessary (€40 à la carte dinner, daily 13:00–16:00 & 20:30–23:30, air-con, Cronista Lecea 11, tel. 921-466-017, reservas@rtejosemaria.com).

Restaurante Casa Chapete, a homey little place filled with smoke, happy locals, and not a tourist in sight, serves traditional lamb and pig dishes—but only for lunch (€22 three-course meals including wine, €35 quarter *cochinillos* for 2–3 people, €9 simple three-course fixed-price meals on weekdays, daily 12:30–16:00, 2 blocks beyond aqueduct, across from recommended Hostal Don Jaime at Calle Ochoa Ondategui 7, tel. 921-421-096).

The Old Center (No Pig)

Plaza Mayor, the main square, provides a great backdrop for a light lunch, dinner, or drink. Prices at the cafés are generally reasonable, and many offer a good selection of tapas and *raciones.* Grab a table at the place of your choice and savor the scene. **Café Jeyma** has a fine setting and cathedral view. **La Concepción Restaurante** is also good (€30 meals, closer to the cathedral).

Narizotas serves more imaginative and non-Castilian alternatives to the gamey traditions. You'll dine outside on a delightful square or inside with modern art under medieval timbers. For a wonderful dining experience, try their chef's choice mystery samplers, either the "Right Hand" (€37, about 10 courses, with wine and dessert) or the

"Left Hand" (€33, about six courses, with wine and dessert). They offer a less elaborate three-course €16 fixed-priced meal, and their à la carte menu is also a treat (daily 13:00–16:30 & 20:30–23:30, midway down Calle Juan Bravo at Plaza de Medina del Campo 1, tel. 921-462-679).

Restaurante Bar San Martín, a no-frills place popular with locals, has a lively tapas bar, great outdoor seating by a fountain on the same square as the recommended Narizotas, and a smoky restaurant in the back. I'd eat here only to enjoy the setting on the square (€10 three-course fixed-price meal on weekdays, tapas bar open Tue–Sun 9:00–24:00, restaurant open Tue–Sun 13:30–16:00 & 20:30–23:00, both closed Mon, Plaza de San Martín 3, tel. 921-462-466).

Cueva de San Esteban serves traditional home cooking with a stress-free photo menu at the door, and hearty, big-enough-to-split plates (daily 11:00–24:00, full meals 13:00–16:00, two blocks past Plaza Mayor on a quiet back street, Calle Valdelaguila 15, tel. 921-460-982).

Rodilla, the popular chain, offers a tasty selection of sandwiches and salads (Mon–Fri 9:30–22:00, Sat–Sun 10:00–22:30, on Calle Juan Bravo, at intersection with Calle de la Herrería).

Breakfast: For breakfast, I like to sit on Plaza Mayor enjoying the cool air and the people scene (many choices). Or, 100 yards down the main drag toward the aqueduct, **Café La Colonial** serves good breakfasts (with seating on a tiny square or inside, Plaza del Corpus).

Nightlife: Inexpensive bars and eateries line Calle de Infanta Isabel, just off Plaza Mayor. For nightlife, the bars on Plaza Mayor, Calle de Infanta Isabel, and Calle Isabel la Católica are packed. There are a number of late-night dance clubs along the aqueduct.

Dessert: **Limon y Menta** offers a good, rich *ponche segoviano (mazapán)* cake by the slice for €2.50, or try the lighter honey-and-almond *crocantinos* (daily 9:30–21:30 but hours can vary, seating inside, Isabel La Católica 2, tel. 921-462-141).

Market: An outdoor produce market thrives on Plaza Mayor on Thursday (8:00–14:00). Nearby, a few stalls are open daily except Sunday on Calle del Cronista Ildefonso Rodríguez.

TRANSPORTATION CONNECTIONS

If side-tripping between Segovia and Madrid, the AVE train takes less than half as long as the bus. However, you'll spend more time getting to the AVE stations in Segovia and Madrid than to the bus stations, so the total time spent in transit is about the same. (In Madrid, the AVE goes to the Chamartín train station, while the bus goes to Príncipe Pío Metro station.) *Cercanías* commuter trains also run to Madrid, but take two hours and don't save you much money.

From Segovia by Bus to: La Granja Palace (14/day, 25 min), **Ávila** (5/day weekdays, 2/day weekends, 1 hr), **Madrid** (2/hr, departing on the half-hour, 1.25 hrs, €6, first departure at 6:30, last return at

21:30, often stops first at Madrid's Metro: Moncloa, but the end of the line is the Príncipe Pío bus terminal and Metro stop, tel. 915-598-955, www.lasepulvedana.es), **Salamanca** (2/day, 3 hrs, transfer in Labajos; it's smart to call ahead to reserve a seat for the Labajos–Salamanca segment—call Madrid's La Sepulvedana office at tel. 915-598-955 to book your seat). Consider busing from Segovia to Ávila for a visit, then continuing to Salamanca by bus or train.

If you're riding the bus from Madrid to Segovia, about 30 minutes after leaving Madrid you'll see—breaking the horizon on the left—the dramatic concrete cross of the Valley of the Fallen. Its grand facade marks the entry to the mammoth underground memorial (described earlier in this chapter).

By Train to: Madrid (via high-speed AVE train: 8/day, 35 min, €9, leaves from Segovia's Guiomar station, arrives at Madrid's Chamartín station; via *cercanías* commuter train: 9/day, 2 hrs, €5.65, leaves from Segovia's inconvenient *cercanías* station, arrives at both Madrid's Chamartín and Atocha stations). AVE trains leave from Segovia's Guiomar station; to get there, take city bus #11 from the base of the aqueduct (20 min, buses usually timed to match arrivals). To reach the sleepy, dead-end *cercanías* station, walk 20 minutes past the bus station along Paseo de Ezequiel González (which turns into Paseo del Conde de Sepulvedana); catch bus #6 (leaves from the bus station) or #8 (leaves from the aqueduct); or take a taxi. Train info: tel. 902-240-202.

Route Tips for Drivers

From Madrid to Segovia: Leave Madrid on A-6. Exit 39 gets you to Segovia via a slow, winding route over the scenic mountain. Exit at 60 (after a long €3 toll tunnel) or get there quicker by staying on the toll road all the way to Segovia (add €2 weekdays or €3 on weekends). At the Segovia aqueduct, follow *casco histórico* signs to the old town (on the side where the aqueduct adjoins the crenellated fortress walls).

Parking in Segovia: Free parking is available in the Alcázar's lot, but you must move your car out by 19:00, when the gates close. Or try the lot northwest of the bus station by the statue of Cándido, along the street called Paseo de Ezequiel González. Outside the old city, there's an Acueducto Parking underground garage kitty-corner from the bus station, and there's free parking just down from the bus station. Although it can be a hard slog up the hill to the Alcázar on a hot day, it beats trying to maneuver uphill through tight bends. A huge garage is planned near the aqueduct (to be completed around 2009).

While there are generally lots of parking spaces in the city center, they're not free. If you want to park in the old town, be legal or risk an expensive ticket. Buy a ticket from the nearby machine to park in areas marked by blue stripes, and place the ticket on your dashboard (€1.40/hr, pay meter every 2 hours 9:00–14:00 & 16:30–20:00; free parking 20:00–9:00, Sat afternoon, and all day Sun).

Segovia to Salamanca (100 miles): Leave Segovia by driving around the town's circular road, which offers good views from below the Alcázar. Then follow signs for Ávila (road N-110). Notice the fine Segovia view from the three crosses at the crest of the first hill. The Salamanca road leads around the famous Ávila walls to the right. The best wall view is from the signposted Cuatro Postes, a mile northwest of town. Salamanca (N-501) is clearly marked, about an hour's drive away.

About 20 miles before Salamanca, you might want to stop at the huge bull on the left side of the road. There's a little dirt lane leading right up to it. As you get closer, it becomes more and more obvious it isn't real. Bad boys climb it for a goofy photo. For a great photo op of Salamanca, complete with river reflection, stop at the edge of the city (at the light before the first bridge). In Salamanca, the only safe parking is in a garage; try the underground lot at Plaza Santa Eulalia, Plaza del Campillo, or Lemans (closer to recommended Petit Palace Las Torres), or even easier, try one of the hotels (such as Hotel Don Juan) with valet parking for comparable fees. See the Salamanca chapter for more information.

Ávila

Yet another popular side-trip from Madrid, Ávila is famous for its perfectly preserved medieval walls, as the birthplace of St. Teresa, and for its yummy *yema* treats. For more than 300 years, Ávila was on the battlefront between the Muslims and Christians, changing hands several times. Today, perfectly peaceful Ávila has a charming old town. With several fine churches and monasteries, it makes for an enjoyable quick stop between Segovia and Salamanca (each about an hour away by car).

ORIENTATION

On a quick stop, everything in Ávila that matters is within a few blocks of the cathedral (actually part of the east end of the wall).

Tourist Information

The TI has fine, free maps and information on walking tours (daily 9:00–14:00 & 17:00–20:00, no afternoon closure July–mid-Sept, on Plaza Pedro Dávila 4, take first right when entering through Puerta del Rastro, tel. 920-211-387). Another TI is located outside the wall, opposite the Basilica of San Vicente (daily April–Oct 10:00–20:00, Nov–March 10:00–18:00, public WCs).

A clunky **tourist train** departs from outside the wall by Puerta de San Vicente, heads into town, exits at the westernmost gate, loops by the Monasterio de la Encarnación (where St. Teresa lived), and then shudders along back to the north wall. Unfortunately, its daytime route doesn't stop at the worthwhile Cuatro Postes viewpoint (though it does stop there for a view of the illuminated wall at 22:00 on Fri–Sat in July–Aug). Check the *próxima salida* sign for departure times, which are usually twice an hour (€4 day, €7 night, daily 9:00–18:00, narration in Spanish unless you specify English, mobile 629-222-218).

Arrival in Ávila

Approaching by bus, train, or car, you'll need to make your way through the nondescript modern part of town to find the walled old town. From the cathedral and wall, the bus station is a 15-minute walk, while the train station is a 20-minute walk. There are lockers at Ávila's bus station, but not at the train station. Drivers can use the public parking east of Puerta del Alcázar, just south of the cathedral, or at Parking Dornier (€1.25/hour).

SIGHTS

▲The Wall—Built from around 1100 on even more ancient remains, Ávila's fortified wall is the oldest, most complete, and best-preserved in Spain. It has three access points: One is two blocks away from the Plaza de Santa Teresa (Puerta del Alcázar); the better one, which leads to a longer walk, starts at the gate closest to the cathedral (Puerta del Peso de la Harina) and takes you to the third, Puerta del Carmen. Look for the door marked *subida a la muralla* (€4, April–mid-Oct Tue–Sun 10:00–20:00, mid-Oct–March 11:00–18:00, closed Mon except July–Aug, last entry 45 min before closing). A night visit gives you the same walk, with the wall beautifully lit (€4, mid-June–mid-Sept Sun–Wed 22:00–24:00). Your ticket has two stubs, which allow you to enter the wall's two sections for the same price. You can use one stub to go up during the day, and save the other to go up at night. By 2009, another section of the wall may be opened, adding a fourth entrance—Puerta del Puente—and allowing visitors the chance to walk almost three-quarters of the wall.

There's an interesting paseo scene along the wall each night—make your way along the southern wall (Paseo del Rastro) to Plaza de

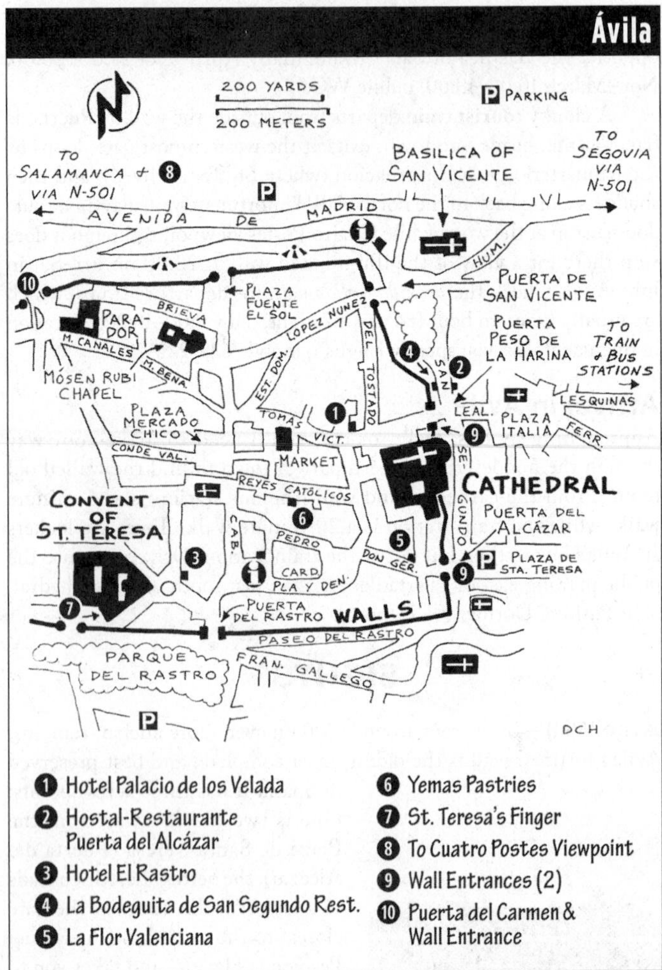

Santa Teresa for spectacular vistas across the plains. The best views of the wall itself are actually from street level (especially along the north side, which drivers will see as they circle to the right from Puerta de San Vicente to catch the highway to Salamanca). The finest overall view of the walled town is about a mile away on the Salamanca road (N-501), at a clearly marked turnout for the Cuatro Postes (four posts).

Cathedral—While it started as Romanesque, Ávila's cathedral, finished in the 16th century, is considered the first Gothic cathedral in Spain. Its position—with its granite apse actually part of the fortified wall—underlines the "medieval alliance between cross and sword." For €4, you can tour the cathedral, its sacristy, cloister, and museum—which includes an El Greco painting (Mon–Sat 10:00–20:00, Sun

12:00–19:00, off-season Mon–Sat 10:00–17:00, Sun 12:00–18:00—but hours often vary, Plaza de la Catedral).

Convent of St. Teresa—Built in the 17th century on the spot where the saint was born, this convent is a big hit with pilgrims (10-min walk from cathedral). A lavishly gilded side chapel marks the actual place of her birth (left of main altar, door may be closed). A separate room of relics (outside, facing the church on your right, Sala de Reliquias) houses a shop that shows off Teresa's finger, complete with a fancy emerald ring, along with one of her sandals and the bones of St. John of the Cross (free, no photos of finger allowed, daily 9:30–13:30 & 15:30–19:30, until 19:00 in winter). A museum in the crypt at the side entrance dedicated to the saint is worth a visit for devotees (€2, April–Oct Tue–Sun 10:00–14:00 & 16:00–19:00, Nov–March Tue–Sun 10:00–13:30 & 15:30–17:30, closed Mon, last entry 30 min before closing).

St. Teresa (1515–1582)—reforming nun, mystic, and writer—bought a house in Ávila and converted it into a convent with more stringent rules than the one she belonged to. She faced opposition in her hometown from rival nuns and those convinced her visions of Heaven were the work of the Devil. However, with her mentor and fellow mystic, St. John of the Cross, she established convents of Discalced (shoeless) Carmelites throughout Spain, and her visions and writings led her to sainthood (canonized 1622).

Yemas—These pastries, made by local nuns, are like soft-boiled egg yolks that have been cooled and sugared. They're sold all over town. The shop Las Delicias del Convento is actually a retail outlet for the cooks of the convent (€3.50 for a small box, Tue–Sat 10:30–14:00 & 17:00–20:00, Sun 10:30–18:30, closed Mon, hours and closed day vary by season, a block from TI, at Calle Reyes Católicos 12, tel. 920-220-293).

SLEEPING

(€1 = about $1.50, country code: 34)

The first hotel is antique and classy, facing the cathedral. The second is simpler and faces the wall's entrance that leads to the cathedral. Àvila is cold in fall, winter, and early spring; both hotels have heating.

$$$ Hotel Palacio de los Velada is a five-centuries-old palace with 145 elegant rooms surrounding a huge and inviting arcaded courtyard (Sb-€150, Db-€190, third person-€30 extra on weekends, lower rates Mon–Thu and for 2-night weekend stays, higher on holidays, air-con, elevator, Plaza de la Catedral 10, tel. 920-255-100, fax 920-254-900, www.veladahoteles.com, reserves.avila@veladahoteles.com).

$$ Hostal-Restaurante Puerta del Alcázar has 27 basic yet spacious rooms right next to the Puerta del Peso de la Harina just outside the wall (Sb-€43, Db-€55, Tb-€77, Qb-€99, includes tax and breakfast, no air-con, San Segundo 38, tel. 920-211-074, fax 920-211-075, www.puertadelalcazar.com, info@puertadelalcazar.com). Also see "Eating," below.

$$ Hotel El Rastro has 26 rooms with a modern country touch—but a stuffy staff—near Puerta del Rastro (Sb-€45, Db-€75, includes breakfast, Calle Cespedas s/n, tel. 920-352-225, fax 920-352-223, www.elrastroavila.com, info@elrastroavila.com, Pilar).

EATING

La Bodeguita de San Segundo is a good bet for a classy light lunch. Owned by a locally famous wine connoisseur, it serves fine wine by the glass with gourmet tapas, including smoked-cod salad and wild-mushroom scrambled eggs (Thu–Tue 12:00–24:00, closed Wed, along the outside of wall near cathedral at San Segundo 19, tel. 920-257-309).

Hostal-Restaurante Puerta del Alcázar, filled with more locals than hotel guests, serves elaborate salads, fixed-price meals (for €12 and €20), and more. You can sit indoors, or even better, outdoors with cathedral views (Mon–Sat 13:30–16:00 & 21:00–23:30, Sun 13:30–16:00, San Segundo 38, tel. 920-211-074).

Dessert: **La Flor Valenciana** is where locals beat the heat on warm days with an ice cream or a *granizado* (slushee) with some unique flavors (daily in summer 10:00–23:00, in winter hours vary according to demand, by Puerta del Alcázar on Calle Don Gerónimo 13, tel. 920-212-254). If the weather's cool, pop in the courtyard of **Hotel Palacio de los Velada** (listed earlier) for a €3 coffee or hot chocolate.

TRANSPORTATION CONNECTIONS

The bus terminal is closed on Sundays, but you can purchase tickets when boarding the bus.

From Ávila to: Segovia (5 buses/day weekdays, 2 on weekends, 1.25 hrs), **Madrid** (1 train/hr until 21:55, 90 min, more frequent connections with Chamartín station than Atocha; 8 buses/day, 4 on weekends, 1.5 hrs; Estación Sur de Autobuses in Madrid, tel. 914-684-200), **Salamanca** (6 trains/day, 1 hr; 4 buses/day, 2 on weekends, 1.5 hrs). Train info: tel. 902-240-202, www.renfe.es. Bus info: tel. 902-222-282, www.lasepulvedana.es.

TOLEDO

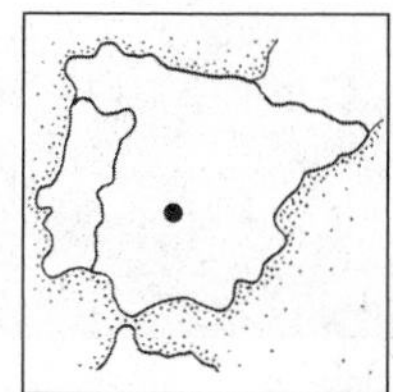

An hour south of Madrid, Toledo teems with tourists, souvenirs, and great art by day, and delicious dinners, echoes of El Greco, and medieval magic by night. Incredibly well preserved and full of cultural wonder, the entire city has been declared a national monument.

Spain's former capital crowds 2,500 years of tangled history—Roman, Jewish, Visigothic, Moorish, and Christian—onto a high, rocky perch protected on three sides by the Tajo River. It's so well preserved that the Spanish government has forbidden any modern exteriors. The rich mix of Jewish, Moorish, and Christian heritages makes it one of Europe's artistic highlights.

Today, Toledo thrives as a provincial capital and a busy tourist attraction. This decade has been an eventful one for Toledo. The advent of the new high-speed AVE train connection makes Toledo a quick, 30-minute ride from Madrid. While locals worried that this link would turn their town into a bedroom community for wealthy Madrileños, the already high real-estate prices minimized the impact. The city is also undergoing a major construction project: the building of a new convention center, complete with a huge escalator that will take visitors from the bus station nearly to the main square, Plaza de Zocodover. When this addition is complete (perhaps in 2009), the city will become largely traffic-free (except for city residents' cars, public transit, and service vehicles).

Toledo remains the historic, artistic, and spiritual center of Spain. Despite tremendous tourist crowds, Toledo sits enthroned on its history, much as it was when Europe's most powerful king and its most famous resident artist, El Greco, called it home.

Planning Your Time

To properly see Toledo's sights—including its museums (great El Greco) and cathedral (best in Spain)—and to experience its medieval atmosphere (wonderful after dark), you'll need two nights and a day. Plan carefully for lunchtime closures and for Toledo's notorious midday heat in summer. Get an early start and stay out late...but take a rest during the unbearable summer afternoons. Note that a few sights are closed on Monday (including Sinagoga del Tránsito).

ORIENTATION

Toledo sits atop a circular hill, with the cathedral roughly dead-center. Lassoed into a tight tangle of streets by the sharp bend of the Tajo River (called the Tejo in Portugal, where it hits the Atlantic at Lisbon), Toledo has Spain's most confusing medieval street plan. But it's a small town within its walls, with only 10,000 inhabitants (80,000 total live in greater Toledo, including its modern suburbs). The major sights are well signposted, and most locals will politely point you in the right direction if you ask.

The top sights stretch from the main square, Plaza de Zocodover (zoh-koh-doh-VEHR), southwest along Calle Comercio (a.k.a. Calle Ancha, "Wide Street") to the cathedral, and beyond to Santo Tomé and more. The visitor's city lies basically along this small but central street, and most tourists never stray from this axis. Make a point to get lost. The town is small and bounded on three sides by the river. When it's time to return to someplace familiar, pull out the map or ask, "*¿Para Plaza de Zocodover?*" From the far end of town, handy bus #12 circles back to Plaza de Zocodover (take "Bus #12 Self-Guided Tour," page 409).

Keep in mind that sights appear closer on maps than they really are, because local maps don't factor into account the slope of the hill. In Toledo, they say everything's uphill—it certainly feels that way.

Tourist Information

Toledo has two TIs: The TI just outside **Bisagra Gate**—in a freestanding brick building—is nearest to the bus and train stations (Mon–Fri 9:00–18:00, Sat 9:00–19:00, Sun 9:00–15:00, longer hours in summer, tel. 925-220-843). The other TI is on Plaza del Ayuntamiento, near the **cathedral** (Mon 10:30–14:30, Tue–Sun 10:30–14:30 & 16:30–19:00, WC, tel. 925-254-030). Pick up the free magazine *t-descubre* (or visit www.t-descubre.com) for a listing of sights, a few walking tours of the city, and a calendar of events.

Toledo

Arrival in Toledo

"Arriving" in Toledo means getting uphill to Plaza de Zocodover. This involves a hike, taxi, or bus ride, but future plans include a proposed escalator running directly from the bus station nearly to Plaza de Zocodover (which would be helpful even for those arriving by train).

By Train: From the train station, it's an ugly 30-minute hike (described below), a €4 taxi ride, or an easy ride on bus #5, #6, or #22 to Plaza de Zocodover (€1, pay on bus, confirm by asking, "*¿Para Plaza de Zocodover?*"). Consider buying a city map at the kiosk; it's better than the free one at the TI. To walk, turn right leaving the station, cross the bridge with the mighty Alcázar on your left, pass the bus station (on right), go straight through the roundabout, and continue uphill to Bisagra Gate (TI), into the old town to Plaza de Zocodover.

Toledo's History

Perched strategically in the center of Iberia, for centuries, Toledo was a Roman transportation hub with a thriving Jewish population. After Rome fell, the city became a Visigothic capital (A.D. 554). In 711, the Moors (Muslims) made it a regional center. In 1085, the city was reconquered by Christians, but many Moors remained in Toledo, tolerated and respected as scholars and craftsmen.

While Jews were commonly persecuted elsewhere in Europe, Toledo's Jewish community—educated, wealthy, and cosmopolitan—thrived from the city's earliest times. Jews of Spanish origin are called Sephardic Jews. The American expression "Holy Toledo" likely originated from the Sephardic Jews who eventually immigrated to America. To them, Toledo was the holiest Jewish city in Europe...Holy Toledo!

During its medieval heyday (c. 1350), Toledo was a city of the humanities, where God was known by many names. In this haven of cultural diversity, people of different faiths lived together in harmony.

Toledo remained Spain's political capital until 1561, when Philip II moved to more-spacious Madrid. Historians fail to agree why the move was made; some say that Madrid was the logical place for a capital in the geographic center of newly formed *España,* while others say that Philip wanted to separate politics from religion. Whatever the reason, Toledo was mothballed, only to be rediscovered by 19th-century Romantic travelers. They wrote of it as a mystical place... which it remains today.

By Bus: If you arrive by bus, go upstairs to the station lobby. You'll find luggage storage and a small bus-information office opposite the cafeteria. Confirm your departure time (probably every half-hour to Madrid). You can put off buying a return ticket until just minutes before you leave Toledo. Specify you'd like a *directo* bus, because the *ruta* trip takes longer (60 min vs. 90 min). If you miss the *directo* bus (or if it's sold out), the *ruta* option offers a peek of off-the-beaten-path Madrid suburbia; you'll arrive at the same time as taking the next *directo* bus. From the bus station, Plaza de Zocodover is a 15-minute walk (see directions from train station, above), a €3 taxi ride, or a short bus ride (catch #5, #12, or #22 downstairs—underneath the lobby, €1, pay on bus).

By Car: If you're arriving by car, you can enjoy a scenic big-picture orientation by following the *Ronda de Toledo* signs on a big circular drive around the city. You'll view the city from many angles along the Circunvalación road across the Tajo Gorge. Stop at a viewpoint or drive to Parador de Toledo, located just south of town, for the view (from the balcony) that El Greco made famous in his portrait of Toledo. The best time for this trip is the magic hour before sunset, when the top

Central Toledo

viewpoints are busy with tired old folks and frisky young lovers.

Upon arrival in Toledo, you can park for free in the streets near the Bisagra Gate escalators, or pay to park (€16/day) in the parking lot across from them. You can also drive into town and park in Garage Alcázar (opposite the Alcázar in the old town—€1.60/hr, €16.20/day).

A car is useless within Toledo's city walls, where the narrow, twisting streets are no fun to navigate. Ideally, see the old town outside of car-rental time. Pick up or drop off your car on the outskirts of town; **Avis** is at the train station (Mon–Fri 9:30–13:30 & 16:30–19:30, Sat 9:30–13:30, closed Sun, tel. 925-214-535).

By Escalator into Town: A series of escalators runs outdoors past Bisagra Gate, giving you a free ride up, up, up into town (Sun–Fri 8:00–22:00, Sat 8:00–24:00). You'll end up near San Ildefonso

Toledo at a Glance

▲▲▲Cathedral One of Europe's best, with a marvelously vast interior and great art. **Hours:** Mon–Sat 10:00–18:30, Sun 14:00–18:30. See page 397.

▲▲Santa Cruz Museum Renaissance building housing wonderful artwork, including 15 El Grecos. **Hours:** Mon–Sat 10:00–18:30, Sun 10:00–14:00. See page 403.

▲Alcázar Imposing former imperial residence that dominates Toledo's skyline. **Hours:** Interior currently closed for installation of the new National Military Museum (may open in late 2009). See page 404.

▲Santo Tomé Simple chapel with El Greco's masterpiece, *The Burial of the Count of Orgaz.* **Hours:** Daily 10:00–18:45, until 17:45 mid-Oct–March. See page 405.

▲Tourist Train Tacky but fun 50-minute trip through Toledo's highlights with great Tajo Gorge views. **Hours:** Daily at top of the hour from 11:00 until into the evening. See page 397.

Sinagoga del Tránsito Museum of Toledo's Jewish past. **Hours:** Mid-Feb–Nov Tue–Sat 10:00–21:00, Sun 10:00–14:00, closed Mon; Dec–mid-Feb Tue–Sat 10:00–18:00, Sun 10:00–14:00, closed Mon. See page 407.

Sinagoga de Santa María la Blanca Synagogue that harmoniously combines Toledo's three religious influences: Jewish, Christian, and Moorish. **Hours:** Daily April–Nov 10:00–18:45, Oct–March 10:00–17:45. See page 408.

Museo Victorio Macho Collection of the 20th-century Toledo sculptor's works, with expansive river-gorge view. **Hours:** Mon–Sat 10:00–19:00, Sun 10:00–15:00. See page 407.

San Juan de los Reyes Monasterio Church/monastery that was to be the final resting place of Isabel and Ferdinand. **Hours:** Daily 10:00–18:45, until 17:45 in winter. See page 408.

El Greco's House Museum that holds 20 works by the painter, but likely closed for renovation in 2009. **Hours:** Check at TI. See page 407.

and far from Plaza de Zocodover, but it's worth it for the novelty. (Sometime in 2009, Toledo hopes to have a more useful escalator in place, taking visitors directly and easily from the bus station nearly to Plaza de Zocodover.)

Helpful Hints

Local Guidebook: Consider the readable *Toledo: Its Art and Its History* (small version for €5, sold all over town). It explains all of the sights (which generally provide no on-site information) and gives you a photo to point at and say, "*¿Dónde está...?*"

Internet Access: Miradero Sicra Internet Locutorio is a good central standby for email, with seven fast terminals. From Plaza de Zocodover, walk a long block down the big street, Calle de las Armas, which becomes Calle de Venancio González, and go to #9 (€2/hr, daily 10:30–23:00).

TOURS

▲Tourist Train—For a great city overview, hop on the cheesy Tren Imperial Tourist Tram. Crass as it feels, you get a 50-minute putt-putt through Toledo and around the Tajo River Gorge. It's a fine way for non-drivers to enjoy views of the city from across the Tajo Gorge (€4.50, buy ticket from convenience store with handy WC at Calle de la Sillería 14, leaves Plaza de Zocodover daily on the hour from 11:00 into the evening, recorded English/Spanish commentary, tel. 925-220-300). There are no photo stops, but it goes slowly—for the best views of Toledo across the gorge, sit on right side, not behind the driver.

For a cheap alternative to the tourist train, try the #7.1 **city bus,** which leaves Plaza de Zocodover hourly (7:50–21:50) and offers the same classic view across the gorge.

Local Guide—Juan José Espadas, a.k.a. Juanjo, is a good local guide who enjoys sharing his hometown in English (€140/3 hrs weekdays, €155/3 hrs weekends, mobile 667-780-475, juanjo@guiadetoledo.es).

SIGHTS

▲▲▲Cathedral

Holy Toledo! Spain's leading Catholic city has a magnificent cathedral. Shoehorned into the old center (on the spot where a mosque once stood), it has an exterior that's hard to appreciate. But the interior is so lofty, rich, and vast that it'll have you wandering around like a Pez dispenser stuck open, whispering "Wow."

Cost and Hours: The cathedral and associated sights (choir, chapter house, sacristy, cloister, and treasury) require a €7 ticket normally sold in the shop opposite the church entrance on Calle Cardenal. But due to recent renovations, tickets may be sold on the other side of the church at temporary stands on the Calle Chapinería (cathedral open Mon–Sat 10:00–18:30, Sun 14:00–18:30, last entry 30 min before closing, audioguides-€3, no photos, tel. 925-222-241).

➲ **Self-Guided Tour:** Wander among all the pillars, thick and sturdy as a redwood forest. Sit under one and imagine a time when the light bulbs were candles and the tourists were pilgrims—before the *No Photo* signs, when every window provided spiritual as well as physical light. The cathedral is primarily Gothic. But since it took more than 250 years to build (1226–1495)—with continuous embellishments after that (every archbishop wanted to leave his imprint)—it's a mix of styles, including Gothic, Renaissance, Baroque, and Neoclassical. Enjoy the elaborate wrought-iron work, lavish wood carvings, window after colorful window of 500-year-old stained glass, and a sacristy with a collection of paintings that would put any museum on the map.

This confusing collage of great Spanish art deserves a close look. Hire a private guide, discreetly freeload on a tour (they come by every few minutes during peak season), rent an audioguide, or follow this quick tour. Here's a framework for your visit:

1. High Altar: First, walk to the high altar to marvel through the iron grille at one of the most stunning altars in Spain. Real gold on wood, by Flemish, French, and local artists, it's one of the country's best pieces of Gothic art. Don't miss the finely worked gold-plated iron grille itself—considered to be the best from the 16th century in Spain. About-face to the...

2. Choir: Facing the high altar, the choir is famous for its fine carving. The rich symbolism of the carving centers on the archbishop's throne in the center. First, look carefully at the fine alabaster relief above the throne: It shows a seventh-century Visigothic miracle, when Mary came down to give the local bishop the holy robe, legitimizing Toledo as the spiritual capital (and therefore political capital) of Spain.

Because of its primacy in Iberia, Toledo was the first city in the crosshairs of the Reconquista Christian forces. They recaptured the city in 1085 (over 400 years before they re-took Granada). A local saying goes, "A carpet frays from the edges, but the carpet of Al-Andalus (Muslim Spain) frayed from the very center" (meaning Toledo). The fall of Toledo marked the beginning of the end of the Muslim domination of Iberia.

Cheap Tricks in Toledo

- Good news: Most of the city's sights charge less than €3 to enter. Or you can beat that price by going to the Sinagoga del Tránsito on Saturday afternoon or Sunday when it's free. El Greco fans can see his art for free at the Santa Cruz Museum.
- Pick up the free *t-descubre* magazine at either TI and follow the walking tours ("t-rutas").
- Use Toledo's public transportation for your tours. Take the bus #12 self-guided tour through town (see page 409). To get to El Greco's famous viewpoint, take bus #7.1, which leaves from Plaza de Zocodover at :50 hourly until 21:50. Its circular route loops around to the vista where you can hop off, snap some photos, and wait at the same stop for the next bus to take you back.
- Shop for picnics at the city market, Mercado Municipal, and choose an atmospheric square for your meal.
- If you're day-tripping from Madrid to Toledo, take the bus, which is half the cost of the AVE train.

The lower wooden stalls are decorated with scenes showing the finale of the one-city-at-a-time Christian victory, when Muslims were slowly pushed back into Africa. Set in the last decade of the Reconquista, these images celebrate the retaking of the towns around Granada: Each idealized castle has the reconquered town's name on it, culminating in the final victory at Granada in 1492 (the reliefs flank the archbishop's throne). While the castles are romanticized, the carvings of the clothing, armor, and weaponry are so detailed and accurate that historians have studied them to learn the evolution of weaponry.

The upper stalls feature Old Testament figures—an alabaster genealogy of the church—starting with Adam and Eve, working clockwise to Joseph and "S. M. Virgo Mater" (St. Mary the Virgin Mother). All this imagery is to remind viewers of the legitimacy of the bishop's claims to religious power. Check out the seat backs, made of carved walnut and featuring New Testament figures—with Peter (key) and Paul (sword)—alongside the archbishop himself.

And, as is typical of choir decoration, the carvings on the misericords (the tiny seats that allowed tired worshippers to lean while they "stand") feature the frisky, folksy, sexy, profane art of the day. Apparently, since you sat on it, it could never be sacred anyway.

Take a moment to absorb the marvelous complexity, harmony, and cohesiveness of the art around you. Look up. There are two fine pipe organs: one early 18th-century Baroque and the other late 18th-century Neoclassical. As you leave the choir, note the serene beauty of the 13th-century Madonna and child at the front, thought to be a gift from the

Toledo's Cathedral

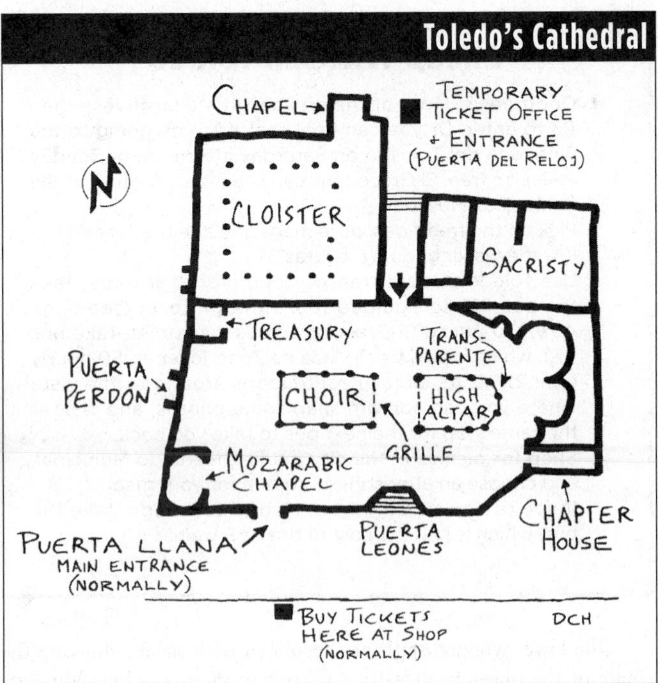

French king to Spain. Its naturalism and intimacy was radical in its day.

The iron grille of the choir is notable for the dedication of the man who built it. Domingo de Céspedes, a Toledo ironworker, accepted the commission to build the grille for 6,000 ducats. The project, which took from 1541 to 1548, was far more costly than he anticipated. The medieval Church didn't accept cost overruns, so to finish it, he sold everything he owned and went into debt. He died a poor—but honorable—man. (It's a charming story, but the artistic iron gate before the altar is the true treasure.)

3. Chapter House (Sala Capitular): Face the altar, and go around it to your right to the chapter house. Under its lavish ceiling, this fresco celebrates the humanism of the Italian Renaissance. There's a Crucifixion, a *pietà,* and a Resurrection on the front wall; they face a fascinating Last Judgment, where the seven sins are actually spelled out in the gang going to hell: arrogance (the guy striking a pose), avarice (holding his bag of coins), lust (the easy woman with the fiery crotch and lovely hair), anger, gluttony (fat guy), envy, and laziness. Imagine how instructive this was in 1600.

Below the fresco, a pictorial review of 1,900 years of Toledo archbishops circles the room. The upper row of portraits dates from the 16th century. Except for the last two, these were not painted from life. The lower portraits were added one at a time from 1515 on and are therefore of more historic than artistic interest. Imagine sitting down to church business surrounded by all this tradition and theology. As you leave, notice the iron-pumping cupids carved into the pear-tree panels lining the walls.

4. *Transparente:* The *transparente,* behind the high altar, is a unique feature of the cathedral. In the 1700s, a hole was cut into the ceiling to let a sunbeam brighten Mass. Melding this big hole with the Gothic church presented a challenge, and the result was a Baroque masterpiece. Gape up at this riot of angels doing flip-flops, babies breathing thin air, bottoms of feet, and gilded sunbursts. Study the altar, which looks chaotic, but is actually structured thoughtfully: The good news of salvation springs from Baby Jesus, up past the archangels (including one who knows how to hold a big fish correctly) to the Last Supper high above, and beyond into the light-filled dome. I like it, as did (I guess) the two long-dead cardinals whose faded red hats hang from the edge of the hole. (A perk that only a cardinal enjoys is to choose a burial place in the cathedral and hang his hat over that spot until the hat rots.)

5. Sacristy: The cathedral's sacristy is a mini-Prado, with 18 El Grecos and masterpieces by Francisco de Goya, Titian, Peter Paul Rubens, Diego Velázquez, Caravaggio, and Giovanni Bellini. First, notice the fine perspective work on the ceiling (frescoed by Lucca Giordano from Naples, c. 1690). Then walk to the end of the room for the most important painting in the collection, El Greco's *The Spoliation* (a.k.a. *Christ Stripped of His Garments*).

Spain's original great painter was Greek, and this is his first masterpiece after arriving in Toledo. El Greco's painting from 1579 hangs exactly where he intended it to—in the room where priests prepared themselves for Mass. It shows Jesus surrounded by a sinister mob and suffering the humiliation of being stripped in public before his execution.

The scarlet robe is about to be yanked off, and the women (lower left) avert their eyes, turning to watch a carpenter at work (lower right) who bores the holes for nailing Jesus to the cross. While the carpenter bears down, Jesus—the other carpenter—looks up to heaven. The contrast between the motley crowd gambling for his clothes and Jesus' noble face underscores the quiet dignity with which he endures this ignoble treatment. Jesus' delicate white hand stands out from the flaming red tunic with an odd gesture that's common in El Greco's paintings. Some say this was the way Christians of the day swore they were true believers, not merely Christians-in-name-only, such as former Muslims or Jews who converted to survive.

On the right is a rare religious painting by Goya, the *Betrayal of Christ,* which shows Judas preparing to kiss Jesus, thus identifying him to the Roman soldiers. Enjoy the many other El Grecos. A small-but-lifelike 17th-century carving of St. Francis by Pedro de Mena is just to the right of the Goya.

6. The Cloister: Take a peaceful detour to a funerary chapel located at the far side of the cloister from the entrance. The ceiling over the marble tomb of a bishop was frescoed by a student of Giotto (a 14th-century Italian Renaissance master).

7. Treasury: The *tesoro* is tiny, but radiant with riches. The highlight is the 10-foot-high, 430-pound monstrance—the tower designed to hold the Holy Communion wafer (the host) during the festival of Corpus Christi ("body of Christ") as it parades through the city. Built in 1517 by Enrique de Arfe, it's made of 5,000 individual pieces held together by 12,500 screws. There are diamonds, emeralds, rubies, and 400 pounds of gold-plated silver. The inner part is 35 pounds of solid gold. Yeow. The base is a later addition from the Baroque period.

To the right of the monstrance is a beautiful, red-coral cross given by the Philippines. To the right of the cross is a facsimile of a 700-year-old Bible hand-copied and beautifully illustrated by French monks; it was a gift from St. Louis, the 13th-century king of France. Imagine looking on these lavish illustrations with medieval eyes—an exquisite experience. The finely painted small crucifix on the opposite side in the corner—by the great Gothic Florentine painter Fra Angelico—depicts Jesus alive on the back and dead on the front. This was a gift from Mussolini to Franco. Underneath, you'll find the rather plain sword of Franco. Hmmm. There's even a gift in this room from Toledo's sister city, Toledo, Ohio.

If you're at the cathedral between 9:00 and 9:15, you can peek into the otherwise-locked **Mozarabic Chapel** (Capilla Mozárabe). The Visigothic Mass (in Latin), the oldest surviving Christian ritual in Western Europe, starts at 9:15 (9:45 on Sun). You're welcome to partake in this stirring example of peaceful coexistence of faiths—but once the door closes, you're a Visigoth for 30 minutes. Toledo's proud Mozarabic community of 1,500 people traces its roots to Visigothic times.

In Central Toledo

Plaza de Zocodover—The main square is Toledo's center and your gateway to the old town. The word "Zocodover" derives from the Arabic for "souk (marketplace) of the beasts" (mostly donkeys and horses).

Because Toledo is the state capital of Castile-La Mancha, the regional government administration building overlooks Plaza de Zocodover. Look for the three flags: one for Europe, one for Spain,

and one for Castile-La Mancha. And speaking of universal symbols—find the low-key McDonald's. A source of controversy, it was finally allowed...with only one small golden arch.

The square is a big local hangout and city hub: Old people arrive in the morning, and young people come in the evening. A goofy, white tourist train leaves from here (see earlier description), as do buses #5 and #22, which lumber to the bus and train stations (bus #6, which also leaves from here, goes only to the train station). Just uphill is the stop for #4.1 (heading to Plaza de Toros), the circular route #12, which travels around the old town to Santo Tomé, as well as the #7.1, which heads out to the panoramic viewpoint made famous by El Greco.

▲▲Santa Cruz Museum—For years, this museum has been in a confused state of renovation—not really open, not really closed. During renovation, the museum's cloister and a room full of its best art are open and free. If the core of the building is filled with a temporary exhibit, you can generally wander in for a free look (Mon–Sat 10:00–18:30, Sun 10:00–14:00; from Plaza de Zocodover, go through arch to Calle Miguel de Cervantes 3).

This stately Renaissance building was an orphanage and hospital, built from money left by the humanist and diplomat Cardinal Mendoza when he died in 1495. The cardinal, confirmed as Chancellor of Castile by Queen Isabel, was so influential that he was called "the third king."

Your visit has three parts: the main building (with temporary exhibit), the fine cloister, and the museum rooms off the cloister.

The building (especially its facade, cloister arches, and stairway leading to the upper cloister) is a fine example of the Plateresque style. This ornate strain of Spanish Renaissance is named for the fancy work of silversmiths of the 16th century. During this time (c. 1500–1550), the royal court moved from Toledo to Madrid—when Madrid was a village, and Toledo was a world power. (You'll see no Plateresque work in Madrid.) Note the Renaissance-era mathematics, ideal proportions, round arches, square squares, and classic columns.

The main building is in the form of a Greek cross. As 1500 was a time of transition, the fine ceiling is an impressive mix of two styles: indigenous Moorish and Italian Renaissance, which was in vogue at the time. After renovation, the wings of the building will be filled with 16th-century art, tapestries, furniture, armor, and documents.

Enjoy the peaceful cloister. In the corner stands an ignored well (now capped), bearing an Arabic inscription and grooves made by generations of Muslims pulling their buckets up by rope. The well was once in the courtyard of an 11th-century mosque that stood where the cathedral does today.

The museum section features a collection of 15 El Grecos. The highlight: the impressive *Assumption of Mary,* a spiritual poem on canvas. This altarpiece, finished one year before El Greco's death in 1614, is the culmination of his unique style, combining all of his techniques to express an otherworldly event.

Study the *Assumption* (which some believe is misnamed, and actually shows the Immaculate Conception). Bound to earth, the city of Toledo sleeps, but a vision is taking place overhead. An angel in a billowing robe spreads his wings and flies up, supporting Mary, the mother of Christ. She floats up through warped space, to be serenaded by angels and wrapped in the radiant light of the Holy Spirit. Mary flickers and ripples, charged from within by her spiritual ecstasy, caught up in a vision that takes her breath away. No painter before or since has captured the supernatural world better than El Greco.

Find the lavish but faded *Astrolabe Tapestry* (c. 1480, Belgian), which shows a new view of the cosmos at the dawn of the Renaissance and the Age of Discovery: God (far left) oversees all, as Atlas (with the help of two women and a crank handle) spins the universe, containing the circular earth. The wisdom gang (far right) heralds the wonders of the coming era. Rather than a map of earth, this is a chart showing the cosmic order of things as the constellations spin around the stationary North Star (center).

Upstairs is a wonderful exhibit for tile- and ceramic-lovers. The private collection of the Carranza family has been "on loan" to the museum for the past 20 years. They began collecting tile and assorted ceramics that date from the end of the Reconquista (1492). Each piece is categorized by the Spanish region where it was made and professionally displayed. In spite of the lack of English explanations, this is the only place in Spain where you can compare regional differences in tile work and pottery.

▲Alcázar—This huge former imperial residence—built on the site of Roman, Visigothic, and Moorish fortresses—dominates the Toledo skyline. It has been closed for years for renovation. When it finally reopens (perhaps in 2009), it will be the National Military Museum. The Alcázar became a kind of right-wing Alamo during Spain's Civil War, when Franco's Nationalists (and hundreds of hostages) were besieged for two months in 1936. Finally, after many fierce but futile Republican attacks that destroyed much of the Alcázar, Franco sent in an army that took Toledo. The place was rebuilt and glorified under Franco (Cuesta de Carlos V 2).

Toledo's Muslim Legacy

You can see the Moorish influence in these sights:

- Mezquita del Cristo de la Luz, the last of the town's mosques
- Sinagoga del Tránsito's Mudejar plasterwork
- Sinagoga de Santa María la Blanca's mosque-like horseshoe arches and pinecone capitals
- Puerta de Sol (Gate of the Sun) and other surviving gates (with horseshoe arches) along the medieval wall
- The city's labyrinthine, medina-like streets

Mezquita del Cristo de la Luz—Of Muslim Toledo's 10 mosques, only this barren little building survives, built in 1000. Looking up, you'll notice the Moorish fascination with geometry—each of the domes is a unique design. The lovely keyhole arch faces Mecca. In 1187, after the Reconquista, the mosque was changed to a church, the Christian apse was added, and the former mosque got its current name. The fine garden with its fountains is a reminder of the Quranic image of heaven (€2.30, daily 10:00–18:45, until 17:45 in winter, Cuesta de las Carmelitas Descalzas 10).

Southwest Toledo

These sights cluster at the southwest end of town. For efficient sightseeing, visit them in this order, then zip back home on bus #12 (described on page 409).

▲Santo Tomé—A simple chapel on the Plaza del Conde holds El Greco's most beloved painting. *The Burial of the Count of Orgaz* couples heaven and earth in a way only The Greek could. It feels so right to see a painting left *in situ,* where the artist placed it 400 years ago (€2.30, daily 10:00–18:45, until 17:45 mid-Oct–March, audioguide-€1.50, tel. 925-256-098). Go early or late to avoid long lines of tour groups.

Take this slow. Stay a while—let it perform. The year is 1323. You're at the burial of the good count, who's being laid to rest right here in this chapel. He

El Greco
(1541–1614)

Born on Crete and trained in Venice, Doménikos Theotokópoulos (tongue-tied friends just called him "The Greek") came to Spain to get a job decorating El Escorial. He failed there, but succeeded in Toledo, where he spent the last 37 years of his life. He mixed all three regional influences into his palette. From his Greek homeland, he absorbed the solemn, abstract style of icons. In Italy, he learned the bold use of color, elongated figures, twisting poses, and dramatic style of the later Renaissance. These elements were then fused in the fires of fanatic Spanish-Catholic devotion.

Not bound by the realism so important to his fellow artists, El Greco painted dramatic visions of striking colors and figures—bodies unnatural and lengthened as though stretched between heaven and earth. He painted souls, not faces. His work is on display at nearly every sight in Toledo. Thoroughly modern in his disregard of realism, he didn't impress the austere Philip II. But his art seems as fresh as contemporary art does today.

was so holy, even saints Augustine and Stephen have come down from heaven to lower his body into the grave. (The painting's subtitle is "Such is the reward for those who serve God and his saints.")

More than 250 years later, in 1586, a local priest hired El Greco to make a painting of the burial to hang over the count's tomb. The funeral is attended by Toledo's most distinguished citizens. (El Greco used local nobles as models.) The painting is divided in two by a serene line of noble faces—heaven above and earth below. Above the faces, the count's soul, symbolized by a little baby, rises up through a mystical birth canal to be reborn in heaven, where he's greeted by Jesus, Mary, and all the saints. A spiritual wind blows through as colors change and shapes stretch. This is Counter-Reformation propaganda—notice Jesus pointing to St. Peter, the symbol of the pope in Rome, who controls the keys to the Pearly Gates. Each face is a detailed portrait. El Greco himself (eyeballing you, seventh figure in from the left) is the only one not involved in the burial. The boy in the foreground—pointing to the two saints as if to say, "One's from the first century, the other's from the fourth...it's a miracle!"—is El Greco's son. On the handkerchief in the boy's pocket is El Greco's signature, written in Greek.

El Greco's House (Museo El Greco)—Really a small art gallery in a house built upon the spot where El Greco lived, this place has no hint of "home." The museum will probably be closed for renovation in 2009; check at the TI for the latest (Calle Samuel Leví, tel. 925-224-046).

Sinagoga del Tránsito (Museo Sefardí)—Built in 1361, this is the best surviving slice of Toledo's Jewish past. Serving as Spain's national Jewish museum, it displays Jewish artifacts, including costumes, menorahs, and books. The synagogue's interior decor looks more Muslim than Jewish. After Christians reconquered the city in 1085, many Moorish workmen stayed on, beautifying the city with their unique style called Mudejar. The synagogue's intricate, geometrical carving in stucco features leaves, vines, and flowers; there are no human shapes, which are forbidden by the Quran as being "graven images." In the frieze (running along the upper wall, just below the ceiling), the Arabic-looking script is actually Hebrew, quoting psalms from the Bible. The side-wall balcony is the traditional separate worship area for women. Scale models of the development of the Jewish quarter (on the ground floor) and video displays (upstairs) give a fuller picture of Jewish life in medieval Toledo.

This 14th-century synagogue was built at the peak of Toledo's enlightened tolerance—constructed for Jews with Christian approval by Muslim craftsmen. Nowhere else in the city does Toledo's three-culture legacy shine brighter than at this synagogue. But in 1391, just a few decades after it was built, the Church and the Spanish kings began a violent campaign to unite Spain as a Christian nation, forcing Jews and Muslims to convert or leave. In 1492, Ferdinand and Isabel exiled Spain's remaining Jews. It's estimated that, in the 15th century, a third of Spain's Jews were killed, a third survived by converting to Christianity, and a third moved elsewhere (€2.40, free Sat afternoon from 14:00 and all day Sun; open mid-Feb–Nov Tue–Sat 10:00–21:00, Sun 10:00–14:00, closed Mon; Dec–mid-Feb Tue–Sat 10:00–18:00, Sun 10:00–14:00, closed Mon; audioguide-€3, near El Greco's House on Calle de los Reyes Católicos).

Museo Victorio Macho—Here you can see *mucho* Macho. Overlooking the gorge and Tajo River, this small, attractive museum—once the home and workshop of the early-20th-century sculptor Victorio Macho—offers several rooms of his bold work interspersed with view terraces (€3, Mon–Sat 10:00–19:00, Sun 10:00–15:00, Plaza de Victorio Macho 2, between the two *sinagogas,* tel. 925-284-225).

Recognized as Spain's first modern sculptor, Victorio Macho's work is heavily influenced by Art Deco. The highlight is *La Madre,* Macho's life-size sculpture of his mother sitting in a chair. It's so lifelike and gentle that it could easily be anyone's mom. But the big draw for many is the air-conditioned theater, featuring a fast-moving nine-minute video that sweeps through Toledo's history (request English showing; the longer 29-minute history video available upon request).

The **river-gorge view** from the Museo Victorio Macho terrace clearly shows how the Tajo River served as a formidable moat protecting the city. Imagine trying to attack from this side. The 14th-century bridge on the right, and the remains of a bridge on the left, connected the town with the region's *cigarrales*—mansions of wealthy families with orchards of figs and apricots that dot the hillside even today.

Sinagoga de Santa María la Blanca—This synagogue-turned-church has Moorish horseshoe arches and wall carvings. It's an eclectic but harmonious gem, and a vivid reminder of the religious cultures that shared this city. While it looks like a mosque, it never was one. Built by Muslims around 1200, it was originally a synagogue, then a church—hence the mix-and-match name. (It's still owned by the Church, and has a Christian altar.) After being used as horse stables by Napoleonic troops, it was further ruined in the 19th century. Today, it's an evocative space, beautiful in its simplicity (€2.30, daily April–Sept 10:00–18:45, Oct–March until 17:45, no flash photos allowed, Calle de los Reyes Católicos 2/4).

Casa de Jacob Libería & Judaica is a Jewish bookshop and cultural center on the street behind Santa María la Blanca. While there are books in English, most are in Spanish and Hebrew. The owners can organize tours in Toledo or throughout Spain focusing on Jewish history (Mon–Fri 10:00–20:00, Sun 11:00–14:00, closed Sat, Calle del Ángel 15, tel. 925-216-454, www.casadejacob.com).

San Juan de los Reyes Monasterio—"St. John of the Monarchs" is a grand monastery, impressive church, and delightful cloistered courtyard. The style is Isabeline, contemporaneous with Portugal's Manueline (c. 1500) and Flamboyant Gothic elsewhere in Europe. It was the intended burial site of the Catholic Monarchs (Isabel and Ferdinand). But after the Moors were expelled in 1492 from Granada, their royal bodies were planted there to show Spain's commitment to maintaining a Moor-free peninsula (€2.30, daily 10:00–18:45, until 17:45 in winter, San Juan de los Reyes 2, tel. 925-223-802).

The **facade,** which has been undergoing restoration, may still be covered with scaffolding. If the facade is visible, notice the chains hanging on it. These were used by the Moors to confine Christians until the time of the Reconquista battles in Granada. It's said that the freed Christians brought these chains to the church, making them a symbol of the Catholic faith.

In the **chapel**—the planned site of Ferdinand and Isabel's tombs—the big coats of arms are repeated obsessively, à la Moorish decor. Had this been used as the burial site, these would have looked down on the most important tombs in Spain.

Napoleon's troops are mostly to blame for the destruction of the church, a result of Napoleon's view that monastic power in Europe was a menace. While Napoleon's biggest error was to invade Russia, his second dumbest move was to alienate the Catholic faithful by destroying monasteries such as this one. This strategic mistake eroded popular support from people who might have seen Napoleon as a welcome alternative to the tyranny of kings and the Church.

▲Bus #12 Self-Guided Tour (with a Sweat-Free Santo Tomé to Plaza de Zocodover Return Trip)—When you're finished with the sights at the Santo Tomé end of town, you can hike all the way back (not fun)—or simply catch bus #12 from in front of Santo Tomé (fun!). Santo Tomé is the end of the line, so buses wait to depart from here twice hourly (at :25 and :55), heading to Plaza de Zocodover. Closer to the synagogues and monastery, you can also catch the same bus at Plaza del Barrio Nuevo. The bus offers tired sightseers a quick, interesting look at the town walls. Here's what you'll see on your way from Santo Tomé:

Leaving Santo Tomé, you'll first ride through Toledo's Jewish section. On the right, you'll pass El Greco's House, Sinagoga del Tránsito, and Sinagoga de Santa María la Blanca, followed by—on your left—the ornate Flamboyant Gothic facade of San Juan de los Reyes Monasterio. After squeezing through the 16th-century city gate, the bus follows along the mighty 10th-century wall. (Toledo was never conquered by force...only by siege.)

Just past the big escalator (which brings people from parking lots up into the city), the wall gets fancier, as demonstrated by the little Old Bisagra Gate. Soon after, you see the big New Bisagra Gate, the main entry into the old town. While the city walls date from the 10th century, this gate was built as an arch of triumph in the 16th century.

The TI is just outside the big gate, at the edge of a well-maintained and shaded park—a picnic-perfect spot and one of Toledo's few green areas. After a detour to the bus-station basement to pick up people coming from Madrid, you swing back around Bisagra Gate and climb into the old town, passing the fine Moorish (14th century) Sun Gate, and then arrive at the main square, Plaza de Zocodover. Push the button to indicate that you'd like to get off at the square (the bus will not automatically stop at Zocodover).

SHOPPING

Toledo probably sells more souvenirs than any city in Spain. This is *the* place to buy medieval-looking swords, armor, maces, three-legged stools, lethal-looking letter-openers, and other nouveau antiques. It's also Spain's damascene center, where, for centuries, craftspeople have inlaid black steel with gold, silver, and copper wire. Spain's top bullfighters wouldn't have their swords made anywhere else.

Knives: At the workshop of English-speaking **Mariano Zamorano,** you can see swords and knives being made. Judging by what's left of Mariano's hand, his knives are among the sharpest (Mon–Fri 10:00–14:00 & 16:00–19:00, Sat–Sun 10:00–14:00—although you may not see work done on weekends, 10 percent discount with this book, behind Ayuntamiento/City Hall at Calle Ciudad 19, tel. 925-222-634, www.marianozamorano.com).

Damascene: Shops selling the shiny inlaid plates and decorative wares are all over town. The damascene is a real tourist racket, but it's fun to pop into a shop and see the intricate handwork in action. The **Simian** shop (just below the cathedral) offers good-quality items and a great chance to see the work (daily 9:30–19:30, Santa Ursula 6, tel. 925-250-546).

El Martes, Toledo's colorful outdoor market and a lively local scene, bustles on Paseo de Merchan, better known to locals as "La Vega" (Tue only 9:00–14:00, outside Bisagra Gate near TI).

SLEEPING

Madrid day-trippers darken the sunlit cobbles, but few stay to see Toledo's medieval moonrise. Spend the night. Spring and fall are high season; November through March and July and August are less busy.

Near Plaza de Zocodover

$$ Hotel Las Conchas, a three-star hotel, gleams with marble. It's so sleek and slick it almost feels more like a hospital than a hotel. Its 35 rooms are plenty comfortable (Sb-€55, Db-€85, Db with terrace-€100, includes tax, 5 percent discount in 2009 with this book, breakfast-€6, air-con, near the Alcázar at Juan Labrador 8, tel. 925-210-760, fax 925-224-271, www.lasconchas.com, lasconchas@ctv.es, Pablo and Yuki).

$ Hotel Imperio is your best budget bet in town—offering 21 basic, air-conditioned rooms with marginal beds in a handy old-town location. Weekends can be noisy; ask for a *tranquilo* room (Sb-€31,

Sleep Code

(€1 = about $1.50, country code: 34)

S = Single, **D** = Double/Twin, **T** = Triple, **Q** = Quad, **b** = bathroom, **s** = shower only. Unless otherwise noted, credit cards are accepted and English is spoken.

To help you easily sort through these listings, I've divided the rooms into three categories, based on the price for a standard double room with bath during high season:

$$$ Higher Priced—Most rooms €90 or more.
$$ Moderately Priced—Most rooms between €60-90.
$ Lower Priced—Most rooms €60 or less.

Db-€46, Tb-€61, includes tax, 5 percent discount in 2009 with this book, elevator, cheery café; from Calle Comercio, at #38 go a block uphill to Calle Cadenas 5; tel. 925-227-650, fax 925-253-183, www.terra.es/personal/himperio, himperio@hotmail.es, friendly Pablo and Esther).

$ Hostal Centro rents 28 modern, clean, and comfy rooms (Sb-€35, Db-€50, Tb-€65, inviting roof terrace; 50 yards off Plaza de Zocodover, first right off Calle Comercio at Calle Nueva 13; tel. 925-257-091, fax 925-257-848, www.hostalcentro.com, hostalcentro@telefonica.net, Asun or David).

$ Hostal Nuevo Labrador, with 12 clean, shiny, and spacious rooms, is quiet and modern—another good value (Sb-€30, Db-€45, bigger Db-€50, Tb-€65, Qb-€80, includes tax, no breakfast, air-con, elevator, Juan Labrador 10, tel. 925-222-620, fax 925-226-278, www.nuevolabrador.com, nuevolabrador@telefonica.net, César).

$ Pensión Castilla, a family-run cheapie, has seven basic non-smoking rooms (S-€18, Db-€29, cash only, fans, needs notice in advance if you'll be in after 1:00 in the morning, Calle Recoletos 6, tel. 925-256-318, Teresa doesn't speak English).

$ Hostal Palacios has 15 clean, renovated rooms at a decent price above Restaurante-Mesón Palacios (Sb-€30, Db-€50, air-con, Calle Navarro Ledesma 4, can also enter through restaurant on Calle Alfonso X El Sabio 3, for location see map on page 414, tel. 925-280-083, fax 925-253-504, www.hostalpalacios.net, info@hostalpalacios.net, run by ladies' man Jesús).

Near the Bisagra Gate

$$$ Hostal del Cardenal, a 17th-century cardinal's palace built into Toledo's wall, is quiet and elegant, with a cool garden and a stuffy restaurant. This poor-man's parador, at the dusty old gate of Toledo, is closest to the station, but below all the old-town

action. The nearby outdoor escalators take the sweat out of getting into town (Sb-€72, Db-€115, extra bed-€20, 20 percent cheaper mid-Dec–mid-March, 5 percent discount in 2009 with this book, breakfast-€8, air-con, some free parking, *serioso* staff, enter through town wall 100 yards below Bisagra Gate, Paseo de Recaredo 24, tel. 925-224-900, fax 925-222-991, www.hostaldelcardenal.com, cardenal@hostaldelcardenal.com).

$ Hotel Sol, with 15 newly decorated, pastel, non-smoking rooms, is a good value. It's on a quiet street between the Bisagra Gate and Plaza de Zocodover (Sb-€44, Db-€59, Tb-€72, includes tax, 10 percent discount in 2009 with this book, breakfast-€4, air-con, Wi-Fi, private parking-€10/day, leave the busy main drag at Hotel Real and head 50 yards down the lane to Azacanes 8, tel. 925-213-650, fax 925-216-159, www.hotelyhostalsol.com, info@hotelyhostalsol.com, José Carlos). Their 11-room **$ Hostal Sol** annex across the street is just as comfortable, smoke-free, and a bit cheaper (Sb-€36, Db-€49, Tb-€59, Qb-€72, includes tax, 10 percent discount in 2009 with this book, breakfast-€4, same parking and contact info as above).

$ Hospedería de los Reyes has 15 colorful and thoughtfully appointed rooms in a new, attractive, yellow building 100 yards north of the Bisagra Gate, outside the wall (Sb-€40–50, Db-€53–70, includes breakfast, air-con, Wi-Fi, Perala 37, tel. 925-283-667, fax 925-283-668, www.hospederiadelosreyes.com).

Deep in Toledo

$$$ Hotel Pintor El Greco, at the far end of the old town, has 33 plush, rustic-feeling, recently renovated rooms with all the comforts, yet it's in a historic 17th-century building. With a reasonably priced garage (€12/day) immediately opposite the hotel, it's a good bet for drivers (Sb-€103, Db-€130, Tb-€150, Qb-€172, manager José promises 15 percent discount off official rates if you show this book and reserve direct in 2009, breakfast-€8, air-con, elevator to second floor only, a block from Santo Tomé at Alamillos del Tránsito 13, tel. 925-285-191, fax 925-215-819, www.hotelpintorelgreco.com, info@hotelpintorelgreco.com).

$$ La Posada de Manolo rents 14 thoughtfully furnished rooms across from the downhill corner of the cathedral. Manolo Junior recently opened this fine *hostal* according to his father's vision: a comfortable place with each of its three floors themed differently—Moorish, Jewish, and Christian (Sb-€42, Db-€72, big Db-€84, includes buffet breakfast, 10 percent discount when reserved directly in 2009, air-con, no elevator, two nice view terraces, Calle Sixto Ramón Parro 8, tel. 925-282-250, fax 925-282-251, www.laposadademanolo.com, toledo@laposadademanolo.com).

$ Hotel Santa Isabel, in a 15th-century building two blocks from the cathedral, has 42 clean, modern, and comfortable rooms and squeaky tile hallways (Sb-€35, Db-€52, Tb-€70, includes tax, breakfast-€5, air-con, elevator, scenic roof terrace, parking-€10/day, buried deep in old town—take a taxi instead of the bus, drivers enter from Calle Pozo Amargo, Calle Santa Isabel 24, tel. 925-253-120, fax 925-253-136, www.santa-isabel.com, santa-isabel@arrakis.es, Emilio).

Outside of Town, near the Bullring

These places are on a modern street next to the bullring (Plaza de Toros, bullfights only on holidays), just beyond Bisagra Gate. In this area, parking is free on the street. The bus station is a five-minute walk away, and city buses lumber by every few minutes (all go directly to Plaza de Zocodover). There are many other similarly nondescript, comfy, and cheap places in this neighborhood.

$$$ Hotel María Cristina, a sprawling 74-room hotel, has all the comforts under a thin layer of prefab tradition (Sb-€68, Db-€105, Tb-€142, suites-€140–170, tax not included, breakfast-€8, air-con, elevator, restaurant, parking-€10/day, Marqués de Mendigorría 1, tel. 925-213-202, fax 925-212-650, www.hotelmariacristina.com, informacion@hotelmariacristina.com).

The next two listings are good budget bets, but have office-building charm and no English-speaking staff: **$ Hostal Gaviláness II** has 18 renovated rooms (Sb-€35–42, Db-€43–55, Db suite-€85, Tb-€57–63, Qb-€66–85, includes tax, breakfast-€2.50, air-con, parking-€6/day, Marqués de Mendigorría 14, tel. 925-211-628, fax 925-211-635, www.gavilanes.to, hostallosgavilanes2@hotmail.com).

Toledo Hotels and Restaurants

STREET WIDTH IS EXAGGERATED FOR CLARITY

200 YARDS

200 METERS

VIEW

PARKING

BUS STOP

DCH

1. Hostal Palacios & Restaurante-Mesón Palacios
2. Hostal & Rest. del Cardenal
3. Hotel Sol & Hostal Sol Annex
4. To Hospedería de los Reyes
5. Hotel Pintor El Greco
6. La Posada de Manolo
7. Hotel Santa Isabel
8. To Hotel María Cristina, Hostal Gavilánes II & Hostal Madrid
9. To Albergue Juvenil San Servando (Hostel)
10. To Parador de Toledo & Hotel La Almazara
11. Los Cuatro Tiempos Rest.
12. Casa Aurelio I
13. Casa Aurelio II & III (on Sinagoga) & Pizzeria Pastucci
14. Restaurante Casón López de Toledo
15. La Perdiz Restaurante
16. Adolfo Vinoteca
17. Taverna de Amboades
18. Mercado Municipal (Market)

$ Hostal Madrid has two locations on the same street with over 20 rooms and a café next door (at #7: Sb-€28, Db-€40, Tb-€55; at #14: Db-€38, Tb-€52; includes tax, air-con, parking-€8/day, Marqués de Mendigorría 7 and 14, reception at #7, tel. 925-221-114, fax 925-228-113, www.hostal-madrid.net, info@hostal-madrid.net).

Hostel

The 96-bed **Albergue Juvenil San Servando** youth hostel is lavish and newly renovated but cheap, with small rooms for two, three, or four people (€12.80 per bed, €12 obligatory *alberguista* membership can be bought on site, swimming pool, views, cafeteria, good management, located in 10th-century Arab castle of San Servando, 10-min walk from train station, 15-min hike from town center, over Puente Viejo outside town, tel. 925-224-554, reservations tel. 925-221-676, alberguesclm@jccm.es, no English spoken).

Outside of Town with the Grand Toledo View

$$$ Parador de Toledo, with 76 rooms, is one of Spain's best-known inns. Its guests enjoy the same Toledo view El Greco made famous from across the Tajo Gorge. In 2008, the hotel underwent major renovations that could increase these rates in 2009 (Sb-€142, Db-€170, Db with view-€178, Tb-€230, Tb with view-€248, tax included, breakfast-€16, €31 fixed-price meals sans drinks in their fine restaurant overlooking Toledo, 2 windy miles from town at Cerro del Emperador, tel. 925-221-850, fax 925-225-166, www.parador.es, toledo@parador.es).

$ Hotel La Almazara was the summer residence of a 16th-century archbishop of Toledo. A friend of the archbishop and fond of this location's classic Toledo view, El Greco hung out here for inspiration. A lumbering old place with cushy public rooms and 28 simple bedrooms (10 with views), it's truly in the country, but just 1.5 miles out of Toledo (Sb-€33, Db-€45, Db with view-€49, Tb-€62, tax not included, air-con, Carretera de Toledo Arges y Polan at kilometer 3.4, follow signs from circular Ronda de Toledo road, tel. 925-223-866, fax 925-250-562, www.hotelalmazara.com, reservas@hotelalmazara.com). They serve breakfast, but not lunch or dinner.

EATING

Dining in Traditional Elegance

A day full of El Greco and the romance of Toledo after dark puts me in the mood for game. Typical Toledo dishes include partridge *(perdiz),* venison *(venado),* wild boar *(jabalí),* roast suckling pig *(cochinillo asado),* or baby lamb (*cordero*—similarly roasted after a few weeks of mother's milk). After dinner, find a *mazapán* place (such as the Santo Tomé shops) for dessert.

Los Cuatro Tiempos Restaurante ("The Four Seasons") specializes in local game and roasts, proficiently served in a tasteful and elegant setting. They have an extensive and inviting Spanish wine list (€19 three-course lunches, €30 à la carte dinners, Mon–Sat 13:00–16:00 & 20:30–23:00, Sun 13:00–16:00 only, at downhill corner of cathedral, Sixto Ramón Parro 5, tel. 925-223-782).

Toledo's three **Casa Aurelio** restaurants all offer traditional cooking (game, roast suckling pig, traditional soup, €30 dinners) with a classy atmosphere more memorable than the meals (13:00–16:30 & 20:00–23:30, air-con). None have outdoor seating, and all are within three blocks of the cathedral: **Plaza del Ayuntamiento 4** is festive (closed Sun night and Mon, tel. 925-227-716), **Sinagoga 6** is most *típico* (closed Tue night and Wed, tel. 925-222-097), and **Sinagoga 1,** popular with Toledo's political class, is the newest and dressiest, with a wine cellar and more modern cuisine (closed Mon, tel. 925-221-392).

Restaurante Casón López de Toledo, a fancy restaurant located in an old noble palace, specializes in Castilian food, particularly venison and partridge. The more casual ground-floor bar has an €11 lunch special on weekdays (a swinging deal), but its weekend *raciones* tapa menu is creatively expensive. The restaurant's character unfolds upstairs in the formal restaurant (€50 dinners, Tue–Sat 13:30–16:00 & 20:30–23:30, in summer closed Sun–Mon, in winter closed Sun night and Mon, reservations smart, near Plaza de Zocodover at Calle de la Sillería 3, tel. 925-254-774).

Hostal del Cardenal Restaurante, a classic hotel restaurant near Bisagra Gate at the bottom of town, is understandably popular with tourists for its decent traditional roast dishes and lush patio (daily 13:00–16:00 & 20:30–23:00, Puerto de Recaredo 24, tel. 925-220-862). This place is too traditional for some, but the dining in the elegant garden ambience can't be beat.

La Perdiz ("The Partridge") is *the* place for a splurge near the Santa Tomé sights. This classy spot offers partridge (as the name suggests), venison, suckling pig, fish, and the *mazapán* desserts made by the in-house pastry-chef are hard to forget (Tue–Sat 13:00–16:00 & 20:00–23:00, Sun 13:00–16:00 only, closed Mon and first half of Aug, Calle de los Reyes Católicos 7, tel. 925-252-919).

Adolfo Vinoteca is the wine bar of the highly respected local chef Adolfo, who also runs a fine restaurant across the street. His hope is to introduce the younger generation to the culture of fine food and wine. The place offers plenty of style...without pretension. You can't go wrong with their short list of gourmet appetizers (€7–15 each) and fine local wines (€2–3 per glass). I'd just throw myself at the mercy of your waiter, and enjoy the feeling of gourmet slaves in the kitchen bringing you your wildest edible fancies. If the Starship *Enterprise* had a Spanish wine and tapas bar, this would be it. Wine is sold at shop prices with a €3–6 cork fee (daily 12:00–24:00, across from cathedral at Calle Nuncio Viejo 1, tel. 925-224-244).

Eating Simply

For locations, see the maps on pages 412 and 414.

Restaurante-Mesón Palacios is a simple diner, serving good regional food at reasonable prices in a warm and friendly atmosphere. Their bean soup with partridge *(judías con perdiz)* and €14 roast suckling lamb and pig are good (Mon–Sat from 12:00 and from 19:00, Sun from 12:00 only, rents rooms above restaurant—see Hostal Palacios listing in "Sleeping," near Plaza de San Vicente at Alfonso X El Sabio 3, tel. 925-215-972, run by ladies' man Jesús).

Restaurante Maravilla, plain and forgettable, serves a €11 fixed-price meal. Just half a block off Plaza de Zocodover, it has cool air-conditioning (daily 13:00–16:00 & 20:00–23:00, Plaza Barrio Rey 5, tel. 925-228-582).

At **Plaza de Zocodover,** several eateries serve edible food at reasonable prices, considering the wonderful people-watching scene.

At **Taverna de Amboades,** a humble but earnest wine-and-tapas bar near the Bisagra Gate, Miguel Ángel enjoys explaining the differences between Spanish wines. To try some really good wines with quality local cheese and meat (€8 combo-plate), drop by and let Miguel impress you (Wed–Sun 20:00–24:00, also Fri–Sun 13:00–16:30, closed Mon-Tue, non-smoking, Alfonso VI 5, mobile 678-483-749).

Pizzeria Pastucci, while nondescript, is a local favorite for pizza and pasta (€14 feeds two, Tue–Sun 12:00–16:00 & 19:00–24:00, closed Mon, near cathedral at Calle de la Sinagoga 10).

Picnics: Picnics are best assembled at the city market, Mercado Municipal, on Plaza Mayor (on the Alcázar side of cathedral, with a supermarket inside open Mon–Sat 9:00–15:00 & 17:00–20:00 and stalls open mostly in the mornings until 14:00, closed Sun). This is a fun market to prowl, even if you don't need food. If you feel like munching a paper plate–size Communion wafer, one of the stalls sells crispy bags of *obleas*—a great gift for your favorite pastor. For a picnic with people-watching, consider Plaza de Zocodover or Plaza del Ayuntamiento.

And for Dessert: *Mazapán*

Toledo's famous almond-fruity-sweet *mazapán* is sold all over town. Locals say the best is made by **Santo Tomé** (several outlets, including a handy one on Plaza de Zocodover, daily 9:00–22:00). Browse their tempting window displays. They sell *mazapán* goodies individually (two for about €1, *sin relleno*—without filling—is for purists, *de piñon* has pine nuts, *imperiales* is with almonds, others have fruit fillings). Boxes are good for gifts, but sampling is much cheaper when buying by the piece. Their *Toledana* is a nutty, crumbly, not-too-sweet cookie with a subtle thread of squash filling (€1.20 each).

For a sweet and romantic evening moment, pick up a few pastries and head down to the cathedral. Sit on the Plaza del Ayuntamiento's benches (or stretch out on the stone wall to the right of the TI). The fountain is on your right, Spain's best-looking city hall is behind you, and there before you: her top cathedral, built back when Toledo was Spain's capital, shining brightly against the black night sky.

TRANSPORTATION CONNECTIONS

While the new AVE bullet train makes the trip to Madrid in half the time (nearly hourly, 30 minutes), buses depart twice as frequently. Either way, Madrid and Toledo are very easily connected.

From Toledo to Madrid: By bus (2/hr, 1–1.5 hrs, €4.40 one-way, *directo* is faster than *ruta,* use Madrid's Estación sur Autobuses, Metro: Mendez Álvaro, Continental Auto bus company, tel. 925-223-641), **by train** (almost hourly, 30 min, €8.60 one-way, AVE fast train zips to Madrid's Atocha station, www.renfe.es/ave), **by car** (40 miles, 1 hr). Toledo bus info: tel. 925-215-850; train info: tel. 902-240-202.

From Toledo to Other Points: To get to Granada and elsewhere in Spain from Toledo, assume you'll have to transfer in Madrid. See Madrid's "Transportation Connections" for information on reaching various destinations.

Route Tips for Drivers

Granada to Toledo (250 miles, 5 hours): The Granada–Toledo drive is long, hot, and boring. Start early to minimize the heat and make the best time you can. Follow signs for *Madrid/Jaén/N-323* into what some call "the Spanish Nebraska"—La Mancha (see next section). After Puerto Lapice, you'll see the Toledo exit.

Toledo to Madrid (40 miles, 1 hour): It's a speedy *autovía* north, past one last billboard to Madrid (on N-401). The highways converge into M-30, which encircles Madrid. Follow it to the left (*Nor* or *Oeste*) and take the Plaza de España exit to get back to Gran Vía. If you're airport-bound, keep heading into Madrid until you see the airplane symbol (N-II).

To drive to Atocha Station in Madrid, take the exit off M-30 for Plaza de Legazpi, then take Delicias (second on your right off the square). Parking for car return is on the north side of the train station.

La Mancha

La Mancha, which is worth a visit if you're driving between Toledo and Granada, shows a side of Spain that you'll see nowhere else—vast and flat. Named for the Arabic word for "parched earth," it makes you feel small—lost in rough seas of olive-green polka dots. Random buildings look like houses and hotels hurled off some heavenly Monopoly board.

This is the setting of Miguel de Cervantes' *Don Quixote,* published in the early 17th century, after England sank the Armada and the Spanish Empire began its decline. Cervantes' star character fights doggedly for good, for justice, and against the fall of Spain and its traditional old-regime ideals. Ignoring reality, Don Quixote is a hero fighting a hopeless battle. Stark La Mancha is the perfect stage.

The epitome of *Don Quixote* country, the town of **Consuegra** (TI tel. 925-475-731) must be the La Mancha Cervantes had in mind. Drive up to the ruined 12th-century castle and joust with a windmill. It's hot and buggy here, but the powerful view overlooking the village, with its sun-bleached, light-red roofs, modern concrete reality, and harsh, windy silence makes for a profound picnic (a one-hour drive south of Toledo). The castle belonged to the Knights of St. John (12th and 13th centuries) and is associated with their trip to Jerusalem during the Crusades. Originally built from the ruins of a nearby Roman circus, it has been newly restored (€3). Sorry, the windmills are post-Cervantes, only 200 to 300 years old—but you can go inside the one that serves as the TI to see how it works (€1).

If you've seen windmills, the next castle north (above Almonacid, 8 miles from Toledo) is free and more interesting than the Consuegra castle. Follow the ruined lane past the ruined church up to the ruined castle. The jovial locals hike up with kids and kites.

GRANADA

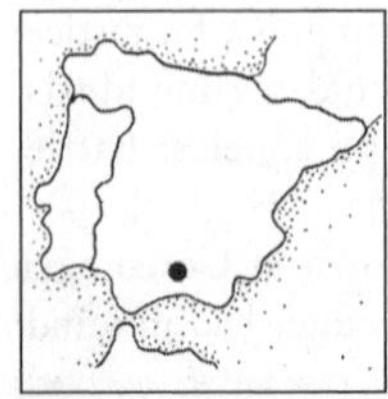

For a time, Granada was the grandest city in Spain. But in the end, with the tumult that came with the change from Moorish to Christian rule, it eventually lost its power and settled into a long slumber. Today, Granada seems to specialize in evocative history and good living. We'll keep things fun and simple, settling down in the old center and exploring monuments of the Moorish civilization and its conquest. And we'll taste the treats of a North African–flavored culture that survives here today.

Granada's magnificent Alhambra fortress was the last stronghold of the Moorish kingdom in Spain. The city's exotically tangled Moorish quarter bustles across from the grand Alhambra, which glows red in the evening while locals stroll, enjoying Granada's cool, late-night charms.

There is an old saying: "Give him a coin, woman, for there is nothing worse in this life than to be blind in Granada." This city has much to see, yet it reveals itself in unpredictable ways. It takes a poet to sort through and assemble the jumbled shards of Granada. Peer through the intricate lattice of a Moorish window. Hear water burbling unseen among the labyrinthine hedges of the Generalife Gardens. Listen to a flute trilling deep in the swirl of alleys around the cathedral. Don't be blind in Granada—open your senses.

Planning Your Time

Granada is worth one day and two nights at a minimum. The Costa del Sol's best beach town, Nerja, is just a two-and-a-half-hour bus ride away. You can also get to white hill towns such as Ronda (by train) in that time; Sevilla is an easy three-hour train ride. To use your

Cheap Tricks in Granada

- Buy some drinks and snacks near Plaza Nueva, and sling them up to the Albayzín. This makes for a great cheap date at San Nicolás or one of the scattered squares and lookout points.
- Have a drink at the Carmen de Aben Humeya—it's an inexpensive way to soak up great Alhambra views.
- Do a tapas crawl on Calle Navas right off of Plaza del Carmen. Claim your "right" to a free tapa with every drink.
- Take your time going up to the Alhambra—the lush and shady garden walkways are inviting and free (bring a picnic if you please).

time efficiently in Granada, reserve in advance for the Alhambra (see sidebar on page 430). Non-direct Madrid–Granada train service is slow (4.5 hours), but passes through beautiful countryside.

Here's the best one-day plan: In the morning, tour the cathedral and Royal Chapel (both closed roughly 13:00–16:00) and stroll the pedestrian-zone shopping scene. Do the Alhambra in the late afternoon. At sunset, take bus #31 or #32 up to the San Nicolás viewpoint in the Moorish quarter (the Albayzín), then find the right place for a suitably late dinner.

ORIENTATION

Modern Granada sprawls (300,000 people), but its sights are all within a 20-minute walk of Plaza Nueva, where dogs wag their tails to the rhythm of modern hippies and street musicians. Most of my recommended hotels are within a few blocks of Plaza Nueva. Make this the hub of your Granada visit.

Plaza Nueva was a main square back when kings called Granada home. This historic center is in the Darro River Valley, which separates two hills (the river now flows under the square). On one hill is the great Moorish palace, the Alhambra, and on the other is the best-preserved Moorish quarter in Spain, the Albayzín. To the southeast are the cathedral, Royal Chapel, and Alcaicería (Moorish market), where the city's two main drags—Gran Vía de Colón (often just called "Gran Vía" by locals) and Calle Reyes Católicos—lead away into the modern city.

Greater Granada

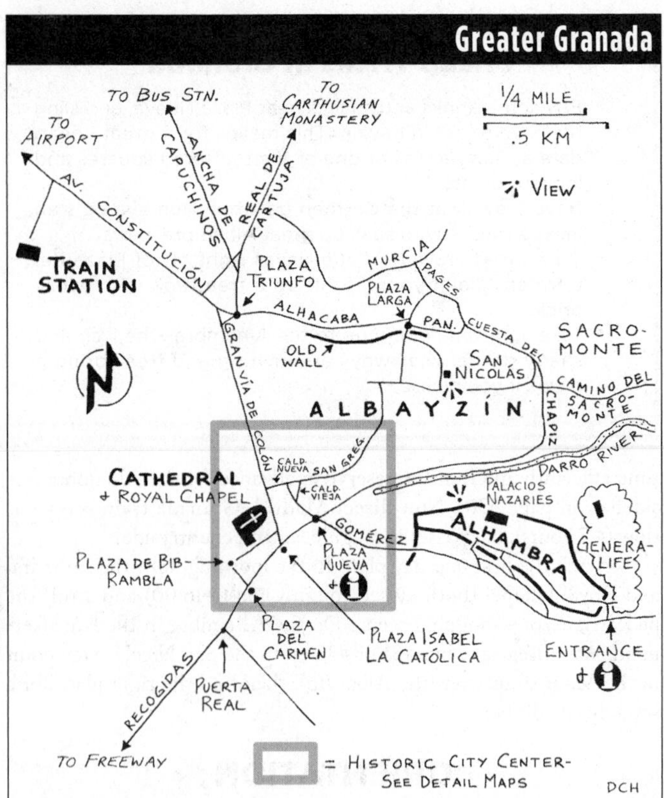

Tourist Information

The main TI is tucked away just above Plaza Nueva on Santa Ana (above the church, Mon–Fri 9:00–19:30, Sat 10:00–19:00, Sun 10:00–14:00, tel. 958-575-202). Another TI is at the entrance of the Alhambra (March–Oct Mon–Sat 8:30–19:30, Nov–Feb until 18:00, year-round Sun 8:30–14:00, tel. 958-544-003). Both cover Granada as well as all Andalucía. At either TI, get a free city map and the *Pocket Guía* magazine in easy Spanish (English magazines not always available), and verify your Alhambra plans. To save yourself a trip to the train or bus stations, get schedule information (both TIs list all departures on the wall). During peak season (April–Oct), TI kiosks sometimes pop up in Plaza Nueva and Plaza de Bib-Rambla.

Arrival in Granada

By Train: Granada's train station is connected to the center by frequent buses, a €5 taxi ride, or a 30-minute walk down Avenida de la Constitución and Gran Vía. The train station doesn't have luggage storage. If your itinerary is set, you can reserve your train out upon arrival.

Exiting the train station, walk straight ahead down the tree-lined Avenida Andaluces. At the first major intersection (Avenida de la Constitución), you'll see a series of bus stops on your right. Buses #3 through #9 (and most other buses—check the easy-to-read map at the stop) go to the cathedral, the nearest stop to Plaza Nueva—confirm by asking the driver, "*¿Catedral?*" (kah-tay-DRAHL). Buy a €1 ticket from the driver. Get off when you see the fountain of Plaza Isabel La Católica in front of the bus at the stop near the cathedral; cross the busy Gran Vía and walk three short blocks to Plaza Nueva.

By Bus: Located on the city outskirts, Granada's bus station, Estación de Autobuses, has a good and cheap cafeteria, ATMs, luggage storage, and info office (tel. 958-185-480; or tel. 902-422-242 for the Alsa company, which serves Barcelona and east-coast destinations). To get to the center, either take a 10-minute taxi ride (€6) or bus #3 or #33 (€1, pay driver). It's about a 20-minute bus ride; nearing the center, the bus goes up Gran Vía. For Plaza Nueva, get off at the stop for the cathedral (cathedral not visible from bus), a half-block before the grand square called Plaza Isabel La Católica (a three-block walk from Plaza Nueva).

By Car: Driving in Granada's historic center is restricted to buses, taxis, and tourists with hotel reservations. Signs are posted to this effect, and entrance is strictly controlled—but generally not by an officer. Hidden cameras snap a photo of your license plate as soon as you enter the restricted zone. Getting into the old center and finding your hotel or a parking garage is a major frustration because of these strict controls and the many one-way streets.

If you want to drive into the restricted zone to get close to downtown, be sure to give your hotel your license-plate number when reserving or confirming your room; your hotelier can contact the local police department (and prevent a nasty surprise when you return your rental car). Some hoteliers have deals with nearby garages and can give you detailed directions to those spots.

The *autovía* (freeway) circles the city with a *circumvalación* road (Ronda Sur). If you're heading for a hotel near Plaza Nueva, take exit #129, direction Centro, Recogidas. Calle Recogidas becomes Calle Reyes Católicos and leads directly into the heart of town. Note that the first traffic-monitor camera is stationed at the intersection of Calle Recogidas and Calle Solarillo de Gracia. Consider parking just outside of the restricted zone, then hiring a taxi to take you to your hotel (try the convenient Garage Rex on Calle Recogidas, €18/day; taxi stand just around corner at Calle Campos, €4 to Plaza Nueva). There might be a police block at Puerta Real (Victoria Hotel) because driving down

Calle Reyes Católicos is now heavily controlled. Technically, you can pull into Plaza Nueva if you have a hotel reservation, but the roadside posts—which have a list of hotels with button buzzers to gain drivers entry—generally do not work.

Granada has several parking garages. Parking San Agustín—near the cathedral, just off Gran Vía—costs more than the others, but is the only lot that's an easy walk to my recommended hotels (€20/day; as you approach Plaza Isabel La Católica on Gran Vía, follow blue *Parking* sign).

By Plane: Granada's airport (code: GRX) is about 10 miles west of the city center. To get between the airport and downtown, you can take a taxi (€25) or, much cheaper, the airport bus, timed to leave when flights arrive and depart (€3, 6/day, 30 min). Use the bus stop at Gran Vía del Colón, nearly across from the cathedral. Airport info: tel. 958-245-223.

Helpful Hints

Theft Alert: Roma (Gypsy) women, usually hanging out near the cathedral and Alcaicería, will probably accost you with sprigs of rosemary. The twig is free...and then they grab your hand and read your fortune for a tip. Coins are bad luck, so the minimum payment they'll accept is €5. Don't make eye contact, don't accept a sprig, and say firmly but politely, *"No, gracias."* While aggressive (especially in the morning), these Spanish Roma are harmless. Locals warn that Roma from Romania (new arrivals who tend to have gold teeth) are more likely to be pickpockets. In general, be on guard for pickpockets, especially late at night in the Albayzín. Your biggest threat is being conned while enjoying drinks and music in Sacromonte.

City Pass: The **Bono Turístico** city pass covers the Alhambra, cathedral, Royal Chapel, Carthusian Monastery, sightseeing bus, and 10 free public-bus trips, plus minor sights and discounts on others (€30, valid for five days). The pass might also include a €2 discount with Cicerone walking tours (inquire at purchase). When you buy your pass, the vendor schedules a time for your Alhambra visit. Passes are sold at a kiosk on Plaza Nueva by the stop for bus #31. You can save time by calling ahead to purchase your pass by credit card, and it will be ready for you when you arrive at the vendor (€2.50 processing fee, tel. 902-100-095; you can also order one online at http://caja.caja-granada.es, but the website is aggravating and confusing to use). During peak season (roughly April–June and Sept–Oct), it's worth ordering the pass in advance to avoid the small risk of not getting into the Alhambra—particularly if you'll only be in town for just one day and haven't already made a reservation. Note that some of the fancier hotels provide one free pass per room for stays of two or more nights during the busy season.

Festivals and Concerts: From late June to early July, the International Festival of Music and Dance offers classical music, ballet, flamenco, and zarzuela (light opera) nightly in the Alhambra at reasonable prices. The ticket office is located in the Corral de Carbón (open mid-April–Oct). Beginning in February, you can also book tickets online at www.granadafestival.org. This festival is one of the most respected and popular in Spain, and tickets for major performers typically sell out months in advance. During the festival, flamenco is free every night at midnight; ask the ticket office or TI for the venue.

From fall through spring, the City of Granada Orchestra offers popular weekly concerts that sell out quickly; reservations are recommended (€5–20, Sept–May only, Auditorio Manuel de Falla, ticket office in Corral de Carbón, Mon–Fri 12:00–14:00 & 17:00–19:00, Sat 12:00–14:00, closed Sun, www.orquestaciudadgranada.es).

Internet Access: There are many Internet points scattered throughout Granada, often part of *locutorios* (call centers). A number of hotels also offer Wi-Fi access (see "Sleeping," page 456).

Post Office: It's on Puerta Real (Mon–Fri 8:30–20:30, Sat 9:30–14:00, closed Sun, tel. 958-221-138).

Travel Agencies: All travel agencies book flights, and many also sell long-distance bus and train tickets. **Viajes Bonanza** sells it all, slow but convenient at Calle Reyes Católicos 30 (Mon–Fri 9:00–13:00 & 17:00–20:00, Sat 10:00–13:30, closed Sun, tel. 958-223-578). Mega-chain **El Corte Inglés** sells plane and train tickets, but doesn't handle bus travel (Mon–Sat 10:00–21:00, closed Sun, Acera del Darro, floor 2).

Getting Around Granada

With cheap taxis, efficient minibuses, good city buses, and nearly all points of interest an easy walk from Plaza Nueva, you'll get around Granada easily.

Tickets for the minibuses and city buses cost €1 per ride (buy from driver). Credibus magnetic cards save you money if you'll be riding often—or, since they're shareable, if you're part of a group (€5/8 trips, €10/17 trips, plus €2 for each card issued, buy from driver, valid on minibuses and city buses, no fee for connecting bus if you transfer within 45 min).

By Minibus: The handy little red minibuses, which cover the city center, depart every few minutes from Plaza Nueva and Plaza Isabel La Católica until late in the evening (about 22:30; bus stops marked on

Granada at a Glance

▲▲▲The Alhambra The last and greatest Moorish palace, highlighting the splendor of that civilization in the 13th and 14th centuries. Reservations recommended. **Hours:** The entire complex is open daily March-Oct 8:30-20:00, Nov-Feb 8:30-18:00. The Palacios Nazaries is open for nighttime visits March-Oct Tue-Sat 22:00-23:30, closed Sun-Mon; Nov-Feb only Fri-Sat 20:00-21:30, closed Sun-Thu. See page 428.

▲▲Royal Chapel Lavish 16th-century Plateresque Gothic chapel with the tombs of Queen Isabel and King Ferdinand. **Hours:** April-Oct Mon-Sat 10:30-13:00 & 16:00-19:00, opens Sun at 11:00; Nov-March Mon-Sat 10:30-13:00 & 15:30-18:30, opens Sun at 11:00. See page 443.

▲▲San Nicolás Viewpoint Breathtaking vista over the Alhambra and the Albayzín. **Hours:** Always open; best at sunset. See page 452.

Cathedral The second-largest cathedral in Spain, unusual for its bright, Renaissance design. **Hours:** April-Oct Mon-Sat 10:45-13:30 & 16:00-20:00, Sun 16:00-20:00; Nov-March Mon-Sat 10:45-13:30 & 16:00-19:00, Sun 16:00-19:00. See page 447.

Alcaicería Tiny shopping lanes filled with a silk and jewelry market. **Hours:** Always open, with shops open long hours. See page 448.

Corral del Carbón Granada's only surviving caravanserai (inn for traveling merchants), with impressive Moorish door. **Hours:** Always viewable. See page 448.

map on page 433). Here are a few handy minibus routes to look for:

Bus #32 is the best for a trip up to the Alhambra, connecting the Alhambra and Albayzín (from Plaza Isabel La Católica, the bus goes up to the Alhambra, returns to Plaza Isabel La Católica, then loops through the Albayzín and back down Gran Vía).

Bus #31 does the Albayzín loop (a few go through Sacromonte), departing from Plaza Nueva.

Bus #34 infrequently goes up into Sacromonte, and also connects to the Alhambra, but by a very circuitous route.

Bus #30 would normally be the most direct and quickest bet for getting up to the Alhambra, but its route—up Cuesta de Gomérez—is closed through 2009 while the Granada Gate is being restored. Although Cuesta de Gomérez is closed to vehicle traffic, eager pedestrians can still hike up to the Alhambra.

Paseo de los Tristes A prime strolling strip above the Darro River lined with eateries and peppered with Moorish history. **Hours:** Always open; best in the evenings. See page 449.

Hammam El Bañuelo Eleventh-century ruins of Moorish baths. **Hours:** Tue-Sat 10:00-14:00, closed Sun-Mon. See page 450.

Hammam Bãnos Árabes Tranquil spot for soaks and massages in Arab baths. **Hours:** Daily 10:00-24:00. See page 450.

Great Mosque of Granada Brand-new Islamic house of worship featuring a minaret with a live call to prayer, an information center for the Muslim perspective on Granada history, and a courtyard with commanding views. **Hours:** Daily 11:00-14:00 & 18:00-21:00. See page 452.

Zambra Dance Flamenco-like dance performance in Sacromonte district. **Hours:** Shows generally at 22:00. See page 454.

Center for the Interpretation of Sacromonte Digs into geology and cave building, as well as Roma (Gypsy) crafts, food, and music. **Hours:** April-Oct Tue-Sun 10:00-14:00 & 17:00-21:00; Nov-March Tue-Sun 10:00-14:00 & 16:00-19:00, closed Mon. See page 455.

Carthusian Monastery Lavish Baroque monastery on the outskirts of town. **Hours:** Daily April-Oct 10:00-13:00 & 16:00-20:00, Nov-March 10:00-13:00 & 15:00-18:00. See page 456.

By City Bus: These are handy if you're visiting the Carthusian Monastery (#8) or going to the bus station (#3 or #33) or train station (#3–#9).

TOURS

Walking Tours—Cicerone, a multi-guide organization run by María and Rosa, offers informative 2.5-hour tours from the City Hall (Ayuntamiento) on Plaza del Carmen (€12, kids under 14 free, March–Oct daily at 10:30, Nov–Feb Wed–Sun at 11:00, small groups; to book a tour, visit the stand labeled *Meeting Points* on Plaza Bib-Rambla, show up on Plaza Carmen, or call mobile 670-541-669 or 600-412-051; www.ciceronegranada.com, info@ciceronegranada.com). Cicerone's excellent guides describe the fitful and fascinating changes the city underwent as it morphed from a Moorish capital to a Christian one 500 years ago. The tour doesn't go inside any sights, but it weaves together bits of the Moorish heritage that survive around the cathedral and the Albayzín. Tours finish on Plaza Nueva. Visits are generally in both English and Spanish, giving you time to take photos when the language switches.

Private Guides—**Margarita Ortiz de Landázuri,** a local English-speaking guide, knows how to teach and has good rates (tel. 958-221-406, www.alhambratours.com, info@alhambratours.com). If Margarita is busy, her partner, Miguel Ángel, is also very good.

Olive Oil Tour—This company helps you explore Granada's countryside and taste some local olive oil. The morning tours include lunch, the afternoon tours don't (€55 with lunch, €38 without, both in English, tel. 958-559-643, mobile 651-147-504, www.oliveoiltour.com, reservas@oliveoiltour.com).

SELF-GUIDED TOUR

▲▲▲The Alhambra

This last and greatest Moorish palace is one of Europe's top sights. Attracting up to 8,000 visitors a day, it's the reason most tourists come to Granada. Nowhere else does the splendor of Moorish civilization shine so beautifully.

The last Moorish stronghold in Europe is, with all due respect, really a symbol of retreat. Granada was only a regional capital for centuries. Gradually the Christian Reconquista moved south, taking Córdoba (1237) and Sevilla (1248). The Nazarids, one of the many diverse ethnic groups of Spanish Muslims, held Granada until 1492. As you tour their grand palace, remember that while Europe slumbered through the Dark Ages, Moorish magnificence blossomed—busy stucco, plaster "stalactites," colors galore, scalloped windows framing Granada views, exuberant gardens, and water, water everywhere. Water—so rare and precious in most of the Islamic world—was the purest symbol of life to the Moors. The Alhambra is decorated with water: standing still, cascading, masking secret conversations, and drip-dropping playfully.

Orientation: The Alhambra, not nearly as confusing as it might seem, consists of four sights clustered together atop a hill:

▲▲▲Palacios Nazaries—Exquisite Moorish palace, the one must-see sight.

▲Generalife Gardens—Fancy, manicured gardens with small summer palace.

▲**Charles V's Palace**—Christian Renaissance palace plopped on top of the Alhambra after the Reconquista (free entry).

Alcazaba—Empty old fort with tower and views.

These sights are described in more detail in "The Alhambra in Four Parts," on page 432.

Cost: The Alcazaba fort, Palacios Nazaries, and Generalife Gardens require a €12 combo-ticket. If the Palacios Nazaries is booked up during the day, consider getting the €6 ticket that covers only the Generalife and Alcazaba, so you can view the garden and fort during the day, and then visit the palace at night (see "The Alhambra by Moonlight," below 428). Only Charles V's Palace is free. A good map is included with your ticket if you ask for it at the ticket window.

Hours: The Alhambra is open daily March–Oct 8:30–20:00, Nov–Feb 8:30–18:00 (ticket office opens at 8:00, last entry one hour before closing, tel. 902-441-221). The Palacios Nazaries is also open most evenings (see below).

The Alhambra by Moonlight: If you're frustrated by the reservation system, or just prefer doing things after dark, late-night visits to the Alhambra are easy (you never need a reservation—just buy your ticket upon arrival) and magical (less crowded and beautifully lit). The night visits only include the Palacios Nazaries (not the Alcazaba fort or the Generalife Gardens)—but, hey, the palace is 80 percent of the Alhambra's thrills anyway. It's open March–Oct Tue–Sat 22:00–23:30 (ticket office open 21:30–22:30), closed Sun–Mon; and Nov–Feb only Fri–Sat 20:00–21:30 (ticket office open 19:30–20:30), closed Sun–Thu.

Getting to the Alhambra: There are three ways to get to the Alhambra:

1. From Plaza Nueva, hike 30 minutes up the street Cuesta de Gomérez. Keep going straight—you'll see the Alhambra high on your left. The ticket pavilion is on the far side of the Alhambra, near the Generalife Gardens.

2. From Plaza Isabel La Católica, catch a red #32 minibus, marked *Alhambra* (€1, runs every 15 min).

3. Take a taxi (€5, taxi stand on Plaza Nueva).

Don't drive. Though there's convenient parking near the entrance of the Alhambra (€1.50/hr), leaving via the one-way streets will send you into the traffic-clogged center of modern Granada.

Planning Your Visit: It's a 15-minute walk from the entry (at the top end) to Palacios Nazaries at the other end. Be sure to arrive at the Alhambra with enough time to make it to the palace before your

Getting a Reservation for the Alhambra

Many tourists never get to see the Alhambra, because tickets sell out. Make a reservation as soon as you're ready to commit to a time (especially during Holy Week, on weekends, or on major holidays). During the off-season (July–Aug and winter), you might be able to walk right in. While things are improving, the crowds can still be unpredictable; luckily, getting a reservation is quite easy.

The Alhambra complex's top sight is the Moorish palace—Palacios Nazaries. Only 350 visitors are allowed to enter per half-hour. You have a 30-minute time slot during which you must go in (printed on your ticket). Once inside the palace, however, you can linger as long as you like. If your entry time to Palacios Nazaries is before 14:00, you can stroll the Alhambra grounds anytime in the morning, see the palace at your appointed time, and leave the Alhambra by 14:00 (although you can get away with staying longer in the fort, gardens, or palace, you won't be allowed to *enter* any of these sites after 14:00). If your ticket is stamped for 14:00 or later, you cannot go inside the Alhambra grounds any earlier than 14:00. For instance, if you have a reservation to visit Palacios Nazaries between 16:30 and 17:00, you can enter the Alhambra grounds starting at 14:00 and see the fort and Generalife Gardens before the palace. (Because of the time restriction on afternoon visits, morning tickets sell out the quickest. But for most travelers, an afternoon is ample time to see the site—the light is perfect, and there are fewer tour groups.)

Reserving in Advance: There are four options, each with a (worth it) €1 surcharge.

1. Order online at www.alhambra-tickets.es. This is easy and just takes a few minutes.

2. Order by phone. Within Spain, dial 934-923-750 (cheaper), 902-888-001, or 902-505-061. To call internationally, dial the international access code first (00 from a European country, 011 from the US or Canada), then 34-934-923-750 (daily 8:30–16:00, can reserve between one day and a year in advance; while waiting for an operator, a recording tells you the date of the next available tickets). Pay with a credit card (Visa, MasterCard, or American Express).

3. If you plan to stay at one of the fancier hotels, ask—when you book your hotel room—if the hotelier can make a reservation for you to visit the Alhambra the day after your arrival.

4. If you buy a Bono Turístico city pass (explained below) in advance, you can also book your Alhambra appointment then.

Picking Up Tickets: On the day of your tour, make sure

GRANADA

you arrive at the Alhambra about an hour before your palace appointment, since the ticket line may require up to a 20-minute wait, and walking from the ticket office to the palace takes 15 minutes. Bring the same debit/credit card that you used to make the reservation. If you have a foreign card, you will need to wait in line at the windows marked *Retirada de Reservas* to pick up your tickets. Bring photo identification and be prepared to enter your credit or debit card's PIN (this is the code required to withdraw cash, not your credit card's security code).

If You're in Granada Without a Reservation: You have a number of alternatives, the least appealing of which involves getting up unnaturally early (#2).

1. Your hotel may be willing to book a reservation for you on short notice. The Alhambra sets aside 400 tickets daily for hotel guests.

2. Wake up early and stand in line. The Alhambra admits 7,800 visitors a day. Six thousand tickets are sold in advance. The remaining 1,800 are sold each day at the Alhambra ticket window labeled *Venta Directa* (near Generalife Gardens and parking lot). The ticket office opens at 8:00, and on busy peak-season days, tickets can sell out quickly. (You'll hear periodic updates over the PA system about how many tickets are left for the day, which can help you judge whether it's worth waiting in line.) Generally if you're in line by about 7:30, you'll get an entry time, probably for later that day. On a slow day, you'll get in right away. (If paying by credit or debit card, you may need to know your cash-withdrawal PIN.) If the Palacios Nazaries is booked up during the day, get the €6 ticket that covers only the Generalife Gardens and the Alcazaba fort, then return to visit the palace at night (see "The Alhambra by Moonlight," page 429).

3. If you'll be staying in Granada at least two days, consider getting the Bono Turístico city pass (see "Helpful Hints," page 424). It costs €30, covers admission to the Alhambra and Granada's other top sights, and includes a reservation for the Alhambra (scheduled when you buy the pass). But there are no guarantees that a time slot will be available (especially during April–June and Sept–Oct).

4. Take a tour of the Alhambra. The pricier hotels can book you on an expensive €49 GranaVisión tour that includes transportation to the Alhambra and a guided tour of the Palacios Nazaries (tel. 958-535-875, www.visitagranada.com).

5. Easiest of all, simply go at night (Palacios Nazaries only; see "The Alhambra by Moonlight," page 429).

allotted half-hour entry time slot ends. The ticket-checkers at Palacios Nazaries are strict. Remember that if you have an appointment for Palacios Nazaries after 14:00, you can't get into the Alhambra any earlier than 14:00. And, as mentioned earlier, once you're inside the palace, you can stay as long as you want.

To minimize walking, see Charles V's Palace and the Alcazaba fort before your visit to Palacios Nazaries. When you finish touring Palacios Nazaries, you'll leave through the Partal Gardens near the Alhambra entrance, not far from the Generalife Gardens. Depending on your time, you can visit the Generalife Gardens before or after seeing Palacios Nazaries. If you have any time to kill before your palace appointment, you can do it luxuriously on the breezy view terrace of the parador bar (actually within the Alhambra walls). You can find drinks, WCs, and guidebooks near the entrance of Palacios Nazaries, but you'll find none inside the actual palace. If you're going to the Albayzín afterwards, catch bus #32, which goes from the Alhambra back through Plaza Isabel La Católica and then up into the Albayzín.

Audioguide: The €3 audioguide brings the palace to life, providing an hour and 45 minutes of description for 48 stops (rent it at the entrance and at Charles V's Palace; you'll need to return it where you picked it up). Audioguides are not available for night visits.

Guidebooks: Consider getting a guidebook in town and reading it the night before to understand the layout and history of this remarkable sight before entering. The classic is *The Alhambra and the Generalife* (€8, includes great map, sold in town and throughout the Alhambra), but even better is the slick *Alhambra and Generalife in Focus,* which is more readable and has vibrant color photos (€8, sold at many bookstores around town). The one called the "official guide" is not as good.

Eating: The only eateries within the Alhambra walls are the restaurant at the parador and a small bar/café kiosk in front of the Alcazaba fort (near entrance of Palacios Nazaries). But there are plenty of options nearby. Restaurante La Mimbre (below the top bus stop) is probably best for a real meal. You'll find snack vending machines at the entrance and the Charles V Palace (at WCs). You're welcome to bring in a picnic as long as you eat it in a public area.

Photography: Photos without a flash are permitted.

The Alhambra in Four Parts

I've listed these sights in the order you're likely to visit them. Note that there are other sights you can visit for free on the Alhambra grounds (see sidebar).

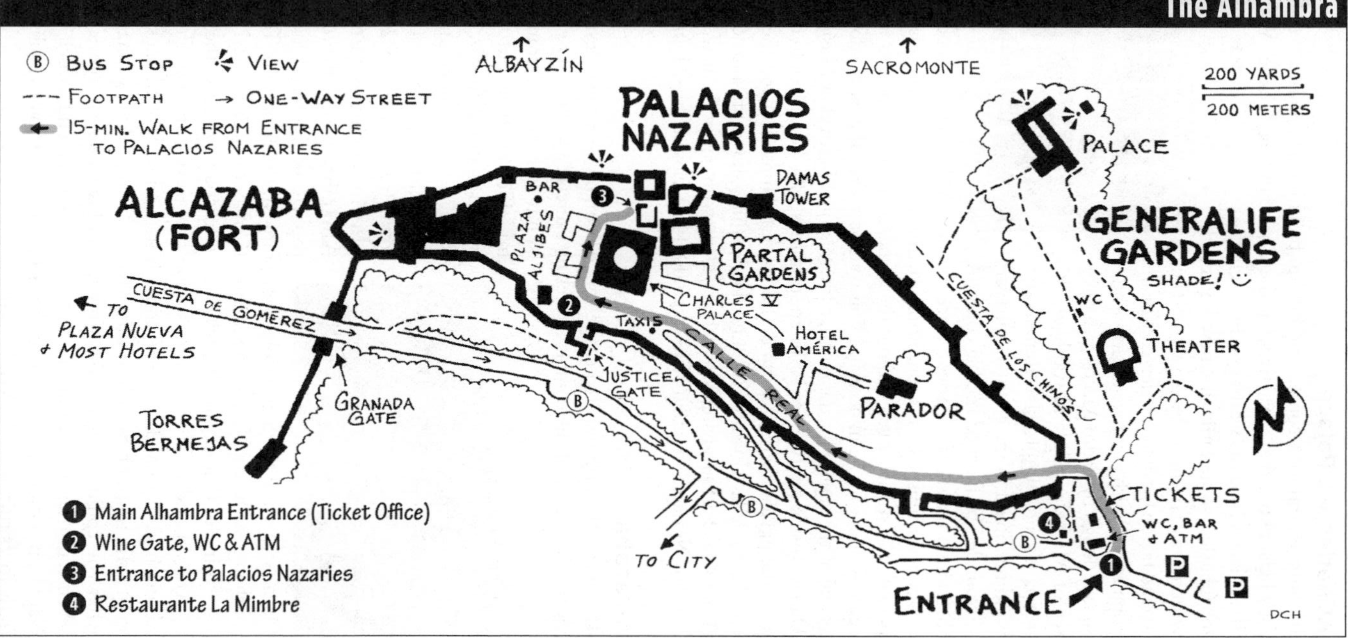
The Alhambra
Bus Stop
View
Footpath
One-Way Street
15-min. Walk from Entrance to Palacios Nazaries
Albayzín
Sacromonte
200 Yards
200 Meters
Palacios Nazaries
Alcazaba (Fort)
Bar
Plaza Aljibes
Damas Tower
Partal Gardens
Charles V Palace
Hotel América
Taxis
Calle Real
Cuesta de Gomérez
To Plaza Nueva & Most Hotels
Justice Gate
Granada Gate
Torres Bermejas
To City
Parador
Cuesta de los Chinos
Palace
Generalife Gardens
Shade! :)
WC
Theater
Tickets
WC, Bar & ATM
Entrance
DCH
1 Main Alhambra Entrance (Ticket Office)
2 Wine Gate, WC & ATM
3 Entrance to Palacios Nazaries
4 Restaurante La Mimbre

▲Charles V's Palace

It's only natural for a conquering king to build his own palace over his foe's palace, and that's exactly what the Christian king Charles V did. The Palacios Nazaries wasn't good enough for Charles, so he built this new home, which was financed by a salt-in-the-wound tax on Granada's defeated Muslim population. With a unique circle within a square design by Pedro Machuca, a devotee of Michelangelo and Raphael, this is Spain's most impressive Renaissance building. Stand in the circular courtyard surrounded by mottled marble columns, then climb the stairs. Charles' palace was designed to have a dome, but it was never finished—his son, Philip II, abandoned it to build his own palace, El Escorial. Even without the dome, acoustics are perfect in the center—stand in the middle and sing your best aria. The palace doubles as one of the venues for the popular International Festival of Music and Dance. Inside are two not-so-interesting museums (both free to enter, as is the palace itself): Museo de Bellas Artes (upstairs) and the better Museo de la Alhambra (ground floor), which shows off some of the Alhambra's best surviving Moorish art, along with one of the lions from Palacios Nazaries' fountain (Tue–Sat 9:00–14:30, closed Sun–Mon).

Alcazaba

This fort—the original "red castle" or "Alhambra"—is the oldest and most ruined part of the complex, offering exercise and fine city views. What you see is from the mid-13th century, but there was probably a fort here in Roman times. Once upon a time, this tower defended a town (or medina) of 2,000 Muslims living within the Alhambra walls. From the top (looking north), find Plaza Nueva and the San Nicolás viewpoint (in the Albayzín). To the south are the Sierra Nevada mountains. Is anybody skiing today?

Think of that day in 1492 when the Christian cross and the flags of Aragon and Castile were raised on this tower, and the fleeing Moorish king Boabdil (Abu Abdullah in Arabic) looked back and wept. His mom chewed him out, saying, "Weep like a woman for what you couldn't defend like a man." With this defeat, more than seven centuries of Muslim rule in Spain came to an end. Much later, Napoleon stationed his troops at the Alhambra, contributing substantially to its ruin when he left.

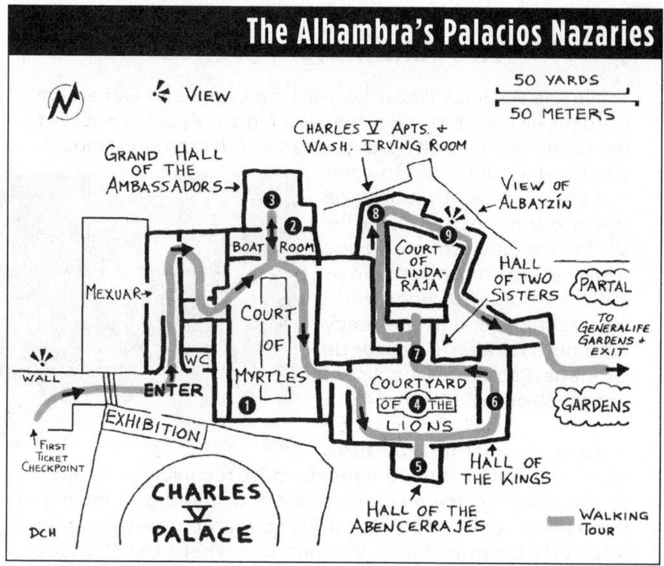

To get to Palacios Nazaries, follow the signs down and around to the entrance. If you're early, duck into the exhibit across from the palace entry. It's in Spanish, but the models of the Alhambra upstairs are easy to appreciate.

▲▲▲Palacios Nazaries

During the 30-minute entry time slot stamped on your ticket, enter the jewel of the Alhambra: the Moorish royal palace. Once you're in, you can relax—there are no more time constraints. You'll walk through three basic sections: royal offices, ceremonial rooms, and private quarters. Built mostly in the 14th century, this palace offers your best possible look at the refined, elegant Moorish civilization of Al-Andalus (Arabic for the Iberian Peninsula).

You'll visit rooms decorated from top to bottom with carved wood ceilings, stucco "stalactites," ceramic tiles, molded-plaster walls, and filigree windows. Open-air courtyards in the palace feature fountains with bubbling water like a desert oasis, the Quran's symbol of heaven. The palace is well-preserved, but the trick is to imagine it furnished and filled with Moorish life...sultans with hookah pipes lounging on pillows upon Persian carpets, tapestries on the walls, heavy curtains on the windows, and ivory-studded wooden furniture. The whole place was painted with bright colors, many suggested by the

The Alhambra Grounds

While the Palacios Nazaries, Alcazaba fort, and Generalife Gardens all have turnstiles, there's a big zone in the middle of the former fortified city that you can wander through (though you need a valid ticket to enter this area). These attractions on the grounds include Charles V's Palace (see listing on page 434); a line of shops showing off traditional woodworking techniques; and the fancy Alhambra parador (Parador de Granada San Francisco, listed under "Sleeping" on page 456).

It's especially fun to snoop around the historic **parador,** which—as a national monument—must technically be open to the public. Once a Moorish palace within the Alhambra, it was later converted into a Franciscan monastery, with a historic claim to fame: Its church is where the Catholic Monarchs (Ferdinand and Isabel) chose to be buried. For a peek, step in through the arch leading to a small garden area and reception. Enter to see the tomb, located in the open-air ruins of the church (just before the reception desk and the guests-only-beyond-this-point sign). The slab on the ground near the altar—a surviving bit from the mosque that was here before the church—marks the place where the greatest king and queen of Spain were buried until 1521 (when they were moved to the Royal Chapel—see page 443). The next room is a delightful former cloister. Renovation plans are currently under way to add a separate restaurant and café for non-guests.

Remember as you wander these grounds that the Alhambra was a fortified city of 2,000 people. This open zone was a medina, a town with a general urban scene. The main road dead-ended at the **Wine Gate** (Puerta del Vino), which protected the fortress. When you pass through the Wine Gate, you enter a courtyard that was originally a moat, then a reservoir (in Christian times). The well—now encased in a bar/kiosk—is still a place for cold drinks. If you're done with your Alhambra visit, you can exit down to the city from the Wine Gate.

Quran—red (blood), blue (heaven), green (oasis), and gold (wealth). And throughout the palace, walls, ceilings, vases, carpets, and tiles were covered with decorative patterns, mostly verses of praise from the Quran written in calligraphy.

As tempting as it might be to touch, stucco is very susceptible to the oils from your hand. If everyone who went through the Alhambra touched a wall, there would be no decoration left for the next generation to treasure.

As you wander, keep the palace themes in mind: water, no images, "stalactite" ceilings—and few signs telling you where you are. Even today, the route constantly changes. Use the map in this chapter to locate the essential stops listed below.

• *Begin by walking through a few administrative rooms (the* mexuar*) with a stunning, Mecca-oriented prayer room and a small courtyard with a round fountain, until you hit the big rectangular courtyard with a fish pond lined by a myrtle-bush hedge.*

❶ Court of Myrtles

Moors loved their patios—with a garden and water, under the sky. Women rarely went out, so they stayed in touch with nature here, in the Court of Myrtles (Patio de los Arrayanes). One exotic theory about the function of this complex is that the living quarters for the women (harem) were upstairs—the Quran let a man have "all the women you can maintain with dignity." Notice the wooden screens (erected by jealous husbands) that allowed the cloistered women to look out without being clearly seen. The less interesting, but more likely, theory is that the upstairs was for winter use, and the cooler ground level was for the hotter summer.

• *Head left from the entry through gigantic wooden doors to the throne room, called the...*

❷ Boat Room

It's understandable that many think the Boat Room (Sala de la Barca) is named for the upside-down-hull shape of its fine cedar ceiling. But the name is actually derived from the Arab word *baraka,* meaning "divine blessing and luck" (which was corrupted to *barca,* similar to the Spanish word for "boat," *barco*). As you passed through this room, blessings and luck are exactly what you'd need—because in the next room, you'd be face-to-face with the sultan.

• *Oh, it's your turn now...*

❸ Grand Hall of the Ambassadors

The palace's largest room, the Gran Salón de los Embajadores, functioned as the throne room. It was here that the sultan, seated on a throne opposite the entrance, received foreign emissaries. Ogle the room—a perfect cube—from top to bottom. The star-studded, domed

Islamic Art

Rather than making paintings and statues, Islamic artists expressed themselves with beautiful but functional objects. Ceramics (often blue and white, or green and white), carpets, glazed tile panels, stucco-work ceilings, and glass tableware are covered with complex patterns. The intricate interweaving, repetition, and unending lines suggest the complex, infinite nature of God, known to Muslims as Allah.

You'll see only a few pictures of humans or animals, since the Islamic religion was wary of any "graven images" or idols forbidden by God. However, secular art by Muslims for their homes and palaces was not bound by this restriction; you'll get an occasional glimpse of realistic art featuring men and women enjoying a garden paradise, a symbol of the Muslim heaven.

Look for floral patterns (twining vines, flowers, and arabesques) and geometric designs (stars and diamonds). The most common pattern is calligraphy—elaborate lettering of an inscription in Arabic, the language of the Quran (and the lettering used even in non-Arabic languages). A quote from the Quran on a vase or lamp combines the power of the message with the beauty of the calligraphy.

ceiling, made of cedar of Lebanon (8,000 inlaid pieces like a giant jigsaw puzzle), suggests the complexity of Allah's infinite universe. Wooden "stalactites" also form the cornice, running around the entire base of the ceiling. The stucco walls, even without their original paint and gilding, are still glorious, decorated with ornamental flowers made by pressing a mold into the wet plaster. The filigree windows once held stained glass and had heavy drapes to block out the heat. Some original 14th-century tiles survive in the center of the floor.

A visitor here would have stepped from the glaring Court of Myrtles into this dim, cool, incense-filled world, to meet the silhouetted sultan. Imagine the alcoves functioning busily as work stations, and the light at sunrise or sunset, rich and warm, filling the room.

Note the finely carved Arabic script. Muslims avoided making images of living creatures—that was God's work. But they could carve decorative religious messages. One phrase—"only Allah is victorious"—is repeated 9,000 times throughout the palace. Find the character for "Allah"—it looks like a cursive W with a nose on its left side. The swoopy toboggan blades underneath are a kind of artistic punctuation setting off one phrase.

In 1492, two historic events likely took place in this room. Culminating a 700-year-long battle, the Reconquista was completed here as the last Moorish king, Boabdil, signed the terms of his surrender before eventually leaving for Africa.

And it was here that Columbus made his pitch to Isabel and Ferdinand to finance a sea voyage to the Orient. Imagine the scene: The king, the queen, and the greatest minds from the University of Salamanca gathered here while Columbus produced maps and pie charts to make his case that he could sail west to reach the East. Ferdinand and the professors laughed and called Columbus mad—not because they thought the world was flat (most educated people knew otherwise), but because they thought Columbus had underestimated the size of the globe, and thus the length and cost of the journey.

But Isabel said *"Sí, señor."* Columbus fell to his knees (promising to pack light, wear a money belt, and use the most current guidebook available), and she gave him an ATM card with a wad of travelers checks as a backup.

Opposite the Boat Room entrance, photographers and tour groups pause for a picture-perfect view of the tower reflected in the Court of Myrtles pool.

• *Continue deeper into the palace, to a court where, 600 years ago, only the royal family and their servants could enter. It's the much-photographed...*

❹ Courtyard of the Lions

The Patio de los Leones features a fountain that's usually ringed with 12 lions; however, they've been missing for the past two years as they undergo restoration (they'll probably be back in place sometime in 2009). One of the lions is on display in the Museo de la Alhambra inside the Charles V Palace.

Why did the fountain have 12 lions? Since the fountain was a gift from a Jewish leader celebrating good relations with the sultan (Granada had a big Jewish community), the lions probably represent the 12 tribes of Israel. During Moorish times, the fountain functioned as a clock, with a different lion spouting water each hour. (Conquering Christians disassembled the fountain to see how it worked, and it's never worked since.) From the center, four streams went out—figuratively to the corners of the earth and literally to various apartments of the royal family. Notice how the court, with its 124 columns, resembles the cloister of a Catholic monastery. The craftsmanship is first-class. For example, the lead fittings between the pre-cut sections of the columns allow things to flex during an earthquake, preventing destruction during shakes.

Six hundred years ago, the Muslim Moors could read the Quranic poetry that ornaments this court, and they could understand the symbolism of this lush, enclosed garden, considered the embodiment of paradise or truth. ("How beautiful is this garden / where the flowers of Earth rival the stars of Heaven. / What can compare with this alabaster fountain, gushing crystal-clear water? / Nothing except the fullest moon, pouring light from an unclouded sky.") Imagine—they appreciated this part of the palace even more than we do today.

• *On the right, off the courtyard, is a square room called the...*

❺ Hall of the Abencerrajes

According to legend, the father of Boabdil took a new wife and wanted to disinherit the children of his first marriage—one of whom was Boabdil. In order to deny power to Boabdil and his siblings, the sultan killed nearly the entire pro-Boabdil Abencerraje family. He thought this would pave the way for the son of his new wife to be the next sultan. He happily stacked 36 Abencerraje heads in the pool under the sumptuous honeycombed stucco ceiling in this hall, called the Sala de los Abencerrajes. But his scheme failed, and Boabdil ultimately assumed the throne. Bloody power struggles like this were the norm here in the Alhambra.

• *At the end of the court opposite where you entered is the...*

❻ Hall of the Kings

Notice the ceilings of the three chambers branching off this gallery, the Hall of the Kings (Sala de los Reyes). Breaking from the tradition of imageless art, paintings on the goat-leather ceiling depict scenes of the sultan and his family. The center room's group portrait shows the first 10 of the Alhambra's 22 sultans. The scene is a fantasy, since these people lived over a span of many generations. The two end rooms display scenes of princely pastimes, such as hunting and shooting skeet. In a palace otherwise devoid of figures, these offer a rare look at royal life in the palace.

• *The next room is the...*

❼ Hall of Two Sisters

The Sala de Dos Hermanas has another oh-wow stucco ceiling lit from below by clerestory windows. The room features geometric patterns and stylized Arabic script quoting verses from the Quran, but no figures. If the inlaid color tiles look "Escher-esque," you've got it backwards: Escher is Alhambra-esque. M. C. Escher was inspired by these very patterns on his visit. Study the patterns—they remind us of the Moorish expertise in math.

• *That's about it for the palace. From here, you wander past the star-domed roofs of the old baths down a hallway to a pair of rooms decorated with a mahogany ceiling. Marked with a large plaque is the...*

❽ Washington Irving Room

This is where Washington Irving wrote *Tales of the Alhambra*. While living in Spain in 1829, Irving stayed in the Alhambra. It was a romantic time, when the palace was home to Gypsies and donkeys. His "tales" kindled interest in the Alhambra, causing it to become recognized as a national treasure. A plaque on the wall thanks Irving, who later served as the US ambassador to Spain (1842–1846). Here's a quote from Irving's "The Alhambra by Moonlight": "On such heavenly nights I would sit for hours at my window inhaling the sweetness of the garden, and musing on the checkered fortunes of those whose history was dimly shadowed out in the elegant memorials around."

• *As you leave, stop at the open-air...*

❾ Hallway with a View

Here you'll enjoy the best-in-the-palace view of the labyrinthine Albayzín—the old Moorish town on the opposite hillside. Find the famous San Nicolás viewpoint (below where the white San Nicolás church tower breaks the horizon). Creeping into the mountains on the right are the Roma (Gypsy) neighborhoods of Sacromonte. Still circling old Granada is the Moorish wall (built in the 1400s to protect the city's population, swollen by Muslim refugees driven south by the Reconquista). For more on Albayzín sights, see page 450.

• *As you leave the Palacios Nazaries, play with the acoustics in the "Secrets Room," located in the brickwork baths (whisper into a corner and your friend—with an ear to the wall—hears you in the opposite corner). Then look for signs to* El Partal *(where you can enjoy the reflecting pond of the Partal Palace), climb a few stairs, continue through the gardens, and follow signs directing you left to the Generalife Gardens or right to the exit. If you're interested in poking around the Alhambra grounds (see sidebar on page 436), exit and do it now before entering the Generalife (because you can't easily backtrack into the Alhambra grounds after leaving the gardens).*

▲Generalife Gardens

If you have a long wait before your entry to the Palacios Nazaries, tour these gardens first, then the Alcazaba fort and Charles V's Palace.

The sultan's vegetable and fruit garden and summer palace, called the Generalife (hen-eh-raw-LEEF-ay), are a short hike uphill past the ticket office. The 2,000 residents of the Alhambra enjoyed the fresh fruit and veggies grown here. But most importantly, the sultan enjoyed a quiet and handy escape from things in the summer: his Generalife Palace.

Walk through the sprawling gardens (planted only in the 1930s—in Moorish times, there were no cypress trees here). The sleek, modern amphitheater has been recently renovated and continues to be an important concert venue for Granada. It sees most activity during the International Festival of Music and Dance (see page 425). Many of the world's greatest artists have performed here, including Arthur Rubenstein, Rudolf Nureyev, and Margot Fonteyn. At the small palace, pass through the dismounting room (imagine dismounting onto the helpful stone ledge, and letting your horse drink in the trough here). Step past the guarded entry into the most perfect Arabian garden in Andalucía.

This summer home of the Moorish kings, the closest thing on earth to the Quran's description of heaven, was planted more than 600 years ago—remarkable longevity for a European garden. Five-hundred-year-old paintings show it looking essentially the same as it does today. The flowers, herbs, aromas, and water are exquisite... even for a sultan. Up the Darro River, the royal aqueduct diverted a life-giving stream of water into the Alhambra. It was channeled through this extra-long, decorative fountain to irrigate the bigger garden outside, then along an aqueduct into the Alhambra for its 2,000 thirsty residents.

At the end of the pond, you enter the sultan's tiny, three-room summer palace. From the end, climb 10 steps into the Christian Renaissance gardens. The ancient, decrepit tree rising over the pond inspired Washington Irving, who wrote that this must be the "only surviving witness to the wonders of that age of Al-Andalus."

Exiting left to the top floor of the palace reveals a stunning view of the Albayzín. Don't climb the *Escalera del Agua* unless you need the exercise...it only goes up and then back down. Pass the turnstile (pausing for a view back down into the palace garden) and follow *salida* (exit) signs as you circle back to where you entered the Generalife.

Your visit to the Alhambra is complete, and you've earned your reward. "Surely Allah will make those who believe and do good deeds enter gardens beneath which rivers flow; they shall be adorned therein with bracelets of gold and pearls, and their garments therein shall be of silk" (Quran 22.23).

SIGHTS

In Central Granada

These sights are within a short walk of each other, in downtown Granada.

Plaza Nueva and Nearby

Plaza Nueva—Along the main square of the city, Plaza Nueva is dominated by the Palace of Justice, hippies, Roma (Gypsies), and a Moroccan ambience. The fountain is capped by a stylized pomegranate—the symbol of the city, always open and fertile. The main action here is the comings and goings of the busy little shuttle buses serving the Alhambra and Albayzín. The local hippie community, nicknamed the *pies negros* (black feet) for obvious reasons, hangs out here and on Calle Elvira. They squat in abandoned caves above those the Roma occupy in Sacromonte. Many are the children of rich Spanish families from the north, hell-bent on disappointing their high-achieving parents.

Plaza Isabel La Católica—Granada's two grand boulevards, Gran Vía and Calle Reyes Católicos, meet a block off Plaza Nueva at Plaza Isabel La Católica. Above the fountain, a fine statue shows Columbus unfurling a long contract with Isabel. It lists the terms of Columbus' MCDXCII voyage: ("Forasmuch as you, Columbus, are going by our command to discover and subdue some Islands and Continents in the ocean....")

Isabel was driven by her desire to spread Catholicism. Columbus was driven by his desire for money. As a reward for adding territory to Spain's Catholic empire, Isabel promised Columbus the ranks of Admiral of the Oceans and Governor of the New World. To sweeten the pie, she tossed in one-eighth of all the riches he brought home. Isabel died thinking that Columbus had found India or China. Columbus died poor and disillusioned.

Calle Reyes Católicos leads from this square to the busy intersection of Puerta Real. From there, Acera del Darro takes you through modern Granada to the river via the huge El Corte Inglés department store and lots of modern commerce. This area erupts with locals out strolling each night. For the best Granada paseo, be here around 19:00.

▲▲Royal Chapel (Capilla Real)

Without a doubt Granada's top Christian sight, this lavish chapel holds the dreams—and bodies—of Queen Isabel and King Ferdinand.

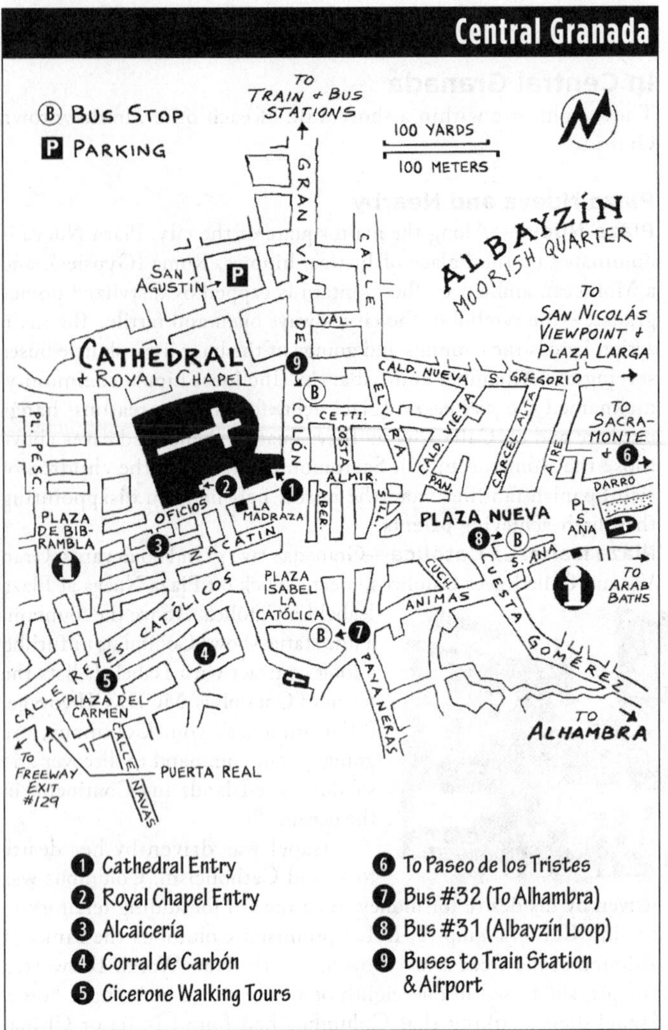

The "Catholic Monarchs" were all about the Reconquista. Their marriage united the Aragon and Castile kingdoms, allowing an acceleration of the Christian and Spanish push south. In its last 10 years, the Reconquista snowballed. This last Moorish capital—symbolic of their victory—was their chosen burial place.

Cost, Hours, Location: €3.50; April–Oct Mon–Sat 10:30–13:00 & 16:00–19:00, opens Sun at 11:00; Nov–March Mon–Sat 10:30–13:00 & 15:30–18:30, opens Sun at 11:00; no photos; entrance on Calle Oficios, just off Gran Vía—go through iron gate; tel. 958-227-848.

➲ **Self-Guided Tour:** In the lobby, before you enter the chapel, notice the **painting of Boabdil** (on the black horse) giving the key of Granada to the conquering King Ferdinand. Boabdil wanted to fall to his knees, but the Spanish king, who had great respect for his Moorish foe, embraced him instead. They fought a long and noble war (for instance, respectfully returning the bodies of dead soldiers). Ferdinand is in red, and Isabel is behind him wearing a crown. The painting is flanked by two large portraits of Ferdinand and Isabel. Two small permanent exhibits behind glass celebrate the 500th anniversaries of Isabel's death in 2005 and Philip the Fair's in 2006.

Isabel decided to make Granada the capital of Spain (and burial place for Spanish royalty) for three reasons: 1) With the conquest of this city, Christianity had finally overcome Islam in Europe; 2) her marriage with Ferdinand, followed by the conquest of Granada, had marked the beginning of a united Spain; and 3) in Granada, she agreed to sponsor Columbus.

Step into the **chapel.** It's Plateresque Gothic—light and lacy silver-filigree style, named for and inspired by the fine silverwork of the Moors. Five hundred years ago, this was the most lavish interior money could buy. Ferdinand and Isabel spent a fourth of their wealth on it. Because of its speedy completion (1506–1521), the architecture is unusually harmonious.

The **four royal tombs** are Renaissance-style. Carved in Italy in 1521 out of Carrara marble, they were sent by ship to Spain. The faces—based on death masks—are considered accurate. If you're looking at the altar, **Ferdinand** and **Isabel** are on the right. (Isabel fans attribute the bigger dent she puts in the pillow to her larger brain.) Isabel's contemporaries described the queen as being of medium height, with auburn hair and blue eyes, and possessing a serious, modest, and gentle personality. (Compare Ferdinand and Isabel's tomb statues with the painted and gilded wood statues of them kneeling in prayer, flanking the altarpiece.)

Philip the Fair and **Juana the Mad** (who succeeded Ferdinand and Isabel) lie on the left. Philip was so "Fair" that it drove the insanely jealous Juana "Mad." Philip died young, and for two years Juana kept his casket at her bedside, kissing his embalmed body good night. Philip and Juana's son, Charles V (known as Carlos I in Spain), was a key figure in European history, as his coronation merged the Holy Roman Empire (Philip the Fair's Habsburg domain) with Juana's Spanish empire. Europe's top king, Charles V ruled a vast empire stretching from Holland to Sicily, from Bohemia to Bolivia (1519–1556, see sight listing for his palace within the Alhambra, page 434).

When Philip II, the son of Charles V, decided to build El Escorial and establish Madrid as the single capital of a single Spain, Granada lost power and importance. More importantly, Spain began to decline. After the reign of Charles V, Spain squandered her awesome wealth trying to maintain this impossibly huge empire. The country's rulers did it not only for material riches, but to defend the romantic, quixotic dream of a Catholic empire—ruled by one divinely ordained Catholic monarch—against an irrepressible tide of nationalism and Protestantism that was sweeping across the vast Habsburg holdings in Central and Eastern Europe. Spain's relatively poor modern history can be blamed, in part, on its people's stubborn unwillingness to accept the end of this old-regime notion. Even Franco borrowed symbols from the Catholic Monarchs to legitimize his dictatorship and keep the 500-year-old legacy alive. Today's Spaniards reflect on how an expansion through marriage sucked their country into centuries of European squabbling, eventually impoverishing it.

Look at the fine carving on the tombs (unfortunately vandalized by Napoleon's troops). It's a humanistic statement, with these healthy, organic, realistic figures rising out of the Gothic age.

From the feet of the marble tombs, step downstairs to see the actual **coffins.** They are plain. Ferdinand and Isabel were originally buried in the Franciscan monastery (in what is today the parador up at the Alhambra). You're standing in front of the two people who created Spain. The fifth coffin (on right, marked *PM*) belongs to a young Prince Michael, who would have been king of a united Spain and Portugal. (A sad—but too long—story...)

The **high altar** is one of the finest Renaissance works in Spain. It's dedicated to two Johns: the Baptist and the Evangelist. In the center, you can see the Baptist and the Evangelist chatting as if over tapas—an appropriately humanistic scene. Scenes from the Baptist's life are on the left: John beheaded after Salomé's fine dancing, and (below) John baptizing Jesus. Scenes from the Evangelist's life are on the right: John's martyrdom (a failed attempt to boil him alive in oil), and John on Patmos (where he wrote the last book of the Bible, Revelation). John is talking to the eagle that flew him to heaven, according to tradition.

A finely carved Plateresque arch, with the royal initials "F" and "Y," leads to a small glass pyramid in the **treasury.** This holds Queen Isabel's silver crown ringed with pomegranates (symbolizing Granada), her scepter, and King Ferdinand's sword. Beside the entry arch you'll see the devout Isabel's prayer book, in which she followed the Mass. The book and its sturdy box date from 1496. The fancy box on the other side of the door is supposedly the one that Isabel (cash-poor because of her military expenses) filled with jewels and gave to Columbus. Columbus sold these to finance his journey. In the corner (and also behind glass) is the cross that Cardinal Mendoza, staunch supporter of Queen Isabel, carried into the Alhambra on that historic day in 1492. Next, the big, silk, silver-and-gold tapestry is the altar banner for the mobile campaign chapel of Ferdinand and Isabel, who always traveled with their army. In the next case, you'll see the original Christian army flags raised over the Alhambra in 1492.

The room holds the first great art collection ever established by a woman. Queen Isabel amassed more than 200 important paintings. After Napoleon's visit, only 30 remained. Even so, this is a fine collection, all on wood, featuring works by Sandro Botticelli, Pietro Perugino, the Flemish master Hans Memling, and some less-famous Spanish masters.

Finally, at the end of the room, the two carved sculptures of Ferdinand and Isabel were the originals from the high altar. Charles V considered these primitive and replaced them with the ones you saw earlier.

To reach the cathedral (described next), exit behind Isabel, out through one iron gate and then immediately through the neighboring iron gate.

Cathedral

One of only two Renaissance churches in Spain (the other is in Córdoba), Granada's cathedral is the second-largest in Spain after Sevilla's.

Cost, Hours, Location: €3.50; April–Oct Mon–Sat 10:45–13:30 & 16:00–20:00, Sun 16:00–20:00; Nov–March Mon–Sat 10:45–13:30 & 16:00–19:00, Sun 16:00–19:00; 45-min audioguide-€3, entrance off Gran Vía through iron gateway, tel. 958-222-959.

➲ Self-Guided Tour: You'll start your visit (step right) in the priests' wardrobe room. Lush and wide-open, the gilded ceilings, mirrors, and wooden cabinets give this room a light, airy feel. Two grandfather clocks made in London (one with Asian motifs) ensured that everyone got dressed on time.

Wandering out, you'll be behind the main altar. A fine series of paintings by Granada's own Alonso Cano (1601–1667), moved from niches high above, now encircle the back of the altar. Their distortion was intentional, since the paintings were designed to look natural when viewed from floor level. As you walk around the pews and gigantic Baroque organs, you'll see the cathedral at its most beautiful.

The cathedral's cool, spacious, bright interior is a refreshing break from the dark Gothic of so many Spanish churches. In a modern move back in the 18th century, the choir walls were taken out so that people could be involved in the worship. At about the same time, a bishop ordered the interior painted with lime (for hygienic reasons, during a time of disease). The people liked it, and it stayed white. As you explore, remember that the abundance of Marys is all part of the Counter-Reformation. Most of the side chapels are decorated in Baroque style. To the right of the high altar is a politically incorrect version of St. James the Moor-Slayer, with his sword raised high and an armored Moor under his horse's hooves. Nearby are gigantic wooden doors that would lead to the Royal Chapel if there weren't a separate entrance fee.

The semicircular main altar is breathtaking and maintains the theme of light and bright. Wander back through the pews toward the cathedral's main doors. A small sacristy museum is tucked away in the right corner (as you face the doors). There may be no detailed descriptions for any of the items, but a beautiful bust of St. Peter (with a flowing beard) by Alonso Cano is worth seeking out. Also on display is the confusing accounting book for the cathedral's construction. As you head out, look for the music sheets behind the main altar; they're mostly 16th-century Gregorian chants. Notice the sliding C clef. Rather than a fixed G or F clef, the monks knew that this clef—which could be located wherever worked best on the staff—marked middle C, and they chanted to notes relative to that. Go ahead—try singing a few verses of the Latin.

Near the Cathedral

Alcaicería—Originally a Moorish silk market with seven gates and 200 shops, the Alcaicería (al-kai-thay-REE-ah) neighborhood around the cathedral still functions as a silk and jewelry market. Silk was a huge industry in Moorish times (silkworm-friendly mulberry trees flourished in the countryside), a product so important that the sultans controlled and guarded it by constructing this fine market. After the Reconquista, the Christians didn't mess with it. But a terrible fire in 1850 destroyed the place. Today's Alcaicería was rebuilt in the late 1800s as a tourist souvenir souk (marketplace) to complement the romantic image of Granada created by the writings of Washington Irving.

Explore the mesh of tiny shopping lanes between the cathedral and Calle Reyes Católicos. Go on a photo and sound safari: popcorn machines popping, men selling balloons, leather goods spread out on streets, kids playing soccer, barking dogs, dogged shoeshine boys, and the whirring grind of bicycle-powered knife sharpeners.

Corral del Carbón—A caravanserai (of silk road fame) is a protected place for merchants to rest their camels, spend the night, get a bite to eat, and spin yarns. The only surviving caravanserai of Granada's original 14 is, logically, just a block away from the silk market. This plain-yet-elegant structure (free, across Calle Reyes Católicos from Alcaicería) is evocative of times when traders would gather here with exotic goods and tales from across Arabia. After the Reconquista, it was a coal storage facility (hence the name "Carbón"). Notice the fine

Moorish door. These days it houses two offices where you can buy tickets for musical events.

Plaza de Bib-Rambla—The exuberant square two blocks behind the cathedral is Plaza de Bib-Rambla. While today it's fine for coffee or a meal amidst the color and fragrance of flower stalls and a Neptune-topped fountain, in Moorish times this was a place of public execution. It remains a multi-generational hang-out where, it seems, everyone is enjoying a peaceful retirement. A block away, the square Pescadería is a smaller, similarly lively version of Bib-Rambla.

Paseo de los Tristes

In the cool of the early evening, consider strolling the street called Paseo de los Tristes, which runs east from Plaza Nueva high above the Darro River. (If you're tired, note that minibuses #31 and #32 stop here.) This "Walk of the Sad Ones" was once the route of funeral processions to the cemetery at the edge of town.

➲ **Self-Guided Walk:** Start at Plaza Nueva. Walk up past the Church of Santa Ana, at the far end of the square. This was originally a mosque—the church tower replaced a minaret. Notice the ceramic brickwork. This is Mudejar art, a technique of Moorish craftsmen later employed by Christians. Inside you'll see a fine Alhambra-style cedar ceiling.

Follow Carrera del Darro high above the River Darro at the base of the Alhambra (look down by the river for a glimpse of feral cats). Six miles upstream, part of the Darro is diverted to provide water for the Alhambra's many fountains. Past the church on your right is the turn-off bridge for the Hammam Baños Árabes (Arab baths, described below). On the left is Santa Catalina de Zafra, a convent of cloistered nuns (they worship behind a screen that divides the church's rich interior in half).

Farther ahead is the broken nub of a once-grand 11th-century bridge over the river, leading to the Alhambra. Notice two slits in the column: One held an iron portcullis to keep bad guys from entering the town via the river. The second held a solid door that was lowered to build up water, then released to flush out the riverbed and keep it clean. Across from the remains of the bridge (and the stop for minibuses #31 and #34) is the evocative brick facade of a Moorish bath, the Hammam El Bañuelo (described below).

Continuing straight ahead, you see the Church of San Pedro, the parish church of Sacromonte's Roma (Gypsy) community (across from the Archaeological Museum). Within its rich interior is an ornate oxcart used to carry the Host on the annual pilgrimage to Rocio near the Portuguese border.

Finally, you reach the end of Paseo de los Tristes, with restaurant tables spilling out under the floodlit Alhambra. From here, the road arcs up into Sacromonte. Also from here, a lane (called Cuesta de los Chinos or Carretera del Rey Chico) leads up to the Alhambra "through the back door."

Baths Along the Paseo de los Tristes

Hammam El Bañuelo (Moorish Baths)—In Moorish times, hammams (public baths) were a big part of the community (private homes didn't have bathrooms). Baths were strictly segregated (as they are today) and functioned as more than a place to wash: Business was done here, and it was a social meeting point. In Christian times, it was assumed that conspiracies brewed in these baths—therefore, few of them survive. This place gives you the chance to explore the stark but evocative ruins of an 11th-century Moorish public bath.

Entering the baths, you pass the house of the keeper and the foyer into the cold room, the warm room (where services like massage were offered), and finally the hot or steam room (where you wore special shoes to protect your feet from the heat). Beyond that, you can see the oven that generated the heat, which flowed under the hypocaust-style floor tiles (getting less hot with distance). The romantic little holes in the ceiling once had glass louvers, which attendants opened and closed with sticks to regulate the heat and steaminess. People weren't totally immersed, but instead, they scooped and splashed water over themselves (free, Tue–Sat 10:00–14:00, closed Sun–Mon, along the Paseo de los Tristes—see above, at first bus stop and big broken bridge—two bridges upstream from Plaza Nueva on Carrera del Darro).

Hammam Baños Árabes (Arab Baths)—For an intimate and subdued experience, consider a visit to these Arab baths. A maximum of 16 people are allowed in the baths at one time. The 90-minute soak and a 15-minute massage cost €26; for a 90-minute bath only, it's €17 (daily 10:00–24:00, appointment times scheduled every even-numbered hour, coed with mandatory swimsuits, quiet atmosphere encouraged, free lockers and towels available, just off Plaza Nueva at Santa Ana 16; from Plaza Nueva, it's the first right, over a bridge and past the church; 50 percent paid reservation necessary—credit card OK, occasional discounts if you reserve online, tel. 958-229-978, www.hammamspain.com/granada).

The Albayzín

Explore Spain's best old Moorish quarter, with countless colorful corners, flowery patios, and shady lanes. Climb high to the San Nicolás church for the best view of the Alhambra. Then wander through the mysterious backstreets. (I've listed these sights roughly in order from the San Nicolás viewpoint.) Warning: Thefts have increased after dark in the Albayzín; take the bus or a taxi back to your hotel if you linger here for a late-night dinner.

Getting to the Albayzín: A handy city **minibus** threads its way around the Albayzín from Plaza Nueva (see "Albayzín Circular Bus Tour," next), getting you scenically and sweatlessly to the San Nicolás viewpoint. You can also **taxi** to the San Nicolás church and explore from there. Consider having your cabbie take you on a Sacromonte detour en route.

To **walk** up, leave the west end of Plaza Nueva on Calle Elvira. After about 200 yards, bear right on Calle Caldereria Nueva. Follow this stepped street past Moroccan eateries and pastry shops, vendors of imported North African goods, *halal* butchers, and *teterías* (Moorish tea rooms). The lane bears right, then passes to the left of the church (now becoming San Gregorio), and slants, winds, and zigzags uphill. San Gregorio eventually curves left and is regularly signposted. When you reach the Moorish-style house, La Media Luna, stop for a photo and a breather, then follow the wall, continuing uphill. At the next intersection, turn right on Aljibe del Gato. Farther on, this street takes a 90-degree turn to the left, becoming Calle Atarasana Vieja. It's confusing, but keep going up, up, up. At the crest, turn right on Camino Nuevo de San Nicolás, then walk 300 yards to the street that curves up left (look for a bus stop sign—this is where the minibus would have dropped you off). Continue up the curve and soon you'll see feet hanging from the plaza wall. Steps lead up to the church's viewpoint. Whew! You made it!

Albayzín Circular Bus Tour—The handy Albayzín minibus #31 gallops the 15-minute loop as if in a race, departing from Plaza Nueva about every 15 minutes (pay driver €1, minibus #32 does the same loop but—depending on where you catch it—goes to the Alhambra first). While good for a lift to the top of the Albayzín (buzz when you want to get off), I'd stay on for an entire circle and return to the Albayzín later for dinner—either on foot or by bus again.

Here's the route: You'll go along up above the Darro River, past the ruins of a bridge and gate and the Paseo de los Tristes square (see page 449). Turning uphill, you pass Sacromonte on the right (entrance to the neighborhood marked by a statue of a popular Roma guide). Then, turning left, you enter the actual Albayzín. After stopping at the church of San Salvador, you plunge into the thick of it, with stops below the San Nicolás church (famous viewpoint, and the jumping-off point for my suggested "Exploring the Albayzín" stroll—described later in this section) and at Plaza San Miguel Bajo (cute square with recommended eateries and another viewpoint). Then you descend, enjoying a commanding view of Granada on the left as you swing through the modern city. Hitting the city's main drag, Gran Vía, you make a U-turn at the Garden of the Triumph, celebrating the Immaculate Conception of the Virgin Mary (notice her statue atop a column). Behind Mary stands the old Royal Hospital—built in the 16th century for Granada's poor by the Catholic kings after the Reconquista, in hopes of winning the favor of the city's conquered residents. From here, you zip past the cathedral and back home to Plaza Nueva.

▲▲San Nicolás Viewpoint (Mirador de San Nicolás)—For one of Europe's most romantic viewpoints, be here at sunset, when the Alhambra glows red and the Albayzín widows share the benches with local lovers, hippies, and tourists (free, always open). In 1997, President Clinton made a point to bring his family here—a favorite spot from a trip he made as a student. For a drink with the same view, step into the El Huerto de Juan Ranas Bar (just below and to the left, at Calle de Atarazana 8).

Great Mosque of Granada—A striking and inviting mosque is just next to the San Nicolás viewpoint (to your left as you face the Alhambra). Local Muslims write, "The Great Mosque of Granada signals, after a hiatus of 500 years, the restoration of a missing link with a rich and fecund Islamic contribution to all spheres of human enterprise and activity." Built in 2003 (with money from the local community and Islamic Arab nations), it has a peaceful view courtyard and a minaret that comes with a live call to prayer five times a day (printed schedule inside). It's stirring to see the muezzin holler "God is Great" from the minaret without amplification (two possible explanations: Muslims wanted it to be authentic, as in the old days; or locals didn't want it amplified). Visitors are welcome in the courtyard, which offers Alhambra views without the hedonistic ambience of the more famous San Nicolás viewpoint (free, daily 11:00–14:00 & 18:00–21:00).

While tourists come to Granada to learn about the expulsion of the Moors in 1492, local Muslims are frustrated by the "errors, nonsense, and lies local guides perpetuate without knowledge nor shame which flocks of passive tourists accept without questioning." A flier at the mosque tries to set the record straight, from the Muslim perspective: Muslims were not foreign invaders of Spain—the Muslims of Granada and Andalucía were as Iberian as the modern Spaniards of today. Islam is not a religion of immigrants. Islam is not a culture of the Orient and Arabs. Muslims and Arabs are different. The Muslims of Al-Andalus were not hedonistic. The Reconquista did not liberate Spain. Harems were not just full of sexy women. (For more on the

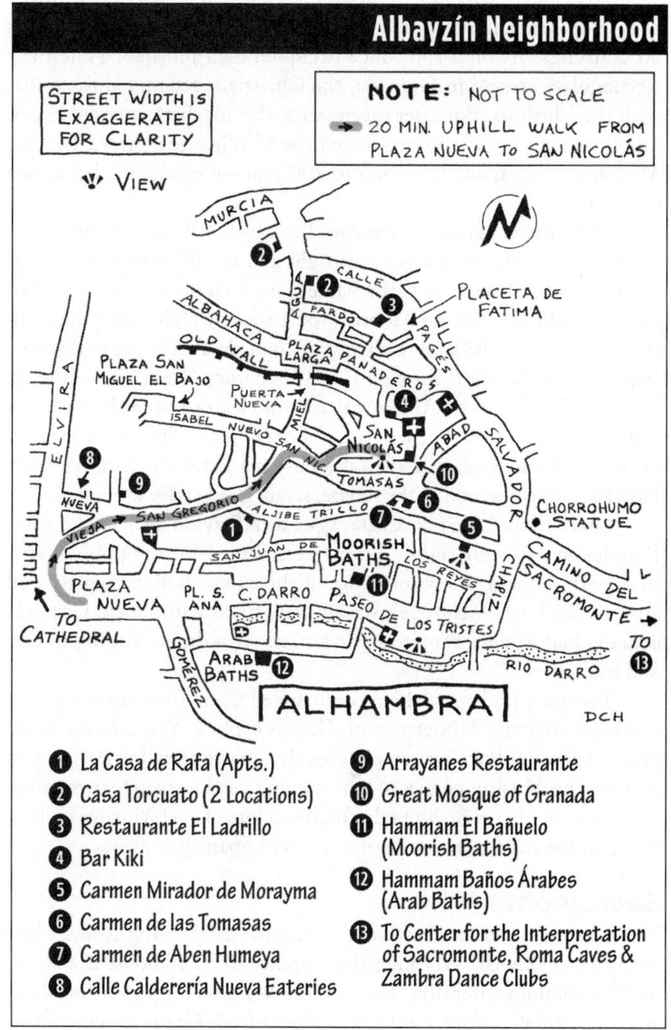

Muslim perspective, visit the info desk at the mosque.)

The European Union sees Granada as a center for Muslim-Christian integration. The city hosts the headquarters of several organizations designed to help the communities live peacefully together. To Muslims, the city is a symbol of the "holocaust" of the Reconquista, when 135,000 of their people were brutally expelled and many more suffered "forced conversion" in the 16th century. Today there are about 700,000 Muslims in Spain (and about 5 million in France).

Exploring the Albayzín—From the San Nicolás viewpoint and the Great Mosque, you're at the edge of a hilltop neighborhood even the people of Granada recognize as a world apart. Each of the district's 20 churches sits on a spot once occupied by a mosque. When the Reconquista arrived in Granada, the Christians attempted to coexist with the Muslims. But after seven years, this idealistic attempt ended in failure, and the Christians forced the Muslims to convert. In 1567, Muslims were expelled, leading to 200 years of economic depression for the city.

From the viewpoint, turn your back to the Alhambra and walk north (passing the church on your right and the Biblioteca Municipal on your left). A lane leads past a white stone arch (on your right)—now a chapel built into the old Moorish wall. You're walking past the scant remains of the pre-Alhambra fortress of Granada. At the end of the lane, step down to the right through the 11th-century "New Gate" (Puerta Nueva—older than the Alhambra) and into **Plaza Larga.** In medieval times, this tiny square (called "long," because back then it was) served as the local marketplace. It still is a busy market each morning. Casa Pasteles, at the near end of the square, serves good coffee and cakes.

Leave Plaza Larga on **Calle Agua de Albayzín** (as you face Casa Pasteles, it's to your right). The street, named for the public baths that used to line it, shows evidence of the Moorish plumbing system: gutters. Back when Europe's streets were filled with muck, Granada actually had Roman Empire–style gutters with drains leading to clay and lead pipes.

This road leads past the recommended Casa Torcuato restaurant (see page 461) to a T-intersection. Or just explore. You're in the heart of the Albayzín. Poke into an old church. They're plain by design to go easy on the Muslim converts, who weren't used to being surrounded by images as they worshipped. You'll see lots of real Muslim culture living in the streets, including many recent Spanish converts.

Sacromonte

The Sacromonte district is home to Granada's thriving Roma community (see sidebar). Marking the entrance to Sacromonte is a statue of Chorrohumo (literally, "Exudes Smoke," and a play on the slang word for "thief"...*chorro*). He was a Roma from Granada, popular in the 1950s for guiding people around the city.

Sacromonte has one main street: Camino del Sacromonte is lined with caves primed for tourists and restaurants ready to fight over the bill. (Don't come here expecting to get a deal on anything.) Intriguing lanes run above and below this main drag.

Zambra Dance—A long flamenco tradition exists in Granada. Sacromonte is a good place to see *zambra*, a flamenco variation with a more Oriental feel in which the singer also dances. Two popular—or at least well-established—*zambra* venues are Zambra Cueva del Rocio (€25, includes a drink and a bus ride from hotel, €20 without transport, show at 22:00, 60 min, Camino del Sacromonte 70, tel. 958-227-129)

Granada's Roma (Gypsies)

Both the English word "Gypsy" and its Spanish counterpart, *gitano,* come from the word "Egypt"—where Europeans used to mistakenly believe these nomadic people originated. Today, the preferred term is "Roma," since the term "Gypsy" has acquired negative connotations (I've used both names throughout this book).

After migrating from India in the 14th century, the Roma people settled mostly in the Muslim-occupied lands in the south (such as the Balkan Peninsula, then controlled by the Ottoman Turks). Under the Muslims, the Roma enjoyed relative tolerance. They were traditionally good with crafts and animals.

The first Roma arrived in Granada in the 15th century—and they've remained tight-knit ever since. Today 50,000 Roma call Granada home, many of them in the district called Sacromonte. In most of Spain, Roma are more assimilated into the general population, but Sacromonte is a large, distinct Roma community. (After the difficult Civil War era, they were joined by many farmers who, like the Roma, appreciated Sacromonte's affordable, practical cave dwellings—warm in the winter and cool in the summer.)

Spaniards, who consider themselves accepting and not racist, claim that in maintaining such a tight community, the Roma segregate themselves. The Roma call Spaniards *payos* ("whites"). Recent mixing of Roma and *payos* has given birth to the term *gallipavo* (rooster-duck), although who's who depends upon whom you ask.

Are Roma thieves? Sure, some of them are. But others are honest citizens, trying to make their way in the world just like anyone else. It's wise to be cautious when dealing with a Roma person—but it's also important to keep an open mind.

and María la Canastera (€25, includes a drink and transportation from hotel, €17 without transport, daily show at 22:00, Camino del Sacromonte 89, tel. 958-121-183). I'd just go and explore late at night (with no wallet and €30 in my pocket) rather than booking an evening through my hotel (they'll likely offer to reserve for you).

Center for the Interpretation of Sacromonte (Centro de Interpretación del Sacromonte)—This facility is a kind of Roma open-air folk museum, offering an insight into Sacromonte's geology and environment, cave building, and Roma crafts, food, and musical traditions (with English explanations). There are also great views over Granada and the Alhambra. As you wander, imagine this in the 1950s, when it was still a bustling community of Roma cave-dwellers. Today, hippies squat in abandoned caves higher up. The center also features €12 flamenco shows and classical guitar concerts in its wonderfully scenic

setting (details at TI), 300 yards up the steep hill from the Venta El Gallo restaurant on the main Sacromonte lane (€5; April–Oct Tue–Sun 10:00–14:00 & 17:00–21:00, Nov–March Tue–Sun 10:00–14:00 & 16:00–19:00, closed Mon; Barranco de los Negros, tel. 958-215-120, www.sacromontegranada.com). The closest a taxi can get you is the Venta El Gallo restaurant. From there, you climb on foot, following the signs.

Near Granada

Carthusian Monastery (La Cartuja)—A church with an interior that looks as if it squirted out of a can of whipped cream, La Cartuja is nicknamed the "Christian Alhambra" for its elaborate white Baroque stucco work. In the rooms just off the cloister, notice the gruesome paintings of martyrs placidly meeting their grisly fates (€3.50, daily April–Oct 10:00–13:00 & 16:00–20:00, Nov–March 10:00–13:00 & 15:00–18:00, tel. 958-161-932). It's a mile north of town on the way to Madrid. Drive north on Gran Vía de Colón and follow the signs, or take bus #8 from Gran Vía.

SLEEPING

In July and August, when Granada's streets are littered with sunstroke victims, rooms are plentiful. Crowded months are April, May, June, September, and October. Except for the hotels in the Albayzín and near the Alhambra, most of my listings are within a five-minute walk of Plaza Nueva (see map on page 458).

Given all the restrictions, it is difficult to drive into Granada even when you know the system (see "Arrival in Granada," page 422). While few of the hotels have parking facilities, any of them can direct you to a garage (such as Parking San Agustín, just off Gran Vía, €20/day).

On or near Plaza Nueva

Each of these is big, professional, plenty comfortable, and perfectly located. Prices vary with the demand.

$$$ Hotel Inglaterra is a modern and peaceful chain hotel, with 36 rooms offering all the comforts (Sb/Db-€77–155, extra bed-€27–61, buffet breakfast-€12, air-con, elevator to third floor only, 20 parking spaces at €13/day, Cetti Merien 6, tel. 958-221-559, fax 958-227-100, www.nh-hotels.com, nhinglaterra@nh-hotels.com).

$$$ Hotel Maciá Gran Vía, right on Granada's main drag, has a stately lobby with 85 Euro-modern, business-class rooms (Sb-€75, Db-€116, Tb-€142, show this book for a 10 percent discount in 2009,

Sleep Code

(€1 = about $1.50, country code: 34)
S = Single, **D** = Double/Twin, **T** = Triple, **Q** = Quad, **b** = bathroom, **s** = shower only. Unless otherwise noted, credit cards are accepted and English is spoken. Breakfast and the 7 percent IVA tax are usually not included.

To help you easily sort through these listings, I've divided the rooms into three categories based on the price for a standard double room with bath during high season:

$$$ Higher Priced—Most rooms €100 or more.
$$ Moderately Priced—Most rooms between €50-100.
$ Lower Priced—Most rooms €50 or less.

breakfast-€8, air-con, elevator, parking-€17/day, 5-min walk from Plaza Nueva, Gran Vía 25—enter on side street called Postigo Veluti, tel. 958-285-464, fax 958-285-591, www.maciahoteles.com, granvia @maciahoteles.com).

$$$ Casa del Capitel Nazarí, just off the church end of Plaza Nueva, is a restored 16th-century Renaissance palace transformed into 17 small but tastefully decorated rooms facing a courtyard (Db-€115, extra bed-€36, breakfast-€8, includes afternoon tea/coffee and pastry, air-con, free Internet access, parking-€18.50/day, Cuesta Aceituneros 6, tel. 958-215-260, fax 958-215-806, www.hotelcasacapitel.com, info @hotelcasacapitel.com).

$$ Hotel Maciá Plaza, right on the colorful Plaza Nueva, has 44 clean, modern, and classy rooms. Choose between an on-the-square view or a quieter interior room (Sb-€67, Db-€95, Tb-€118, 10 percent discount in 2009 when you show this book at check-in or reserve directly through their website, good buffet breakfast-€6, air-con, elevator, free Wi-Fi, Plaza Nueva 4, tel. 958-227-536, fax 958-227-533, www.maciahoteles.com, maciaplaza@maciahoteles.com).

$$ Hotel Anacapri is a bright, cool marble oasis with 49 modern rooms, a quiet lounge, and three spacious, loft-style junior suites (Sb-€55–62, Db-€75–90, Tb-€110, extra bed-€20, includes breakfast with direct bookings in 2009, air-con, elevator, Wi-Fi, 2 blocks toward Gran Vía from Plaza Nueva at Calle Joaquín Costa 7, just a block from cathedral bus stop, tel. 958-227-477, fax 958-228-909, www.hotelanacapri.com, reservas@hotelanacapri.com, helpful Kathy speaks Iowan).

Cheap Sleeps on Cuesta de Gomérez

These are inexpensive and ramshackle lodgings on the street leading from Plaza Nueva up to the Alhambra. A restoration project is

Granada Hotels and Restaurants

1. Hotel Inglaterra
2. Hotel Maciá Gran Vía
3. Casa del Capitel Nazarí
4. Hotel Maciá Plaza
5. Hotel Anacapri
6. Pensión Landazuri
7. Hostal Residencia Britz
8. Pensión Gomérez
9. Hostal Viena & Hotel Austria
10. To Hotel Navas; Los Diamantes & Bar Las Copas Fish Bars
11. Hotel Lisboa
12. To Hotel Reina Cristina
13. Hotel Los Tilos
14. Bodegas Castañeda
15. Restaurante Sevilla
16. Vinoteca Salinas II
17. Los Italianos Ice Cream
18. To Paseo de los Tristes Eateries

currently blocking the end of the road, making it quieter and almost traffic-free. There are plans to make this a pedestrian-only street, but for now you can still access these places by car.

$ Pensión Landazuri is run by friendly, English-speaking Matilda Landazuri and her son, Manolo. Some of their 18 rooms are well-worn, while others are renovated. It boasts hardworking, helpful management and a great roof garden with an Alhambra view (S-€24, Sb-€36, D-€34, Db-€45, Tb-€60, cheap eggs-and-bacon breakfast, cash only, parking-€10/day, Cuesta de Gomérez 24, tel. & fax 958-221-406). The Landazuris also run a good, cheap café.

$ Hostal Residencia Britz, overlooking Plaza Nueva, is simple and no-nonsense. All of its 22 basic rooms are streetside—bring earplugs (S-€23, D-€35, Db-€46, includes tax, elevator, Plaza Nueva y Gomérez 1, tel. & fax 958-223-652).

$ Pensión Gomérez is run by English-speaking Sigfrido Sanchez de León de Torres (who'll explain to you how Spanish surnames work if you have the time). This basic nine-room *hostal,* listed in nearly every country's student-travel guidebook to Spain, is another fine cheapie. Quieter rooms are in the back (S-€18, D-€30, T-€40, Q-€45, includes tax, cash only, Cuesta de Gomérez 10, 1 floor up, tel. & fax 958-223-022).

$ Hostal Viena, run by English-speaking Austrian Irene (ee-RAY-nay), rents 32 basic backpacker-type rooms on a quiet side street (S-€28, Sb-€38, D-€38, Db-€48, T-€55, Tb-€65, family rooms, includes tax, air-con, next-door bar noisy on weekends, 10 yards off Cuesta de Gomérez at Hospital de Santa Ana 2, tel. & fax 958-221-859, www.hostalviena.com, hostalviena@hostalviena.com). Some of these rooms are in nearby and similar **Hotel Austria,** also run by Irene.

Near Plaza del Carmen

The pleasant Plaza del Carmen and the beginning of Calle Navas are pedestrian areas offering a couple of good values (and two deep-fried-fish bars: Los Diamantes and Bar Las Copas, both close to Hotel Navas and very popular with locals).

$$$ Hotel Navas, a block down Calle Navas, is a modern, well-run, tour-friendly, business-class hotel with 49 spacious rooms and no character (Sb-€80, Db-€110, deals in low season, includes tax, breakfast buffet-€8, air-con, elevator, Calle Navas 24, tel. 958-225-959, fax 958-227-523, www.hotelesporcel.com, navas@hotelesporcel.com).

$ Hotel Lisboa, which overlooks Plaza del Carmen opposite Granada's city hall, offers 28 simple but well-maintained rooms with friendly owners (S-€23, Sb-€34, D-€34, Db-€48, T-€44, Tb-€64, includes tax, elevator, free Internet access, Plaza del Carmen 27, tel. 958-221-414, fax 958-221-487, www.lisboaweb.com, Mary and Juan José).

Near the Cathedral

$$$ Hotel Reina Cristina has 58 quiet, elegant rooms a few steps off Plaza Trinidad, a park-like square near the lively Pescadería and Bib-Rambla squares. Check out the great Mudejar ceiling and the painting at the entrance of this house, where the famous Spanish poet Federico García Lorca hid until he was captured and executed by the Guardia Civil (Sb-€53–75, Db-€75–114, Tb-€107–135, breakfast-€12, air-con, elevator, Internet access-€2/hr, free Wi-Fi, near Plaza de la Trinidad at Tablas 4, tel. 958-253-211, fax 958-255-728, www.hotelreinacristina.com, clientes@hotelreinacristina.com).

$$ Hotel Los Tilos offers 30 comfortable rooms (some with balconies) on the charming, traffic-free Plaza de Bib-Rambla behind the cathedral. All clients are welcome to use the fourth-floor view terrace overlooking the great café, shopping, and people-watching neighborhood. The hall carpets are well-trafficked, but the in-room flooring has been renovated (Sb-€40–55, Db-€55–80, Tb-€77–100, prices may be cheaper if you reserve online, includes tax and breakfast with this book in 2009, air-con, parking-€18/day, Plaza de Bib-Rambla 4, tel. 958-266-712, fax 958-266-801, www.hotellostilos.com, clientes@hotellostilos.com, friendly José María).

In the Albayzín

$$ La Casa de Rafa is a traditional house in the heart of the Albayzín that's been converted into four small, funky kitchenette apartments with an eclectic, ever-evolving artistic feel (Chicago-raised owner Rafa lives on-site). You'll share two tiny patios and a rooftop terrace with a spectacular in-your-face view of the Alhambra (Sb-€35–45, Db-€45–60, extra person-€10–12.50, 2-night minimum, includes tax, 5-min walk from Plaza Nueva at Plaza Virgen del Carmen—see map page 453, tel. 958-220-682, mobile 610-322-216, www.elnumero8.com, casaocho@gmail.com). Call Rafa to get (initially tricky) directions and set up a time to meet and check in.

In or near the Alhambra

If you want to stay on the Alhambra grounds, there are two popular options—famous, overpriced, and generally booked up long in advance. These are a half-mile up the hill from Plaza Nueva.

$$$ Parador de Granada San Francisco offers 40 designer rooms in a former Moorish palace that was later transformed into a 15th-century Franciscan monastery. It's considered Spain's premier parador...and that's saying something (Db-€310, includes tax, breakfast-€18, air-con, free parking, Calle Real de la Alhambra, tel. 958-221-440, fax 958-222-264, www.parador.es, granada@parador.es). You must book months ahead to spend the night in this lavishly located, stodgy, and historic palace. Any peasant, however, can drop in for a coffee, drink, snack, or meal (daily 13:00–16:00 & 20:30–23:00). For details about the history of the building, see sidebar on page 436.

$$$ Hotel América is classy and cozy, with 17 rooms next to the parador (Sb-€70, Db-€115, includes tax, breakfast-€8, closed Dec–Feb, Calle Real de la Alhambra 53, tel. 958-227-471, fax 958-227-470, www.hotelamericagranada.com, reservas@hotelamericagranada.com). Book three months ahead in high season.

EATING

Some of Granada's bars still serve a small tapas plate free with any beer or wine—a tradition that's dying out in most of Spain.

In search of an edible memory? A local specialty, *tortilla Sacromonte,* is a spicy omelet with pig's brain and other organs. *Berenjenas fritas* (fried eggplant) and *habas con jamón* (small green fava beans cooked with cured ham) are worth seeking out. *Tinto de verano*—a red-wine spritzer with lemon and ice—is refreshing on a hot evening. For tips on eating near the Alhambra, see "Eating" on page 432.

In the Albayzín

The most interesting meals hide out deep in the Albayzín (Moorish quarter). The easy way to get there is by taking minibus #31 from Plaza Nueva or #32 from Plaza Isabel La Católica. To find a particular square, ask any local, or follow my directions and the map on page 453. If dining late, take the minibus or a taxi back to your hotel; Albayzín back streets can be dangerous because of pickpockets.

Casa Torcuato is a hardworking eatery serving straightforward yet creative food in a smart upstairs dining room. They serve a good €8 fixed-price meal. Plates of fresh fish run €8–12 and their tropical salad includes a Tahitian wonderland of fruits (Mon–Sat 13:00–16:00 & 20:00–24:00, closed Sun, 2 blocks beyond Plaza Larga at Calle Aqua 20, second location on nearby Calle Pagés, tel. 958-202-039).

Restaurante El Ladrillo, with outdoor tables on a peaceful square, is *the* place for piles of fish. Their popular €9 *barco* ("boatload" of mixed fried fish) is a fishy feast that stuffs two to the gills. The smaller €7.50 *canoa* fills one person adequately, or, when combined with a salad, can feed two (daily 12:00–24:00, on Plaza Fátima, just off Calle Pages).

Near the San Nicolás Viewpoint: The **Bar Kiki,** a laid-back and popular bar/restaurant on an unpretentious square, serves simple tapas. Try their tasty fried eggplant (long hours, closed Wed, just behind viewpoint at Plaza de San Nicolás 9).

On Plaza San Miguel el Bajo: While it's the farthest hike into the Albayzín, this neighborhood square boasts my favorite funky, local scene—with kids kicking soccer balls, old-timers warming benches, and women gossiping under the facade of a humble church. Tables spill into the square from its four bars (serious tapas) and good little restaurant (€10 fixed-price meal). This is a fine spot to end your Albayzín visit, as there's a viewpoint overlooking the modern city a block away. Minibuses #31 and #32 rumble by every few minutes, ready to zip you back to Plaza Nueva.

Carmens: For a more memorable but expensive experience, consider fine dining with Alhambra views in a *carmen,* a typical Albayzín house with a garden (buzz to get in). **Carmen Mirador de Morayma** boasts great atmosphere and fine rustic cuisine. This is where famous visitors—from local celebrities to President Clinton—dine to the sounds of classical guitar. For seating, choose between outdoor (on one of three dreamy garden terraces) or inside the noble mansion (with an intimate, garden-view ambience). With one night in Granada, I'd eat here. Reservations are smart (€30 tasting *menus*, Mon–Sat 13:30–15:30 & 20:30–23:30, closed Sun, read the romantic history on the card, Calle Pianista García Carrillo 2, tel. 958-228-290). **Carmen de las Tomasas** serves gourmet traditional Andalusian cuisine with killer views in a dressy/stuffy atmosphere (€40 meals, Wed–Sun 21:00–24:00, generally closed Mon–Tue, call ahead as they sometimes close on Sun instead, reservations required, Carril de San Agustín, tel. 958-224-108, Cristina). **Carmen de Aben Humeya** is the least expensive and least stuffy. Its outdoor-only seating lets you enjoy a meal or just a long cup of coffee while gazing at the Alhambra (€10–15 plates, daily 13:00–24:00, food served 13:00–16:00 & 19:30–22:30—or until 24:00 in heat of summer, Cuesta de las Tomasas 12, tel. 958-226-665).

Near Plaza Nueva

For people-watching, consider the many restaurants on Plaza Nueva or Bib-Rambla (south of cathedral). For a happening scene, check out the bars on and around Calle Elvira. It's best to wander and see where the biggest crowds are.

Bodegas Castañeda is the best mix of lively, central, untouristy, and cheap among the tapas bars I visited. Just a block off Plaza Nueva, it requires a bit of self-service: When crowded, you need to power your way to the bar to order; when quiet, you can order at the bar and grab a little table (same budget prices). Consider their *tablas combinadas*—variety plates of cheese, meat, and *ahumados* (four different varieties of smoked fish)—and tasty *croquetas* (breaded and fried mashed potatoes and ham). The big kegs tempt you with different local sherries. Tapas can be ordered from an easy menu and cost €2–3 apiece (daily 11:30–16:30 & 17:00–24:00, Calle Almireceros 1, tel.

958-215-464). Don't be confused by a different "Castaneda" restaurant nearby (unless you're hankering for stuffed potatoes).

Restaurante Sevilla, with its tight and charming little dining room, has been a favorite of well-dressed natives for 75 years. Specialties include paella, other rice dishes, soups, and salads. You'll eat surrounded by old photos of local big shots who've dined here. On hot nights, tables pour out onto the little square facing the Royal Chapel. It's a local-feeling, elegant, urban scene (€15 plates; summer Tue–Sat 13:00–16:00 & 20:00–23:30, Mon 20:00–23:30, closed Sun; rest of year Tue–Sat 13:00–16:00 & 20:00–23:30, Sun 13:00–16:00, closed Mon; across from Royal Chapel at Calle Oficios 12, tel. 958-221-223).

Vinoteca Salinas II is mod rather than traditional, serving tapas and wines a cut above the other bars. You'll sit on stools at tables made of wine barrels, while enjoying a good selection of sophisticated €2 *montaditos* (open-face sandwiches), tapas, and the best selection of fine wine by the glass in town—a little pricier, but still reasonable. A crisp glass of Albariño (white wine from Galicia) cools down a hot day (daily 12:30–24:00, Calle Almireceros).

Hippie Options on Calle Caldereria Nueva: From Plaza Nueva, walk two long blocks down Calle Elvira and turn right onto the wonderfully hip and Arabic-feeling Calle Caldereria Nueva, which leads uphill into the Albayzín. The street is lined with trendy *teterías.* These small tea shops, open all day, are good places to linger, chat, and imagine you're in Morocco. Some are conservative and unmemorable, and others are achingly romantic, filled with incense, beaded cushions, live African music, and effervescent young hippies. They sell light meals such as crêpes, and a worldwide range of teas, all marinated in a candlelit snakecharm. At **Arrayanes,** Mostafa will help you choose among the Moroccan salads, the *pastela* (a chicken-and-cinnamon pastry appetizer), the couscous, or *tajin* dishes. He treats you like an old friend...especially the ladies (Wed–Mon 13:30–16:30 & 19:30–23:30, closed Tue, Cuesta Marañas 4, where Calles Caldereria Nueva and Vieja meet, tel. 958-228-401).

Dessert: **Los Italianos,** teeming with locals, is popular for its ice cream, *horchata* (*chufa*-nut drink), and shakes (mid-March–mid-Oct daily 8:00–24:00, closed mid-Oct–mid-March, across the street from cathedral and Royal Chapel at Gran Vía 4, tel. 958-224-034).

Markets: Though heavy on meat, the **Mercado San Agustín** also sells fruits and veggies. If nothing else, it's as refreshingly cool as a meat locker (Mon–Sat 8:00–15:30, closed Sun, has small café/bar, a block north of cathedral and a half-block off Gran Vía on Calle Cristo San Agustín). The **Pescadaría** square, a block from Plaza de Bib-Rambla, usually has some fruit stalls on its northern end, along with inviting restaurants on the square itself.

TRANSPORTATION CONNECTIONS

From Granada by Train to: Barcelona (1/day Wed, Fri, and Sun only, 11.5 hrs; also 1/night daily, 12 hrs), **Madrid** (3/day, 5 hrs), **Toledo** (all service is via Madrid, nearly hourly AVE connections to Toledo), **Algeciras** (3/day, 4.25–5 hrs), **Ronda** (3/day, 2.5 hrs), **Sevilla** (4/day, 3 hrs), **Córdoba** (2/day, 2.5 hrs), **Málaga** (3/day, 2.5–3.25 hrs, transfer in Bobadilla). Train info: tel. 902-240-202. Many of these connections have a more frequent (and sometimes much faster) bus option—see below.

By Bus to: Nerja (5/day, 2.5 hrs, more with transfer in Motril), **Sevilla** (11/day, 3 hrs *directo,* 4 hrs *ruta*), **Córdoba** (8/day, 2.5–3 hrs), **Madrid** (13/day, 5.25 hrs), **Málaga** (hourly, 1.5–2 hrs), **Algeciras** (6/day, 4–5.5 hrs, some are *directo,* others are the slow *ruta*), **La Línea/Gibraltar** (2/day, 5 hrs), **Jerez** (1/day, 4.5 hrs). All of these buses are run by the Alsina Graells company (tel. 958-185-480).

To better handle the winding roads, some tourists like to reserve a seat at the front of the bus (generally seats #1–20, request when you book). You (or your hotel or travel agency) can call the station to book a seat—they'll hold it until 40 minutes before departure (tel. 958-185-480; or 902-422-242 for Alsa, serving Barcelona or east-coast destinations, www.alsa.es). If you don't want to show up early to claim your seat, you can buy your ticket in advance with a credit card (tel. 902-330-400). During peak season, the bus to Nerja can fill up; purchase tickets as far in advance as possible to snare a spot.

By Car: To drive to Nerja (1.5 hours away), take the exit for the coastal town of Motril. You'll wind through 50 scenic miles south of Granada, then follow signs for Málaga.

SEVILLA

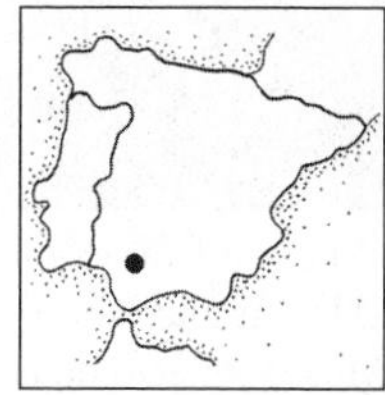

Sevilla is the flamboyant city of Carmen and Don Juan, where bullfighting is still politically correct and where little girls still dream of growing up to become flamenco dancers. While Granada has the great Alhambra and Córdoba has the remarkable Mezquita, Sevilla has a soul. (Soul—or *duende*—is fundamental to flamenco.) It's a wonderful-to-be-alive-in kind of place.

The gateway to the New World in the 16th century, Sevilla boomed when Spain did. The explorers Amerigo Vespucci and Ferdinand Magellan sailed from its great river harbor, discovering new routes and sources of gold, silver, cocoa, and tobacco. In the 17th century, Sevilla was Spain's largest and richest city. Local artists Diego Velázquez, Bartolomé Murillo, and Francisco de Zurbarán made it a cultural center. Sevilla's Golden Age—and its New World riches—ended when the harbor silted up and the Spanish empire crumbled.

In the 19th century, Sevilla was a big stop on the Romantic "Grand Tour" of Europe. To build on this tourism and promote trade among Spanish-speaking nations, Sevilla planned a grand exposition in 1929. Bad year. The expo crashed along with the stock market. In 1992, Sevilla got a second chance at a world's fair. This expo was a success, leaving the city with an impressive infrastructure: a new airport, train station, sleek bridges, and the super AVE bullet train (making Sevilla a 2.5-hour side-trip from Madrid). In 2007, the main boulevards—once thundering with noisy traffic and cutting the city mercilessly in two—were pedestrianized, giving Sevilla even more charm.

Today, Spain's fourth-largest city (pop. 700,000) is Andalucía's leading destination, buzzing with festivals, orange and jacaranda trees, sizzling summer heat, color, guitars, and castanets. James Michener wrote, "Sevilla doesn't *have* ambience, it *is* ambience." Sevilla has its share of impressive sights, but the real magic is the city itself, with its tangled Jewish Quarter, riveting flamenco shows, thriving bars, and teeming evening paseo.

Planning Your Time

If ever there was a big Spanish city to linger in, it's Sevilla. On a three-week trip, spend two nights and two days here. On even the shortest Spanish trip, I'd zip here on the slick AVE train for a day trip from Madrid.

The major sights are few and simple for a city of this size; the cathedral and the Alcázar are worth about three hours, and a wander through the Santa Cruz district takes about an hour. You could spend half a day touring its other sights. Stroll along the bank of the Guadalquivir River and cross the Bridge of Triana for a view of the cathedral and Golden Tower. An evening is essential for the paseo and a flamenco show.

Bullfights take place on most Sundays in May and June, on Easter, and daily through the April Fair. Sevilla's Alcázar and Museo de Bellas Artes are closed on Monday, while the Museo Palacio de la Condesa de Lebrija is closed on Sunday. Tour groups clog the Alcázar and cathedral in the morning; go late in the day to avoid the lines.

Córdoba (see next chapter) is a convenient and worthwhile side-trip from Sevilla, or a handy stopover if you're taking the AVE to or from Madrid.

ORIENTATION

For the tourist, this big city is small. Sevilla's major sights—including the lively Santa Cruz district and the Alcázar—surround the cathedral. The central north–south pedestrian boulevard, Avenida de la Constitución (with TIs, banks, and a post office), leads past the cathedral to Plaza Nueva (gateway to the shopping district). Nearly everything is within easy walking distance. The bullring is a few blocks west of the cathedral, and Plaza de España is a few blocks south. The area on the west bank of the Guadalquivir River is working-class and colorful, but lacks tourist sights. With taxis so friendly, easy, and reasonable (€3

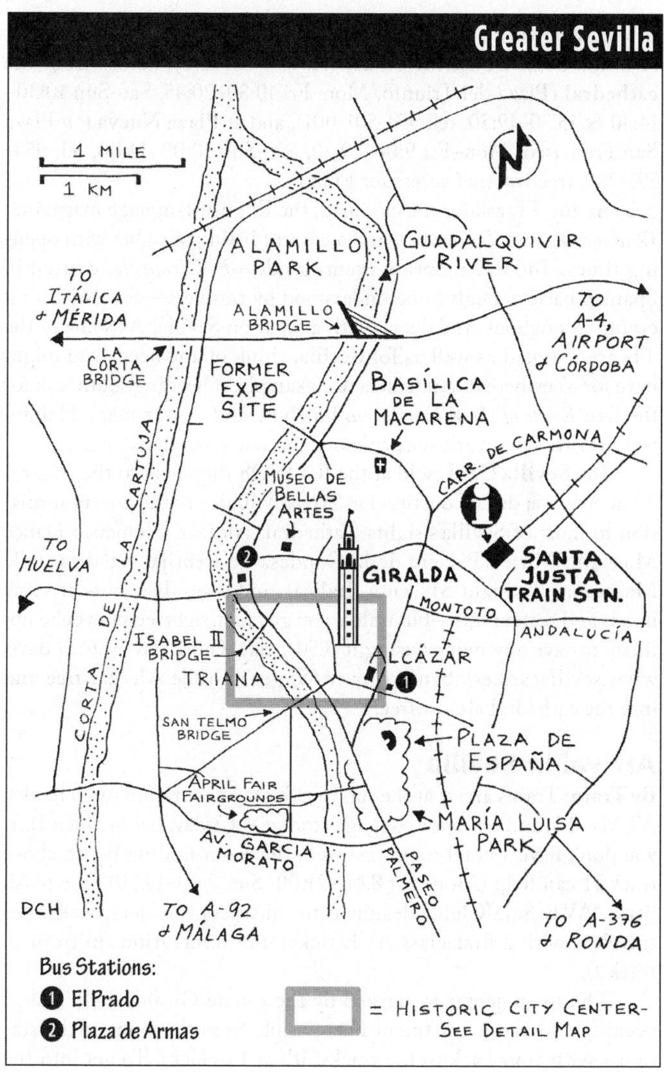

for a short ride), I rarely bother with the bus—though a bus pass can be worthwhile for those on a tight budget.

Tourist Information

Sevilla has tourist offices wherever you need them—at the **airport** (Mon–Fri 9:00–21:00, Sat–Sun 11:00–15:00, tel. 954-449-128), **train station** (overlooking track 6, Mon–Fri 8:30–20:30, Sat–Sun 10:00–14:00, tel. 954-782-003), and three along Avenida de la Constitución: at the river side of the **Alcázar** (posts a handy list of daily events in town, Mon–Fri 9:00–19:30, Sat 10:00–19:00, Sun 10:00–14:00, Avenida de la Constitución 21, tel. 954-787-578); across from the **cathedral** (Plaza del Triunfo, Mon–Fri 10:30–20:45, Sat–Sun 10:30–14:30 & 15:30–19:30, tel. 954-501-001); and at **Plaza Nueva** (on Plaza San Francisco, Mon–Fri 9:00–19:30, Sat–Sun 10:00–14:00, tel. 954-595-288, free Internet access for 1 hour).

At any TI, ask for the city map, the English-language magazines *Welcome Olé* and *The Tourist,* and a current listing of sights with opening times. The free monthly events guide—*El Giraldillo,* written in Spanish basic enough to be understood by travelers—covers cultural events throughout Andalucía, with a focus on Sevilla. As some of the TIs are regional as well as for Sevilla, think of any needs you might have for elsewhere in Andalucía (for example, if heading south, ask for the free *Route of the White Towns* brochure and a Jerez map). Helpful websites are www.turismosevilla.org and www.andalucia.org.

The **Sevilla Card** (sold at the ICONOS shop next to the Alcázar TI at Avenida de la Constitución 21, daily 10:00–19:00) covers admission to most of Sevilla's sights (cathedral, Alcázar, Flamenco Dance Museum, Museo Palacio de la Condesa de Lebrija, Basílica de la Macarena, Bullfight Museum, Itálica), and gives discounts at some hotels and restaurants—but unless you go crazy sightseeing, you're not likely to save any money using it (€50/1 day, €60/2 days, €65/3 days, www.sevillacard.es). Seniors (over 65) get into the Alcázar free and into the cathedral almost free.

Arrival in Sevilla

By Train: Trains arrive at the sublime Santa Justa station (with banks, ATMs, TI, and *consigna*/baggage storage—€3/day, below track 1). If you don't have a hotel room reserved, the room-finding booth above track 11 can help (Mon–Sat 8:00–21:00, Sun 8:00–14:30). The plush little "AVE Sala Club," designed for business travelers, welcomes travelers with a first-class AVE ticket and reservation (in front of track 1).

The town center is marked by the ornate Giralda Bell Tower, peeking above the apartment flats (visible from the front of the station—with your back to the tracks, it's at 1 o'clock). To get into the center, it's a flat and boring 20-minute walk (longer if you get lost), a €5 taxi ride, or a short bus ride. Bus #C2 runs from 100 yards in front of the train station to Plaza de la Encarnación, but not to recommended hotels (€1.10, pay driver).

By Bus: Sevilla's two major bus stations both have information offices, cafeterias, and luggage storage. The **El Prado station** covers most of Andalucía (daily 7:00–22:00, information tel. 954-417-111, no English spoken; luggage storage at back of station, €2/day, daily 9:00–21:00). To get downtown from the station, it's a 10-minute walk (use the color map in the front of this book).

The **Plaza de Armas station** (near the river, opposite the Expo '92 site) serves long-distance destinations such as Madrid, Barcelona, Lagos, and Lisbon. Luggage lockers are across from the ticket counters (€3/day). As you exit onto the main road (Calle Arjona), the bus stop is to the left, in front of the taxi stand (bus #C4 goes downtown, €1.10, pay driver, get off at Puerta de Jerez near main TI). Taxis to downtown cost around €5.

By Car: To drive into Sevilla, follow *centro ciudad* (city center) signs and stay along the river. For short-term parking on the street, the riverside Paseo de Cristóbal Colón has two-hour meters and hard-working thieves. Ignore the bogus traffic wardens who direct you to an illegal spot, take a tip, and disappear later when your car gets towed. For long-term parking, hotels charge as much as a normal garage. For simplicity, I'd just park at a central garage and catch a taxi to my hotel. Try the big one under the bus station at Plaza de Armas (€10/day), the Cristóbal Colón garage (by the bullring and river, €1.15/hr, €13/day), or the one at Avenida Roma/Puerta de Jerez (€14/24 hrs, cash only). For hotels in the Santa Cruz area, the handiest parking is the Cano y Cueto garage near the corner of Calle Santa María la Blanca and Menéndez Pelayo (€16/day, open 24/7, at edge of big park, unsigned and underground).

By Plane: The Especial Aeropuerto (EA) bus connects the airport with the train station and town center (€2.10, 30 min, 2/hr, generally departs from airport at :15 and :45, buy ticket from driver). If going from downtown Sevilla *to* the airport, ask your hotel or the TI where to catch it (the bus stop constantly changes because of religious processions, construction, and other factors); in 2008, the stop was in front of the El Prado bus station on Calle Jose María Osborne. You can also catch the bus at the Santa Justa train station. Taxis have a fixed €20–23 rate between the airport and town center (but confirm price anyway). For flight information, call 954-449-000.

Getting Around Sevilla

By Bus: On a hot day, buses in Sevilla can be a blessing. A single trip costs €1.10 (pay driver), or you can buy a Bonobus pass, which gives you 10 trips for €6 (shareable, sold at kiosks). The various #C buses make a circular loop that covers María Luisa Park and Basílica de la Macarena. The #C3 stops in Murillo Gardens, Triana (district south of the river), then Macarena. The #C4 goes the opposite direction without entering Triana. Spunky little #C5 is a minibus that winds through the old center of town, providing a fine and relaxing joyride (pick it up at Plaza Nueva).

By Taxi: Sevilla is a great taxi town. You can hail them anywhere (€3 drop, or €4 at night and on weekends, €20–23 to airport). While I'm quick to take advantage of a taxi, because of one-way streets and traffic congestion, you can often hoof it just as fast between central points.

Helpful Hints

Festivals: Sevilla's peak season is April and May, and it has two one-week festival periods when the city is packed: Holy Week and April Fair.

While **Holy Week** *(Semana Santa)* is big all over Spain, it's biggest in Sevilla. It's held the week between Palm Sunday and Easter Sunday (April 5–12 in 2009). Locals start preparing for the big event up to a year in advance. What would normally be a five-minute walk could take you an hour and a half if a procession crosses your path. But even these hassles seem irrelevant as you listen to the *saetas* (spontaneous devotional songs) and let the spirit of the festival take over.

Then, two weeks after Easter—after taking enough time off to catch its communal breath—Sevilla holds its **April Fair** (April 28–May 3 in 2009, described on page 498). This is a celebration of all things Andalusian, with plenty of eating, drinking, singing, and merrymaking (though most of the revelry takes place in private parties at a large fairground).

Book rooms well in advance for these festival times. Warning: Prices can go sky-high, food quality at touristy restaurants plummets, and many hotels have four-night minimums.

Internet Access: Sevilla has plenty of places to get online. Near the recommended Santa Cruz hotels, head for **Internetia,** a thriving-with-students place with a fine café and 30 terminals (€2.20/hr, Wi-Fi, disc-burning, daily 11:00–23:00, Avenida Menéndez Pelayo 43–45, tel. 954-534-003). Between the Alcázar and the river, try **Internet Workcenter** (daily 9:00–14:00 & 16:00–21:00, San Fernando 1, tel. 954-220-487). The **TI at Plaza Nueva** (on Plaza San Francisco) offers up to one hour of free Internet access from eight terminals (Internet available Mon–Fri 10:00–14:00 & 17:00–20:00, closed Sat–Sun).

Post Office: The post office is at Avenida de la Constitución 32, across from the cathedral (Mon–Fri 8:30–20:30, Sat 9:30–14:00, closed Sun).

Laundry: Lavandería Roma offers quick and economical drop-off service (€6/load wash and dry, Mon–Fri 9:30–14:00 & 17:30–20:30, Sat 9:00–15:00, closed Sun, 2 blocks inland from bullring at Castelar 2, tel. 954-210-535). Near the recommended Santa Cruz hotels, **La Segunda Vera Tintorería** has two machines for self-service (€10/load wash and dry, drop-off service also available, Mon–Fri 9:30–13:45 & 17:30–20:00, closed Sat–Sun, across from Internetia cybercafé, Avenida Menéndez Pelayo 11, tel. 954-534-219).

Train Tickets: The RENFE offices give out train schedules and sell train tickets. There's a RENFE Travel Center at the **train station** (daily 8:00–22:00, take a number and wait, tel. 902-240-202 for

Cheap Tricks in Sevilla

- For an inexpensive lunch, many regular bar-cafeterias will make you a *bocadillo*. These are often simply ham and cheese (or *tortilla española*—potato omelet) on a baguette, with no fixings. But at €3–4, they are perfect for a picnic in one of the many squares and parks. Plaza Doña Elvira is especially picturesque and shady.
- Instead of taking a guided tour, head to the Golden Tower and enjoy a walk along the Guadalquivir River. There's a bike path and plenty of sunbathers stretched out along the grassy sections. Spot the Giralda Bell Tower from a distance, look over at Triana, and watch rowers go down the river. You can also walk around a large, sand-colored sculpture by the Basque artist Eduardo Chillida near the Isabel II Bridge.
- Need to get online? The Plaza Nueva TI on Plaza San Francisco offers free Internet access for up to one hour.

reservations and info) and one near **Plaza Nueva** in the center (Mon–Fri 9:30–14:00 & 17:30–20:00, Sat 10:00–13:30, closed Sun, Calle Zaragoza 29, tel. 954-211-455). Many travel agencies sell train tickets for the same price as the train station (look for train sticker in agency window).

TOURS

Five Guided City Walks by Concepción—Concepción Delgado, an enthusiastic teacher and a joy to listen to, takes small groups on English-language walks. Using me as her guinea pig, Concepción designed a fine two-hour **Sevilla Cultural Show & Tell.** This introduction to her hometown, sharing important insights the average visitor misses, is worthwhile, even on a one-day visit (€12/person, Sept–July Mon–Sat at 10:30; Aug Mon, Wed, and Fri at 10:30; starting from statue in Plaza Nueva).

For those wanting to really understand the city's two most important sights—which are tough to fully appreciate—Concepción also offers in-depth tours of the **cathedral** and the **Alcázar** (both tours last 75 minutes, cost €6, and meet at 13:00 at the statue in Plaza del Triunfo; cathedral tours—Mon, Wed, and Fri; Alcázar tours—Tue, Thu, and Sat; no Alcázar tours in Aug).

SEVILLA

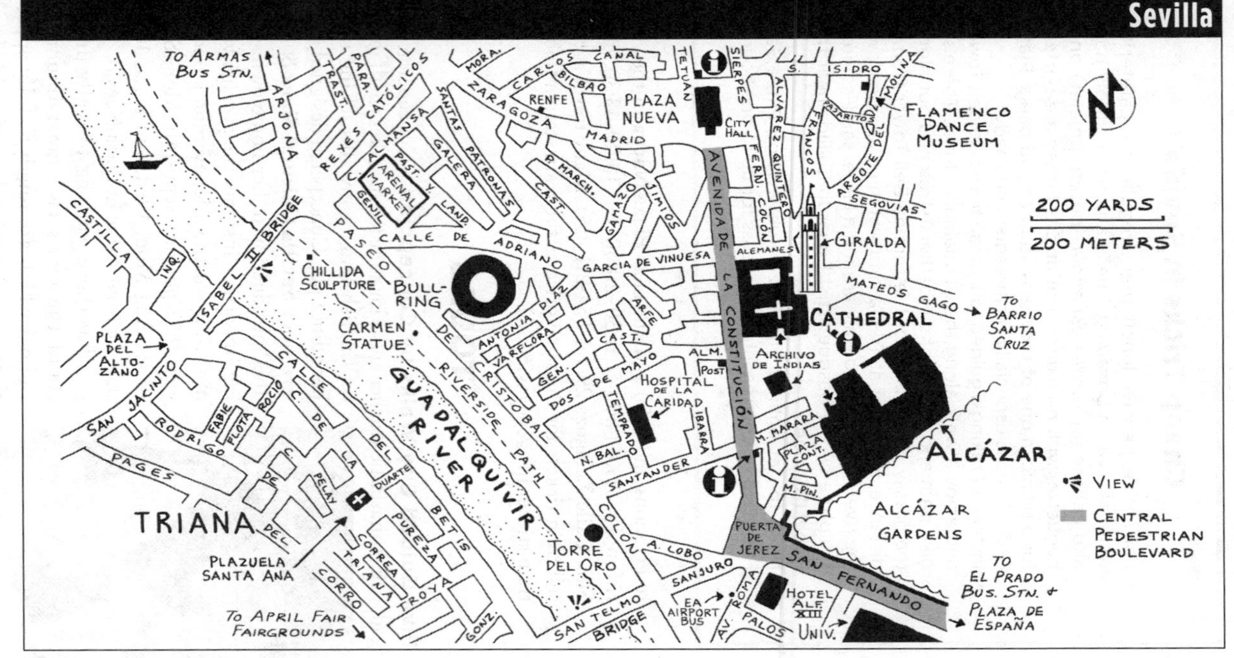
Sevilla
To Armas Bus Stn.
Plaza Nueva
City Hall
Renfe
Flamenco Dance Museum
200 Yards
200 Meters
Giralda
Cathedral
To Barrio Santa Cruz
Archivo de Indias
Hospital de la Caridad
Avenida de la Constitución
Arenal Market
Chillida Sculpture
Bull-ring
Carmen Statue
Isabel II Bridge
Plaza del Altozano
Guadalquivir River
Riverside Path
Paseo de Cristobal Colón
Torre del Oro
Alcázar
Alcázar Gardens
View
Central Pedestrian Boulevard
Puerta de Jerez
San Fernando
To El Prado Bus. Stn. & Plaza de España
Hotel Alf. XIII
Univ.
EA Airport Bus
San Telmo Bridge
Triana
Plazuela Santa Ana
To April Fair Fairgrounds
Calle Betis
Pureza
Castilla
San Jacinto
Pages

Her newest tour is the **bullring** (16:00, €5 plus admission) followed by a two-hour walk through the **Triana** neighborhood (the gritty other side of the river, 17:00, €12). These tours go Mondays and Thursdays (mid-March–June and Sept–mid-Nov) and come with a small discount if you take both.

While you can just show up for Concepción's tours, it's smart to confirm the departure times and reserve a place (tel. 902-158-226, mobile 616-501-100, www.sevillawalkingtours.com, info@sevillawalkingtours.com). Concepción does no tours on Sundays or holidays.

Hop-on, Hop-off Bus Tours—Two competing city bus tours leave from the curb near the riverside Golden Tower. You'll see the buses parked with salespeople handing out fliers. Each does about an hour-long swing through the city with a recorded narration (green route slightly better because it includes María Luisa Park, €15, daily 10:00–21:00). The tours, which allow hopping on and off at four stops, are heavy on Expo '29 and Expo '92 neighborhoods—both zones of little interest in '09. While the narration does its best, Sevilla is most interesting where buses can't go.

Horse and Buggy Tours—A carriage ride is a classic, popular way to survey the city and a relaxing way to enjoy María Luisa Park (about €40 for a 45-min clip-clop, if shared by 2 couples the ride is actually quite inexpensive, find a likable English-speaking driver for better narration). Look for rigs at Plaza América, Plaza del Triunfo, Golden Tower, Alfonso XIII Hotel, and Avenida Isabel la Católica.

Boat Cruises—Boring one-hour panoramic tours leave every 30 minutes from the dock behind Torre de Oro. The low-energy recorded narration is hard to follow, but there's little to see anyway (overpriced at €15, tel. 954-561-692).

Andalusian Minibus Tours—Aussie Paul McGrath, who's lived in Sevilla for eight years, takes small groups on all-day tours in his nine-seat minivan. You'll head to the villages south of Sevilla, which are difficult to reach without a car. Paul provides some commentary en route. This is an efficient, economic way to explore the great whitewashed towns along the "Route of the Pueblos Blancos." You'll leave in the morning and visit Olvera, Zahara, Grazalema, and Setenil de las Bodegas; the tour also includes a stop at the Moorish castle Aguzaderas, an olive-oil mill, and a swimming-stop option in the summer (€53, leaves daily from Torre de Oro at 9:00, returns about 19:30, call or email to reserve, mobile 657-889-875, www.theotherspain.galeon.com, the-other-spain@hotmail.com).

Sevilla at a Glance

▲▲▲Flamenco Flamboyant, riveting music-and-dance performances, offered at clubs throughout town. **Hours:** Shows start as early as 19:30. See page 501.

▲▲Cathedral and Giralda Bell Tower The world's largest Gothic church, with Columbus' tomb, a treasury, and climbable tower. **Hours:** July–mid-Sept Mon–Sat 9:30–17:00, Sun 14:30–18:00; mid-Sept–June Mon–Sat 11:00–18:00, Sun 14:30–19:00. See page 480.

▲▲Alcázar Palace built by the Moors in the 10th century, revamped in the 14th century, and still serving as royal digs. **Hours:** Peak season Tue–Sat 9:30–19:00, Sun 9:30–17:00, closed Mon; off-season Tue–Sat 9:30–17:00, Sun 9:30–13:30, closed Mon. See page 488.

▲▲Flamenco Dance Museum High-tech museum explaining the history and art of Sevilla's favorite dance. **Hours:** Daily 9:00–19:00. See page 492.

▲▲Basílica de la Macarena Church and museum with the much-venerated Weeping Virgin statue and two significant floats from Sevilla's Holy Week celebrations. **Hours:** Daily 9:30–14:00 & 17:00–20:00. Possibly closed until Easter 2009. See page 495.

More Tours—Visitours, a typical big-bus tour company, does €85 all-day trips to Córdoba Tuesday, Thursday, and Saturday (tel. 954-460-985, mobile 686-413-413, www.visitours.es.mn, visitours@terra.es). For other guides, contact the **Guides Association of Sevilla** (tel. 954-210-037, www.apitsevilla.com, visitas@apitsevilla.com).

SELF-GUIDED WALK

Barrio Santa Cruz

Of Sevilla's once-thriving Jewish Quarter, only the tangled street plan and a wistful Old World ambience survive. This classy maze of lanes (too narrow for cars), small plazas, tile-covered patios, and whitewashed houses with wrought-iron latticework draped with flowers is a great refuge from the summer heat and bustle of Sevilla. The narrow streets—some with buildings so close they're

▲▲**Evening Paseo** Locals strolling in the cool of the evening, mainly along Avenida de la Constitución, Barrio Santa Cruz, the Calle Sierpes and Tetuán shopping pedestrian zone, and the Guadalquivir River. **Hours:** Spring through fall, until very late at night in summer. See page 501.

▲▲**Bullfight Museum** Guided tour of the bullring and its museum. **Hours:** Daily 9:30-19:00, May-Oct until 20:00, on fight days until 14:00. See page 498.

▲**Museo Palacio de la Condesa de Lebrija** A fascinating 18th-century aristocratic mansion. Hours: Mon-Fri 10:00-19:30, Sat 10:00-14:00, closed Sun. See page 493.

▲**Museo de Bellas Artes** Andalucía's top paintings, including Spanish masters Murillo and Zurbarán. **Hours:** Tue 14:30-20:30, Wed-Sat 9:00-20:30, Sun 9:00-14:30, closed Mon. See page 494.

▲**Bullfights** Some of Spain's best bullfighting, held at Sevilla's arena. **Hours:** Fights on most Sundays in May and June, on Easter, daily through the April Fair, and daily in late Sept; generally at 18:30. Rookies fight small bulls on Thursdays in July. See page 497.

called "kissing lanes"—were actually designed to maximize shade. Even today, locals claim the Barrio Santa Cruz is three degrees cooler than the rest of the city.

Orange trees abound. Since they never lose their leaves, they provide constant shade. But forget about eating any of the oranges. They're bitter and used only to make vitamins, perfume, cat food, and that marmalade you can't avoid in British B&Bs.

The Barrio is made for wandering. Getting lost is easy, and I recommend doing just that. But to get started, here's a plaza-to-plaza walk that loops you through the *corazón* (heart) of the neighborhood and back out again. Ideally, don't do the walk in the morning, when the Barrio's charm is trampled by tour groups. Early evening (around 18:00) is ideal. Start in front of the cathedral.

❶ **Plaza de la Virgen de los Reyes:** This square is dedicated to the Virgin of the Kings. See her tile on the wall. She's big here because she was brought by the Spanish king when he retook the town from the Moors in 1248. The fountain dates from 1929. From this peaceful square (part of the new traffic-free charm of 21st-century Sevilla), look up the street leading away from the cathedral and notice the characteristic (government-protected) 19th-century architecture. The

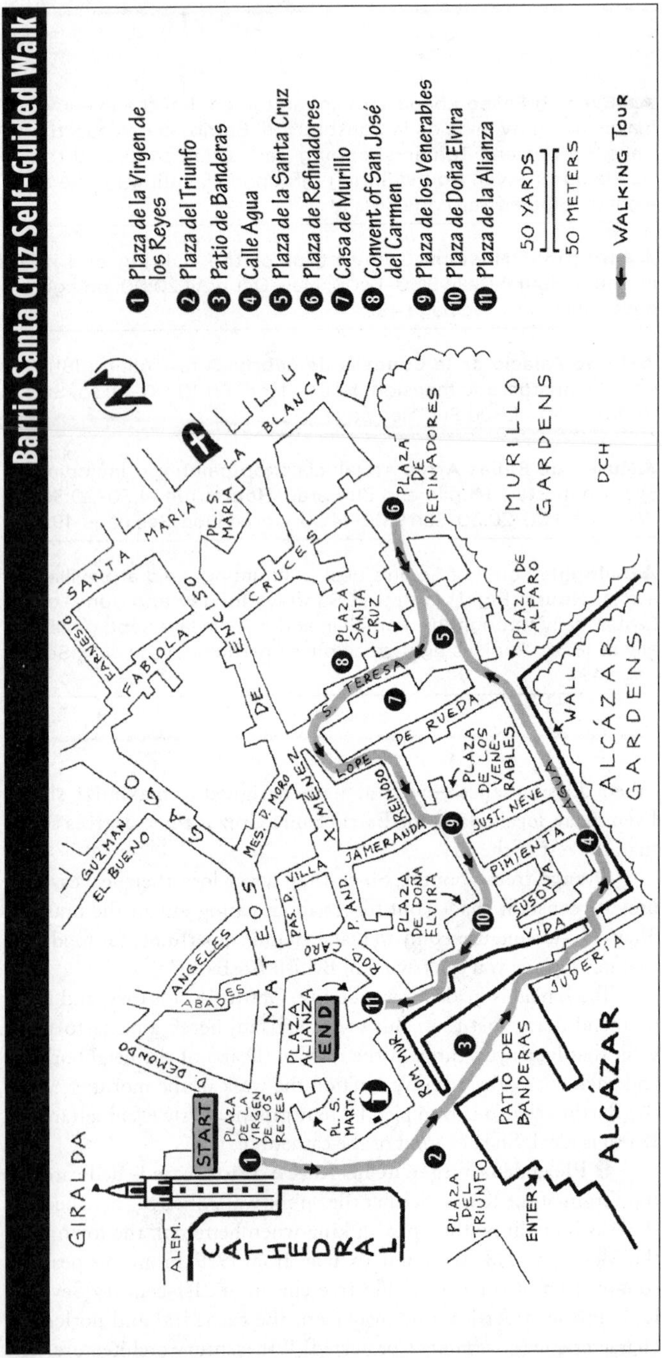

Barrio Santa Cruz Self-Guided Walk
1 Plaza de la Virgen de los Reyes
2 Plaza del Triunfo
3 Patio de Banderas
4 Calle Agua
5 Plaza de la Santa Cruz
6 Plaza de Refinadores
7 Casa de Murillo
8 Convent of San José del Carmen
9 Plaza de los Venerables
10 Plaza de Doña Elvira
11 Plaza de la Alianza
50 YARDS
50 METERS
WALKING TOUR
GIRALDA
CATHEDRAL
ALEM.
START
PLAZA DE LA VIRGEN DE LOS REYES
PLAZA DEL TRIUNFO
ENTER
PATIO DE BANDERAS
ALCÁZAR
PL. S. MARTA
PLAZA ALIANZA
END
ROM. MUR.
ROD. CARO
D. DEMONIO
ABADES
ANGELES
GUZMAN EL BUENO
MATEOS GAGO
MES. D. MORO
XIMÉNEZ
PAS. D. VILLA
P. AND.
PLAZA DE DOÑA ELVIRA
JAMERANDA
REINOSO
LOPE DE RUEDA
PLAZA DE LOS VENE-RABLES
JUST. NEVE
PIMIENTA
SUSONA
VIDA
JUDERÍA
AGUA
WALL
ALCÁZAR GARDENS
S. TERESA
PLAZA SANTA CRUZ
PLAZA DE ALFARO
PLAZA DE REFINADORES
MURILLO GARDENS
DCH
FARNESIO
FABIOLA
SANTA MARIA LA BLANCA
PL. S. MARIA
DE ENCISO
CRUCES
DE

iron work is typical of Andalucía, and the pride of Sevilla. You'll see it and these traditional colors all over the town center.

• *Walk with the cathedral on your right (passing the guard who allows only real worshippers into the royal chapel).*

❷ **Plaza del Triunfo:** The "Plaza of Triumph" is named for the 1755 earthquake that destroyed Lisbon, but didn't rock Sevilla or its tower. Notice the statue, thanking the Virgin.

• *Pass through an opening in the Alcázar wall under the arch. You'll emerge into a courtyard called...*

❸ **Patio de Banderas:** Named for "flags," not Antonio, the Banderas Courtyard was once a kind of military parade ground for the royal guard. The barracks surrounding the square once housed the king's bodyguards. Today it offers a postcard view of the Giralda Bell Tower.

• *Exit the courtyard at the far corner, through the Judería arch. Walking alongside the Alcázar wall, take the first left, then right, through a small square and follow the narrow alleyway called...*

❹ **Calle Agua:** This street is named for the water pipes in the wall that flowed into the Alcázar (you can see them at the end of the lane—they follow the wall of the Alcázar gardens). On the left, peek through iron gates for the occasional glimpse of the flower-smothered patios of exclusive private residences. The patio at #2 is a delight—ringed with columns, filled with flowers, and colored with glazed tiles. The tiles are not only decorative; they keep buildings cooler in the summer heat. At the end of the street (look back to see the old plumbing) is an entrance into the pleasant Murillo Gardens (to the right), formerly the fruit-and-vegetable gardens for the Alcázar.

• *Don't enter the gardens now, but instead cross the square and continue 20 yards down a lane to...*

❺ **Plaza de la Santa Cruz:** Arguably the heart of the Barrio, this was once the site of a synagogue (there were three, now there are none), which Christians destroyed. They replaced the synagogue with a church, which the French (under Napoleon) then demolished. It's a bit of history that locals remember when they see the red, white, and blue French flag marking the French consulate, now overlooking this peaceful square. The painter Murillo, who was buried in the now-gone church, now lies somewhere below you. On the square you'll find the recommended Los Gallos flamenco bar (described on page 502) and Bar El Tamboríl (which combusts nightly after midnight with impromptu flamenco; see page 502).

• *Follow Calle Mezquita farther east to the nearby...*

❻ **Plaza de Refinadores:** Sevilla's most famous (if fictional) 17th-century citizen is honored here with a statue. Don Juan Tenorio—the original Don Juan—was a notorious sex addict and atheist who thumbed his nose at the stifling, Church-driven morals of his day.

• *Backtrack to Plaza de la Santa Cruz and turn right (north) on Calle*

Sevilla's Jews

In the summer of 1391, smoldering anti-Jewish sentiment flared up in Sevilla. On June 6, the city's Jewish Quarter (Judería) was ransacked by Christian mobs. Four thousand Jews were killed, 5,000 Jewish families driven from their homes, synagogues were stripped and transformed into churches, the Star of David came down, and the former Judería eventually became the neighborhood of the Holy Cross—Barrio Santa Cruz. Sevilla's uprising spread through Spain (and Europe), the first of many nasty pogroms during the next century.

Before the pogrom, Jews had lived in Sevilla for centuries as the city's respected merchants, doctors, and bankers. They flourished under the Muslim Moors. When Sevilla was "liberated" by King Ferdinand (1248), Jews were given protection by Spain's kings and allowed a measure of self-government, though they were confined to the Jewish neighborhood.

But by the 14th century, Jews were increasingly accused of everything from poisoning wells to ritually sacrificing Christian babies. Mobs killed suspected Jews, some of Sevilla's most respected Jewish citizens had their fortunes confiscated, and Jewish kids were mocked and bullied on the playground.

After 1391, Jews faced a choice: Be persecuted (even killed), relocate, or convert to Christianity. Those who converted—called *conversos,* New Christians, or *marranos* ("swine")—were always under suspicion of practicing their old faith in private, undermining true Christianity. Fanning the suspicion was the fact that Old Christians were threatened by this new social class of converted Jews who now had equal status.

To root out the perceived problem of underground Judaism, the "Catholic Monarchs" Ferdinand and Isabel established the Inquisition in Spain (1478). Under the direction of Grand Inquisitor Tomás de Torquemada, these religious courts arrested and interrogated *conversos* suspected of practicing Judaism. Using long solitary confinement and torture, they extracted confessions.

On February 6, 1481, Sevilla hosted Spain's first *auto da fé* ("act of faith"), a public confession and punishment for heresy. Six accused *conversos* were paraded barefoot into the cathedral, made to publicly confess their sins, then were burned at the stake. Over the next three decades, thousands of *conversos* (some historians say hundreds, some say tens of thousands) were tried and killed in Spain.

In 1492, the same year the last Moors were driven from Spain, Ferdinand and Isabel decreed that all remaining Jews convert or be expelled (to Portugal and ultimately to Holland). Spain emerged as a nation unified under the banner of Christianity.

Bartolomé Murillo
(1617–1682)

The son of a barber of Seville, Bartolomé Murillo got his start selling paintings meant for export to the frontier churches of the Americas. In his 20s, he became famous after he painted a series of saints for Sevilla's Franciscan monastery. By about 1650, Murillo's sugary, simple, and accessible religious style was spreading through Spain and beyond.

Murillo painted street kids with cute smiles and grimy faces, and radiant young Marías with Ivory-soap complexions and rapturous poses (Immaculate Conceptions). His paintings view the world through a soft-focus lens, wrapping everything in warm colors and soft light, with a touch (too much, for some) of sentimentality.

Murillo became rich, popular, a family man, and the toast of Sevilla's high society. In 1664, his wife died, leaving him heartbroken, but his last 20 years were his most prolific. At age 65, Murillo died painting, falling off a scaffold. His tomb is lost somewhere under the bricks of Plaza de la Santa Cruz.

Santa Teresa. At #8 is...

❼ **Casa de Murillo:** One of Sevilla's famous painters lived here, soaking in the ambience of street life and reproducing it in his paintings of cute beggar children (see sidebar).

• *Directly across from Casa de Murillo is the...*

❽ **Convent of San José del Carmen:** This is where Saint Teresa stayed when she visited from her hometown of Ávila. The convent (closed to the public) keeps relics of the mystic nun, such as the manuscript of her treatise *Las Moradas* ("The Interior Castle," "where truth dwells").

Continue north on Calle Santa Teresa, then take the first left (west) on Calle Lope de Rueda, then right on **Calle Reinoso.** This street—so narrow that the buildings almost touch—is one of the Barrio's "kissing lanes."

• *The street spills into...*

❾ **Plaza de los Venerables:** This square is another candidate for "heart of the Barrio." The streets branching off it ooze local ambience. The large, harmonious, Baroque-style Hospital of the Venerables (1675), once a priests' retirement home (the "venerables"), is now a museum (€4.75). The highlight is the church and courtyard, featuring a round, sunken fountain.

• *Continuing west on Calle Gloria, you soon reach...*

⑩ **Plaza de Doña Elvira:** This small square—with orange trees, tile benches, and a stone fountain—sums up our Barrio walk. Shops sell work by local artisans, such as ceramics, embroidery, and fans.

• *Cross the plaza and head north along Calle Rodrigo Caro into...*

⑪ **Plaza de la Alianza:** Ever consider a career change? Gain inspiration at the John Fulton Studio, a former art gallery featuring the work of the American who pursued two dreams. Though born in Philadelphia, Fulton got hooked on bullfighting. He trained in the tacky bullrings of Mexico, then in 1956 he moved to Sevilla, the world capital of the sport. His career as matador was not top-notch, and the Spaniards were slow to warm to the Yankee, but his courage and persistence earned their grudging respect. After retirement, he put down the cape and picked up a brush, making the colorful paintings in this studio.

• *From Plaza de la Alianza, you can return to the cathedral by turning left (west) on Calle Romero Murube (along the wall). Or head east/northeast on Callejón de Rodrigo Caro, which intersects with Calle Mateos Gago, a street lined with atmospheric tapas bars.*

SIGHTS

▲▲Cathedral and Giralda Bell Tower

Sevilla's cathedral is the third-largest church in Europe (after St. Peter's at the Vatican and St. Paul's in London), and the largest Gothic church anywhere. When they ripped down a mosque of brick on this site in 1401, the Reconquista Christians bragged, "We'll build a cathedral so huge that anyone who sees it will take us for madmen." They built for 120 years. Even today, the descendants of those madmen proudly display an enlarged photocopy of their *Guinness Book of Records* letter certifying, "The cathedral with the largest area is: Santa María de la Sede in Sevilla, 126 meters long, 82 meters wide, and 30 meters high."

Cost and Hours: €7.50; July–mid-Sept Mon–Sat 9:30–17:00, Sun 14:30–18:00; mid-Sept–June Mon–Sat 11:00–18:00, Sun 14:30–19:00; last entry one hour before closing, WC and drinking fountain inside near entrance and in courtyard near exit, tel. 954-214-971.

Tours: My self-guided tour (below) covers the basics. The €3 audioguide explains each side chapel for anyone interested in all the old paintings and dry details. For €6, you can enjoy Concepción Delgado's tour instead (described on page 471).

➲ **Self-Guided Tour:** Enter the cathedral at the south end (closest to the Alcázar, with a full-size replica of the Giralda's weathervane statue in the patio).

• *First, head to the...*

Art Pavilion and Restoration: Just past the turnstile, you step into a pavilion of paintings that once hung in the church, including works by Sevilla's two 17th-century masters—Bartolomé Murillo *(St. Ferdinand)* and Francisco de Zurbarán *(St. John the Baptist in the Desert)*. Also find a painting showing the two patron saints of Sevilla—Santa Justa and Santa Rufina. They are easy to identify for their pots and palm branches, and for the bell tower symbolizing the town they protect. As you tour the cathedral, keep track of how many depictions of this dynamic and saintly duo you spot. They're everywhere.

Walking past a rack of church maps and a WC, enter the actual church. The first things you'll see are the **restoration braces** supporting huge pillars. These are intended to help keep the building from collapsing as people search for an answer to the problem of the pillars' cracking. (But I'd move right along.)

• *In the center of the church, sit down in front of the...*

High Altar: Look through the wrought-iron Renaissance grille at what's called the largest altarpiece *(retablo mayor)* ever made—65 feet tall, with 44 scenes from the life of Jesus carved out of walnut and chestnut, blanketed by a staggering amount of gold leaf (and dust). The work took three generations to complete (1481–1564). The story is told left to right, bottom (birth of Jesus) to top (Pentecost), with the Crucifixion at the dizzying summit.

• *Turn around and check out the...*

Choir: Facing the high altar, the choir features an organ of 7,000 pipes (played at the 10:00 Mass Mon–Fri, not in July–Aug, free for worshippers). A choir area like this one (an enclosure within the cathedral for more intimate services) is common in Spain and England, but rare in churches elsewhere. The big, spinnable book holder in the middle of the room held giant hymnals—large enough for all to chant from in a pre-Xerox age when there weren't enough books for everyone.

• *Now turn 90 degrees to the left and march to find the...*

Tomb of Columbus: In front of the cathedral's entrance for pilgrims are four kings who carry the tomb of Christopher Columbus. His pallbearers represent the regions of Castile, Aragon, León, and Navarre (identify them by their team shirts). Columbus even traveled a lot posthumously. He was buried first in Spain, then in Santo Domingo in the Dominican Republic, then Cuba, and finally—when Cuba gained independence from Spain, around 1900—he sailed home again to Sevilla. Are the remains actually his? Sevillans like to think so. (Columbus died in 1506. Five hundred years later, to help celebrate

Sevilla's Cathedral

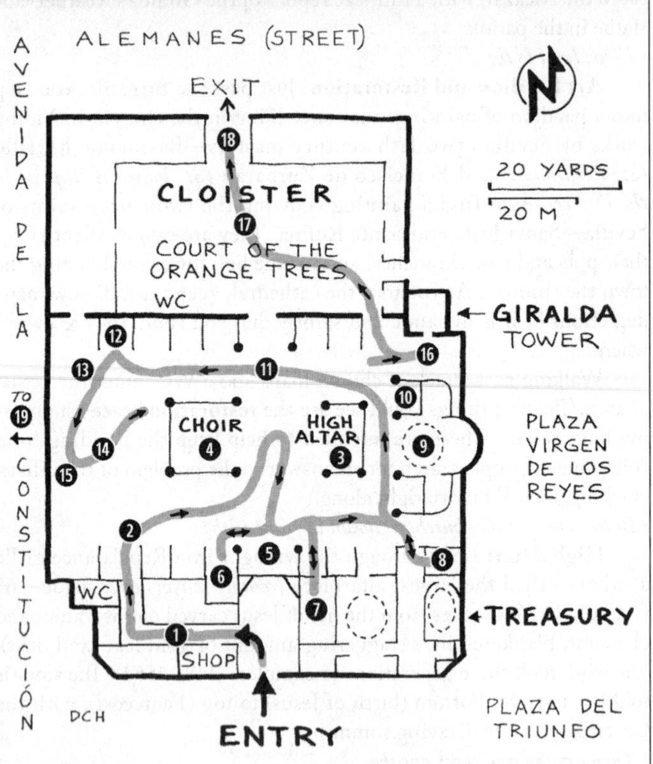

ALEMANES (STREET)

AVENIDA DE LA CONSTITUCIÓN

EXIT

CLOISTER

COURT OF THE ORANGE TREES

WC

GIRALDA TOWER

20 YARDS

20 M

CHOIR

HIGH ALTAR

TO 19

PLAZA VIRGEN DE LOS REYES

WC

TREASURY

SHOP

DCH

ENTRY

PLAZA DEL TRIUNFO

1. Art Pavilion
2. Pillar Restoration Braces
3. High Altar
4. Choir
5. Tomb of Columbus
6. Antigua Chapel
7. Sacristy
8. Treasury
9. Royal Chapel
10. Chapel of St. Peter
11. View of Plateresque Ceiling
12. Chapel of St. Anthony
13. Pennant of Fernando III
14. Back of the Nave
15. MURILLO – Guardian Angel
16. Giralda Tower Climb Entrance
17. Court of the Orange Trees
18. Moorish-Style Doorway
19. To Nun-Baked Goodies

the anniversary of his death, DNA samples gave Sevillans the evidence they needed to substantiate their claim.) High above on the left is a mural of St. Christopher—patron saint of travelers—from 1584. The clock above has been ticking since 1788.

• *Head to the next chapel on the right to find the...*

Antigua Chapel: Within this chapel is the gilded fresco of the Virgin Antigua, the oldest art in the church. It was actually painted onto a horseshoe-shaped prayer niche of the former mosque on this site. After Sevilla was reconquered in 1248, the mosque served as a church for about 120 years—until it was torn down to make room for this huge cathedral. Builders, captivated by the beauty of the Virgin holding the rose and the Christ Child holding the bird (and knowing that she was considered the protector of sailors in this port city), decided to save the fresco.

• *Exiting the chapel, we'll tour the cathedral counterclockwise. As you explore, note that its many chapels are described in English, and many of the windows have their dates worked into the design. Just on the other side of Columbus, step into the...*

Sacristy: This space is used each morning before Mass. The Goya painting above the altar features Justa and Rufina—the two patron saints of Sevilla, who were martyred in ancient Roman times. In addition to the town bell tower, they're always shown with their trademark items. I say they each hold a bowl of *gazpacho* (particularly refreshing on hot summer days) and sprigs of rosemary from local Gypsies (an annoyance even back then). Art historians claim that since they were pottery-makers, they are shown with earthenware, and the sprigs are palm leaves—symbolic of their martyrdom. Whatever.

• *A few rooms over is the...*

Treasury: The *tesoro* fills several rooms in the corner of the church. Start by marveling at the ornate, 16th-century Plateresque dome of the main room, a grand souvenir from Sevilla's Golden Age. The intricate masonry resembles lacy silverwork (it's named for *plata*—silver). God is way up in the cupola. The three layers of figures below him show the heavenly host; relatives in purgatory—hands folded—looking to heaven and hoping you do them well; and the wretched in hell, including a topless sinner engulfed in flames and teased cruelly by pitchfork-wielding monsters. Locals use the 110-pound silver monstrance, which dominates this room, to parade the holy host (communion bread) through town during Corpus Christi festivities.

Wander deeper into the treasury to find a unique oval dome. It's in the 16th-century chapter room *(sala capitular)*, where monthly meetings take place with the bishop (he gets the throne, while the others share the bench). The paintings here are by Murillo: a fine *Immaculate Conception* (1668, above the bishop's throne) and portraits of saints important to Sevillans.

The wood-paneled "room of ornaments" shows off gold and silver

reliquaries, which hold hundreds of holy body parts, as well as Spain's most valuable crown. The Corona de la Virgen de los Reyes sparkles with 11,000 precious stones and the world's largest pearl—used as the torso of an angel. Opposite the crown is a reliquary featuring "a piece of the true cross."

• *Leave the treasury and cross through the church to see...*

More Church Sights: First you'll pass the closed-to-tourists **Royal Chapel,** the burial place of several of the kings of Castile (open for worship only—access from outside); then the **Chapel of St. Peter,** which is dark but filled with paintings by Francisco de Zurbarán (showing scenes from the life of St. Peter). At the far corner—past the glass case displaying the *Guinness* certificate declaring that this is indeed the world's largest church by area—is the entry to the Giralda Bell Tower. You'll finish your visit here. But for now, continue your counterclockwise circuit. Near the middle (and high) altar, crane your neck skyward to admire the Plateresque tracery on the ceiling.

The **Chapel of St. Anthony** (Capilla de San Antonio), the last chapel on the right, is used for baptisms. The Renaissance baptismal font has delightful carved angels dancing along its base. In Murillo's painting, *Vision of St. Anthony* (1656), the saint kneels in wonder as a baby Jesus comes down surrounded by a choir of angels. Anthony is one of Iberia's most popular saints. As he is the patron saint of lost things, people come here to pray for Anthony's help in finding jobs, car keys, and life partners. Above that is the *Baptism of Christ,* also by Murillo. You don't need to be an art historian to know that the stained glass dates from 1685. And by now, you must know who the women are...

Nearby, a glass case displays the **pennant of Fernando III,** which was raised over the minaret of the mosque on November 23, 1248, as Christian forces finally expelled the Moors from Sevilla. For centuries, it was paraded through the city on special days.

Continuing on, stand at the **back of the nave** (behind the choir) and appreciate the ornate immensity of the church. Can you see the angels trumpeting on their Cuban mahogany? Any birds?

Turn around. The massive candlestick holder dates from 1560. To the left is a niche with Murillo's *Guardian Angel* pointing to the light, and showing an astonished child the way.

Immaculate Conception

Throughout Sevilla and Spain, you'll see paintings titled *The Immaculate Conception,* all looking quite similar (see example on page 479). Young, lovely, and beaming radiantly, these virgins look pure, untainted...you might even say "immaculate." According to Catholic doctrine, Mary, the future mother of Jesus, entered the world free from the original sin that other mortals share. When she died, her purity allowed her to be taken up directly to heaven (the Assumption).

The doctrine of Immaculate Conception can be confusing, even to Catholics. It does not mean that the Virgin Mary herself was born of a virgin. Rather, Mary's mother and father conceived her in the natural way. But at the moment Mary's soul animated her flesh, God granted her a special exemption from original sin. The doctrine of Immaculate Conception had been popular since medieval times, though it was not codified until 1854. It was Sevilla's own Bartolomé Murillo (1617–1682) who painted the model that so many lesser artists copied of this goddess-like Mary. In Counter-Reformation times (when Murillo lived), paintings of a fresh-faced, ecstatic Mary made abstract doctrines like the Immaculate Conception and the Assumption tangible and accessible to all.

An easy way to recognize an image of the Immaculate Conception is to look for the following clues: a radiant crown, a crescent moon at Mary's feet, and often a pose showing Mary stepping on cherubs' heads. Paintings by Murillo frequently portray Mary in a blue robe with long, wavy hair—young and innocent.

• *Backtrack the length of the church toward the Giralda Bell Tower, and notice the back of the choir's Baroque pipe organ. The* exit *sign leads to the Court of the Orange Trees and the exit. But first, for some exercise...*

Giralda Tower Climb: Your church admission includes entry to the bell tower. Notice the beautiful Moorish simplicity as you climb to its top, 330 feet up, for a grand city view. The spiraling ramp was designed to accommodate riders on horseback, who galloped up five times a day to give the Muslim call to prayer.

• *Go back down the stairs and visit the...*

Court of the Orange Trees: Today's cloister was once the mosque's Court of the Orange Trees (Patio de los Naranjos). Twelfth-century Muslims stopped at the fountain in the middle to wash their hands, face, and feet before praying. The ankle-breaking lanes between

Christopher Columbus
(1451–1506)

This Italian wool-weaver ran off to sea, was shipwrecked in Portugal, married a captain's daughter, learned Portuguese and Spanish, and convinced Spain's monarchs to finance his bold scheme to trade with the East by sailing west. On August 3, 1492, Columbus set sail from Palos (near Huelva, 60 miles west of Sevilla) with three ships and 90 men, hoping to land in Asia, which Columbus estimated was 3,000 miles away. Three thousand miles later—with the superstitious crew ready to mutiny, having seen evil omens like a falling meteor and a jittery compass—Columbus landed on an island in the Bahamas (October 12, 1492), convinced he'd reached Asia. They traded with the "Indians" and returned home to Palos harbor, where they were received as heroes.

Columbus made three more voyages to the New World and became rich with gold. He gained a bad reputation among the colonists, was arrested, and returned to Spain in chains. Though pardoned, Columbus fell out of favor with the court. On May 20, 1506, he died in Valladolid. His son said he was felled by "gout and by grief at seeing himself fallen from his high estate," but historians speculate that diabetes or syphilis may have contributed. Columbus died thinking he'd visited Asia, unaware he'd opened up Europe to a New World.

the bricks were once irrigation streams—a reminder that the Moors introduced irrigation to Iberia. The mosque was made of bricks; the church is built of stone. The only remnants of the mosque today are the Court of the Orange Trees, the Giralda Bell Tower, and the site itself.

As you exit the Court of the Orange Trees (and the cathedral), notice the arch over the **Moorish-style doorway.** As with much of the Moorish-looking art in town, it's actually Christian—the two coats of arms are a giveaway. The relief above the door (looking in from outside) shows the Bible story of Jesus ridding the temple of the merchants...a reminder to contemporary merchants that there will be no retail activity in the church. The plaque on the right is one of many scattered throughout town showing a place mentioned in the books of Miguel de Cervantes, the great 16th-century Spanish writer. (In this case, the topic was pickpockets.) The huge green doors predate the church. They are a bit of the surviving pre-1248 mosque—wood covered with bronze. Study the fine workmanship.

Giralda Tower Exterior: Step across the street from the exit gate and look at the bell tower. Formerly a Moorish minaret from which Muslims were called to prayer, it became the cathedral's bell

tower after the Reconquista. It's crowned by a 4,500-pound bronze statue symbolizing the Triumph of Faith (specifically, the Christian faith over the Muslim one) that caps it and serves as a weathervane (*giraldillo* in Spanish). In 1356, the original top of the tower fell. You're looking at a 16th-century Christian-built top with a ribbon of letters proclaiming, "The strongest tower is the name of God" (you can see *Fortísima*—"strongest"—from this vantage point).

Needing more strength than their bricks could provide for the lowest section of the tower, the Moors used Roman-cut stones. Now circle around for a close look at the corner of the tower at ground level; you can actually read the Latin chiseled onto one of the stones 2,000 years ago. The tower offers a brief recap of the city's history—sitting on a Roman foundation, a long Moorish period capped by our Christian age. Today, by law, no building can be higher than the statue atop the tower.

• *If you've worked up an appetite, finish your cathedral tour with some...*

Nun-Baked Goodies: Stop by the "El Torno" Pasteleria de Conventos, a co-op where the various orders of cloistered nuns sell their handicrafts (such as baby's baptismal dresses) and baked goods. "El Torno" is the lazy Susan that the cloistered nuns spin to sell their cakes and cookies without being seen. This is a humble little hole-in-the-wall, but it's worth a peek (Sept–July Mon–Fri 10:00–13:30 & 17:00–19:30, Sat–Sun 10:30–14:00, closed Aug, across Avenida de la Constitución, immediately in front of the cathedral's biggest door, follow *dulces de convento* sign down a little covered lane to Plaza Cabildo 21, tel. 954-219-190).

Near the Cathedral

Avenida de la Constitución—Old Sevilla is bisected by its grand boulevard. It was named to celebrate the 1978 democratic constitution the Spanish people adopted as they moved quickly after the 1975 death of Franco to establish their freedom. Long a commercial street, it was made into a pedestrian boulevard in 2007. Overnight, the city's paseo route took on a new dimension. And suddenly cafés and shops here had an appeal. (Two Starbucks moved in, placed strategically like bookends on the boulevard, but are having a tough time winning the loyalty of locals who like small coffees for €1 rather than mammoth ones for €4.) The tram line (which is infamous for being short—only three-quarters of a mile long) is controversial as it violates what might have been a more purely people zone.

Alcázar and Nearby

▲▲Alcázar—Originally a 10th-century palace built for the governors of the local Moorish state, this building still functions as a royal palace...the oldest in use in Europe. What you see today is an extensive 14th-century rebuild, done by Moorish (Mudejar) workmen for the Christian king Pedro I. Pedro was nicknamed either "the Cruel" or "the Just," depending on which end of his sword you were on.

Cost and Hours: €7; peak season Tue–Sat 9:30–19:00, Sun 9:30–17:00, closed Mon; off-season Tue–Sat 9:30–17:00, Sun 9:30–13:30, closed Mon; tel. 954-502-323. Tour groups clog the palace and rob it of any mystery in the morning (especially on Tue); come as late as possible.

Tours: The fast-moving, easy-to-use €3 audioguide gives you an hour of information as you wander—if you want that much (drop it off at the exit). Again, rather then renting the audioguide, you could follow my self-guided tour (below), or consider Concepción Delgado's €6 Alcázar tour (described on page 471).

➲ Self-Guided Tour: The Alcázar is a thought-provoking glimpse of a graceful Al-Andalus (Moorish) world that might have survived its Castilian conquerors...but didn't. The floor plan is intentionally confusing, part of the style designed to make experiencing the place more exciting and surprising. While Granada's Alhambra was built by Moors for Moorish rulers, what you see here is essentially a Christian ruler's palace, built in the Moorish style.

Just past the turnstiles, walk through the Patio of the Lions and stop under the arch of the wall to orient yourself. Facing the Patio de la Montería, you see the palace's three wings: the wing on the right is the 16th-century Admiral's Apartments; straight ahead is King Pedro the Cruel's Palace; and on the left is the 13th-century Gothic wing. You'll tour them in that order (entering the Gothic wing from within Pedro's palace).

Before starting, notice the public WCs in the far-left corner, and a staircase in the far-right corner leading up to the lived-in Royal Apartments. (These are available by tour only. They're similar to what you'll see downstairs, but with furniture. If interested, go there now to book an available spot—€4 for a 25-min escorted walk through 15 rooms with an audioguide, 15 people per tour, lockers provided for your visit.)

• *Start by heading to the...*

Alcázar

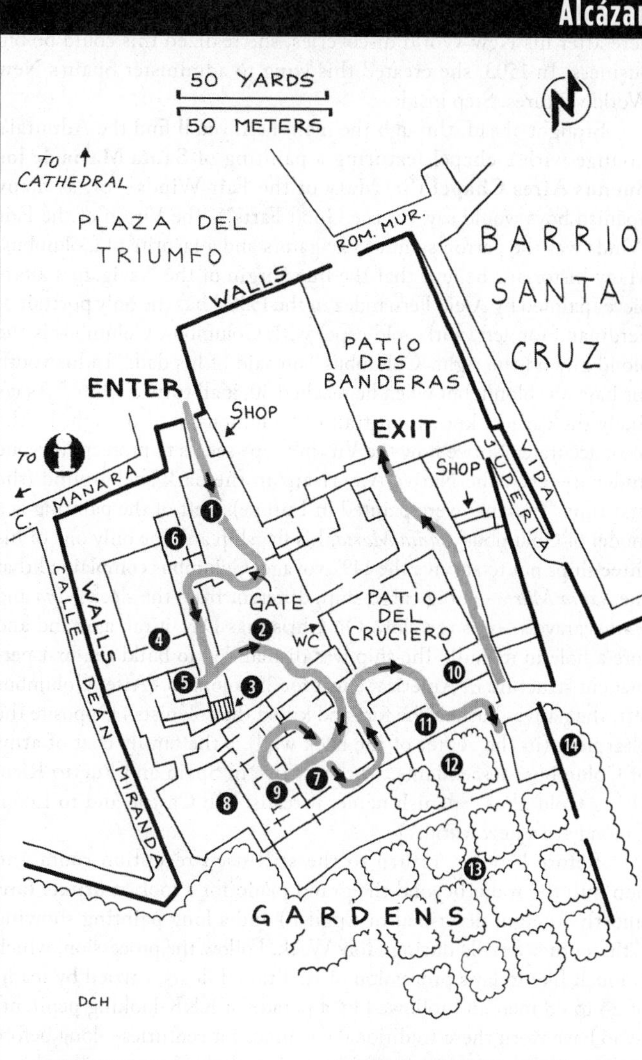

1. Patio of the Lions
2. Patio de la Montería
3. Stairs to Royal Apartments
4. Admiral's Apartments
5. Painting of Santa María de los Buenos Aires Chapel
6. Ornate Fans
7. Court of the Maidens
8. King Pedro the Cruel's Palace
9. Dolls' Court
10. Gothic Wing
11. Big Tapestries
12. Moorish Garden
13. Christian Garden
14. Elevated Walkway

Admiral's Apartments: When Queen Isabel debriefed Columbus here after his New World discoveries, she realized this could be big business. In 1503, she created this wing to administer Spain's New World ventures. Step inside.

Straight ahead, through the main hall, you'll find the Admiral's Lounge with a chapel featuring a painting of **Santa María de los Buenos Aires Chapel** (St. Mary of the Fair Winds—or, as many Spanish boys would say, "of the Good Farts"). The Virgin of the Fair Winds was the patron saint of navigators and a favorite of Columbus. Many historians believe that the fine Virgin of the Navigators altarpiece (painted by Alejo Fernández in the 1530s) has the only portrait of Ferdinand (on left, with gold cape) with Columbus. Columbus is the blond guy on the right. Columbus' son said of his dad: "In his youth his hair was blond, but when he reached 30, it all turned white." As it's likely the earliest known portrait of Columbus, it also might be the most accurate. Notice how the Virgin's cape seems to protect everyone under it—even the Native Americans in the dark background (the first time "Indians" were painted in Europe). Left of the painting is a model of Columbus' *Santa María,* his flagship and the only one of his three ships not to survive the 1492 voyage. Columbus complained that the *Santa María*—a big cargo ship, different from the sleek *Niña* and *Pinta* caravels—was too slow. On Christmas Day, it ran aground and tore a hole in its hull. The ship was dismantled to build the first permanent structure in America, a fort for 39 colonists. (After Columbus left, the natives burned the fort and killed the colonists.) Opposite the altarpiece (in the center of the back wall) is the family coat of arms of Columbus' descendants, who now live in Spain and Puerto Rico. Using Columbus' Spanish name, it reads: "To Castile and to León, Colón gave a new world."

Before leaving, return to the still-used reception room and pop into the room beyond the grand piano for a look at **ornate fans** (mostly foreign, described in English) and a long painting showing 17th-century Sevilla during Holy Week. Follow the procession, which is much like today's procession of traditional floats, carried by teams of 24 to 48 men and followed by a parade of KKK-looking penitents (who have worn these traditional costumes for centuries—long before such hoods became associated with racism in the American South).

• *Return to the main courtyard, enter the middle wing, and walk to the left through the vestibule until you hit the big courtyard called the* ***Court of the Maidens*** *(Patio de las Doncellas).*

King Pedro the Cruel's Palace: This 14th-century nucleus of the complex—the real Alcázar—is centered around the elegantly proportioned Court of the Maidens, decorated in 14th-century Moorish style below and a 16th-century Renaissance style above.

As you explore this wing, circulate counterclockwise through rooms branching off of this central courtyard and imagine day-to-day life in the palace (with VIP guests tripping on the tiny but jolting steps). King Pedro (1334–1369) cruelly abandoned his wife and moved into the Alcázar with his mistress. He hired Muslim workers from Granada to re-create the romance of that city's Alhambra in Sevilla's stark Alcázar. The designers created a microclimate engineered for coolness: water, plants, pottery, thick walls, and darkness. Even with the inevitable hodgepodge of style that comes with 600 years of renovation, this is considered Spain's best example of the Mudejar style. Notice the sumptuous ceilings; you'll see peacocks, castles, and kings that you wouldn't find in religious Muslim decor, which avoids images. The stylized Arabic script survives, creating a visual chant of verses from the Quran seen in Moorish buildings (including the Alhambra). The artisans added propaganda phrases such as, "Dedicated to the magnificent Sultan Pedro—thanks to God!"

The second courtyard, the smaller and more delicate **Dolls' Court** (Patio de las Muñecas) was for the king's private and family life. Originally, the center of the courtyard had a pool, cooling the residents and reflecting the decorative patterns once brightly painted on the walls.

• *Leave this wing from the big courtyard. Head to the staircase opposite from where you entered, and climb up into the...*

Gothic Wing: This wing of the palace shows fine **tapestries** from Brussels (1554). Find the second hall—with the biggest tapestries. These celebrate Emperor Charles V's 1535 victory in Tunis over the Turks (described both in Spanish along the top and in Latin along the bottom). The map tapestry comes with an unusual perspective—with Africa at the top (it's supposed to be from a Barcelona aerial perspective). Find the big fortified city in the middle (Barcelona, just above eye level), Santiago de Compostela, Lisboa (Lisbon), Gibraltar, the west edge of Italy, Rome, Sicily, and the Mediterranean islands. Don't try to navigate by this early map. Montserrat, which is just a few miles outside of Barcelona, is shown all the way over by Lisbon. The artist paints himself holding the legend—with a scale in both leagues and miles. This is an 18th-century copy of the original.

• *Head outside to...*

The Garden: This space is full of tropical flowers, wild cats, cool fountains, and hot tourists. The intimate geometric zone nearest the palace is the Moorish garden. The far-flung garden beyond that was the backyard of the Christian ruler. The elevated walkway along the left side of the gardens (access at both ends) provides fine views. You can explore the gardens and return via this walkway, or vice versa.

Archivo de Indias—The Lonja Palace (across the street from Alcázar) was designed by the same person who designed El Escorial. Originally a market, it's the top building in Sevilla from its 16th-century glory days. Today, it houses the archive of documents from the discovery and conquest of the New World. This could be fascinating, but little of importance is on display (old maps of Havana). The displays are in Spanish, but you can pick up English brochures describing both permanent and temporary exhibits (free, Mon–Sat 9:00–16:00, Sun 10:00–14:00, tel. 954-500-528).

Between the River and the Cathedral

Hospital de la Caridad—This Charity Hospital was founded by a nobleman in the 17th century. Peek into the fine courtyard. On the left, the chapel has some gruesome art (above both doors) illustrating that death is the great equalizer, and an altar so sweet only a Spaniard could enjoy it. The Dutch tiles depicting scenes of the Old and New Testament are a reminder of the time when the Netherlands were under Spanish rule in the mid-16th century (€5, erratic hours, but typically Mon–Sat 9:00–13:30 & 15:30–19:30, Sun 9:00–13:00, last entry 30 min before closing, tel. 954-223-232).

Golden Tower (Torre del Oro) and Naval Museum—Sevilla's historic riverside Golden Tower was the starting point and ending point for all shipping to the New World. It's named for the golden tiles that once covered it—not for all the New World booty that landed here. Since the Moors built it in the 13th century, it has been part of the city's fortifications, with a heavy chain draped across the river to protect the harbor. Today it houses a dreary little naval museum. Looking past the dried fish and charts of knots, find the mural showing the world-spanning journeys of Vasco da Gama, the model of Columbus' *Santa María* (the first ship to land in the New World), and an interesting mural of Sevilla in 1740. Enjoy the view from the balconies upstairs. The Guadalquivir River is now just a trickle of its former self, after canals built in the 1920s siphoned off most of its water to feed ports downstream (€2, includes audioguide, Sept–July Tue–Fri 10:00–14:00, Sat–Sun 11:00–14:00, closed Mon and Aug, tel. 954-222-419).

North of the Cathedral, near Plaza Nueva

▲▲Dance Museum (Museo del Baile Flamenco)—If you want to understand more about the dance that embodies the spirit of southern Spain, this museum—while overpriced at €10—does the trick. The grande dame of flamenco, Cristina Hoyos, has collected a few artifacts and costumes and put together a series of videos explaining the art of flamenco. One particularly interesting film illustrates the key elements of the dance form: pain, joy, elegance, seduction, soul, and—I believe—love of ham (daily 9:00–19:00,

Calle Manuel Rojas Marcos 3, about three blocks east of Plaza Nueva, tel. 954-340-311, www.museoflamenco.com). Watch a dance class when visiting the museum, or participate in a one-hour lesson and take a little *olé* home with you (€60 max per person, prices go down with more people, shoes provided). There are also dance shows on Thursday, Friday, and Saturday nights at 19:30 (€25, 10 percent discount with this book in 2009).

▲Museo Palacio de la Condesa de Lebrija—This aristocratic mansion takes you back into the 18th century like no other place in town. The Countess of Lebrija was a passionate collector of antiquities. Her home's ground floor is paved with Roman mosaics (that you actually walk on) and lined with musty old cases of Phoenician, Greek, Roman, and Moorish artifacts—mostly pottery. To see a plush world from a time when the nobility had a private priest and their own chapel, take a quickie tour of the upstairs, which shows the palace as the countess left it when she died in 1938 (€4 for unescorted visit of ground floor, €8 includes tour of "lived-in" upstairs offered every 45 min, likely open Mon–Fri 10:00–19:30, Sat 10:00–14:00, closed Sun, free and obligatory bag check, Calle Cuna 8, tel. 954-227-802).

South of the Cathedral, near Plaza de España

University—Today's university was yesterday's *fábrica de tabacos* (tobacco factory), which employed 10,000 young female *cigareras*—including the saucy femme fatale of Bizet's opera *Carmen*. In the 18th century, it was the second-largest building in Spain, after El Escorial. Wander through its halls as you walk to Plaza de España. The university's bustling café is a good place for cheap tapas, beer, wine, and conversation (Mon–Fri 8:00–21:00, Sat 9:00–13:00, closed Sun).

Plaza de España—This square, the surrounding buildings, and the nearby María Luisa Park are the remains of the 1929 international fair, where for a year the Spanish-speaking countries of the world enjoyed a mutual-admiration fiesta. When they finish the construction work here (it's taking years), this delightful area—the epitome of world's fair–style architecture—will once again be great for people-watching (especially during the 19:00–20:00 peak paseo hour). The park's highlight is the former Spanish Pavilion. Its tiles (a trademark of Sevilla) show historic scenes and maps from every province of Spain (arranged in alphabetical order, from Álava to Zaragoza). Climb to one of the balconies for a fine view. Beware: This is a classic haunt of thieves and con artists. Believe no one here. Thieves, posing as lost tourists, will come at you with a map unfolded to hide their speedy, greedy fingers.

Away from the Center

▲Museo de Bellas Artes

Sevilla's passion for religious art is preserved and displayed in its Museum of Fine Art. While most Americans go for El Greco, Goya, and Velázquez (not a forte of this collection), this museum gives a fine look at the other, less-appreciated Spanish masters: Zurbarán and Murillo. Rather than exhausting, the museum is pleasantly enjoyable.

Cost, Hours, Location: €1.50, Tue 14:30–20:30, Wed–Sat 9:00–20:30, Sun 9:00–14:30, closed Mon, last entry 15 min before closing, 15-min walk from the cathedral, Plaza Museo 9, tel. 954-220-790. Pick up the English-language floor plan, which explains the theme of each room. If coming from La Macarena (described on next page), take bus #C4 to the Torneo stop and walk inland four blocks.

Background: Several of Spain's top artists—Zurbarán, Murillo, and Velázquez—lived in Sevilla. This was Spain's wealthy commercial capital, like New York City, while Madrid was a newly built center of government, like Washington DC. In the early 1800s, Spain's liberal government was disbanding convents and monasteries, and secular fanatics were looting churches. Thankfully, the region's religious art was rescued and hung safely here in this convent-turned-museum.

Spain's economic Golden Age (the 1500s) blossomed into the Golden Age of Spanish painting (the 1600s). Artists such as Zurbarán combined realism with mysticism. He painted balding saints and monks with wrinkled faces and sunburned hands. The style suited Spain's spiritual climate, as the Catholic Church used this art in its Counter-Reformation battle against the Protestant rebellion.

➲ **Self-Guided Tour:** The core of the collection is in Rooms 3 through 10. Most of the major works are displayed in Room 5, the convent's former chapel. It's difficult not to say "Wow!" when entering. Tour the collection starting upstairs in Room 10 (head into the cloister and climb the grand staircase). Then, after exploring the first floor according to your interests, finish in the big former church (Room 5).

Francisco de Zurbarán (thoor-bar-AHN, 1598–1664) paints saints and monks, and the miraculous things they experience, presented with unblinking, crystal-clear, brightly lit, highly detailed realism. Monks and nuns could meditate upon Zurbarán's meticulous paintings (Room 10 and the room leading to 10) for hours, finding God in the details.

Zurbarán shines a harsh spotlight on his subject, creating strong shadows. Like the secluded monks themselves, Zurbarán's people stand starkly isolated against a dark, single-color background. He was the ideal painter of the austere religion of 17th-century Spain.

In Zurbarán's ***St. Hugo Visiting the Carthusian Monks at Supper*** (Room 10), white-robed monks gather together for their simple meal in the communal dining hall. Above them hangs a painting of Mary, Baby Jesus, and John the Baptist. Zurbarán created paintings for monks' dining halls like this. His audience: celibate men and women who lived in isolation, as in this former convent, devoting their time to quiet meditation, prayer, and Bible study.

In ***The Virgin of the Caves*** (also in Room 10, just to the right), study the piety and faith in the monks' rustic faces. Zurbarán shows a protective Mary with her hands on the heads of the two top monks of that order. Note the loving detail on the cape embroidery, the brooch, and the flowers at her feet. But also note the angel babies holding the cape—painfully double-jointed arms. Zurbarán was no Leonardo.

The ***Apotheosis of St. Thomas Aquinas*** (ground level, Room 5) is considered Zurbarán's most important work. It was done at the height of his career, when stark realism was all the rage. Here again Zurbarán presents the miraculous moment (when the saint gets his spiritual awakening) in a believable, down-to-earth way.

Bartolomé Murillo (mur-EE-oh, 1617–1682) was another hometown boy (see page 479). In Room 5, his ***Madonna and Child*** (*La Servilletta,* 1665; facing the front of the room, it's in a small room around the corner on the right) shows the warmth and appeal of his work. By about 1650, Murillo's easy-to-appreciate style had replaced Zurbarán's harsh realism.

The Immaculate Conception (several versions in the museum, ground floor, Room 5) was Murillo's favorite subject. To many Spaniards, Mary is their main connection to heaven. They pray directly to her, asking her to intercede for them with God. Murillo's *Mary*s are always receptive and ready to help.

▲▲Basílica de la Macarena

Sevilla's Holy Week (Semana Santa) celebrations are Spain's grandest. During the week leading up to Easter, the city is packed with pilgrims witnessing 50 processions carrying about 100 religious

floats. Get a feel for this event by visiting Basílica de la Macarena (built in 1947) to see the two most impressive floats and the darling of Holy Week, the Weeping Virgin (Virgen de la Macarena, a.k.a. La Esperanza). The museum may be closed for restoration until Easter 2009 (or possibly longer)—before making the trip, confirm at the TI that it's open.

Cost, Hours, Location: church free, museum-€3.50, buy ticket at shop by entrance, daily 9:30–14:00 & 17:00–20:00, taxi to Puerta Macarena or bus #C3 or #C4 from Puerta de Jerez or Menéndez Pelayo, tel. 954-901-800.

➲ **Self-Guided Tour:** Grab a pew and study Mary, complete with crystal teardrops. She's like a 17th-century doll with human hair and articulated arms, and even dressed with underclothes. Her beautiful expression—halfway between smiling and crying—is moving, in a Baroque way. Her weeping can be contagious—look around you. Filling a side chapel (on left) is the Christ of the Sentence (from 1654), showing Jesus the day he was condemned.

The two most important floats of the Holy Week parades—the floats that Jesus and Mary ride every Good Friday—are parked behind the altar (through the door left of the altar, museum ticket required).

The three-ton float that carries Jesus is slathered in gold leaf and shows a commotion of figures acting out the sentencing of Christ (whose statue—the one you saw in the church—is placed in the front of this crowd). Pontius Pilate is about to wash his hands. Pilate's wife cries as a man reads the death sentence. While pious Sevillan women wail in the streets, relays of 48 men carry this on the backs of their necks—only their feet showing under the drapes—as they shuffle through the streets from midnight until 14:00 in the afternoon every Good Friday. (The photo on the wall behind Pilate shows the float—with the bound "Christ of the Sentence" in place—pulling out of the church on Good Friday in 1986.) Shuffle upstairs for another perspective.

La Esperanza follows the Sentencing of Christ in the procession. Mary's smaller (1.5-ton) float, in the next room, seems all silver and candles—"strong enough to support the roof, but tender enough to quiver in the soft night breeze." Mary has a wardrobe of three huge mantles (each displayed here) worn in successive years. They are about 100 years old. Her six-pound gold crown/halo (in a glass case in the wall) is from 1913. This float has a mesmerizing effect on the local crowds. They line up for hours, clapping, weeping, and throwing roses as it slowly works its way through the city. My Sevillan friend explained, "She knows all the problems of Sevilla and its people. We've been confiding in her for centuries. To us, she is hope. That's her name—Esperanza."

Before leaving, find the case of matador garb (also upstairs) given to the church by bullfighters over the years. They are a token of thanks for the protection they feel they received from La Macarena. Considered the protector of bullfighters, she's big in bullring chapels. In 1912, the bullfighter José Ortega, hoping for protection, gave her the five emerald brooches she wears. It worked for eight years...until he was gored to death in the ring. (This was such a big deal that La Macarena was dressed in black—the only time that has happened.)

Outside, notice the best surviving bit of Sevilla's old walls. Originally Roman, what remains today is 12th-century Moorish, a reminder that off and on for centuries Sevilla was the capital of the Islamic kingdom in Iberia.

And yes, it's from this city that a local dance band (Los del Río) changed the world by giving us "The Macarena."

Near Sevilla

Itálica—One of Spain's most impressive Roman ruins is found outside the sleepy town of Santiponce, about six miles northwest of Sevilla. Founded in 206 B.C. for wounded soldiers recuperating from the Second Punic War, Itálica became a thriving town of great agricultural and military importance. It was the birthplace of famous Roman emperors Trajan and Hadrian. Today its best-preserved ruin is its amphitheater—one of the largest in the Roman Empire—with a capacity for 30,000 spectators. Other highlights include beautiful floor mosaics, such as the one in Casa de los Pájaros (House of the Birds) that shows more than 30 species of birds. To avoid the midday heat, plan your visit to arrive early or late, and definitely bring water (€1.50; April–Sept Tue–Sat 8:30–20:30, Sun 9:00–15:00, closed Mon; Oct–March 9:00–17:30, Sun 10:00–16:00, closed Mon; tel. 955-997-376).

Getting There: You can get to Itálica on bus #M172 (30-min trip, frequent departures from Sevilla's Plaza de Armas station). Drivers leave Sevilla heading west in the direction of Huelva; after you cross the second branch of the river, turn north on N-630, and after a few miles, get off at Santiponce. Drive past pottery warehouses and through the town to the ruins at the far (west) end.

EXPERIENCES

Bullfighting

▲Bullfights—Some of Spain's best bullfighting is done in Sevilla's 14,000-seat bullring, Plaza de Toros. Fights are held (generally at 18:30) on most Sundays in May and June; on Easter; during the April Fair (April 28–May 3 in 2009); and daily at the end of September (during the Feria de San Miguel). These serious fights, with adult matadors, are called *corrida de toros* and often sell out in advance. On

many Thursday evenings in July, there are *novillada* fights, with teenage novices doing the killing and smaller bulls doing the dying. *Corrida de toros* seats range from €20 for high seats looking into the sun to €140 for the first three rows in the shade under the royal box; *novillada* seats are half that—and easy to buy at the arena a few minutes before show time (ignore scalpers outside; get information at TI, your hotel, or call 954-210-315).

▲▲Bullfight Museum—Follow a bilingual (Spanish and English), 25-minute guided tour through the bullring's strangely quiet and empty arena, its museum, and the chapel where the matador prays before the fight. (Thanks to readily available blood transfusions, there have been no deaths in nearly three decades.) The two most revered figures of Sevilla, the Virgin of Macarena and the Christ of Gran Poder (All Power), are represented in the chapel. In the museum, you'll see great classic scenes and the heads of a few bulls—awarded the bovine equivalent of an Oscar for a particularly good fight. They were so appalled when the famous matador Manolete was killed in 1947 that they even destroyed the mother of the bull who gored him. Matadors—dressed to kill—are heartthrobs in their "suits of light." Many girls have their bedrooms wallpapered with posters of cute bullfighters. See page 651 for more on the "art" of bullfighting (€5, entrance with escorted tour only—no free time inside, 3/hr, daily 9:30–19:00, May–Oct until 20:00, until 14:00 on fight days, when chapel and horse room are closed). While they take groups of up to 50, it's still wise to call or drop by to reserve a spot in the busy season (tel. 954-210-315).

The April Fair

For seven days each April (April 28–May 3 in 2009), much of Sevilla is packed into its vast fairgrounds for a grand party. The fair, seeming to bring all that's Andalusian together, feels friendly, spontaneous, and very real. The local passion for horses, flamenco, and sherry is clear—riders are ramrod straight, colorfully clad girls ride sidesaddle, and everyone's drinking sherry spritzers. Women sport outlandish dresses that would look clownish all alone but are somehow brilliant here en masse. Horses clog the streets in an endless parade until

about 20:00, when they clear out and the streets fill with exuberant locals. The party goes for literally 24 hours a day for the entire week.

Countless private party tents, or *casetas,* line the lanes. Each tent is the private party zone of a family, club, or association. You need to know someone in the group—or make friends quickly—to get in. Because of the exclusivity, it has a real family-affair feeling. In each *caseta,* everyone knows everyone. It seems like a thousand wedding parties being celebrated at the same time.

Any tourist can have a fun and memorable evening by simply crashing the party. The city's entire fleet of taxis (who'll try to charge double) and buses seems dedicated to shuttling people from downtown to the fairgrounds. With the traffic jams, you may be better off hiking: From the Golden Tower, cross the San Telmo Bridge to Plaza de Cuba and hike down Calle Asunción. You'll see the towering gate to the fairgrounds in the distance. Just follow the crowds (there's no admission charge). Arrive before 20:00 to see the horses, but stay later, as the ambience improves after they giddy-up on out. Some of the larger tents are sponsored by the city and open to the public, but the best action is in the streets, where party-goers from the livelier *casetas* spill out. While private tents have bouncers, everyone is so happy, it's not tough to strike up an impromptu friendship, become a "special guest," and be invited in. The drink flows freely, and the food is fun and cheap.

SHOPPING

For the best local shopping experience, follow my shopping stroll (see below). The popular pedestrian streets Sierpes, Tetuán, and Velázquez—as well as the surrounding lanes near Plaza Nueva—are packed with people and shops. While small shops close between 13:30 and 16:00 or 17:00, big ones such as El Corte Inglés stay open (and air-conditioned) right through the siesta. El Corte Inglés also has a supermarket downstairs and a good but expensive restaurant (Mon–Sat 10:00–22:00, closed Sun). Popular souvenir items include ladies' fans, ceramics, and items from flamenco (castanets, guitars, costumes) and bullfighting (posters).

Collectors' markets hop on Sunday: stamps and coins at Plaza del Cabildo (near the cathedral) and art on Plaza del Museo (by the Museo de Bellas Artes).

Mercado del Arenal, the covered fish-and-produce market, is perfect for hungry photographers (Mon–Sat 9:00–14:30, closed Sun, least lively on Mon, on Calle Pastor y Landero at Calle Arenal, just beyond bullring). For suggestions on dining here (including a small café/bar for breakfast and a fish restaurant inside), see page 509 in "Eating."

▲▲Shopping Paseo Tour

While many tourists never get beyond the cathedral and the Santa Cruz neighborhood, it's important to wander west into the lively pedestrian shopping center of town. These streets—on Calle Tetuán, Calle Sierpes, and Calle Cuna—also happen to be part of the oldest section of Sevilla. A walk here is a chance to join one of Spain's liveliest paseos—that bustling celebration of life that takes place before dinner each evening, when everyone is out strolling. Locals stroll to show off their fancy shoes and make the scene. This walk (if done between 18:00 and 20:00) gives you a look at the paseo scene and the town's most popular shops. You'll pass windows displaying the best in both traditional and trendy fashion. The walk ends at a plush mansion of a local countess (open to the public).

Start on the pedestrianized **Plaza Nueva,** a 19th-century square facing the ornate city hall, which features a statue of Ferdinand III, a local favorite because he freed Sevilla from the Moors in 1248. From here, wander the length of Calle Tetuán (notice the latest in outrageous shoes). Calle Tetuán becomes Velázquez, and ends at La Campana (a big intersection and popular meeting point, with the super department store, El Corte Inglés, just beyond). At La Campana, tempt yourself with sweets at the venerable Confitería La Campana. Then take two rights to get to Calle Sierpes, great for shopping and strolling. Calle Sierpes is the main street of the Holy Week processions—imagine it packed with celebrants and with balconies bulging with spectators.

At the corner of Sierpes and Jovellanos/Sagasta, you're near several fine shops featuring Andalusian accessories. Drop in to see how serious local women are about their fans, combs, shawls, and *mantillas* (ornate head scarves). Andalusian women have various fans to match different dresses. The *mantilla* comes in black (worn only on Good Friday and by the mother of the groom at weddings) and white (worn at bullfights during the April Fair).

From here, turn left down Calle Sagasta. Notice that the street has two names—the modern version and a medieval one: Antigua Calle de Gallegos ("Ancient Street of the Galicians"). With the Christian victory in 1248, the Muslims were given one month to evacuate. To consolidate Christian control, settlers from the north were planted here. This street was home to the Galicians.

Finally, at the charming Plaza del Salvador, backtrack left along Calle Cuna, famous for its exuberant flamenco dresses and classic wedding dresses. (Flamenco miniskirts have been popular in recent years, but now hemlines are falling again.) If all this shopping makes you feel like a countess, Calle Cuna leads to the Museo Palacio de la Condesa de Lebrija (see listing on page 493).

NIGHTLIFE

▲▲Evening Paseo—Sevilla is meant for strolling. The areas along either side of the river between the San Telmo and Isabel II bridges (Paseo de Cristóbal Colón and Triana district; see "Eating," page 509), up Avenida de la Constitución, around Plaza Nueva, at Plaza de España, and throughout the Barrio Santa Cruz thrive every non-winter evening. On hot summer nights, even families with toddlers are out and about past midnight. Spend some time rafting through this sea of humanity. Savor the view of floodlit Sevilla by night from the far side of the river—perhaps over dinner.

▲▲▲Flamenco—This music-and-dance art form has its roots in the Roma (Gypsy) and Moorish cultures. Even at a packaged "flamenco evening," sparks fly. The men do most of the flamboyant machine-gun footwork. The women concentrate on graceful turns and a smooth, shuffling step. Watch the musicians. Flamenco guitarists, with their lightning-fast finger-roll strums, are among the best in the world. The intricate rhythms are set by castanets or the hand-clapping (called *palmas*) of those who aren't dancing at the moment. In the raspy-voiced wails of the singers, you'll hear echoes of the Muslim call to prayer.

Like jazz, flamenco thrives on improvisation. Also like jazz, good flamenco is more than just technical proficiency. A singer or dancer with "soul" is said to have *duende*. Flamenco is a happening, with bystanders clapping along and egging on the dancers with whoops and shouts. Get into it. For a tourist-oriented flamenco show, your hotel can get you nightclub show tickets (happily, since they snare a hefty commission for each sale). But it's easy to book a place on your own.

Casa de la Memoria de Al-Andalus ("House of the Memory of Al-Andalus"), run by Andalusian-culture devotees Sebastián and Rosana, offers more of an intimate concert with a smaller cast and more classic solos. Other, touristy flamenco shows give you all the clichés, and they can feel crass; here, you'll enjoy an elegant and classy musical experience. In an alcohol-free atmosphere, 90 tourists sit on three rows of folding chairs circling a small stage for shows featuring flamenco and other Andalusian music performed by young, professional local musicians. It's all acoustic, and the nightly musical mix varies according to the personalities of the performers. It's also a perfect place to practice your Spanish fan *(abanico)* skills on warm nights. Concerts are nightly all year at 21:00. With demand, shows are added at 22:30 in summer (€14, one-hour shows, reservations smart, box office open 11:00–14:00 and from 18:00, same-day tickets generally available, arrive early for front-row seats, in Barrio Santa Cruz, adjacent to Hotel Alcántara at Ximénez de Enciso 28, tel. 954-560-670, memoria@terra.es).

Los Gallos presents nightly two-hour shows at 20:00 and 22:30 (€30 ticket includes a drink, €3/person discount with this book in 2009—but limited to two admissions, arrive 30 min early for best seats, noisy bar but no food served, Plaza de la Santa Cruz 11, tel. 954-216-981, managers José and Nuria promise goose bumps).

El Arenal has arguably more professional performers and a classier setting for its show—but dinner customers get the preferred seating, and waiters are working throughout the performance (€35 including a drink, €69 with dinner, shows at 20:00 and 22:00, near bullring at Calle Rodó 7, tel. 954-216-492).

El Patio Sevillano is more of a variety show (€35 including a drink, 15 percent discount with Sevilla Card, shows at 19:30 and 22:00, next to bullring at Paseo de Cristóbal Colón, tel. 954-214-120).

The packaged shows described above can be a bit sterile, and an audience of tourists doesn't help. But I find both Los Gallos and El Arenal entertaining and riveting. While El Arenal may have a slight edge on talent, Los Gallos has a cozier setting, with cushy rather than hard chairs—and it's a bit cheaper.

Impromptu flamenco still erupts spontaneously in bars throughout the old town after midnight. Just follow your ears as you wander down Calle Betis, leading off Plaza de Cuba across the bridge. The **Lo Nuestro** and **Rejoneo** bars are local favorites (at Calle Betis 31A and 31B). Or find these:

Bar El Tamboríl is a funky local bar dedicated to the Virgin Mary—buried in the touristy Santa Cruz neighborhood, yet somehow still overlooked. It comes to life each midnight with a sung prayer. This kicks off the impromptu flamenco music (tourists welcome, no cover—just buy a drink, €4 wine, €7 cocktails, 50 yards in front of the Los Gallos flamenco show at Plaza de Santa Cruz, mobile 652-188-244).

La Carbonería Bar is the sangria equivalent of a beer garden. If the Beach Boys sang flamenco, they'd hang out here. It's a sprawling place with a variety of rooms leading to a big, open, tented area filled with young locals, casual guitar strummers, and nearly nightly flamenco music after midnight (no dancing). Located just a few blocks from most of my recommended hotels, this is worth finding if you're not quite ready to end the day (no cover, €2 sangria, daily 20:00–3:00

in the morning; near Plaza Santa María: find Hotel Fernando III, the side alley Céspedes dead-ends at Levies, head left to Levies 18, unsigned door; for location, see map on page 505).

SLEEPING

All of my listings are centrally located, mostly within a five-minute walk of the cathedral. The first are near the charming but touristy Santa Cruz neighborhood. The last group is just as central but closer to the river, across the boulevard in a more workaday, less touristy zone.

Room rates as much as double during the two Sevilla fiestas (Holy Week—April 5–12 in 2009; and the weeklong April Fair, held 2 weeks after Easter—April 28–May 3 in 2009). In general, the busiest and most expensive months are April, May, September, and October. Hotels put rooms on the discounted push list in July and August—when people with any sense avoid this furnace—and from November through February. Prices rarely include the 7 percent IVA tax. A price range indicates low- to high-season prices (but I have not listed festival prices). Ground-floor rooms come with more noise. Ask for upper floors *(piso alto)*. Always telephone to reconfirm what you think is a reservation. If you do visit in July or August, the best values are central business-class places. They offer summer discounts and provide a necessary cool, air-conditioned refuge.

But be warned that Spain's air-conditioning often isn't the icebox you're used to, especially in Sevilla. The best setup is an individual, remote-controlled air-conditioner. If you have central air-conditioning, owners often turn it off during the day—and even when it's on, they control the temperature.

Santa Cruz Neighborhood

These places are off Calle Santa María la Blanca and Plaza Santa María. The most convenient parking lot is the underground Cano y Cueto garage near the corner of Calle Santa María la Blanca and Menéndez Pelayo (€16/day, open 24/7, at edge of big park, unsigned). A fine Internet café and self-service laundry place are a block away up Menéndez Pelayo (see "Helpful Hints" on page 470).

$$$ Hotel Las Casas de la Judería has quiet, elegant rooms and suites tastefully decorated with hardwood floors and a Spanish flair. The rooms, which surround a series of peaceful courtyards, are a romantic splurge (Sb-€93–105, Db-€140–180, extra bed-€41; low-season prices—July, Aug, and late-Nov–Feb—are discounted a further 10 percent to those with this book who ask in 2009, but check their website for even better rates; expensive but great buffet breakfast-€17, air-con, elevator, valet parking-€18/day, on small traffic-free lane off Plaza Santa María, Callejón de Dos Hermanas 7, tel. 954-415-150, fax 954-422-170, www.casasypalacios.com, juderia@casasypalacios.com).

Sleep Code

(€1 = about $1.50, country code: 34)
S = Single, **D** = Double/Twin, **T** = Triple, **Q** = Quad, **b** = bathroom, **s** = shower only. Unless otherwise noted, credit cards are accepted, hoteliers speak enough English, and breakfast generally costs extra.

To help you easily sort through these listings, I've divided the rooms into three categories, based on the price for a standard double room with bath during high season:

$$$ Higher Priced—Most rooms €100 or more.
$$ Moderately Priced—Most rooms between €60-100.
$ Lower Priced—Most rooms €60 or less.

$$ Hotel Amadeus is a little gem that music-lovers will appreciate (it even has a couple of soundproofed rooms with pianos—something I've never seen anywhere else in Europe). It's lovingly decorated with a music motif around a little courtyard and a modern glass elevator that takes you to a roof terrace. While small, this 14-room place is classy and comfortable, with welcoming public spaces and a very charming staff (Db-€90, big Db-€103, 2 suites-€110 and €135, cheaper July–Aug, air-con, elevator, free Internet access, laundry-€15; the €7 breakfast comes on a trolley—enjoy it in your room, in the lounge, or on the delightful roof garden; Calle Farnesio 6, tel. 954-501-443, fax 954-500-019, www.hotelamadeussevilla.com, reservas@hotelamadeussevilla.com, wonderfully run by María Luisa and her staff—Zaida and Cristina). Their next-door annex is every bit as charming and a similarly good value: **$$$ La Música de Sevilla** offers six additional, beautifully appointed rooms; three rooms face the interior patio, and three are streetside with small balconies (patio Db-€103, exterior Db-€125, air-con, reserve and check in at Hotel Amadeus).

$$ Hotel Alcántara offers more no-nonsense comfort than character. Well located but strangely out of place in the midst of the Santa Cruz jumble, it rents 21 slick rooms at a good price (Sb-€66, small Db-€78, bigger Db twin-€87, fancy Db-€110, 10 percent cash discount with this book in 2009, breakfast-€5, air-con, elevator, free Wi-Fi, rentable laptop, Ximénez de Enciso 28, tel. 954-500-595, fax 954-500-604, www.hotelalcantara.net, info@hotelalcantara.net). The hotel is adjacent to Casa de la Memoria de Al-Andalus, which offers concerts (see page 501).

$$ YH Giralda, once an 18th-century abbots' house, is now a charming 14-room hotel tucked away on a little street right off Mateo Gagos, just a couple blocks from the cathedral. The exterior rooms have windows onto a pedestrian street, and a few of the interior rooms

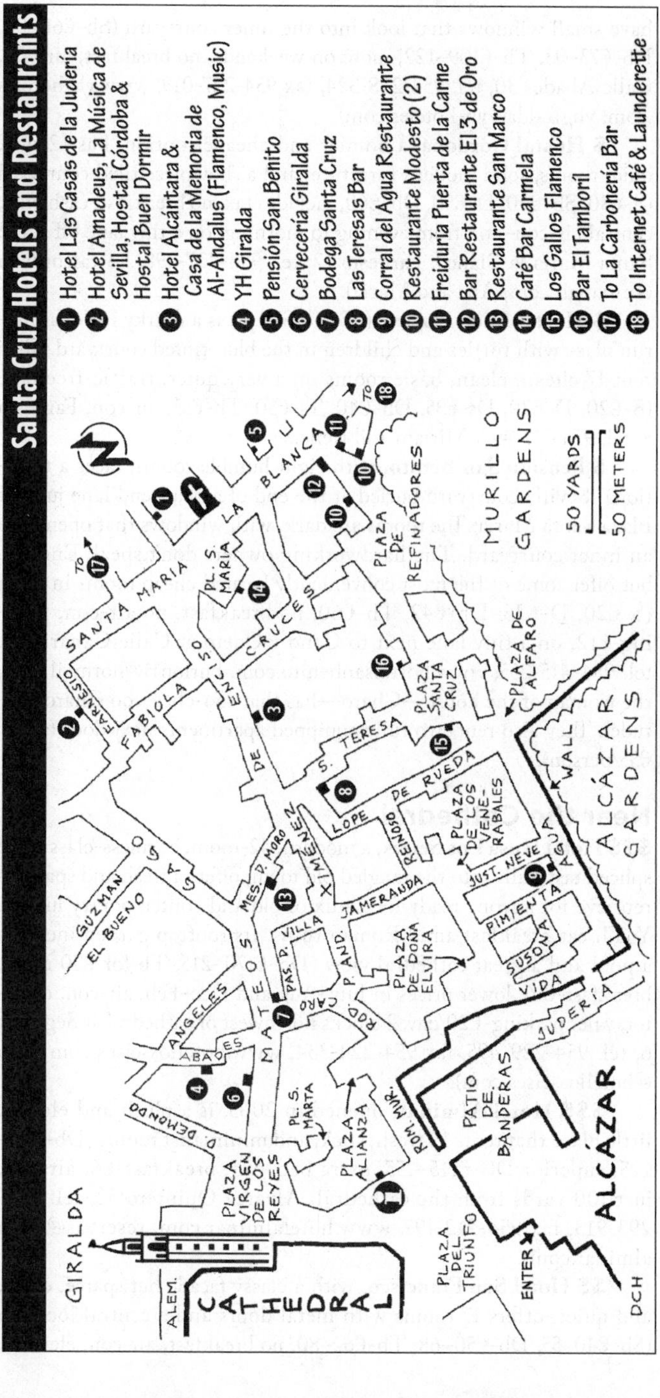
Santa Cruz Hotels and Restaurants
1 Hotel Las Casas de la Judería
2 Hotel Amadeus, La Música de Sevilla, Hostal Córdoba & Hostal Buen Dormir
3 Hotel Alcántara & Casa de la Memoria de Al-Andalus (Flamenco, Music)
4 YH Giralda
5 Pensión San Benito
6 Cervecería Giralda
7 Bodega Santa Cruz
8 Las Teresas Bar
9 Corral del Agua Restaurante
10 Restaurante Modesto (2)
11 Freiduría Puerta de la Carne
12 Bar Restaurante El 3 de Oro
13 Restaurante San Marco
14 Café Bar Carmela
15 Los Gallos Flamenco
16 Bar El Tamboril
17 To La Carbonería Bar
18 To Internet Café & Launderette
GIRALDA
CATHEDRAL
ALEM.
PLAZA VIRGEN DE LOS REYES
PLAZA DEL TRIUNFO
ENTER
DCH
ALCÁZAR
PATIO DE BANDERAS
PL. S. MARTA
PLAZA ALIANZA
ROM. MUR.
ABADES
ANGELES
GUZMAN EL BUENO
MATEOS GAGO
FABIOLA
FARNESIO
SANTA MARIA LA BLANCA
PL. S. MARIA
ENCISO
DE CRUCES
MES. D. MORO
XIMENEZ DE ENCISO
PAS. D. VILLA
P. AND.
ROD. CARO
PLAZA DE DOÑA ELVIRA
JAMERANDA
LOPE DE RUEDA
S. TERESA
REINOSO
PLAZA DE LOS VENERABALES
JUST. NEVE
PIMIENTA
SUSONA
VIDA
JUDERÍA
AGUA
WALL
PLAZA SANTA CRUZ
PLAZA DE ALFARO
PLAZA DE REFINADORES
MURILLO GARDENS
ALCÁZAR GARDENS
50 YARDS
50 METERS
TO

SEVILLA

have small windows that look into the inner courtyard (Sb-€66–80, Db-€73–93, Tb-€109–122, more on weekends, no breakfast, air-con, Calle Abades 30, tel. 954-228-324, fax 954-227-019, www.yh-hoteles.com, yhgiralda@yh-hoteles.com).

$ Hostal Córdoba, a homier and cheaper option, has 12 tidy, quiet rooms, solid modern furniture, and a showpiece tiled courtyard (S-€30, Sb-€40, D-€50, Db-€60, includes tax, no breakfast, cash only, central air-con—on from evening to morning, on a tiny lane off Calle Santa María la Blanca, Farnesio 12, tel. 954-227-498, hostalcordoba@mixmail.com, Ana and María).

$ Hostal Buen Dormir ("Good Sleep") is a quirky little family-run place with turtles and children in the blue-tinted courtyard. They rent 17 cheap, clean, basic rooms on a very quiet, traffic-free lane (S-€20, D-€30, Ds-€35, Db-€40, Ts-€50, Tb-€55, air-con, Farnesio 8, tel. 954-217-492, Miriam and Rene).

$ Pensión San Benito, with eight humble rooms, faces a traditional Sevilla courtyard buried at the end of a dead-end lane just off Plaza Santa María. The rooms are dark, with windows that open onto an inner courtyard. The hardworking owners don't speak English, but offer some of the most conveniently located cheap rooms in town (S-€20, D-€36, Db-€42, Tb-€60, no breakfast, no air-con, parking-€12, on a tiny lane next to Cano y Cueto at Calle Canarios 4, tel. 954-415-255, www.hostalsanbenito.com, burlon11@hotmail.com, the woman of the house—Charo—has that coo-chee-coo Charo attitude). They also rent two fully equipped apartments next door (about €35/person).

Near the Cathedral

$$$ Hotel Husa Los Seises, a modern, 42-room, business-class place spliced tastefully into the tangled old town, offers a fresh and spacious reprieve for anyone ready for a mix of old and contemporary luxury. You'll eat breakfast amid Roman ruins. Its rooftop garden includes a pool and a great cathedral view (Db-€170–215, Tb for €30 more, breakfast-€16, lower prices in July–Aug and Dec–Feb, air-con, elevator, valet parking-€20/day, 2 blocks northwest of cathedral at Segovias 6, tel. 954-229-495, fax 954-224-334, www.hotellosseises.com, info@hotellosseises.com).

$$$ Hotel Alminar, opened in 2005, is a plush and elegant little place that rents 12 fresh, slick, and minimalist rooms (Db-€95–125, superior Db-€115–155, extra bed-€25, breakfast-€6, air-con, just 100 yards from the cathedral, Álvarez Quintero 52, tel. 954-293-913, fax 954-212-197, www.hotelalminar.com, reservas@hotelalminar.com).

$$ Hotel San Francisco, with a classy facade but sparse, clean, and quiet, offers 17 rooms with metal doors and a central location (Sb-€40–55, Db-€50–68, Tb-€62–80, no breakfast, air-con, elevator,

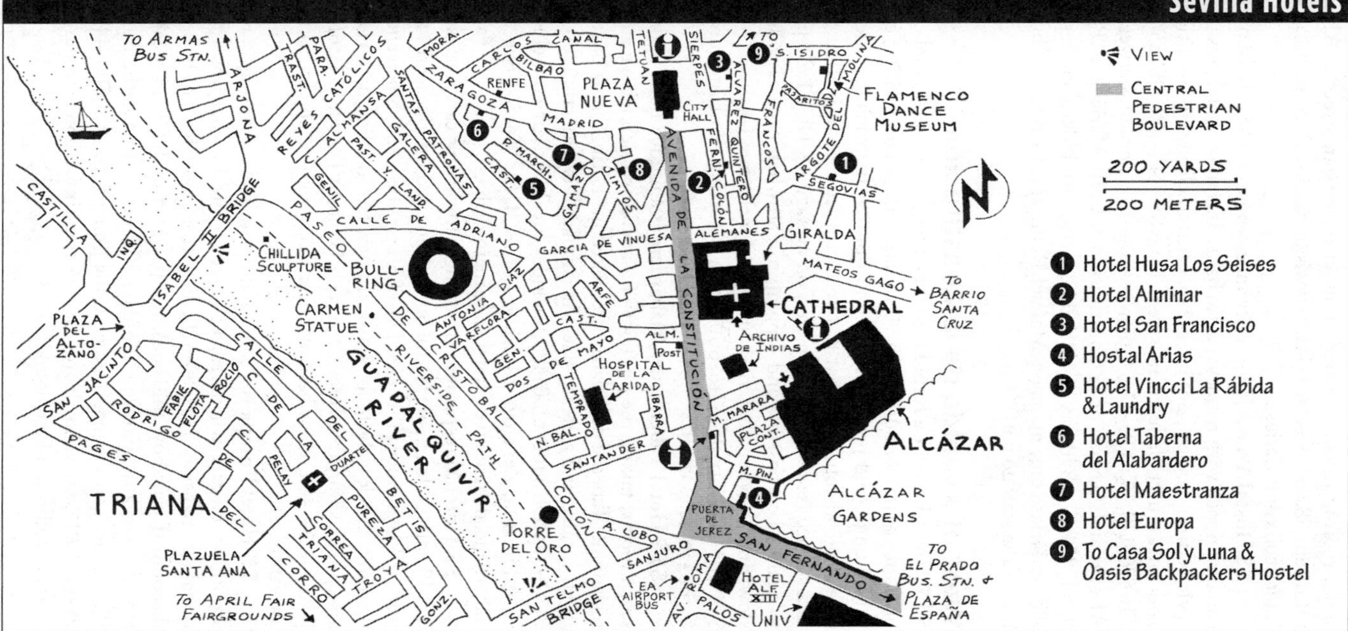
Sevilla Hotels
View
Central Pedestrian Boulevard
200 Yards
200 Meters
1 Hotel Husa Los Seises
2 Hotel Alminar
3 Hotel San Francisco
4 Hostal Arias
5 Hotel Vincci La Rábida & Laundry
6 Hotel Taberna del Alabardero
7 Hotel Maestranza
8 Hotel Europa
9 To Casa Sol y Luna & Oasis Backpackers Hostel
To Armas Bus Stn.
Arjona
Reyes Católicos
Zaragoza
Renfe
Plaza Nueva
Madrid
Tetuan
Sierpes
City Hall
To S. Isidro
Alvarez Quintero
Francos
Argote del Molina
Pajaritos
Flamenco Dance Museum
Segovias
Giralda
Alemanes
Mateos Gago
To Barrio Santa Cruz
Cathedral
Archivo de Indias
Alcázar
Alcázar Gardens
Avenida de la Constitución
Hospital de la Caridad
Puerta de Jerez
San Fernando
Hotel Alf. XIII
Univ.
EA Airport Bus
To El Prado Bus. Stn. & Plaza de España
Torre del Oro
San Telmo Bridge
Guadalquivir River
Riverside Path
Paseo de Cristobal Colón
Bull-Ring
Calle de Adriano
Garcia de Vinuesa
Carmen Statue
Chillida Sculpture
Isabel II Bridge
Plaza del Altozano
Castilla
San Jacinto
Pages del Corro
Triana
Plazuela Santa Ana
To April Fair Fairgrounds
Betis
Pureza
Correa
Troya

SEVILLA

small rooftop terrace, located on quiet pedestrian street at Álvarez Quintero 38, tel. 954-501-541, www.sanfranciscoh.com, info@sanfranciscoh.com, Carlos).

$$ Hostal Arias is low-service and no-nonsense. Its 14 basic rooms come equipped with medieval disco balls. This funky hotel gets mixed reviews from readers, but it's cheap, central, clean, air-conditioned, and on a quiet pedestrian street (big Sb-€45–68, Db-€56–99, Tb-€76–120, Qb-€85–134, Quint/b-€100–156, elevator, between the Alcázar and Avenida de la Constitución at Calle Mariana de Pineda 9, tel. 954-226-840, fax 954-211-649, www.hostalarias.com, reservas@hostalarias.com, manager Manuel Reina speaks English, but the rest of the staff do not).

West of Avenida de la Constitución

$$$ Hotel Vincci La Rábida, part of a big, impersonal hotel chain, offers four-star comforts with 90 rooms, a huge and inviting courtyard lounge, and powerful air-conditioning. Its pricing is dictated by a magical computer that has perfect price discrimination down to a science (see website for prices; on average it's Db-€132, spiking to €200 when possible and dipping to €80 when necessary during slow times—when that air-con is most welcome; Castelar 24, tel. 954-501-280, fax 954-216-600, www.vinccihoteles.com, larabida@vinccihoteles.com).

$$$ Hotel Taberna del Alabardero is a unique hotel with only seven rooms, taking the top floor of a poet's mansion (above a classy restaurant, Taberna del Alabardero, listed in "Eating," next page). It's nicely located and a great value. The ambience is perfectly 1900 (Db-€130–160, Db suite-€150–190, includes breakfast, air-con, elevator, closed in Aug, Zaragoza 20, tel. 954-502-721, fax 954-563-666, www.tabernadelalabardero.es, hotel.alabardero@esh.es).

$$ Hotel Maestranza, sparkling with loving care and charm, has 18 small, clean, simple rooms well located on a peaceful street just off Plaza Nueva (Sb-€53, Db-€87, extra bed-€20, 5 percent cash discount, check website for seasonal rates, family suite, no breakfast, air-con, elevator, free Internet access, Gamazo 12, tel. 954-561-070, fax 954-214-404, www.hotelmaestranza.es, sevilla@hotelmaestranza.es, Antonio).

$$ Hotel Europa is a somber and sturdy place renting 16 rooms around an elegant wicker furniture courtyard in what was a traditional old mansion (Db-€80–120, 40 percent more for Tb, 10 percent discount if you show this book and pay cash in 2009, no breakfast, air-con, elevator, parking-€16/day, 200 yards from cathedral and Plaza Nueva on a tranquil street, Calle Jimios 5, tel. 954-500-443, fax 954-210-016, www.hoteleuropasevilla.com, info@hoteleuropasevilla.com, Claudio and Francisco).

North of Plaza Nueva, Between Plaza de la Encarnación and Plaza de la Alfalfa

$ Casa Sol y Luna is quaint, with a cordial staff. Run by an Englishman named Geno and his Spanish wife, Esther, it's inexpensive, but a bit farther (10-min walk) from the cathedral (S-€22, D-€38, Db-€45, Calle Pérez Galdós 1A, tel. 954-210-682, www.casasolyluna1.com, info@casasolyluna1.com).

$ Oasis Backpackers Hostel is the best new spot for cheap beds and a fine place to hang out and connect with young backpackers. Each room, with four double bunks, comes with a modern bathroom and individual lockers. The rooftop terrace—with lounge chairs, a small pool, and adjacent kitchen—is well used (64 bunk beds in 8 rooms, €20 per bed, includes breakfast and Internet access, just off Plaza de la Encarnación behind the church at #29 1/2 on the tiny and quiet lane, tel. 954-293-777, www.hostelsoasis.com). They also have popular branches in Lisbon and Granada.

EATING

Local soups, such as *salmorejo* (Córdoba-style super-thick *gazpacho*) and *ajo blanco* (almond-based with garlic), are tasty. A popular Andalusian meal is fried fish, particularly marinated *adobo.* I liked *taquitos de merluza* (hake fish), but for a mix of fish, ask for *frito variado.*

If you're hungry for dinner before the Spaniards are, do the tapas tango, using the tapas tips on page 22. Wash down your tapas with *fino* (chilled dry sherry) or the more refreshing *tinto de verano* ("summer red wine"), an Andalusian red wine with soda, like a mild sangria. A good light white wine is *barbadillo.* And for a heavy red, always go for the Rioja.

Eating in Triana, Across the River

The colorful Triana district—south of the river, between the San Telmo and Isabel II bridges—is filled with rustic and fun eateries. The riverside and traffic-free Calle Betis is lined with a variety of places to eat, from fine riverside restaurants to sloppy fish joints, and comes with good picnic and take-out opportunities for romantic urchins.

Tapas in a Triana Neighborhood Joint

Bars along the river and the parallel street one block inland are good for tapas. Before sitting down, walk to the Santa Ana church (midway between the bridges, 2 blocks off the river), where tables spill into the square (Plazuela de Santa Ana) in the shadow of the floodlit church spire. It feels like the whole neighborhood is out celebrating.

Restaurante Bistec, with most of the square's tables, does grilled fish with gusto. They're enthusiastic about their cod cakes and

Restaurants and Flamenco in Sevilla

1. Rest. Bistec & Taberna La Plazuela
2. Bar Santa Ana
3. Restaurante Río Grande
4. El Faro de Triana & La Taberna del Pescador
5. Bodega Restaurante La María
6. Los Chorritos
7. Horno San Buenaventura
8. Bodega Morales & Freiduría La Isla
9. Bodega Paco Góngora
10. Taberna Torre de la Plata
11. Cafetería Mesón Serranito
12. Marisquería Arenal Sevilla
13. Bar Restaurante Pepe Hillo
14. Restaurante Enrique Becerra
15. Taberna del Alabardero
16. El Arenal (Flamenco)
17. El Patio Sevillano (Flamenco)
18. Lo Nuestro & Rejoneo Bars

calamari. Consider their indoor seating and the fun at the bar before sitting out on the square (€7 half-*raciones,* €13 full *raciones,* Thu–Tue 11:30–16:00 & 20:00–24:00, closed Wed, also closed Sun afternoons in winter, Plazuela de Santa Ana, tel. 954-274-759).

Taberna La Plazuela is self-service, doing simpler fare with enticing €12 *tostones* (giant, fancy Andalusian bruschetta, good for 3–4 people) and €2 *montaditos* (little sandwiches). Get what you want and grab a table on the leafy square. Ignore the printed menu and read the daily specials board (same hours and owners as Restaurante Bistec, above).

Bar Santa Ana, just a block away on the side of the church, is a rustic neighborhood sports-and-bull-bar with great seating on the street. Peruse the interior, draped in bullfighting and Weeping Virgin memorabilia. It's always busy with the neighborhood gang, who enjoy a fun list of tapas like *delicia de solomillo* (tenderloin) and the bar's willingness to serve even cheap tapas at the outdoor tables (long hours, typically closed one day per week—closed Sun during April Fair, facing the side of the church at Pureza 82, tel. 954-272-102).

Riverside Dinners in Triana

Restaurante Río Grande is your stuffy, candlelit-fancy option—*the* place for a restaurant dinner with properly attired waiters and a full menu rather than tapas. Their terrace is less expensive and more casual (€35 dinners, daily 13:00–16:00 & 20:00–24:00, air-con, paella and rice dishes are the house specialty, next to the San Telmo Bridge, tel. 954-273-956).

El Faro de Triana is actually the old yellow bridge tower overlooking the Isabel II Bridge. While professional, it's less formal and quirkier than Río Grande. They offer inexpensive tapas, €15 à la carte dishes, and grand views over the river from the top floor. Choose from four dining zones: rooftop, outdoor terrace just below the rooftop (perhaps the best), riverside metal tables on the sidewalk, and the bar. There's no cover charge, but they don't serve tapas on the roof or riverside (open Tue–Sun, bar—8:00–24:00, restaurant—13:00–17:00 & 20:15–24:00, closed Mon, tel. 954-336-192).

La Taberna del Pescador, with tablecloths on its riverside tables, is fancier and more expensive (€12 and up *raciones* on the river, Wed–Mon 12:00–16:00 & 20:00–24:00, closed Tue, 50 yards from Puente de Isabel II on Calle Betis, tel. 954-330-069).

Bodega Restaurante La María also offers fine tablecloth-type restaurant seating on the riverside, but with a formal menu rather than tapas (€18 fish and meat plates, Wed–Mon 13:30–16:00 & 20:00–24:00, closed Tue, Calle Betis 12, tel. 954-338-461).

Los Chorritos is a carefree and sloppy riverside eatery—my choice for hearty seafood, great prices, and a fun atmosphere. They are enthusiastic about what the menu calls "roast" sardines—grilled rather than fried. Their banner reads, roughly, "Sardines rule. They don't bite. Can't eat just one. Go for it" (€6 half-*raciones*, €10 full *raciones*, closed Mon, about midway between the two bridges on Calle Betis, tel. 954-331-499).

Near Recommended Hotels in Barrio Santa Cruz

These eateries—for tapas, dining, and cheap eats—are handy to my recommended Barrio Santa Cruz accommodations.

Tapas in Barrio Santa Cruz

For tapas, the Barrio Santa Cruz is trendy and *romántico.* Plenty of atmospheric-but-touristy restaurants fill the neighborhood near the cathedral and along Calle Santa María la Blanca. From the cathedral, walk up Mateos Gago, where several classic old bars—with the day's tapas scrawled on chalkboards—keep tourists and locals well fed and watered. (Turn right at Mesón del Moro for several more.)

Cervecería Giralda is a long-established meeting place for locals. It's famous for its fine tapas (confirm prices, stick with straight items on menu rather than expensive trick specials proposed by waiters; open long hours daily, no food served 16:00–20:00, Mateos Gago 1).

A block farther, you'll find **Bodega Santa Cruz** (a.k.a. **Las Columnas**), a popular standby with good, cheap tapas and *montaditos* (little sandwiches). You can keep an eye on the busy kitchen from the bar, or hang out like a cowboy at the tiny stand-up tables out front. Separate chalkboards list €2 tapas and €2 *montaditos.*

Las Teresas, a block off Mateos Gago, is a characteristic small bar draped in fun photos. It serves good tapas from a tight little user-friendly menu. Prices at the bar and outside tables (for fun tourist-watching) are the same, but they serve tapas only at the bar. The hams (with little upside-down umbrellas to catch the dripping fat) are a reminder that they are enthusiastic about their cured-meat dishes (open daily but closed for the siesta, Calle Santa Teresa 2, tel. 954-213-069).

Dining in Barrio Santa Cruz

Corral del Agua Restaurante, a romantic pink-tablecloth place with a smart interior and charming courtyard seating, serves fine Andalusian cuisine deep in the Barrio Santa Cruz (€18 entrées, 3-course lunch special with wine for €20, Mon–Sat 12:00–16:00 & 20:00–24:00, closed Sun, arrive early or reserve ahead, Calle Agua 6, tel. 954-224-841).

Restaurante Modesto is a local favorite serving pricey but top-notch Andalusian fare—especially fish—with a comfortable dining room and atmospheric outdoor seating in the bright, bustling square just outside the Barrio Santa Cruz. They offer creative, fun meals—look around before ordering—and a good €20 fixed-price lunch or dinner with energetic, occasionally pushy waiters. Their mixed salad is a meal (inside open daily 12:00–17:00 & 20:00–24:00, outside tables open daily 12:00–24:00, near Santa María la Blanca at Cano y Cueto 5, tel. 954-416-811). Note that they have two indoor dining areas on both sides of the street (busy bar at one, non-smoking zone—in other words, tourists—at the other).

Eating Cheaply in Barrio Santa Cruz and Plaza Santa María la Blanca

Freiduría Puerta de la Carne and **Bar Restaurante El 3 de Oro** is a fried-fish-to-go place, with great outdoor seating and a restaurant across the street that serves fine wine or beer. You can order a cheap cone of tasty fried fish, sip a nice drink (served by a waiter from the restaurant), and enjoy a great outdoor setting—almost dining for the cost of a picnic. Study the photos of the various kinds of seafood available—*un quarto* (250 grams for about €5) serves one (Mon–Sat until 24:00, Sun lunch only, Santa María la Blanca 34, tel. 954-426-820).

Restaurante San Marco offers cheap pizza and fun, basic Italian cuisine under the arches of what was a Moorish bath in the Middle Ages (and a disco in the 1990s). The atmosphere is air-conditioned and easygoing—family-friendly, yet not cheesy (good salads, pizza, and pasta for €8, daily 13:15–16:30 & 20:15–24:00, Calle Mesón del Moro 6, tel. 954-564-390).

Breakfast on Plaza Santa María la Blanca: Several nondescript places seem to keep travelers happy at breakfast time on the sunny main square near most of my recommended hotels. I like **Café Bar Carmela.** For the cost of a continental breakfast at your hotel (€6), you can have a hearty American-style breakfast on the square (easy menus, metal tables, open from 9:30, Calle Santa María la Blanca 6, tel. 954-540-590).

Between the Cathedral and the River

I don't like the restaurants surrounding the cathedral, but many good places are just across Avenida de la Constitución. In the area between the cathedral and the river, you can find tapas, cheap eats, and fine dining.

Tapas Between the Cathedral and the River

Calle García de Vinuesa leads past several colorful and cheap tapas places to a busy corner surrounded with happy eateries.

Horno San Buenaventura, across from the cathedral, is slick, chrome-filled, spacious, and handy for tapas, coffee, pastries, and ice cream. They are understandably happy to be booming now, thanks to the newly pedestrianized boulevard (open daily, light meals are posted by the door, good quiet seating upstairs).

Bodega Morales is farther up Calle García de Vinuesa, at #11. While the front area is more of a drinking bar, go in the back section (around the corner) to munch tiny sandwiches *(montaditos)* and tapas, and sip wine among huge kegs. Everything is the same price (€2 *montaditos,* €2 tapas, €6 half-*raciones*—order at the bar), with the selections chalked onto giant adobe jugs (Mon–Sat 12:00–16:00 & 20:00–24:00, closed Sun, tel. 954-22-1242).

Freiduría La Isla, next door, has been frying fish since 1938 (they just renovated...and changed the oil). Along with *pescado frito,* they also sell wonderful homemade potato chips and fried almonds. It's family-friendly, with an easy English menu. Try their €5 *adobo* (marinated shark) or *frito variado* for a fish sampler. It's all fried fish, except for a tomato and pepper dish and their €1.20 *gazpacho,* offered only in the summer (Mon 20:00–23:30, Tue–Sat 13:00–15:30 & 20:00–23:30, closed Sun).

Bodega Paco Góngora is colorful and a bit classier than most tapas bars, with a tight dining area and delightful tapas dishes served at the bar. Its sit-down meals are well-presented and reasonably priced (daily 13:00–16:00 & 20:00–24:00, ask for the English menu, off Plaza Nueva at Calle Padre Marchena 1, tel. 954-214-139).

Cheap Eats Between the Cathedral and the River

Taberna Torre de la Plata is a handy-to-the-Alcázar eatery close to the sights, but tucked away enough that it's mostly patronized by locals who appreciate its tasty dishes. Local guides take lunch here in the cool, quiet back courtyard (€9 plates, wine list, midway between the cathedral and the Torre del Oro at Calle Santander 1, tel. 954-228-761).

Cafetería Mesón Serranito is a family-friendly diner full of bull lore and happily munching locals (€9 *platos combinados,* Antonia Díaz 11, tel. 954-211-243).

Mercado del Arenal, the covered fish-and-produce market, is ideal for both snapping photos and finding a cheap lunch. As with most markets, you'll find characteristic little diners with prices designed to lure in savvy shoppers, not to mention a crispy fresh world of picnic goodies—and a riverside promenade with benches just a block away (Mon–Sat 9:00–14:30, closed Sun, sleepy on Mon, on Calle Pastor y Landero at Calle Arenal, just beyond bullring). There's also a fancier fish restaurant in the market with a great lunch deal (see Taberna del Alabardero, below).

Dining Between the Cathedral, Plaza Nueva, and the River

Marisquería Arenal Sevilla is a popular fish restaurant that thrives in the middle of the Arenal Market. When the market closes (daily at 14:30), this eatery stays open. You'll be eating in the empty Industrial Age market with workers dragging their crates around. It's a great, family-friendly, finger-licking-good scene much appreciated by its enthusiastic local following (€8–20 fish plates, generally open

13:00–17:00 & 21:00–24:00, in summer closed Sat night and all day Sun, rest of year closed Mon, reservations smart for dinner, Mercado Arenal, enter on Calle Pastor y Landero 9, tel. 954-220-881).

Bar Restaurante Pepe Hillo serves upscale bar food with a bull motif, across from the bullring (and, therefore, riotous after fights). One side is a youthful tapas bar. But the other side is a delightful oasis serving big half-*raciones* from an inviting menu with creative house specialties and a good wine list (enter on Calle Pastor y Landero, Adriano 24, tel. 954-215-390).

Restaurante Enrique Becerra is a fancy little 10-table place popular with local foodies. It's well-known for its gourmet Andalusian cuisine and fine wine. Muscle past the well-dressed locals at their tapas bar for gourmet snacks and wine by the glass. While the restaurant satisfies its guests with quality food, given the tight seating and its popularity with tourists, it can feel like a trap (€40 dinners, Mon–Sat 13:00–16:30 & 20:00–24:00, closed Sun, reservations essentially required, Gamazo 2, tel. 954-213-049).

Taberna del Alabardero, one of Sevilla's finest restaurants, serves refined Spanish cuisine in chandeliered elegance just a couple of blocks from the cathedral. If you order à la carte it will add up to about €45 a meal, but for €60 you can have a fun, seven-course fixed-price meal with lots of little surprises from the chef. Or consider their €18 (per person—no sharing) starter sampler, followed by an entrée. The service in the fancy upstairs dining rooms gets mixed reviews (carefully read and understand your bill)...but the setting is stunning (daily 13:00–16:30 & 20:00–24:00, closed Aug, air-con, reservations smart, Zaragoza 20, tel. 954-502-721).

Taberna del Alabardero Student-Served Lunch: Their ground-floor dining rooms (elegant but nothing like upstairs) are popular with local office workers for their great-value, student-chef fixed-price sampler (daily 13:00–16:30, €13 for three delightful courses Mon–Fri, €18 Sat–Sun). To avoid a wait, arrive before 14:00 (no reservations possible).

TRANSPORTATION CONNECTIONS

Note that many destinations are well-served by both trains and buses.

From Sevilla by AVE Train to Madrid: The AVE express train is expensive (€72, €6 cheaper in off-peak times, €10 reservation fee with railpass) but fast (2.5 hrs to Madrid; departures 7:00–21:45 on the hour, see page 356 for more on the Sevilla–Madrid train route). Departures between 16:00 and 19:00 can book up far in advance, but surprise holidays and long weekends can totally jam it up—book as far ahead as possible.

From Sevilla by Train to Córdoba: The fast 45-minute AVE train goes hourly, but it's pricey for such a short journey (€24, €38 round-trip—must reserve both ways when you book, with railpass you still must pay €10 reservation fee). The slower train to Córdoba takes 80 minutes, costs only €8 each way, and comes with no reservation headaches.

Other Trains from Sevilla: Málaga (11/day, 2 hrs on AVE or AVANT, 2.5 hrs on other trains), **Ronda** (2/day, 4 hrs, transfer in Bobadilla), **Granada** (4/day, 3 hrs), **Jerez** (12/day, 1.25 hrs), **Barcelona** (3/day, 6.5–10 hrs), **Algeciras** (3/day, 5 hrs, change at Córdoba, Antequera, or Bobadilla). Trains run to **Lisbon,** Portugal, but they take a long time, since they go through Madrid; buses to Lisbon are far better (see below). Train info: tel. 902-240-202, www.renfe.es.

From Sevilla by Bus to: Madrid (departures generally on the hour, 6 hrs, €19, tel. 902-229-292), **Córdoba** (9/day, 2 hrs), **Málaga** (9/day, 7 direct, 2.5–3.5 hrs, connects to Nerja), **Ronda** (5/day, 2.5 hrs, less on weekends), **Tarifa** (4/day, 3 hrs), **La Línea/Gibraltar** (4/day, 4 hrs), **Granada** (11/day, 3 hrs *directo,* 4 hrs *ruta*), **Arcos** (2/day, 2 hrs, more departures with a change in Jerez, **Jerez** (7/day, 1.5 hrs), **Barcelona** (2/day), **Algeciras** (11/day, 2 direct, less on weekends, 2.25–2.5 hrs). Bus info: tel. 954-908-040 but rarely answered, go to TI for latest schedule info.

By Bus to Portugal: The best way to get to **Lisbon,** Portugal, is by bus (Alsa and Eurolines share a service offering 2/day, departures at 15:00 and 24:00, 7 hrs, €40 by way of Faro, departs Plaza de Armas station, tel. 954-907-800 or 902-422-242, www.alsa.es). The midnight departure continues past Lisbon to **Coimbra** (arriving 9:45) and **Porto** (arriving 11:30). Sevilla also has a direct bus service to **Lagos,** Portugal, on the Algarve (4/day in summer, 2/day off-season, about 6 hrs, €19, buy ticket a day or two in advance May–Oct, tel. 954-907-737, www.damas-sa.es). The bus departs from Sevilla's Plaza de Armas bus station and arrives at the Lagos bus station. If you'd like to visit Tavira on the way to Lagos, purchase a bus ticket to Tavira, have lunch there, then take the train to Lagos.

CÓRDOBA

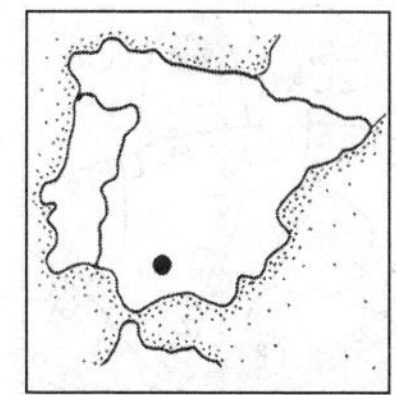

Straddling a sharp bend of the Guadalquivir River, Córdoba has a glorious Roman and Moorish past, once serving as a regional capital for both empires. It's home to Europe's best Islamic sight after Granada's Alhambra: the Mezquita, a mosque that dates from A.D. 784. When you step inside the mosque, which is magical in its grandeur, you can imagine Córdoba as the center of a thriving and sophisticated culture. During the Dark Ages, when much of Europe was barbaric and illiterate, Córdoba was a haven of enlightened thought—famous for religious tolerance, artistic expression, and dedication to philosophy and the sciences.

Planning Your Time

Ideally, Córdoba is worth two nights and a day. Don't rush the magnificent Mezquita, but also stick around to experience the city's other pleasures: Wander the evocative Jewish Quarter, enjoy the tapas scene, and take the TI's guided town walk in the evening.

However, if you're tight on time, it's possible to do Córdoba more quickly—especially since it's conveniently located on the AVE bullet-train line (and because, frankly, Córdoba is less interesting than the other two big Andalusian cities, Sevilla and Granada). To see Córdoba as an efficient stopover between Madrid and Sevilla (or as a side-trip from Sevilla—hourly trains, 45-min trip), focus on the Mezquita: Taxi from the station, spend two hours there, explore the old town for an hour...and then scram.

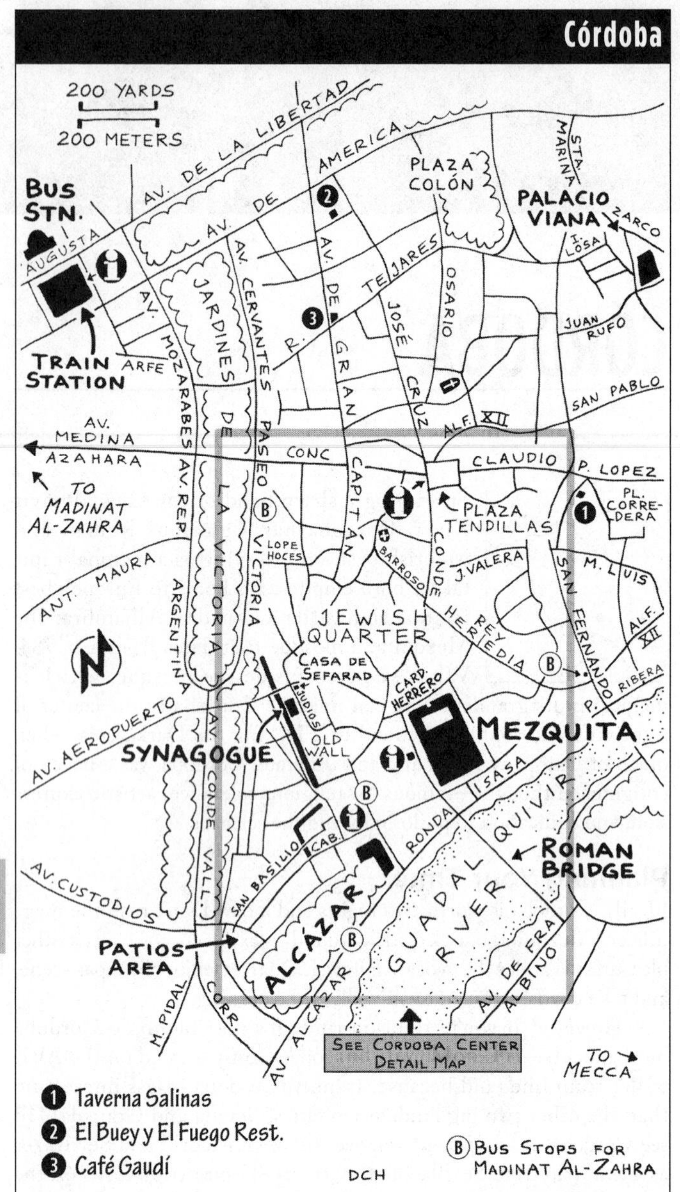
Córdoba
200 YARDS
200 METERS
AV. DE LA LIBERTAD
AV. DE AMERICA
PLAZA COLÓN
STA. MARINA
BUS STN.
AUGUSTA
PALACIO VIANA
ZARCO
I. LOSA
AV. MOZARABES
JARDINES DE LA VICTORIA
AV. CERVANTES
AV. DE GRAN CAPITÁN
TEJARES
JOSÉ CRUZ CONDE
OSARIO
JUAN RUFO
TRAIN STATION
ARFE
R.
SAN PABLO
ALF. XII
AV. MEDINA AZAHARA
TO MADINAT AL-ZAHRA
CONC
CLAUDIO
P. LOPEZ
PASEO VICTORIA
PLAZA TENDILLAS
PL. CORRE-DERA
AV. REP. ARGENTINA
LOPE HOCES
BARROSO
J. VALERA
M. LUIS
SAN FERNANDO
ANT. MAURA
JEWISH QUARTER
REY HEREDIA
ALF. XII
CASA DE SEFARAD
JUDIOS
CARD. HERRERO
P. RIBERA
AV. AEROPUERTO
SYNAGOGUE
OLD WALL
MEZQUITA
ISASA
AV. CONDE VALL.
CAB.
RONDA
GUADALQUIVIR RIVER
ROMAN BRIDGE
AV. CUSTODIOS
SAN BASILIO
ALCÁZAR
PATIOS AREA
M. PIDAL
CORR.
AV. ALCÁZAR
AV. DE FRA ALBINO
SEE CORDOBA CENTER DETAIL MAP
TO MECCA
1 Taverna Salinas
2 El Buey y El Fuego Rest.
3 Café Gaudí
DCH
B Bus Stops for Madinat Al-Zahra

ORIENTATION

Córdoba's big draw is the mosque-turned-cathedral called the Mezquita. Most of the town's major sights are nearby, including the Alcázar, a former royal castle. While the town ignores its river, a Roman triumphal arch with a stout "Roman Bridge" spans the marshy Guadalquivir River (a prime bird-watching area), across from the town's old fortified gate. The Mezquita is buried in the characteristic medieval town. North of that stretches the Jewish Quarter, then the modern city—which feels much like any other in Spain, but with some striking Art Deco buildings at Plaza de las Tendillas and lots of Art Nouveau lining Avenida del Gran Capitán.

Tourist Information

Córdoba has three helpful TIs: at the **train station,** at the **Mezquita,** and at the **Alcázar** (all open daily 9:30–14:00 & 16:30–19:30, Alcázar TI open through midday break Fri–Sun, tel. 902-201-774, toll-free within Spain, www.turismodecordoba.org). There's also a small TI kiosk on **Plaza de las Tendillas** (daily 10:00–14:00 & 16:30–19:30, summer 10:00–14:00 & 18:00–21:30).

The TIs sell a **Córdoba Card** (€30–45, good for one year), which is unlikely to be a good value for any short visit. Both the Alcázar and Tendillas TIs rent good **audioguide** walking tours of the city's main attractions (see "Tours," page 520).

Arrival in Córdoba

By Train or Bus: Córdoba's train station is located on Avenida de América. The bus station is across the street from the train station (on Avenida Vía Augusta, to the north). It's about a 25-minute walk from either station to the old town. There is currently no luggage storage at the train station (for security reasons), but you can stow your bag at the bus station for €3.20.

Built in 1991 to accommodate the high-speed AVE train line, the train station has ATMs, restaurants, a variety of shops, a TI booth, an information counter, and a small lounge for first-class AVE passengers. Taxis and local buses are just outside.

A **taxi** to the Mezquita costs about €6.

The only local **bus** from the train station to the old town (#3) does a long, slow loop through most of Córdoba (eventually stopping one block from the Mezquita); a better option is to ride it to Plaza de las Tendillas and walk 15 minutes from there. Because this bus does a one-way loop, it's much quicker to take it from the old town back to the stations.

To **walk** the 25 minutes from the train station to the Mezquita, turn left onto Avenida de América, then right on Avenida del Gran Capitán, which becomes a pedestrian zone. At the end, ask someone,

"*¿Dónde está la Mezquita?*" You'll be directed downhill, through the whitewashed old Jewish Quarter.

Helpful Hints

Closed Days: Many sights—the synagogue, the Alcázar, and Madinat Al-Zahra—are closed on Monday, while the Palacio de Viana is closed Sunday. The Mezquita is open daily (but some parts are closed during Sun morning Mass).

Festival: During the first half of May, Córdoba hosts the Concurso Popular de Patios Cordobeses—a patio contest (see "Patios" sidebar on page 532).

Cheap Tricks: Some minor sights, including the Baths of the Caliphate Alcázar and the Alcázar de los Reyes Cristianos, are free all day Friday. The Mezquita is free Monday through Saturday, but only if you get there before 10:00. If you don't eat or sleep, your visit to Córdoba might just cost you zero.

Internet Access: Chat-is is a block down from Plaza de las Tendillas at Calle Claudio Marcelo 15 (Mon–Fri 9:30–13:30 & 17:00–20:30, closed Sat–Sun, tel. 957-475-500).

Laundry: The helpful staff at **Sol y Mar** will wash, dry, and fold your laundry (€12.50/load, usually same-day service, cheaper for self-service, Mon–Fri 9:00–13:30 & 17:00–20:30, Sat 9:30–13:30, closed Sun, Dr. Fleming 8).

TOURS

Guided Walks—In summer, two-hour nighttime walks start at the TI on Plaza de las Tendillas and finish at the Mezquita (€15, includes a drink and tapa at a typical bar, April–Oct daily at 21:30, no tours Nov–March, prepay at TI, request English).

City Audioguide—This audioguide tour provides interesting walking itineraries that take you into the main monuments. Simply follow along on the provided map. It's a much better option than the dry Alcázar and Mezquita audioguides, and you can start and stop the device as you please (€15, €30 refundable deposit, available from Alcázar and Plaza de las Tendillas TIs, rent for 24 hours, two headphones included—or use your own).

Private Guide—**Angel Lucena** is both a good teacher and a joy to be with (€95/2.5 hrs, mobile 607-898-079, aluc@eresmas.com).

SIGHTS

Many sights may be changing their visiting hours in 2009, so confirm opening and closing times at any TI.

▲▲▲The Mezquita

This massive former mosque—now with a 16th-century church rising up from the middle—was once the center of Western Islam and a wonder of the medieval world. It's remarkably well-preserved, giving today's visitors a chance to soak up the ambience of Islamic Córdoba in its 10th-century prime.

Cost and Hours: €8, ticket kiosk inside the Patio de los Naranjos, free entry until 10:00 (because they don't want to charge a fee to attend Mass), dry €3.50 audioguide; open Mon–Sat 8:30–19:00, Sun 8:30–10:30 & 14:00–19:00, Christian altar accessible only after 10:30 unless you attend Mass, try to avoid midday crowds (11:00–15:00) by coming early or late; tel. 957-470-512. Only some parts of the cathedral are accessible during Sunday-morning Mass (8:30–10:00); entry is free at that time).

➲ **Self-Guided Tour:** Before entering the patio, take in the exterior of the Mezquita. The mosque's massive footprint is clear when you survey its sprawling walls from outside. At 590 feet by 425 feet (more than 250,000 square feet), it seems to dominate the higgledy-piggledy medieval town that surrounds it.

Patio de los Naranjos: The Mezquita's big and welcoming courtyard is free to enter. When this was a mosque, the Muslim faithful would gather in this courtyard in the shade of olive and palm trees (the *naranjos*—orange trees—came with the Christians) to perform ablution—ritual washing before prayer, as directed by Muslim law. Gaze up through the trees for views of the **Baroque bell tower,** which encases the original Muslim minaret (you can see its red bricks behind the bells). For three centuries, five times a day, a cleric (called a *muezzin*) would climb the minaret to call Muslims to face Mecca and pray.

• *Face Mecca now and pass through the end key-hole gate (present your ticket here and pick up an English map-brochure as you enter).*

Interior: Entering the former mosque from the patio, you pass from an orchard of orange trees into a forest of delicate columns. The 850 red-and-blue columns are topped with double arches—a round Romanesque arch above a Visigothic horseshoe arch—made from alternating red brick and white stone. Many of the columns and capitals (made of marble, granite, and alabaster) were

The Mezquita

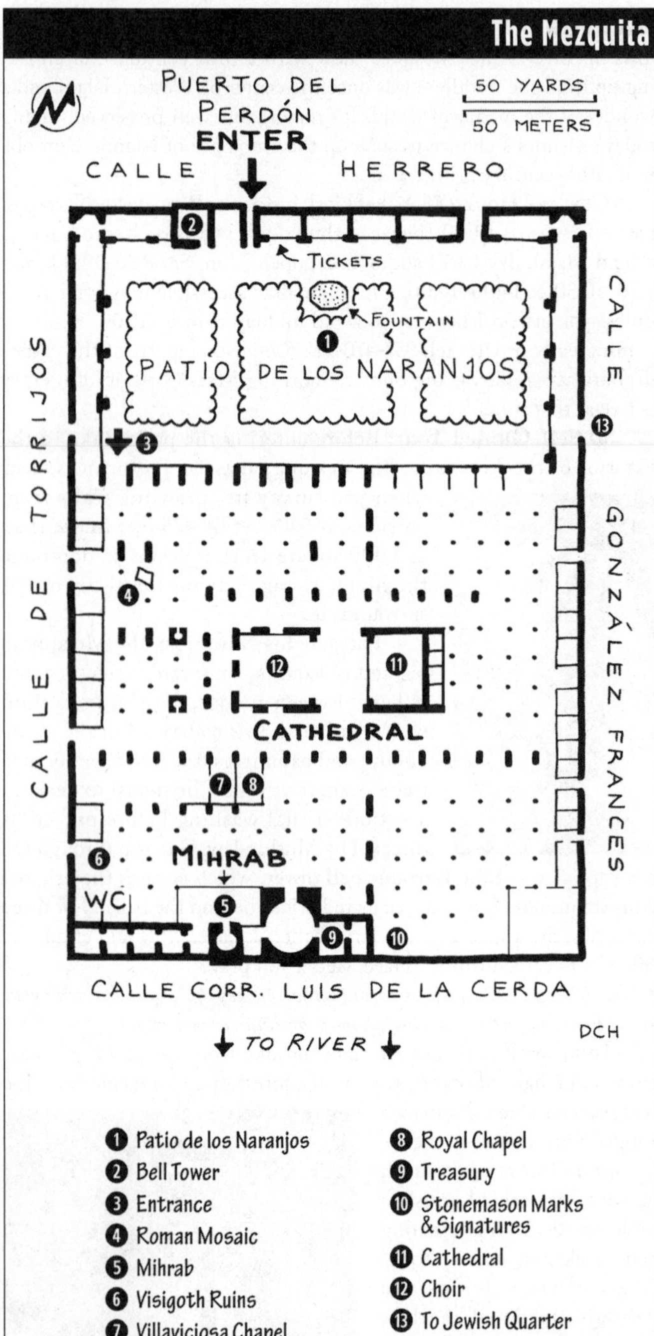

recycled from ancient Roman ruins and conquered Visigothic churches. The columns seem to recede to infinity, as if reflecting the immensity and complexity of Allah's creation. Supporting such a tall ceiling with thin columns required extra bracing with the double arches you see—a beautiful solution to a practical problem.

Although it's a vast room, the low ceilings and dense columns create an intimate and worshipful atmosphere. The original mosque was brighter before Christians renovated the place for their use and closed in the arched entrances from the patio and street. The giant cathedral sits in the center of the mosque. For now, pretend it doesn't exist. We'll visit it after exploring the mosque.

The mosque sits on the site of an early-Christian church built during the late Roman period. Five columns in from the entrance, a wooden railing marks a hole where you can look down to see an ancient **Roman mosaic** from that original church. Roman Córdoba was the leading city of southern Spain in its day.

• *Walk to the center of the far wall (opposite the entrance), where you'll find the focal point of the mosque, the...*

Mihrab: The mosque equivalent of a church's high altar, this was the focus of the original mosque and is the highlight of the Mezquita today. Picture the mosque at prayer time. Each floor stone is about the size of a prayer rug...more than 20,000 people could pray at once here. Imagine the multitude kneeling in prayer, facing the mihrab, rocking forward to touch their heads to the ground, and saying, *"Allahu Akbar, La illa a il Allah, Muhammad razul Allah"*—"Allah is great, there is no god but Allah, and Muhammad is his prophet."

The mihrab, a feature found in all mosques, is a decorated "niche"—in this case, more like a small room with a golden-arch entrance. During a service, the imam (prayer leader) would stand here to read scripture and give sermons. Built in the mid-10th century by Al-Hakam II, the exquisite room reflects the wealth of Córdoba in its prime. Three thousand pounds of multicolored glass-and-enamel cubes panel the walls and domes in mosaics designed by Byzantine craftsmen, depicting flowers and quotes from the Quran. Gape up. Overhead rises a colorful, starry dome with skylights and interlocking lobe-shaped arches.

• *In the far-right corner, you'll find...*

Visigoth Ruins: On display in the corner to the right of the mihrab are bits of carved stone from the Visigothic Christian church of San Vicente that stood here in the fifth century. (The Christian symbolism was scratched off so the stones could be reused by Muslims.) Abd Al-Rahman I bought the church from his Christian subjects before leveling it to build the mosque. From here, pan 90 degrees to enjoy a view that reveals the vastness of the mosque. (Perhaps you might also enjoy a hidden WC—in the corner.)

• *Immediately in front of the mihrab, in about the center of the mosque, is an open area that was the...*

Islamic Córdoba (756-1236): Medieval Europe's Cultural Capital

After his family was slaughtered by political rivals (A.D. 750), 20-year-old Prince Abd Al-Rahman fled the royal palace at Damascus, headed west across North Africa, and went undercover among the Berber tribesmen of Morocco. For six years, he avoided assassination while building a power base among his fellow Arab expatriates and the local Muslim Berbers. As an heir to the title of "caliph," or ruler of Islam, he sailed north and claimed Moorish Spain as his own, confirming his power by decapitating his enemies and sending their salted heads to the rival caliph in Baghdad. This split in Islam is much like the divide in Christianity between Protestants and Catholics.

Thus began an Islamic flowering in southern Spain under Abd Al-Rahman's family, the Umayyads. They dominated Sevilla and Granada, ruling the independent state of "Al-Andalus," with their capital at Córdoba.

By the year 950—when the rest of Europe was mired in poverty, ignorance, and superstition—Córdoba was Europe's greatest city, rivaling Constantinople and Baghdad. It had more than 100,000 people (Paris had a third that many), with hundreds of mosques, palaces, and public baths. The streets were paved and lighted at night with oil lamps, and running water was piped in from the outskirts of the city. Medieval visitors marveled at the size and luxury of the Mezquita mosque, a symbol that the

Villaviciosa Chapel: In 1236, Saint-King Ferdinand III conquered the city and turned the mosque into a church. Still, the locals continued to call it "La Mezquita," and left the structure virtually unchanged (70 percent of the original structure survives to this day). Sixteen columns were removed and replaced by Gothic arches to make this chapel. It feels as if the church architects appreciated the opportunity to incorporate the sublime architecture of the preexisting mosque into their church. Notice how the floor was once almost entirely covered with the tombs of nobles and big shots eager to make this their final resting place.

• *Behind the wall, face the mihrab and look to the left to see the...*

Royal Chapel: The chapel is completely closed off, but the tall, well-preserved Mudejar walls and dome are easily visible. The lavish Arabic-style decor dates from the 1370s, done by Muslims still living in the city after the Reconquista. Designed for the tombs of Christian kings, it was never open to the public.

• *Return to the mihrab. To your immediate left, enter the Baroque...*

Treasury (Tesoro): The treasury is filled with display cases of religious artifacts and the enormous monstrance that was paraded through the streets of Córdoba each Corpus Christi, 60 days after Easter. The

Umayyads of Spain were the equal of the caliphs of Baghdad.

This Golden Age was marked by a remarkable spirit of tolerance and cooperation among the three great monotheistic religions: Islam, Judaism, and Christianity. The university rang with voices in Arabic, Hebrew, and Latin, sharing their knowledge of *al-jibra* (algebra), medicine, law, and literature. The city fell under the enlightened spell of the ancient Greeks, and Córdoba's 70 libraries bulged with translated manuscripts of Plato and Aristotle, works that would later inspire medieval Christians.

Ruling over the Golden Age were two energetic leaders—Abd Al-Rahman III (912-961) and Al-Hakam II (961-976)—who conquered territory, expanded the Mezquita, and boldly proclaimed themselves caliphs.

Córdoba's Y1K crisis brought civil wars that toppled the caliph (1031), splintering Al-Andalus into several kingdoms. Córdoba came under the control of the Almoravids (Berbers from North Africa), who were less sophisticated than the Arab-based Umayyads. Then a wave of even stricter Islam swept through Spain, bringing the Almohads to power (1147) and driving Córdoba's best and brightest into exile. The city's glory days were over, and it was replaced by Sevilla and Granada as the centers of Spanish Islam. In 1236, Christians conquered the city, it declined in importance, and "Ave Marias" soon echoed through the columns of the mosque.

monstrance was an attempt by 16th-century Christians to create something exquisite enough to merit being the holder of the Holy Communion wafer. As locals believed the wafer actually was the body of Christ, this trumped any relics. The monstrance is designed like a seven-scoop ice cream cone, held together by gravity. While the bottom is silver-plated 18th-century Baroque, the top is solid silver with gold plating.

The big canvas nearest the entrance shows Saint-King Ferdinand III, who conquered Córdoba in 1236, accepting the keys to the city's fortified gate from the vanquished Muslims. The victory ended a six-month siege and resulted in a negotiated settlement: The losers' lives were spared, providing they evacuated. Most went to Granada, which remained Muslim for another 250 years. The next day (exhibiting the same spirit of military glee enjoyed by American troops who set up camp in Saddam Hussein's palace), the Spaniards celebrated Mass in a makeshift chapel right here in the great mosque.

Among the other Catholic treasures, don't miss the ivory crucifix carved in 1665. Get close to study Jesus' mouth—it's incredibly realistic. The artist? No one knows.

Just outside the treasury exit, a glass case shows off casts of the many **stonemason marks and signatures** found in this one building.

Try to locate the actual ones on nearby columns. (I was five for six.) This part of the mosque has the best light for photography, thanks to skylights put in by 18th-century Christians.

The mosque grew over several centuries under a series of rulers. Remarkably, each ruler kept to the original vision—rows and rows of multicolored columns topped by double arches. Then came the Christians...

Cathedral: Rising up in the middle of the forest of columns is the cathedral, oriented in the Christian tradition, with its altar at the east end. Gazing up at the rich decoration, it's easy to forget that you were in a former mosque just seconds ago. While the mosque is about 30 feet high, the cathedral's ceiling soars 130 feet up. Look at the glorious ceiling. (Unfortunately, ongoing renovation will keep access limited through 2009.)

In 1523, Córdoba's bishop proposed building this grand church in the Mezquita's center. The town council opposed it, but King Charles V ordered it done. According to a false but believable legend, when the king saw the final product, he declared that they'd destroyed something unique to build something ordinary.

The basic structure is late Gothic with fancy Isabelline-style columns. The nave's towering Renaissance arches and dome emphasize the triumph of Christianity over Islam in Córdoba. The twin pulpits feature a marble bull, lion, angel, and eagle—symbols of the four evangelists.

Choir: The Baroque-era choir stalls were added much later—made in 1750 of New World mahogany. While beautiful, the choir cluttered up a previously open Gothic space. Each of the 109 stalls (108 plus the throne—*catedra*—of the bishop) features a scene from the Bible: Mary's life on one side facing Jesus' life on the other. The medieval church strayed from the inclusiveness taught by Jesus. Choirs (which seem to consume otherwise-spacious church interiors throughout Spain) were only for cannons, priests, and the bishop. Those days are long gone. In fact, a public Mass is now held right here (Mon–Sat at 9:30 in the morning).

Near the Mezquita

Just downhill from the mosque is the Guadalquivir River (which flows on to Sevilla and eventually out to the Atlantic). While silted up today, it was once navigable from here. The town seems to turn its back on the Guadalquivir, but the Roman triumphal arch that faces the "Roman Bridge" (with its ancient foundation surviving) and the fortified gate on the far bank evoke a day when the river was key to the city's existence.

Baths of the Caliphate Alcázar (Banos Califales)—The scant but evocative remains of these 10th-century royal baths date from a time when the city had hundreds of baths and a population of several hundred thousand. The exhibit teaches about Arabic baths in general and the caliph's in particular. A 10-minute video (normally in Spanish, English on request) tells the story well (€2, May–June and Sept–mid-Oct Tue–Sat 10:00–14:00 & 17:30–19:30; July–Aug Tue–Sat 8:30–14:30; mid-Oct–April Tue–Sat 10:00–14:00 & 16:30–18:30; year-round: Sun 9:30–14:30, closed Mon; just outside the wall near the Alcázar).

Jewish Córdoba

Córdoba's Jewish Quarter dates from the late Middle Ages, after Muslim rule and during the Christian era. Now little remains. For a sense of it in its thriving heyday, visit the synagogue and the cultural center located a few steps away (both described below). For a pretty picture, find **Calle de las Flores** (a.k.a. "Blossom Lane"). This narrow, flower-bedecked street frames the cathedral's bell tower as it hovers in the distance (the view is a favorite for local guidebook covers).

Synagogue (Sinagoga)—The small yet beautifully preserved synagogue was built in 1315, under Christian rule, but the Islamic decoration has roots way back to Abd Al-Rahman I (see "Islamic Córdoba" sidebar on page 524). During Muslim times, Córdoba's sizable Jewish community was welcomed, though they paid substantial taxes to the city—money that enlarged the Mezquita and generated good will. That good will came in handy when Córdoba's era of prosperity and mutual respect came to an end with the arrival of the intolerant Almohad Berbers. Christians and Jews were repressed, and brilliant minds—such as the rabbi and philosopher Maimonides—fled for their own safety.

The Christian Reconquista of Córdoba (1236) brought another brief period of religious tolerance. That's when this synagogue was built—the result of a joint effort by Christians, Jews, and Muslim (Mudejar) craftsmen. By the end of the 14th century, however, Spain's Jews were again persecuted. They were finally expelled or forced to convert in 1492; this is one of only three surviving synagogues in Spain built before that year.

Rich Mudejar decorations of intertwined flowers, arabesques, and Stars of David plaster the walls. What appear to be quotes from the Quran in Arabic are actually quotes from the Bible in Hebrew. On the east wall (the symbolic direction of Jerusalem), find the niche for the Ark, which held the scrolls of the Torah (the Jewish scriptures). The upstairs gallery was reserved for women. This synagogue, the only one that survives in Córdoba, was left undisturbed because it was used as a church until the 19th century—in fact, you can see a cross

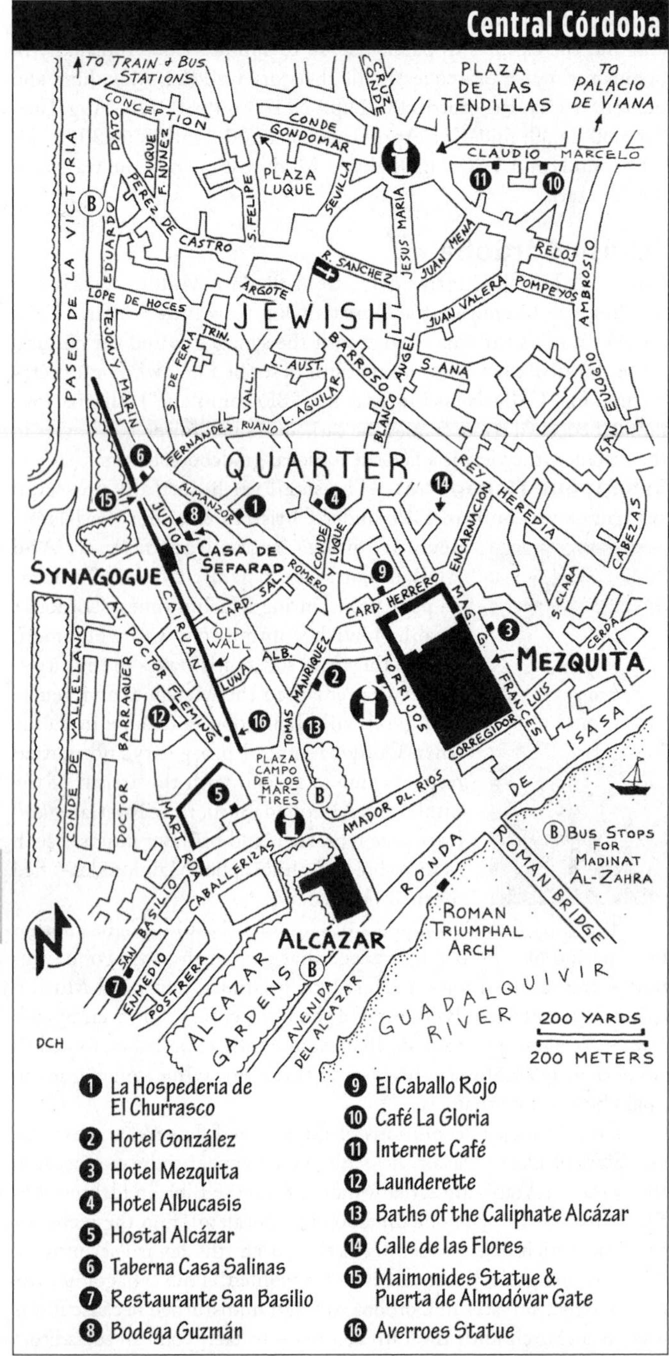

1. La Hospedería de El Churrasco
2. Hotel González
3. Hotel Mezquita
4. Hotel Albucasis
5. Hostal Alcázar
6. Taberna Casa Salinas
7. Restaurante San Basilio
8. Bodega Guzmán
9. El Caballo Rojo
10. Café La Gloria
11. Internet Café
12. Launderette
13. Baths of the Caliphate Alcázar
14. Calle de las Flores
15. Maimonides Statue & Puerta de Almodóvar Gate
16. Averroes Statue

painted into a niche (€0.30, Tue–Sat 9:30–14:00 & 15:30–17:30, Sun 9:30–13:30, closed Mon, Calle de los Judíos 20, tel. 957-202-928). To learn more about the synagogue and its community, head next to the Casa de Sefarad (described next), just 10 steps uphill.

Casa de Sefarad—Set inside a restored 14th-century home directly across from the synagogue, this interpretive museum brings to life Córdoba's rich Jewish past. Five rooms around a central patio are themed to help you understand different aspects of daily life for Spain's former Jewish community. The rooms focus on contributions from women in the community, Jewish holidays, musical traditions, and more. Upstairs is an interpretive center for the synagogue, along with rooms dedicated to Maimonides and to the synagogue. The Casa de Sefarad is a cultural center for Sephardic (the Hebrew word for "Spanish") Jewish heritage. The staff here stresses that the center's purpose is not political or religious, but cultural. Along with running this small museum, they teach courses, offer a library, and promote an appreciation of Córdoba's Sephardic heritage (€4, Mon–Sat 11:00–19:00, Sun 11:00–14:00, 30-minute guided tours in English on most days—drop by and ask when, next to the synagogue at the corner of Calle de los Judíos and Calle Averroes, tel. 957-421-404, www.casadesefarad.es). The Casa de Sefarad hosts **weekly concerts**—acoustic, Sephardic, and Andalusian, but no flamenco—on its patio (€10, most Fridays at 21:00, reservations smart).

Statues of Maimonides and Averroes—Statues honor two of Córdoba's deepest-thinking homeboys—one Jewish, one Muslim, both driven out during the wave of Islamic intolerance after the fall of the Umayyad caliphate. (Maimonides is 30 yards downhill from the synagogue; Averroes is at the end of the old wall, where Cairuan and Doctor Fleming streets meet.)

Maimonides (1135–1204) was born in Córdoba and raised on both Jewish scripture and Aristotle's philosophy. Like many tolerant Córdobans, he saw no conflict between the two. Maimonides—sometimes called the "Jewish Aquinas"—wrote the *Guide of the Perplexed* (in Arabic), in which he asserted (as the Christian philosopher St. Thomas Aquinas later would) that secular knowledge and religious faith could go hand-in-hand.

Córdoba changed in 1147, when the fundamentalist Almohads assumed power. (Imagine Pat Robertson taking over the US.) Maimonides was driven out, eventually finding work in Cairo as the sultan's doctor. Today tourists, Jewish scholars, and fans of Aquinas rub the statue's foot for good luck.

Córdoba's Jewish Quarter: A Ten-Point Scavenger Hunt

While most of the area around the big mosque is commercial and touristy, the neighborhood to the east seems somehow almost untouched by tourism and the modern world (as you leave the Mezquita, turn right and exit the orange-grove patio). To catch a whiff of Córdoba before the onslaught of tourism and the affluence of the 21st century, explore this district. Just wander and observe. Here are a few characteristics to look for:

1. **Narrow streets.** Skinny streets make sense in hot climates, as they provide much-appreciated shade.
2. **Thick, whitewashed walls.** Both features serve as a kind of natural air-conditioning.
3. **Colorful doors and windows.** The vibrancy helps counter the boring whitewash.
4. **Iron grills.** Historically, these were more artistic, but modern ones are more practical. Their continued presence is a reminder of the persistent gap through the ages between rich and poor.
5. **Stone bumpers on corners.** These protected buildings against reckless drivers. Scavenged, second-hand ancient Roman pillars worked well.
6. **Scuff guards.** Made of harder materials, these guards sit at the base of the whitewashed walls—and, from the looks of it, are serving their purpose.
7. **Riverstone cobbles.** These stones were cheap and local, and provided drains down the middle of a lane. They were flanked by smooth stones that stayed dry for walking.
8. **Open front doors.** Córdobans are proud of their patios. Walk up to the inner iron gate and peek in (see "Patios" sidebar on page 532).
9. **Remnants of old towers from minarets.** Muslim Córdoba peaked in the 10th century with an estimated 400,000 people, which meant lots of neighborhood mosques.
10. **A real neighborhood.** People really live here. There are no tacky shops, and just about the only tourist...is you.

The story of **Averroes** (1126–1198) is a mirror image of Maimonides', except that Averroes was a Muslim lawyer, not a Jewish doctor. He became the medieval world's number-one authority on Aristotle, influencing Aquinas. Averroes' biting tract *The Incoherence of the Incoherence* attacked narrow-mindedness, asserting that secular philosophy (for the elite) and religious faith (for the masses) both led to truth. The Almohads banished him from the city and burned his books, ending four centuries of Córdoban enlightenment.

More Sights in Córdoba

Alcázar de los Reyes Cristianos—Tourists line up to visit Córdoba's fortress, the "Castle of the Christian Monarchs," which sits strategically on the Guadalquivir River. Upon entering, look to the right to see a big, beautiful garden rich with flowers and fountains. To the left is a modern-feeling, unimpressive fort. While it was built along the Roman walls in Visigothic times, constant reuse and recycling has left it sparse and barren (with the exception of a few interesting Roman mosaics on the walls). Crowds squeeze up and down the congested spiral staircases of "Las Torres" for meager views. The castle was rebuilt and expanded by the Moors, who added the gardens. They loved to build gardens that evoked the Quranic description of heaven. Ferdinand and Isabel donated the castle to the Inquisition in 1482, and it became central in the church's effort to discover "false converts to Christianity"—mostly Jews who had decided not to flee Spain in 1492 (€4, €2.50 for gardens, €3.50 for audioguide; May–mid-June Tue–Sun 10:00–14:00 & 17:30–19:30; mid-June–mid-Sept Tue–Sun 8:30–14:30; closed Mon; erratic hours in winter—check with TI; gardens open 20:00–24:00, weather permitting).

Plaza de las Tendillas—While most tourists leave Córdoba having seen just the Mezquita and the cute medieval quarter that surrounds it, the modern city offers a good peek at urban Andalucía. Perhaps the best way to sample this is to browse Plaza de las Tendillas and the surrounding streets. The square, with an Art Deco charm, acts like there is no tourism in Córdoba. On the hour, a clock here chimes the guitar chords of Juan Serrano, a Córdoban classic.

Characteristic cafés and shops abound. For example, **Café La Gloria** provides an earthy Art Nouveau experience. Located just down the street from Plaza de las Tendillas, it has an unassuming entrance, but a sumptuous interior. Carved floral designs wind around the bar, mixing with *feria* posters and bullfighting memories. Pop in for a quick beer or coffee (daily from 8:30, quiet after lunch crowd clears out, Calle Claudio Marcelo 15, tel. 957-477-780).

Palacio de Viana—Decidedly off the beaten path, this former palatial estate is a 20-minute walk northeast from the cluster of sights near the Mezquita. A guided tour whisks you through each room of an exuberant 16th-century estate, while an English handout drudges through the dates and origin of each important piece. But the house is best enjoyed by ignoring the guide and gasping at the massive collection of—for lack of a better word—stuff. Decorative-art fans will have a field day.

Patios

In Córdoba, patios are taken very seriously, as shown by the fiercely fought contest that takes place the first half of every May to pick the city's most picturesque. Patios, a common feature of houses throughout Andalucía, have a long history here. The Romans used them to cool off, and the Moors added lush, decorative touches. The patio functioned as a quiet outdoor living room, an oasis from the heat. Inside elaborate ironwork gates, roses, geraniums, and jasmine spill down whitewashed walls, while fountains play and caged birds sing. Some patios are owned by individuals, some are communal courtyards for several homes, and some grace public buildings like museums or convents.

Today, homeowners take pride in these mini-paradises, and have no problem sharing them with tourists. Keep an eye out for square metal signs that indicate historic homes. As you wander Córdoba's back streets, pop your head into any wooden door that's open. The proud owners (who keep inner gates locked) enjoy showing off their picture-perfect patios. A concentration of previous patio-contest award-winners runs along Calle San Basilio and Calle Martín Roa, just across from the Alcázar gardens.

The sight is known as the "patio museum" for its 12 connecting patios, each with a different theme (house-€6, patios only-€3; June–Sept Mon–Sat 9:00–14:00, closed Sun; Oct–May Mon–Fri 10:00–13:00 & 16:00–18:00, Sat 10:00–13:00, closed Sun; no photos inside, Plaza Don Gome 2, tel. 957-496-741).

Away from the Center

Madinat Al-Zahra (Medina Azahara)—Five miles northwest of Córdoba, these ruins of a once-fabulous palace of the caliph were completely forgotten until excavations began in the early 20th century. Built in A.D. 929 as a power center to replace Córdoba, Madinat Al-Zahra was both a palace and an entirely new capital city—the "City of the Flower"—covering nearly half a square mile (only about

10 percent has been uncovered). Extensively planned with an orderly design, Madinat Al-Zahra was meant to symbolize and project a new discipline on an increasingly unstable Moorish empire in Spain. It failed. Only 75 years later, the city was looted and destroyed.

The site is a jigsaw puzzle waiting to be reassembled by patient archaeologists. Upper terrace excavations have uncovered stables and servants' quarters. Farther downhill, the house of a high-ranking official has been partially reconstructed. At the lowest level, you'll come to the remains of the mosque—placed at a diagonal, facing true east. The highlight of the visit is an elaborate reconstruction of the caliph's throne room, capturing a moody world of horseshoe arches and delicate stucco. Legendary accounts say the palace featured waterfall walls, lions in cages, and—in the center of the throne room—a basin filled with mercury, reflecting the colorful walls. The effect likely humbled anyone fortunate enough to see the caliph.

Cost and Hours: €1.50, Tue–Sat 10:00–20:30, Sun 10:00–14:00, closed Mon.

Getting There: Madinat Al-Zahra is located on a back road five miles from Córdoba. By **car,** head to Avenida de Medina Azahara (one block south of the train station), following signs for A-431; the site is well-signposted from the highway. Though the ruins aren't accessible via regular public transportation, the TI runs a **shuttle bus** that leaves each morning and returns two hours later (€6.50, buy ticket at Alcázar or Plaza Tendillas TIs, runs year-round Tue–Fri at 11:00, Sat–Sun at 10:00 and 11:00, informative English booklet provided). Catch the bus near the Mezquita at Avenida Alcázar, along the river.

SLEEPING

All these listings are within a five-minute stroll of the Mezquita (see map on page 528). If it's hot and you've got a lot of luggage, don't bother with the inconvenient city buses; just hop in a taxi.

$$$ La Hospedería de El Churrasco is a nine-room jewel box of an inn, featuring plush furniture, tasteful traditional decor, and hardwood floors. It's quiet, romantic, and just enough away from the tourist storm, yet still handy (Sb-€110–130, Db-€130–150, superior Db-€170–190, €35 for extra bed in superior Db, €20 more per room in April–May and Oct, website shows off each distinct room, no twin rooms, includes breakfast, air-con, Internet access, parking-€20, midway between Puerta de Almodóvar and the Mezquita at Calle

Sleep Code

(€1 = about $1.50, country code: 34)
S = Single, **D** = Double/Twin, **T** = Triple, **Q** = Quad, **b** = bathroom, **s** = shower only. Unless otherwise noted, credit cards are accepted, English is spoken, and breakfast generally costs extra.

To help you easily sort through these listings, I've divided the rooms into three categories, based on the price for a standard double room with bath during high season:

$$$ Higher Priced—Most rooms €100 or more.
$$ Moderately Priced—Most rooms between €60-100.
$ Lower Priced—Most rooms €60 or less.

Romero 38, tel. 957-294-808, fax 957-421-661, www.elchurrasco.com, hospederia@elchurrasco.com).

$$ Hotel González, with many of its 17 basic rooms facing its plant-filled patio, provides a bit of budget charm in Córdoba. It's sparse but clean, quiet, and well-run, with a fine location and price. Some rooms have renovated bathrooms with small windows, while others have simpler bathrooms that overlook the inner courtyard for better light—let them know if you have a preference (Sb-€43, Db-€78, Tb-€110, includes breakfast, Manríquez 3, tel. 957-479-819, fax 957-486-187, www.hotel-gonzalez.com, hotelgonzalez@wanadoo.es).

$$ Hotel Mezquita, just across from the main entrance of the Mezquita, rents 21 modern and comfortable rooms. The grand entrance lobby elegantly recycles an upper-class mansion (Sb-€36, Db-€69, Tb-€96, breakfast-€3.50, air-con, Plaza Santa Catalina 1, tel. 957-475-585, fax 957-476-219, www.hotelmezquita.com, hotelmezquita@wanadoo.es).

$$ Hotel Albucasis, at the edge of the tourist zone, features 15 basic, clean rooms, all of which face quiet interior patios. The friendly, accommodating staff and cozy setting make you feel right at home (Sb-€55, Db-€85, breakfast-€6, air-con, parking-€12, Calle Buen Pastor 11, tel. 957-478-625, www.hotelalbucasis.com, hotelalbucasis@hotmail.com).

$ Hostal Alcázar is a cheap bet. Run-down and budget-priced, without a real reception desk, this place is just outside the old city wall on a quiet, cobbled, traffic-free street. Its 16 rooms are split between two homes on opposite sides of the lane, conveniently located 50 yards from a taxi and bus stop (Sb-€18, small Db-€30, bigger Db-€45, Tb-€45–54, two-room apartment-€60 for two or €80 for four, breakfast-€3, air-con, parking-€6, near the Alcázar at Calle San Basilio 2, tel. 957-202-561, www.hostalalcazar.com, hostalalcazar@hotmail.com, ladies' man Fernando and family, son Demitrio speaks English).

EATING

There are plenty of touristy options around the Mezquita. I've listed places a bit farther afield, where you're likely to dine with locals who add to the ambience (rather than tour groups who detract from it). Many smaller places have "bar menus" with *raciones* and half- *(media) raciones* rather than typical first and second courses. Enjoy this as an opportunity to explore the local cuisine. Ordering half-*raciones* may cost a bit more per ounce, but you'll broaden your tasting experience. Don't be intimidated by the language barrier. Ask for the *lista de tapas* in English. There's usually one around somewhere. Don't miss *salmorejo,* Córdoba's version of *gazpacho*. It's creamier, with more bread and olive oil and generally served with pieces of ham and hard-boiled egg. Most places serve sherry from the nearby Montilla-Moriles region; these *finos* are slightly less dry but more aromatic than those produced in Jerez de la Frontera.

Near the Mezquita

Taberna Casa Salinas, buried in the Jewish Quarter a block in from Puerta de Almodóvar, serves delicious and inexpensive plates. Whether you sit in the pub in front or the restaurant in back, order from the same simple-yet-enticing bar menu (lovely little €2.50 tapas, a good place to try *salmorejo,* daily 12:00–16:00 & 20:00–24:00, tel. 957-290-846).

Restaurante San Basilio is the local diner on Calle San Basilio, just outside the wall. While there's no seating outside, the restaurant still offers great "patio ambience"—with a view of the kitchen action. No tourists, no pretense...it's understandably the neighborhood favorite (classic €18 fixed-priced meal, €9 fixed-price meal weekdays, lots of €10 fish dishes, 13:00–16:00 & 21:00–24:00 with one night off a week, Calle San Basilio 19, tel. 957-297-007).

Bodega Guzmán, which proudly displays the heads of brave-but-unlucky bulls, serves tapas to locals who burst into song when they feel the flamenco groove. Arrive early to get a table. While it feels like a drinking place, you can ask for an English list of dishes if you're hungry. Choose a table or belly up to the bar and try a dry sherry (Fri–Wed 11:30–16:00 & 20:00–24:00, closed Thu, if entering the old town from Puerta de Almodóvar take the first right—it's 100 yards from the gate at Calle de los Judíos 7).

El Caballo Rojo is venerable, elegant, and professional. Located next to the Mezquita, it's been making tourists happy with regional cuisine for 45 years. While the modern, ground-floor bar serves tapas and drinks (€5–10 *raciones*), the action and charm are upstairs. It's dressy, yet not stuffy, with black-suited waiters serving nicely presented dishes. On a hot summer evening, their rooftop terrace with bell-tower views is a hit (€30 meals, lunch from 13:00, dinner from 20:00, reservations smart, Cardenal Herrero 28, tel. 957-475-375).

In the Modern City

These restaurants are located north of the Jewish Quarter, in the modern city (see map on page 518).

At **Taverna Salinas,** you'll find the classic Córdoba scene. While all the seating is indoors, it's still pleasantly patio-esque, and popular with locals for its traditional cuisine and exuberant bustle. The fun menu features a slew of enticing €5 plates. Study what locals are eating before ordering. There's no drink menu—just basic beer or inexpensive wine. They don't take reservations. If there's a line (as there often is later in the evening), leave your name and throw yourself into the adjacent tapas-bar mosh pit for a drink (Mon–Sat 12:00–16:00 & 20:00–24:00, closed Sun; from Plaza de las Tendillas walk 3 blocks to the Roman temple, then go 1 more block and turn right to Tendidores 3; tel. 957-480-135).

El Buey y El Fuego is designed for steak-lovers, serving enormous portions of anything that can be grilled. As it's far away from anything touristy, getting here involves a short taxi ride. Its regular diners enjoy the fancy but convivial atmosphere (€15 fixed-price lunches, dinners average €35/person, Mon–Sat 14:00–17:00 & 21:00–24:00, closed Sun, reservations smart on Fri–Sat, Benito Pérez Galdós 1, tel. 957-491-012). Walk off dinner by strolling down Art Nouveau–rich Avenida del Gran Capitán.

Café Gaudí boasts a faded Modernista interior with a smoky, old-school ambience. The bar is perfectly local, and the sidewalk tables look out on Córdoba's main drag. There's just a simple bar menu, so the food's basic. You come here for the people-watching (Mon–Sat 8:00–23:00, Sun 10:00–22:00, Avenida del Gran Capitán 22, tel. 957-471-736).

TRANSPORTATION CONNECTIONS

From Córdoba by Train: Córdoba is on the slick AVE train line (reservations required), making it an easy stopover between **Madrid** (30/day, 1.75 hrs) and **Sevilla** (hourly, 45 min, €24 one-way, €38 round-trip—must reserve both ways when you book, with railpass you still must pay €10 reservation fee). The slow train to **Sevilla** doesn't require a reservation and is much cheaper (80 min, €8 one-way). Other trains go to **Granada** (2/day, 2.5 hrs), **Ronda** (2/day direct, 1.75 hrs; more with transfer in Bobadilla, 3.5 hrs), **Málaga** (10/day, 1 hr on fast AVE train; 2/day, 3 hrs on slower train), and **Algeciras** (4/day, 4.5–5 hrs, transfer in Bobadilla). Train info: tel. 902-240-202.

By Bus to: Granada (8/day, 2.5–3 hrs), **Sevilla** (9/day, 2 hrs), **Córdoba** (1/day, 4.5 hrs), **Madrid** (6/day, 5 hrs), **Málaga** (5/day, 3–3.5 hrs *directo*), **Barcelona** (2/day, 10 hrs). The efficient staff at the information desk prints bus schedules for you. Bus info: tel. 957-404-040.

ANDALUCÍA'S WHITE HILL TOWNS

Arcos de la Frontera • Ronda • Zahara • Grazalema • Jerez

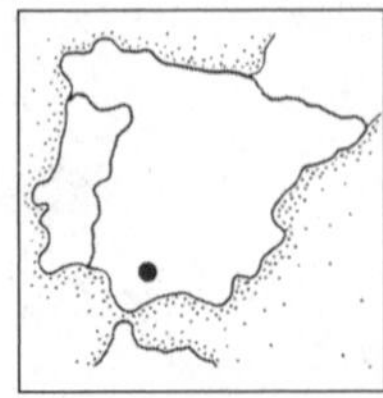

Just as the American image of Germany is Bavaria, the Yankee dream of Spain is Andalucía. This is the home of bullfights, flamenco, gazpacho, pristine whitewashed hill towns, and glamorous Mediterranean resorts. The big cities of Andalucía (Granada, Sevilla, and Córdoba) and the South Coast (Costa del Sol) are covered in separate chapters. This chapter explores its hill-town highlights.

The Route of the White Hill Towns (Ruta de los Pueblos Blancos), Andalucía's charm bracelet of cute towns perched in the sierras, gives you wonderfully untouched Spanish culture. Spend a night in the romantic queen of the white towns, Arcos de la Frontera. Towns with "de la Frontera" in their names were established on the front line of the centuries-long fight to recapture Spain from the Muslims, who were slowly pushed back into Africa. The hill towns—no longer strategic, no longer on any frontier—are now just passing time peacefully. Join them. Nearby, the city of Jerez, while teeming with traffic and lacking in charm, is worth a peek for its famous horses and a glass of sherry.

To study ahead, visit www.andalucia.com for information on hotels, festivals, museums, nightlife, and sports in the region.

Planning Your Time

On a three-week vacation in Spain, the region is worth two nights and up to two days sandwiched between visits to Sevilla and Tarifa. Arcos makes the best home base, as it's near Jerez, close to interesting smaller towns, and conveniently situated halfway between Sevilla and Tarifa. The towns can also be (and often are) accessed from the Costa del Sol resorts via Ronda.

See Jerez on your way in or out, spend a day hopping from town

Southern Andalucía

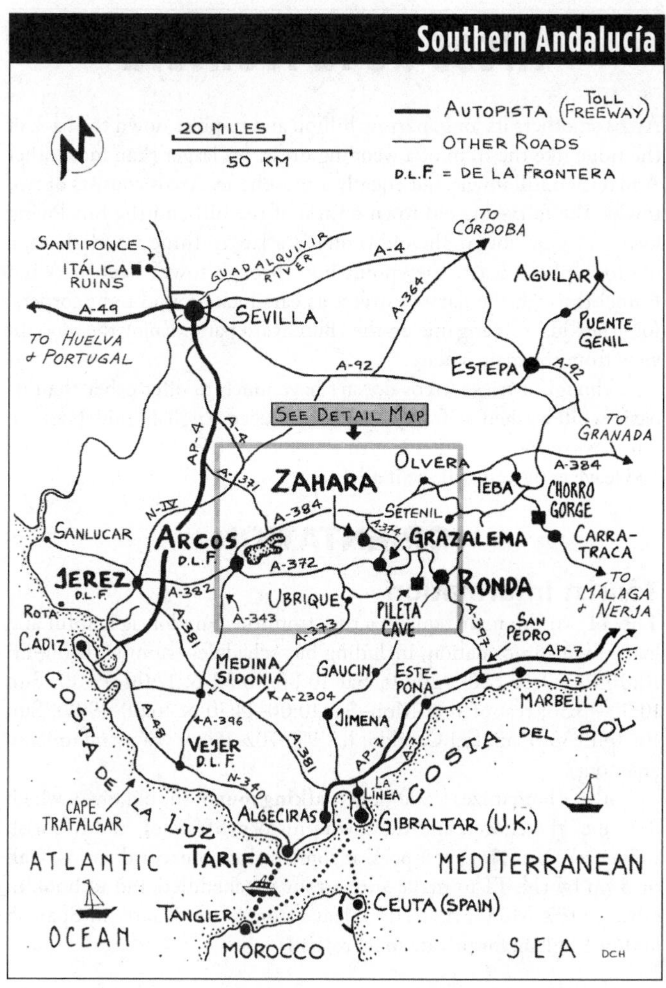

to town in the more remote interior (Grazalema and Zahara, at a minimum), and enjoy Arcos early and late in the day. For more details on exploring this region by car, see "Route Tips for Drivers" at the end of this chapter.

Without a car, you might keep things simple and focus only on Arcos and Jerez (both well-served by public buses). Another option, if you're staying in Sevilla, is to use Andalusian Minibus Tours for an all-day excursion to Olvera, Zahara, Grazalema, and Setenil de las Bodegas (see page 473).

Spring and fall are high season throughout this area. In summer you'll find intense heat, but empty hotels and no crowds.

Arcos de la Frontera

Arcos smothers its long, narrow hilltop and tumbles down the back of the ridge like the train of a wedding dress. It's larger than most other Andalusian hill towns, but equally atmospheric. Arcos consists of two towns: the fairy-tale old town on top of the hill and the fun-loving lower, or new, town. The old center is a labyrinthine wonderland, a photographer's feast. Viewpoint-hop through town. Feel the wind funnel through the narrow streets as cars inch around tight corners. Join the kids' soccer game on the churchyard patio. Enjoy the moonlit view from the main square.

Though it tries, Arcos doesn't have much to offer other than its basic whitewashed self. The locally produced English guidebook on Arcos waxes poetic and at length about very little. You can arrive late and leave early and still see it all.

ORIENTATION

Tourist Information

The TI, on the main square across from the parador, is helpful and loaded with information, including bus schedules (summer Mon–Fri 10:00–14:30 & 17:00–20:00, Sat 10:00–13:30 & 17:00–19:00, Sun 10:30–13:30; rest of year Mon–Sat 10:00–14:30 & 16:00–19:00, Sun 10:30–13:30; Plaza del Cabildo, tel. 956-702-264, www.ayuntamientoarcos.org).

The TI organizes a one-hour **walking tour** of the old town, which describes the church and the town's history, lifestyles, and Moorish influences. You also get a peek at some private courtyard patios. Call or drop by the TI to make sure a tour is scheduled and to book in advance (€7, Mon–Fri at 11:00, leave from main square, in Spanish and/or English; for private tours call TI).

Arrival in Arcos

By Bus: The bus station is on Calle Corregidores, at the foot of the hill. To get up to the old town, catch the shuttle bus marked *Centro* (€1, pay driver, 2/hr, Mon–Sat 8:15–21:15, doesn't run on Sun), hop a taxi (€5 fixed rate), or hike 20 uphill minutes (see map).

By Car: The old town is a tight squeeze with a one-way traffic flow from west to east (coming from the east, circle south under town). The TI and my recommended hotels are in the west. If you miss your target, you must drive out the other end, double back, and try again. Driving in Arcos is like threading needles. Turns are tight, parking is frustrating, and congestion can lead to long jams.

Small cars can park in the main square of the old town at the top of the hill (Plaza del Cabildo). Get a €3.50 all-day pass from your

Cheap Tricks in the White Hill Towns

Good news: In general, the south of Spain is cheaper than the north (especially in the small towns).

In Arcos de la Frontera
For a cheap (€1) and scenic loop around town, take the minibus joyride described in "Getting Around Arcos" (below).

In Ronda
Instead of going for the big meal with views, either grab a *bocadillo* (sandwich) from a bar or get picnic fixings at the supermarket, and eat your lunch in the Alameda del Tajo park. Then have a coffee at the Hotel Don Miguel terrace, where you feel like you're falling into the gorge.

In Jerez
Rather than attending the horse show, watch the cheaper training sessions. Afterwards, take the Sandeman sherry tour (without tapas), or just go to the Sandeman shop and buy a bottle to chill and drink at your hotel.

hotel or buy a ticket from the machine (€0.70/hr, 2-hr maximum, only necessary Mon–Fri 9:00–14:00 & 17:00–21:00 and Sat 9:00–14:00—confirm times on machine). If checking in, tell the uniformed parking attendant the name of your hotel. If there's no spot, wait until one opens up (he'll help). Once you grab a spot, tell him you'll be back from your hotel with a ticket.

It's less stressful (and better exercise) to park in the modern underground lot at Plaza de España in the new town. From this lot, catch a taxi or the shuttle bus up to the old town (2/hr; as you're looking uphill, the bus stop is to the right of the traffic circle), or hike 15 minutes.

Getting Around Arcos

The old town is easily walkable, but it's fun and relaxing to take a circular **minibus** joyride. The little shuttle bus constantly circles through the town's one-way system and around the valley (€1, 2/hr, Mon–Sat 8:15–21:15, doesn't run on Sun). For a 30-minute tour, hop on. You can catch it just below the main church in the old town near the mystical stone circle (generally departs at :20 and :50 past the hour). Sit in the front seat for the best view of the tight squeezes and the school kids hanging out in the plazas as you wind through the old town. After passing under a Moorish gate, you enter a modern residential neighborhood, circle under the eroding cliff, and return to the old town by way of Plaza de España.

Helpful Hints

Internet Access: Try the single computer at the TI (€1/15 min).

Post Office: It's in the old town at Paseo de los Boliches 24, a few doors up from Hotel Los Olivos (Mon–Fri 8:30–14:30, Sat 9:30–13:00, closed Sun).

Viewpoint: For drivers, the best town overlook is from a tiny park just beyond the new bridge on the El Bosque road. In town, there are some fine viewpoints (for instance, from the main square), but the church towers are no longer open to the public.

SELF-GUIDED WALK

Welcome to Arcos' Old Town

This walk will introduce you to virtually everything worth seeing in Arcos.

• *Start at the top of the hill, in the main square dominated by the church. (Avoid this walk during the hot midday siesta.)*

Plaza del Cabildo: Stand at the viewpoint opposite the church on the town's main square. Survey the square, which in the old days doubled as a bullring. On your right is the parador, a former palace of the governor. It flies three flags: Europe, Spain, and the green Andalusian flag. On your left are the City Hall and the TI, below the 11th-century Moorish castle where Ferdinand and Isabel held Reconquista strategy meetings (castle privately owned and closed to the public).

Now belly up to the railing and look down. The people of Arcos boast that only they see the backs of the birds as they fly. Ponder the parador's erosion concerns (it lost part of its lounge in the 1990s—dropped right off), the orderly orange groves, and fine views toward Morocco. The city council considered building an underground parking lot to clear up the square, but nixed it because of the land's fragility. You're 330 feet above the Guadalete River. This is the town's suicide departure point for men (women jump from the other side).

• *Looming over the square is the...*

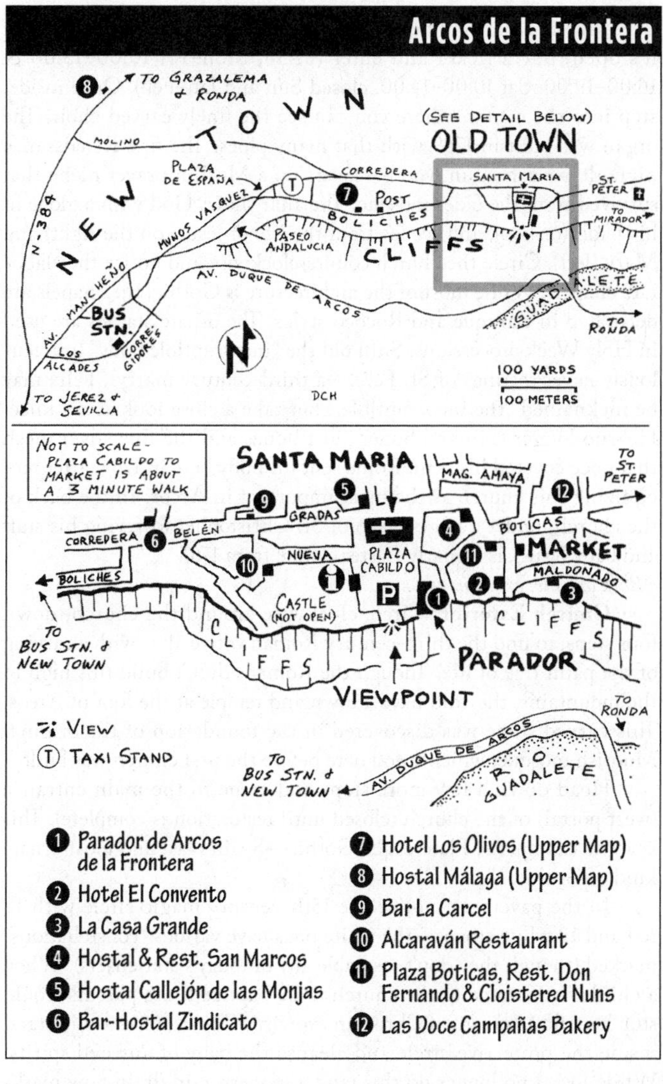

Church of Santa María: After Arcos was retaken from the Moors in the 13th century, this church was built atop a mosque. Notice the church's fine but chopped-off bell tower. The old one fell in the earthquake of 1755 (famous for destroying Lisbon). The replacement was intended to be the tallest in Andalucía after Sevilla's—but money ran out. It looks like someone lives on an upper floor. Someone does—the church guardian resides there in a room strewn with bell-ringing ropes.

The church may be closed for restoration through 2009; if it's open, buy a ticket and enter (€1.50, Mon–Fri 10:00–13:00 & 16:00–19:00, Sat 10:00–14:00, closed Sun and Jan–Feb). Once inside, step into the center, where you can see the finely carved choir. The organ was built in 1789 with that many pipes. The fine Renaissance high altar—carved in wood—covers up a Muslim prayer niche that survived from the older mosque. The altar shows God with a globe in his hand (on top), and scenes from the life of Jesus (on the right) and Mary (left). Circle the church counterclockwise and notice the elaborate chapels. While most of the architecture is Gothic, the chapels are decorated in Baroque and Rococo styles. The ornate statues are used in Holy Week processions. Sniff out the "incorruptible body" (miraculously never rotting) of St. Felix—a third-century martyr. Felix may be nicknamed "the incorruptible," but take a close look at his knee. He's no longer skin and bones...just bones and the fine silver mesh that once covered his skin. Rome sent his body here in 1764, after recognizing this church as the most important in Arcos. In the back of the church, under a huge fresco of St. Christopher (carrying his staff and baby Jesus), is a gnarly Easter candle from 1767.

• *Back outside, examine the...*

Church Exterior: Circle clockwise around the church, down four steps, to find the third-century Roman votive altar with a carving of the palm tree of life. Though the Romans didn't build this high in the mountains, they did have a town and temple at the foot of Arcos. This carved stone was discovered in the foundation of the original Moorish mosque, which stood here before the first church was built.

Head down a few more steps and come to the main entrance (west portal) of the church (closed until restoration is complete). This is a fine example of Plateresque Gothic—Spain's last and most ornate kind of Gothic.

In the pavement, notice the 15th-century magic circle with 12 red and 12 white stones—the white ones have various "constellations" marked (though they don't resemble any of today's star charts). When a child would come to the church to be baptized, the parents would stop here first for a good Christian exorcism. The exorcist would stand inside the protective circle and cleanse the baby of any evil spirits. While locals no longer do this (and a modern rain drain now marks the center), Sufis, members of a sect of Islam, still come here in a kind of pilgrimage every November. (Down a few more steps and 10 yards to the left, you can catch the public bus for a circular minibus joyride through Arcos; see "Getting Around Arcos," page 541.)

Continue around the church to the intersection below the flying buttresses. These buttresses were built to shore up the church when it was damaged by an earthquake in 1699. Thanks to these supports, the church survived the bigger earthquake of 1755. The spiky security grille (over the window above) protected cloistered nuns when this building was a convent. Look at the arches that prop up the houses downhill on the left; all over town, arches support earthquake-damaged structures.

At the corner, **Sr. González Oca's tiny barbershop** has some exciting posters of bulls running Pamplona-style through the streets of Arcos during Holy Week—an American from the nearby Navy base at Rota was killed here by a bull in 1994. (Sr. González Oca is happy to show off his posters; drop in and say, "Hola." Need a haircut, guys? €9.) Downstairs in his son's bar, you can see a framed collection of euro coins from each of the 12 original participating nations (under the TV in the corner). Continuing along under the buttresses, notice the scratches of innumerable car mirrors on each wall (and be glad you're walking).

• *Now make your way...*

From the Church to the Market: Completing your circle around the church, turn left under more arches built to repair earthquake damage and walk east down the bright, white Calle Escribanos. From now to the end of this walk, you'll basically go straight until you come to the town's second big church (St. Peter's). After a block, you hit **Plaza Boticas.**

On your right is the last remaining **convent** in Arcos. Notice the no-nunsense window grilles high above, with tiny peepholes in the latticework for the cloistered nuns to see through. Step into the lobby under the fine portico to find their one-way mirror and a spinning cupboard that hides the nuns from view. Push the buzzer, and one of the eight sisters (several are from Kenya and speak English well) will spin out some €5 boxes of excellent, freshly baked pine-nut cookies for you to consider buying (open daily but not reliably 8:30–14:30 & 17:00–19:00; be careful—if you stand big and tall to block out the light, you can actually see the sister through the glass). If you ask for *magdalenas,* bags of cupcakes will swing around (€1.50). These are traditional goodies made from natural ingredients. Buy some cupcakes to support their church work, and give them to kids as you complete your walk.

The **covered market** *(mercado)* at the bottom of the plaza (down from the convent) resides in an unfinished church. At the entry, notice what is half of a church wall. The church was being built for the Jesuits, but construction stopped in 1767 when King Charles III, tired of the Jesuit appetite for politics, expelled the order from Spain. The market is closed on Sunday and Monday—since they rest on Sunday, there's no produce, fish, or meat ready for Monday. Poke inside. It's tiny but has everything you need. Pop into the *servicio público* (public WC)—no gender bias here.

• *Continue straight down Calle Boticas...*

From the Market to the Church of St. Peter: As you walk, peek discreetly into private patios. These wonderful, cool-tiled courtyards filled with plants, pools, furniture, and happy family activities are typical of Arcos. Except in the mansions, these patios are generally shared by several families. Originally, each courtyard served as a catchment system, funneling rainwater to a drain in the middle, which filled the well. You can still see tiny wells in wall niches with now-decorative pulleys for the bucket.

Look for **Las Doce Campañas bakery,** where Juan Miguel sells traditional and delicious sultana cookies (€1.20 each). These big, dry macaroons (named for the wives of sultans) go back to Moorish times. At the next corner, squint back above the bakery to the corner of the tiled rooftop. The tiny stone—where the corner hits the sky—is a very eroded mask, placed here to scare evil spirits from the house. This is Arcos' last surviving mask from a tradition that lasted until the mid-19th century.

Also notice the ancient columns on each corner. All over town, these columns—many actually Roman, appropriated from their original ancient settlement at the foot of the hill—were put up to protect buildings from reckless donkey carts and tourists in rental cars.

As you continue straight, notice that the walls are scooped out on either side of the windows. These are a reminder of the days when women stayed inside but wanted the best possible view of any people action in the streets. These "window ears" also enabled boys in a more modest age to lean inconspicuously against the wall to chat up eligible young ladies.

Across from the old facade ahead, find the **Association of San Miguel.** Duck right, past a bar, into the oldest courtyards in town—you can still see the graceful Neo-Gothic lines of this noble home from 1850. The bar is a club for retired men—always busy when a bullfight's on TV or during card games. The guys are friendly, and drinks are cheap (a stiff Cuba Libre costs €1.50). You're welcome to flip on the light and explore the old-town photos in the back room.

Just beyond, facing the elegant front door of that noble house, is Arcos' second church, **St. Peter's** (€1 donation, Mon–Fri 10:30–14:00 & 17:00–19:00, Sat 10:30–14:00, closed Sun). You know it's St. Peter's because St. Peter, mother of God, is the centerpiece of the facade. Let me explain. It really is the second church, having had an extended battle with Santa María for papal recognition as the leading church in Arcos. When the pope finally favored Santa María, St.

Peter's parishioners changed their prayers. Rather than honoring "María," they wouldn't even say her name. They prayed "St. Peter, mother of God." Like Santa María, it's a Gothic structure, filled with Baroque decor, many Holy Week procession statues, humble English descriptions, and relic skeletons in glass caskets (two from the third century A.D.).

In the cool of the evening, the tiny square in front of the church—about the only flat piece of pavement around—serves as the old-town soccer field for neighborhood kids. Until a few years ago, this church also had a resident bellman—notice the cozy balcony halfway up. He was a basket-maker and a colorful character, famous for bringing a donkey into his quarters, which grew too big to get back out. Finally, he had no choice but to kill and eat the donkey.

Twenty yards beyond the church, step into the fine **Galería de Arte San Pedro,** featuring artisans in action and their reasonably priced paintings and pottery. Walk inside. Find the water drain and the well.

Across the street, a sign directs you to **Mirador**—a tiny square 100 yards away that affords a commanding view of Arcos. The reservoir you see to the east of town is used for water sports in the summertime, and forms part of a power plant that local residents protested—to no avail—based on environmental issues.

From the Church of St. Peter, circle down and around back to the main square, wandering the tiny neighborhood lanes. Just below St. Peter's is a delightful little Andalusian garden (formal Arabic style, with aromatic plants such as jasmine, rose, and lavender, and water in the center). The lane, called Higinio Capote—below Santa María—is particularly picturesque with its many geraniums. Peek into patios, kick a few soccer balls, and savor the views.

NIGHTLIFE

Evening Action in the New Town—The newer part of Arcos has a modern charm. In the cool of the evening, all generations enjoy life out around Plaza de España (10-min walk from the old town). Several fine tapas bars border the square or are nearby.

The big park (Recinto Ferial) below Plaza de España is the late-night fun zone in the summer (June–Aug) when *carpas* (restaurant tents) fill with merrymakers, especially on weekends. The scene includes open-air tapas bars, disco music, and dancing. Throughout the summer, there are free evening events here, including live concerts on Fridays and open-air cinema on Sundays.

Flamenco—On Plaza del Cananeo in the old town and three other venues, amateur flamenco sizzles on Thursday evenings (free, July–Aug from 22:00, check TI for locations).

SLEEPING

Hotels in Arcos consider April, May, August, September, and October to be high season. Note that some hotels double their rates during the motorbike races in nearby Jerez (usually April or May, varies yearly, call TI or ask your hotel) and during Holy Week (April 5–12 in 2009); these spikes are not reflected in the prices below.

In the Old Town

$$$ Parador de Arcos de la Frontera is royally located, with 24 elegant, recently refurbished, and reasonably priced rooms (8 have balconies). If you're going to experience a parador, this is a good one (Sb-€115, Db-€144, Db with terrace-€173, cheaper Nov–Feb, breakfast-€14, air-con, elevator, minibar, free parking, Plaza del Cabildo, tel. 956-700-500, fax 956-701-116, www.parador.es, arcos@parador.es).

$$ Hotel El Convento, deep in the old town just beyond the parador, is the best value in town. Run by a hardworking family and their wonderful staff, this cozy hotel offers 13 fine rooms—all with great views, most with balconies. In 1998, I enjoyed a big party with most of Arcos' big shots as they dedicated a fine room with a grand-view balcony to "Rick Steves, Periodista Turístico." Guess where I sleep when in Arcos... (Sb with balcony-€55, Sb with terrace-€68, Db with balcony-€70, Db with terrace-€85, extra person-€18, includes tax; 10 percent discount in 2009 when you book direct, pay in cash, and show this year's book; cheaper Nov–Feb; parking on Plaza del Cabildo-€3.50, Maldonado 2, tel. 956-702-333, fax 956-704-128, www.hotelelconvento.es, reservas@hotelelconvento.es). Over an à la carte breakfast, bird-watch on their view terrace, with all of Andalucía spreading beyond your *café con leche.*

$$ La Casa Grande is a lovingly appointed *Better Homes and Moroccan Tiles* kind of place that rents eight rooms with big-view windows. Like in a lavish bed-and-breakfast, you're free to enjoy its fine view terrace, homey library, and classy courtyard, where you'll be served a traditional breakfast (Db-€65–75, Db suite-€82–90, Tb-€110–115, Qb suite-€120–131, air-con, free Internet access and Wi-Fi, Maldonado 10, tel. 956-703-930, fax 956-717-095, www.lacasagrande.net, info@lacasagrande.net, Elena).

$ Hostal San Marcos, run from a bar in the heart of the old town, offers four air-conditioned rooms and a great sun terrace with views of the reservoir above a neat little bar (Sb-€25, Db-€35,

Sleep Code

(€1 = about $1.50, country code: 34)
S = Single, **D** = Double/Twin, **T** = Triple, **Q** = Quad, **b** = bathroom, **s** = shower only. Unless otherwise noted, you can assume credit cards are accepted, English is spoken, and breakfast and the 7 percent IVA tax are not included.

To help you easily sort through these listings, I've divided the rooms into three categories, based on the price for a standard double room with bath during high season.

$$$ Higher Priced—Most rooms €100 or more.
$$ Moderately Priced—Most rooms between €50-100.
$ Lower Priced—Most rooms €50 or less.

Tb-€45, includes tax, Marqués de Torresoto 6, tel. 956-700-721, mobile 615-375-077, sanmarcosarcos@mixmail.com, Loli and Lola speak no English).

$ Hostal Callejón de las Monjas, with a tangled floor plan and nine simple rooms, offers the best cheap beds in the old town. It's on a sometimes-noisy street behind the Church of Santa María (Sb-€20, D-€27, Db-€33, Db with terrace-€39, Tb-€44, Qb apartments-€66, includes tax, air-con, Calle Deán Espinosa 4, tel. & fax 956-702-302, padua@mesonelpatio.com, staff speak no English). Sr. González Oca, a ladies' man, runs a tiny barbershop in the foyer (see page 545) and a restaurant in the cellar.

$ At **Bar-Hostal Zindicato,** the bar comes first, but they also rent four tidy air-conditioned rooms really cheap out back on the ground floor (Db-€30, just below the old town gate at Calle Corredera 2, tel. 956-701-841, mobile 657-911-851).

In the New Town

$$ Hotel Los Olivos is a bright, cool, and airy place with 19 rooms, an impressive courtyard, roof garden, generous public spaces, bar, view, friendly folks, and easy parking. The seven view rooms can be a bit noisy in the afternoon, but—with double-paned windows—are usually fine at night (Sb-€45, Db-€75, Tb-€87, extra bed-€12, breakfast-€8, includes tax, 10 percent discount with cash and this year's book, free Internet access and Wi-Fi, Paseo de los Boliches 30, tel. 956-700-811, fax 956-702-018, http://hotel-losolivos.es, reservas@hotel-losolivos.es, Raquel and Miguel Ángel).

$ Hostal Málaga is surprisingly nice, if for some reason you want to stay on the big, noisy road at the Jerez edge of town. Nestled on a quiet lane between truck stops on A-382, it offers 18 clean, attractive rooms and a breezy two-level roof garden (Sb-€20–25, Db-€35–38, Qb apartment-€50, air-con, easy parking, Ponce de León 5, tel. & fax 956-702-010, saturno1004@hotmal.com, Josefa speaks German if that helps).

EATING

Dining in Arcos

The **Parador** (described under "Sleeping," above) has an expensive restaurant with a cliff-edge setting. Its €36 11-course sampler menu is an interesting option. A costly drink on the million-dollar-view terrace can be worth the price (€25–30 fixed-price meal at lunch, open for lunch and dinner daily, on main square).

Tapas in Arcos' Old Town

There are four decent rustic bar/restaurants in the old town within a block or two of the main square and church. Most serve tapas at the bar and *raciones* at their tables. Prices are fairly consistent (€2 tapas, €5 half-*raciones*, €8 *raciones*).

Bar La Carcel ("The Prison") is run by a hardworking family that brags about its exquisite tapas and *montaditos* (small, open-faced sandwiches). I agree. The menu is accessible; prices are the same at the bar or at the tables; and the place has a winning energy, giving the traveler a fun peek at this community (Tue–Sun 12:00–16:00 & 20:00–24:00, closed Mon, Calle Deán Espinosa 18, tel. 956-700-410).

Alcaraván tries to be a bit trendier yet *típico,* with a hibachi hard at work out front. A flamenco ambience fills its medieval vault in the castle's former dungeon. This place attracts French and German tourists who give it a cool vibe. Francisco and his wife cook from 21:00 on (closed Mon, Calle Nueva 1).

Restaurante San Marcos is a tiny, homey bar with five tables, an easy-to-understand menu offering hearty, simple home-cooking, and cheap €5 plates (14:00–16:00 & after 20:00, Marqués de Torresoto 6).

Restaurante Don Fernando gives rustic a feminine twist with an inviting bar, and both indoor and great outdoor seating on the square just across from the little market (13:00–15:30 & after 20:30 for food, longer hours for drinks on the square, on Plaza Boticas).

Tapas in the New Town

Plaza de España, in the lower new town, is lined with tapas bars and restaurants. There's even an Egyptian restaurant if you're in the mood for a change. For a great perch while enjoying the local family scene, consider the busy **Restaurante Bar Terraza** (€12 plates) at the end of Plaza de España. Just beyond that is **Casa Juan Bernal,** a little bar that's enthusiastic about its "prizewinning" tapas (the local gang injects energy after 21:00, Calle Munoz Vazquez 11).

TRANSPORTATION CONNECTIONS

By Bus

Leaving Arcos by bus can be frustrating (especially if you're going to Ronda)—buses generally leave late, the schedule information boards are often inaccurate, and the ticket window usually isn't open (luckily, you can buy your tickets on the bus). But local buses do give you a glimpse at *España profunda* ("deep Spain"), where everyone seems to know each other, no one's in a hurry, and despite any language barriers, people are quite helpful when approached.

Two bus companies (Los Amarillos and Comes) share the Arcos bus station. Call the Jerez offices for departure times, or ask your hotelier for help. If you want to find out about the Arcos–Jerez schedule, make it clear you're coming from Arcos (Los Amarillos tel. 956-341-063; Comes tel. 902-199-208, www.tgcomes.es). Also try the privately run www.movelia.es for bus schedules and routes.

From Arcos by Bus to: Jerez (hourly, 30 min), **Ronda** (3/day, 2 hrs, or 4 hrs if you transfer in Villamartín; when transferring, confirm with driver what the final destination is—bus could be headed to Ronda or Sevilla, and dashboard destination signs are often inaccurate), **Cádiz** (4/day, 75 min), **Sevilla** (2/day, 2 hrs, more departures with transfer in Jerez). The closest train station to Arcos is Jerez.

Route Tips for Drivers

The trip to **Sevilla** takes just over an hour if you pay €5 for the toll road. To reach **southern Portugal,** follow the freeway to Sevilla, skirt the city by turning west on C-30 in the direction of Huelva, and it's a straight shot from there.

For more driving tips for the region, see the end of this chapter.

Ronda

With 40,000 people, Ronda is one of the largest white hill towns. It's also one of the most spectacular, thanks to its gorge-straddling setting. While day-trippers from the touristy Costa del Sol clog Ronda's streets during the day, locals retake the town in the early evening, making nights peaceful. If you liked Toledo at night, you'll love the local feeling of evenings in Ronda. Since it's served by train and bus, Ronda makes a relaxing break for non-drivers traveling between Granada, Sevilla, and Córdoba. Drivers can use Ronda as a convenient base to explore many of the other *pueblos blancos*.

Ronda's main attractions are its gorge-spanning bridges, the oldest bullring in Spain, and an interesting old town. The cliffside setting, dramatic today, was practical back in its day. For the Moors, it provided a tough bastion, taken by the Spaniards only in 1485, seven years before Granada fell. Spaniards know Ronda as the cradle of modern bullfighting and the romantic home of 19th-century *banditos.* The real joy of Ronda these days lies in exploring its back streets and taking in its beautiful balconies, exuberant flowerpots, and panoramic views.

ORIENTATION

Ronda's breathtaking ravine divides the town's labyrinthine Moorish quarter and its new, noisier, and more sprawling Mercadillo quarter. A massive-yet-graceful 18th-century bridge connects these two neighborhoods. Most things of touristic importance (TI, post office, hotels, bullring) are clustered within a few blocks of the bridge. The paseo (early evening stroll) happens in the new town, on Ronda's major pedestrian street, Carrera Espinel. The Alameda del Tajo park can be lively before lunch, filling up with seniors who are taking a break from the nearby *geriatrico.*

Tourist Information

The central TI is on the main square, Plaza de España, opposite the bridge (Mon–Fri 9:00–19:30, Sat–Sun 10:00–14:00, longer hours in summer, tel. 952-871-272). Get the free Ronda map, the excellent Andalusian road map, and a listing of the latest museum hours. Consider picking up free maps of Granada, Sevilla, or the Route of the White Towns. Another TI is located opposite the bullring at Paseo Blas Infante (Mon–Fri 10:00–19:15, Sat–Sun 10:15–14:00 & 15:30–18:30, tel. 952-187-119, www.turismoderonda.es).

Local Guide: Energetic and knowledgeable **Antonio Jesús Naranjo** will take you on a two-hour walking tour of the city's sights (from €90 Mon–Fri, from €110 Sat–Sun and holidays, reserve early, tel. 952-879-215, mobile 639-073-763, guiajesus@yahoo.es). The TI has a list of other local guides.

Arrival in Ronda

By Train: The station is a 15-minute walk from the center: Turn right out of the station on Avenida de Andalucía, and go through the roundabout (you'll see the bus station on your right). Continue straight down the street (now called San José) until it dead-ends. Turn left and walk downhill past a church and the Alameda. Keep going down this street, passing the bullring, to get to the TI and the famous bridge. A **taxi** to the center costs about €5.

By Bus: To get to the center from the bus station (lockers inside, buy token at kiosk by exit), leave the station walking to the right of

Ronda

TO PILETA CAVES, ARCOS, SEVILLA & 2
BUS STATION
ANDALUCÍA
TO TRAIN STATION & 13
MONTEREJAS
LAURIA
MADRID
CALLE JEREZ
SAN JOSÉ
SEVILLA
POZO
MOLINO
SOUBIRON
ALMENDRA
200 YARDS
200 METERS
VIEW
PARKING
PLAZA MERCED
VIRGEN DE LA PAZ
CRUZ VERDE
WC
ALAMEDA
POST
PLAZA SOCORRO
ESPINEL
NARANJA
MERCADILLO
CORTES
CABRERA
BULLRING
PEDEST. ST.
QUARTER
NUEVA
PLAZA C. ABELA (TAXIS)
PLAZA DE ESPAÑA
ROSARIO
LOS REMEDIOS
CANTOS
PEÑAS
REAL
GUADALEVÍN RIVER
OLD BRIDGE
PUENTE NUEVO
S. DOMINGO
TENORIO
ARMIÑÁN
ARAB BRIDGE
TRAIL TO PUERTO DE LOS MOLINOS
MOORISH
ARAB BATHS MUSEUM
PLAZA DE MARÍA AUXILIADORA
QUARTER
MONDRAGÓN PALACE
BANDOLERO MUSEUM
CITY WALL
SANTA MARÍA LA MAYOR
TO COSTA DEL SOL & 14
1 Parador de Ronda
2 To Hotel Reina Victoria
3 Hotel San Gabriel
4 Hotel & Rest. Alavera de los Baños
5 Hotel Don Miguel
6 Hotel en Frente Arte Ronda
7 Hotel El Tajo
8 Hotel San Francisco
9 Hotel Ronda
10 Hotel Royal
11 Hostal Ronda Sol
12 Hostal Biarritz
13 To Hostal Andalucía
14 To Los Pastores
15 Restaurante Pedro Romero
16 Rest. Casa Santa Pola
17 Restaurante Tragabuches
18 Restaurante del Escudero
19 Café & Bar Faustino
20 Spar Supermarket
21 Casa del Rey Moro Garden
22 Palacio del Marqués de Salvatierra
23 Museo Joaquín Peinado

RONDA

the roundabout, then follow the directions for train travelers (above), heading down San José.

By Car: The handiest place to park in Ronda is the underground lot at Plaza del Socorro (1 block from bullring, €18/24 hrs).

SIGHTS

Ronda's New Town

▲▲▲The Gorge and New Bridge (Puente Nuevo)—The ravine, called El Tajo—360 feet down and 200 feet wide—divides Ronda into the whitewashed old Moorish town (La Ciudad) and the new town (El Mercadillo) that was built after the Christian reconquest in 1485. The New Bridge mightily spans the gorge. A different bridge was built here in 1735, but fell after six years. This one was built from 1751 to 1793. Look down...carefully. Legend has it the architect fell to his death while inspecting it, and during Spain's brutal Civil War, hundreds from both sides were thrown off this bridge.

You can see the foundations of the original bridge (and a super view of the New Bridge) from the Jardines de Cuenca park (daily in summer 9:30–21:30, winter 9:30–18:30): From Plaza de España, walk down Calle Rosario, turn right on Calle Los Remedios, and then take another right at the sign for the park.

▲▲Bullring—Ronda is the birthplace of modern bullfighting, and this was the first great Spanish bullring. While Philip II initiated bullfighting as war training for knights in the 16th century, it wasn't until the early 1700s that Francisco Romero established the rules of modern bullfighting and introduced the scarlet cape, held unfurled with a stick. His son Juan further developed the ritual (or art), and his grandson Pedro was one of the first great matadors (killing nearly 6,000 bulls in his career).

To see the bullring, stables, chapel, and museum, buy a ticket from the booth at the main entrance—it's at the back of the bullring, the farthest point from the main drag (€6, daily April–Sept 10:00–20:00, March and Oct 10:00–19:00, Nov–Feb 10:00–18:00, on main drag in new town, 2 blocks up from the New Bridge on the left, tel. 952-874-132).

The bullfighters' **chapel** greets you at the entrance. Before going into the ring, every matador would stop here to pray to Mary for safety—and hope to see her again.

Just after the chapel is the **museum,** split in two separate sections (and with translations in English). Trot quickly through the left section to see fine French saddles worn by royal horses in the 18th century. Backtrack to visit the museum's other section. With plenty of stuffed bull heads, photos, artwork, posters, and costumes, it is a shrine to bullfighting and the historic Romero family.

Take advantage of the opportunity to walk in the actual two-tiered **arena,** with plenty of time to play *toro,* surrounded by 5,000 empty seats. The arena was built in 1784. Notice the 176 classy Tuscan columns. With your back to the entry, look left to see the ornamental columns and painted doorway where the dignitaries sit (over the gate where the bull enters). On the right is the place for the band—in the case of a small town like Ronda, a high school band.

Bullfights are scheduled only for the first weekend of September during the *feria* (fair) and occur rarely in the spring. While every other *feria* in Andalucía celebrates a patron saint, the Ronda fair glorifies legendary bullfighter Pedro Romero. For September bullfights, tickets go on sale the preceding July (ticket-sales concession changes yearly, call TI for current year's office and phone number—TI does not sell tickets). *Sol* means "sun" (cheap seats) and *sombra* means "shade" (pricier seats).

Alameda del Tajo—One block away from the bullring, this park is a fine place for people-watching, a snooze in the shade, or practicing your Spanish with seniors from the old folks' home.

Parador de Ronda—Walk around and through this newest of Spain's fabled paradors, located on Plaza de España. The views from the walkway just below the outdoor terrace are magnificent. Anyone is welcome at the cafés (outdoor—with terraces and views—open daily 11:00–17:00, indoor 17:00–24:00). However, you have to be a guest (see "Sleeping") to use the pool.

Ronda's Old Town

Santa María la Mayor Collegiate Church—This 15th-century church shares a fine park-like square with orange trees and the City Hall. Its Renaissance bell tower still has parts of the old minaret. It was built on and around the remains of Moorish Ronda's main mosque (which was itself built on the site of a temple to Julius Caesar). In the same room where you purchase your ticket, look for the only surviving mosque archway. Partially destroyed by an earthquake, the reconstruction of the church resulted in the Moorish/Gothic/Renaissance/Baroque fusion (or confusion) you see today. Enjoy the bright frescoes, elaborately carved choir and altar, and the new bronze sculpture depicting the life of the Virgin Mary. The treasury displays vestments that look curiously like matadors' brocaded outfits (€3, daily June–Oct 10:00–20:00, March–May 10:00–19:00, Nov–Feb 10:00–18:00, Plaza Duquesa de Parcent in old town).

Mondragón Palace (Palacio de Mondragón)—This beautiful Moorish building was erected in the 14th century, possibly as the residence of Moorish kings, and was carefully restored in the 16th century. Wander through its many rooms to find the enjoyable prehistory museum, with exhibits on Neolithic toolmaking and early metallurgy (many captions in English). If you plan to visit the Pileta Cave (see page 558), find the panels that describe the cave's formation and shape. Even if you have no interest in your ancestors or speleology, the palace is worth a visit for the architecture alone. Don't miss the topographic model of Ronda at the entrance (€3, May–Sept Mon–Fri 10:00–19:00, Sat 10:00–13:45 & 15:00–18:00, Sun 10:00–15:00, Oct–April closes an hour earlier, on Plaza Mondragón in old town, tel. 952-878-450). Linger in the two small gardens, especially the shady one.

Wander left out to the nearby Plaza de María Auxiliadora for more views and a look at the two rare *pinsapos* (resembling extra-large Christmas trees) in the middle of the park; this is the only region in Europe where these ancient trees are found. For an intense workout but a picture-perfect view, find the *Puerta de los Molinos* sign and head down, down, down. Just remember you have to walk back up, up, up. Not for the faint of heart or for the heat of the afternoon sun, this pathway leads down to the viewpoint where windmills once stood. Photographers go crazy reproducing the most famous postcard view of Ronda—the entirety of the New Bridge. Wait until just before sunset for the best light and the coolest temperatures.

Museo del Bandolero—This tiny museum, while not as intriguing as it sounds, is an interesting assembly of *bandito* photos, guns, clothing, and knickknacks. The Jesse Jameses and Billy el Niños of Andalucía called this remote area home, and brief but helpful English descriptions make this a fun detour. One brand of romantic bandits fought Napoleon's army—often more effectively than the regular Spanish troops (€3, daily May–Sept 10:30–20:00, Oct–April 10:30–18:00, across main street below Church of Santa María la Mayor at Calle Armiñan 65, tel. 952-877-785, www.museobandolero.com).

▲Museo Joaquín Peinado—Housed in an old palace, this fresh museum features a professional overview of the life's work of Joaquín Peinado, a Ronda native and pal of Picasso. His style ranges from Expressionist to Cubist, and even to erotic. Some of the most famous 20th-century depictions of Don Quixote and Sancho Panza were painted by Peinado. You'll have an interesting modern-art experience without the crowds of Madrid's museums (€3; summer Mon–Sat 10:00–14:00 & 17:00–20:00, Sun 10:00–14:00; rest of year Mon–Sat 10:00–14:00 & 16:00–19:00, Sun 10:00–14:00; Plaza del Gigante, tel. 952-871-585).

Walk Through Old Town—From the New Bridge, you can descend down Cuesta de Santo Domingo into a world of whitewashed houses, tiny grilled balconies, and winding lanes—the old town.

The **Casa del Rey Moro** garden may be in jeopardy if a five-star hotel occupies this mansion as planned (or so they've been saying for the past 10 years). Designed during the belle époque by a French landscape architect, the original 1912 project has been nicely preserved. It offers access to "the Mine," an exhausting series of 280 slick, narrow stairs (like climbing down and then up a 20-story building) leading to the floor of the gorge. The Moors cut this zigzag staircase into the wall of the gorge in the 14th century to access water when under siege, then used Spanish slaves to haul water to the thirsty town (€4, generally daily 10:00–19:00 but often closed).

Fifty yards downhill from the garden is **Palacio del Marqués de Salvatierra** (closed to public). As part of the "distribution" following the Reconquista here in 1485, the Spanish king gave this fine house to the Salvatierra family. The facade is rich in colonial symbolism from Spanish America—note the pre-Columbian-looking characters flanking the balcony above the door and below the family coat of arms.

From the palace pillory, look out to the fine view. A series of square vats are what remains of the old tanneries. At the bottom of the hill is a small, rectangular horse arena. If you are doing this walk in the morning or late afternoon, you'll likely spy a few horses as well. The young colts are being trained for bullfighting. The stables and arena are owned by La Maestranza—Sevilla's giant bullring. The Ronda bullring was once used to train horses, but La Maestranza moved to this location when the bullring became mainly a tourist attraction.

Continuing downhill you come to the **Puente Viejo** (Old Bridge), built in 1616 upon the ruins of an Arabic bridge. Enjoy the views, then continue down the zigzag, cobblestone stairs. From the base of the staircase, look back up to glimpse some of the surviving, highly fortified Moorish city walls. You've now reached the oldest bridge in Ronda, the Arab Bridge (also called the San Miguel Bridge). Sometimes given the misnomer of Puente Romano (Roman Bridge), it was more likely built long after the Romans left.

Before heading back to the main town, stop in to visit the **Arab Baths,** a restored archaeological site located at one of the former city gates to the Moorish town. You would traditionally stop here on arrival to wipe away the grime of traveling. For the moment, skip the cold, warm, and hot rooms, and head directly to the last room. An interpretive 10-minute video explains the entire layout using 3-D computer animation. Wait for the English version (5-minute interval between English and Spanish videos) and imagine how good a massage would feel right now (€2, Mon–Fri 10:00–19:00, Sat 10:00–13:45 & 15:00–18:00, Sun 10:00–15:00, Nov–April closes Mon–Fri at 18:00).

Crossing the bridge, you'll see stairs on the left, leading scenically along the gorge back to the New Bridge. Straight ahead bubbles the welcoming Eight Springs fountain. In Ronda, what goes down must come up, so continue climbing (veering left) on Calle Penas to reach the new Mercadillo part of town and the pedestrian strip.

Near Ronda: Pileta Cave

The Pileta Cave (Cueva de la Pileta) is the best and probably the most intimate look a tourist can get at prehistoric cave paintings in Spain. Because the famous caves at Altamira in northern Spain are closed (though you can tour a replica cave nearby—see page 268), this is your only way to see real Neolithic and Paleolithic paintings that are up to 25,000 years old. Set in a dramatic, rocky limestone ridge at the eastern edge of Sierra de Grazalema Natural Park, Pileta Cave is 14 miles from Ronda, past the town of Benaoján, at the end of an access road.

Farmer José Bullón and his family live down the hill from the cave, and because they strictly limit the number of visitors, Pileta's rare paintings are among the best-preserved in the world. Sr. Bullón and his son lead up to 25 people at a time through the cave, which was discovered by Sr. Bullón's grandfather in 1905. Call the night before to make sure no groups are scheduled for the time you want to visit—otherwise you'll have to wait. Note that if the 13:00 tour is full, it'll be another three hours before the next one starts (€8, 60-min tours on the hour, daily 10:00–13:00 & 16:00–18:00, closes Nov–mid-April at 17:00, closing times indicate last tour, no reservations taken—just join the line, €10 guidebook, no photos, tel. 952-167-343, www.cuevadelapileta.org). Bring a flashlight, sweater, and good shoes. You need a good sense of balance to take the tour. The 10-minute hike to the cave entrance is moderately steep. Inside the cave, there are no handrails, and it can be difficult to keep your footing on the slippery, uneven floor while being led single-file, with only a lantern light illuminating the way.

Sr. Bullón is a master at hurdling the language barrier. As you walk the cool half-mile, he'll spend an hour pointing out lots of black, ochre, and red drawings, which are five times as old as the Egyptian pyramids. Mostly it's just lines or patterns, but there are also horses, goats, cattle, and a rare giant fish, made from a mixture of clay and fat by finger-painting prehistoric *hombres*. The 200-foot main cavern is impressive, as are some weirdly recognizable natural formations such as the Michelin man and a Christmas tree.

Getting There: It's possible to get here without wheels, but I wouldn't bother (you'd have to take the Ronda–Benaoján bus—2/day, departs at 8:30 and 13:00, 30 min—and then it's a 2-hour, 3-mile uphill hike). You can get from Ronda to the cave by taxi (€25) and try to hitch a ride back with another tourist, or hire the taxi for a round-trip (€55). If you're driving, it's easy: Leave Ronda through the new part of town, and take A-376. After a few miles, passing Cueva del Gato, exit left toward Benaoján on MA-555. Go through Benaoján and follow the numerous signs to the cave. Leave nothing of value in your car.

Eating near the Cave: Nearby Montejaque has a great outdoor restaurant, **La Casita** (tel. 952-167-120).

Sleeping near the Cave: A good base for visiting Ronda and the Pileta Cave (as well as Grazalema) is **$$ El Cortijo de las Piletas.** Nestled at the edge of Sierra de Grazalema Natural Park, this spacious, family-run country estate has opportunities for swimming, hiking, horseback riding, and exploring the surrounding area. Access is easy from the main highway (Sb-€68–74, Db-€84–90, extra bed-€15–18, includes breakfast, tel. 605-080-295, www.cortijolaspiletas.com, info@cortijolaspiletas.com, Pablo and Elisenda). Another countryside option is **$$ Finca La Guzmana,** run by expat Brits Peter and Claire. Five beautifully appointed pastel rooms surround an open patio at this renovated estate house. Bird-watching, swimming, and trekking are possible (Db-€80, includes tax and breakfast, tel. 600-006-305, www.laguzmana.com, info@laguzmana.com).

SLEEPING

(€1 = about $1.50, country code: 34)

Ronda has plenty of reasonably priced, decent-value accommodations. It's crowded only during Holy Week (the week leading up to Easter, April 5–12 in 2009) and the first week of September. Most of my recommendations are in the new town, a short stroll from the New Bridge and about a 10-minute walk from the train station. (The exceptions are Hostal Andalucía, across from the train station, and Hotel Reina Victoria, at the edge of town—and at the edge of the gorge.) In the cheaper places, ask for a room with a *ventana* (window) to avoid the few interior rooms. Breakfast and the 7 percent IVA tax are usually not included in the price.

$$$ Parador de Ronda, on Plaza de España, is hard to miss. It's an impressive integration of stone, glass, and marble. All 78 rooms have hardwood floors, and most have fantastic view balconies (ask about family-friendly duplexes). There's also a pool overlooking the bridge (Sb-€120–128, Db-€150–160, higher prices are for views, breakfast-€15, air-con, on-site garage-€20, Plaza de España, tel. 952-877-500, fax 952-878-188, www.parador.es, ronda@parador.es). Consider at least a drink on the terrace.

$$$ Hotel Reina Victoria, with its 89 rooms, hangs royally over the gorge at the edge of town and has a marvelous view—Hemingway loved it (Sb-€89–100, Db-€110–150, extra bed-€24, breakfast-€12, air-con, elevator, pool, free parking, 10-min walk from city center; easy to miss—look for intersection of Avenida Victoria and Calle Jerez, Jerez 25; tel. 952-871-240, fax 952-871-075, www.hotelhusareinavictoria ronda.com, reinavictoriaronda@husa.es).

$$$ Hotel San Gabriel has 21 pleasant rooms, a kind staff, public rooms filled with art books, a cozy wine cellar, and a fine garden terrace. If you're a cinephile, kick back in the charming TV room—with seats from Ronda's old theater—then head to the breakfast room to check out photos of big movie stars who have stayed here (Sb-€68, Db-€96–106, Db suite-€117, breakfast-€6.50, air-con, just off Plaza Poeta Abul-Beca at Calle Marqués de Moctezuma 19, tel. 952-190-392, fax 952-190-117, www.hotelsangabriel.com, info@hotel sangabriel.com, family-run by José Manuel and Ana).

$$ Alavera de los Baños, located next to ancient Moorish baths at the bottom of the hill, has nine clean and colorful rooms, with an appropriately Moorish decor. This hotel offers a swimming pool, a peaceful Arabic garden, a wonderful restaurant (see page 562), and a nice rural-feeling setting within the city—a unique combination in Ronda (Sb-€60, Db-€80–95, Db with terrace-€90–105, includes tax and breakfast, closed Dec–Jan, Calle San Miguel, tel. & fax 952-879-143, www.alaveradelosbanos.com, alavera@telefonica.net, personable Christian and Imma).

$$ Don Miguel, facing the gorge, is just left of the bridge and has all the charm of a tour-group hotel. Of its 30 sparse but comfortable rooms, 20 have balconies and/or gorgeous views at no extra cost, but street rooms come with a little noise (Sb-€55, Db-€85, includes buffet breakfast, air-con, elevator, parking garage a block away-€9/day, Plaza de España 4, tel. 952-877-722, fax 952-878-377, www.dmiguel.com, reservas@dmiguel.com).

$$ Hotel en Frente Arte Ronda is relaxed, funky, and friendly. The 14 rooms are spacious and exotically decorated, but dimly lit. There's also a peaceful bamboo garden, game room, small swimming pool, sauna, views, and terraces. Guests can enjoy themed dinners on certain nights (€15, confirm with reception). It's in all the guidebooks, so reserve in advance (Sb-€70, Db-€80–100, extra bed-€35, includes buffet breakfast and drinks from their bar, air-con, elevator, Internet access, Real 40, tel. 952-879-088, fax 952-877-217, www.enfrentearte.com, reservations@enfrentearte.com).

$$ Hotel El Tajo has 33 decent, quiet rooms—once you get past the tacky, faux-stone Moorish decoration in the foyer (Sb-€45, Db-€65, air-con, parking-€10/day, Calle Cruz Verde 7, a half-block off the pedestrian street, tel. 952-874-040, fax 952-875-099, www.hoteleltajo.com, reservas@hoteleltajo.com).

$$ Hotel San Francisco offers 27 small, nicely decorated rooms a block off the main pedestrian street in the town center (Sb-€40, Db-€60–70, Tb-€80, includes tax, breakfast-€3, air-con, 6 parking spaces-€15, María Cabrera 20, tel. 952-873-299, fax 952-874-688, hotelronda@terra.es).

$$ Hotel Ronda provides an interesting mix of minimalist and traditional Spanish decor, with five rooms located in the old town. Although there are no views, the refurbished mansion is quiet and homey (Sb-€50, Db-€65, additional bed-€20, includes tax, air-con, free Internet access, Ruedo Doña Elvira 12, tel. 952-872-232, www.hotelronda.net, laraln@telefonica.net, no English spoken).

$$ Hotel Royal has 29 clean, spacious, simple rooms—many on the main street that runs between the bullring and bridge. Thick glass keeps out most of the noise, while the tree-lined Alameda del Tajo park across the street is a treat (Sb-€34, Db-€57, Tb-€66, air-con, includes self-serve breakfast, Calle Virgen de la Paz 42, 3 blocks off Plaza de España, tel. 952-871-141, fax 952-878-132, www.ronda.net/usuar/hotelroyal, hroyal@ronda.net, some English spoken).

$ Hostal Ronda Sol has a homey atmosphere with 15 cheap but monkish rooms (S-€13, D-€20, cash only, parking-€14/day, Almendra 11, tel. 952-874-497, friendly María or Rafael). The same owner runs **Hostal Biarritz** next door, which offers 21 similar rooms, some with private bathrooms (S-€13, D-€20, Db-€28, T-€30, Tb-€42, includes tax, cash only, parking-€14/day, Almendra 7, tel. 952-872-910, no English spoken).

$ Hostal Andalucía has 11 clean, comfortable, and recently renovated rooms immediately across the street from the train station (Sb-€24, Db-€40, includes tax, air-con, easy street parking, Martínez Astein 19, tel. 952-875-450).

Near Ronda

$$ Los Pastores, 2.5 miles southwest of Ronda on A-369, is a pleasant renovated farmhouse in the countryside (Db-€60–75, four-person apartments-€60–95, one-night stay-€10 extra, breakfast-€6–10, Apartado de Correos 167, on A-369, tel. 952-798-305 or 952-114-464, www.lospastores.com, info@lospastores.com, Martin). When the hotel is at least half-full, it offers a four-course dinner for €15.

EATING

Dodge the tourist traps. Locals say one of the best meals in Ronda is at the **parador** (*muy elegante,* figure €35 per person). **Plaza del Socorro,** a block in front of the bullring, is a wonderful scene, where families enjoy the square and its restaurants. Join the paseo down pedestrian-only **Carrera Espinel,** and choose a place with tables spilling out into the action. The best drinks and views in town are enjoyed on the terraces of **Hotel Don Miguel** or the parador.

Restaurante Pedro Romero—assuming a shrine to bullfighting draped in *el toro* memorabilia doesn't ruin your appetite—gets good reviews but is touristy and priced to match. Rub elbows with the local bullfighters or dine with the likes (well, photographic likenesses) of Orson Welles, Ernest Hemingway, and Francisco Franco (€17 fixed-price meals, or €30 à la carte, daily 12:30–16:00 & 19:00–23:00, air-con, across the street from bullring at Calle Virgen de la Paz 18, tel. 952-871-110).

Restaurante Casa Santa Pola offers gourmet versions of traditional food with friendly, professional service—and outdoor terrace tables for an extra 10 percent charge. Reservations are smart (€30 fixed-price meal, €40 three-course dinners; good oxtail stew, roasted lamb, and honey-tempura eggplant; lunch 13:00–16:00, dinner 20:00–22:15; after crossing New Bridge from the bullring, take the first left downhill and you'll see the sign, Calle Santo Domingo 3; tel. 952-879-208).

Alavera de los Baños, located in the hotel of the same name, serves tasty Moorish specialties such as lamb and chicken *tajine,* along with vegetarian dishes. It also offers great outdoor dining. Reservations are required and hotel guests have priority (open to public for dinner Thu–Fri 20:00–22:30, closed Dec–Jan along with hotel, Calle San Miguel, tel. 952-879-143).

Trendy, spendy **Restaurante Tragabuches** serves "nouvelle cuisine Andalouse," prepared by Spain's renowned chef, Daniel García (€85 multi-course fixed-price meal—drinks not included, à la carte around €35 for main course, Tue–Sat 13:30–15:30 & 20:30–22:30, Sun 13:30–15:30, closed Mon, José Aparicio 1, tel. 952-190-291, www.tragabuches.com).

Restaurante del Escudero serves tasty Spanish food with a posh, modern touch on a terrace over the gorge. From the owners of Restaurante Tragabuches, it offers a more affordable version of their excellent cuisine (worth-it €15 and €33 gourmet fixed-price meals for lunch or dinner, extensive à la carte choices, Mon–Sat 12:00–16:00 & 19:00–23:00, Sun 12:00–16:00, behind bullring at Paseo Blas Infante 1, tel. 952-871-367).

The no-frills **Café & Bar Faustino** offers the cheapest tapas in town (€1) to a lively crowd of students, blue-collar workers, and tourists (Tue–Sun 12:00–24:00, closed Mon, just off Plaza Carmen Abela at Santa Cecilia 4, tel. 952-190-307).

Supermarket: Picnic shoppers find the **Spar** supermarket convenient, at Calle Cruz Verde 18 opposite Hotel El Tajo (Mon–Sat 9:00–21:30, closed Sun). The Alameda del Tajo park (with WC) near the bullring is a good picnic spot.

TRANSPORTATION CONNECTIONS

Note that some destinations are linked with Ronda by both bus and train. Direct bus service to other hill towns can be sparse (as few as one per day), and train service usually involves a transfer in Bobadilla. It's worth spending a few minutes in the bus or train station on arrival to plan your departure. Your options improve from major transportation hubs such as Málaga.

From Ronda by Bus to: Algeciras (6/day, 2 hrs), **La Línea/Gibraltar** (no direct bus, transfer in Algeciras; Algeciras to Gibraltar—2/hr, 45 min), **Arcos** (3/day, 2 hrs), **Benaoján** (2/day, 30 min), **Jerez** (4/day, 3 hrs), **Grazalema** (2/day, 45 min), **Zahara** (1/day, Mon–Fri only, 1 hr), **Sevilla** (5/day, 2.5 hrs, fewer on weekends; also see trains below), **Málaga** (10/day, 1.75 hrs *directo,* 3 hrs *ruta*; access other Costa del Sol points from Málaga), **Marbella** (6/day, 75 min), **Fuengirola** (5/day, 2 hrs), **Nerja** (4 hrs, transfer in Málaga; can take train or bus from Ronda to Málaga). If traveling to **Córdoba,** it's easiest to take the train since there are no direct buses (see below). There's no efficient way to call "the bus company" because four share the same station; one of them is at tel. 952-187-061. It's best to just drop by and compare schedules (on Plaza Concepción García Redondo, several blocks from train station).

By Train to: Algeciras (6/day, 2 hrs), **Bobadilla** (4/day, 1 hr), **Málaga** (1/day direct, 1 hr; 6/day with transfer in Bobadilla, 2.5 hrs), **Sevilla** (2/day, 4 hrs, transfer in Bobadilla), **Granada** (3/day, 2.5 hrs), **Córdoba** (2/day direct, 1.75 hrs; more with transfer in Bobadilla, 3.5 hrs), **Madrid** (2/day, 4 hrs). Transfers are a snap and time-coordinated in Bobadilla; with four trains arriving and departing simultaneously, double-check that you're jumping on the right one. Train info: tel. 902-240-202.

More Hill Towns: Zahara and Grazalema

There are plenty of undiscovered and interesting hill towns to explore. About half of the towns I visited were memorable. Unfortunately, public transportation is frustrating, so I'd do these towns only by car. Or you could consider a tour—Andalusian Minibus Tours stops at Zahara and Grazalema on their all-day trip from Sevilla (see page 473). Useful information on the area is rare. Fortunately, a good map, the tourist brochure (pick it up in Sevilla or Ronda), and a spirit of adventure work fine. Along with Arcos, Zahara and Grazalema are my favorite white villages.

Zahara

This tiny town in a tingly setting under a Moorish castle (worth the climb) has a spectacular view. While the big church facing the town square is considered one of the richest in the area, the smaller church has the most-loved statue. The Virgin of Dolores is Zahara's answer to Sevilla's Virgin of Macarena (and is similarly paraded through town during Holy Week). Zahara is a fine overnight stop for those who want to hear only the sounds of the wind, birds, and elderly footsteps on ancient cobbles.

ORIENTATION

Tourist Information

The TI is located in the main plaza (daily 9:00–14:00 & 16:00–19:00, gift shop, Plaza del Rey 3, tel. 956-123-114). It has a single computer with Internet access (€1.50, one-hour limit). Upstairs from the TI are Spanish-only displays about the flora and fauna of nearby Sierra de Grazalema Natural Park (see page 566). Drivers can park for free in the main plaza, or continue up the hill (just past the cliffside Hotel Arco de la Villa) to reach a large, free parking lot.

For outdoor adventures in Sierra de Grazalema Natural Park, such as hiking, horseback riding, caving, and kayaking in the Zahara reservoir, contact **Zahara Catur** (daily 9:00–14:00 & 16:00–19:00, tel. 956-123-114, mobile 657-926-394, www.zaharacatur.com, centro@zaharacatur.com), or **Horizon** in Grazalema (see page 568).

SIGHTS

▲Zahara Castle—During Moorish times, Zahara lay within the fortified castle walls above today's town. It was considered the gateway to Granada and a strategic stronghold for the Moors by the Christian forces of the Reconquista. Locals tell of the Spanish conquest of the Moors' castle (in 1482) as if it happened yesterday: After the Spanish failed several times to seize the castle, a clever Spanish soldier noticed that the Moorish sentinel would

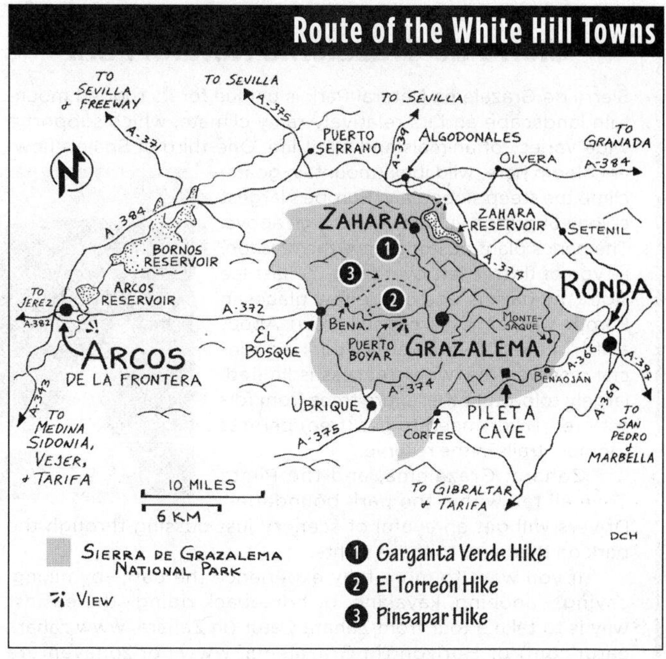

check if any attackers were hiding behind a particular section of the wall by tossing a rock and setting the pigeons in flight. If they flew, the sentinel figured there was no danger. One night a Spaniard hid there with a bag of pigeons and let them fly when the sentinel tossed his rock. Upon seeing the birds, the guard assumed he was clear to enjoy a snooze. The clever Spaniard then scaled the wall and opened the door to let in his troops, who conquered the castle. Ten years later Granada fell, the Muslims were back in Africa, and the Reconquista was complete.

It's a fun climb up to the remains of the castle (free, tower always open). Start at the paved path across from the town's upper parking lot. It's a moderately easy 15-minute hike past newly discovered Roman ruins and along a cactus-rimmed ridge to the top, where you can enter the tower. Use your penlight or feel along the stairway to reach the roof, and enjoy spectacular views from this almost impossibly high perch far above the town. As you pretend you're defending the tower, realize that what you see is quite different from what the Moors saw: The huge lake dominating the valley is a reservoir—before 1991, the valley had only a tiny stream.

El Vínculo—This family-run olive mill welcomes visitors for a look at its traditional factory, as well as a taste of some homemade sherry and olive oil, produced on this site for centuries by the Urruti family. Juan will treat you to a glass of sherry if you show the 2009 edition of this book

Sierra de Grazalema Natural Park

Sierra de Grazalema Natural Park is unique for its rugged mountain landscape and its relatively rainy climate, which support a wide variety of animals and plant life. One-third of Spain's flowers bloom here, wild ibex (mountain goats) climb the steep slopes, and Europe's largest colony of griffon vultures soars high above. The park's plant poster child is the *pinsapo,* a type of fir tree left over from the last Ice Age (the park is one of the few places in Europe where these trees still grow). About a fifth of the 200-square-mile park is a special reserve area, where access is limited, largely to protect these rare trees from forest fires. Hikers need to get (free) permits for most trails in the reserve.

Zahara, Grazalema, and the Pileta Cave all fall within the park boundaries. Drivers will get an eyeful of scenery just passing through the park on their way to these sights.

If you want to more fully experience the park—by hiking, caving, canoeing, kayaking, or horseback riding—the easiest way is to take a tour from Zahara Catur (in Zahara, www.zaharacatur.com) or Horizon (in Grazalema, www.horizonaventura.com). They handle the permit procedure for you.

If you want to hike in the park on your own, you'll need a park map, a permit for most hikes within the reserve area (see permit procedure on next page), and a car to get to the trailhead. And from July through September, you may have to go with a guided

(€6, daily 9:30–20:00, on CA-531 just outside Zahara, tel. 956-123-002, mobile 696-404-368, www.molinoelvinculo.com, molinoelvinculo@telefonica.net). Juan also rents various houses on his estate, which include access to a big swimming pool and great views surrounded by fragrant olive trees (you can rent anything from a large house that sleeps up to 12 for €430 to a small house for €86, July–Aug €96; includes tax).

SLEEPING AND EATING

(€1 = about $1.50, country code: 34)

Also see El Vínculo, above, for accommodations.

$$ Hotel Arco de la Villa—long on efficiency, short on character—has 17 rooms, all with stunning views. It's located high above the reservoir, just up the hill past the main square. Avoid noisy single room #1 (Sb-€37, Db-€60, extra bed-€15, restaurant, Camino Nazarí, tel. 956-123-230, fax 956-123-244, www.tugasa.com, arco-de-la-villa@tugasa.com).

group anyway, if you want to hike in the reserve (about €12-16/person for a half-day hike, offered by Zahara Catur and Horizon).

Popular hikes in the reserve (all requiring permits) include:

Garganta Verde: Explore a canyon with a huge open cave near vulture breeding grounds (1.5 miles each way, initially gentle hike then very steep descent, allow 4-5 hours).

El Torreón: Climb the park's highest mountain, at 5,427 feet (1.75 miles each way, steep incline to summit, allow 4-5 hours).

Pinsapar: Hike on mountain slopes forested with *pinsapar* (8.5 miles each way, steep climb for first third of trail then downhill, allow 6 hours).

Information: The TIs in Grazalema and Zahara sell a Spanish-only park guide with descriptions and trail maps (€15).

Getting a Hiking Permit: A permit is free but required; a ranger will fine you if you don't have one. To get a permit, call or visit the park office in the town of El Bosque, a gateway to the park. You can request a permit for a specific hike up to 15 days in advance. Pick up the permit in El Bosque, or have them fax it to the TI in Grazalema or Zahara (office hours generally Mon-Sat 10:00-14:00 & 16:00-18:00, Sun 9:00-14:00, tel. 956-727-029, passport number required, Avenida de la Diputación, allow plenty of time for this process). If you're staying at the recommended La Mejorana Guest House in Grazalema, your host can call for you.

Hikes from Grazalema (No Permit Required): If you'd rather not hassle with getting a permit, or if you don't have a car to reach the trailheads, try one of several solid hikes that start from the town of Grazalema. You'll find descriptions in pamphlets available at the Grazalema TI or Horizon (€1).

$ Pensión Los Tadeos is a quiet place in the lower part of town by the municipal swimming pool *(piscina)*. It offers 10 good rooms—and is adding more—with great views of fields and orchards in an expansive valley (Db-€50, Tb-€65, includes tax, restaurant, Paseo de la Fuente, tel. 956-123-086, lostadeos@terra.es, Ruíz family doesn't speak English).

Eating: The cafés around the main square are popular for tapas, and the recommended Pensión Los Tadeos has a good restaurant.

Grazalema

A beautiful postcard-pretty hill town, Grazalema offers a royal balcony for a memorable picnic, a square where you can watch old-timers playing cards, and plenty of quiet, whitewashed streets and shops to explore. Grazalema, situated within Sierra de Grazalema Natural Park, is graced with lots of scenery and greenery. While the park is known as the rainiest place in Spain, the clouds seem to

wring themselves out before they reach the town—I've only ever had blue skies.

The **TI** is on Plaza de España (May–Aug Mon–Fri 10:00–14:00 & 17:00–21:00, Sat–Sun 10:00–21:00; Sept–April Mon–Fri 10:00–14:00 & 16:00–20:00, Sat–Sun and holidays 10:00–20:00; gift store upstairs, tel. 956-132-073).

A free, well-signed parking lot is at the view terrace, with two additional free parking lots up the hill on the right past Plaza de Andalucía.

Plaza de Andalucía, the main plaza a block off the view terrace, is the hub for day-trippers. Shops sell the town's beautiful and famous handmade wool blankets and good-quality leather items from nearby Ubrique.

Popular with Spaniards, the town makes a good home base for exploring Sierra de Grazalema Natural Park—famous for its spectacularly rugged limestone landscape of cliffs, caves, and gorges (see sidebar). For outdoor gear and adventures, including hiking, caving, and canoeing, contact **Horizon** (summer Tue–Sat 9:00–14:00 & 17:00–19:00, rest of year Tue–Sat 9:00–14:00 & 16:00–19:00, closed Sun–Mon year-round, off Plaza de España at Corrales Terceros 29, tel. & fax 956-132-363, mobile 655-934-565, www.horizonaventura.com, grazalema@horizonaventura.com).

SLEEPING

$$ La Mejorana Guest House is the best bet in town—if you can manage to get one of its five rooms. You won't want to leave this beautifully perched garden villa, overlooking the valley from the upper part of town. Helpful Ana and Andres will call to get you a hiking permit in the park (Db-€52, includes breakfast and tax, pool, located on tiny lane below Guardia Civil headquarters at Santa Clara 6, tel. 956-132-327, mobile 649-613-272, www.lamejorana.net, info@lamejorana.net).

$$ Villa Turística de Grazalema is a big, popular national-park-lodge kind of place. It's good for kids, and has a huge lobby and fireplace. Its 38 apartments and 24 regular hotel rooms open onto either the swimming-pool garden from the ground floor, or balconies if you're on the first floor (Sb-€37, Db-€60, extra person-€15, apartments-€70–123, extra bed-€23, includes breakfast, restaurant, turn right just before crossing the bridge into town, tel. 956-132-136, fax 956-132-213).

$$ Hotel Peñón Grande, named for a nearby mountain, is just off the main square and offers comfortable business-class rooms (Sb-€38, Db-€55, extra bed-€14, includes tax, air-con, Plaza Pequeña

7, tel. 956-132-434, fax 956-132-435, www.hotelgrazalema.es, hotel@hotelgrazalema.es).

$ Casa de Las Piedras has 16 comfortable rooms just a block from the main square—ask for a room in their newer wing. The beds feature the town's locally made wool blankets. Local hiking guidebooks are available here (Sb-€35, D-€40 with access to kitchen, Db-€47, two €55 one-room and €100 two-room apartments with kitchen and fireplace, includes tax, discounts for kids, 10 percent discount with this book and two-night minimum stay in 2009, buffet breakfast-€6, Calle Las Piedras 32, tel. & fax 956-132-014, Katy and Rafi).

EATING

Grazalema offers many restaurants and bars—tiny Plaza de Andalucía has several good bars for tapas, including **Zulema** (tel. 956-132-402) and **La Posadilla** (tel. 956-132-051).

El Torreón specializes in local lamb and game dishes, and also has many vegetarian options (Calle Agua 44, tel. 956-132-313).

El Pinsapar, up the hill from the main plaza, features meat and trout dishes and other local specialties (closed Wed, air-con, Dr. Mateos Gago 22, tel. 956-132-202).

TRANSPORTATION CONNECTIONS

Bus service to Grazalema is provided by Los Amarillos (www.touristbus.es).

From Grazalema by Bus to: Ronda (2/day, 45 min), **El Bosque** (2/day, 45 min).

Jerez

With nearly 200,000 people, Jerez is your typical big-city mix of industry and dusty concrete suburbs, but it has a lively old center and two claims to touristic fame: horses and sherry.

Jerez is ideal for a noontime visit on a weekday. See the famous horses, sip some sherry, wander through the old quarter, and swagger out.

ORIENTATION

There is no easy way to feel oriented in Jerez due to the complicated, medieval street plan, so ask for directions liberally.

Tourist Information

The helpful TI, on Plaza Alameda Cristina, gives out free maps and info on the sights (Mon–Fri 10:00–15:00 & 17:00–19:00, Sat–Sun 9:30–14:30, tel. 956-324-747, www.turismojerez.com).

Arrival in Jerez

By Bus or Train: Both the bus and train stations are by the enormous headless statue at Glorieta del Minotauro. Unfortunately, you can't store luggage at either one. However, you can stow bags for free in the Royal Andalusian School's *guardaropa,* or coat room, if you attend their Horse Symphony show (see "Sights," below).

The center of town and the TI are a 20-minute walk from both stations. When exiting either station, keep the large parking lot on your left. You'll soon be greeted by the gigantic Glorieta del Minotauro statue at a traffic circle. Take the crosswalk straight over to Calle Medina and follow it faithfully. At the confusing five-way intersection, angle right on Honda, continue past a small roundabout decorated with empty sherry barrels, and go straight until you reach Plaza Alameda Cristina—the TI is tucked away on your right.

By Car from Arcos: Driving in Jerez can be frustrating. The outskirts are filled with an almost endless series of roundabouts. Continuing straight through each one will eventually bring a rail bridge into sight, with Bodegas Harvey on the right side. Continue to follow traffic and signs to *centro ciudad.* The route may seem circuitous (it is) but will eventually take you past the main TI on Plaza Alameda Cristina.

If you're going straight to see the horses, follow the directions below (under "Getting There"); otherwise it's best to park in one of the many underground garages and catch a cab or walk. Plaza Arenal (€1.30/hr) is the most centrally located lot, or there's the handy underground parking lot at Plaza Alameda Cristina. For street parking, blue-line zones require prepaid parking tickets on your dashboard (Mon–Fri 9:00–13:30 & 17:00–20:00, Sat 9:00–14:00, Sun and July–Aug afternoons free).

SIGHTS

▲▲Royal Andalusian School of Equestrian Art—If you're into horses, this is a must. Even if you're not, this is art like you've never seen. The school does its Horse Symphony show Tuesday and Thursday at 12:00 during most of the year (also on Fri in Aug, Nov–Feb Thu only; €18 general seating, €24 "preference" seating, 90 min with 15-min intermission;

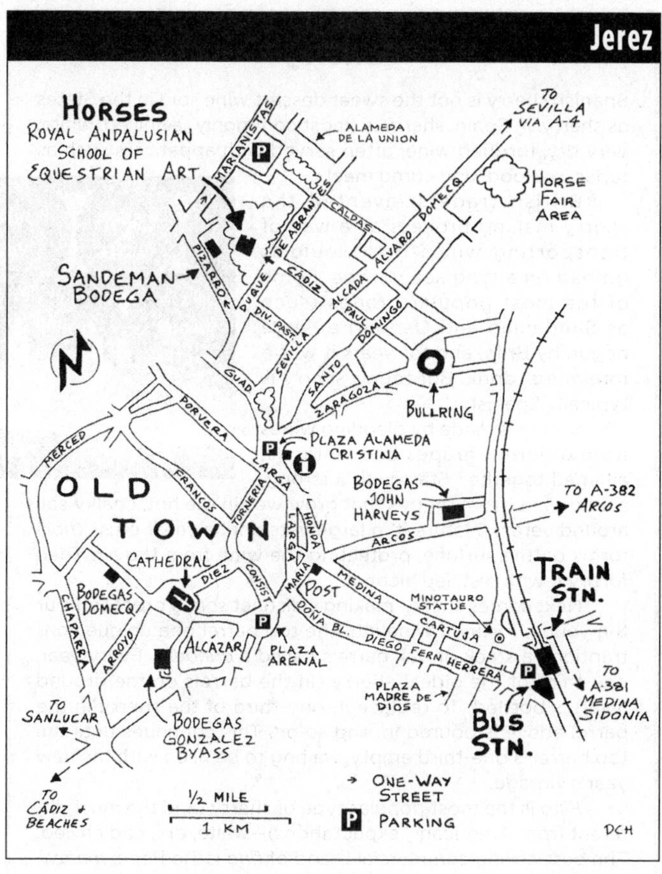

no photos in show, stables, or museum; tel. 956-318-008, fax 956-318-015, tickets available online at www.realescuela.org). General seating is fine; some "preference" seats are too close for good overall views. The show explanations are in Spanish.

This is an equestrian ballet with choreography, purely Spanish music, and costumes from the 19th century. The stern riders and their talented, obedient steeds prance, jump, hop on their hind legs, and do-si-do in time to the music, all to the delight of an arena filled with mostly tourists and local horse aficionados.

The riders, trained in dressage (dreh-SAZH), cue the horses with the slightest of commands, whether verbal or with body movements. You'll see both purebred Spanish horses (of various colors, with long tails, calm personalities, and good jumping ability) and the larger mixed breeds (with short tails and a walking—not prancing—gait). The horses must be three years old before their three-year training begins, and most performing horses are male (stallions or geldings),

Sherry

Spanish sherry is not the sweet dessert wine sold in the States as sherry. In Spain, sherry is (most commonly) a chilled, white, very dry, fortified wine, often served with appetizers such as tapas, seafood, and cured meats.

British traders invented the sherry-making process as a way of transporting wines that wouldn't go bad on a long sea voyage. Some of the most popular brands (such as Sandeman and Osbourne) were begun by Brits, and for years it was a foreigners' drink. But today, sherry is typically Spanish.

Sherry is made by blending wines from different grapes and vintages, all aged together. Start with a strong, acidic wine (from grapes that grow well in the hot, chalky soil around Jerez). Mature it in large vats until a yeast crust *(flor)* forms on the surface, protecting the wine from the air. Then fortify it with distilled alcohol.

Next comes sherry-making's distinct *solera* process. Pour the young, fortified wine into the top barrel of a unique contraption—a stack of oak barrels called a *criadera.* Every year, one-third of the oldest sherry (in the barrels on the ground level) is bottled. To replace it, one-third of the sherry in the barrel above is poured in, and so on. This continues until the top barrel is one-third empty, waiting to be filled with the new year's vintage.

Fino is the most popular type of sherry (and the most different from Americans' expectations)—white, dry, and chilled. The best-selling commercial brand of *fino* is Tío Pepe; *manzanilla* is a regional variation of *fino*—best from Córdoba. Darker-colored and sometimes sweeter varieties of sherry include *amontillado* and *oloroso.* And yes, Spain also produces the thick, sweet cream sherries served as dessert wines. A good, raisin-y, syrupy sweet variety is Pedro Ximénez, made from sun-dried grapes of the same name.

since mixing the sexes brings problems.

The equestrian school is a university, open to all students in the EU, and with all coursework in Spanish. Although still a male-dominated activity, there have recently been a few female graduates. Tight-fitted mushroom hats are decorated with different stripes to show each rider's level. Professors often team with students and evaluate their performance during the show.

Training sessions on non-performance days offer the public a sneak preview (€10; Mon, Wed, and Fri—except no Fri in Aug, also on Tue in Nov–Feb; arrive anytime between 11:00–13:00). Big tour groups crowd in at 11:00 and schedules may vary, so it's wise to call ahead. Sessions can be exciting or dull, depending on what the trainers are working on. After the training session, you can take a 90-minute guided tour of the stables, horses, multimedia and carriage museums, tack room, gardens, and horse health center. Sip sherry in the arena's bar to complete this Jerez experience.

Getting There: After passing the TI on Plaza Alameda Cristina, follow pink signs with arrows pointing to the *Real Escuela de Arte Ecuestre*. Parking is located behind the horse school, and one-way streets mean there is only one way to arrive. Expect to make at least one wrong turn, so give yourself a little extra time.

From the bus or train stations to the horses, it's about a €5 taxi ride or a 40-minute walk.

▲▲Sherry Bodega Tours—Spain produces more than 10 million gallons per year of this fortified wine. The name "sherry" comes from English attempts to pronounce Jerez. While traditionally the drink of England's aristocracy, today it's more popular with Germans. Your tourist map of Jerez is speckled with *venencia* symbols, each representing a sherry bodega that offers tours and tasting. *Venencias* are specially designed ladles for dipping inside the sherry barrel, breaking through the yeast layer, and getting to the good stuff.

Sandeman Sherry: Just around the corner from the horse school is the venerable Sandeman winery, which has been producing sherry since 1790 and is the longtime choice of English royalty. This tour is the aficionado's choice for its knowledgeable guides and their quality explanations of the process. Each stage is explained in detail, with visual examples of *flor* (the yeast crust) in backlit barrels, graphs of how different blends are made, and a quick walk-through of the bottling plant. The finale is a chance to taste three varieties (€6, light tapas lunch with tour-€12.50, English tours on the half-hour Mon, Wed, and Fri 10:30–15:00, Sat 11:00–15:00, Tue and Thu 10:00–16:00, closed Sun, tour times adjust with the horse show, call to confirm, reservations not required, tel. 956-151-700, www.sandeman.com). It's efficient to see the Horse Symphony, which ends at 13:30, and then walk to Sandeman's for the next English tour.

Harveys Bodega: Their English-language tours aren't substantial, but they do include a 15-minute video, a visit to the winery, and all the sherry you like in the tasting room (€8, Mon–Fri at 12:00, 90-min tour, reservations recommended one day in advance,

Calle Pintor Muñoz Cebrian, tel. 956-151-551, fax 956-349-427, www.bodegasharveys.es, bodegasharveys@beamglobal.com).

González Byass: The makers of the famous Tío Pepe offer a tourist-friendly tour, with more pretense and less actual sherry-making on display (it's done in a new, enormous plant outside of town). The tourist train through fake vineyards and a video presentation are forgettable, but the grand circle of sherry casks signed by a *Who's Who* of sherry-drinkers is worthwhile. Taste two sherries at the end of the 90-minute tour (€10, light tapas lunch with tour-€15, tours run hourly at :30 past the hour, Mon–Sat 11:30–17:30, extra tour at 14:00; July–Sept no tours at 14:00 and 15:30, extra tour at 18:30; Sun 11:30–14:00; Manuel María González 12, tel. 956-357-000, fax 956-357-046).

Alcázar—This gutted castle looks tempting, but don't bother. The €3 entry fee doesn't even include the Camera Obscura (€6.30 combo-ticket covers both, Mon–Sat 10:00–18:00, Sun 10:00–15:00). Its underground parking is convenient for those touring González Byass (€1.30/hr).

TRANSPORTATION CONNECTIONS

Jerez's bus station is shared by six bus companies, each with its own schedule. Some specialize in certain destinations, while others share popular destinations such as Sevilla and Algeciras. The big ones serving most southern Spain destinations are Los Amarillos (tel. 902-210-317, www.losamarillos.es), Comes (tel. 902-199-208, www.tgcomes.es), and Linesur (tel. 956-341-063). Shop around for the best departure time and most direct route. While here, clarify routes for any further bus travel you may be doing in Andalucía—especially if you're going through Arcos de la Frontera, where the ticket office is often closed. Also try the privately run www.movelia.es for bus schedules and routes.

From Jerez by Bus to: Tarifa (2/day on Algeciras route with Comes, 2 hrs, more frequent with transfer in Cádiz), **Algeciras** (2/day with Comes, 9/day with Linesur, 2.5 hrs), **Arcos** (hourly, 30 min), **Ronda** (4/day, 3 hrs), **La Línea/Gibraltar** (2/day, 3 hrs), **Sevilla** (7/day, 1.5 hrs), **Málaga** (3/day, 4.5–5 hrs), **Granada** (1/day, 4.5 hrs), **Madrid** (3/day, more service on weekends, 7 hrs).

By Train to: Sevilla (12/day, 1.25 hrs), **Madrid** (2/day, 5 hrs), **Barcelona** (2/day, one overnight, 12 hrs). Train info: tel. 902-240-202.

By Car: It's a zippy 30 minutes from Jerez to Arcos.

Easy Stops for Drivers

If you're driving between Arcos and Tarifa, here are several sights to explore.

Yeguada de la Cartuja

This breeding farm, which raises Hispanic Arab horses according to traditions dating back to the 15th century, offers shows on Saturday at 11:00 (€18 for best seats in *tribuna* section, Finca Fuente del Suero, Ctra. Medina–El Portal, km 6.5, Jerez de la Frontera, tel. 956-162-809, www.yeguadacartuja.com). From Jerez, take the road to Medina Sidonia, then turn right in the direction of El Portal—you'll see a cement factory on your right. Drive for five minutes until you see the farm. A taxi from Jerez will cost about €14 one-way.

Medina Sidonia

This town is as whitewashed as can be, surrounding its church and hill, which is topped with castle ruins. I never drive through here without a coffee break and a quick stroll. Signs to *centro urbano* route you through the middle to Plaza de España (lazy cafés, bakery, plenty of free parking just beyond the square out the gate). If it's lunchtime, consider buying a picnic, as all the necessary shops are nearby and the plaza benches afford a fine workaday view of a perfectly untouristy Andalusian town. According to its own TI, the town is "much appreciated for its vast gastronomy." Small lanes lead from the main square up to Plaza Iglesia Mayor (church and TI open in summer daily 10:00–14:00 & 17:00–19:00; in winter Tue–Sun 10:00–14:00 & 16:00–18:00, closed Mon; tel. 956-412-404). At the church, a man will show you around for a tip. Even without a tip, you can climb yet another belfry for yet another vast Andalusian view. The castle ruins just aren't worth the trouble.

Vejer de la Frontera

Vejer, south of Jerez and just 30 miles north of Tarifa, will lure all but the very jaded off the highway. Vejer's strong Moorish roots give it a distinct Moroccan (or Greek Island) flavor—you know, black-clad women whitewashing their homes, and lanes that can't decide if they're roads or stairways. Only a generation ago, women here wore veils. The town has no real sights—other than its women's faces—and very little tourism, making it a pleasant stop (**TI** open June–Sept daily 8:00–14:30 & 18:00–22:00; Oct–May Mon–Fri 10:00–14:00 & 17:00–19:00, closed Sat–Sun; Marqués de Tamarón 10, tel. 956-451-736).

The coast near Vejer has a lonely feel, but its fine, windswept beaches are popular with windsurfers and sand flies. The Battle of Trafalgar was fought just off Cabo de Trafalgar (a nondescript lighthouse today). I drove the circle so you don't have to.

Sleeping in Vejer: A newcomer on Andalucía's tourist map, the old town of Vejer has just a few hotels.

$$ Hotel La Botica de Vejer, a boutique place high in the old town, provides 13 comfortable rooms in what was once a local apothecary. Homey decor and view patios—tailor-made for an afternoon beer—add to the charm (interior Db-€60, exterior Db-€70, €20 more in June–Aug, extra bed-€15–20, includes taxes and breakfast, air-con, Wi-Fi, 200 yards above Plaza de España—go through the gate and left to Canalejas 13, tel. 956-450-225, mobile 617-477-636, www.laboticadevejer.com, info@laboticadevejer.com). If Josip isn't home, call his mobile number and he will be.

$$ Convento de San Francisco is a poor man's parador in a refurbished convent with pristine, spacious rooms and elegant public lounges (Sb-€46, Db-€66, breakfast-€4, prices soft off-season, air-con, La Plazuela, tel. 956-451-001, fax 956-451-004, convento-san-francisco@tugasa.com).

$$ Hotel El Bandolero is for nature-lovers. Settle into the rustic rooms, go hiking and bird-watching, or take a dip in their pool (Sb-€45–50, standard Db-€64–101, superior Db-€73–111, Db suite-€90–128, restaurant, Avenida Havaral 43, tel. 952-183-660, www.hotelbandolero.com, reservas@hotelbandolero.com).

$ Hostal La Posada's 10 clean and charming rooms, in a modern apartment flat, are cheap and funky. This family-run place has no reception (S-€20, Db-€45, cheaper off-season, Los Remedios 21, tel. & fax 956-450-258, no English spoken).

Route Tips for Drivers

Sevilla to Arcos (55 miles): The remote hill towns of Andalucía are a joy to tour by car with Michelin map 578 or any other good map. Drivers can zip south on N-IV from Sevilla along the river, following signs to *Cádiz*. Take the fast toll expressway (blue signs, E-5, A-4); the toll-free N-IV is curvy and dangerous. About halfway to Jerez, at Las Cabezas, take CA-403 to Villamartín. From there, circle scenically (and clockwise) through the thick of the Pueblos Blancos—Zahara and Grazalema—to Arcos.

It's about two hours from Sevilla to Zahara. You'll find decent but winding roads and sparse traffic. It gets worse (but very scenic) if you take the tortuous series of switchbacks over the 4,500-foot summit of Puerto de Las Palomas (Pass of the Pigeons, climb to the viewpoint) on the direct but difficult road from Zahara to Grazalema (you'll see several hiking trailheads into Sierra de Grazalema Natural Park, though most require free permits—see sidebar on page 566).

Another scenic option through the park from Grazalema to Arcos is the road that goes up over Puerto del Boyar (Pass of the Boyar), past the pretty little valley town of Benamahoma, and down to El Bosque. The road from Ronda to El Gastor, Setenil (cave houses and great olive oil), and Olvera is another picturesque alternative.

Arcos to Tarifa (80 miles): You can drive from Arcos to Jerez in 30 minutes. If you're going to Tarifa, take the tiny C-343 road at the Jerez edge of Arcos toward Paterna and Vejer. Later, you'll pick up signs to *Medina Sidonia,* and then to *Vejer* and *Tarifa*.

Costa del Sol to Ronda and Beyond: Drivers coming up from the coast catch A-397 at San Pedro de Alcántara and climb about 20 miles into the mountains. A-369 offers a much longer, winding, but scenic alternative that takes you through a series of whitewashed villages.

Beware if you have old maps. The road numbering system from the coast into Sevilla was changed a couple of years ago: From Marbella to Ronda, take A-397 (formerly A-376). From Ronda to Jerez, start on A-374 (formerly A-376) then get on A-384 (which at Arcos may still be labeled with its old number, A-382). To head to Seville, branch off from A-384 onto A-375.

SPAIN'S SOUTH COAST

Nerja • Gibraltar • Tarifa

Spain's famous Costa del Sol is so bad, it's interesting. To northern Europeans, the sun is a drug, and this is their needle. Anything resembling a quaint fishing village has been bikini-strangled and Nivea-creamed. Oblivious to the concrete, pollution, ridiculous prices, and traffic jams, tourists lie on the beach like game hens on skewers—cooking, rolling, and sweating under the sun.

Where Europe's most popular beach isn't crowded by high-rise hotels, most of it's in a freeway choke hold. Wonderfully undeveloped beaches between Tarifa and Cádiz, and east of Almería, are ignored, while human lemmings make the scene where the coastal waters are so polluted that hotels are required to provide swimming pools. It's a fascinating study in human nature.

Laugh with Ronald McDonald at the car-jammed resorts. But if you want a place to stay and play in the sun, unroll your beach towel at **Nerja.** And don't forget that you're surprisingly close to jolly olde England. The land of tea and scones, fish-and-chips, pubs and bobbies awaits you—in **Gibraltar.** Beyond "The Rock," the white-washed port of **Tarifa**—the least-developed piece of Spain's generally overdeveloped southern coast—provides an enjoyable springboard for a quick trip to Morocco (see next chapter). These three places alone—Nerja, Gibraltar, and Tarifa—make the Costa del Sol worth a trip.

Costa del Sol

Planning Your Time

My opinions on the "Costa del Turismo" are valid for peak season (mid-July–mid-Sept). If you're there during a quieter time and you like the ambience of a beach resort, it can be a pleasant stop. Off-season it can be neutron-bomb quiet.

The whole 150 miles of coastline takes six hours by bus or three hours to drive with no traffic jams. You can resort-hop by bus across the entire Costa del Sol and reach Nerja for dinner. If you want to party on the beach, it can take as much time as Mazatlán.

To day-trip to Tangier, Morocco, take a tour from Tarifa.

Nerja

While cashing in on the fun-in-the-sun culture, Nerja (NEHR-hah) has actually kept much of its quiet, Old World charm. It has good beaches, a fun evening paseo (strolling scene) that culminates in the proud Balcony of Europe terrace, enough pastry shops and nightlife, and locals who get more excited about their many festivals than the tourists do.

Thanks to cheap airfares and the completion of the

expressway, real estate is booming (property values have doubled in six years). Because of "residential tourism," Nerja's population of 22,000 swells to about 90,000 in the summer. For an insight into the mostly English expat community, read the free local expat magazines. Spanish visitors complain that some restaurants have only English menus. You'll find beans on your breakfast plate and Tom Jones for Muzak. Pensioners from northern Spain also retire here—enjoying long lives thanks to low blood pressure from the diet of fish and wine. As elsewhere along the Costa del Sol, real estate, construction, and tourism motor the economy.

ORIENTATION

The tourist center of Nerja is right along the water and crowding close to its famous bluff, the "Balcony of Europe." Two fine beaches flank the bluff. The old town is just inland from the Balcony, while the more modern section slopes up and away from the water.

Tourist Information

The helpful, English-speaking TI has bus schedules, tips on beaches and side-trips, and brochures for nearby destinations such as Málaga and Gibraltar (April–Oct Mon–Fri 10:00–14:00 & 17:00–20:00, Sat 10:00–13:30, closed Sun; Nov–March Mon–Sat 10:00–14:00 & 16:30–19:00, closed Sun; just off Balcony of Europe at Puerta del Mar 2, tel. 952-521-531, www.nerja.org, turismo@nerja.org). Ask for a free city map (or buy the more detailed version for €0.80) and the *Leisure Guide,* which has a comprehensive listing of activities. Their booklet on hiking is good, and you can reach some of the trailheads by bus.

To get a free flier with the latest theater and musical events, stop by the Villa de Nerja Cultural Center at Granada 45 (shows take place here, tel. 952-523-863). In the third week of July, they host the music festival in the Caves of Nerja.

Arrival in Nerja

By Bus: The Nerja bus station is actually just a bus stop with an info booth on Avenida de Pescia (daily 6:00–21:00, schedules posted, tel. 952-521-504). To travel from Nerja, you have to buy tickets at the info kiosk, not on the bus. Since many buses leave at the same times, arrive at least 15 minutes before departure to avoid elbowing other tourists.

By Car: Follow signs to *Balcón de Europa,* and then into the big, expensive (€1/hr) underground parking lot (which deposits you 200 yards from the Balcony of Europe). As an alternative, an enormous parking lot (entrance off Calle Frigiliana) provides excellent free parking for tour buses, locals, and you.

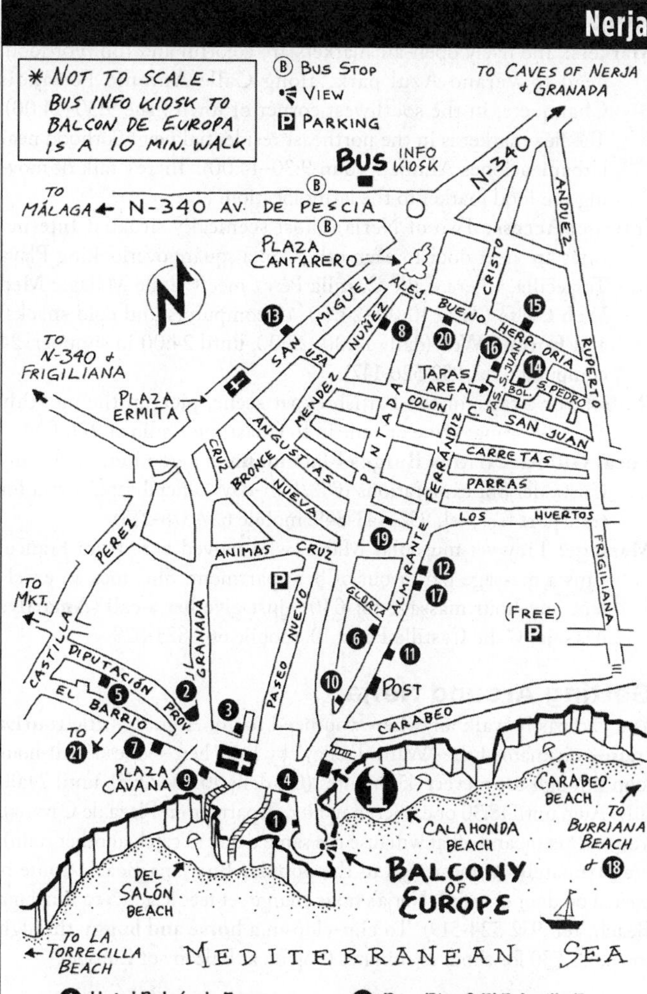

1. Hotel Balcón de Europa
2. Hotel Plaza Cavana
3. Hotel Puerta del Mar
4. Hostal Marissal & Cochran's Terrace
5. Hostal Don Peque
6. Hostal Miguel
7. Pensión Mena
8. Hostal Lorca
9. Casa Luque Restaurante
10. Los Mariscos Restaurante
11. Pepe Rico & El Pulguilla Rest.
12. Pinocchio Restaurante
13. Mercadona Supermarket
14. El Chispa Restaurante
15. Los Cuñaos Restaurante
16. La Puntilla Bar Restaurante
17. Haveli Restaurante
18. To Ayo's Café
19. Bar El Molino
20. Bodega Los Bilbainos
21. To Internet Cafés (2)

Helpful Hints

Markets: The lively open-air markets are colorful and fun. For food, head to Verano Azul park, along Calle Antonio Ferrandis Chanquete, in the southwest corner of town (Tue 9:30–14:00). The flea market is in the northeast residential neighborhood near Urbanizaciones Almijara (Sun 9:30–14:00). There's talk of moving the food market to the latter location.

Internet Access: Two of Nerja's most scenically situated Internet cafés are next door to each other, on a square overlooking Playa Torrecilla, where Calle Castilla Pérez meets Calle Málaga: **Med Web C@fé** (daily 10:00–24:00, 18 computers and cold snacks) and **Europ@Web** (daily 10:00–22:00, until 24:00 in summer, 24 computers, tel. 952-526-147).

Radio: For a taste of the British expat scene, pick up the monthly *Street Wise* magazine or tune in to Coastline Radio at 97.6 FM.

Local Guide: Cristina Burgos Flachmann is a good guide for any Costa del Sol explorations (€98/half-day "official rate," extra for transport fees, tel. 952-443-849, mobile 627-378-215).

Massage: Tiny yet muscular Marie, who moved here from France, runs a massage parlor out of her apartment. She does an excellent one-hour massage for €40—just give her a call (**Amarilys Masaje,** Calle Castilla Perez 10, mobile 667-825-828).

Getting Around Nerja

You can easily walk anywhere you need to go. A goofy little **tourist train**—nicknamed the "Wally Trolley" by Brits here—does a half-hour loop through town every 45 minutes (€4, daily 10:30–22:30, until 24:00 July–Aug, until 18:30 or earlier in winter, departs from Plaza de Cavana). You can get on and off at will (use the same ticket to catch another train). Unfortunately, it doesn't go to the popular Burriana Beach (route is posted on door of train). Nerja's **taxis** charge set fees (e.g., €5 to Burriana Beach, tel. 952-524-519). To clip-clop in a **horse and buggy** through town, it's €30 for about 25 minutes (hop on at Balcony of Europe).

SIGHTS AND ACTIVITIES

In Nerja

▲▲Balcony of Europe (Balcón de Europa)—The bluff, jutting happily into the sea, is the center of Nerja's paseo and a magnet for street performers. The mimes, music, and puppets can draw bigger crowds than the Balcony itself, which overlooks the Mediterranean, miles of coastline, and little coves and caves below. In the ninth century, a Moorish castle stood here, but was later partially destroyed by the English in a battle against Napoleon's French troops. Now it's a people-friendly view terrace.

The cute statue of King Alfonso XII reminds locals of how this

Costa del Sol History

Many Costa del Sol towns come in pairs: the famous beach town with little history, and its smaller yet much more historic partner established a few miles inland—safely out of reach of the Barbary pirate raids that plagued this coastline for centuries. Nerja is a good example of this pattern. While it has almost no history and was just an insignificant fishing village until tourism hit, its more historic sister, Frigiliana, hides out in the nearby hills. The Barbary pirate raids were a constant threat. In fact, the Spanish slang for "the coast is clear" is *"no hay moros en la costa"* (there are no Moors on the coast).

Nerja was overlooked by the tourism scene until about 1980, when the phenomenal Spanish TV show *Verano Azul (Blue Summer)* was set here. This post-Franco program featured the until-then off-limits topics of sexual intimacy, marital problems, adolescence, and so on in a beach-town scene (imagine combining *All in the Family, Baywatch,* and *The Hills*). Today when Spaniards hear the word "Nerja," they think of this TV hit.

Despite the fame, development didn't really hit until about 2000, when the expressway finally and conveniently connected Nerja with the rest of Spain. Thankfully, a building code prohibits any new buildings higher than three stories in the old town.

popular sovereign (the great-grandfather of today's King Juan Carlos) came here after a devastating earthquake in which a huge number of locals died. He mobilized the local rich to dig out the community and put things back together. Standing on this promontory, he coined its now-famous name, "Balcón de Europa."

Scan the horizon. Until recently, this was a favored landing spot (just beyond the tighter security zone near Gibraltar) for illegal immigrants and drug runners coming in from Africa. Thanks to a new high-tech satellite-scanning system, the Guardia Civil can now detect floating objects as small as makeshift rafts and intercept them before they reach land.

Walk below the Balcony for views of the scant remains (bricks and stones) of the Moorish castle. Locals claim an underground passage connected the Moorish fortress with the mosque that stood where the San Sebastián church stands today.

Promenades—Pleasant seaview promenades lead in opposite directions from the Balcony of Europe, going east to Burriana Beach and west to Torrecilla Beach. An early-morning walk along the delightful Paseo de los Carabineros from the Balcony of Europe to Burriana Beach past several coves is a great way to start your day (10-min walk, farther to get to Ayo's for breakfast—see page 589). In Spain, all beaches (except the one in Rota, which is reserved for American soldiers) are open to the public...by law.

Beaches (Playas)—Nerja has several good beaches. They are well-equipped, with bars and restaurants, free showers, and rentable lounges and umbrellas (about €4, same cost for 10 minutes or all day). Watch out for red flags on the beach, which indicate that the seas are too rough for safe swimming.

The sandiest—and most crowded—is **Del Salón Beach** (Playa del Salón), down the walkway to the right of the Restaurante Marissal, just off the Balcony of Europe. For great drinks-with-a-view, stop by either Cochran's Terrace or Casa Luque on the way down (see page 588). Continuing farther west, you'll reach another sandy beach, **Playa La Torrecilla,** at the end of Calle Málaga.

The pebblier **Calahonda Beach** (Playa Calahonda) is full of fun pathways, crags, and crannies (head down through the arch to the right of the TI). The humble Papagayo restaurant is open all day. Antonio can be seen each morning working with his nets and sorting through his fish. His little pre-tourism beach hut is wonderfully photogenic.

Burriana Beach (Playa de Burriana) is Nerja's leading beach (a 10-min walk from the Balcony of Europe along the Paseo de los Carabineros). It's fun for families, with paddleboats and entertainment options. It's also a destination for those visiting Ayo's paella-feast restaurant (see page 589).

Cantarriján Beach, a 15-minute drive east of Nerja (4.5 miles), is the nudists' choice (see next page).

Near Nerja

▲Caves of Nerja (Cuevas de Nerja)—These caves, 2.5 miles east of Nerja (exit 295), have the most impressive array of stalactites and stalagmites I've seen anywhere in Europe. The huge caverns are filled with expertly backlit formations and appropriate music. The visit involves a 30-minute unguided ramble deep into the mountain, up and down lots of dark stairs congested with Spanish families. At the end, you reach the Hall of the Cataclysm, where you'll circle the world's largest stalactite column (certified by the *Guinness Book of World Records*). Someone figured out that it took one trillion drops to make the column (€7, daily 10:00–14:00 & 16:00–18:30, July–Aug until 19:30, tel. 952-529-520).

The free exhibit in the Centro de Interpretación explains the cave's history and geology (orange house next to bus parking; exhibit in Spanish, but includes free English brochure).

To get to the caves, catch a bus from the Nerja bus stop on Avenida de Pescia (€1, 13/day, 10 min). During the festival held here the third week of July, the caves provide a cool venue for hot flamenco and classical concerts (tickets sold out long in advance). The restaurant offers a view and three-course fixed-price meals for €8. But the picnic spot (just up from and behind the ticket office) is even better, with pine trees, benches, and a kids' play area.

Frigiliana—This picture-perfect whitewashed village, only four miles inland from Nerja, is easy to reach by car or bus (€1, 9/day, 15 min, none on Sun). It's a worthwhile detour from the beach, particularly if you don't have time for the Pueblos Blancos hill towns. To bring the town to life, catch the 90-minute town walk by David Riordan, an American who has lived here for more than a decade (€7.50, Fri at 11:30; also does tours of nearby Almuñécar, Tue and Thu at 10:30; reserve by phone or email, mobile 625-986-065, vaquerodave@gmail.com).

Cantarriján Beach—For a more desolate beach, those with a car can drive 12 miles east (direction Herradura) to the Cerro Gordo exit, and follow signs (paved road, just before the tunnel) to *Playa Cantarriján*. You might be able to park at the beach, but more likely you'll park at the viewpoint and ride down in a shuttle van. At the beach, rocks and two restaurants separate two pristine beaches—one for people with bathing suits, the other for nudists.

Hiking—Europeans visiting the region for a longer stay generally use Nerja as a base from which to hike. The TI (and your hotel) can describe a variety of hikes. One of the most popular includes a refreshing and delightful two- to three-hour walk up a river (up to your shins in water). Another, more demanding hike takes you to the 5,000-foot summit of El Cielo for the best memorable king-of-the-mountain feeling this region offers.

NIGHTLIFE

If you're out late, consider **Bar El Molino** for folk singing after 23:00; it's touristy but fun (no cover, just buy a drink, Calle San José 4). For a more colorful hole-in-the-wall, consider the **Bodega Los Bilbainos,** a favorite with local men and communists (tapas and drinks, Calle Alejandro Bueno 8). For more trendy and noisy nightlife, check out the bars and dance clubs on Antonio Millón and Plaza Tutti Frutti.

SLEEPING

The entire Costa del Sol is crowded during August and Holy Week (April 5–12 in 2009), when prices are at their highest. Reserve in advance for peak season—basically mid-July through mid-September—which is prime time for Spanish workers to hit the beaches. Any other time of year, you'll find that Nerja has plenty of comfy, low-rise, easygoing, resort-type hotels and rooms. Room rates are generally three-tiered: low season (Nov–March), middle season (April–June and Oct), and high season (July–Sept).

Compared to the pricier hotels, the better *hostales* are an excellent value, and the Don Peque and Mena are within three blocks of the Balcony of Europe.

Breakfast: Ayo's on Burriana Beach is a great place for breakfast (see page 589).

Close to the Balcony of Europe

$$$ Hotel Balcón de Europa is the most central place in town. It's right on the water and the square, with the prestigious address Balcón de Europa 1. It has 110 rooms with all the modern comforts, including a pool and an elevator down to the beach. Groups love this spot, so the management speaks perfect British English. All the suites have sea-view balconies, and most regular rooms also come with views (Sb-€69/79/103, standard Db-€95/111/135, about €30 extra for sea view and balcony, breakfast-€11, air-con, elevator, parking-€9/day—signs posted for drivers, tel. 952-520-800, fax 952-524-490, www.hotelbalconeuropa.com, reservas@hotelbalconeuropa.com).

$$$ Hotel Plaza Cavana, with 39 rooms, overlooks a plaza lily-padded with cafés. If you like a central location, marble floors, modern furnishings, an elevator, and a small rooftop swimming pool, dive in (Sb-€50–80, Db-€75–125, extra bed-€20, 10 percent discount with this book in 2009, breakfast-€7, some view rooms, air-con, second small pool in basement, parking-€12/day, 2 blocks from Balcony of Europe at Plaza de Cavana 10, tel. 952-524-000, fax 952-524-008, www.hotelplazacavana.com, info@hotelplazacavana.com).

$$ Hotel Puerta del Mar, just around the corner from Hotel Plaza Cavana and run by the same owners, offers 24 newer rooms at a better value (Sb-€35–60, Db-€55–95, Tb-€75–120, Qb-€85–135, 15 percent discount with this book in 2009, includes breakfast next door and use of all Cavana facilities, air-con, Calle Gómez, tel. 952-527-304, www.hotelpuertadelmar.com, info@hotelpuertadelmar.com).

Sleep Code

(€1 = about $1.50, country code: 34)

S = Single, **D** = Double/Twin, **T** = Triple, **Q** = Quad, **b** = bathroom, **s** = shower only. Unless otherwise noted, credit cards are accepted and English is spoken. Breakfast and the 7 percent IVA tax are not included (unless noted).

To help you easily sort through these listings, I've divided the rooms into three categories, based on the price for a standard double room with bath during high season:

$$$ Higher Priced—Most rooms €100 or more.
$$ Moderately Priced—Most rooms between €50–100.
$ Lower Priced—Most rooms €50 or less.

$$ Hostal Marissal has an unbeatable location next door to the fancy Balcón de Europa hotel, and 23 modern, spacious rooms—some with small view balconies overlooking the action on the Balcony of Europe (Sb-€30/35/45, Db-€40/50/60, apartment for up to 4 people-€80–150, breakfast with beans-€5, double-paned windows, air-con, elevator, Internet access, Balcón de Europa 3, reception at Marissal café, tel. 952-520-199, fax 952-526-654, www.hostalmarissal.com, reserva@hostalmarissal.com, Carlos and María).

$$ Hostal Don Peque has ten bright and cheery rooms, eight with balconies. Owners Roberto and Clara moved here from France and have infused the place with their personality. They rent beach equipment at reasonable prices, but their bar-terrace with fantastic views may be more enticing (Sun–Thu: Sb-€33/43/60, Db-€38/48/60, Tb-€50/60/72; Fri–Sat: Sb/Db-€50/60/72, Tb-€62/72/84; includes tax, breakfast-€6, air-con, Diputación 13, tel. 952-521-318, www.hostaldonpeque.com, info@hostaldonpeque.com).

$ Hostal Miguel offers nine bright and airy rooms in the heart of "Restaurant Row." Top-floor rooms have mountain views, and breakfast is served on the pretty green terrace. The owners—British expats Ian, Jane, and Hannah—are long-time Nerja devotees (Sb-€29–38, Db-€38–55, 4 percent more if paying with credit card, beach equipment available on request, Almirante Ferrándiz 31, tel. 952-521-523, mobile 661-228-250, www.hostalmiguel.com, hostalmiguel@gmail.com).

$ Pensión Mena is erratically run but has 11 fine rooms—four with terraces and sea views—and a quiet, breezy garden (Sb-€18–28, Db-€27–43, €5 extra for terrace, includes tax, some street noise, El Barrio 15, tel. & fax 952-520-541, hostalmena@hotmail.com, María). During the off-season, check-in is only available when reception is open (Nov–March daily 9:30–13:30 & 17:00–20:30).

In a Residential Neighborhood

$ Hostal Lorca is located in a quiet residential area five minutes from the center, three blocks from the bus stop, and close to a small, handy grocery store and free parking lot. Run by a friendly young Dutch couple, Femma and Rick, this *hostal* has nine modern, comfortable rooms and an inviting, compact backyard with a terrace, palm tree, and small pool. You can use the microwave and take drinks (on the honor system) from the well-stocked fridge. This quiet, homey place is a winner (Sb-€29–33, Db-€33–50, extra bed-€12, includes tax, cash only, look for yellow house at Mendez Nuñez 20, tel. 952-523-426, www.hostallorca.com, info@hostallorca.com).

EATING

There are three Nerjas: the private domain of the giant beachside hotels; the central zone, packed with fun-loving (and often tipsy) expats and tourists enjoying great food from trilingual menus; and the back streets, where local life goes on as if there were no tourists. The whole old town (around the Balcony of Europe) sizzles with lively restaurants. Wander around and see who's eating best.

Close to the Water

Drinks with a View: For drinks or a meal with a sea view, **Cochran's Terrace** does the trick (open daily anytime for drinks, 12:00–15:00 & 19:00–23:00 for meals, just behind Hostal Marissal). Its great view tables overlook the Del Salón Beach.

Casa Luque is a worthwhile splurge, featuring a terrace in back with wicker furniture, sea views, and enough ambience to justify the price (€20 plates, €2–5 tapas, wines can be purchased by the glass, Thu–Tue 13:30–15:30 & 20:00–23:30, closed Sun lunch and all day Wed, tel. 952-521-004).

"Restaurant Row": You'll find lots of options on Calle Almirante Ferrándiz (which changes its name farther uphill to "Cristo"). Consider **Los Mariscos,** a traditional, family-style fish restaurant (at #17); **Pepe Rico,** another popular spot, with local specialties and atmosphere (#28); and **Pinocchio,** a big, popular eatery serving good Spanish food (#51). **El Pulguilla,** which specializes in seafood—with clams so fresh they squirt—is a delight. It's got a lively tapas bar up front and a breezy, casual terrace way out back. Though not listed on the menu, half-portions *(media raciones)* are available for many items, allowing you to easily sample different dishes (€10–15 dinners, Tue–Sun 13:00–16:00 & 19:00–24:00, closed Mon, Almirante Ferrándiz 26, tel. 952-521-384).

Supermarket: To pick up picnic items, visit the **Mercadona supermarket** (Mon–Sat 9:15–21:15, closed Sun, past the Plaza Ermita on Calle San Miguel).

Tapas and Colorful Holes-in-the-Wall Farther Inland

A 10-minute uphill hike takes you into the residential thick of things, where the sea views come thumbtacked to the walls, prices are lower, and locals fill the tables.

Tapas near Herrera Oria: These two eateries are within a block of each other around Herrera Oria. Each specializes in seafood and is fine for a sit-down meal, or for a stop on a tapas crawl. Remember—tapas are snack-size portions; to turn them into more of a meal, ask for a *ración,* a *media* (half) *ración,* or a menu. These places maintain the wonderful tradition of serving free tapas with each drink you order at the bar. They're generally open all day for tapas and drinks; I've included just their serving hours in case you're hungry for a sit-down meal: **El Chispa** is big on seafood, with an informal terrace. Their *tomate ajo* (garlic tomato) is tasty, and their *berenjenas* (fried and salted eggplant) is also worth considering (Tue–Sun 11:00–16:00 & 19:30–24:00, closed Mon, San Pedro 12, tel. 952-523-697). **Los Cuñaos** is the most fun late in the evening, when families munch tapas, men watch soccer on TV, women chat, and kids wander around like it's home (good seafood and prices, Sun–Fri 12:00–16:00 & 19:00–23:00, closed Sat, Herrera Oria 19, tel. 952-521-107).

La Puntilla Bar Restaurante is a boisterous little place, with its rickety, plastic Pepsi furniture spilling out onto the cobbles on hot summer nights (cheap and good fish, tapas at bar, daily 12:00–24:00, a block in front of Los Cuñaos at Calle Bolivia 1, tel. 952-528-951).

Haveli, run by Amit and his Swedish wife Eva, serves good Indian food in a big and happening atmosphere. This is a hit with vacationing Brits (€10–12 plates, daily 19:00–24:00 in summer, closed Mon off-season, Cristo 42, tel. 952-524-297).

On Burriana Beach

Ayo's is famous for its characteristic owner and its €5 beachside all-you-can-eat paella feast. For 30 years, Ayo—a lovable, ponytailed bohemian who promises to be here until he dies—has been feeding locals. The paella fires get stoked up at about noon. Grab one of a hundred tables under the canopy next to the rustic, open-fire cooking zone, and enjoy the beach setting in the shade with a jug of sangria (daily 9:00–17:00, breakfast at 9:00—see below, not open in the evenings, Playa de Burriana, tel. 952-522-289). It's a 20-minute walk from the Balcony of Europe to the east end of Burriana Beach—look for Ayo's orange rooftop pyramid.

Breakfast at Ayo's: Consider hiking the deserted beach early and arriving at Ayo's at 9:00 for breakfast. Locals order the *tostada con aceite de oliva* (toast with olive oil and salt-€0.50); Ayo also serves omelets and good coffee.

TRANSPORTATION CONNECTIONS

Nerja

From Nerja by Bus to: Nerja Caves (13/day, 10 min), **Frigiliana** (9/day, 15 min, none on Sun), **Granada** (6/day, 2.5 hrs, more with transfer in Motril—but check the departure time from Motril to Granada to make sure you're really saving time; Nerja to Motril-1 hr, Motril to Granada-1.75 hrs), **Córdoba** (1/day, 4.5 hrs), **Sevilla** (3/day, 4 hrs). Remember to double-check the codes on bus schedule—for example, 12:00*S* means 12:00 daily except Saturday.

To the Málaga Airport (about 40 miles west): Catch the bus to Málaga (€4, 18/day, 1.25–1.5 hrs), then take a local bus to the airport (€1, about 2/hr, 30 min); or pay €55 for a taxi from Nerja (airport tel. 952-048-804).

Málaga

This seaside city's busy airport is the gateway to the Costa del Sol, and is undergoing a major renovation. The closest train station to Nerja is in Málaga.

Málaga's train and bus stations—a block apart—both have pickpockets and lockers (train station lockers are more modern; both cost €3/day). You can rent a car at the train station from Atesa or Europcar. If you have time to kill, the train station is connected to a modern shopping mall, and another mall is located across from the bus station roundabout. Both have decent food courts.

From Málaga by Train to: Ronda (6/day, 2.5 hrs, transfer in Bobadilla), **Algeciras** (4/day, 4 hrs, transfer in Bobadilla), **Madrid** (12/day, 2.25–3 hrs on AVE), **Córdoba** (15/day, 1 hr on fast AVE or AVANT trains; 3/day, 2.25–3 hrs on slower trains), **Granada** (3/day, 2.5–3.25 hrs on AVE, transfer in Bobadilla or Antequera), **Sevilla** (11/day, 2 hrs on AVE or AVANT, 2.5 hrs on other trains), **Barcelona** (3/day, fast AVE train leaves at 17:00—6.5 hrs, 13 hrs on slow trains). Train info: tel. 902-240-202, www.renfe.es.

Buses: Málaga's bus station, a block from the train station, has a helpful information office with bus schedules (daily 7:00–22:00, tel. 952-350-061) and a TI (daily 11:00–19:00, Internet access, ATM, and lockers, on Paseo de los Tilos).

By Bus to: Algeciras (17/day, 1.75 hrs *directo,* 3 hrs *ruta*), **Nerja** (18/day, 1.25–1.5 hrs), **Ronda** (14/day, 1.75 hrs *directo,* 3 hrs *ruta*), **La Línea/Gibraltar** (4/day, 3 hrs), **Tarifa** (2/day, 3.5 hours), **Sevilla** (9/day, 7 direct, 2.5–3.5 hrs), **Jerez** (3/day, 4.5–5 hrs), **Granada** (hourly, 1.5–2 hrs), **Córdoba** (5/day, 3–3.5 hrs), **Madrid** (11/day, 6 hrs). Bus info: www.estabus.emtsam.es.

Between Nerja and Gibraltar

Buses take five hours to make the Nerja–Gibraltar trip, including a transfer in Málaga, where you may have to change bus companies (they leave nearly hourly from Nerja to Málaga). Along the way, buses stop at each of the following towns (see map on page 579).

Fuengirola and Torremolinos—The most built-up part of the region, where those most determined to be envied settle down, is a bizarre world of Scandinavian package tours, flashing lights, pink flamenco, multilingual menus, and all-night happiness. Fuengirola is like a Spanish Mazatlán with a few older, less-pretentious budget hotels between the main drag and the beach. The water here is clean and the nightlife fun and easy. James Michener's idyllic Torremolinos has been strip-mauled and parking-metered.

Marbella—This is the most polished and posh town on the Costa del Sol. High-priced boutiques, immaculate streets set with intricate pebble designs, and beautifully landscaped squares testify to Marbella's arrival on the world-class-resort scene. Have a *café con leche* on the beautiful Plaza de Naranjas in the old city's pedestrian section. Wander down to new Marbella and the high-rise beachfront apartment buildings to walk along the wide promenade lined with restaurants. Check out the beach scene. Marbella is an easy stop on the Algeciras–Málaga bus route (as you exit the bus station, take a left to reach the center of town). You can also catch a handy direct bus here from the Málaga airport (20/day, fewer off-season, 45 min, www.ctsa-portillo.com).

San Pedro de Alcántara—This town's relatively undeveloped sandy beach is popular with young travelers. San Pedro's neighbor, Puerto Banús, is "where the world casts anchor." This luxurious, Monaco-esque jet-set port, complete with casino, is a strange mix of Rolls-Royces, yuppies, boutiques, rich Arabs, and budget browsers.

Gibraltar

One of the last bits of the empire upon which the sun never set, Gibraltar is a quirky mix of Anglican propriety, "God Save the Queen" tattoos, English bookstores, military memories, and tourist shops. In 20 years the economy has gone from one dominated by the military to one based on tourism (as, it seems, happens to many empires). On summer days and weekends, the tiny colony is inundated by holiday-goers, primarily Spanish (who come here for tax-free cigarettes and booze) and British (who want a change in weather but not in culture).

While it's hard to imagine a community of 30,000 that feels like its own nation, real Gibraltarians, as you'll learn when you visit, are a proud bunch. They were evacuated during World War II, and it's said that after their return, a national spirit was forged. If you doubt that, be here on Gibraltar's national holiday, September 10, when everyone's decked out in red and white, the national colors.

Gibraltarians have a mixed and interesting heritage. Spaniards call them Llanitos (yah-NEE-tohs), meaning "flat" in Spanish, though the residents live on a rock. The locals—a fun-loving and tolerant mix of British, Spanish, and Moroccan—call their place "Gib."

A passport is required to cross the border (you'll only get a stamp if you need a visa—otherwise, you'll just get a wave-through).

Planning Your Time

Make Gibraltar a side-trip (or just an overnight); rooms are expensive compared to Spain.

For the best day trip to Gibraltar, consider this plan: Walk across the border, catch bus #3, and ride it to the end, following my self-guided tour (see page 597). Ride bus #3 back to the cable-car station, then catch the cable car to the peak for Gibraltar's ultimate top-of-the-rock view. From there, either walk down or take the cable car back into town. From the cable-car station, follow my self-guided town walk all the way to Casemates Square. Spend your remaining free time in town before returning to Spain.

Tourists who stay overnight find Gibraltar a peaceful place in the evening, when the town can just be itself. No one's in a hurry. Families stroll, kids play, seniors window-shop, and everyone chats, but the food is still pretty bad.

There's no reason to side-trip into Morocco from Gibraltar—for many reasons, it's better from Tarifa (specifics covered in next chapter).

Gibraltar

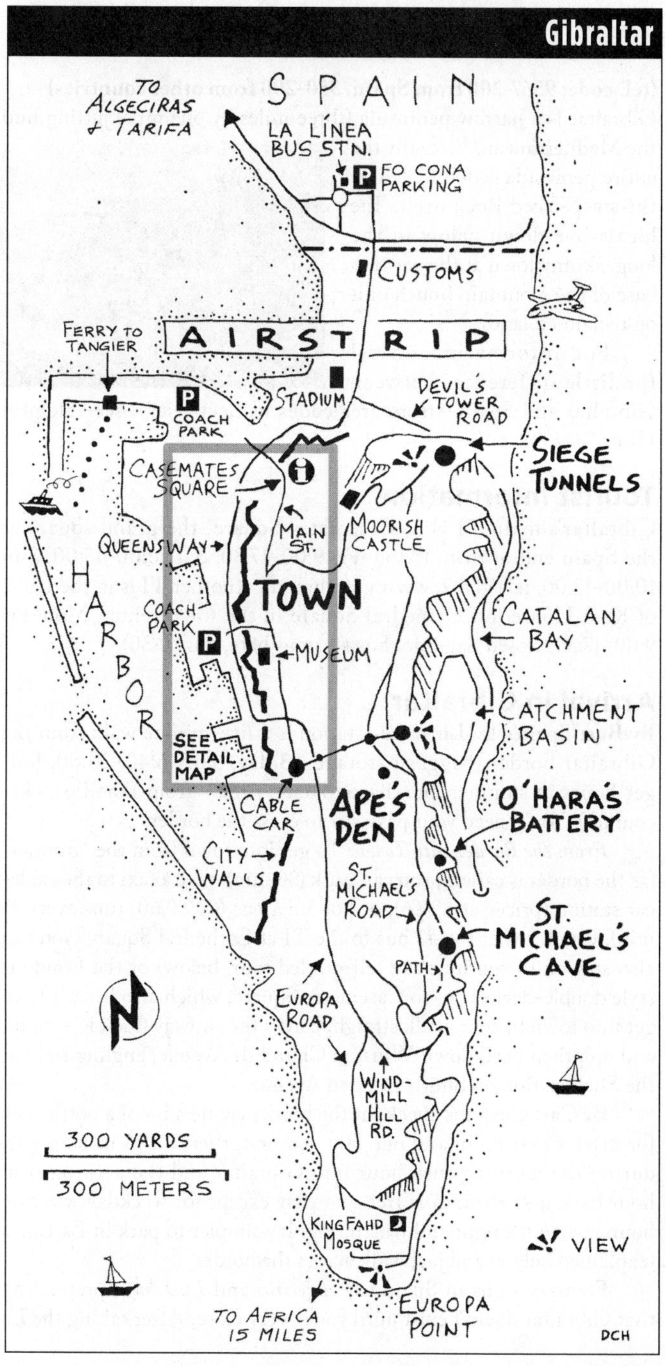

SPAIN
TO ALGECIRAS & TARIFA
LA LÍNEA BUS STN.
FO CONA PARKING
CUSTOMS
AIRSTRIP
FERRY TO TANGIER
COACH PARK
STADIUM
DEVIL'S TOWER ROAD
SIEGE TUNNELS
CASEMATES SQUARE
MAIN ST.
MOORISH CASTLE
QUEENSWAY
TOWN
HARBOR
COACH PARK
MUSEUM
CATALAN BAY
CATCHMENT BASIN
SEE DETAIL MAP
CABLE CAR
APE'S DEN
O'HARA'S BATTERY
CITY WALLS
ST. MICHAEL'S ROAD
ST. MICHAEL'S CAVE
PATH
EUROPA ROAD
WIND-MILL HILL RD.
300 YARDS
300 METERS
KING FAHD MOSQUE
VIEW
TO AFRICA 15 MILES
EUROPA POINT
DCH

ORIENTATION

(tel. code: 9567-200 from Spain, 350-200 from other countries)
Gibraltar is a narrow peninsula (three miles by one mile) jutting into the Mediterranean. Virtually the entire peninsula is dominated by the steep-faced Rock itself. The locals live down below in the long, skinny town at the western base of the mountain (much of it on reclaimed land).

For information on all the little differences between Gibraltar and Spain—from area codes to electricity—see "Helpful Hints," next page).

Tourist Information

Gibraltar's main TI is at Casemates Square, the grand square at the Spain end of town (Mon–Fri 9:00–17:30, Sat 10:00–15:00, Sun 10:00–13:00, tel. 74982, www.gibraltar.gi). Another TI is in the Duke of Kent House (off Cathedral Square in the town center, Mon–Fri 9:00–17:30, closed Sat–Sun, bus #3 stops here, tel. 74950).

Arrival in Gibraltar

By Bus: Spain's La Línea bus station is a five-minute walk from the Gibraltar border (baggage storage-€3/day, daily 6:40–20:00, longer hours in summer, purchase token—*ficha*—from Portillo ticket counter). You'll need your passport to cross the border.

From the Border into Town: To get into town from the "frontier" (as the border is called), you can walk (30 min), take a taxi to the cable-car station (pricey at €9/£6), or hop on a bus (€1/£0.60, runs every 15 min). Catch either the #3 bus to the TI at Cathedral Square (you can also stay on to continue my self-guided tour, below) or the London-style double-decker bus to Casemates Square, which also has a TI. To get into town by foot, walk straight across the runway (look left, right, and up), then head down Winston Churchill Avenue, angling right at the Shell station on Smith Dorrien Avenue.

By Car: Customs checks at the border create a bit of a bottleneck for drivers getting in and out. But at worst, there's a 15-minute wait during the morning rush hour into Gibraltar and the evening rush hour back out. Parking is free and easy except for weekday working hours, when it's tight and frustrating. It's simpler to park in La Línea (explained below) and just walk across the border.

Freeway signs in Spain say *Algeciras* and *La Línea,* pretending that Gibraltar doesn't exist until you're very close. After taking the La

Spain vs. Gibraltar

Spain has been annoyed about Gibraltar ever since Great Britain snagged this prime 2.5-square-mile territory through the 18th-century Treaty of Utrecht (1713) at the end of the War of the Spanish Succession. Although Spain long ago abandoned efforts to reassert its sovereignty by force, it still tries to make Gibraltarians see the error of their British ways. Over the years, Spain has limited Gibraltar's air and sea connections, choked traffic at the three-quarter-mile border, and even messed with the local phone system in efforts to convince Gibraltar to give back the Rock. Still, given the choice—which they got in referenda in 1967 and 2002—Gibraltar's residents steadfastly remain Queen Elizabeth's loyal subjects, voting overwhelmingly (99 percent in the last election) to continue as a self-governing British dependency. Gibraltar's governor, who is serving his third four-year term, is popular for dealing forcefully and effectively with Spain on these issues.

Línea–Gibraltar exit off the main Costa del Sol road, continue as the road curves left (with the Rock to your right). Enter the left-hand lane at the traffic circle before the border and you'll end up in La Línea. The Fo Cona underground parking lot is handy (€1/hr, €6/day, on "20th of April" street). You'll also find blue-lined parking spots in this area (€1/hr from meter, 6-hr limit 9:00–20:00, free before and after that, bring coins, leave ticket on dashboard). From La Línea, it's a five-minute stroll to the border, where you can catch a bus or taxi into town (see "From the Border into Town," above).

If driving into Gibraltar, drive along the sea side of the ramparts (on Queensway—but you'll see no street name). There are big parking lots here and at the cable-car terminal. Parking is generally free—if you can find a spot. By the way, while you'll still find the English-style roundabouts, cars here stopped driving on the British side of the road in the 1920s.

Helpful Hints

Gibraltar Spain: Gibraltar, a British colony, uses different coins, currency (see below), stamps, and phone cards than those used in Spain. Note that British holidays such as the Queen's Birthday (June 16) and Bank Holidays (May 4, May 26, and Aug 25 in

2009) are observed, along with local holidays such as Gibraltar's National Day (Sept 10).

Use Pounds, not Euros: Gibraltar uses the British pound sterling (£1 = about $2). They also accept euros...but for about a 20 percent extra cost to you. Gibraltar is expensive even at fair pound sterling rates. You'll save money by hitting up an ATM and taking out what you'll need. But before you leave, stop at an exchange desk and change back what you don't spend (at about a 5 percent loss), since Gibraltar currency is hard to change in Spain. (If you'll be making only a few purchases, you can try to avoid this problem by skipping the ATM and buying things with your credit card.) Be aware that if you pay for anything in euros, you may get pounds back in change.

Hours: This may be the United Kingdom, but Gibraltar follows a siesta schedule, with some businesses closing 13:00–15:00 on weekdays, and shutting down at 14:00 on Saturdays until Monday morning.

Electricity: If you have electrical gadgets, note that Gibraltar uses the British three-pronged plugs (not the European two-pronged ones). Your hotel may be able to loan you an adapter.

Telephone: To telephone Gibraltar from anywhere in Europe, dial 00-350-200 and the five-digit local number. To call Gibraltar from the US or Canada, dial 011-350-200-local number.

Internet Access: Café Cyberworld has pricey Internet access (daily 12:00–24:00, Queensway 14, in Ocean Heights Gallery, an arcade 100 yards toward the water from Casemates Square, tel. 51416). **Western Union** has an Internet center on Main Street (£0.75/hr; at #269, right before Convent Square). Another cheap place for Internet access is the cultural center listed next.

John Mackintosh Cultural Centre: This is your classic British effort to provide a cozy community center. The upstairs library, without a hint of tourism, welcomes drop-ins to enjoy all the local newspapers and publications, and to check their email cheaply and easily (£0.75/30 min, Mon–Fri 9:30–19:30, closed Sat–Sun).

Weekend Trip to Tangier, Morocco: Travel agencies in Gibraltar sell weekend trips to Tangier. Ferries leave Gibraltar only on Friday at 19:00 and depart Tangier only on Sunday at 20:00 (Morocco time). This weekend ferry schedule was adopted so the large number of Moroccans working in Gibraltar can spend the weekend with their families (£23 one-way, £41 round-trip). Because Gibraltar is expensive compared to Spain, it makes sense to use your time here to see the Rock, and day-trip to Morocco from Tarifa instead (see page 610).

SELF-GUIDED BUS TOUR

Gibraltar Town Bus #3 Orientation Tour

Upon arrival at the "frontier," pick up a map at the TI window. Then walk straight ahead for 200 yards to the bus stop on the right. Catch bus #3 and enjoy this three-mile orientation ride that takes you from one end of the colony to the other (every 15 min, buy ticket from driver, ride 20 min to the end of the line: Europa Point). A single ticket gives you on-and-off privileges for an hour (€1/£0.60). To save money, ask the driver for a round-trip ticket (€1.50/£0.90) instead of purchasing two separate fares.

Here's the tour. It goes quickly. Read fast...

Airstrip: You enter Gibraltar by crossing an airstrip. Three or four times a day, the entry road into Gibraltar is closed to allow planes to land or take off. Originally a horse-racing stadium, this area was later filled in with stones excavated from the 30 miles of military tunnels carved into the Rock. This airstrip was a vital lifeline in the days when Spain and Britain were quarreling over Gibraltar (especially 1970–1985) and the border was closed. If you look at the face of the Rock, you can see tiny windows (which used to be perches from where big cannons could fire) marking the Siege Tunnels—now open as a tourist attraction.

Moorish Castle: Just after the airstrip, at the first roundabout, the bus passes a road leading left (which heads clockwise around the Rock to the town of Catalan Bay, peaceful beaches, and the huge mountainside rainwater-catchment wall). The Moorish Castle above dates back over a thousand years. On the right is land reclaimed in 1989, filled mostly with government-subsidized apartments.

Ramparts: You'll cross the bridge and drive onto the ramparts. Water once came all the way up to the ramparts—50 percent of the city is on reclaimed land. Gibraltar's heritage shows in the architecture: tiles (Portuguese), shutters (Genoa, Italian), and wrought iron (Georgian English).

On the right after the next stop, you'll see World War memorials. The first is the American War Memorial (a building-like structure with a gold plaque and arch), built in 1932 to commemorate American sailors based here in World War I. Farther along you'll see 18th-century cannons and a memorial to Gibraltarians who died in World War II.

Downtown: The following sights come up quickly: Passing the NatWest House office tower on the left, you'll immediately see a **synagogue** (only the top peeks out above a wall; the wooden doors in the wall bear the Star of David). In the 19th century, half of Gibraltar was Jewish. The Jewish community now numbers 600. Just after the synagogue is little **Cathedral Square,** with a playground, TI, and the Moorish-looking Anglican cathedral (behind the playground). Gibraltar is the European headquarters of the Anglican Church.

Now you'll pass a long wall; most of it is the back of the Governor's Residence (a.k.a. The Convent).

Charles V Wall: The next bus stop is at the old Charles V wall, built in response to a 1552 raid in which the pirate Barbarossa captured 70 Gibraltarians into slavery. Immediately after you pass under the wall, you'll see a green park on your left that contains the **Trafalgar cemetery.** Buried here are some British sailors who died defeating the French off the coast of Spain's Cape Trafalgar in 1805.

Botanical Gardens: The next stop is at the big parking lot for the **cable car** to the top of the Rock, as well as for the **botanical gardens** (free, daily 8:00–sunset), located at the base of the lift. You can get off to do this now—or finish the tour, and come back here later, on the way back into town.

Out of Town: Heading uphill out of town, your best views are on the right. It's believed that the body of Admiral Nelson was pickled in a barrel of spirits in a harbor just below you after his victorious (yet fatal) Battle of Trafalgar. You pass the big former naval hospital and barracks. Reaching the end of the Rock, you pass modern apartments and the mosque.

King Fahd Mosque: This $20 million gift from the Saudi sultan was completed in 1997, and Gibraltar's 900 Muslims worship here each Friday. Five times a day—as across the strait in Morocco—an imam sings the call to prayer.

Europa Point: The lighthouse marks windy Europa Point—the end of the line. Buses retrace the route you just traveled, departing about every 15 minutes. Europa Point, up the mound from the bus stop and tourist shop (on right), is an observation post. A plaque here identifies the mountains of Morocco 15 miles across the strait. The glow of the lighthouse (150 feet tall, from 1841, closed to visitors) can be seen from Morocco.

Your tour is finished. Enjoy the views before catching a bus back into town. Get off at the cable-car station to ride to the top of the Rock, tour the botanical gardens, or begin the town walk described next.

SELF-GUIDED WALK

Welcome to Gibraltar

Gibraltar town is long and skinny, with one main street (called Main Street). Stroll the length of it from the cable-car station to Casemates Square, following this little tour. A good British pub and a room-temperature pint of beer await you at the end.

Just past the cable-car terminal is the **Trafalgar cemetery,** a reminder of the colony's English military heritage. Next you come to the **Charles V wall**—a reminder of its Spanish military heritage—built in 1552 by the Spanish to defend against marauding pirates. Gibraltar was controlled by Moors (711–1462), Spain (1462–1704), and then the British (1704 until now). Passing through the Southport Gates, you'll see one of the many red history plaques posted about town.

Heading into town, you pass the tax office, then the **John Mackintosh Cultural Centre,** which has cheap Internet access and a copy of today's *Gibraltar Chronicle* upstairs in its library. The *Chronicle* comes out Monday through Friday and has covered the local news since 1801. The Methodist church sponsors the cheap and cheery **Carpenter's Arms** tearoom just above one of several fish-and-chips joints (rare in Iberia).

The pedestrian portion of Main Street begins near the **Governor's Residence.** The British governor of Gibraltar took over a Franciscan convent, hence the name of the local white house: The Convent. The **Convent Guard Room,** facing the Governor's Residence, is good for photos.

Gibraltar's courthouse stands behind a **small tropical garden,** where John and Yoko got married back in 1969 (as the ballad goes, they "got married in Gibraltar near Spain"). Sean Connery did, too. Actually, many Brits like to get married here because weddings are cheap, fast (only 48 hours' notice required), and legally recognized as British.

Main Street now becomes a **shopping drag.** You'll notice lots of colorful price tags advertising tax-free booze, cigarettes, and sugar (highly taxed in Spain). Lladró porcelain, while made in Valencia, is popular here (because it's sold without the 16 percent Spanish VAT—Value-Added Tax). The big **Marks & Spencer department store** helps vacationing Brits feel at home, while the Catholic cathedral retains a whiff of Arabia (as it was built upon the remains of a mosque).

The town (and this walk) ends at **Casemates Square.** While a lowbrow food circus today, it originated as a barracks and place for ammunition storage. When Franco closed the border with Spain in 1969, Spanish guest workers could no longer commute into Gibraltar, so the colony countered by inviting Moroccan workers to take their place. This ended a nearly 500-year Moroccan absence, which began when the Moors fled in 1462. As a result, today's Moroccan community dates only from the 1970s. While the previous Spanish labor force just commuted into work, the Moroccans needed apartments, so Gibraltar converted the Casemates barracks for that purpose. Cheap Spanish labor has crept back in, causing many locals to resent store clerks who can't speak proper English. On Casemates Square, there's a crystal shop that makes its own crystal right there (you can watch). They claim it's the only thing actually "made in Gibraltar." But just upstairs, on the upper floor of the barracks, you'll find a string of local crafts shops. Beyond the square (behind the TI) is the covered **produce market.**

SIGHTS

In Gibraltar Town

▲Gibraltar Museum—Built atop a Moorish bath, this museum tells the story of a chunk of land that has been fought over for centuries. Start with the fine 15-minute video overview of the story of the Rock—a worthwhile prep for the artifacts (such as ancient Roman anchors made of lead) you'll see in the museum. Then, wander through the scant remains of the 14th-century Moorish baths. Upstairs you'll see military memorabilia, a 15-foot-long model of the Rock, wonderful century-old photos of old Gibraltar, paintings by local artists, and, in a cave-like room off the art gallery, a collection of prehistoric remains and artifacts. The famous skull of a Neanderthal woman found in Forbes' Quarry is a copy (the original is in the British Museum in London). Found in Gibraltar in 1848, this was the first Neanderthal skull ever discovered. No one realized its significance until a similar skull found years later in Germany's Neanderthal Valley was correctly identified—stealing the name, claim, and fame from Gibraltar (£2, Mon–Fri 10:00–18:00, Sat 10:00–14:00, closed Sun, no photos, on Bomb House Lane near the cathedral).

Up on the Rock

The actual Rock of Gibraltar is the colony's best sight. Its attractions: the stupendous view from the very top, quirky apes, a hokey cave (St. Michael's), and the impressive Siege Tunnels drilled through the rock face for military purposes. The Rock, which is technically called the "Upper Rock Nature Reserve," is open daily 9:30–19:00.

You have two £8 options for touring the Rock: Ride the cable car or take a 90-minute taxi tour. The taxi tour includes a couple of extra stops and the running commentary of your licensed cabbie/guide. Hikers can ride the lift up and walk down, connecting the various sights (you'll walk on paved military lanes, not trails).

In either case, to tour St. Michael's Cave or the Siege Tunnels, you'll need to pay £8 extra for a combo-ticket. Because the cable car doesn't get you very close to the cave and tunnels, take the taxi tour if you'll be visiting these sights. On the other hand, the cable car takes you to the very top of the Rock (which the taxi tours don't). Frankly, the sights are not much, but the Rock's best attractions—enjoying views from the top and playing with the monkeys—are free.

There's certainly no reason to take a big bus tour (advertised and sold all over town) considering how fun, cheap, and easy the taxi tours are. Private cars are not allowed high on the Rock.

Taxi Tours: Minibuses driven by cabbies trained and licensed to lead these little trips are standing by at the border and on Cathedral Square in town. They charge £32 per carload or £8 per person, whichever is more. (Remember, you'll pay an additional £8 for

admission to the cave and the tunnels; if you opt out, you'll have to sit in the car while the other passengers make these little visits.) Taxi tours and big buses do the same 90-minute loop tour with four stops: a Mediterranean viewpoint (called the Pillar of Hercules), St. Michael's Cave (15-min visit), a viewpoint near the top of the Rock where you can get up close to the monkeys, and the Siege Tunnels (20-min visit). Buddy up with other travelers and share the cost.

Cable Car to the Summit: The ride costs £8 (6/hr, daily 9:30–17:15, last ride down at 17:45, closed Sun in winter and when windy or rainy—ask at TI if cable car is running when weather is questionable, pick up map with ticket). Your cable-car ride includes a multimedia device that explains the spectacular views (pick it up at the well-marked booth when you disembark at the top). The cable car stops halfway down, for those who want to get out, see the monkeys, and take a later car down. From there, many hike to the Cave of St. Michael (skippable and described below).

To see all the sights, you'll end up hiking down, rather than taking the cable car back. Approximate hiking times: from the top of the cable car to St. Michael's Cave—25 minutes; from the cave to the Apes' Den—20 minutes; from the Apes' Den to the Siege Tunnels—30 minutes; from the tunnels back into town, passing the Moorish Castle—20 minutes. Total from top to bottom: about 90 minutes (on paved roads with almost no traffic), not including sightseeing.

▲▲▲The Summit of the Rock—The cable car takes you to the real highlight of Gibraltar: the summit of the spectacular Rock itself. (Taxi tours do not go here—they stop on a ridge below the summit, where you enjoy a commanding view...but one that's nowhere near as good.) The limestone massif, or large rock mass, is nearly a mile long, rising 1,400 feet high with very sheer faces. According to legend, this was one of the Pillars of Hercules (paired with Djebel Musa, another mountain across the strait in Morocco), marking the edge of the known world in ancient times. Local guides say that these pillars are the only places on the planet where you can see two seas and two continents at the same time.

In A.D. 711, the Muslim chieftain Tarik ibn Ziyad crossed over from Africa and landed on the Rock, beginning the Moorish conquest of Spain and naming the Rock after himself—"The Rock of Tarik," or Djebel-Tarik, which became Gibraltar.

At the top of the Rock (the cable-car terminal), there's a view terrace and a restaurant. From here, you can explore old ramparts and drool at the 360-degree view of Morocco (including the Rif Mountains and Djebel Musa), the Strait of Gibraltar, the bay stretching west toward Algeciras, and the twinkling Costa del Sol arcing eastward. The views are especially crisp on brisk off-season days. Below you (to the east) stretches the giant catchment system that the British built to collect rainwater in the not-so-distant past, when Spain allowed neither water nor tourists to cross its disputed border. Broad sheets catch the rain, sending it through channels to reservoirs located inside the rock.

O'Hara's Battery—While it's closed to visitors, some travelers still hike up here (20 min from the top of the cable-car lift). At 1,400 feet, this is the actual highest point on the Rock. A 100-ton, nine-inch gun sits on the summit where a Moorish lookout post once stood. It was built after World War I, and the last test shot was fired in 1974. Locals are glad it's been mothballed—during test firings, if they didn't open their windows to allow air to move freely after the concussion, the windows could shatter. The iron rings you see every 30 yards or so along the military lanes around the Rock once anchored pulleys used to haul up guns such as the huge one at O'Hara's Battery.

▲St. Michael's Cave—Studded with stalagmites and stalactites, eerily lit, and echoing with classical music, this cave is dramatic, corny, and slippery when wet. Considered a one-star sight since Neolithic times, these caves were alluded to in ancient Greek legends—when the caves were believed to be the Gates of Hades (or the entrance of a tunnel to Africa). All taxi tours stop here. This sight requires a long walk for cable-car riders.

▲Apes of Gibraltar—The Rock is home to about 200 "apes" (actually, tailless Barbary macaques—a type of monkey). Taxi tours come with great monkey fun. Those riding the cable car can get off halfway down to photograph the apes. The males are bigger, females have beards, and newborns are black. They live about 15–20 years. Legend has it that as long as the apes remain here, so will the Brits. Keep your distance from the apes. (Guides say that for safety reasons, "They can touch you, but you can't touch them.") Beware of their kleptomaniac tendencies; they'll ignore the peanut in your hand and claw after the full bag in your pocket. If there's no ape action, wait for a banana-toting taxi tour to stop by and stir some up.

▲Siege Tunnels—Also called the Upper Galleries, these chilly tunnels were blasted out of the rock by the Brits during the Spanish and French siege (1779–1783). The clever British, safe inside the Rock, used hammers and gunpowder to carve these tunnels in order to plant four big guns on the north face and drive off the French. During World War II, 30 more miles of tunnels were blasted out. Hokey but fun dioramas help recapture a time when Brits were known more for conquests than for crumpets.

Moorish Castle—Actually more a tower than a castle, this building offers a tiny museum of Moorish remnants and carpets. (In the interest of political correctness, the tourist board is trying to change the name to "Medieval Castle"...but it is Moorish.) It was constructed on top of the original castle built in A.D. 711 by the Moor Tarik ibn Ziyad, who gave his name to Gibraltar. The tower marks the end of the Upper Rock Nature Reserve. A short hike downhill drops you back in town.

NIGHTLIFE

Gibraltar is quiet at night. You can sip a drink on the waterfront at the Queensway Quay Marina (see below). Other than that, it's music in the pubs and lounges. O'Callaghan Eliott Hotel hosts free live jazz on Monday and Thursday evenings, and Casemates Square is everyone's choice for live music in the pubs. The Queen's Cinema (by the cable car) is the colony's only movie theater.

SLEEPING

Gibraltar is not a good value for hotels. Except at the hostel, the beds are either bad or overpriced. Remember, you'll pay a 20 percent premium with euros—pay with local cash or your credit card.

$$$ O'Callaghan Eliott Hotel, with four stars, boasts a rooftop pool with a view, a fine restaurant, bar, terrace, inviting sit-a-bit public spaces, and 120 modern if sterile rooms (sky-high rack rates of Db-£240–270, but often around Db-£100 with Web booking during non-peak days, breakfast-£13, non-smoking floors, air-con, elevator, free parking, centrally located at Governor's Parade up Library Street from main drag, tel. 70500, fax 70243, www.ocallaghanhotels.com, reservations@ocallaghanhotels.com).

$$$ Bristol Hotel offers basic English rooms in the heart of Gibraltar (Sb-£57–62, Db-£74–79, Tb-£85–93, higher prices for

Sleep Code

(£1 = about $2, tel. code: 350-200)
S = Single, **D** = Double/Twin, **T** = Triple, **Q** = Quad, **b** = bathroom, **s** = shower only. All of these places accept credit cards and speak English. To help you easily sort through these listings, I've divided the rooms into three categories, based on the price for a standard double room with bath during high season:

$$$ Higher Priced—Most rooms £75 or more.
$$ Moderately Priced—Most rooms between £35–75.
$ Lower Priced—Go back to Spain.

exterior rooms, breakfast-£5, air-con, elevator, swimming pool, free parking, Cathedral Square 10, tel. 76800, fax 77613, www.bristolhotel.gi, reservations@bristolhotel.gi).

$$ Queen's Hotel, near the cable-car lift, has 62 comfortable, remodeled rooms in a noisy location (Sb-£50, Db-£65, seaview Db-£75–95, Tb-£85, Qb-£90, includes English breakfast, 20 percent discount for students with ISIC cards and paying cash, elevator, free parking, at #3 bus stop, Boyd Street 1, tel. 74000, fax 40030, www.queenshotel.gi, queenshotel@gibtelecom.net).

$$ Continental Hotel isn't fancy, but it has a friendly feel. Its 17 high-ceilinged, air-conditioned rooms border an unusual elliptical atrium (Sb-£52, Db-£70, Tb-£85, Qb-£95, includes continental breakfast, elevator, a couple of blocks south of Casemates TI in Main Street pedestrian area, Engineer Lane, tel. 76900, fax 41702, contiho@gibtelecom.net).

$$ Cannon Hotel is a run-down dive. But it's also well-located, friendly, and has the only cheap hotel rooms in town. Its 18 rooms (most with wobbly cots and no private bathrooms) look treacherously down on a little patio (S-£26, D-£38, Db-£46, T-£47, Tb-£54, includes full English breakfast, behind cathedral at Cannon Lane 9, tel. 51711, fax 51789, www.cannonhotel.gi, cannon@gibnet.gi).

$ Emile Hostel, charming and the cheapest place in town, welcomes people of any age (44 beds, dorm bed-£15, S-£20, D-£35, includes breakfast, lockout only for dorm rooms from 10:30–17:00, on Montagu Bastion diagonally across the street from a petrol station, ramped entrance on Line Wall Road, tel. & fax 51106, www.emilehostel.com, emilehostel@yahoo.co.uk).

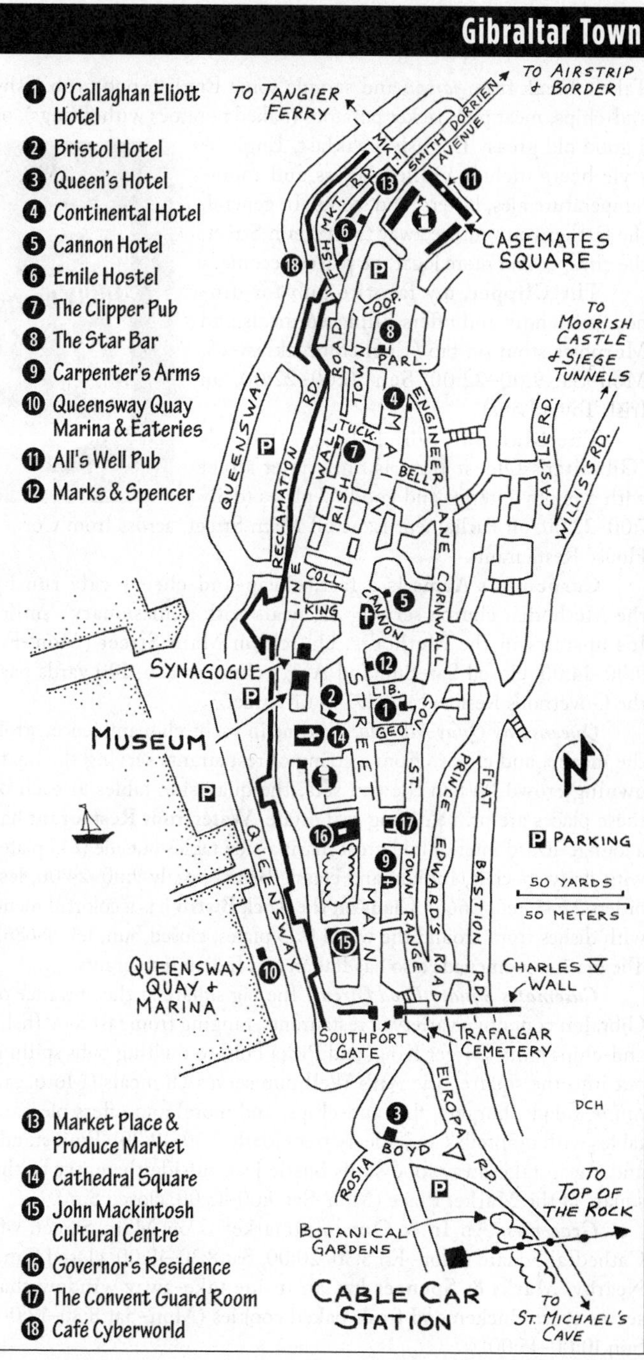
Gibraltar Town
1 O'Callaghan Eliott Hotel
2 Bristol Hotel
3 Queen's Hotel
4 Continental Hotel
5 Cannon Hotel
6 Emile Hostel
7 The Clipper Pub
8 The Star Bar
9 Carpenter's Arms
10 Queensway Quay Marina & Eateries
11 All's Well Pub
12 Marks & Spencer
13 Market Place & Produce Market
14 Cathedral Square
15 John Mackintosh Cultural Centre
16 Governor's Residence
17 The Convent Guard Room
18 Café Cyberworld
TO TANGIER FERRY
TO AIRSTRIP & BORDER
SMITH DORRIEN AVENUE
MKT. RD.
FISH MKT. RD.
CASEMATES SQUARE
TO MOORISH CASTLE & SIEGE TUNNELS
COOP.
PARL.
QUEENSWAY
RECLAMATION RD.
LINE WALL RD.
TOWN
IRISH
TUCK.
BELL
MAIN
ENGINEER LANE
CASTLE RD.
WILLIS'S RD.
COLL.
KING
CANNON
CORNWALL
SYNAGOGUE
MUSEUM
LIB.
GEO.
GOV. ST.
PRINCE EDWARD'S ROAD
FLAT BASTION RD.
STREET
TOWN RANGE
MAIN
P PARKING
50 YARDS
50 METERS
QUEENSWAY
QUEENSWAY QUAY & MARINA
CHARLES V WALL
SOUTHPORT GATE
TRAFALGAR CEMETERY
EUROPA RD.
DCH
BOYD
ROSIA
TO TOP OF THE ROCK
BOTANICAL GARDENS
CABLE CAR STATION
TO ST. MICHAEL'S CAVE

GIBRALTAR

EATING

Take a break from *jamón* and sample some English pub grub: fish-and-chips, meat pies, jacket potatoes (baked potatoes with fillings), or a good old greasy English breakfast. English-style beers include chilled lagers and room-temperature ales, bitters, and stouts. In general, the farther you venture away from Main Street, the cheaper and more local the places become.

The Clipper, my favorite pub for dinner, is friendly and offers filling £6 meals and Murphy's stout on tap (English breakfast-£5, Mon–Sat 9:00–22:00, Sun 10:00–22:00, on Irish Town Lane).

The Star Bar, which brags that it's "Gibraltar's Oldest Bar," is on a quiet street with a pubby interior and good £7 plates (daily 7:00–22:00, on Parliament Lane off Main Street, across from Corner House Restaurant).

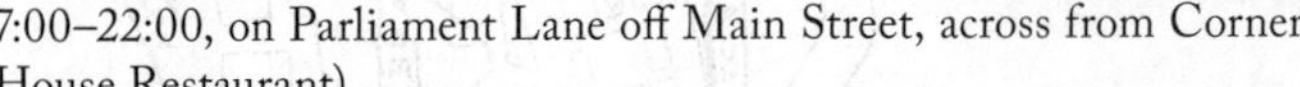

Carpenter's Arms is a fast, cheap-and-cheery café run by the Methodist church serving £3 meals with a missionary's smile. It's upstairs in the Methodist church on Main Street (Mon–Fri 9:00–14:00, closed Sat–Sun and Aug, volunteer-run, 100 yards past the Governor's Residence at 297 Main Street).

Queensway Quay Marina: To dine in yacht-club ambience, stroll the marina and choose from a string of restaurants serving the boat-owning crowd. When the sun sets, the quay-side tables at each of these places are prime dining real estate. **Waterfront Restaurant** has a lounge-lizard interior and great marina-side tables outside (£15 plates with daily specials, Indian, and classic British, daily 9:00–24:00, last orders 22:45, tel. 45666). **Claus on the Rock Bistro** has a colorful menu with dishes from around the world (£15 plates, closed Sun, tel. 48686). The marina promenade also has Italian and Indian restaurants.

Casemates Square Food Circus: The big square at the entrance of Gibraltar contains a variety of restaurants, ranging from fast food (fish-and-chips joint, Burger King, and Pizza Hut) to inviting pubs spilling out into the square. The **All's Well** pub serves £8 meals (Moroccan *tajine,* salads, burgers, fish-and-chips, and more) and offers pleasant tables with umbrellas under leafy trees (daily 9:30–19:00). Fruit stands and cheap take-away food stalls bustle just outside the entry to the square at the **Market Place** (Mon–Sat 9:00–15:00, closed Sun).

Groceries: An **In & Out** minimarket is on Main Street, off Cathedral Square (Mon–Fri 8:30–20:00, Sat 8:30–18:00, closed Sun). Nearby, **Marks & Spencer** has an inside take-away window that serves roast chicken and fresh-baked cookies (Mon–Sat 8:30–19:00, Sun 10:00–15:00).

TRANSPORTATION CONNECTIONS

Gibraltar is expanding its flight schedule. Currently there are daily Iberia Airlines flights to Madrid and about four British Air flights a day between London/Gatwick and Madrid. The discount airline Monarch flies to London's Luton Airport.

Bus travelers walk five minutes from Gibraltar's border into Spain to reach La Línea, the nearest bus station (tel. 902-199-208 or 956-172-396). The nearest train station is at Algeciras, which is the region's main transportation hub (for Algeciras connections, see page 617).

From La Línea by Bus to: Algeciras (2/hr, 45 min, can buy ticket on bus), **Tarifa** (8/day direct, 60 min), **Málaga** (4/day, 3 hrs), **Ronda** (no direct bus, transfer in Algeciras; Algeciras to Ronda: 6/day, 2 hrs), **Granada** (2/day, 5 hrs), **Sevilla** (4/day, 4 hrs), **Jerez** (2/day, 3 hrs), **Huelva** (1/day, 6 hrs), **Madrid** (2/day, 8 hrs).

Tarifa

Europe's southernmost town is whitewashed and Arab-looking, with a lovely beach, an old castle, restaurants swimming in fresh seafood, inexpensive places to sleep, enough windsurfers to sink a ship, and best of all, hassle-free boats to Morocco.

As I stood on Tarifa's town promenade under the castle, looking out at almost-touchable Morocco across the Strait of Gibraltar, I regretted only that I didn't have this book to steer me clear of gritty Algeciras on earlier trips. Tarifa, with daily 35-minute boat transfers to Tangier, is the best jumping-off point for a Moroccan side-trip.

Tarifa has no blockbuster sights (and can be quiet off-season), but it's a town where you just feel good to be on vacation. Given its lofty status as a breezy mecca among windsurfers, it's mobbed with young German and French adventure-seekers in July and August.

ORIENTATION

The old town, surrounded by a wall, slopes gently up from the water's edge. The modern section stretches farther inland from Tarifa's fortified gate.

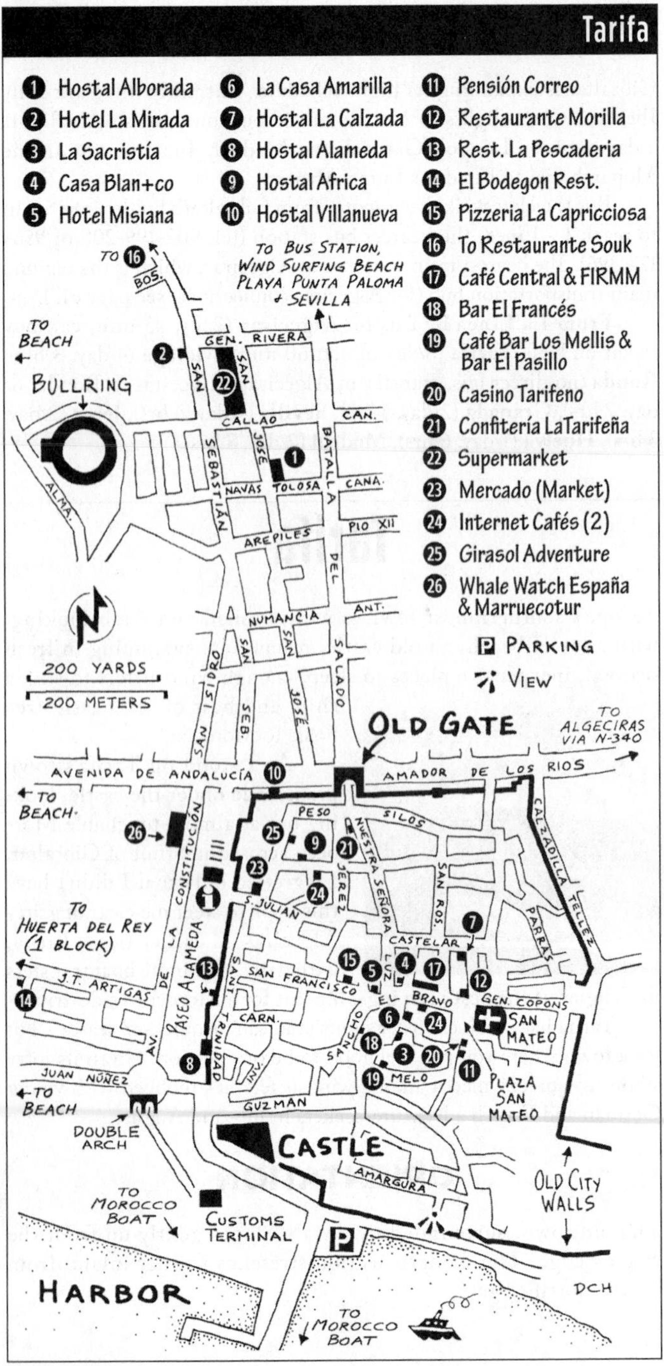

Tarifa

1 Hostal Alborada
2 Hotel La Mirada
3 La Sacristía
4 Casa Blan+co
5 Hotel Misiana
6 La Casa Amarilla
7 Hostal La Calzada
8 Hostal Alameda
9 Hostal Africa
10 Hostal Villanueva
11 Pensión Correo
12 Restaurante Morilla
13 Rest. La Pescaderia
14 El Bodegon Rest.
15 Pizzeria La Capricciosa
16 To Restaurante Souk
17 Café Central & FIRMM
18 Bar El Francés
19 Café Bar Los Mellis & Bar El Pasillo
20 Casino Tarifeno
21 Confitería La Tarifeña
22 Supermarket
23 Mercado (Market)
24 Internet Cafés (2)
25 Girasol Adventure
26 Whale Watch España & Marruecotur

P Parking
View

To 16
Bos.
To Bus Station, Wind Surfing Beach Playa Punta Paloma & Sevilla
To Beach
Bullring
Gen. Rivera
San
San
Callao
Can.
José
Batalla
Sebastián
Navas Tolosa
Cana.
Alma.
Pio XII
Arepiles
Del
Numancia
Ant.
San
San
Salado
San Isidro
Seb.
José
200 Yards
200 Meters
Old Gate
To Algeciras via N-340
Avenida de Andalucía
Amador de los Rios
To Beach
Peso
Silos
Nuestra Señora
Calzadilla
Tellez
San Ros.
Jerez
S. Julian
Parras
Constitución
To Huerta del Rey (1 block)
Castelar
Luz
Paseo Alameda
De la
Av.
J.T. Artigas
San Francisco
El Bravo
Gen. Copons
San Mateo
Carn.
Sancho
Santa Trinidad
IV
Melo
Plaza San Mateo
Juan Núñez
To Beach
Guzman
Double Arch
Castle
Amargura
Old City Walls
To Morocco Boat
Customs Terminal
Harbor
DCH
To Morocco Boat

Tourist Information

The TI is on Paseo de la Alameda (June–Sept daily 10:00–13:30 & 18:00–20:00; Oct–May Mon–Fri 10:00–13:30 & 16:00–18:00, Sat–Sun 10:00–14:00; hours may vary slightly on slow or bad-weather days, tel. 956-680-993, turismo@aytotarifa.com).

Arrival in Tarifa

By Bus: The bus station (actually a couple of portable buildings with an outdoor sitting area) is on Batalla del Salado, about a five-minute walk from the old town. (The more-central TI also has bus schedules.) Buy tickets directly from the driver if the ticket booth is closed (Mon–Fri 7:30–9:30 & 10:00–11:00 & 14:30–18:30, Sat–Sun 15:00–19:45, tel. 902-199-208). To reach the old town, walk away from the wind generators perched on the mountain ridge.

By Car: If you're staying in the center of town, follow signs for *Alameda* or *Puerto,* and continue along Avenida de Andalucía. Follow signs to make an obligatory loop to the port entrance, and park at Calle Juan Núñez (on the harbor, at the base of the castle, reasonable cost, generally a place available). Note that Avenida de la Constitución is one-way (going away from the port). There's plenty of free parking just outside Tarifa's old town walls. Blue lines indicate paid parking.

Helpful Hints

Internet Access: Pandor@, in the heart of the old town, is across from Café Central and near the church (long hours, 15 computers). **Evasión** is near the old-town gate (summer Mon–Sat 11:00–24:00, rest of year Mon–Sat 11:00–14:00 & 17:00–22:00, closed Sun, María Antonia Toledo 38).

Excursions: Girasol Adventure offers a variety of outdoor excursions, including mountain bike rentals (€18/day with helmet), guided bike tours, hikes in the national park, beginners' rock-climbing classes, and, when you're all done...a massage (€45/hr). The various activities generally last a half-day and cost around €25. Ask Sabine or Chris for details (Mon–Fri 10:15–14:00 & 18:30–20:30, Sat 11:00–14:00, closed Sun, Calle Colón 12, tel. 956-627-037, www.girasol-adventure.com).

SIGHTS AND ACTIVITIES

Church of St. Matthew (Iglesia de San Mateo)—Tarifa's most important church, facing its main drag, is richly decorated for being in such a small town. Most nights, it seems life squirts from the church out the front door and into the fun-loving Calle El Bravo. Wander inside (daily 9:00–13:00 & 17:30–20:30; there may be English-language leaflets inside on the right).

Find the fragment of an ancient tombstone—a tiny square

▲▲▲Side-Tripping to Morocco

For me, Tangier is the main reason to go to Tarifa. The fast, modern catamaran ride (a huge car ferry that zips over every two hours all year long) takes less than an hour. You walk from the Tangier port into a remarkable city—the fifth-largest in Morocco—which is no longer the Tijuana of Africa, but a booming town enjoying the enthusiastic support and can-do vision of a new and activist king.

Most tourists do the mindless belly-dancing-and-shopping excursion (which costs about €56—essentially the same as the €55 round-trip ferry ride). They're met by a guide, taken on a bus tour and a walk through the old town market, offered a couple of crass Kodak moments with snake charmers and desert dancers, and given lunch with live music and belly-dancing. Then they visit a big shop and are hustled back down to their boat where—five hours after they landed—they return to the First World thankful they don't have diarrhea.

The alternative is to simply take the ferry on your own and leave the tourist track. Things are cheap and relatively safe. Since more than 90 percent of visitors choose the comfort of a tour, independent adventurers rarely see another tourist and avoid all the kitsch. You can catch the first boat (9:00) and spend the entire day, returning that evening; extend with an overnight in Tangier; or even head deeper into Morocco.

If you're planning a day trip or an overnight stay, see the Tangier chapter for all the details. If you're going to stay longer in Morocco, you'll need the help of another guidebook.

(eye-level, about the size of this book) in the wall just before the transept on the right side. Probably the most important historical item in town, this stone fragment proves there was a functioning church here during Visigothic times, before the Moorish conquest. The tombstone reads, in a kind of Latin Spanish (try reading it), "Flaviano lived as a Christian for 50 years, a little more or less. In death he received forgiveness as a servant of God on March 30, 674. May he rest in peace." If that gets you in the mood to light a candle, switch on an electric "candle" by dropping in a coin. (It works.)

Step into the side chapel around the corner in the right transept. The centerpiece of the **altar** is a boy Jesus. By Andalusian tradition, he used to be naked, but these days he's clothed with outfits that vary with the Church calendar. Cherubs dance around on the pink-and-purple interior above an exquisite chandelier.

A statue of **St. James the Moor-Slayer** (missing his sword) is on the right wall of the main central altar. Since the days of the Reconquista, James has been Spain's patron saint. For more on this important figure—and why he's fighting invaders that came to Spain centuries after his death—see page 247.

The left side of the nave harbors several **statues**—showing typically over-the-top Baroque emotion—that are paraded through town during Holy Week. The **Captive Christ** (with hands bound, on left wall) evokes a time when Christians were held captive by Moors. The door on the left side of the nave is the **"door of pardons."** For a long time, Tarifa was a dangerous place—on the edge of the Reconquista. To encourage people to live here, the Church offered a second helping of forgiveness to anyone who lived in Tarifa for a year. One year and one day after moving to Tarifa, they would have the privilege of passing through this special "door of pardons," and a Mass of thanksgiving would be held in that person's honor.

Castle of Guzmán el Bueno—This castle is a concrete hulk in a vacant lot, interesting only for the harbor views from its ramparts (closed indefinitely for restoration). It was named after a 13th-century Christian general who gained fame in a sad show of courage while fighting the Moors. Holding Guzmán's son hostage, the Moors demanded he surrender the castle or they'd kill the boy. Guzmán refused, even throwing his own knife down from the ramparts. It was used on his son's throat. Ultimately, the Moors withdrew to Africa, and Guzmán was a hero. *Bueno* (when open: €1.20, Tue–Sat 11:00–14:00 & 18:00–20:00, Sun 11:00–14:00, closed Mon).

If you can't get into the castle, you'll get equally good views from the plaza just left of the town hall. Follow *ayto* signs to the ceramic frog fountain in front of the Casa Constitorial and continue left.

Bullfighting—Tarifa has a third-rate bullring where novices botch fights on occasional Saturdays through the summer. Professional bullfights take place the first week of September. The ring is a short walk from town. You'll see posters everywhere.

▲Whale-Watching—Daily whale- and dolphin-watching excursions are offered by several companies in Tarifa. In little more than 40 years, people in this area went from eating whales to protecting them and sharing them with 20,000 visitors a year. Talks are under way between Morocco and Spain to protect the Strait of Gibraltar by declaring it a national park.

For any of the tours, it's wise (but not always necessary) to reserve one to three days in advance. You'll get a multilingual tour and a two-hour boat trip (usually no WC on board). Sightings occur more than 90 percent of the time. Dolphins and pilot whales frolic here any time of year (they like the food), sperm whales visit May through July, and orcas pass through in July and August. In bad weather, boats may leave instead from Algeciras—drivers follow in a convoy, people without cars usually get rides from staff, and you'll stand a lesser chance of seeing whales.

The best company is the Swiss nonprofit **FIRMM** (Foundation for Information and Research on Marine Mammals), which gives a 25-minute educational talk before departure (€30/person, 1–5 trips/day April–Oct, sometimes also Nov, also offers courses, around the corner from Café Central—one door inland at Pedro Cortés 4, tel. 956-627-008, mobile 619-459-441, www.firmm.org, firmm98@aol.com). If you don't see any whales or dolphins on your tour, you can join another trip for free.

Another good option is **Whale Watch España** (Avenida de la Constitución 6, tel. 956-627-013, mobile 639-476-544, www.whalewatchtarifa.net, run by Lourdes and Flor).

▲▲Windsurfing—Tarifa's vast, sandy beach stretches west for about five miles. You can walk the beach from Tarifa or those with a car can explore farther (following Cadiz Road). On windy summer days, the sea is littered with sprinting windsurfers, while kitesurfers flutter in the sky. It's a fascinating scene: A long string of funky beach resorts is packed with vans and fun-mobiles from northern Europe under mountain ridges lined with modern energy-generating windmills. The various resorts each have a sandy access road, parking, a cabana-type hamlet with rental gear, beachwear shops, a bar, and a hip, healthy restaurant. I like Valdevaqueros beach (five miles from Tarifa), with a wonderful thatched restaurant serving hearty salads, paella, and burgers. Camping Torre de la Peña also has some fun beach eateries.

Camping—In July and August, inexpensive buses do a circuit of nearby campgrounds, all on the waterfront (€2, departures about every 2 hours, confirm times with TI). Trying to get a parking spot in August can take the joy out of this experience.

SLEEPING

Room rates vary with the season. For many hotels, I've listed the three seasonal tiers (highest prices—mid-June–Sept; medium prices—spring and fall; and lowest prices—winter).

Outside the City Wall

These hotels are about five blocks from the old town, right off the main drag, Batalla del Salado, in the plain, modern part of town. They are close to the beach and the bus station with free and easy street parking.

Sleep Code

(€1 = about $1.50, country code: 34)
S = Single, **D** = Double/Twin, **T** = Triple, **Q** = Quad, **b** = bathroom, **s** = shower only. Unless otherwise noted, credit cards are accepted and English is spoken. Breakfast and the 7 percent IVA tax are not included (unless noted).

To help you easily sort through these listings, I've divided the rooms into three categories, based on the price for a standard double room with bath during high season:

$$$ Higher Priced—Most rooms €100 or more.
$$ Moderately Priced—Most rooms between €50–100.
$ Lower Priced—Most rooms €50 or less.

$$ Hostal Alborada is a squeaky-clean, family-run, 37-room place with two attractive courtyards and modern conveniences. Carlos, Quino, and family offer a great Morocco ferry-booking service. Simply buy your ticket from them (same cost as buying direct), and they'll give you a free lift to the port (Sb-€35/45/60, Db-€48/60/75, Tb-€70/80/95, get your price and then show this book in 2009 for a 10 percent discount—*except* during high season, includes tax, breakfast-€2.50–5, air-con, Internet access and free Wi-Fi, laundry-€12, Calle San José 40, tel. 956-681-140, fax 956-681-935, www.hotelalborada.com, alborada@cherrytel.com).

$$ Hotel La Mirada has 25 recently renovated rooms, most with sea views at no extra cost (Sb-€45/50/60, Db-€60/75/90, breakfast-€3.60, includes tax, elevator, Wi-Fi, expansive sea views from large roof terrace with inviting lounge chairs, Calle San Sebastián 41, tel. 956-684-427, fax 956-681-162, www.hotel-lamirada.com, reservas@hotel-lamirada.com, Antonio and Salvador).

On or Inside the City Wall

$$$ La Sacristía, formerly a Moorish stable, now houses travelers who want stylish surroundings. It offers 10 fine rooms, each decorated differently: chic Spanish on the first floor, Asian-style on the second floor. They offer spa treatments, custom tours of the area, and occasional special events—partake in the party or you won't sleep (Db-€115, superior Db-€135, extra bed-€35, same prices all year, includes breakfast, fans, massage room, roof terrace, very central at San Donato 8, tel. 956-681-759, fax 956-685-182, www.lasacristia.net, tarifa@lasacristia.net, helpful Teresa).

$$$ Casa Blan+co, where minimalist meets Moroccan, is the newest reasonably priced designer hotel on the block. Each of its seven rooms is decorated (and priced) differently. The place is decked out with practical amenities (mini-fridge and stovetop) as well as romantic touches—loft beds, walk-in showers, and subtle lighting. The reception is 50 yards away at Hotel Misiana (Db-€59–134, includes tax and breakfast, small roof terrace, off main square at Calle Nuestra Señora de la Luz 2, tel. & fax 956-681-515, www.casablan-co.com, info@casablan-co.com).

$$$ Hotel Misiana has 13 comfortable, newly remodeled, spacious rooms. Their designer gave the place a mod, pastel, boutique-ish ambience (Sb-€40/60/75, Db-€70/90/120, fancy top-floor Db suite-€120/160/230, includes tax and breakfast, double-paned windows, elevator, 100 yards directly in front of the church at Calle Sancho IV El Bravo 18, tel. 956-627-083, fax 956-627-055, www.misiana.com, reservas@misiana.com).

$$ La Casa Amarilla ("The Yellow House") offers 10 posh apartments plus three regular rooms with modern decor and tiny kitchens (three Db-€43/63/80, larger apartment Db-€55/77/102, secure reservation with credit card, across street from Café Central, Calle Sancho IV El Bravo 9, tel. 956-681-993, fax 956-684-029, www.lacasaamarilla.net, info@lacasaamarilla.net).

$$ Hostal La Calzada has eight airy, well-appointed rooms right in the lively, old-town thick of things (Db-€50–80, extra bed-€10, includes tax, closed Nov–March, air-con, 20 yards from church at Calle Justino Pertinez 7, tel. 956-681-492, fax 956-680-366, www.hostallacalzada.com, Diego).

$$ Hostal Alameda, overlooking a square where the local children play, glistens with pristine marble floors and dark red decor. The main building has 11 bright rooms and the annex has 16 more-modern rooms; both face the same delightful square (Db-€60/70/90, extra bed-€20–30, can gouge in Aug, includes tax, air-con, Paseo de la Alameda 4, tel. 956-681-181, fax 956-680-264, www.hostalalameda.com, reservas@hostalalameda.com, Antonio).

$$ Hostal Africa, with 13 bright rooms and an inviting roof garden, is buried on a very quiet street in the center of town. Its dreamy blue-and-white color scheme and stripped-down feel give it a Moorish ambience (S-€20/25/35, Sb-€25/35/50, D-€30/40/50, Db-€35/50/65, Tb-€50/75/100, includes tax, laundry-€10, storage for boards and bikes, Calle María Antonia Toledo 12, tel. 956-680-220, mobile 606-914-294, hostal_africa@hotmail.com, Miguel and Eva keep the reception desk open only from 9:00–24:00).

$ Hostal Villanueva offers 12 remodeled rooms at budget prices. It's simple, clean, and friendly, and includes an inviting terrace that overlooks the old town. On a busy street, it's dominated by its restaurant, with no lounge or public area. Pepe asks that you reconfirm your reservation by phone the day before you arrive (Sb-€25–30, Db-€35–45, higher rates in July–Aug, includes tax, cash only, just west of the old-town gate at Avenida de Andalucía 11, access from outside the wall, tel. & fax 956-684-149).

$ Pensión Correo rents 12 simple rooms at a good value—especially Room 8, with its private roof terrace (S-€15–25, Db-€30–50, extra bed-€15–20, reservations accepted within 24 hours of arrival, roof garden, Coronel Moscardo 8, tel. 956-680-206, www.pensioncorreo.com, pensioncorreo@hotmail.com, María José and Lucca).

EATING

I've grouped my recommendations below into two categories: Sit down to a real restaurant meal, or enjoy a couple of the many characteristic tapas bars in the old town.

Restaurant Dining in Tarifa

Restaurante Morilla, facing the church and on the town's prime piece of people-watching real estate, serves tasty local-style fish—grilled or baked. This is a real restaurant (no tapas) with good indoor and outdoor seating. A list of the day's available fish is scribbled on a piece of paper that the waiter reviews with you; it's sold by weight, so confirm the price carefully (€12 fish plates, daily 13:00–23:00, Calle Sancho IV El Bravo, tel. 956-681-757).

Restaurant La Pescaderia is a thriving fish place with an inviting menu and great seating, both inside and on delightful Paseo de la Alameda. Their specialty is a paella-style rice and fish stew (€10–15 fish plates, daily 13:00–16:30 & 20:00–23:30, no reservations, tel. 956-627-078).

El Bodegon Restaurante is a neighborhood favorite, run by one big family (Antonio speaks English). With not a hint of tourism, it offers great fish and honest prices (€12 meals, Sun–Wed 12:00–16:30, Fri–Sat 12:00–16:30 & 20:00–24:00, closed Thu; from Paseo de la Alameda, head down Joaquin Tena Artigas two blocks to Bda. Huerta del Rey 23; tel. 956-680-911).

Pizzeria La Capricciosa, cozy and fun, is one of the numerous pizza-and-pasta joints supported by the large expat Italian community. It serves creative, hearty dinner salads and €8 pizzas and pastas under a wall full of Sergio's bike trophies (daily 20:00–24:00, July–Aug also open 13:00–16:00, at the beginning of Calle San Francisco, tel. 956-685-040).

Outside of Town

Restaurante Souk serves a tasty fusion of Moroccan, Indian, and Thai cuisine in a dark, exotic, and romantic ambience. This is a fine place to spend €20—if you don't mind a 10-minute walk out of town. Head up Calle San Sebastian until you see a big staircase on the right, which you'll take to Mar Tirreno 46 (daily 18:00–24:00, closed Tue in Sept–June, also closed in Feb, good wine list, tel. 956-627-065, friendly Patricia).

Tapas in Tarifa

Café Central is *the* happening place nearly any time of day—it's the perch for all the cool tourists. The tapas are priced at €1.20; just go to the bar and point. They also offer breakfast with eggs; great, ingenious €6 salads (study the menu); and impressively therapeutic, healthy fruit drinks (daily 9:00–24:00, off Plaza San Mateo, near church, tel. 956-680-560).

Bar El Francés is a thriving hole-in-the-wall where "Frenchies" (as the bar's name implies) Marcial and Alexandra serve tasty little plates of tapas. From Café Central, follow the cars 100 yards to the first corner on the left to reach this simple, untouristy, standing-and-stools-only eatery. This spot is popular for its fine *raciones* (€4–8) and tapas (generally €1.30)—especially oxtail *(rabo del toro),* pork with tomato sauce *(carne con tomate),* and pork with spice *(chicharrones).* The outdoor terrace with restaurant-type tables (no tapas served here) is an understandably popular spot to enjoy a casual meal (Mon–Fri open long hours, especially April–Sept; closed Sat–Sun and Jan; show this book and Marcial will be happy to bring you a free sherry, Calle Sancho IV El Bravo 21A).

Café Bar Los Mellis is a local favorite for feasts on rickety tables set on cobbles. This family-friendly place offers a good chorizo sandwich and *patatas bravas*—potatoes with a hot tomato sauce served on a wooden board (Thu–Tue 13:00–16:00 & 20:00–24:00, closed Wed, run by brothers José and Ramón; from Bar El Francés, cross parking lot and take Calle del Legionario Ríos Moya up 1 block). **Bar El Pasillo,** next to Los Mellis, also serves tapas (closed Mon).

Casino Tarifeno is just to the sea side of the church. It's an old-boys' social club "for members only," but it offers a musty Andalusian welcome to visiting tourists, including women. Wander through. There's a low-key bar with tapas, a TV room, a card room, and a lounge. There's no menu, but prices are standard. Just point and say the size you want: tapa, half-*ración,* or *ración.*

Dessert: **Confitería La Tarifeña** serves super pastries and flan (closed Mon, at the top of Calle Nuestra Señora de la Luz, near the main old-town gate).

Windsurfer Bars: If you have a car, head to the string of beaches. Many have bars and thatched fun-loving restaurants that keep the wet-suited gang fed and watered (see "Windsurfing" on page 612).

Picnics: Stop by the *mercado municipal* (farmers market, Mon–Sat 8:00–14:00, closed Sun, in old town, inside gate nearest TI), any grocery, or the **Eroski Center supermarket** (Mon–Sat 9:15–21:15, closed Sun, has simple cafeteria, near the hotels in the new town at Callao and San José).

TRANSPORTATION CONNECTIONS

Tarifa

From Tarifa by Bus to: La Línea/Gibraltar (6/day direct, 60 min; 10/day with transfer in Algeciras), **Algeciras** (10/day, 30 min, first departure from Tarifa weekdays at 6:30, on Sat 8:00, on Sun 10:00; return from Algeciras as late as 21:00), **Jerez** (2/day, 2 hrs, more frequent with transfer in Cádiz), **Sevilla** (4/day, 3 hrs), **Huelva** (for those Portugal-bound, 1/day, 5 hrs), and **Málaga** (2/day, 3.5 hrs). All bus service from Tarifa is by Comes (tel. 902-199-208, www.tgcomes.es).

Algeciras

Algeciras is only worth leaving. It's useful to the traveler mainly as a transportation hub, offering ferries to Tangier and trains and buses to destinations in southern and central Spain. The **TI** is on Juan de la Cierva, a block inland from the port. It's on the same street as both the train and bus station, which runs frequent service to Tarifa and La Línea.

Trains: The train station is four blocks inland, opposite Hotel Octavio (tel. 956-630-202). If arriving by train, head down San Bernardo toward the sea to Juan de la Cierva for the TI and port. As an alternative, you can also purchase ferry tickets at the train station branch of Viajes Algemar Travel (open daily, follows train schedules, tel. 956-657-311).

From Algeciras by Train to: Madrid (2/day, 6 hrs, arrives at Atocha), **Ronda** (6/day, 2 hrs), **Granada** (3/day, 4.25–5 hrs), **Sevilla** (3/day, 5 hrs, transfer at either Córdoba, Antequera, or Bobadilla), **Córdoba** (4/day, 4.5–5 hrs, transfer in Bobadilla), **Málaga** (4/day, 4 hrs, transfer in Bobadilla). With the exception of the route to Madrid, these are particularly scenic trips; the best is the mountainous journey to Málaga via Bobadilla.

Buses: Algeciras is served by three different bus companies (Comes, Portillo, and Linesur), all located in the same terminal next to Hotel Octavio and directly across from the train station. The companies generally serve different destinations, but there is some overlap. Compare schedules and rates to find the most convenient bus for you. By the ticket counter you'll find an easy red letter board listing departures. Lockers are by the platforms—purchase a token at the machines.

Comes (tel. 902-199-208, www.tgcomes.es) runs buses to **La Línea** (2/hr, 45 min, from 7:00–22:30), **Tarifa** (10/day, 30 min), **Sevilla** (4/day, 3.5 hrs), **Jerez** (2/day, 2.5 hrs), **Huelva** (1/day, 6 hrs), and **Madrid** (4/day, 8 hrs).

Portillo (tel. 956-654-304, www.ctsa-portillo.com) offers buses to **Málaga** (17/day, 1.75 hrs *directo*, 3 hrs *ruta*, some buses run by Alsina Graells) and **Granada** (5/day, 4–5.5 hrs).

Linesur (tel. 956-667-649, www.linesur.com) runs the most

frequent direct buses to **Sevilla** (11/day, 2 direct, fewer on weekends, 2.25–2.5 hrs) and **Jerez** (9/day, 2.5 hrs).

Ferries from Algeciras to Tangier, Morocco: If you plan to sail from Algeciras, buy your ticket at the port instead of one of the many divey-looking travel agencies littering the town. To find the ticket office, go to the farthest building at the port, which is labeled in large letters: *Estación Marítima Terminal de Pasajeros* (luggage storage available here, easy parking at port-€6). The official offices of the seven boat companies are inside this main port building, directly behind the helpful little English-speaking info kiosk (8–22 ferries/day, port open daily 6:45–21:45, tel. 956-585-463).

Route Tips for Drivers

Tarifa to Gibraltar (45 min): This short drive takes you past a silvery-white forest of windmills, from peaceful Tarifa past Algeciras to La Línea (the Spanish town bordering Gibraltar). Passing Algeciras, continue in the direction of Estepona. At San Roque, take the La Línea–Gibraltar exit.

Gibraltar to Nerja (130 miles): Barring traffic problems, the trip along the Costa del Sol is smooth and easy by car—much of it on a new highway. Just follow the coastal highway east. After Málaga, follow signs to *Almería* and *Motril*.

Nerja to Granada (80 miles, 1.5 hrs, 100 views): Drive along the coast to Motril, catching N-323 north for about 40 miles to Granada. While scenic side-trips may beckon, don't arrive late in Granada without a confirmed hotel reservation.

MOROCCO

MOROCCO

Al-Maghreb

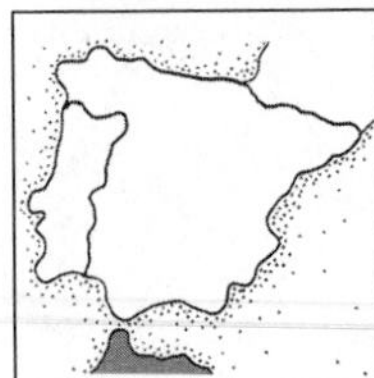

A young country with an old history, Morocco is a photographer's delight and a budget traveler's dream. It's cheap, exotic, and easier and more appealing than ever. Along with a rich culture, Morocco offers plenty of contrast—from beach resorts to bustling desert markets, from jagged mountains to sleepy, mud-brick oasis towns. And there's a distinct new energy as its popular activist king asserts his vision.

Morocco (*Marruecos* in Spanish; *Al-Maghreb* in Arabic) also provides a good dose of culture shock—both bad and good. It makes Spain and Portugal look meek and mild. You'll encounter oppressive friendliness, brutal heat, the Arabic language, the Islamic faith, ancient cities, and aggressive beggars.

While Morocco is clearly a place apart from Mediterranean Europe, it doesn't really seem like Africa either. It's a mix, reflecting its strategic position between the two continents. Situated on the Strait of Gibraltar, Morocco has been flooded by waves of invasions over the centuries. The Berbers, the native population, have had to contend with the Phoenicians, Carthaginians, Romans, Vandals, and more.

The Arabs brought Islam to Morocco in the seventh century A.D. and stuck around, battling the Berbers in various civil wars. A series of Berber and Arab dynasties rose and fell; the Berbers won out and still run the country today.

From the 15th century on, European countries carved up much of Africa. By the early 20th century, most of Morocco was under French control, and the country wasn't granted independence until 1956. In the late 1970s, Morocco itself became an invading country, grabbing Spain's Western Sahara territory and causing the relatively few inhabitants to clamor for independence. Western Sahara's claim still has not been settled by the United Nations.

Unfortunately, most of the English-speaking Moroccans whom the typical tourist meets are

hustlers. Most visitors develop some intestinal problems by the end of their visit. Most women are harassed on the streets by horny but generally harmless men. Things don't work smoothly. In fact, compared to Morocco, Spain resembles Sweden in terms of efficiency.

When you cruise south across the Strait of Gibraltar, leave your busy itineraries and split-second timing behind. Morocco must be taken on its own terms. In Morocco things go smoothly only *"Inshallah"*—if God so wills.

Helpful Hints

Politics: Americans pondering a visit understandably wonder how they'll be received in this Muslim nation. Al Jazeera blares from televisions in all the bars—with graphic anti–Iraq war video clips demonizing the American war effort. Regardless, I saw no angry graffiti or posters and felt no animosity towards American individuals there. Western visitors feel a warm welcome in post-9/11 Morocco. And it's culturally enriching for Westerners to experience Morocco—a Muslim monarchy with women still in traditional dress and roles, succeeding on its own terms without embracing American "norms."

Hustler Alert: While Moroccans are some of Africa's wealthiest people, you are still incredibly rich to them. This imbalance causes predictable problems. Wear your money belt. Assume con artists are more clever than you. Haggle when appropriate (prices skyrocket for tourists). You'll attract hustlers like flies at every famous tourist sight. In the worst-case scenario, they'll lie to you, get you lost, blackmail you, and pester the heck out of you. Never leave your car or baggage where you can't get back to it without someone else's "help." Anything you buy in a guide's company gets him a 20 percent commission. Normally locals, shopkeepers, and police will come to your rescue if the hustlers' heat becomes unbearable. Consider hiring a guide, since it's helpful to have a translator, and once you're "taken," the rest seem to leave you alone.

Marijuana Alert: In Morocco, marijuana *(kif)* is as illegal as it is popular, a fact that many Westerners in local jails would love to remind you of. As a general rule, just walk right by those hand-carved pipes in the marketplace. Some dealers who sell it cheap make their profit after you get arrested. Cars and buses are stopped and checked by police routinely throughout Morocco—especially in the north and in the Chefchaouen region, which is Morocco's *kif* capital.

Health: Morocco is much more hazardous to your health than Spain or Portugal. Eat in clean—not cheap—places. Peel fruit, eat only cooked vegetables, and drink reliably bottled water (Sidi Harazem or Sidi Ali). When you do get diarrhea—and you should plan on it—adjust your diet (small and bland meals, no milk or grease) or fast for a day, but make sure you replenish lost fluids. Relax: Most diarrhea is not serious, just an adjustment that will run its course.

Closed Days: Friday is the Muslim day of rest, when most of the country (except Tangier) closes down.

Ramadan: During this major, month-long religious holiday (Aug 21–Sept 20 in 2009), Muslims focus on prayer and reflection. Following Islamic doctrine, they refrain during daylight hours from eating, drinking (including water), smoking, and having sex. On the final day of Ramadan, Muslims celebrate *Eid* (an all-day feast and gift-giving party, similar to Christmas) and travelers may find some less-touristy stores and restaurants closed.

Money: Euros work here (as do dollars and pounds). If you're on a five-hour tour, bring along lots of €1 and €0.50 coins for tips, small purchases, and camel rides. But if you plan to do anything independently, change some money into Moroccan dirhams upon arrival (8 Moroccan dirhams = about $1). Banks and ATMs have uniform rates. If you use an exchange desk, just be sure you can see the buying and selling rates; they should be within 10 percent of each other with no extra fees. Don't leave the country with Moroccan money unless you want a souvenir, since few places in Spain are willing to change dirhams to euros or dollars.

Information: Travel information, English or otherwise, is rare here. For an extended trip, bring guidebooks from home or Spain. Lonely Planet and Rough Guide both publish good ones, and the green Michelin *Morocco* guidebook is worthwhile (if you read French). Buy the best map you can find locally—names are always changing, and it's helpful to have towns, roads, and place names written in Arabic.

Language: It's unusual to be in a country where a trilingual sign or menu doesn't include English. English ranks fourth here after Arabic, French, and Spanish. The Arabic squiggle-script, its many difficult sounds, and the fact that French is Morocco's second language combine to make communication tricky for English-speaking travelers. A little French goes a long way, but learn a few words in Arabic. Have your first local friend help you with the pronunciation:

English	Arabic	Pronounced
Hello. ("Peace be with you")	*Salaam alaikum.*	sah-LAHM ah-LAY-koom
Hello. (response: "Peace also be with you")	*Wa alaikum salaam.*	wah ah-LAY-koom sah-LAHM
Please.	*Min fadlik.*	meen FAHD-leek
Thank you. (like "sugar on")	*Shokran.*	SHOH-kron
Excuse me.	*Ismahli.*	ees-SMAH-lee
Yes.	*Yeh.*	EE-yeh
No.	*Lah.*	lah
Give me five. (kids like this…not above but straight ahead)	*Ham sah.*	hahm sah
OK.	*Wah hah.*	wah hah
Very good.	*Miz yen biz ef.*	meez EE-yehn beez ehf
Goodbye.	*Maa salama.*	mah sah-LEM-ah

Moroccans are more touchy-feely than their Spanish neighbors. Expect lots of hugs if you make an effort to communicate. When greeting someone, a handshake is customary, followed by a fist over your heart. Listen carefully and write new words phonetically. Bring an Arabic phrase book. In markets, I sing, "la la la la la" to my opponents. *Lah shokran* means, "No, thank you."

Getting Around Morocco: Moroccan trains are quite good. Second class is cheap and comfortable. Buses connect all smaller towns quite well. By car, Morocco is easy, but drive defensively and never rely on the oncoming driver's skill. Night driving is dangerous. Pay a guard to watch your car overnight.

Keeping Your Bearings: Navigate the labyrinthine *medinas* (old towns) by altitude, gates, and famous mosques or buildings. Write down what gate you came in, so you can enjoy being lost—temporarily. *Souk* is Arabic for a particular market (such as leather, yarn, or metalwork).

TANGIER

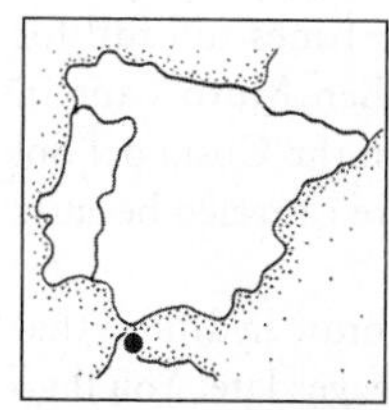

Go to Africa. As you step off the boat, you realize that the crossing (less than an hour) has taken you further culturally than did the trip from the US to Spain. Morocco needs no museums; its sights are living in the streets. For decades, its coastal city of Tangier deserved its image as the "Tijuana of Africa." But that has changed. The new king is enthusiastic about Tangier, and there's a fresh can-do spirit in the air. The town is as Moroccan as ever...yet more enjoyable and less stressful.

Morocco in a Day?

While Morocco certainly deserves more than a day, many visitors touring Spain see it in a quick side-trip. And, though such a short sprint through Tangier is only a tease, it's far more interesting than another day in Spain. A day in Tangier gives you a good introduction to Morocco, a legitimate taste of North Africa, and a non-threatening slice of Islam. All you need is a passport (no visa or shots required) and €55 for the round-trip ferry crossing. Your big decisions: where to sail from; whether to go on your own or buy a ferry/guided tour day-trip package; and whether to make it a day trip or spend the night.

Time Difference: Morocco is on Greenwich Mean Time (like Great Britain), and does not observe Daylight Savings Time. This means it's two hours behind Spain in summer, and one hour behind in winter.

Terminology: Note that the Spanish refer to Morocco as "Marruecos" (mar-WAY-kohs) and Tangier as "Tanger" (pronounced with a guttural "g" at the back of the throat, sounding like TAHN-hair).

Going on Your Own, by Ferry from Tarifa

While the trip from Spain to Tangier can be made from three different ports (Tarifa, Algeciras, or Gibraltar), it's easiest, fastest, and cheapest from Tarifa. I'll describe the trip assuming you're sailing from Tarifa, which is most logical for the typical traveler.

Ferry Crossing: Just buy a ferry ticket (at the port, through your Tarifa hotel, or from a local travel agency). There is only one ferry company (FRS), and prices should be the same everywhere (€31 one-way, €55 round-trip). The ferry departs daily from Tarifa to Tangier at 9:00, 11:00, 13:00, 15:00, 17:00, 19:00, 21:00, and 23:00; and from Tangier to Tarifa at 7:00, 9:00, 11:00, 13:00, 15:00, 17:00, 19:00, and 21:00. Because of its popularity with tours, the 9:00 ferry in July and August is sometimes too full for walk-ons. Boats are most crowded in July (when Moroccans in Spain go home for holiday), and in August (when the Costa del Sol groups come en masse). A few crossings a year are canceled because of storms, mostly in winter.

Procedure: The ferry from Tarifa is a fast Nordic hydrofoil that theoretically takes 35 minutes to cross. It often leaves late. You'll go through Spanish customs at the port and Moroccan customs on the ferry. Whether taking a tour or traveling on your own, you *must* get a stamp (available on board) from the Moroccan immigration officer. After you leave Spain, find the customs desk on the boat, line up, and get your passport and entry paper stamped. If you're coming back the same day and know your return time, the immigration official will also give you an exit stamp (for your return from Morocco)—this prevents delays at the port at departure time. (If your return is open, you will have to go through a passport check and get your exit stamp on the way back to Spain.) The ferry is equipped with WCs, a shop, and a snack bar. Tarifa's modern little terminal has a cafeteria and WCs.

Hiring a Guide: Even if you're visiting Morocco independently, I recommend hiring a local guide to show you around Tangier (for tips, see "Guides," page 633).

Taking a Tour

Taking a tour is easier but less rewarding than doing it on your own. A typical day-trip tour includes a round-trip crossing and a guide who meets you at a prearranged point in Tangier, then hustles you through the hustlers and onto your tour bus. Several guides await the arrival of each ferry in Tangier and assemble their groups. (Tourists wear stickers identifying which tour they're with.) All offer essentially the same five-hour Tangier experience: a city bus tour, possibly a trip to the desolate Atlantic Coast for some rugged African scenery, the famous ride-a-camel stop (five-minute camel ride for a couple of euros), a drive through the ritzy palace neighborhood, a walk through the medina (old town), and a too-thorough look at a sales-starved carpet shop (where prices include a roughly 20 percent commission for your guide and tour company). The tour wraps up with lunch in a palatial Moroccan setting with live music (and non-Moroccan belly dancing), topped off by a final walk back to your boat through a gauntlet of desperate merchants.

Sound cheesy? It is. But no amount of packaging can gloss over this exotic and different culture. This kind of cultural voyeurism is almost embarrassing, but it's nonstop action. The shopping is... Moroccan. Bargain hard!

The day trip is so tightly organized that tourists have hardly any time alone in Tangier. For many people, that's just fine. But frankly, seeing a line of day-trippers clutching their bags nervously like paranoid kangaroos reminded me of the Tehran hostage crisis—the big difference being this one is self-imposed. It was pathetic.

You rarely need to book a tour more than a day in advance, even during peak season. Tours generally cost about €56, roughly the same price as a ferry ticket alone—the tour company makes its money off commissions if you shop, and gets a group rate on the ferry tickets. Prices are roughly the same at the various travel agencies. I wouldn't worry about which tour company you select. (They're all equally bad.)

Tours generally leave Tarifa on the 9:00 ferry and return at 13:00 (15:00 Spanish time), or they depart on the 13:00 ferry and return at 17:00 (19:00 Spanish time).

Those taking the tour have an option to spend the night at a fancy Tangier hotel (about €35 extra, includes dinner). If you stay overnight, the first day is the same as the one-day tour, but rather than catching the boat that afternoon, you take the same boat—on your own—24 hours later.

Independent types can also take the one-day tour (you'll need to stay with your group until you return to the ferry dock) and then just slip back into town thinking, "Freedom!" You're welcome to use your return ferry ticket on any later boat (departures every two hours).

Travel Agencies Offering Tours: Travel agencies throughout southern Spain sell Tangier ferry and ferry/tour tickets. Here are two in Tarifa: Marruecotur (daily in summer 7:40–21:00, across from the TI at Avenida de la Constitución 5, tel. 956-681-242) and Speedlines Tours (Batalla del Salado 10, tel. 956-627-048, www.speedlinestours.com). Many hotels are happy to book a ticket for you (ask when you reserve). If they offer this service, I'd take it.

You can also just drop by the port in Tarifa and buy your ticket directly from the ferry company (FRS Maroc at Tarifa's dock, tel.

956-681-830, www.frs.es). FRS also offers a **"VIP tour"** for up to four people. For an additional €60 (after buying individual ferry tickets), your group receives a private guide and vehicle, plus lunch. This is actually quite economical if you're traveling as a foursome.

Tangier

Artists, writers, and musicians have always loved Tangier. Matisse was drawn to the evocative light. The Beat generation, led by William S. Burroughs and Jack Kerouac, sought the city's multicultural, otherworldly feel. Paul Bowles found his sheltering sky here. From the 1920s through the 1950s, Tangier was an "international city," too strategic to give to any one nation, and jointly governed by France, Spain, Britain, and Italy. It attracted playboy millionaires, bon vivants, globetrotting scoundrels, con artists, and expat romantics.

Tangier is always defying expectations. Ruled by Spain in the 19th century and France in the 20th, it's a rare place, where signs are in three languages...and English doesn't make the cut. In this Muslim city, you'll find a synagogue, Catholic and Anglican churches, and the town's largest mosque within close proximity.

Because of its "international zone" status, Morocco's previous king neglected the city, denying it national funds for improvements. Neglected Tangier became the armpit of Morocco. But when the new king—Mohammed VI—was crowned in 1999, the first city he visited was Tangier. His vision is to restore Tangier to its former glory.

Thanks to King Mohammed VI, Tangier (with a population of 700,000 and growing) is experiencing a rebirth. Restorations are taking place on a grand scale: The beach has been painstakingly cleaned, pedestrian promenades are popping up everywhere, and gardens bloom with lush new greenery. In the works are a new soccer stadium and a project to move the shipping port beyond the bay where the ferry docks are (which will clear current traffic congestion and make Tangier's ferry terminal much more welcoming).

I'm uplifted by the new Tangier because it's affluent and modern without having abandoned its roots and embraced Western values. A visit here lets a Westerner marinated in anti-Muslim propaganda see what Islam aspires to be, and can be—and realize it is not a threat.

Planning Your Time

If you're on your own, either hire a guide upon arrival (see "Guides," later in this chapter), or stop by the TI first thing to get oriented (you can walk or catch a Petit Taxi from the port to the TI). Exit the TI to the right and continue up to Place de Faro, with its cannons and views back to Spain. Beyond that, at the Place de France (at Café du Paris), turn right on Rue de la Liberté, which leads directly into the Grand Socco square, the hub of old Tangier. Orient from here with the map on page 635. For the quickest visit, first cover the old town (Museum of the Kasbah, Dar el-Makhzen palace, Old American Legation Museum, and Petit Socco). Then catch a taxi to the beach (Plage de Corniche), and sightsee along the beach and then along Avenue Mohammed VI back to the port. You'll rarely see other tourists outside the tour-group circuit.

After Dark: Nighttime is great in Tangier. If spending the night, don't relax in a fancy hotel restaurant. Get out and about in the old town after dark. It's an entirely different experience and a highlight of any visit.

ORIENTATION

Like almost every city in Morocco, Tangier is split in two. From the ferry dock, you'll see the old town (medina)—encircled by its medieval wall—on your right, behind Hotel Continental. The old town has the markets, the Kasbah (with its palace and the mosque of the Kasbah—marked by the higher of the two minarets you see), cheap hotels, homes both decrepit and recently renovated, and 2,000 wannabe guides. The twisty, hilly streets of the old town are caged within a wall accessible by keyhole gates. The larger minaret (on the left) belongs to the modern Mohammed V mosque—the biggest one in town.

The new town, where the TI and fancy hotels reside, sprawls past the industrial port zone to your left. The big square, Grand Socco, is the link between the old and new parts of town.

Because Tangier is the fifth-largest city in Morocco, many assume they'll get lost here. Although the city could use more street signs, it's laid out simply. Nothing listed under "Sights" (page 634) is more than a 15-minute walk from the port. Petit Taxis (described under "Getting Around Tangier," below) are a godsend for the hot and tired tourist. Use them liberally.

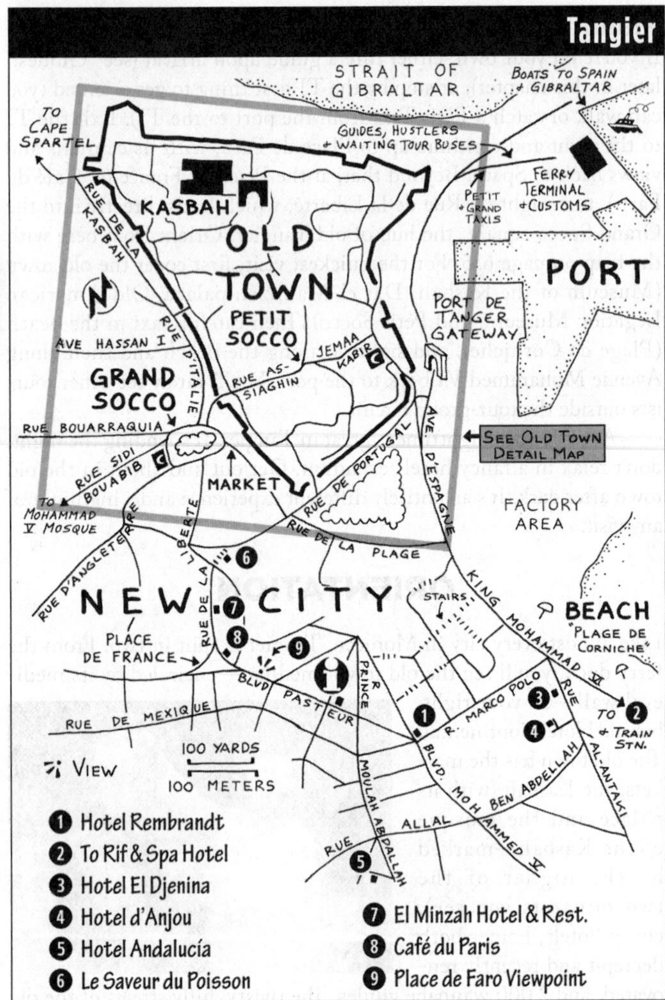

Tourist Information

Get a free map and advice at the TI. A little bit of French goes a long way here (Mon–Fri 9:00–16:30, closed Sat–Sun, in new town at Boulevard Pasteur 29, tel. 94-80-50). They try to have a few guides standing by in the morning when boats arrive.

Arrival in Tangier

If you're taking a tour, just follow the leader.

Independent travelers will walk five minutes from the ferry past trucks and warehouses (follow signs to *sortie*), and through the gate at the end of the port. Change money at any little exchange desk (those at the gate are good—they have a straight and fair buy-and-sell rate and are open long hours).

The big Port de Tanger gateway (a few hundred yards from the ferry dock) defines the end of the port area and the start of the city. Leave mental breadcrumbs, so you can find your way back to your boat. Your first glimpse of the city will be a line of decent fish restaurants; restored French colonial buildings; and a fancy, palm-tree–lined pedestrian boulevard arcing along the beach into the new town. From this delightful square, stairs (on the right) lead up into the old town and the market.

A Petit Taxi is your easiest way into town (described under "Getting Around Tangier," next); unfortunately, prices are not regulated from the port. An honest cabbie will charge you 10 dirhams (about $1.25) for a ride from the ferry into town, while less scrupulous drivers will try to charge closer to 100 dirhams. Set your price before hopping in.

Getting Around Tangier

There are two types of taxis: Avoid the big, beige Mercedes "Grand Taxis," which are most aggressive and don't use their meters. Look instead for Petit Taxis—blue with a yellow stripe (they fit up to three people). These generally use their meters, are very cheap, and only circulate within the city. However, at the port, Petit Taxis are allowed to charge whatever you'll pay without using the meter, so it's essential to agree on a price up front (should be around 10 dirhams into town).

Helpful Hints

Money: The exchange rate is 8 dirhams = about $1; 12 dirhams = about €1. The most convenient banks with ATMs are opposite the TI along Boulevard Pasteur. There are also several in the Grand Socco. While most businesses happily take euros or dollars, it's classier to use the local currency—and you'll save money. If you're on a tour, they'll rip you off anyway, so just stick with euros. If you're on your own, it's fun to get a pocket full of dirhams. ATMs work as you expect them to. Exchange desks are quick, easy, and fair. (Just understand the buy and sell rates—there should be no other fee. If you change €50 into dirhams and immediately change the dirhams back, you should have about €45.) Convert your dirhams back to euros before catching the ferry—it's cheap and easy to do here (change desks at the port keep long hours), but very difficult once you're back in Spain.

Telephone: To call Tangier from Spain, dial 00 (international access code), 212 (Morocco's country code), 5 (for land lines) or 6 (for cell phones), 39 (Tangier's city code), then the local six-digit number.

Navigation: Tangier's maps and street signs are frustrating. I ask in French for the landmark: *"oo ay Medina?"*, *"oo ay Kasbah*?", and so

Women in Morocco

Most visitors to Tangier expect to see the women completely covered head-to-toe by their kaftan. In fact, only about one-quarter of Moroccan women still adhere strictly to this religious code. Some just cover their head (allowing their face to be seen), while others eliminate the head scarf altogether. Some women wear only Western-style clothing. This change in dress visibly reflects deeper, more fundamental shifts in women's rights.

Morocco happens to be one of the most progressive Muslim countries around. As in any border country, contact with other cultures fosters the growth of new ideas. Bombarded with Spanish television and visitors like you, change is inevitable. Another proponent of change is King Mohammed VI, who was only 35 years old when he rose to the throne in 1999. For the first time in the country's history, the king personally selected a female advisor to demonstrate his commitment to change. The king also married a commoner for...get this...*love*. And even more shocking, she's seen in public. (It's a first—locals don't even know what King Mohammed VI's mother looks like, as she is never in the public view.)

Recent times have brought even more sweeping transformations to Moroccan society. In order to raise literacy levels and understanding between the sexes, schools are now co-ed—something taken for granted in the West for decades. In 2004 the Mudawana, or judiciary family code, was shockingly overhauled. The legal age for women to marry is now 18 (just like men) instead of 15. Other changes make it more difficult to have a second wife. Verbal divorce and abandonment are no longer legal—disgruntled husbands must now take their complaints to court before divorce is granted. And for the first time, women can divorce their husbands. If children are involved, whoever takes care of the kids gets the house. Of course, not everyone has been happy with the changes, and Islamic fundamentalists were blamed for a series of bombings in Casablanca in 2003. But the reforms became law, and Morocco became a trendsetter for women's equality in the Islamic world.

on. Ask for directions from people who can't leave what they're doing (such as the only clerk in a shop) or from women who aren't near men. There are fewer hustlers in the new (but less interesting) part of town. It's fun to meet people this way. In case you get the wrong directions, ask three times and go with the consensus.

Mosques: Mosques are not open to non-Muslim visitors in Tangier (unlike mosques in some other Muslim cities).

Guides

If you're on your own, you'll be to street guides what a horse's tail is to flies...all day. In order to have your own translator and a shield from less scrupulous touts who hit up tourists constantly throughout the old town, I recommend hiring a guide. Stress your interest in the people and culture rather than shopping. Guides, hoping to get a huge commission from your purchases, can cleverly turn your Tangier day into the equivalent of the Shopping Channel. Truth be told, some of these guides would work for free, considering all the money they make on commissions when you buy stuff.

That said, I've had good luck with the private guides who meet the boat. If you are a decent judge of character, interview guides when you get off the ferry, find one you click with, and negotiate a good price. These hardworking, English-speaking, and licensed guides offer their services for the day for €15.

To avoid the stress of being mobbed by potential guides at the port, book one before you arrive, and arrange for the guide to meet you at the port (through FRS in Tarifa, or through the guides' association—tel. 93-13-72, dttanger@menara.com). Once in town, the TI (tel. 94-80-50) can often set you up with a guide.

Aziz Begdouri is a great local guide who will show you the very best of his hometown. He enjoys teaching about Moroccan society and culture. Aziz can also arrange ferry tickets from Tarifa in advance. He meets you at the boat (5-hour walking tour-€15 per person, groups limited to 4–5 people; 8-hour grand tour with minibus ride to resorts, the Caves of Hercules, and Cape Spartel-€35 per person; easier to reach him from Spain on his Spanish mobile—tel. 607-897-967—than his Moroccan mobile, tel. 00-212-61-63-93-32, aziztour@hotmail.com). Aziz is a friend. Even if you're not hiring him, give him a call if you're in a jam.

SIGHTS

▲▲Grand Socco—This big, noisy square is a transportation hub, market, and gateway to the medina (old town). Five years ago, it was a pedestrian nightmare and a perpetual traffic jam. Use the map to orient yourself from here, as this is the center of the visitor's Tangier. On the downhill side, a fancy gate leads into the medina. An incredible market is opposite the mosque.

Anglican Church—St. Andres Anglican Church was built in a Moorish style, but is still Christian. The Lord's Prayer rings the arch in Arabic, as verses of the Quran would in a mosque. The land on which the church sits was a gift from the sultan to the British community in 1881, during Queen Victoria's era. The church was built shortly thereafter. Knock on the door—Mustapha will greet you and give you a "thank you very munch" tour. Leave a donation in the church's alms box.

The Medina and Petit Socco—A maze of winding lanes and tiny alleys weave through the old-town market area. Petit Socco, a little square (souk) in the old town, is lined with tea shops. A casual first-time visitor cannot stay oriented. I just wander, knowing that uphill will eventually get me to the Kasbah and downhill will eventually lead me to the port. Expect to get a little lost... going around in circles is part of the fun. Pop in to see artisans working in their shops: mosaic tile-makers, thread spinners, tailors. Many people can't afford private ovens, phones, or running water, so there are economical communal options: phone desks, baths, and bakeries. Notice locals dropping off their ready-to-cook flour at bakeries. Ornate "keyhole" doors lead to neighborhood mosques. Green doors are the color of Islam and symbolize peace. The Petit Socco is a people- (and now tourist-) friendly little square, great for a mint tea and some casual people-watching.

The **Market,** just off the Grand Socco, is a highlight. Wander past piles of fruit, veggies, and olives, countless varieties of bread, and fresh goat cheese wrapped in palm leaves. Phew! Venturing right, you'll eventually come to less perishable (and less aromatic) items—clothing, recordable CDs, and lots of electronics. You'll find everything but pork. The chickens are plucked and hung to show they

Tangier's Old Town

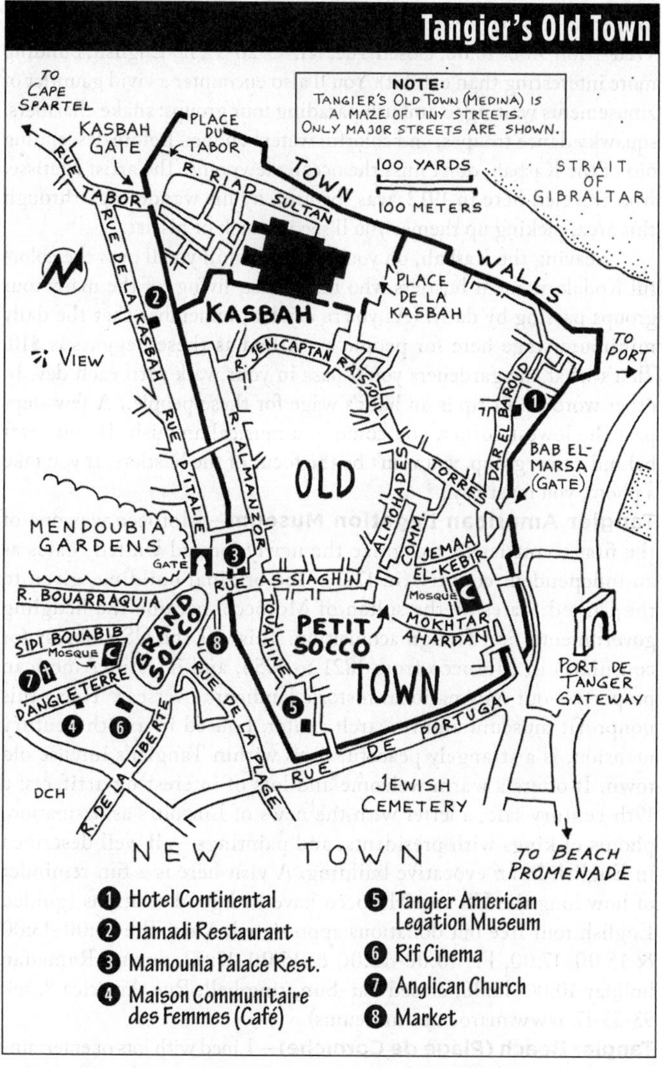

have been killed according to Islamic guidelines (Halal): Animals are slaughtered with a sharp knife in the name of Allah, head to Mecca, and drained of their blood.

• *When you've soaked in enough old-town atmosphere, make your way to the Kasbah (see map). Within the medina, head uphill, or exit the medina gate and go right on Rue de la Kasbah, which follows the old wall uphill to Porte de la Kasbah, a gateway into the Kasbah.*

Kasbah—This is the fortress (now a residential area) atop old Tangier. On Place de la Kasbah, you'll find the Dar el-Makhzen, a former sultan's palace that now houses a history museum (10 dirhams, Wed–Mon 9:00–16:00, closed Tue, tel. 93-20-97, no English, building more interesting than exhibit). You'll also encounter a vivid gauntlet of amusements waiting to ambush parading tour groups: snake charmers, squawky dance troupes, and colorful water vendors. Before descending out of the Kasbah, don't miss the ocean viewpoint. The artist Matisse, who traveled here in 1912, was inspired by his wanderings through this area, picking up themes you'll see in much of his art.

Leaving the Kasbah, on your way downhill you'll pass the colorful Kodak-moment hustlers who make their living off the many tour groups passing by daily. (As you're cajoled, remember that the daily minimum wage here for people as skilled as these beggars is $10. That's what the gardeners you'll pass in your walk earn each day. In other words, a €1 tip is an hour's wage for these people.) A few steps past the lowest corner, you come to a musical ambush. If you draft behind a tour group, you won't be the focus of the hustlers. If you take a photo, you must pay.

Tangier American Legation Museum—Morocco was one of the first countries to recognize the newly formed United States as an independent country (in 1777). The original building, given to the United States by the sultan of Morocco, became the fledgling government's first foreign acquisition. This was the US embassy (or consulate) in Morocco from 1821 to 1956, and it's still American property—our only national historic landmark overseas. Today this nonprofit museum and research center, housed in a 19th-century mansion, is a strangely peaceful oasis within Tangier's intense old town. It offers a warm welcome and lots of interesting artifacts: a 19th-century safe, a letter with the news of Lincoln's assassination, photos of kings with presidents, and paintings—all well described in English in an evocative building. A visit here is a fun reminder of how long the US and Morocco have had good relations (guided English tour free but donations appreciated, Mon–Thu 10:00–13:00 & 15:00–17:00, Fri 10:00–12:00 & 15:00–17:00, during Ramadan holiday 10:00–15:00, closed Sat–Sun, ring bell, Rue America 8, tel. 93-53-17, www.maroc.net/museums).

Tangier Beach (Plage de Corniche)—Lined with lots of entertaining and fishy eateries, this fine, wide, white-sand crescent beach stretches eastward from the port. It's packed with locals doing what people around the world do at the beach—with a few variations. Traditionally clad moms let their kids run wild. Along with lazy camels, you'll see people—young and old—covered in hot sand to combat rheumatism. Early, late, and off-season, the beach becomes a popular venue for soccer teams. The palm-lined pedestrian street along the waterfront was renamed for King Mohammed VI, in appreciation for recent restorations.

Just past the beach on the port side is a zone of nondescript factories. Here local women sew clothing for big, mostly European companies that pay $8 a day. Each morning and evening rush hour, the street is filled with these women commuters...on foot.

Evenings in Tangier—Most important: Be out in the **medina** around 21:00. In the cool of the evening, the atmospheric squares and lanes become even more evocative. Then at about 22:00 things get dark, lonely, and foreboding.

El Minzah Hotel hosts **traditional music** most nights (see "Eating," next page; 85 Rue de la Liberté, tel. 93-58-85).

The **Rif Cinema** shows movies in French—which the younger generation must learn—and Arabic. The cinema is worth popping into, if only to see the Art Deco interior. As movies cost only 15 dirham, consider dropping by to see a bit of whatever's on...in Arabic (on the Grand Socco, tel. 93-46-83).

SLEEPING

These hotels are centrally located, near the TI, and within walking distance of the market. The first two are three-star hotels and take credit cards; the others are cash-only. To reserve from Europe, dial 00 (Europe's international access code), 212 (Morocco's country code), 39 (Tangier's city code), then the local number. July through mid-September is high season, when rooms may be a bit more expensive and reservations are wise. Most hotels charge an extra tax of 10 dirhams per person per night.

$$$ Hotel Rembrandt just feels like the 1940s, with a restaurant, bar, and swimming pool surrounded by a great grassy garden. Its 75 rooms are clean and comfortable, and some come with views (Sb-510–620 dirhams, Db-660–780 dirhams, higher prices are for June–Aug, sea view-100 dirhams extra, includes tax, breakfast-70 dirhams, air-con, elevator, Boulevard Mohammed VI 1, tel. 93-78-70, fax 93-04-43, www.hotel-rembrandt.com, hotelrembrandt@menara.ma).

$$$ Rif & Spa Hotel, recently restored to its 1970s glamour, is a worthy splurge. Offering 130 plush, modern rooms, sprawling public spaces, a garden, a pool, and grand views, it feels like an oversized boutique hotel. The great Arabic lounge with harbor view is a momentum-buster (Sb-1,060–1,150 dirhams, Db-1,220–1,460 dirhams, includes tax, see website for specials, breakfast-100 dirhams, air-con, elevator, 3 restaurants, Avenue Mohammed VI 152, tel. 34-93-00, fax 32-19-04, www.hotelsatlas.com, riftanger@menara.ma).

$$ Hotel Continental is the Humphrey Bogart option, a grand old place sprawling along the old town. It overlooks the port, with lavish, atmospheric public spaces, a chandeliered breakfast room, and 70 spacious bedrooms with rough hardwood floors. Jimmy, who's always around and runs the shop adjacent to the lobby, says he offers everything but Viagra. When I said, "I'm from Seattle," he said, "206." Test him—he knows your area code (Sb-386 dirhams, Db-462 dirhams, 10 percent

Sleep Code

(8 dirhams = about $1, country code: 212, area code: 39)
S = Single, **D** = Double/Twin, **T** = Triple, **Q** = Quad, **b** = bathroom, **s** = shower only. Unless otherwise noted, credit cards are accepted, English is spoken, and breakfast is included.

To help you easily sort through these listings, I've divided the rooms into three categories, based on the price for a standard double room with bath (during high season):

$$$ Higher Priced—Most rooms 500 dirhams or more.
$$ Moderately Priced—Most rooms between 300–500 dirhams.
$ Lower Priced—Most rooms 300 dirhams or less.

more July–Sept, includes tax and breakfast, cash only, Dar Baroud 36, tel. 93-10-24, fax 93-11-43, hcontinental@iam.net.ma).

$$ Hotel El Djenina is a local-style business-class hotel—extremely plain, reliable, safe, and well-located. Its 30 rooms are a block off the harbor, midway between the port and the TI. Request a room on the back side to escape the street noise (Sb-220–320 dirhams, Db-270–420 dirhams, higher prices are for June–Aug, cash only, tel. 94-22-44, fax 94-22-46, Rue al-Antaki 8, eldjenina@menara.ma).

$ Hotel d'Anjou is a sleepable dive—the best dirt-cheap option I could find—renting 20 safe-feeling rooms on a quiet street two blocks off the harbor (Sb-140 dirhams, Db-160 dirhams, Tb-220 dirhams, 10 percent more in summer, cash only, just off Rue al-Antaki at Rue Ibn Albanna 3, tel. & fax 94-27-84, Hakim speaks English).

$ Hotel Andalucía is solid, clean, and minimal. It's in the new town, about a 20-minute walk from the Grand Socco. It has 19 rooms, a small reception, and a peaceful lobby (Sb-195 dirhams, Db-230 dirhams, cash only, Rue Ibn Hazim 14, tel. 94-13-34, Azdeen speaks a little English).

EATING

For the local equivalent of a yacht club restaurant, survey the places along the beach. The first two places I list below are buried in the medina and are disgustingly touristy. As they're designed for groups, the only locals you'll see here are the waiters. Still, they offer travelers a safe, comfortable break. The last three include a seafood paradise hole-in-the-wall; a big, fancy hotel restaurant with live traditional music; and a charity-run refuge that provides a quality, low-stress, and safe lunch.

Tourist Traps: **Hamadi** is as luxurious a restaurant as a tourist can find in Morocco, with good food at reasonable prices (Rue Kasbah 2, tel. 93-45-14). **Mamounia Palace** is right on Petit Socco and more in the middle of the action. A meal here will cost you about 100 dirhams for three courses—less if you order from the menu. Both of these places are tour-group hell and make you thankful to be free.

Le Saveur du Poisson is an excellent choice for the more adventurous, featuring one Tiki Hut–type room with a busy kitchen. There are no choices here. Just sit down and let owner Muhammad or his son, Hassan, take care of the rest. You get a rough one-use spoon and fork carved just for you...a fine souvenir. Surrounded by lots of locals and unforgettable food, you'll be treated to a multi-course menu. Savor the delicious fish dishes—Tangier is one of the few spots in Morocco where seafood is a major part of the diet. The fruit punch—a mix of seasonal fruits brewed overnight in a vat—simmers in the back room. Ask for an explanation, or even a look. After trying their dessert, Nuts 'n' Honey will never be the same. The big sink in the room is for locals who prefer to eat with their fingers (150-dirham fixed-price meal, Sat–Thu 12:00–16:00 & 19:00–22:00, closed Fri and during Ramadan; walk down Rue de la Liberté until you reach the stairs, then go down until you see fish on the grill, Escalier Waller 2, tel. 33-63-26).

El Minzah Hotel offers a fancier yet still authentic experience. The atmosphere is classy but low-stress. It's where unadventurous tourists and local elites dine. Dress up and choose between a continental (French) dining area or the Moroccan lounge, where you'll be serenaded by live traditional music (music nightly 20:00–23:00, belly dance show at 21:30 and 22:30, no extra charge for music). Entrées (including *tajines* and couscous) in either restaurant average 140 dirhams. There's also a cozy wine bar here—a rarity in a Muslim country. Light meals and salads are served poolside (daily 13:00–16:00 & 20:00–22:00, Rue de la Liberté 85, tel. 93-58-85, www.elminzah.com).

Maison Communitaire des Femmes, a community center for women, hides an inexpensive, hearty lunch spot that's open to everyone. A tasty three-course lunch is only 50 dirhams. Profits support the work of the center (Mon–Sat 12:00–16:00, last order at 15:30, closed Sun, near the slipper market just outside the Grand Socco, Place du 9 Avril).

TRANSPORTATION CONNECTIONS

In Tangier, all train traffic comes and goes from the suburban Gare Tanger Ville train station, one mile from the city center and a short Petit Taxi ride away (10–20 dirhams). If you're traveling inland, check the information booth at the entrance of the train station for schedules (www.oncf.ma).

From Tangier by Train to: Rabat (5/day, 5 hrs), **Casablanca**

(station also called **Casa Voyageurs,** 6/day, 5 hrs), **Marrakech** (4/day, 12 hrs), **Fès** (4/day, 4.5 hrs).

From Tangier by Bus to: Ceuta and **Tétouan** (hourly, 1 hr).

From Fès to: Casablanca (9/day, 4.5 hrs), **Marrakech** (7/day, 7 hrs), **Rabat** (9/day, 4 hrs), **Meknès** (10/day, 45 min), **Tangier** (5/day, 5.5 hrs).

From Rabat to: Casablanca (2/hr, 45 min), **Fès** (9/day, 3.5 hrs), **Tétouan** (2 buses/day, 4.5 hrs, 3 trains/day, 6 hrs).

From Casablanca to: Marrakech (9/day, 3.5 hrs).

From Marrakech to: Meknès (7/day, 7 hrs), **Ouarzazate** (4 buses/day, 4 hrs).

By Plane: Flights within Morocco are convenient and reasonable (about $150 one-way from Tangier to Casablanca).

Extended Tour of Morocco

Morocco gets much better as you go deeper into the interior. The country is incredibly rich in cultural thrills, though you'll pay a price in hassles and headaches—it's a package deal. But if adventure is your business, Morocco is a great option. Invest in a good Morocco guidebook to make this trip. Below are a few tips and insights to get you started.

To get a fair look at Morocco, you must get past the hustlers and con artists of the north coast (Tangier, Tétouan). It takes a minimum of four or five days to make a worthwhile visit—ideally seven or eight. Plan at least two nights in either Fès or Marrakech. A trip over the Atlas Mountains gives you an exciting look at Saharan Morocco. If you need a vacation from your vacation, check into one of the idyllic Atlantic beach resorts on the south coast. Above all, get past the northern day-trip-from-Spain, take-a-snapshot-on-a-camel fringe. (Oops, that's us. Oh, well.)

If you're relying on public transportation for your extended tour, sail to Tangier, blast your way through customs, ignore any hustler who tells you there's no way out until tomorrow, and hop into a Petit Taxi for the Tanger Ville train station one mile away. From there, set your sights on Rabat, a dignified, European-type town with fewer hustlers, and make it your get-acquainted stop in Morocco. Trains go farther south from Rabat.

If you're driving a car, crossing the border can be a bit unnerving, since you'll be forced to jump through several bureaucratic hoops. You'll go through customs at both borders, buy Moroccan insurance for your car (cheap and easy), and feel at the mercy of a bristly bunch of shady-looking people you'd rather not be at the mercy of. Don't pay anyone on the Spanish side. Consider tipping a guy on the Moroccan side if you feel he'll shepherd you through. Relax and let him grease those customs wheels. He's worth it. As soon as possible, hit the road and drive to Chefchaouen, the best first stop for those with their own wheels.

SIGHTS

Moroccan Towns

▲▲Chefchaouen—Just two hours by bus or car from Tétouan, this is the first pleasant town beyond the north coast. Monday and Thursday are colorful market days. Stay in the classy old Hotel Chaouen on Place el-Makhzen. The Hotel Parador (historic inn, but not the same as the Spanish-government-run chain) faces the old town and offers fine meals and a refuge from hustlers. Wander deep into the whitewashed old town from here.

▲▲Rabat—Morocco's capital and most European city, Rabat is the most comfortable and least stressful place to start your North African trip. You'll find a colorful market (in the old neighboring town of Salé), bits of Islamic architecture (Mausoleum of Mohammed V), the king's palace, mellow hustlers, and fine hotels.

▲▲▲Fès—More than just a funny hat that tipsy Shriners wear, Fès is Morocco's religious and artistic center, bustling with craftspeople, pilgrims, shoppers, and shops. Like most large Moroccan cities, it has a distinct new town from the French colonial period, as well as an exotic (and stressful) old, walled Arabic town (the medina), where you'll find the market.

For 12 centuries, traders have gathered in Fès, founded on a river at the crossroads of two trade routes. Soon there was an irrigation system, a university, resident craftsmen from Spain, and a diverse population of Muslims, Christians, and Jews. When France claimed Morocco in 1912, they made their capital in Rabat, and Fès fizzled. But the Fès marketplace is still Morocco's best.

▲▲▲Marrakech—Morocco's gateway to the south, Marrakech is where the desert, mountain, and coastal regions merge. This market city is a constant folk festival, bustling with Berber tribespeople and a colorful center. The new city has the train station, and the main boulevard (Mohammed V) is lined with banks, airline offices, a post office, a tourist office, and comfortable hotels. The old city features the mazelike market and the huge Djemaa el-Fna, a square seething with people—a 43-ring Moroccan circus.

▲▲▲Over the Atlas Mountains—Extend your Moroccan trip several days by heading south over the Atlas Mountains. Take a bus from Marrakech to Ouarzazate (short stop), and then to Tinerhir (great oasis town, comfy hotel, overnight stop). The next day go to Er Rachidia and take the overnight bus to Fès.

By car, drive from Fès south, staying in the small mountain town of Ifrane, and then continue deep into the desert country past Er Rachidia and on to Rissani (market days: Sun, Tue, and Thu). Explore nearby mud-brick towns still living in the Middle Ages. Hire a guide to drive you past where the road stops, and head cross-country to an oasis village (Merzouga), where you can climb a sand dune and watch the sun rise over the vastness of Africa. Only a sea of sand separates you from Timbuktu.

SPAIN: PAST AND PRESENT

The distinctive Spanish culture has been shaped by the country's history. Roman emperors, Muslim sultans, hard-core Christians, conquistadors, French dandies, and Fascist dictators have all left their mark on Spain's art, architecture, and customs. Start by understanding the country's long history of invasions and religious wars, and you'll better appreciate the churches, museums, and monuments you'll visit today.

HISTORY

In 1492, Columbus sailed the ocean blue—and Spain became a nation, too. Iberia's sunny weather, fertile soil, and Mediterranean ports made it a popular place to call home. The original "Iberians" were a Celtic people, who crossed the Pyrenees around 800 B.C. The Phoenicians established the city of Cádiz around 1100 B.C., and Carthaginians settled around 250 B.C.

Romans (c. 200 B.C.–A.D. 400)

The future Roman Emperor Augustus finally quelled the last Iberian resistance (19 B.C.), making the province of "Hispania" an agricultural breadbasket (olives, wine) to feed the vast Roman empire. The Romans brought the Latin language, a connection to the wider world, and (in the fourth century) Christianity. When the empire crumbled around A.D. 400, Spain made a peaceful transition, ruled by Christian Visigoths from Germany who had strong Roman ties. Roman influence remained for centuries after, in the Latin-based Spanish language, irrigation, and building materials and techniques. The Romans' large farming estates would change hands over the years, passing from Roman senators to Visigoth kings to Islamic caliphs to Christian nobles. And, of course, the Romans left wine.

Spaniards Throughout History

Hadrian (A.D. 76–138)—Roman Emperor, one of three born in Latin-speaking "Hispania" (along with Trajan, reigned 98–117, and Marcus Aurelius, reigned 161–180), who ruled Rome at its peak of power.

El Cid (1040?–1099)—A real soldier-for-hire who inspired fictional stories and Spain's oldest poem, El Cid (literally, "The Lord"), fought for both Christians and Muslims during the wars of the Reconquista. He's best known for liberating Valencia from the Moors.

St. Teresa of Ávila (1515–1582)—Mystic nun whose holiness and writings led to convent reform and to her sainthood. Religiously intense Spain produced other saints, too, including **Dominic** (1170–1221), who founded an order of wandering monks, and **Ignatius of Loyola** (1491–1556), who founded the Jesuits, an order of "intellectual warriors."

Ferdinand (1452–1516) and Isabel (1451–1504)—Their marriage united most of Spain, ushering in its Golden Age. The "Catholic Monarchs" drove out Moors and Jews, and financed Columbus' lucrative voyages to the New World.

Hernán Cortés (1485–1547)—Conquered Mexico in 1521. Along with Vasco Núñez de Balboa, who discovered the Pacific, and Francisco Pizarro, who conquered Peru, Cortés and other Spaniards explored and exploited the New World.

El Greco (1541–1614)—The artist is known for his ethereal paintings of "flickering" saints.

Diego Velázquez (1599–1660)—Velázquez painted camera-eye realistic portraits of the royal court.

Moors (711–1492)

In A.D. 711, 12,000 zealous members of the world's newest religion—Islam—landed on the Rock of Gibraltar and, in three short years, conquered the Iberian Peninsula. These North African Muslims—generically called "Moors"—dominated Spain for the next 700 years. Though powerful, they were surprisingly tolerant of the people they ruled, allowing native Jews and Christians to practice their faiths, so long as the infidels paid extra taxes.

The Moors were themselves an ethnically diverse culture, including both crude Berber tribesmen from Morocco and sophisticated rulers from old Arab families. From their capital in Córdoba, various rulers of the united Islamic state of "Al-Andalus" pledged allegiance to foreign caliphs in Syria, Baghdad, or Morocco.

With cultural ties that stretched from Spain to Africa to Arabia to Persia and beyond, the Moorish culture in Spain (especially around A.D. 800–1000) was perhaps Europe's most advanced, a beacon of

Francisco Goya (1746–1828)—The artist is best known for his expressionistic nightmares (see page 322 for more).

Francisco Franco (1892–1975)—General who led the military uprising against the elected Republic, sparking Spain's Civil War (1936–1939). After victory, he ruled Spain for more than three decades as an absolute dictator, maintaining its Catholic, aristocratic heritage while slowly modernizing the country.

Salvador Dalí (1904–1989)—A flamboyant, waxed-mustachioed Surrealist painter, Dalí and a fellow Spaniard, filmmaker Luis Buñuel, made one of the first art films, *Andalusian Dog* (see sidebar on page 104).

Pablo Picasso (1881–1973)—Though he lived most of his adult life in France, the 20th century's greatest artist explored Spanish themes, particularly in his famous work *Guernica,* which depicts Civil War destruction (see sidebar on page 332).

Placido Domingo (b. 1941)—The son of zarzuela singers in Madrid (but raised in Mexico), this operatic tenor is just one of many classical musicians from Spain, including fellow "Three Tenors" singer José Carreras, composer Manuel de Falla, cellist Pablo Casals, and guitarist Andrés Segovia.

Spaniards in the News Today—King Juan Carlos I and his Greek-born wife, Queen Sofía; their son Felipe and his wife, Letizia; left-of-center prime minister José Luis Rodríguez Zapatero; bicyclists Oscar Pereiro, Igor Astarloa, Tour de France cyclist Alberto Contador; soccer star Raúl; golfer Sergio Garcia; tennis player Rafael Nadal; pop singer Julio Iglesias (father of pop singer Enrique Iglesias); and Oscar Award–winning actor Javier Bardem and movie directors Pedro Almodóvar and Pedro Amenábar.

learning in Europe's so-called "Dark" Ages. Mathematics, astronomy, literature, and architecture flourished. Even winemaking was encouraged, though for religious reasons Muslims weren't allowed to drink alcohol. The Moorish legacy lives on today in architecture (horseshoe arches, ceramic tiles, fountains, and gardens), language (e.g., Spanish *el* comes from Arabic *al*)...and wine.

Reconquista (711–1492)

The Moors ruled for more than 700 years, but throughout that time they were a minority ruling a largely Christian populace. Pockets of independent Christians remained, particularly in the mountains in the peninsula's north. Local Christian kings fought against the Moors whenever they could, whittling away at the Muslim empire, "re-conquering" more and more land in what's known as the "Reconquista." The last Moorish stronghold, Granada, fell to the Christians in 1492.

The slow, piecemeal process of the Reconquista split the peninsula into many independent kingdoms and dukedoms, some Christian, some Moorish. The Reconquista picked up steam after A.D. 1000, when Al-Andalus splintered into smaller regional states—Granada, Sevilla, Valencia—ruled by local caliphs. Toledo fell to the Christians in 1085. By 1200, the neighboring Christian state of Portugal had the borders it does today, making it the oldest unchanged state in Europe. The rest of the peninsula was a battleground, a loosely knit collection of small kingdoms, some Christian, some Muslim. Heavy stone "castles" dotted the interior region of "Castile," as lords and barons duked it out. Along the Mediterranean coast (from the Pyrenees to Barcelona to Valencia), three Christian states united into a sea-trading power, the kingdom of Aragon.

In 1469, Isabel of Castile married Ferdinand II of Aragon, uniting the peninsula's two largest kingdoms, and instantly making united Spain a European power. In 1492, while Columbus explored the seas under Ferdinand and Isabel's flag, the Catholic Monarchs drove the Moors out of Granada and expelled the country's Jews, creating a unified, Christian, militaristic nation-state, fueled by the religious zeal of the Reconquista.

The Golden Age (1500–1600)

Spain's bold sea explorers changed the economics of Europe, opening up a New World of riches and colonies. The Spanish flag soon flew over most of South and Central America. Gold, silver, and agricultural products (grown on large estates with cheap labor) poured into Spain. In return, the stoked Spaniards exported Christianity, converting the American natives with kind Jesuit priests and cruel conquistadors.

Ferdinand and Isabel's daughter (Juana the Mad) wed a German prince (Philip the Fair), and their son inherited both crowns. Charles V (1500–1558, called Carlos I in Spain) was the most powerful man in the world, ruling an empire that stretched from Holland to Sicily, and from Bohemia to Bolivia. The aristocracy and the clergy were swimming in money. Art and courtly life flourished during this Golden Age, with Spain hosting the painter El Greco and the writer Miguel de Cervantes.

Six Dates that Changed Spain

711 Muslims from North Africa invade and occupy Iberia.

1492 Columbus sails Spain into a century of wealth and power.

1588 Spain's Armada is routed by the British, and the country's slow decline begins.

1898 Thrashed by the US in the Spanish-American War, Spain reaches a low ebb.

1936 The Civil War begins, killing hundreds of thousands during its three-year span, and brings on more than three decades of Franco's fascist rule.

1975 King Juan Carlos I leads the nation to democracy and the European Union.

But Charles V's Holy Roman Empire was torn by different languages and ethnic groups, and by protesting Protestants. He spent much of the nation's energies at war with Protestants, encroaching Muslim Turks, and Europe's rising powers. When an exhausted Charles announced his abdication (1555) and retired to a monastery, his sprawling empire was divvied up among family members, with Spain and its possessions going to his son, Philip II (1527–1598).

Philip II conquered Portugal (1580, his only successful war), moved Spain's capital to Madrid, built El Escorial, and continued fighting losing battles across Europe (the Netherlands, France) that drained the treasury of its New World gold. In the summer of 1588, Spain's seemingly unbeatable royal fleet of 125 ships—the Invincible Armada—sailed off to conquer England, only to be unexpectedly routed in battle by bad weather and Sir Francis Drake's cunning. Just like that, Britannia ruled the waves, and Spain spiraled downward, becoming a debt-ridden, overextended, flabby nation.

Slow Decline (1600–1900)

The fast money from the colonies kept Spain from seeing the dangers at home. They stopped growing their own wheat and neglected their fields. Great Britain and the Netherlands were the rising sea-trading powers in the new global economy. During the centuries when science and technology developed as never before in other European countries, Spain was preoccupied by its failed colonial politics. (Still, Spain in the 1600s produced the remarkable painter Diego Velázquez.)

By 1700, once-mighty Spain lay helpless while rising powers France, England, and Austria fought over the right to pick Spain's next king in the War of the Spanish Succession (1701–1714), which was fought partly on Spanish soil (e.g., Britain holding out against the French in the Siege of Gibraltar). The rightful next-in-line was Louis XIV's son, who was set to inherit both France and Spain. The rest of Europe didn't want powerful France to become even stronger. The war ended in compromise, preventing Louis XIV from controlling both countries, but allowing his grandson to become King of Spain (Spain lost several possessions). The French-born, French-speaking Bourbon King Philip V (1683–1746) ruled Spain for 40 years. He and his heirs made themselves at home building the Versailles-like Royal Palace in Madrid and La Granja near Segovia.

The French Revolution spilled over into Spain, bringing French rule under Napoleon. In 1808, the Spaniards rose up (chronicled by Goya's paintings of the second and third of May, 1808), sparking the Peninsular War—called the War of Independence by Spaniards—that finally won Spain's independence from French rule.

Nineteenth-century Spain was a backward nation, with internal wars over which noble family should rule (the Carlist Wars), liberal revolutions put down brutally, and political assassinations. Spain gradually lost its global possessions to other European powers and to South American revolutionaries. Spain hit rock bottom in 1898, when the upstart United States picked a fight and thrashed them in the Spanish-American War, taking away Spain's last major possessions: Cuba, Puerto Rico, and the Philippines.

The 20th Century

A drained and disillusioned Spain was ill-prepared for modern technology and democratic government.

The old ruling class (the monarchy, church, and landowners) fought new economic powers (cities, businessmen, labor unions) in a series of coups, strikes, and sham elections. In the '20s, a military dictatorship under Miguel Primo de Rivera kept the old guard in power. In 1930, he was ousted and an open election brought a modern democratic Republic to power. But the right wing regrouped under the Falange (fascist) party, fomenting unrest and sparking a military coup against the Republic in 1936, supported by General Francisco Franco (1892–1975).

For three years (1936–1939), Spain fought a bloody Civil War between Franco's Nationalists (also called Falangists) and the Republic (also called Loyalists). Some 600,000 Spaniards died (due to all causes), and Franco won. (For more on the Civil War, see "Valley of the Fallen," page 370.) For nearly the next four decades, Spain was ruled by Franco, an authoritarian, church-blessed dictator who tried to modernize the backward country while shielding it from corrupting modern influences. Spain was neutral in World War II, and the country spent much of the postwar era as a world apart. (On my first visit to Spain in 1973, I came face-to-face with fellow teenagers—me in backpack and shorts, the Spaniards in military uniforms, brandishing automatic weapons.)

Before Franco died, he handpicked his protégé, King Juan Carlos I, to succeed him. But to everyone's surprise, the young, conservative, mild-mannered king stepped aside, settled for a figurehead title, and guided the country quickly and peacefully toward democratic elections (1977).

Spain had a lot of catching up to do. Culturally, the once-conservative nation exploded and embraced new ideas, even plunging to wild extremes. In the 1980s, Spain flowered under the left-leaning Prime Minister Felipe González. Spain showed the world its new modern face in 1992, hosting both a World Exhibition at Sevilla and the Summer Olympics at Barcelona.

Spain Today

From 1996 to 2004, Spain was led by the centrist Prime Minister José María Aznar. He adopted moderate policies to minimize the stress on the country's young democracy, fighting problems such as unemployment and foreign debt with reasonable success. However, his support of George W. Bush's pre-emptive war in Iraq was extremely unpopular with the vast majority of Spaniards. In spring of 2004, the retiring Aznar supported a similarly centrist successor, Mariano Rajoy, who seemed poised to win the election. On the eve of the election, on March 11, three Madrid train stations were bombed at the height of rush hour, killing 200 people. The terrorist group claiming responsibility denounced Spain's Iraq policy, and three days later, Aznar's party lost the election. The new prime minister, left-of-center José Luis Rodríguez Zapatero, quickly began pulling Spain's troops out of Iraq, as well as enacting sweeping social changes in Spain.

Its political squabbles and heightened security aside, Spain is striding into the future. Though not considered wealthy or powerful, Spain is prospering, thanks in part to you and tourism.

ARTISTS

El Greco (1541–1614) exemplifies the spiritual fervor of much Spanish art. The drama, the surreal colors, and the intentionally unnatural distortion have the intensity of a religious vision. (For more on El Greco, see page 327.)

Diego Velázquez (1599–1660) went to the opposite extreme. His masterful court portraits are studies in camera-eye realism and cool detachment from his subjects. Velázquez was unmatched in using a few strokes of paint to suggest details.

Francisco de Goya (1746–1828) lacked Velázquez's detachment. He let his liberal tendencies shine through in unflattering portraits of royalty, and in emotional scenes of abuse of power. He unleashed his inner passions in the eerie, nightmarish canvases of his last, "dark paintings" stage. (For more on Goya, see page 322.)

Bartolomé Murillo (1617–1682) painted a dreamy world of religious visions. His pastel, soft-focus works of cute baby Jesuses and radiant Virgin Marys helped make Catholic doctrine palatable to the common folk at a time when many were defecting to Protestantism. (For more on Murillo, see page 479.)

You'll also find plenty of foreign art in Spain's museums. During its Golden Age, Spain's wealthy aristocrats bought wagonloads of the most popular art of the time—Italian Renaissance and Baroque works by Titian, Tintoretto, and others. They also loaded up on paintings by Peter Paul Rubens, Hieronymus Bosch, and Pieter Brueghel from the Low Countries, which were then under Spanish rule.

In the 20th century, **Pablo Picasso** (see his inspirational antiwar *Guernica* mural in Madrid, described on page 332), **Joan Miró,** and Surrealist **Salvador Dalí** (see sidebar on page 104) made their marks. Great museums featuring all three are in or near Barcelona.

ARCHITECTURE

Spanish History Set in Stone

The two most fertile periods of architectural innovation in Spain were during the Moorish occupation and in the Golden Age. Otherwise, Spanish architects marched obediently behind the rest of Europe. Modern architects have finally brought Spain back to the forefront of construction and design.

Spain's history is dominated by 700 years of pushing the Muslim Moors back into Africa (711–1492). Throughout Spain, it seems every old church was built upon a mosque (Sevilla's immense cathedral, for one). Granada's Alhambra is the best example of the secular Moorish style. It's an *Arabian Nights* fairy tale: finely etched domes, lacey arcades, keyhole arches, and lush gardens. At its heart lies an elegantly proportioned courtyard, where the designers created an ingenious microclimate: water, plants, pottery, thick walls, and darkness...all to be cool. The stuccoed walls are ornamented with a stylized Arabic script, creating a visual chant of verses from the Quran.

As the Christians slowly reconquered Iberian turf, they turned their fervor into stone, building churches in the lighter, heaven-reaching, stained-glass Gothic style (Toledo and Sevilla). Gothic was an import from France, trickling into conservative Spain long after it had swept through Europe.

As Christians moved in, many Muslim artists and architects stayed, giving the new society the Mudejar style. (Mudejar means "those who stayed.") In Sevilla's Alcázar, the Arabic script on the walls relates not the Quran, but New Testament verses and Christian propaganda, such as "Dedicated to the magnificent Sultan, King Pedro—thanks to God!" (The style of Christians living under Moorish rule is called Mozarabic.)

The money reaped and raped from Spain's colonies in the Golden Age spurred new construction. Churches and palaces borrowed from the Italian Renaissance and the more elaborate Baroque. Ornamentation reached unprecedented heights in Spain, culminating in the Plateresque style of stonework, so called because it resembles intricate silver *(plata)* filigree work (see, for example, the facade of the University of Salamanca).

The 1500s was also the era of religious wars. The monastery/palace of El Escorial, built in sober geometric style, symbolizes the austerity of a newly reformed Catholic Church ready to strike back. King Philip II ruled his empire and directed the Inquisition from here, surrounded by plain white walls, well-scrubbed floors, and simple furnishings. Built at a time when Catholic Spain felt threatened by Protestant heretics, its construction dominated the Spanish economy for a generation (1563–1584). Because of this bully in the national budget, Spain has almost nothing else to show from this most powerful period of her history.

For the next three centuries (1600–1900), backward-looking Spain recycled old art styles.

As Europe leapt from the 19th century into the 20th, it celebrated a rising standard of living and nearly a century without a major war. Art Nouveau architects forced hard steel and concrete into softer organic shapes. Barcelona's answer to Art Nouveau was Modernisme, and its genius was Antoni Gaudí, with his asymmetrical, "cake-in-the-rain" buildings like Casa Milà and Sagrada Família.

Much of Spain's 20th-century architecture follows patterns seen elsewhere in Europe—the minimal fascist style of the Valley of the Fallen and ugly concrete apartments. But Spain today produces some of Europe's most interesting structures. Santiago Calatrava (from Valencia, born 1951) uses soaring arches and glass to create bridges (such as the new one in Venice), airports, and performance halls (including Valencia's Opera House). One of the world's most striking buildings in recent years—Frank Gehry's Guggenheim Museum—is in Bilbao, and similarly innovative structures are popping up everywhere.

BULLFIGHTING

A Legitimate Slice of Spain, or a Cruel Spectacle?

The Spanish bullfight is as much a ritual as it is a sport. Not to acknowledge the importance of the bullfight is to censor a venerable part of Spanish culture. But it also makes a spectacle out of the cruel killing of an animal. Should tourists boycott bullfights? I don't know.

Today bullfighting is less popular among locals. If this trend continues, bullfighting may survive more and more as a tourist event. When the day comes that bullfighting is kept alive by our tourist dollars rather than by the local culture, then I'll agree with those who say bullfighting is immoral and that tourists shouldn't encourage it by buying tickets. Consider the morality of supporting this gruesome aspect of Spanish culture before buying a ticket. If you do decide to attend a bullfight, here is what you'll see.

While no two bullfights are the same, they unfold along a strict pattern. The ceremony begins punctually with a parade of participants across the ring. Then the trumpet sounds, the "Gate of Fear" opens, and the leading player—*el toro*—thunders in. A ton of angry animal is an awesome sight, even from the cheap seats (with the sun in your eyes).

The fight is divided into three acts. Act I is designed to size up the bull and wear him down. With help from his assistants, the matador ("killer") attracts the bull with the shake of the cape, then directs the animal past his body, as close as his bravery allows. The bull sees only things in motion and (some think) in red. After a few passes, the *picadores* enter, mounted on horseback, to spear the swollen lump of muscle at the back of the bull's neck. This tests the bull, while the matador watches studiously. It also lowers the bull's head and weakens the thrust of his horns. (Until 1927, the horses had no protective pads, and were often killed.)

In Act II, the matador's assistants *(banderilleros)* continue to enrage and weaken the bull. They charge the charging bull and—leaping acrobatically across its path—plunge brightly colored barbed sticks into the bull's vital neck muscle.

After a short intermission, during which the matador may, according to tradition, ask permission to kill the bull and dedicate the kill to someone in the crowd, the final and lethal Act III begins.

The matador tries to dominate and tire the bull with hypnotic cape work. A good pass is when the matador stands completely still while the bull charges past. Then the matador thrusts a sword between the animal's shoulder blades for the kill. A quick kill is not always easy, and the matador may have to make several bloody thrusts before the sword stays in and the bull finally dies. Mules drag the dead bull out, and his meat is in the market *mañana* (barring "mad cow" concerns—and if ever there was a mad cow...). *Rabo del toro* (bull-tail stew) is a delicacy.

Throughout the fight, the crowd shows its approval or impatience. Shouts of "*¡Olé!*"

or "*¡Torero!*" mean they like what they see. Whistling or rhythmic hand-clapping greets cowardice and incompetence.

You're not likely to see much human blood spilled. In 200 years of bullfighting in Sevilla, only 30 fighters have died (and only three were actually matadors). If a bull does kill a fighter, the next matador comes in to kill him. Historically, even the bull's mother is killed, since the evil qualities are assumed to have come from the mother.

After an exceptional fight, the crowd may wave white handkerchiefs to ask that the matador be awarded the bull's ear or tail. A brave bull, though dead, gets a victory lap from the mule team on his way to the slaughterhouse. Then the trumpet sounds, and a new bull charges in to face a fresh matador.

Fights are held on most Sundays Easter through September (at 18:30 or 19:30). Serious fights with adult matadors are called *corrida de toros*. These are often sold out in advance. Summer fights are often *novillada,* with teenage novices doing the killing. *Corrida de toros* seats range from €20 for nosebleed seats in the sun to €140 for front-row seats in the shade. *Novillada* seats are half that, and generally easy to get at the arena a few minutes before showtime. Many Spanish women consider bullfighting sexy. They swoon at the dashing matadors who are sure to wear tight pants (with their *partas nobles*—noble parts—in view, generally organized to one side, farthest from the bull).

A typical bullfight lasts about two hours and consists of six separate fights—three matadors (each with his own team of *picadores* and *banderilleros*) fighting two bulls each. For a closer look at bullfighting by an American aficionado, read Ernest Hemingway's classic, *Death in the Afternoon.*

APPENDIX

CONTENTS

RESOURCES

Tourist Offices

In the US

National tourist offices in the US are a wealth of information. Before your trip, scan their websites. If you call, get the free general information packet and request any specific information you want (such as regional and city maps and festival schedules).

Spain Tourist Office: www.spain.info, tel. 212/265-8822.

Gibraltar Information Bureau: www.gibraltar.gov.uk, tel. 202/452-1108.

Moroccan National Tourist Office: www.visitmorocco.com.

In Spain

Your best first stop in a new city is the Turismo (tourist information office—abbreviated as **TI** in this book). Try to arrive, or at least telephone, before it closes. Get a city map and advice on public transportation (including bus and train schedules), special events, and recommendations for nightlife. Many TIs have information on the entire country or at least the region, so try to pick up maps for towns you'll be visiting later in your trip.

While TIs are eager to book you a room, use their room-finding service only as a last resort (bloated prices, fees, no opinions, and they take a cut from your host). You'll get a far better value by using the listings in this book and booking direct.

Resources from Rick Steves

Guidebooks and Online Updates

This book is updated every year in person. The telephone numbers and hours of sights listed in this book are accurate as of mid-2008—but even with annual updates, things change. For the latest, visit www.ricksteves.com/update. Also at my website, you'll find a valuable list of reports and experiences—good and bad—from fellow travelers (www.ricksteves.com/feedback).

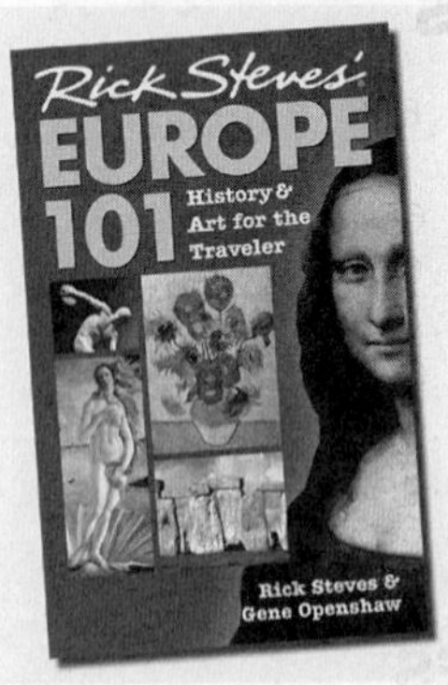

Spain 2009 is one of more than 30 titles in my series on European travel, which includes country guidebooks, city and regional guidebooks, and my budget-travel skills handbook, *Rick Steves' Europe Through the Back Door*. My phrase books—for Spanish, Portuguese, French, Italian, and German—are practical and budget-oriented. My other books are *Europe 101* (a crash course on art and history, newly expanded and in full color), *European Christmas* (on traditional and modern-day celebrations), and *Postcards from Europe* (a fun memoir of my travels). For a complete list of my books, see the inside of the last page of this book.

Public Television and Radio Shows

My TV series, *Rick Steves' Europe,* covers European destinations in 70 shows, with four episodes on Spain. My weekly public radio show, *Travel with Rick Steves,* features interviews with travel experts from around the world, including several hours on Spain and Spanish culture. All the TV scripts and radio shows (which are easy and free to download to an iPod or other MP3 player) are at www.ricksteves.com.

Free Audiotours

If you're traveling beyond Spain to France or Italy, you could take advantage of free self-guided audiotours of the major sights in Paris, Florence, Rome, and Venice. The audiotours,

Begin Your Trip at www.ricksteves.com

At our travel website, you'll find a wealth of free information on European destinations, including fresh monthly news and helpful tips from thousands of fellow travelers.

Our **online Travel Store** offers travel bags and accessories specially designed by Rick Steves to help you travel smarter and lighter. These include Rick's popular carry-on bags (wheeled and rucksack versions), money belts, totes, toiletries kits, adapters, other accessories, and a wide selection of guidebooks, planning maps, and DVDs.

Choosing the right **railpass** for your trip—amidst hundreds of options—can drive you nutty. We'll help you choose the best pass for your needs, plus give you a bunch of free extras.

Rick Steves' Europe Through the Back Door travel company offers **tours** with more than two dozen itineraries and about 450 departures reaching the best destinations in this book...and beyond. Our 15-day Best of Spain & Portugal tour includes the big-city thrills of Barcelona, Madrid, Sevilla, and Lisbon, as well the small-town gems of Ronda and the whitewashed village of Arcos. The eight-day Best of Barcelona & Madrid tour explores Spain's top two cities, while the seven-day Best of San Sebastián & the Basque Countryside tour takes you to an often overlooked, idyllic corner of Europe. You'll enjoy great guides, a fun bunch of travel partners (with small groups of generally around 26), and plenty of room to spread out in a big, comfy bus. You'll find European adventures to fit every vacation length. For all the details, and to get our Tour Catalog and a free Rick Steves Tour Experience DVD (filmed on location during an actual tour), visit www.ricksteves.com or call the Tour Department at 425/608-4217.

produced by Rick Steves and Gene Openshaw (the co-author of seven books in the Rick Steves series), are available through iTunes and at www.ricksteves.com. Simply download them onto your computer and transfer them to your iPod or other MP3 player. (Remember to bring a Y-jack and extra set of earbuds for your travel partner.)

Maps

The black-and-white maps in this book, designed by my well-traveled staff, are concise and simple. The maps are intended to help you locate recommended places and reach TIs, where you'll find more in-depth (and often free) maps of cities or regions. Better maps are sold at newsstands—take a look before you buy to be sure the map has the level of detail you want.

Michelin maps are available—and cheaper than in the US—throughout Spain at bookstores, newsstands, and gas stations. Train travelers can do fine with a simple rail map (such as the one that comes with a train pass) and city maps from the tourist information offices. For drivers, I'd recommend a 1:200,000- or 1:300,000-scale map.

Other Guidebooks

If you're like most travelers, this book is all you'll need. But if you're heading beyond my recommended destinations, you might want some supplemental information. Considering the improvements they'll make in your $5,000 vacation, $30 or $40 for extra maps and books is money well spent. Note that none of the following guidebooks are updated annually; check the copyright date before you buy.

Lonely Planet's guide to Spain is well researched, with good maps and hotel recommendations for low- to moderate-budget travelers. The similar *Rough Guide to Spain* is hip and insightful, written by British researchers. Students and vagabonds like the highly opinionated *Let's Go: Spain & Portugal,* updated by Harvard students. *Let's Go* is best for backpackers who stay at hostels, use railpasses, and dive into the youth and nightlife scene.

The Eyewitness series has about a dozen editions covering Spain, including Barcelona, Madrid, and Sevilla/Andalucía. They're extremely popular for great, easy-to-grasp graphics and photos, but the written content in Eyewitness is relatively skimpy, and the books weigh a ton. I simply borrow them for a minute from other travelers at certain sights to make sure I'm aware of that place's highlights. *Time Out* travel guides provide good, detailed coverage of Madrid, Barcelona, and Andalucía, particularly on arts and entertainment.

The popular, skinny Michelin Green Guides to Spain are excellent, especially if you're driving. They're known for their city and sightseeing maps, dry but concise and helpful information on major sights, and good cultural and historical background. English editions, covering most of the regions you'll want to visit, are sold in Spain.

Visiting Valencia?

This guidebook is designed to be selective, covering the best Spanish destinations in depth. But plenty of visit-worthy places didn't make it in the book, including sunny Valencia.

Valencia—famous for paella and home to El Cid—is Spain's third-largest city and throws its biggest street party, Las Fallas. The thriving city is a cultural center with a popular Mediterranean promenade. It's a leader in Spanish avant-garde architecture—thanks to works by Sir Norman Foster and native son Santiago Calatrava. Equidistant (220 miles) from both Madrid and Barcelona, and located on Spain's east coast, Valencia can be a handy stop with a good day's worth of sightseeing within its characteristic Old Town.

My friend Tooraj Fooladi, who lives in Valencia (and guides tours of Spain for my company), loves his town and has written a fine chapter on Valencia that is available for free at www.ricksteves.com/valencia. If you're visiting Valencia, I hope you can download this chapter, pack it along, and take advantage of Tooraj's hard work. Happy Valencian travels!

I like Cadogan guides for their well-presented background information and coverage of cultural issues. Their recommendations suit upscale travelers. Older travelers enjoy Frommer's Spain guides even though those, like the Fodor's guides, ignore alternatives that enable travelers to save money by dirtying their fingers in the local culture. The encyclopedic Blue Guides to Spain are dry as the plains in Spain, but just right for scholarly types.

Recommended Books and Movies

Spain is overwhelmingly rich in history, art, and culture. For information on Spain past and present, consider reading some of these books or seeing these films:

Non-Fiction

Spain has undergone incredible changes since the death of Franco in 1975. *The New Spaniards* (Hooper) is a survey of all aspects of modern Spain, including its politics, economy, demographics, education, religion, and popular culture.

For a sympathetic cultural history of the Basque people, their language, and contributions from Roman times to the present, read *The Basque History of the World* (Kurlansky).

George Orwell traded his press pass for a uniform, fought against Franco's Fascists in the Spanish Civil War of 1936–39, and then wrote an account of his experiences in his gripping *Homage to Catalonia*. *The Battle for Spain* (Beevor) re-creates the political climate during the Civil War.

James Michener traveled to Spain for several decades, and his tribute, *Iberia*, describes how Spain's dark history created a contradictory and passionately beautiful land.

Hemingway shows his journalistic side in two books on bullfighting: *Death in the Afternoon* and *The Dangerous Summer.*

Travelers' Tales: Spain (McCauley) offers dozens of essays about Spain and its people from numerous authors.

Penelope Casas has written many popular books on the food of Spain, including tapas, paella, and regional cooking. Her *Discovering Spain: An Uncommon Guide* blends references to history, culture, and food with travel information. For deciphering menus in restaurants, foodies like *The Marling Menu-Master for Spain.*

The nature of pilgrimage is explored along the famous Camino de Santiago trail in northern Spain in *Following the Milky Way* (Aviva) and *On Pilgrimage* (Lash).

The eccentricities of village life in the mountains south of Granada are lovingly detailed in a British expat's 1920s experiences in *South from Granada* (Brenan). A contemporary family's adjustments to living in the same region are described in *Driving Over Lemons: An Optimist in Spain* (Stewart) and his later books.

Fiction

Fans of classic literature will want to read Cervantes' *Don Quixote.* Another classic, Irving's *Tales of the Alhambra,* weaves fact, mythical tales, and descriptions of Granada and its beautiful Moorish castle complex—the Alhambra—during his 19th-century visit.

Hemingway fans will enjoy *The Sun Also Rises,* his story of expats living in post-WWI Spain that introduced bullfighting to the world. His *For Whom the Bell Tolls,* a tale of idealism and harsh reality, is set against the complexity of the Spanish Civil War.

The brutality and intolerance of the dark years of the Spanish Inquisition are illuminated in Winstein's *The Heretic,* with Sevilla as the backdrop. *The Last Jew* (Gordon) is one man's story of survival in Inquisition-era Spain. *Stories from Spain* (Barlow and Stivers) relates well-known Spanish legends that chronicle nearly 1,000 years of Spanish history.

The 2005 best-selling thriller *The Shadow of the Wind* (Zafon) takes place in 1950s Barcelona. Robert Wilson's popular police thrillers, including *The Blind Man of Seville,* are set in Spain and Portugal.

Films

In *The Mystery of Picasso* (1956), Picasso is filmed painting, allowing a look at his creative process.

Peter O'Toole and Sophia Loren star in the musical version of Don Quixote, *Man of La Mancha* (1972).

In the first of Carlos Saura's flamenco dance trilogy, *Blood*

Wedding (1981), he adapts Federico García Lorca's play about a wedding imposed on a bride in love with another man. *Carmen* (1983) shows a Spanish cast rehearsing the well-known French novel and opera. *El Amor Brujo* (1986) is a ghostly love story.

In *Barcelona* (1994), two Americans in Spain try to navigate the Spanish singles scene and the ensuing culture clash.

The Spanish film *Open Your Eyes* (1997) inspired the 2001 Tom Cruise thriller *Vanilla Sky*, where a car accident sets off an intricate series of events.

Pedro Almodóvar's films about relationships usually garner piles of awards, including Oscars. Spanish actors Javier Bardem, Penélope Cruz, and Antonio Banderas have starred in his films. Almodóvar's best-known films range from *Women on the Verge of a Nervous Breakdown* (1988) to his most recent, *Volver* (2006).

TELEPHONES, EMAIL, AND MAIL

Telephones

Smart travelers learn the phone system and use it daily to reserve or reconfirm rooms, get tourist information, reserve restaurants, confirm tour times, or phone home.

Types of Phones

You'll encounter various kinds of phones in Spain.

Card-operated phones—in which you insert a locally bought phone card into a public pay phone—are common.

Coin-operated phones, the original kind of pay phone (but becoming increasingly rare), require you to have enough change to complete your call.

Hotel room phones are sometimes cheap for local calls (confirm at the front desk first), but can be a rip-off for long-distance calls ($1–2/minute unless you use an international phone card—described below). But incoming calls are free, making this a cheap way for friends and family to stay in touch, provided they have a good long-distance plan for calls to Europe.

American mobile phones work in Europe if they're GSM-enabled, tri-band or quad-band, and on a calling plan that includes international calls. They're convenient, but pricey. For example, with a T-Mobile phone, you'll pay $1 per minute for calls, and about $0.35 for text messages.

European mobile phones run about $40–75 (for the most basic models) and come without contracts. If you don't speak Spanish, the mechanics of using these phones are almost impossible, but any young Spaniard can bail you out in a snap. These phones are loaded with prepaid calling time that you can recharge as you use up the minutes. As long as you're not "roaming" outside the phone's home country, incoming calls are free. For more information on mobile phones, see www.ricksteves.com/plan/tips/mobilephones.htm.

Using Phone Cards

Get a phone card for your calls. Prepaid phone cards come in two types: international and insertable. Both are described below. Either type of phone card works only in Spain.

International phone cards, called *tarjetas telefónicas con código,* are the cheapest way to make international calls from Spain. You can use these cards from nearly any phone, including the one in your hotel room (check to make sure that your phone is set on tone instead of pulse, and ask at the desk about hidden fees for toll-free calls). Cards are marked as national (for Spain) or international. All cards work for domestic or international calls, but you get better rates if you use the card for the purpose it was intended—so if you plan to use your card mostly for calls home, ask for an international card.

International cards all work the same way and are simple to use (English instructions provided). Scratch off the back to reveal your PIN (Personal Identification Number). Dial the number listed on the card, reaching an automated operator. When prompted, dial in the PIN code. Then dial your number.

You can buy an international phone card at most kiosks and newsstands, but the best selection is usually at hole-in-the-wall shops catering to immigrants, who are the leading experts on calling home cheaply. You can also find them at call centers (*locutorios*). These cards, made by numerous (sometimes fly-by-night) companies, offer good rates but don't consistently work well. Try to confirm that the card can be used for calls to America (the salesclerk may not know), and buy a lower-denomination card in case the card is a dud.

Remember that you don't need the actual card to use a card account, so it's shareable. You can write down the access number and PIN code in your notebook and share it with friends. Give the number of a still lively card to another traveler if you're leaving the country.

Insertable phone cards, called *tarjetas telefónicas,* can only be used at pay phones. These cards are sold at post offices and many newsstand kiosks. Spanish pay phones are easy to find but refuse to be rushed. After you *"inserta"* your *"tarjeta"* into the phone, wait until the digital display says *"Marque número"* and then dial. Dial slowly and deliberately. Push the square R button to get a dial tone for a new call. The phone doesn't beep to remind you that you've left the card in, so don't forget to remove it when you're done. The cost of the call is automatically deducted from your card.

Using Hotel-Room Phones, Metered Phones, VoIP, or US Calling Cards

The phone in your **hotel room** is convenient...but expensive. While incoming calls (made by folks back home) can be an affordable way to keep in touch, charges for *outgoing* calls can be a very unpleasant surprise. Before you dial, get a clear explanation from the hotel staff of the charges, even for local and (supposedly) toll-free calls.

Dialing direct from your hotel room—without using an international phone card (described above)—is usually quite expensive for international calls. If your family has an inexpensive way to call Europe, either through a long-distance plan or prepaid calling card, have them call you in your hotel room. Give them a list of your hotels' phone numbers before you go. Then, as you travel, send them an email or make a quick pay-phone call to set up a time for them to give you a ring.

Metered phones are sometimes available in phone centers *(locutorios)* and bigger post offices. You can talk all you want, then pay the bill when you leave—but be sure you know the rates before you have a lengthy conversation.

If you're traveling with a laptop, consider trying **VoIP (Voice over Internet Protocol).** With VoIP, two computers act as the phones, allowing for a free Internet-based call. The major providers are Skype (www.skype.com) and Google Talk (www.google.com/talk).

US calling cards (such as the ones offered by AT&T, MCI, or Sprint) are the worst option. You'll nearly always save a lot of money by paying with a phone card (see above).

How to Dial

Calling from the US to Europe, or vice versa, is simple—once you break the code. The European calling chart on the next page will walk you through it.

Dialing Domestic Calls

About half of all European countries use area codes; the other half use a direct-dial system without area codes.

All phone numbers in Spain are nine digits (no area codes) that can be dialed direct throughout the country. For example, to call a recommended Madrid hotel, you'd dial the same number (tel. 915-212-941) whether you're calling from the Madrid train station or from Barcelona.

Note that numbers that start with 900 are toll-free; numbers that start with 901 and 902 can be expensive to call.

Dialing Internationally

If you want to make an international call, follow these three steps:

1. Dial the international access code (00 if you're calling from Europe, 011 from the US or Canada).

2. Dial the country code of the country you're calling (see calling chart on the next page).

European Calling Chart

Just smile and dial, using this key:
AC = Area Code, LN = Local Number.

European Country	Calling long distance within...	Calling from the US or Canada to...	Calling from a European country to...
Austria	AC + LN	011 + 43 + AC (without the initial zero) + LN	00 + 43 + AC (without the initial zero) + LN
Belgium	LN	011 + 32 + LN (without initial zero)	00 + 32 + LN (without initial zero)
Bosnia-Herzegovina	AC + LN	011 + 387 + AC (without initial zero) + LN	00 + 387 + AC (without initial zero) + LN
Britain	AC + LN	011 + 44 + AC (without initial zero) + LN	00 + 44 + AC (without initial zero) + LN
Croatia	AC + LN	011 + 385 + AC (without initial zero) + LN	00 + 385 + AC (without initial zero) + LN
Czech Republic	LN	011 + 420 + LN	00 + 420 + LN
Denmark	LN	011 + 45 + LN	00 + 45 + LN
Estonia	LN	011 + 372 + LN	00 + 372 + LN
Finland	AC + LN	011 + 358 + AC (without initial zero) + LN	999 + 358 + AC (without initial zero) + LN
France	LN	011 + 33 + LN (without initial zero)	00 + 33 + LN (without initial zero)
Germany	AC + LN	011 + 49 + AC (without initial zero) + LN	00 + 49 + AC (without initial zero) + LN
Greece	LN	011 + 30 + LN	00 + 30 + LN
Hungary	06 + AC + LN	011 + 36 + AC + LN	00 + 36 + AC + LN
Ireland	AC + LN	011 + 353 + AC (without initial zero) + LN	00 + 353 + AC (without initial zero) + LN

APPENDIX

European Country	Calling long distance within...	Calling from the US or Canada to...	Calling from a European country to...
Italy	LN	011 + 39 + LN	00 + 39 + LN
Montenegro	AC + LN	011 + 382 + AC (without initial zero) + LN	00 + 382 + AC (without initial zero) + LN
Netherlands	AC + LN	011 + 31 + AC (without initial zero) + LN	00 + 31 + AC (without initial zero) + LN
Norway	LN	011 + 47 + LN	00 + 47 + LN
Poland	LN	011 + 48 + LN (without initial zero)	00 + 48 + LN (without initial zero)
Portugal	LN	011 + 351 + LN	00 + 351 + LN
Slovakia	AC + LN	011 + 421 + AC (without initial zero) + LN	00 + 421 + AC (without initial zero) + LN
Slovenia	AC + LN	011 + 386 + AC (without initial zero) + LN	00 + 386 + AC (without initial zero) + LN
Spain	LN	011 + 34 + LN	00 + 34 + LN
Sweden	AC + LN	011 + 46 + AC (without initial zero) + LN	00 + 46 + AC (without initial zero) + LN
Switzerland	LN	011 + 41 + LN (without initial zero)	00 + 41 + LN (without initial zero)
Turkey	AC (if no initial zero is included, add one) + LN	011 + 90 + AC (without initial zero) + LN	00 + 90 + AC (without initial zero) + LN

- The instructions above apply whether you're calling a land line or mobile phone.
- The international access codes (the first numbers you dial when making an international call) are 011 if you're calling from the US or Canada, or 00 if you're calling from virtually anywhere in Europe (except Finland, where it's 999).
- To call the US or Canada from Europe, dial 00, then 1 (the country code for the US and Canada), then the area code and number. In short, 00 + 1 + AC + LN = Hi, Mom!

3. Dial the entire phone number, keeping in mind that calling many countries requires dropping the initial zero of the phone number (see chart on previous page for specifics per country).

For example, to call the Madrid hotel from the US, dial 011 (the US international access code), 34 (Spain's country code), then 915-212-941.

To call my office in Edmonds, Washington, from Spain, I dial 00 (Europe's international access code), 1 (the US country code), 425 (Edmonds' area code), and 771-8303.

Europeans often write their phone numbers with + at the front—it's just a placeholder for the international access code (again, that's 011 from the US or Canada, 00 from Europe).

Useful Phone Numbers

Emergency/Medical Needs

Police: Spain—tel. 091, Morocco—tel. 19
Emergency Medical Assistance: Spain—tel. 112

Consulates and Embassies

US Embassy in Madrid, Spain: tel. 915-872-240, after-hours emergency tel. 915-872-200 (Calle Serrano 75, www.embusa.es/cons/services.html)
US Embassy in Gibraltar: Call US Embassy in Madrid.
US Embassy in Casablanca, Morocco: tel. 22/26-45-50 or 22/26-71-51, after-hours emergency tel. 61/17-23-67 (Boulevard Moulay Youssef 8, www.usembassy.ma)
Canadian Embassy in Madrid, Spain: tel. 914-233-250 (Núñez de Balboa 35, www.canada-es.org)

Travel Advisories

US Department of State: tel. 202/647-5225, www.travel.state.gov
US Centers for Disease Control and Prevention: tel. 877-FYI-TRIP, www.cdc.gov/travel
Canadian Department of Foreign Affairs: Canadian tel. 800-267-6788, www.dfait-maeci.gc.ca

Directory Assistance

In Spain, dial 11811 (€0.40/min) or 11818 (€0.55/call from private numbers, free from phone booths).

Trains

Train (RENFE) Reservation and Information: tel. 902-240-202, www.renfe.es

Airports

The following airports share a customer assistance line,

The Spanish Language Barrier

Spain presents the English-speaking traveler with one of the most formidable language barriers in Western Europe. Locals visibly brighten when you know and use some key Spanish words (see "Spanish Survival Phrases" later in the appendix). Learn the key phrases. Travel with a phrase book, particularly if you want to interact with local people. You'll find that doors open quicker and with more smiles when you can speak a few words of the language.

tel. 902-404-704, and a website, www.aena.es.
Barcelona: El Prat de Llobregat Airport—tel. 932-983-838
Madrid: Barajas Airport—tel. 913-936-000
Sevilla: San Pablo Airport—tel. 954-258-548

Email and Mail

Email: Many travelers set up a free email account with Yahoo, Microsoft (Hotmail), or Google (Gmail). Internet cafés and little hole-in-the-wall Internet-access shops (offering a few computers, no food, and cheap prices) are popular in most cities. Email use among Spanish hoteliers is quite common, and most prefer to receive bookings online rather than by fax or phone. More and more hotels now offer (slow) Internet access in their lobbies for guests for free or for a minimal fee. Ask if your hotel has access. If it doesn't, your hotelier will direct you to the nearest place to get online.

Wireless access (Wi-Fi) is becoming more common throughout Spain. Telefónica, the Spanish telecom, has begun offering Wi-Fi hotspots at some hotels, restaurants, and cafés (www.telefonicaonline.com/on/es/wifi).

Mail: While you can arrange for mail delivery to your hotel (allow 10 days for a letter to arrive), phoning and emailing are so easy that I've dispensed with mail stops altogether.

TRANSPORTATION

By Car or Train?

Cars are best for three or more traveling together (especially families with small kids), those packing heavy, and those scouring the countryside; but are an expensive headache in bigger cities. Trains and buses are best for solo travelers, blitz tourists, and city-to-city travelers.

Overview of Trains and Buses

Public transportation in Spain is becoming slick, modern, and efficient. The best option is to mix bus and train travel. Always verify schedules before your departure. Don't leave a station without your next day's schedule options in hand. To ask for a schedule at an information window, say, *"Horario para* (fill in names of cities), *por favor."* (The local TI will sometimes have schedules available for you to take or copy.) To study train schedules in advance, visit Germany's excellent all-Europe website, http://bahn.hafas.de/bin/query.exe/en, or Spain's site, www.renfe.es. For Comes buses in southern Spain, check www.tgcomes.es. Or try www.movelia.es, a private site listing several bus companies.

Trains

You can buy a Spain "flexi" railpass that allows travel for a given number of days over a longer period of time, but you'll pay separately ($7.50–37.50) for seat reservations on all trains. Buying individual train tickets in advance or as you go in Spain can be less expensive, and gives you better access to seat reservations (which are limited for railpass-holders). Some individual ticket prices already include seat reservations when required (i.e., for fast trains).

If your trip also includes a neighboring country, consider the France–Spain, Portugal–Spain, or Italy–Spain passes (see chart on page 670). A Eurail Selectpass lets you travel even farther. Spain also offers a rail-and-drive pass, which gives you the ease of big-city train hops and the flexibility of a car for rural areas such as the Andalusian hill towns. These passes are sold only outside of Europe. For specifics, check the railpass chart on page 670, contact your travel agent, or see my *Guide to Railpasses* at www.ricksteves.com/rail. Even if you have a railpass, use buses when they're more convenient and direct than the trains. Remember to reserve ahead for the fast AVE trains and overnight journeys.

RENFE (the acronym for the Spanish national train system) used to mean "Really Exasperating, and Not For Everyone," but it has moved into the 21st century. For information and reservations, dial RENFE's national number (tel. 902-157-507) from anywhere in Spain. For tips on buying tickets, see the "Buying Train Tickets" sidebar.

Spain categorizes trains this way:

The high-speed train called the **AVE** (AH-vay, stands for Alta Velocidad Española) whisks travelers between Madrid and Toledo in 30 minutes, Madrid and Sevilla or Madrid and Barcelona in less than three hours, and Madrid and Málaga in three hours. Franco left Spain a train system that didn't fit Europe's gauge, and AVE trains run on European-gauge tracks. AVE trains can be priced differently according to their time of

Buying Train Tickets

As trains can sell out, it's smart to buy your tickets a day in advance even for short rides. You generally have three options for buying train tickets: at the station, at a travel agency, or online. Since station ticket offices can get very crowded, most travelers will find it easiest to go to a travel agency.

At the Station: You will likely have to wait in a line to buy your ticket. First find the correct line—at bigger stations, there might be separate windows for short-distance, long-distance, advance, and "today" *(para hoy)* tickets. To avoid wasting time in the wrong line, read the signs carefully, and ask a local (or a clerk at an information window) which line you need. You might have to take a number—watch locals and follow their lead. To avoid waiting, you can sometimes use your credit card at an automated machine (which looks like an ATM)—but only for trains between major destinations.

As another option, you could buy tickets or reservations at the RENFE offices located in more than 100 city centers. These are more central and multilingual—and also less crowded and confusing—than the train station.

Travel Agency: The best choice for most travelers is to buy tickets at an English-speaking travel agency. The El Corte Inglés department stores (with locations in most Spanish cities) often have handy travel agencies inside. I've recommended these and other travel agencies throughout this book.

Online: You can buy tickets online for any type of train except local commuter trains *(cercanías)*. Use the RENFE site at www.renfe.es (choose "English" in the drop-down box labeled *Seleccione su idioma*). Long-distance trains require reservations, which are automatic when you buy online. Some discounts are available if you book early, starting 60 days in advance of travel (see "The Fine Print," below). First-time users must pick up tickets in person at the station and show ID. Repeat users can print tickets at home. When the online form asks for your Spanish national ID number, enter your passport number. The only drawback for buying tickets online is that if your plans change, you can only change your ticket at one of the automated machines at the station (which you might not find at some small-town stations).

The Fine Print: First-class tickets cost 50 percent more than second class—often as much as a domestic flight (see "Cheap Flights," page 677). Some advance-purchase discounts are available when you purchase point-to-point tickets through RENFE. Discounted tickets come with restrictions, such as being nonrefundable and nonchangeable. Be sure to read all the details carefully at time of purchase.

Railpasses

Prices listed are for 2009 and are subject to change. For the latest prices, details, and train schedules (and easy online ordering), see my comprehensive *Guide to Eurail Passes* at www.ricksteves.com/rail.

"Saver" prices are per person for two or more people traveling together. "Youth" means under age 26. The fare for children 4–11 is half the adult individual fare or Saver fare. Kids under age 4 travel free.

SPAIN RAIL & DRIVE PASS

Any 3 rail days and 2 car days in 2 months.

Car Category	1st Class	2nd Class	Extra car day
Economy car	$333	$275	$46
Compact car	340	282	54
Intermediate car	366	308	80
Intermediate auto. car	401	343	114
Full size	427	370	140

Prices are per person, two traveling together. Solo travelers pay about $100 extra. Third and fourth people sharing car buy only the railpass. Extra rail days (max 7) cost $35-$42 per day. To order Rail & Drive passes, call your travel agent or Rail Europe at 800-438-7245. *This pass is not sold by Europe Through the Back Door.*

SPAIN PASS

	1st Class	2nd Class
3 days in 2 months	257	$205
Extra rail days (max 7)	$38-40	$30-32

SPAIN-PORTUGAL PASS

	Individual 1st Class	Saver 1st Class
3 days in 2 months	$295	$251
Extra rail days (max 7)	40	$35

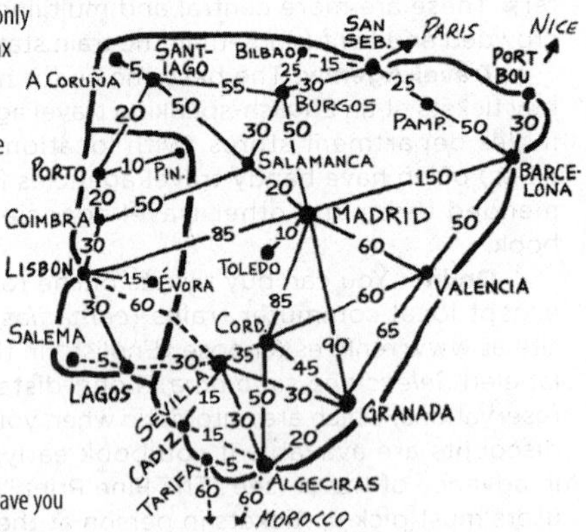

Map key:

Approximate point-to-point one-way second-class rail fares in US dollars. First class costs 50 percent more. Add up fares for your itinerary to see whether a railpass will save you money. Dashed lines are buses.

SELECTPASS

This pass covers travel in three adjacent countries. Please visit **www.ricksteves.com/rail** for four- and five-country options.

	Individual 1st Class	Saver 1st Class	Youth 2nd Class
5 days in 2 months	$435	$370	$284
6 days in 2 months	481	410	315
8 days in 2 months	570	487	370
10 days in 2 months	660	559	427

FRANCE–SPAIN PASS

	Individual 1st Class	Individual 2nd Class	Saver 1st Class	Saver 2nd Class	Youth 2nd Class
4 days in 2 months	$351	$307	$307	$271	$232
Extra rail days (max 6)	42	35	35	30	27

APPENDIX

departure. Peak hours *(punta)* are most expensive, followed by *llano* and *valle* (quietest and cheapest times). AVE is almost entirely covered by the Eurailpass (book ahead, a seat reservation fee from Madrid to Sevilla costs Eurailers about $23 in second class; $38 for first class, includes meal). A new Madrid–Barcelona link is now in operation, and other lines such as Córdoba–Málaga are set to open soon.

The **TALGO** is fast, air-conditioned, and expensive, and runs on AVE rails. **Intercity** and **Electro** trains fall just behind TALGO in speed, comfort, and expense. **Rápido, Tranvía, Semidirecto,** and **Expreso** trains are generally slower. **Cercanías** are commuter trains for big-city workers and small-town tourists. **Regional** and **Correo** trains are slow, small-town milk runs. Trains get more expensive as they pick up speed, but all are cheaper per mile than their northern European counterparts. Spain loves to name trains, so you may encounter types of trains not listed here. The names Euromed, Alaris, Altaria, and Arco all indicate faster trains that require reservations.

Salidas means "departures" and *llegadas* is "arrivals." On train schedules, "LMXJVSD" stand for the days of the week in Spanish, starting with Monday. A train that runs "LMXJV-D" doesn't run on Saturdays. *Laborables* can mean Monday through Friday or Monday through Saturday.

Overnight Trains: For long trips, I go overnight on the train or I fly (domestic shuttle flights are generally less than $100). Overnight trains (and buses) are usually less expensive and slower than the daytime rides. Most overnight trains have berths and beds that you can rent (not included in the cost of your train ticket or railpass). A sleeping berth *(litera)* costs extra, with the price depending on the route and type of compartment. Night trains are popular, so it's smart to reserve in advance, even from home. Travelers with first-class reservations are entitled to use comfortable "Intercity" lounges in train stations in Spain's major cities.

Hotel Trains: The term "Hotel Train" *(Trenhotel)* usually means fancy and expensive. The pricey overnight Hotel Train between Madrid and Lisbon is called the Lusitania (first class-$205, including a bed in a double compartment; second class-$117 in a quad; pay $54 or more for a sleeper if you have a railpass, additional cost for singles or a shower in your compartment). Unfortunately, no cheaper rail option exists between these two capital cities. You can save money by taking a bus, or save time by taking a plane. Hotel Train prices are at least as high between other major cities, such as Barcelona–Valencia or Barcelona–Madrid.

Pricey international Hotel Trains connect France, Italy, and Switzerland with Spain. All of these spendy overnight trains (known collectively as Elipsos) have names: Francisco de Goya (Madrid–Paris), Joan Miró (Barcelona–Paris), Pau Casals (Barcelona–Zürich), and Salvador Dalí (Barcelona–Milan). Full fares range from $268 in a quad to $748 for a Gran Clase single compartment. Travelers with any railpass that covers at least one country on the route of travel (including Swiss Passes but not Swiss Cards) can use a railpass travel day and pay about half the full fare. For more information on international Hotel Trains, see www.elipsos.com. If you can easily afford to take a Hotel Train, consider flying instead to save time (see "Cheap Flights," page 677).

To avoid the expensive luxury of an international Hotel Train, you can take a cheaper train trip that involves a transfer at the Spanish border (at Irún on Madrid–Paris runs, at Cerbère on the eastern side). You'll connect to a normal night train with $30 *literas* (*couchette* berths) on one leg of the trip. This plan is more time-consuming, and may take two days of a flexipass.

Buses

Spain's bus system is confusing. There are a number of different bus companies (though usually clustered within one building), sometimes running buses to the same destinations and using the same transfer points. If you have to transfer, make sure to look for a bus with the same name/logo as the company you bought the ticket from. The larger stations have an information desk with all of the schedules. In smaller stations, check the destinations and schedules posted on each office window. Bus service on holidays, Saturdays, and especially Sundays can be less frequent.

If you arrive in a city by bus and plan to leave by bus, upon your arrival at the bus station check your departure options and buy a ticket in advance if necessary (and possible). If you're downtown, need a ticket, and the bus station isn't central, save time by asking at the tourist office about travel agencies that sell bus tickets.

Smoking is no longer allowed on buses, and most people respect this new law. This is the best evidence that Spain isn't stuck in the past—even though people are complaining all the way into the future. You can (and most likely will be required to) stow your luggage under the bus. For longer rides, give some thought to which side of the bus will get the most sun, and sit on the opposite side, even if the bus is air-conditioned and has curtains. Your ride will likely come with a soundtrack: taped Spanish pop music, a radio, or sometimes videos. If you prefer silence, bring earplugs.

Drivers and station personnel rarely speak English. Buses generally lack WCs, but they stop every two hours or so for a break (usually 15 min, but can be up to 30). Drivers announce how long the stop will be, but if in doubt, ask the driver, "How many minutes here?" (*"¿Cuántos minutos aquí?"*) so you know if you have time to get out. Listen for the bus horn as a final call before departure. Bus stations have WCs (rarely with toilet paper) and cafés that offer quick and slightly overpriced food.

Public Transportation Routes in Iberia

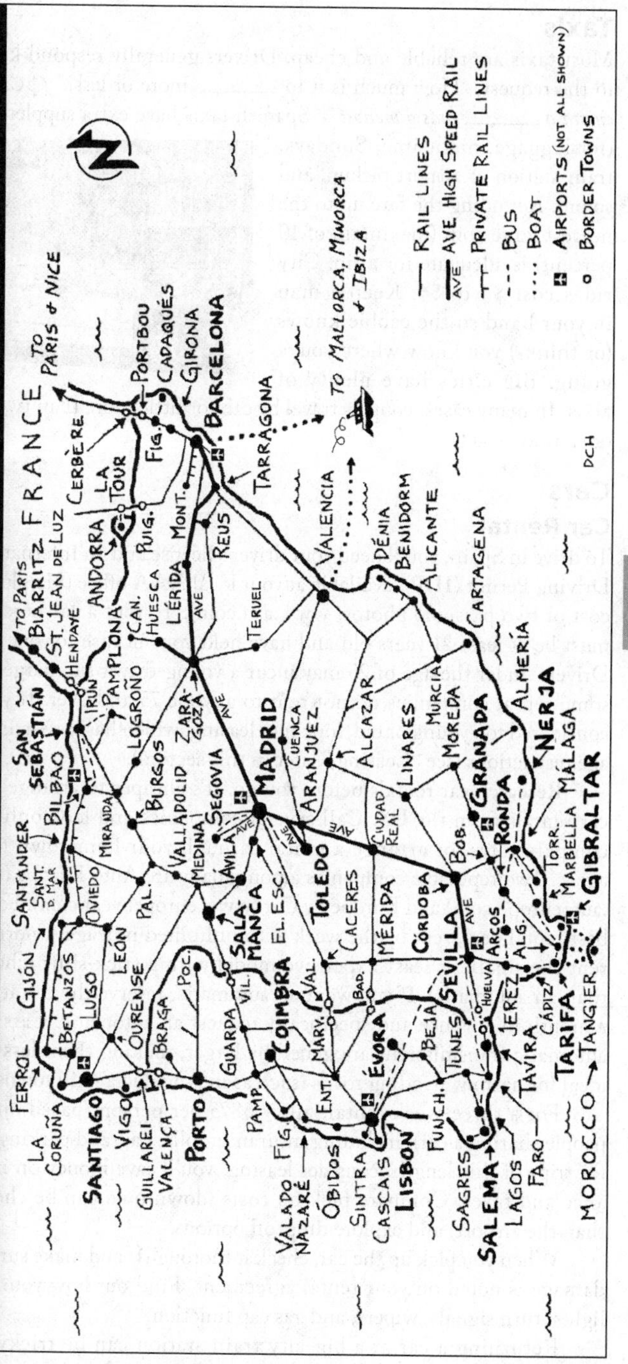

— RAIL LINES
AVE AVE HIGH SPEED RAIL
PRIVATE RAIL LINES
--- BUS
.... BOAT
AIRPORTS (NOT ALL SHOWN)
o BORDER TOWNS

DCH

APPENDIX

Taxis

Most taxis are reliable and cheap. Drivers generally respond kindly to the request, "How much is it to ______, more or less?" *("¿Cuánto cuesta a ______, más o menos?")*. Spanish taxis have extra supplements (for luggage, nighttime, Sundays, train-station or airport pickup, and so on). Rounding the fare up to the nearest large coin (maximum of 10 percent) is adequate for a tip. City rides cost $4 to $6. Keep a map in your hand so the cabbie knows (or thinks) you know where you're going. Big cities have plenty of taxis. In many cases, couples travel by cab for little more than two bus or subway tickets.

Cars

Car Rental

To drive in Spain, you'll need your driver's license and an International Driving Permit (IDP), available at your local AAA office ($15 plus the cost of two passport photos, www.aaa.com). To rent a car here, you must be at least 21 years old and have held your license for one year. Drivers under the age of 25 may incur a young-driver surcharge, and some rental companies do not rent to anyone 75 and over. If you're considered too young or old, look into leasing, which has less-stringent age restrictions (see "Leasing," later in this section).

Research car rentals before you go. It's cheaper to arrange most car rentals from the US. Call several companies and look online to compare rates, or arrange a rental through your hometown travel agent. Two reputable companies among many are Auto Europe (www.autoeurope.com) and Europe by Car (www.europebycar.com). For the best rental deal, rent by the week with unlimited mileage. I normally rent the smallest, least-expensive model with a stick-shift (cheaper than an automatic). If you want an automatic, reserve the car at least a month in advance and specifically request an automatic. Cars with automatic transmissions are generally larger, making them less than ideal for narrow, winding roads (such as in Andalucía's hill towns).

For a three-week rental, allow $875 per person (based on two people sharing a car), including insurance, tolls, gas, and parking. But for trips of this length, consider leasing; you'll save money on insurance and taxes. Compare pick-up costs (downtown can be cheaper than the airport) and explore drop-off options.

When you pick up the car, check it thoroughly and make sure any damage is noted on your rental agreement. Find out how your car's lights, turn signals, wipers, and gas cap function.

Returning a car at a big-city train station can be tricky; get precise details on the car drop-off location and hours. Note that rental offices usually close from midday Saturday until Monday. When you return the car, make sure the agent verifies its condition with you.

Car Insurance Options

When you rent a car, you are liable for a very high deductible, sometimes equal to the entire value of the car. There are various ways you can limit your financial risk in case of an accident. For Spain, you have three options: buy Collision Damage Waiver (CDW) coverage from the car-rental company, get coverage through your credit card (free, if your card automatically includes zero-deductible coverage), or buy coverage through Travel Guard.

CDW includes a very high deductible (typically $1,000–1,500). When you pick up the car, you'll be offered the chance to "buy down" the deductible to zero (for $10–30/day; this is often called "super CDW").

If you opt for credit-card coverage, there's a catch. You'll technically have to decline all coverage offered by the car-rental company, which means they can place a hold on your card for the full deductible amount. In case of damage, it can be time-consuming to resolve the charges with your credit-card company. Before you decide on this option, quiz your credit-card company about how it works and ask them to explain the worst-case scenario.

Buying CDW insurance (plus "super CDW") is the easier but pricier option. Using the coverage that comes with your credit card saves money, but can involve more hassle.

Finally, you can buy CDW insurance from Travel Guard ($9/day plus a one-time $3 service fee covers you up to $35,000, $250 deductible, tel. 800-826-4919, www.travelguard.com). It's valid throughout Europe, but some car-rental companies refuse to honor it (especially in Italy and the Republic of Ireland). Oddly, residents of Washington State aren't allowed to buy this coverage.

For more fine print about car-rental insurance, see www.ricksteves.com/cdw.

Leasing

For trips of three weeks or more, consider leasing (which automatically includes zero-deductible collision and theft insurance). By technically buying and then selling back the car, you save lots of money on tax and insurance. Leasing provides you a brand-new car with unlimited mileage and a 24-hour emergency assistance program. You can lease for as little as 17 days to as long as 6 months. Car leases must be arranged from the US. One of many reliable companies offering affordable lease packages is Europe by Car (US tel. 800-223-1516, www.europebycar.com).

Driving

Driving in Spain is great—sparse traffic and generally good roads—but a pain in big cities such as Madrid. Good maps are available and inexpensive throughout Spain. Freeways come with tolls (about $4/hr) but save huge amounts of time. Always pick up a ticket as you enter a toll freeway. On freeways, navigate by direction *(norte, oeste, sur, este)*. Also, since road numbers can be puzzling and inconsistent, navigate by city names.

Mileage signs are in kilometers (see page 680 for conversion formula into miles). In smaller towns, following signs to *centro ciudad* or *centro urbano* will get you to the heart of things.

Drive defensively. If you're involved in an accident, you will be blamed and will be in for a monumental headache. Seatbelts are required by law. Children under 12 must ride in the back seat, and children up to age 3 must have a child seat. You must put on a reflective safety vest any time you get out of your car on the side of a highway or unlit road (most rental-car companies provide one—but check when you pick up the car). Those who use eyeglasses are required by law to have a spare pair in the car.

STOP AND LEARN THESE ROAD SIGNS

Speed Limit (km/hr) | Yield | No Passing | End of No Passing Zone

One Way | Intersection | Main Road | Freeway

Danger | No Entry | No Entry for Cars | All Vehicles Prohibited

Parking | No Parking | Customs | Peace

Watch for traffic radars and expect to be stopped for a routine check by the police (be sure your car-insurance form is up-to-date). Small towns come with speed traps and corruption. Tickets, especially for foreigners, are issued and paid for on the spot. Insist on a receipt, so the money is less likely to end up in the cop's pocket.

Gas and diesel prices are controlled and the same everywhere—about $6 a gallon for gas, less for diesel. *Gasolina* is either *normal* or *super;* unleaded *(sin plomo)* is now widely available. Note that diesel is called *diesel* or *gasóleo.*

Choose parking places carefully. Leave valuables in the trunk

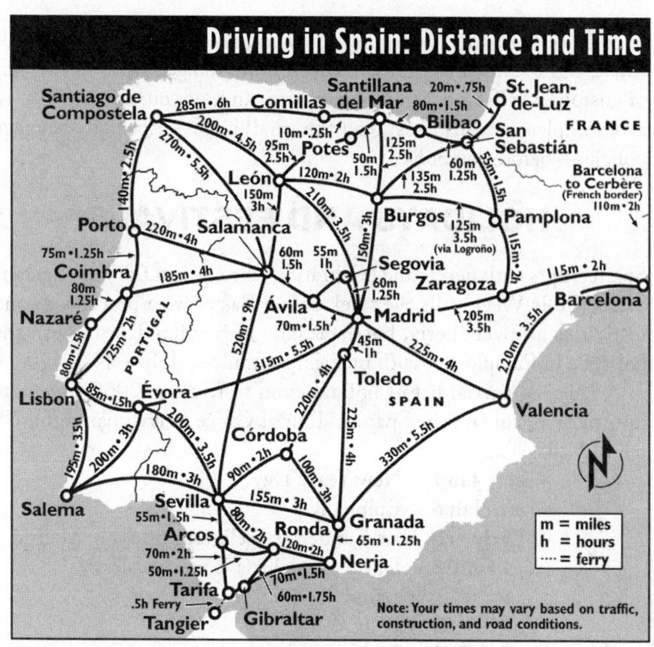

during the day and leave nothing worth stealing in the car overnight. While you should avoid parking lots with twinkly asphalt, thieves break car windows anywhere, even at stoplights. If your car's a hatchback, take the trunk cover off at night so thieves can look in without breaking in. Try to make your car look locally owned by hiding the "tourist-owned" rental-company decals and putting a local newspaper in your front or back window. Parking attendants all over Spain holler, *"Nada en el coche"* ("Nothing in the car"). And they mean it. Ask your hotelier for advice on parking. In cities, you can park safely but expensively in guarded lots.

Cheap Flights

If you're visiting one or more cities on a longer European trip, you might want to look into the affordable intra-European airlines. While trains are still the best way to connect places that are close together, a flight can save both time and money on long journeys.

One of the best websites for comparing inexpensive flights is www.skyscanner.net. Other comparison search engines include www.mobissimo.com and www.wegolo.com.

For flights within Spain, try www.vueling.com, www.iberia.com, or www.spanair.com. Other well-known cheapo airlines include easyJet (www.easyjet.com) and RyanAir (www.ryanair.com). Be aware of the potential drawbacks of flying on the cheap: nonrefundable and nonchangeable tickets, rigid baggage restrictions (and fees if you have more than what's officially allowed), use of airports far outside town, tight schedules that can mean more delays, little in the way of customer assistance if problems arise, and, of course, no frills. To avoid unpleasant surprises, read the small print—especially baggage policies—before you book.

HOLIDAYS AND FESTIVALS

Spain erupts with fiestas and celebrations throughout the year. Semana Santa (Holy Week) fills the week before Easter with processions and festivities all over Iberia, but especially in Sevilla. To run with the bulls, be in Pamplona—with medical insurance—July 6–14.

This is a partial list of holidays and festivals in 2009. For more information, contact the Spanish Tourist Office (www.spain.info, US tel. 212/265-8822).

Jan 1	New Year's Day
Jan 6	Epiphany
Early Feb	La Candelaria (religious festival), Madrid
Feb 28	Day of Andalucía (some closures), Andalucía
April 5–12	Holy Week
April 12	Easter Sunday
April 28–May 5	April Fair, Sevilla
May 1	Labor Day (closures)
May 2	Day of the Autonomous Community, Madrid
Mid-May	Feria del Caballo (horse pageantry), Jerez
Throughout May	San Isidro (religious festival on May 15; also bullfights and zarzuelas all month long), Madrid
June 11	Corpus Christi
Late June	La Patum (Moorish battles), Barcelona
June 24	St. John the Baptist's Day
Late June–Early July	International Festival of Music and Dance, Granada
July 6–14	Running of the Bulls (Fiesta de San Fermín), Pamplona
Aug	Gràcia Festival, Barcelona
Mid-Aug	Verbena de la Paloma (folk festival), Madrid
Aug 15	Assumption of Mary (religious festival)
Mid-Sept–Mid-Oct	Autumn Festival (flamenco, bullfights), Jerez

2009

JANUARY

S	M	T	W	T	F	S
				1	2	3
4	5	6	7	8	9	10
11	12	13	14	15	16	17
18	19	20	21	22	23	24
25	26	27	28	29	30	31

FEBRUARY

S	M	T	W	T	F	S
1	2	3	4	5	6	7
8	9	10	11	12	13	14
15	16	17	18	19	20	21
22	23	24	25	26	27	28

MARCH

S	M	T	W	T	F	S
1	2	3	4	5	6	7
8	9	10	11	12	13	14
15	16	17	18	19	20	21
22	23	24	25	26	27	28
29	30	31				

APRIL

S	M	T	W	T	F	S
			1	2	3	4
5	6	7	8	9	10	11
12	13	14	15	16	17	18
19	20	21	22	23	24	25
26	27	28	29	30		

MAY

S	M	T	W	T	F	S
					1	2
3	4	5	6	7	8	9
10	11	12	13	14	15	16
17	18	19	20	21	22	23
24/31	25	26	27	28	29	30

JUNE

S	M	T	W	T	F	S
	1	2	3	4	5	6
7	8	9	10	11	12	13
14	15	16	17	18	19	20
21	22	23	24	25	26	27
28	29	30				

JULY

S	M	T	W	T	F	S
			1	2	3	4
5	6	7	8	9	10	11
12	13	14	15	16	17	18
19	20	21	22	23	24	25
26	27	28	29	30	31	

AUGUST

S	M	T	W	T	F	S
						1
2	3	4	5	6	7	8
9	10	11	12	13	14	15
16	17	18	19	20	21	22
23/30	24/31	25	26	27	28	29

SEPTEMBER

S	M	T	W	T	F	S
		1	2	3	4	5
6	7	8	9	10	11	12
13	14	15	16	17	18	19
20	21	22	23	24	25	26
27	28	29	30			

OCTOBER

S	M	T	W	T	F	S
				1	2	3
4	5	6	7	8	9	10
11	12	13	14	15	16	17
18	19	20	21	22	23	24
25	26	27	28	29	30	31

NOVEMBER

S	M	T	W	T	F	S
1	2	3	4	5	6	7
8	9	10	11	12	13	14
15	16	17	18	19	20	21
22	23	24	25	26	27	28
29	30					

DECEMBER

S	M	T	W	T	F	S
		1	2	3	4	5
6	7	8	9	10	11	12
13	14	15	16	17	18	19
20	21	22	23	24	25	26
27	28	29	30	31		

Late Sept	La Mercé (parade), Barcelona
Oct 12	Spanish National Day
Nov 1	All Saints' Day
Nov 9	Virgen de la Almudena, Madrid
Mid-Nov	International Jazz Festival, Madrid
Dec 6	Constitution Day
Dec 8	Feast of the Immaculate Conception
Dec 13	Feast of Santa Lucía
Dec 25	Christmas
Dec 31	New Year's Eve

CONVERSIONS AND CLIMATE

Numbers and Stumblers

- Europeans write a few of their numbers differently than we do. 1 = 1, 4 = 4, 7 = 7.
- In Europe, dates appear as day/month/year, so Christmas is 25/12/09.
- Commas are decimal points and decimals commas. A dollar and a half is 1,50, and there are 5.280 feet in a mile.
- When pointing, use your whole hand, palm down.
- When counting with fingers, start with your thumb. If you hold up your first finger to request one item, you'll probably get two.
- What Americans call the second floor of a building is the first floor in Europe.
- On escalators and moving sidewalks, Europeans keep the left "lane" open for passing. Keep to the right.

Metric Conversions (approximate)

1 foot = 0.3 meter
1 yard = 0.9 meter
1 mile = 1.6 kilometers
1 centimeter = 0.4 inch
1 meter = 39.4 inches
1 kilometer = 0.62 mile
1 square yard = 0.8 square meter
1 square mile = 2.6 square kilometers
1 ounce = 28 grams
1 quart = 0.95 liter
1 kilogram = 2.2 pounds
32°F = 0°C

Climate

First line, average daily high; second line, average daily low; third line, days of no rain.

	J	F	M	A	M	J	J	A	S	O	N	D
SPAIN • Madrid												
	47°	52°	59°	65°	70°	80°	87°	85°	77°	65°	55°	48°
	35°	36°	41°	45°	50°	58°	63°	63°	57°	49°	42°	36°
	23	21	21	21	21	25	29	28	24	23	21	21
SPAIN • Barcelona												
	55°	57°	60°	65°	71°	78°	82°	82°	77°	69°	62°	56°
	43°	45°	48°	52°	57°	65°	69°	69°	66°	58°	51°	46°
	26	23	23	21	23	24	27	25	23	22	24	25
SPAIN • Almería (Costa del Sol)												
	60°	61°	64°	68°	72°	78°	83°	84°	81°	73°	67°	62°
	46°	47°	51°	55°	59°	65°	70°	71°	68°	60°	54°	49°
	25	24	26	25	28	29	31	30	27	26	26	26
MOROCCO • Marrakech												
	65°	68°	74°	79°	84°	92°	101°	100°	92°	83°	73°	66°
	40°	43°	48°	52°	57°	62°	67°	68°	63°	57°	49°	42°
	24	23	25	24	29	29	30	30	27	27	27	24

Temperature Conversion: Fahrenheit and Celsius

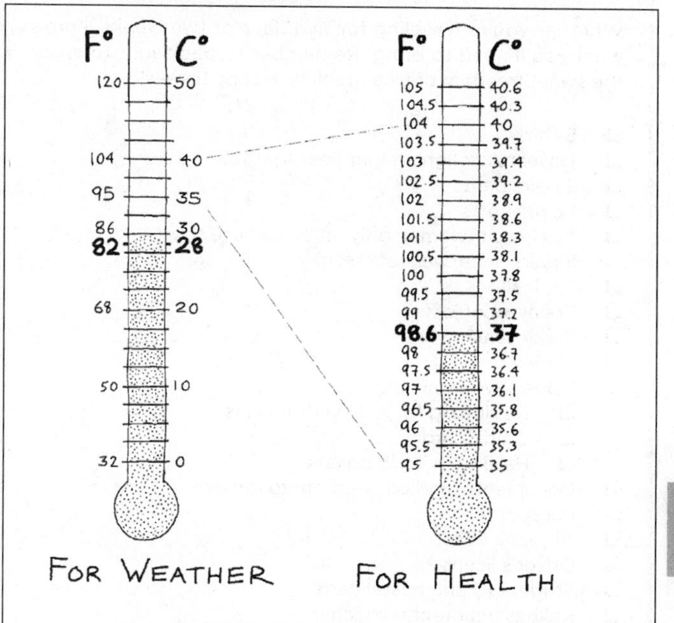

Europe takes its temperature using the Celsius scale, while we opt for Fahrenheit. For a rough conversion from Celsius to Fahrenheit, double the number and add 30. For weather, remember that 28°C is 82°F—perfect. For health, 37°C is just right.

Essential Packing Checklist

Whether you're traveling for five days or five weeks, here's what you'll need to bring. Remember to pack light to enjoy the sweet freedom of true mobility. Happy travels!

- ❑ 5 shirts
- ❑ 1 sweater or lightweight fleece jacket
- ❑ 2 pairs pants
- ❑ 1 pair shorts
- ❑ 1 swimsuit (women only—men can use shorts)
- ❑ 5 pairs underwear and socks
- ❑ 1 pair shoes
- ❑ 1 rain-proof jacket
- ❑ Tie or scarf
- ❑ Money belt
- ❑ Money—your mix of:
  - ❑ Debit card for ATM withdrawals
  - ❑ Credit card
  - ❑ Hard cash in US dollars
- ❑ Documents (and back-up photocopies)
- ❑ Passport
- ❑ Airplane ticket
- ❑ Driver's license
- ❑ Student ID and hostel card
- ❑ Railpass/car rental voucher
- ❑ Insurance details
- ❑ Daypack
- ❑ Sealable plastic baggies
- ❑ Camera and related gear
- ❑ Empty water bottle
- ❑ Wristwatch and alarm clock
- ❑ Earplugs
- ❑ First-aid kit
- ❑ Medicine (labeled)
- ❑ Extra glasses/contacts and prescriptions
- ❑ Sunscreen and sunglasses
- ❑ Toiletries kit
- ❑ Soap
- ❑ Laundry soap (if liquid and carry-on, limit to 3 oz.)
- ❑ Clothesline
- ❑ Small towel
- ❑ Sewing kit
- ❑ Travel information
- ❑ Necessary map(s)
- ❑ Address list (email and mailing addresses)
- ❑ Postcards and photos from home
- ❑ Notepad and pen
- ❑ Journal

Hotel Reservation

To: _________________________ _________________________
hotel *email or fax*

From: _________________________ _________________________
name *email or fax*

Today's date: _____ /_____ /_____
day *month* *year*

Dear Hotel ______________________________________,
Please make this reservation for me:

Name: ______________________________________

Total # of people: _______ # of rooms: _______ # of nights: _______

Arriving: _____ /_____ /_____ My time of arrival (24-hr clock): _______
day *month* *year* (I will telephone if I will be late)

Departing: _____ /_____ /_____
day *month* *year*

Room(s): Single___ Double___ Twin___ Triple___ Quad___

With: Toilet___ Shower___ Bath___ Sink only___

Special needs: View___ Quiet___ Cheapest___ Ground Floor___

Please email or fax confirmation of my reservation, along with the type of room reserved and the price. Please also inform me of your cancellation policy. After I hear from you, I will quickly send my credit-card information as a deposit to hold the room. Thank you.

____
Name

____
Address

____
City ***State*** ***Zip Code*** ***Country***

Before hoteliers can make your reservation, they want to know the information listed above. You can use this form as the basis for your email, or you can photocopy this page, fill in the information, and send it as a fax (also available online at www.ricksteves.com/reservation).

Spanish Survival Phrases

Spanish has a guttural sound similar to the J in Baja California. In the phonetics, the symbol for this clearing-your-throat sound is the italicized ***h***.

Good day.	**Buenos días.**	**bway**-nohs **dee**-ahs
Do you speak English?	**¿Habla usted inglés?**	**ah**-blah oo-**stehd** een-**glays**
Yes. / No.	**Sí. / No.**	see / noh
I (don't) understand.	**(No) comprendo.**	(noh) kohm-**prehn**-doh
Please.	**Por favor.**	por fah-**bor**
Thank you.	**Gracias.**	**grah**-thee-ahs
I'm sorry.	**Lo siento.**	loh see-**ehn**-toh
Excuse me.	**Perdóneme.**	pehr-**doh**-nay-may
(No) problem.	**(No) problema.**	(noh) proh-**blay**-mah
Good.	**Bueno.**	**bway**-noh
Goodbye.	**Adiós.**	ah-dee-**ohs**
one / two	**uno / dos**	**oo**-noh / dohs
three / four	**tres / cuatro**	trays / **kwah**-troh
five / six	**cinco / seis**	**theen**-koh / says
seven / eight	**siete / ocho**	see-**eh**-tay / **oh**-choh
nine / ten	**nueve / diez**	**nway**-bay / dee-**ayth**
How much is it?	**¿Cuánto cuesta?**	**kwahn**-toh **kway**-stah
Write it?	**¿Me lo escribe?**	may loh ay-**skree**-bay
Is it free?	**¿Es gratis?**	ays **grah**-tees
Is it included?	**¿Está incluido?**	ay-**stah** een-kloo-**ee**-doh
Where can I buy / find...?	**¿Dónde puedo comprar / encontrar...?**	**dohn**-day **pway**-doh kohm-**prar** / ayn-kohn-**trar**
I'd like / We'd like...	**Quiero / Queremos...**	kee-**ehr**-oh / kehr-**ay**-mohs
...a room.	**...una habitación.**	**oo**-nah ah-bee-tah-thee-**ohn**
...a ticket to ___.	**...un billete para ___.**	oon bee-**yeh**-tay **pah**-rah
Is it possible?	**¿Es posible?**	ays poh-**see**-blay
Where is...?	**¿Dónde está...?**	**dohn**-day ay-**stah**
...the train station	**...la estación de trenes**	lah ay-stah-thee-**ohn** day **tray**-nays
...the bus station	**...la estación de autobuses**	lah ay-stah-thee-**ohn** day ow-toh-**boo**-says
...the tourist information office	**...la oficina de turismo**	lah oh-fee-**thee**-nah day too-**rees**-moh
Where are the toilets?	**¿Dónde están los servicios?**	**dohn**-day ay-**stahn** lohs sehr-**bee**-thee-ohs
men	**hombres, caballeros**	**ohm**-brays, kah-bah-**yay**-rohs
women	**mujeres, damas**	moo-***heh***-rays, **dah**-mahs
left / right	**izquierda / derecha**	eeth-kee-**ehr**-dah / day-**ray**-chah
straight	**derecho**	day-**ray**-choh
When do you open / close?	**¿A qué hora abren / cierran?**	ah kay **oh**-rah **ah**-brehn / thee-**ay**-rahn
At what time?	**¿A qué hora?**	ah kay **oh**-rah
Just a moment.	**Un momento.**	oon moh-**mehn**-toh
now / soon / later	**ahora / pronto / más tarde**	ah-**oh**-rah / **prohn**-toh / mahs **tar**-day
today / tomorrow	**hoy / mañana**	oy / mahn-**yah**-nah

In the Restaurant

I'd like / We'd like...	**Quiero / Queremos...**	kee-**ehr**-oh / kehr-**ay**-mohs
...to reserve...	**...reservar...**	ray-sehr-**bar**
...a table for one / two.	**...una mesa para uno / dos.**	**oo**-nah **may**-sah **pah**-rah **oo**-noh / dohs
Non-smoking.	**No fumadores.**	noh foo-mah-**doh**-rays
Is this table free?	**¿Está esta mesa libre?**	ay-**stah ay**-stah **may**-sah **lee**-bray
The menu (in English), please.	**La carta (en inglés), por favor.**	lah **kar**-tah (ayn een-**glays**) por fah-**bor**
service (not) included	**servicio (no) incluido**	sehr-**bee**-thee-oh (noh) een-kloo-**ee**-doh
cover charge	**precio de entrada**	**pray**-thee-oh day ayn-**trah**-dah
to go	**para llevar**	**pah**-rah yay-**bar**
with / without	**con / sin**	kohn / seen
and / or	**y / o**	ee / oh
menu (of the day)	**menú (del día)**	may-**noo** (dayl **dee**-ah)
specialty of the house	**especialidad de la casa**	ay-spay-thee-ah-lee-**dahd** day lah **kah**-sah
tourist menu	**menú de turista**	meh-**noo** day too-**ree**-stah
combination plate	**plato combinado**	**plah**-toh kohm-bee-**nah**-doh
appetizers	**tapas**	**tah**-pahs
bread	**pan**	pahn
cheese	**queso**	**kay**-soh
sandwich	**bocadillo**	boh-kah-**dee**-yoh
soup	**sopa**	**soh**-pah
salad	**ensalada**	ayn-sah-**lah**-dah
meat	**carne**	**kar**-nay
poultry	**aves**	**ah**-bays
fish	**pescado**	pay-**skah**-doh
seafood	**marisco**	mah-**ree**-skoh
fruit	**fruta**	**froo**-tah
vegetables	**verduras**	behr-**doo**-rahs
dessert	**postres**	**poh**-strays
tap water	**agua del grifo**	**ah**-gwah dayl **gree**-foh
mineral water	**agua mineral**	**ah**-gwah mee-nay-**rahl**
milk	**leche**	**lay**-chay
(orange) juice	**zumo (de naranja)**	**thoo**-moh (day nah-**rahn**-*h*ah)
coffee	**café**	kah-**feh**
tea	**té**	tay
wine	**vino**	**bee**-noh
red / white	**tinto / blanco**	**teen**-toh / **blahn**-koh
glass / bottle	**vaso / botella**	**bah**-soh / boh-**tay**-yah
beer	**cerveza**	thehr-**bay**-thah
Cheers!	**¡Salud!**	sah-**lood**
More. / Another.	**Más. / Otro.**	mahs / **oh**-troh
The same.	**El mismo.**	ehl **mees**-moh
The bill, please.	**La cuenta, por favor.**	lah **kwayn**-tah por fah-**bor**
tip	**propina**	proh-**pee**-nah
Delicious!	**¡Delicioso!**	day-lee-thee-**oh**-soh

For hundreds more pages of survival phrases for your trip to Spain, check out *Rick Steves' Spanish Phrase Book*.

INDEX

C

Rick Steves®

www.ricksteves.com

TRAVEL SKILLS

Europe Through the Back Door

EUROPE GUIDES

Best of Europe
Eastern Europe
Europe 101
European Christmas
Postcards from Europe

COUNTRY GUIDES

Croatia & Slovenia
England
France
Germany
Great Britain
Ireland
Italy
Portugal
Scandinavia
Spain
Switzerland

CITY & REGIONAL GUIDES

Amsterdam, Bruges & Brussels
Athens & The Peloponnese NEW IN 2009
Budapest NEW IN 2009
Florence & Tuscany
Istanbul
London
Paris
Prague & The Czech Republic
Provence & The French Riviera
Rome
Venice
Vienna, Salzburg & Tirol NEW IN 2009

PHRASE BOOKS & DICTIONARIES

French
French, Italian & German
German
Italian
Portuguese
Spanish

RICK STEVES' EUROPE DVDs

Austria & The Alps
Eastern Europe
England
Europe
France & Benelux
Germany & Scandinavia
Greece, Turkey, Israel & Egypt
Ireland & Scotland
Italy's Cities
Italy's Countryside
Rick Steves' European Christmas
Spain & Portugal
Travel Skills & "The Making Of"

PLANNING MAPS

Britain, Ireland & London
Europe
France & Paris
Germany, Austria & Switzerland
Italy
Spain & Portugal

JOURNALS

Rick Steves' Pocket Travel Journal
Rick Steves' Travel Journal

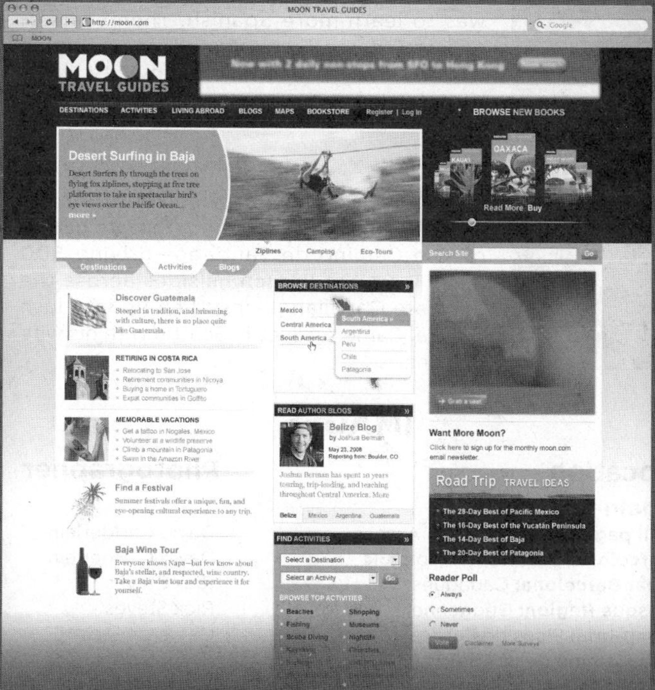

CREDITS

Researchers

To help update this book, Rick relied on...

Amanda Buttinger

Amanda moved to Madrid in 1998 thinking she'd be there a year. Her first reason to stay was to learn more Spanish. Then she discovered the perfect *café con leche,* Iberian wines, travel writing, and sunny city walks with her dog and her man.

Cameron Hewitt

Cameron updated Barcelona and Basque Country, and wrote this book's new chapter on the Camino de Santiago—driving 500 miles from the French hillsides across the desolate Castilian plains, then up into lush Galicia. Cameron lives in Seattle with his wife Shawna.

IMAGES

Location	Photographer
Spain	
Full page image: Moorish Arches	David C. Hoerlein
Barcelona: Barcelona's Montjuïc	David C. Hoerlein
Near Barcelona: Cadaqués	Rick Steves
Basque Region: Guggenheim Bilbao	Rick Steves
Cantabria: Picos de Europa	Cameron Hewitt
The Camino de Santiago: Puente de la Reina	Cameron Hewitt
Santiago de Compostela: Santiago's Cathedral	Cameron Hewitt
Salamanca: Salamanca's Plaza Mayor	Rick Steves
Madrid: Madrid's Retiro Park	David C. Hoerlein
Northwest of Madrid: Segovia's Aqueduct	Rick Steves
Toledo: Toledo Overview	Rick Steves
Granada: The Alhambra	Robert Wright
Sevilla: Sevilla Skyline	Rick Steves
Córdoba: Córdoba's Mezquita	Robert Wright
Andalucía's White Hill Towns: Arcos	David C. Hoerlein
Spain's South Coast: Nerja	Rick Steves
Morocco	
Full page image: Moroccan Woman, Tangier	Rick Steves
Tangier: Market Vendor	Rick Steves

Rick Steves' Guidebook Series

Country Guides

Rick Steves' Best of Europe
Rick Steves' Croatia & Slovenia
Rick Steves' Eastern Europe
Rick Steves' England
Rick Steves' France
Rick Steves' Germany
Rick Steves' Great Britain
Rick Steves' Ireland
Rick Steves' Italy
Rick Steves' Portugal
Rick Steves' Scandinavia
Rick Steves' Spain
Rick Steves' Switzerland

City and Regional Guides

Rick Steves' Amsterdam, Bruges & Brussels
Rick Steves' Athens & the Peloponnese (new in 2009)
Rick Steves' Budapest (new in 2009)
Rick Steves' Florence & Tuscany
Rick Steves' Istanbul
Rick Steves' London
Rick Steves' Paris
Rick Steves' Prague & the Czech Republic
Rick Steves' Provence & the French Riviera
Rick Steves' Rome
Rick Steves' Venice
Rick Steves' Vienna, Salzburg & Tirol (new in 2009)

Rick Steves' Phrase Books

French
French/Italian/German
German
Italian
Spanish
Portuguese

Other Books

Rick Steves' Europe Through the Back Door
Rick Steves' Europe 101: History and Art for the Traveler
Rick Steves' Postcards from Europe
Rick Steves' European Christmas

(Avalon Travel)

Avalon Travel
A member of the Perseus Books Group
1700 Fourth Street
Berkeley, CA 94710

Printed in the US by Worzalla. Third printing May 2009.

Thanks to Cameron Hewitt for writing the original versions of the Camino de Santiago, Santiago de Compostela, and Cantabria chapters; and to Gene Openshaw for his writing on the Prado, Picasso's *Guernica,* and other topics throughout the book.

For the latest on Rick Steves' lectures, guidebooks, tours, public television series, and public radio show, contact Europe Through the Back Door, Box 2009, Edmonds, WA 98020, tel. 425/771-8303, fax 425/771-0833, www.ricksteves.com, rick@ricksteves.com.

ISBN (10) 1-59880-124-4
ISBN (13) 978-1-59880-124-8
ISSN 1551-8388

Europe Through the Back Door Lead Editor: Cameron Hewitt
ETBD Editors: Jennifer Madison Davis, Cathy Lu, Tom Griffin, Gretchen Strauch
ETBD Managing Editor: Risa Laib
Avalon Travel Senior Editor and Series Manager: Madhu Prasher
Avalon Travel Project Editor: Kelly Lydick
Avalobn Travel Editorial Assistant: Jamie Andrade
Research Assistance: Amanda Buttinger, Cameron Hewitt
Copy Editor: Judith Brown
Proofreader: Janet Walden
Indexer: Carl Wikander
Production and Typesetting: McGuire Barber Design
Cover Design: Kimberly Glyder Design
Maps and Graphics: David C. Hoerlein, Lauren Mills, Laura VanDeventer, Barb Geisler, Mike Morgenfeld
Front Matter Color Photos: Title page photo, Mezquita, Córdoba © Robert Wright, other front color photos © ETBD
Front Cover Photo: © JIB/DRR.net
Photography: David C. Hoerlein, Rick Steves, Cameron Hewitt, Robert Wright, Steve Smith, and Cathy McDonald